POLITICS AND FINANCE
IN THE EIGHTEENTH CENTURY

Lucy Stuart Sutherland
(1903-1980)

POLITICS AND FINANCE
IN THE EIGHTEENTH CENTURY

LUCY SUTHERLAND

Edited by Aubrey Newman

THE HAMBLEDON
PRESS

The Hambledon Press 1984
35 Gloucester Avenue, London NW1 7AX

History Series 34

ISBN 0 907628 46 X

British Library Cataloguing in Publication Data

Sutherland, *Dame* Lucy Stuart
  Politics and finance in the eighteenth century.
  — (History series: 34)
  1. Business enterprises — Great Britain — Political
  activity   2. Great Britain — Politics and
  government — 18th century
  I. Title   II. Newman, Aubrey N.   III. Series
  320.941   JN210

Printed and bound in Great Britain by
Robert Hartnoll Ltd Bodmin Cornwall

CONTENTS

I
Business Records and the Law Merchant

II
The City of London and Politics

III
The East India Company and Politics

IV

Edmund Burke

V

Merchants and Financiers

VI

Junius

VII

Eighteenth-Century Oxford

LIST OF ILLUSTRATIONS

PREFACE

The contribution made by Dame Lucy Sutherland to eighteenth-century studies is to be found in her books and her articles, and in the way that she inspired other historians. Her books stand by themselves and need no further comment here; her articles, however, constituted a major part of her work but were spread among a large number of periodicals and books and are consequently difficult to find. It was therefore felt appropriate that they should be brought into a single, coherent volume for the use of scholars. Fugitive pieces such as reviews, and articles that were in effect transcriptions of documents have been excluded.

It has been decided to group the articles together by topic rather than reprinting them in the chronological order of their original publication. Where appropriate reference has been made to subsequent scholarship that has thrown light upon the topics discussed in these essays. The texts are reproduced in all cases from the originals as first printed. For technical reasons it has not been possible to do more than adjust the cross-references; nor has it been possible to incorporate into the text references to later editions of a number of the works cited.

The editor of this volume and the literary executor of the late Dame Lucy Sutherland wish to express their gratitude to the publishers of the books and journals in which these articles originally appeared for giving permission for them to be reprinted, to those who were joint-authors with Dame Lucy for agreeing to the inclusion of their work in this volume, to John Bromley for allowing his appreciation of Dame Lucy's work as an historian to reappear, to Ian Doolittle, Ann Kennedy, Paul Langford and Peter Marshall for help with bibliographical references, and to Gill Goode for her work in compiling the index.

AUBREY NEWMAN

LUCY SUTHERLAND AS HISTORIAN

Historians make their reputations in several ways, some by sheer weight of output or literary seduction, others by evolving a new technique or discovering sensationally fresh evidence, more still nowadays as darlings of the media and as retail salesmen beloved of publishers. Dame Lucy Sutherland's achievement does not fall conveniently into any of these categories. She was no publicist and never wrote a paperback; she once selected nine lectures for publication in that form, but they were British Academy performances and none by herself. Her technique, so far as it was not based on traditional methods of scholarly evaluation, she derived from Sir Lewis Namier. Three books, one of them an edition of Burke's correspondence for 1768-1774, and some two dozen learned articles are a short tally by contemporary standards, especially for one who achieved professional eminence early in life. Yet her accomplishment was of a kind most historians envy. For she was one of that select company who reveal, if not a whole forgotten age, at least a large dimension of it, a world we had lost and have recovered, so that it is now a familiar corner of the vast landscape of history.

Of Namier, Dame Lucy said that he cast "a new and dazzling light on the political institutions of mid-eighteenth century England". She did the same for the City of London in the framework of national politics at that time; and it is some rough indication of the scope of this work that even a brief, and perhaps premature, assessment ideally requires the collaboration of several specialists. No economic historian of the period possesses her mastery of its intricate politics, while none of the distinguished school of "Namierites" can match her easy familiarity with the art of banking, the subtleties of stock-jobbery, the jargon of 'Change. To this we must add a lifelong fascination with Edmund Burke, whose many-sided activity and Shakespearian imagination are the subject of an academic industry in themselves. As if this did not suffice, she set herself in retirement the truly forbidding task, as editor and contributor, of rewriting the controversial history of eighteenth-century Oxford, combing university and college archives with the same zest that had once sent her to the Record Office, the old "India Office", the British Museum, the Sheffield Central Library, and a dozen country houses. The publication of this major enterprise, well advanced at the time of her death, will prove more than a postscript to her previous *oeuvre*. It was a new adventure, though at the same time one for which her long experience of backstairs politics and respect for antiquarian scholarship, to say nothing of her prominence in university affairs, perfectly equipped her.

In 1933, when "Lucy Sutherland, M.A." published her first and most often cited monograph — it was reprinted in 1962 — there was a rapidly rising tide of interest in British economic history. *The Economic History Review* had been started only six years earlier, *The Economic Journal* itself, principal organ of economics in this country, was embarking on a supplement, *Economic History*. To both of these periodicals she contributed, although her main allegiance was to be given to *The English Historical Review*, whose editors in later years often fell back on her advice. The translation is explained by that intersection of business and politics which came to preoccupy her. It all sprang from the journals and ledgers of a William Braund, the significance of whose career — as a woollen exporter and then a bullion importer trading with Portugal, finally a specialist in shipping insurance and a Director of the East India Company — resided "in its very mediocrity"[1]: he had the virtue of being a type. Braund and his brother, who belonged to the influential group of East India "Ships' husbands", occupy no more than an illustrative position in *A London Merchant, 1695-1774*, which in effect is a series of set pieces on various aspects, particularly marine insurance and the India shipping interest, of what struck the author as a flowering-time in the growth of English commercial capitalism, "inherently individual but inherently associationist", an aggregate of many markets. She regretted that Braund provided no opportunity for an exploration of the more embryonic and obscure stock market; but his mixed and moderate record gave her that insight into the mentality of the mass of very ordinary merchants, brokers, ship-chandlers, shopkeepers and craftsmen who voted in City elections, met in coffee-houses, read newspapers, and could by fits and starts make themselves felt at Westminster.

These studies, which read as freshly to-day as when they were published, acquainted Lucy with a large "practical literature" of directories, dictionaries and handbooks, some of them foreign and as old as the sixteenth century. She was impressed by the relative dependence of the English market on mercantile custom, in contrast with the corpus of mercantile law available on the Continent. On 12 April 1934 Miss L. Stuart Sutherland read a paper to the Royal

1   See below, Chapter 16, pp. 365-85.

Historical Society on "The Law Merchant in England in the Seventeenth and Eighteenth Centuries",[2] largely forgotten now but as remarkable as anything she wrote later – one cannot say, in her her maturity, for this was already apparent. It is remarkable as containing more about the seventeenth century than the eighteenth, since she was concerned to show how much the reception of mercantile custom into the common law, notably through the judgements of Lord Mansfield, was indebted to the gropings of English civilians to domesticate Grotius and his predecessors, as well as to the practical handbooks of Molloy and others. Miss Stuart Sutherland moved with easy grace through this legal jungle and displayed a talent for theoretical argument such as there was seldom occasion for afterwards. Her quick sense of the contours of any complicated development, that lucidity which seemed effortless but must have been the reward of a creative struggle, was never more in evidence, if only because it stretched over two centuries, rather than the quarter-century which became her favourite stamping ground. It is the more worth recalling since she did not enjoy the advantage of the many detailed studies of sixteenth-century merchant practice which began to appear twenty years later. Had her interests not already been deflected, she might have given us, for instance, a history of Doctors' Commons or of the Admiralty Court, both still lacking, so congenial were legal records and so fearless her approach.

Instead the future was announced two years earlier, in her very first publication, an article on Burke and the first Rockingham ministry.[3] Its short career, in 1765-6, marked "the most definite step in the rise of merchants to political power": with the repeal of the Stamp Act and other measures for shaping policy in the interests of organised trade, it denoted a younger Whiggism willing to undertake "commercial agitation" for tactical purposes, under Burke's inspiration. Of him the author was already confident enough to state that his methods and opinions were to change remarkably little, from that time forward, indeed that he "never originated but always idealized and intensified the thought which he found about him". The "support out of doors" which he invoked came, in the event, less from the trading towns in general than from the diversified but comparatively well organised rank and file of London's 12,000 freemen, of whom Braund was the prototype. They were poles apart from the monied interest of the City, of the type of the Jewish financier Samson Gideon, the subject of two later articles (1946, 1953),[4] praised by a former President of the Jewish

2   See below, Chapter 2, pp. 9-36.
3   See below, Chapter 14, pp. 299-325.
4   See below, Chapters 17 and 18, pp. 387-98 and 399-413.

Historical Society for their understanding of Gideon's denominational background. Lucy certainly illustrated the mutual dependence of public administration and private credit, but it was the intrusion of the average merchant into politics which continued to preoccupy her. In one respect these two aspects of the City's role were connected, for she was able to show that the normal anti-establishment reflexes of ordinary middlemen were fed by resentment of the monied interest, especially in its monopoly of government loans. London's precocious popular radicalism, however, was a fabric of many colours. In her widely read contribution to *Essays presented to Sir Lewis Namier* (1956)[5] she offered a kind of barometric reading of its surges and retreats in the mid-eighteenth century. Her Raleigh Lecture (British Academy, 1960),[6] a good example of her flair for demarcating the phases of a crisis (and her adroit use of newspapers), explored the phenomenon of Pitt's popularity in the City; her Creighton Lecture (University of London, 1959),[7] the paradox of a Wilkes who was never a Wilkite. Here she reached forbidden ground: "the reasons and feelings underlying public opinion are always both too complex and too inarticulate for precise analysis, and nowhere more than at the point at which principles and aspirations merge with questions of personality." She preferred specific if avowedly incomplete explanations, the fragile links between City and Parliamentary interests, in short, her contribution to the structural analysis of politics. She had only to glance at a list of East India shareholders in order to recognize the distribution of voting rights between affiliations, and for that matter between business interests.

This, in the historians' jargon, was "Namierism". Who can assert that she might not have found her way to it had Sir Lewis's *The Structure of Politics at the Accession of George III* (1929) not been the book of her life? Its publication coincided with her growing interest in what we might now call the politicization of the country's major trading organisation, John Company, and she became the first of the Namierites. When war broke out and she was carried off to Whitehall, substantial portions of *The East India Company in Eighteenth-Century Politics* (1952), her masterpiece, were already in draft. It owed something to Namier's practical kindness — there were reciprocal flows of information as long as he lived — but still more to the inspiration of his method, which she described in a word uncommon with her: it was "revolutionary". So far from being limited to a moment in time, as *The Structure* was, it supplied a philosophy of historical change.

5   See below, Chapter 3, pp. 41-66.
6   See below, Chapter 4, pp. 67-113.
7   See below, Chapter 5, pp. 115-47.

Its enemies were to complain that it devalued political mankind by subordinating large ideas and passionate convictions to personal, family and party self-interest. For Lucy, saturated in Burke's speeches and letters, where noble vision co-existed with violent party prejudice, the implications were altogether different. She stated them briefly in a paper read to a meeting of British and French historians in Paris in 1946 (and printed in *The Economic History Review* for 1947),[8] inviting her audience to consider what it meant to be bereft of that "underlying belief in purposive progress" which, for their predecessors, had allowed "great forces and ideas" insidiously to become in themselves the agents of historical change, fulfilling "the great evolutionary trend". In 1946, on the contrary, the historian was "feeling his way" among "the ruins of former assumptions". It is the practical decisions of many individuals which give coherence to conflicting social forces — "a much more intricate and detailed system of causation". Every specific act has a specific cause. The "circumstances surrounding an event" are therefore worthy of close study in themselves, provided one seeks to decode their "inner history", the "springs of action". This calls for the exercise of imagination. In her Academy *éloge* of Namier (1963) Dr. Sutherland stressed his "powerful historical imagination", in re-creating "a remote and self-contained world". Likewise, in the introduction she wrote to a posthumous collection of papers by her admired contemporary, Richard Pares, *The Historian's Business* (1961), she referred not only to the discovery and analysis of the past, but also to its re-creation. By the laborious detour of structural analysis (one is tempted to comment), the Namierites were returning to the grand aim of Romantic historians, though the comparison would shock them; both word-painting and the dramatization of events were deeply foreign to Lucy's classical temper and quiet, unforced language.

The East India Company, Lucy's chief legacy as a historian, is one of those deliberately circumscribed yet deeply satisfying professional books that make it unlikely that anyone, even supposing him or her to possess the necessary stamina, will need to traverse the same ground again. Reacting against the traditional treatment of Anglo-Indian affairs in terms of spectacular personalities and episodes, the author set herself the task of pursuing an unbroken path through "the maze of East India politics" from 1758 to 1784, with as much attention to the lines of force at Westminster as to the even more kaleidoscopic factions of Leadenhall Street. Step by step, we are invited to participate in a chess contest at high tension. Parliamentary and Company cabals combine and subdivide and re-form under the pressure of events at home and in India. There are the arenas of Bengal and the Carnatic; the Court of

8   See below, Chapter 7, pp. 165-176.

Directors and the General Court of Proprietors, with its frequent and often unpredictable votes; Downing Street and the House of Commons; public opinion and not least the stock market. To hold all these in control, at different stages of a rapidly changing environment, demanded perspicacity and finesse of the highest order. The Company alone was a "vast network of interests", the methods employed "necessarily intricate and laborious". Footnotes stand as mute witnesses now to a "truly formidable mass of material both in print and in manuscript"; some three hundred volumes of Hastings correspondence, to start with, and nearly a thousand of Newcastle and Hardwicke — for examination, assessment, selective transcription, cross-reference. Much of the material, moreover, was poisoned by partisanship. When the author paid tribute to Pares's "subjugation of a vast variety of detailed, first-hand material", and to Namier's "creative effort of mastering his material", she was drawing on her own experience. Those words are simple, perhaps obvious, but they come from the depths.

It must have been difficult, even for Lucy Sutherland, to gather the threads of pre-war research after a distracting five-year secondment to the Board of Trade. That interval may nevertheless have strengthened the powers of political and moral judgement which her subject inexorably exercised. She was too sophisticated not to be on guard against nineteenth-century standards of "official rectitude"; unwilling, unlike many clever women, to condemn mediocrity trapped in a system that had to be made to work somehow; amused, rather than estranged, by the solemnities of male vanity. Nevertheless, although she used words no stronger than "disreputable", realism had to come to terms with an exceptional moral sensibility. One suspects she wished, quite ardently, for an uncontaminated Warren Hastings and Edmund Burke, both of whom "touched pitch". There is no denying the anxiety that haunted her in both cases. An article of 1957, "New Evidence on the Nandakuma Trial,"[9] searches the barely intelligible notes of a friend of Hastings for proof that he was guilty of judicial murder; his friends indeed were, she decided, and he of "economy of truth". Similarly, the Appendix to her impeccable edition (1960) of Burke's letters, on the purchase of Gregories, looks anxiously at Burke's denial of a loan from Lord Verney: had he "told a lie to the detriment of one who had been his benefactor"?[10] That would have been "a particularly discreditable and distasteful charge." Far more sordid charges were properly levelled at the "nabobs", but on these fortune-hunters she turned a judicious

9   See below, Chapter 11, pp. 241-68.
10   See below, Chapter 15, pp. 327-60.

eye — they "were neither idle nor incompetent as a class". Her "superficial and imperfect" understanding of the Indian scene (as she put it) may well have increased her caution there; but it is not hard to believe that the wartime Civil Service subscribed an augmentation of charity. Certainly the heroes of *The East India Company* are the hard-working, well-informed "men of business", the Robinsons and Jenkinsons behind Lord North's administration, of which she wrote that it was "one in which major decisions are seldom taken at the right time, but in which, in default of them, there is much careful consideration of interests and a series of partial solutions, often ingenious and valuable...". At the conference in Paris, she had thought that the turmoil of her time had taught us respect for stable governments with limited aims.

Even without the relentless calls of public life, and especially those of her beloved college, the task of editing Burke must have kept the Principal until 1960 from writing the sequel to her East India book which was contemplated: an extended study of London in national politics. Burke was an exacting letter-writer for his editors, if only because of his intense political activity and wide circle of political friends, shady relatives, and literary connections; he usually wrote in a hurry too, so there are textual problems. Anyone who has edited a text must be aware of his exposure to casual allusions and unidentified names, to say the least. He must expect to be at the mercy of hidden currents and baffling winds. In this kind of undertaking, it is true, Lucy was assisted by an able and kindly General Editor, the late Thomas W. Copeland, and others connected with the enterprise, especially Dr. J.A. Woods and Dr. John Brooke, all of whom contributed to her Festschrift in 1973: *Statesmen, Merchants and Scholars*. Above all she had the advantage of her own intimate knowledge of the years 1768-1774. This shines through numerous footnotes, including quite trivial ones: thus a line to note that Lord Rockingham spent the night of 12 October 1769 at Sir G. Savile's, another to explain the Lord Mayor's health — "Brass Crosby was suffering from the gout". In particular, the editor's well-stored mind frequently pounces on half a sentence in which the innocent reader would see no occasion for comment. It goes without saying that she would run to earth every one of the Latin tags with which Burke buttered his correspondents, but one is agreeably surprised to find her annotating theatrical and racing events. Her authorities were multitudinous, from Dublin newspapers to West Indian genealogies and New York biographies.

Whether Dame Lucy was, after all, fully equipped for that full-length study of London politics of which we have the three fragments already touched upon, may be arguable. It would have required more of a seventeenth-century background than the Company: of that she would have been amply capable. But might it not also have entailed more of that sympathy with common clay, with "mobs", which she admired in Richard Cobb and George Rudé? She was uncomfortable with demagogues, at ease in counter and council chamber rather than workshop or street. It was rather like her to refer to the student restlessness of our day as "curious outbursts": this in spite of a deep penetration of its causes. There is even one ingredient missing from her account of East India politics – the verbal violence in which much of it was conducted. It is often hinted at, never projected. On the other hand, the rumbustious life of male society in eighteenth-century Oxford held no terrors for her.

It is of course a tragedy that she did not live to see her history of Oxford, so much the centre of her thought when she was very ill, to completion. She gave us some foretastes of it: one a dryly humorous and at the same time deadly serious narrative of the fearful academic imbroglio surrounding the foundation of Worcester College (*Oxoniensa*, 1979)[11]; another a James Bryce Memorial Lecture at Somerville in 1972 (O.U.P., 1973) on "The University of Oxford in the Eighteenth Century: A Reconsideration".[12] The subtitle here was well justified, for this wide-ranging lecture neatly and substantially modifies, without altogether suppressing, the accepted picture of hard-drinking dons and idle undergraduates exchanging empty exercises on a scrap-heap of dead learning. But there is more to it than that. Lucy never gave a more spirited performance. It is spiced with a wit (and exquisite choice of quotation) that she had not always allowed herself. For anyone who never met her, this short cut to her sociable personality may be strongly recommended.

For those who had the great fortune to know Dame Lucy, her personality must always transcend her writings, on the whole somewhat taut and reserved in manner. Yet it is unthinkable that she could ever have been other than a passionate student of history. It was meat and drink to her, probably a solace at troubled times, certainly a guide in Namier's sense of imparting an instinctive knowledge of how things do not happen. She was endlessly reviewing, endlessly supplying advice and hard information to other historians, delighted and moved when they did the same for her. Much of her own work, indeed, was fulfilled by the writing of her pupils, on public finance, on India, on politics, perhaps on Oxford too.

11   See below, Chapter 24, pp. 531-49.
12   See below, Chapter 22, pp. 491-518.   **J.S. BROMLEY**

BIBLIOGRAPHY OF DAME LUCY SUTHERLAND

A complete bibliography, up to 1973, is to be found in *Statesmen, Scholars and Merchants: Essays in Eighteenth-Century History presented to Dame Lucy Sutherland*, ed. Anne Whiteman, J.S. Bromley and P.G.M. Dickson (Oxford, 1973). This bibliography is continued, so far as articles are concerned, up to her death in the forthcoming memoir by Anne Whiteman in the *Proceedings of the British Academy*.

I. BOOKS

1933

A London Merchant 1695-1774 (Oxford Historical Series. Reprinted 1962.

1952

The East India Company in Eighteenth-Century Politics (Oxford, Clarendon Press). Reprinted 1962.

Forthcoming

History of the University of Oxford, Volume V (1688-1800), edited by Dame Lucy up to her death in 1980. Chapter V, 'Political Respectability, 1751-71'; Chapter VII, 'The Laudian Statutes'; Chapter VIII, 'The Administration of the University'; Chapter XV, 'The Curriculum'.

II. BOOKS EDITED

1937

M.V. Clarke, *Fourteenth Century Studies*, with May McKisack (Oxford, Clarendon Press).

1938

A.E. Levett, *Studies in Manorial History*, with Helen M. Cam and Mary Coate (Oxford, Clarendon Press).

1960

The Correspondence of Edmund Burke, vol. ii: July 1768-June 1774, general editor, Thomas W. Copeland (Cambridge and Chicago).

1962

Sir Lewis Namier's Ford Lectures (1934), with J. Brooke. Sir Lewis Namier, *Crossroads of Power*, 73-117.

1966

Studies in History. British Academy Lectures, selected and introduced by Lucy S. Sutherland (Oxford).

III. ARTICLES NOT IN THIS COLLECTION

1950

'Universities and Schools', *Universities Quarterly*, v. 20-5.

1953

'Two Letter-books of Richard Barwell 1769-73. Letter-book I', *Indian Archives*, vii. 115-45.

1954

'Pembroke College' and 'Somerville College' (part), in *V.C.H., Oxfordshire*, vol. iii: *The University of Oxford*, 288-97; 343-5.
'Two Letter-books of Richard Barwell, 1769-73. Letter-book II', *Indian Archives*, viii. 14-42.
'The Hanoverian Kings' (last section with J.H. Rose), *sub* 'English History', in *Encyclopaedia Britannica*, viii. 523-31.

1955

'The Ostend Company', in *Encyclopaedia Britannica*, xvi. 955.

1960

'Lady Margaret Hall', *American Oxonian*, xlvii. 70-5.
'The New Status of Women', *Oxford*, xvi, no. 3. 72-6.
Obituary of Sir Lewis Namier, *Oxford Magazine*, 20 Oct. 31-2.

1961

Biographical introduction to Richard Pares, *The Historian's Business and other Essays*, ed. R.A. and Elisabeth Humphreys, ix-xiv.
'Sir Lewis Namier' (translated into Italian by Pino Fino), *Rivista Storica Italiana*, lxxiii. 415-18.

1962

'In Memoriam Lucy Barbara Hammond (*née* Bradby), 1875-1961', *The Brown Book*, 28-9.

1963

'Sir Lewis Namier, 1888-1960', *Proceedings of the British Academy*, xlviii. 371-85.

1964

Contributions to *The History of Parliament. The House of Commons 1754-1790*, ed. Sir Lewis Namier and John Brooke.

1967

'Lewis Namier and Institutional History', *Annali della Fondazione Italiana per la Storia Amministrativa*, iv. 35-43.

1969

'William Miller Macmillan: an Appreciation', *St. Antony's Papers*, no. 21, *African Affairs*, no. 3 (ed. Kenneth Kirkwood), 9-24.

1970

'Maria Edgeworth's Tree Paeony', *The Brown Book*, 63-4.

ACKNOWLEDGEMENTS

The articles reprinted here appeared first in the following places and are reprinted by the kind permission of the original publishers.

1   *Bulletin of the Institute of Historical Research*, xiii (1935), 69-72.

2   *Transactions of the Royal Historical Society*, 4th Series, xvii (1934), 149-76.

3   *Essays Presented to Sir Lewis Namier*, ed. Richard Pares and A.J.P. Taylor (Macmillan, London, 1956), 49-74.

4   The Raleigh Lecture on History (1960). *Proceedings of the British Academy*, xlvi (1961), 147-93.

5   The Creighton Lecture in History (1958); published by The Athlone Press, London (1959).

6   *The Economic History Review*, xvii (1947), 15-26.

7   *English Historical Review*, lxii (1947), 179-90.

8   *English Historical Review*, xlix (1934), 450-86.

9   *English Historical Review*, xc (1975), 523-35.

10 *The Indian Archives*, x (1956), 1-12.

11 *English Historical Review*, lxxii (1957), 438-65.

12 *Bengal Past and Present*, lxxvi (1957), 22-9.

13 *Studies in Burke and his Time*, x (1968), 1005-21.

14 *English Historical Review*, xlvii (1932), 46-72.

15 *Proceedings of the Leeds Philosophical and Literary Society*, xi (1966), 183-216.

16 *Economic History Review*, iii (1932), 367-87.

17 *Transactions of the Jewish Historical Society of England*, xvii (1953), 79-90.

18 *Economic History Review*, xvi (1946), 15-29.

19 *English Historical Review*, lxx (1955), 229-57.

20   *Economic History*, iii (1936), 237-58.

21   *Bulletin of the Institute of Historical Research*, xlii (1969), 158-72.

22   Bryce Lecture, Somerville College (1972).

23   *Bodleian Library Record*, x (1980), 166-77.

24   *Oxoniensia*, xliv (1979), 62-80.

25   *Evidence in Literary Scholarship: Essays in Memory of James Marshall Osborn*, ed. René Wellek and Alvaro Ribiero (Clarendon Press, Oxford, 1979), 229-40.

26   *Christ Church Annual Report*, (1975), 35-9.

'Lucy Sutherland as Historian', by J.S. Bromley first appeared in *The Brown Book* of Lady Margaret Hall, Oxford, *Dame Lucy Sutherland Memorial Supplement* (May 1981), pp. 8-13.

I
Business Records and the
Law Merchant

BIBLIOGRAPHICAL NOTE

CHAPTER 2

See now, J.H. Baker, 'The Law Merchant and the Common Law before 1700', *C.L.J.*, 295 (1979), which contains extensive footnotes dealing with material on the subject since the publication of Dame Lucy's article.

William Murray, 1st Earl of Mansfield (1705-93)
(Jean Baptiste van Loo, 1732)
(National Portrait Gallery)

1

THE USE OF BUSINESS RECORDS
IN THE STUDY OF HISTORY

WHAT archaeological records do for ancient and mediaeval history, business records do for some aspects of mediaeval and modern history. In a concrete, finite way they show us ' how the wheels went round.' But the study does not owe its popularity solely to the precision of its materials or to the propositions which they may be used to prove ; for that matter genealogical records also, by bringing together masses of information about innumerable more or less insignificant persons, show the social influences at work. Yet the study of business records has at the present time an attraction for many who remain indifferent to the charms of genealogy, because the wheels which business records show us going round are those of industrial processes, and the atmosphere of contemporary historiography is so highly charged with economic determinism that such processes have a particular significance for us. Thus the study of business records seems likely to be an activity characteristic of our age, both because it satisfies our need for concrete information and because it produces material illustrative of the reigning philosophy of history.

' Business history ' may be defined as the historical study of the structure of the units of production and exchange of wealth ; with the corollary, that its sources are chiefly to be sought in the working business records of these units. It will be noticed that this definition includes the study of agriculture as well as of trade and industry : it is noticeable that modern studies in the history of agriculture tend increasingly to treat the farm, manor, or vill less as a judicial or sociological unit, and more as a unit of production and exchange.

The importance of business records in the study of history is in the first place that they enable us to reconstruct the actual workings of these units. That such knowledge is of the utmost value for its own sake in reconstructing the history of any period is now no longer doubted. To understand the working of a fifteenth-century Venetian *banco del giro*, of the business of a seventeenth-century English cloth merchant, or the problems of an early factory owner, is to possess valuable historical knowledge of the society in which these units

[1] This paper was read at a group meeting of the interim Anglo-American Historical Conference held at the Institute on 5 July 1935.

occur.   It is also now clearly recognized that this knowledge is not isolated in its usefulness, but that those movements which historians are accustomed to call the ' great ' movements can rarely be understood without reference to a vast variety of minor interests lying behind them.   Among minor interests, those of an economic character are always important, and their full comprehension is often impossible without a close analysis of the structure of those units of production and exchange which go to make them up.   Thus, the history of Genoese predominance and colonial aggrandizement in the late middle ages was never fully comprehensible until the nature of the great bank of San Giorgio was worked out in detail.   Thus, too, the eighteenth-century mercantile system in England, which had so clearly ceased to be a system of control of trade in the interest of policy, and had become on the contrary one of control of policy in the interest of organized trades, can only be understood when the network of trade relationships between individual firms has been elucidated.   What is commonly called political history is not the ordered manifestation of great principles, but the pursuit of expediency, though these principles themselves may sometimes determine for political rulers what is expedient.   In this study of the pursuit of expediency business records have much of value to offer the historian.

The value of business records lies in the fact that they alone can give us certain information about historical facts which are interesting in themselves and important in relation to other historical facts.   In the past little use has been made even of those few records which are known and accessible, and though more recently a number of valuable monographs have been written, only the fringes of the subject have been touched.   In the first place we do not yet know how extensive business records are.   We know that they exist in larger numbers than might have been expected, even for early periods.   But to draw conclusions from such records sheer bulk is essential, and the innumerable subdivisions of business activity cover an enormous field.   These deficiencies are still uncertain.   For instance, we have not got, so far as I am aware, any run of papers of an early stockjobber or broker, since those of the famous eighteenth-century Jewish broker, Sampson Gideon, preserved at least until the nineteenth century by the family, have disappeared.   The light that could be thrown on the floating of eighteenth-century government loans, the part played by the Jewish interest on the money-market, and the early organization of the stock market may well be extinguished for ever.   The records, moreover, are not only deficient at present, but also in many cases difficult of access, scattered in private hands, often in the care of firms which have absorbed older units without preserving the old titles, and frequently quite unknown even to the owners.

Business records are not only incomplete and inaccessible but also difficult to interpret, a serious matter where their numbers are few and the organization of business is far removed from that which we know and understand.   They are always purely utilitarian in origin, and are only intended for the use of those who are already expert in that business.   Thus, for instance, mediaeval and renaissance finance presents serious difficulties in interpretation.   This difficulty is not, however, more serious than that which presents itself in the interpretation of most documentary evidence.   Merchants, traders, and industrialists have generally been a literate and vocal class : their representations and petitions to the government, on the one hand—on the other, the books of reference that were produced for their own use from very early periods, provide literary sources supplementary to the records and usually some clue to technical difficulties.

Such organizations as the Council for the Preservation of Business Archives in this country are doing their best to minimize the difficulties of incompleteness and inaccessibility by helping to preserve threatened records, and by listing those which are safely kept in public or private hands.   But business records are bound to be badly kept in comparison with other forms of record, whatever effort we may make.   In the first place, the average unit of exchange and production is unstable and short-lived in comparison with departments of state or great corporations.   While a few great incorporated companies like the Bank of England may stand like a rock, the various partnerships and private ventures are as shifting as the sands.   Hence luck plays an even greater part in deciding what business records shall survive than it does in the preservation of most records.   Moreover, since the records are purely utilitarian, they have no chance of surviving for their literary interest, nor are they likely to be collected by their contemporaries for their future historical interest.   They are not to be found, as a proclamation may be, embedded in the pages of a mediaeval chronicle, nor, like a modern cabinet minute, inserted in the notebooks of a contemporary diarist.   When once their period of usefulness is over (a period which varies with the business) they rarely, if ever, owe their preservation to anything more positive than inertia or routine.   Pride in ancient records may come later, but only after they have already been preserved.   The superb collections of business records made by such families as the Fuggers and the Medicis are the products of routine among the members of an unusually enduring and stable unit of production and exchange ; as are also the records of the English banks.   The casual collections of old ledgers, account books, and papers, found from time to time in the cellars or attics of business units, are usually preserved by mere inertia, and are thus in a precarious state, for they may be swept out at any time in the interest of space and order.

The routine which preserves business records need not necessarily, however, be the routine of the unit itself.   It may the routine of another institution. Most important here are the courts of law.   In several foreign centres, as, for instance, Amsterdam and Hamburg, the bankruptcy courts preserve most important material.   In England the courts of chancery and exchequer preserve in their records great masses of business accounts and correspondence, copied out and attached to bills and answers as exhibits.   It is to the routine of chancery that we owe the most famous English business correspondence of the fifteenth century, the Cely papers, with the aid of which we have been able to reconstruct the organization of the fifteenth-century English wool trade. Innumerable less valuable finds await the searcher of legal records.

2

THE LAW MERCHANT IN ENGLAND

THE study of Law Merchant in England in the seventeenth
and eighteenth centuries which I venture to read to the
Society to-day arose out of some work upon the business
of eighteenth-century merchants. I approach the complex
problem of the Law Merchant therefore not from the point
of view of the law courts but as the merchant himself
approached it, by way of the problems of commercial intercourse.

The eighteenth century can be considered, from the point
of view of Economic History, either as the zenith of an old
system of capitalism, where the merchant was the " spring
and centre of traffic," or as the forerunner of a new age when
the merchant prince saw his place usurped by the industrial
magnate. It is when one considers the eighteenth century
not in the latter, but in the former aspect that the problem
of the Law Merchant arises. The merchant is predominant
in the economic structure, has forced his way into politics,
and is making his mark on the law. The same period that
is marked so deeply in politics and economics with the
stamp of the great mercantile exporting interests sees mercantile customs capturing the strongholds of the common
law by the twofold assault of custom and theory. The
outlines of the process are well known. In the eighteenth
century English law definitely lost the character it had inherited from the Middle Ages of a predominantly land law
by the addition of a great body of commercial law. Lord

Mansfield, the most famous lawyer of the century, deliberately set out to achieve this.   Sometimes he is spoken of as if he had, single-handed, created English commercial law and that his detachment from the common law traditions held by men like his successors Kenyon and Eldon had made this possible.   But great as was the part he played, he could never have achieved his end had there not stood behind him a strong social need, a willingness in the courts to follow his lead, and a body of commercial custom which was the product of long development.

The intention of this paper is to show what precisely was this need, and to suggest whence the merchants' knowledge of the mercantile custom of their time was drawn.   The material used here consists chiefly of the contemporary publications which sought either to guide lawyers in their dealings with trade, or, more often, to guide merchants in their dealings with the law.

The Law Merchant of the seventeenth and eighteenth centuries, the body of theory and custom that forced its way into the law of the land, has an interest wider than the concerns of trade, for in its development came together the tendencies making for the growth of the theory of the Law of Nations on the one hand, and the evolution of fuller national laws on the other.   Contemporaries were anxious to stress its mediæval heredity, and to speak of it as a " Lex Mercatoria Rediviva," and writers were wont from the seventeenth century onwards to raise on high the " ancient name of Lex Mercatoria."   But just as the customs they administered were more complex than those of their mediæval predecessors, so was their theoretical exposition of the nature of their Law Merchant far more advanced. Just as the seventeenth century meant something far more definite and concrete by the Law of Nations than the fifteenth meant by the Law of Nature ; so when a fifteenth-century Chancellor said in the Star Chamber that a merchant stranger could sue "solonques le ley de Nature en le Chancery, viz. ley marchant que est ley universal par tout le monde " [1] he meant something far less definite than did Malynes when he repeated the commonplaces of 1622 and maintained that the Law Merchant was a known body of customs which " hath alwaies been found *semper eadem*, that is constant and permanent . . . concurring with the law of nations in all countries." [2] The completed theory of the Law Merchant was, in fact, typical less of mediæval thought than that of the sixteenth and seventeenth centuries, when civilians were concerned with the nature of the Law of Nations, and were laying the foundations of International Law.

Historians have studied the Law Merchant of the Middle Ages from two points of view ; in the first place they have collected such material as has survived and examined it to discover what business was carried out in the merchant courts ; in the second place they have tried to find out what contemporaries actually thought it to be, and what were its relations with the common law of the land. [3] In the second attempt they have been perhaps less successful than in the former, partly because they appear to have paid too little attention to chronology and the changing needs of merchants. This paper is an attempt to trace the chronological development. It is useless to quote, as so many have done, seventeenth-century writers such as Davies [4] or Wiseman, [5] Malynes [6] or Zouch, [7] or even Coke himself, to prove that the merchant courts of the Middle Ages had anything like

[1] Year Book. 13 Ed. IV, p. 9. Quoted A. T. Carter, *Early History of the Law Merchant in England.* *Law Quarterly*, XVII, pp. 232 *seq.*

[2] G. Malynes, *Consuetudo vel Lex Mercatoria*, 1622, Epistle Dedicatorie, p. 2.

[3] For instance, C. Gross and H. Hall, *Select Cases on the Law Merchant*, 3 vols. (Selden Society). A. H. Thomas, *Calendar of Select Pleas and Memoranda of the City of London*, especially 1381–1412, to which there is a valuable introduction.

[4] Sir John Davies, *The Question Concerning Impositions.* Published in 1656 but written much earlier and dedicated to James I.

[5] Sir Robert Wiseman, *The Law of Laws*, London, 1657.

[6] *Op. cit.*

[7] R. Zouch, *Jurisdiction of the Admiralty of England Asserted*, London, 1663.

the idea of a " recognised body of private international law " which had been compiled for seventeenth-century Europe, and which was coming into general knowledge with the new strength of the learning of the Law of Nations behind it. There is indeed something to be said for the heretics who maintain that the merchant customs in the Middle Ages were too indefinite to be called by the name of Law Merchant at all, and who complain with Ewart that " Frequent use of the word has almost produced the impression that, as there was a Civil Law and a Canon Law, so also there was somewhere a " Law Merchant " of very peculiar authority and sanctity." [1] No one could deny, of course, that there were merchant courts, and that merchant customs were administered in them. Some, though not all, of these customs were more than local in their application, and it was held that all merchants recognised, if not the precedent behind them, at least the commercial conscience within them. Particularly in the sea laws of the ports, but also in many concerns of trade as well as in the law of partnership, contract and sale (much of which early won recognition in the common law), these universal customs were strong and prominent. Yet mediæval courts merchant were not established with a jurisdiction independent of the Courts of Common Law. Their position is not comparable with that of the courts administering the Canon Law. On the contrary, as the thirteenth-century tract *Lex Mercatoria* says, it was held that " Lex communis . . . est mater legis mercatorie et . . . suam filiam ex certis privilegiis et in certis locis dotavit." [2] To the mediæval lawyer the jurisdiction of the merchant courts was little more than a limited devolution of authority made in the interest of speed and simplicity. The common law courts did not hesitate to try cases involving merchants if occasion arose. It was generally recognised, as in the Ordinances of the Staple, that the parties had their choice of pleading in the merchant or common law courts,

[1] Quoted in *Anglo-American Legal Essays*, iii, 34.
[2] *Little Red Book of Bristol*, ed. F. B. Bickley, 1900, i, 68.

though the King's Council and the Chancery proved the most convenient non-mercantile mediæval courts to deal with difficult cases.

The Law Merchant, in fact, had none of the independent existence that Canon Law had in the Ecclesiastical Courts; there was no border war between the Common Law and the Merchant Courts as there was between it and the Courts Christian. Moreover, if it were not comparable with the Canon Law, no more was it with the Civil Law. It was long before merchant customs had more than a customary and mainly oral existence. Many of its rules were no doubt purely local—even in the eighteenth century Lord Mansfield had to make this distinction very sharply. The various sea laws, reduced to writing and each commanding a certain territorial sphere, such as the Laws of Oleron and later Wisby and the Hanse cities in the north and the Laws of Amalfi and the Consulate of the Sea in the Mediterranean, were the earliest customs of more than local importance to take a fixed form.[1]

It was not till the sixteenth and seventeenth centuries that the great law books of Straccha [2] and Scaccia [3] did for the customs of the merchants what the civilians and canonists had done long before in standardising practice and stating theory, for the great extra-territorial laws. And it is not till this period that the great international claims begin to be systematically advanced for Law Merchant as a body of customs which can be examined and worked upon. The full flowering of the international theory of the Law Merchant is not in short the product of the Middle Ages, but of the great age of the civil law, the sixteenth and seventeenth centuries, and in particular of the great concept developed by that age, the Law of Nations.

In the Middle Ages for certain purposes the common lawyers recognised a summary jurisdiction resting with

[1] For their texts, v. J. M. Pardessus. *Collection de Lois Maritimes,* 1828–45.

[2] Benvenuto Straccha, *Tractatus de Mercatura, seu Mercatore,* 1550.

[3] Sigismundo Scaccia, *Tractatus de Commerciis et Cambio,* 1618.

certain local trading bodies, which might even be created by statute or ordinance as in the case of the Staple under Edward III. Thereby they recognised that some customs whereby they might adjudicate existed and that some of these customs were universal, but such recognition allows little room for the claim that merchant courts were held to be acting according to a well-known and universal body of law, with mysteries with which the common law of the land could not cope. Had the English merchant courts flourished and grown, as did those of some foreign countries, they would no doubt have benefited by the sixteenth- and seventeenth-century compilations of their customs and exaltation of their jurisdiction, and the problem of their relations with the common law courts would have arisen. As they were already in decay, the future of the English courts merchant lay less with the so-called Merchant Law, which was to force its way into the common law of the future, than with the slow decay of the humble pie-powder courts of the fairs.

This lack of development in the merchant courts of England is curious, and is very different from what is found among some other trading and maritime peoples, where courts administering merchant customs were obtaining an independent place among the national legal institutions just at the time when the English courts which might have had a similar development were falling into decay. It is customary to attribute all such differences in English and continental development to the strength of the Common Law, but important as the Civil Law was in the development of commercial customs, this would not seem here to be a full explanation. There were two aspects of merchant customs which were growing vigorously at the time ; the sea laws (especially those dealing with new problems of importance such as marine insurance) and the law or custom of exchange. There were correspondingly two main reasons why the courts administering Law Merchant in England became insignificant just as they were increasing in strength elsewhere. The first is the growth of the Admiralty Court, which, rising to its greatest strength in the sixteenth century, had begun even earlier to take within the orbit of its own jurisdiction those forces which owed their strength to the fact that they were more than local.[1] With its incorporation of the mediæval sea laws of Oleron, its control of all matters in any way concerning shipping, its use (increasing as the Prerogative Courts gave, it the support of their example) of the processes of the Civil Law, the Admiralty, far more than any court merchant of England at any time, had a share by the seventeenth century in the " private international law of Europe."[2] Thus English constitutional development prevented the early strong union of merchant and maritime law, which was essential even to the conception, let alone the legal expression of a commercial custom transcending purely national bounds, and which lay behind the compilations and expositions in some of the continental nations. There, as Malynes said :

Even as the roundnesse of the Globe of the World is composed of the Earth and Waters. So is the Bodie of Lex Mercatoria made and framed of the Merchants' Customes and the Sea-Lawes, which are involved together as the Seas and Earth.[3]

As a consequence, at the time when the commercial jurisdiction was taking shape abroad, the characteristic product of English conditions was something different. It was the elaboration of the practice, and, when the Admiralty power was first seriously challenged, of a theory of the Sea Law as opposed to the Land Law, which bore on it many of the features of the Law Merchant as it was being formulated elsewhere.[4] It was only as the control of the Admiralty was crumbling away, undermined by the assaults of the

[1] See R. G. Marsden, *Select Pleas of the Admiralty*, Selden Society, 2 vols. Sir T. Twiss, *The Black Book of the Admiralty*, Rolls Series.

[2] F. Maitland, *Select Pleas in the Manorial Courts*, Selden Soc., i. 133.

[3] G. Malynes, *op. cit.*, " The Epistle to the Reader."

[4] See, for instance, J. Exton, *The Maritime Dicaeologie ; or Sea-Jurisdiction of England, 1664*, p. 135. Justice is compared to a bird with two wings, the Sea and the Land Laws. Corresponding with " that happy

common law courts and by the growing complexity of the merchant affairs which it was trying to handle, that in England the idea of a unified body of merchant custom could be formulated comparable to that given legal recognition in some countries abroad. It is significant that the only attempt to introduce continental merchant tribunals into England, the abortive institution of the Commissioners of Assurance in 1601, was the result of the incapacity of the Admiralty jurisdiction to deal adequately with the new problems of marine insurance.

The other cause of the failure of the English Law Merchant to develop, was that English economic conditions separated sharply the trader and merchant proper, as the distinction was recognised by the end of the sixteenth century. The merchant was to the English essentially the exporter, with his organised markets abroad. For this reason an English centre of exchange was slow to develop, and when it did was only a small offshoot of the great exchange markets abroad. Seventy years after the founding of the Royal Exchange, Lewes Roberts in his *Merchants' Mappe of Commerce* points out that

The Exchanges practised in England, and principally in London, are confined within a narrow scantling, being but as a Rivolet issuing out of the great streame of those Exchanges that are used beyond the Seas.[1]

Though there must always have been cases, some of them very complicated, decided in London, the sixteenth-century evidence seems to show that it was in the foreign staples or fairs, or in the courts of the exporting companies abroad that the merchant developed the new customs with regard

Government of all Land affairs by its municipal laws," the nation had " Navies, Trade and Commerce under that exact Government which hath ordered and guided all Maritime businesses and Sea affairs, by the Civil and Maritime Laws and Customes (corresponding, agreeing and according with the Laws of Forreign Nations, being suitable to the nature and negotiations of the people that are subject to them) . . ." (Epistle Dedicatory).

[1] First published in 1638, p. 256.

to credit instruments and negotiable securities which the greater scope of his trade made necessary, and certainly these new developments scarcely touched the moribund merchant courts in England. Exchange on the one hand, the sea laws and in particular marine insurance on the other, were the two aspects of the merchant customs which were at that time most international in their scope. Since the old usages of contract, partnership and sale had long since become imbedded in the precedents of national law, it was the development of these new usages which was making out of the customs of merchants a body of written international customs, and it was an adequate expression of these newer customs in law which England almost entirely lacked.

The seventeenth century saw, however, a change coming over the position in England. It was an inevitable change; on the one hand the Admiralty control, and on the other the dominance of the regulated companies was breaking down, and English trade was always expanding. The change itself was twofold; it consisted firstly, in the growingly powerful and systematic expression of merchant customs; secondly, in the beginning of the reception of those customs into the Common Law. The two movements together make up the change of the century and prepare the way for the full reception of the Law Merchant in the next century, the climax of the commercial period.

The first change was in the realm of theory. For Englishmen in the seventeenth and sixteenth centuries the Law Merchant was a theory, and a compilation of customs, which were both of foreign growth, though there had crept into them certain specifically English traditions. From the beginning of the century it is noticeable that English legal theorists, and civilians in particular, begin to lay a new stress on a theoretical systematisation of merchant customs, to give increasing attention to the Merchant Law or Custom, as something known and existent outside the Common Law. Statements of this kind can, of course, be found much

earlier.   The change lies in their increasing frequency, and
in the much clearer indications writers can give of what this
custom is and its association with the Law of Nations.   The
seventeenth century was an age not only of many practical
problems but of legal learning.   It was fitting work for the
seventeenth-century jurists and scholars to give completeness
to the theory of a Law Merchant based on the *Jus Gentium*,
and to expound in systematic manner that inchoate mass
of merchant customs which they found at home or had
adopted abroad, and which were now beginning to play
an important part in national life.

This systematisation of both the theory and technique
of merchant intercourse had to be brought about by adaptation from foreign sources, for adequate English background
there was none.   Here the learning of the Admiralty Courts,
even at the time when they were losing their power over
trade, played a part which cannot be overestimated.   In
the first place, the Admiralty Courts made one of the most
important links between English scholarship, the Civil Law
and the growing theory of Law of Nations, and in the idea
of Law of Nations lay the basis of a theoretical exposition
of the Law Merchant.   In the second place, in its struggles
against the Common Law and its formulation of the Sea
Law the Admiralty did much to introduce to England the
comparative study of the sea laws of Europe and their
history, and this also was of the greatest importance in
the systematic exposition of merchant custom.

The growth of the theory of *Jus Gentium*, and from it
of the Law of Nations, was firstly an attempt to separate
from the Law of Nature such customs and laws as existed
between nations for their mutual relations, public and
private.   It was, also, an attempt to develop these laws
and customs according to the direction of Natural Law,
shown in man's reason and sense of equity.   A stimulus
was therefore given at the same time to an *a priori* and an
empirical development ;   to the old equitable conception of
the Law of Nature and reason which were to flourish greatly

in the age of enlightenment ahead ; and also to a careful concrete study of those international customs already in existence. For that reason the jurisconsults of the Continent, in particular the Dutch, fell with avidity not only on the question of the dominion of the seas, but on all those of commerce of which they had experience. Though many of the theorists dealt, like Grotius, almost exclusively with the public law of nations, concentrating on questions of war and peace, and dominion of the seas, others such as Loccenius [1] paid a good deal of attention to trade and private law in general. The best English statement of the relations between the public and private law of nations at the time is to be found in Sir R. Wiseman's *Law of Laws*, published in 1657. Their theory grew, of course, directly out of the Civil Law, but English theory had missed the whole development of the later civilians and canonists of Italy, France and Spain which lay behind the theoretical structures of the Low Country jurists. Selden and the other English scholars worked backwards to these writers, whence the thought which now affected them had worked forward. The form in which English commercial development was rationalised for legal purposes was fixed by continental moulds of thought.

It is to the influence of the Law of Nations that we must turn, therefore, for the impetus towards the seventeenth-century theory of Law Merchant in England. In spite of the earlier work of the Scottish civilian, William Welwod, which had a European reputation, the first strong direct influence of the Law of Nations on the development of English thought came through Selden's controversy with Grotius on the dominion of the seas. Since the object of this controversy was the public relations of states, its bearing on the subject of Law Merchant was not very obvious. It was the succeeding controversies carried on by the Admiralty against the Common Law Courts which began to bring more to the fore the specific questions of trade. For the Admiralty

[1] J. Loccenius, *De Jure Maritimo et Navali*, Stockholm, 1650.

Court, among other things, was fighting for the retention of its control over trade.   The seventeenth century, which saw the fall of the strong centralised administration built up in the preceding century, saw also the successful attack of the Common Law Courts on all rival jurisdictions.   While the brunt of the attack fell in the earlier part of the century on the Prerogative Courts which were so closely bound up with the Royal Administration, the older rivals of the Common Law, the Ecclesiastical Courts and the Admiralty had their own and longer battles to fight.   Throughout the century all the knowledge of the Admiralty lawyers was massed to resist the inroads of the common lawyers into their jurisdiction.

In the struggles of the Sea Law against the Land Law, questions of trade were only a part.   But the learning of the Admiralty civilians was quickly adapted to the needs of trade by writers of a new type.   Commerce had become a subject of enquiry for men of letters.   Some were pamphleteers, now the recognised classics of mercantilism, who rationalised and systematised the diverse economic experience of the preceding century, infusing into it the while the revolutionary element of individualism which replaced the old ideal of the " ordered trade " by the new ideal of enterprise.   Others more important to us here were the writers of purely descriptive works, merchants' handbooks, guides to the customs and conditions of trade.   In these we find writers who use the legal learning around them and turn it to their own purpose.   This they do in various ways —Malynes in his *Lex Mercatoria* ingeniously but casually, Roberts in his *Merchants Mappe of Commerce* with the diffidence of a very practical man, and Charles Molloy [1] in his *De Jure Maritimo et Navali* with the legal scholarship for which the Admiralty writers such as Godolphin and Zouch [2] had set the example.

[1] C. Molloy, *De Jure Maritimo et Navali*, 1676.   The name would appear to be taken from the title of Loccenius' work.

[2] J. Godolphin, *A View of the Admiral Jurisdiction*, 1661.   R. Zouch, *The Jurisdiction of the Admiralty of England Asserted*, 1663.

If familiarity with the continental method of treating the Law Merchant as part of the Law of Nations had a considerable importance in moulding the growing self-consciousness of English commercial customs, continental studies of the content of merchant customs played a still more important part in developing them. Here, too, the Admiralty learning is to be seen. William Welwod, the Scottish civilian, in his *Abridgement of all Sea-Lawes*,[1] a work which but inadequately fulfils its name, was the first English writer to lay stress on the comparative treatment of the sea laws of Europe. His study, though important in its time, was slight. Selden made a more careful study of the English material, but it was not till the Admiralty struggles of the 'sixties that wider knowledge was popularised. By that time, if only through Loccenius [2] and the commentary of Vinnius on Peckius,[3] the importance of the comparison of the Laws of Oleron and Wisby, the Hanse Laws and the Mediterranean Code, the Consulate of the Sea, was fully understood, and the texts were for the most part available for scholars. Such comparative treatment was of the highest value in expanding the range and applicability of English merchant custom ; of how great value can be seen by examining Molloy's *De Jure Maritimo et Navali*. Molloy, with his learning, makes use in this treatise of all these authorities for purposes of comparison, and also of the laws on insurance holding in Antwerp. His work is indeed of an importance which has seldom been recognised, for it is the practical starting-point for the work of the writers on Law Merchant in the following century, and still further for the first time in England, it definitely lays down

[1] 1st ed., 1613. It was inspired by the intention of Simon Shardius, prevented by his death to produce such a work (Welwod, *op. cit.*, p. 6). Shardius in his *De Varia Temporum in Iure Civili observatione . . . libellus Item Leges Rhodiorum Navales . . .* 1561, had already made the first edition of the Rhodian Laws. (Cf. W. Ashburner, *The Rhodian Sea Law*, Oxford, 1909, p. xli.)

[2] Loccenius, *op. cit.*

[3] A. Vinnius, *V. Cl. Petri Peckii In Titt. Dig. et Cod. Ad Rem Nauticam Pertinentes Commentarii*, 1647.

a body of law and custom in use at home or apposite abroad which covers not only Sea-Law but also Exchange. In Molloy the learning of the Sea Law is definitely turned to the rising claims of trade, and for the first time something in the nature of a body of merchant custom was laid down in England by an able lawyer.

The theoretical systematisation of merchant customs and their reduction to writing was in seventeenth-century England most rapid in the sphere of sea law, where the greatest concrete problem was the growing importance of marine insurance and the disputes arising from it. It was definitely a work of comparative learning. The elaboration of the established practice of Law Merchant was even greater in Exchange. The theory of exchange lay already in the past, in the work of the canonists who since the fourteenth century had striven to confine within the fabric of the usury laws the growing forces of exchange. Their importance was already held, in England at any rate, to be merely academic. The English thought these writers were men " by the reading whereof Merchants are like rather to meta-morphise their profession and become lawyers, than truely to attaine to the particuler knowledge of the . . . Law-merchant." [1] It was the concrete not the theoretical aspects of the work of Straccha, Scaccia and Molina [2] which gained an influence in England. When England herself first pro-duced a writer on the exchanges, he joined the ranks of those who sought to expound, not a theory of exchange and its lawfulness, but the nature of the rapidly developing exchange system. John Marius wrote his *Advice concerning Bills of Exchange* in 1651 ; in 1682 it was followed by John Scarlett's *Stile of Exchanges*. Nothing could be more ruthlessly practical than these works. Marius's work contains no mention of the equity, or reason of a Law Merchant national or international. Instead it is a complete exposition of the

---

[1] G. Malynes, *op. cit.*, p. 5.
[2] B. Straccha, *op. cit.* S. Scaccia, *op. cit.* L. Molina, *De Justitiae, Jure*, 1593.

Law Merchant in action. Without the intervention of law he shows the business of exchange dominated by rules national and international which have, through custom alone, the binding force of law.

The existence of such a body of customs was the very foundation on which the theory of Law Merchant was built. English writers had but to bring together the theory they had elaborated around the sea laws and the practice which they had recorded in Exchange to make up a full statement of the Law Merchant. It was Malynes who first dealt with these two aspects together ; Molloy who first handled them clearly and practically, and finally Alexander Justice in the introduction to his *General Treatise of Money and Exchanges*, 1707,[1] raised to a predominant part within the Law Merchant, the Law or Custom of Exchange.

By these means there had, by the end of the century, grown up in England a fairly consistent and complete exposition of merchant customs as they then existed ; an exposition which saw in them an expression of the Law of Nature and Nations, and which by the use of analogy and rationalisation had brought together a coherent statement of their practice.

What then, to turn to the second change of the seventeenth century, was the place of these customs in law ? The establishment of a theory of the nature of the Law Merchant and the reduction to writing of many of its customary workings were the outcome of real developments and serious needs. However excellent the customs, and however full the knowledge of them might be, they were useless unless they could be enforced. That is why the full theoretical formulation of the international Law Merchant so closely preceded or even coincided with its reception in one form or another into the national legal systems of Europe.

As commerce had grown, and with it the complications

---

[1] This work was based on S. Ricard's *Traité Général du Commerce*, 1702, but was greatly elaborated. See Justice's own preface, and Wm. Forbes, *A Methodical Treatise Concerning Bills of Exchange*, 1718 ; 1st edn., 1703. The later editions mention Justice's work with approbation, p. vii.

of business, the traditions, national and international, of the big markets had become of fundamental importance to its very existence. Where they could find no place in law these traditions had grown by convention and by the rulings of arbitrators.[1] The rulings of the arbitrators were based, like all law, on a mixture of equity (in which the Civil Law had its place) and of precedent, and the range they covered was extraordinary. To the honest merchant, whom the credit of the bourse bound as closely as any power of coercion, the rulings of arbitrators had all the weight of law. Yet there is no doubt that the absence of legal compulsion was often felt. It was this need that had led to the earliest legal developments in such trading centres as the Italian cities,[2] the French fairs,[3] and the English Staples. Even in England, indeed, where no court dealt with these new mercantile transactions, they had not been until the early seventeenth century entirely without contact with the law of the land. Though their cases found little room in Common Law and received little sympathy from the Courts of Equity and the Admiralty except on certain well-marked lines, the elasticity of the King's prerogative justice stood them in good stead. In the sixteenth century the appeals to the King's Council on subjects of trade became very common " forasmuche as the matter . . . consistethe and standeth muche uppon the orders and usages of merchauntes by whom rather than by course of law yt may be forwarded and determyned,"[4] and the council on many occasions gave legal force to commercial decisions by granting orders for arbitration by merchants or for *ad hoc* commissions. Moreover, this elastic and convenient method,

[1] For the early history of arbitration in England, cf. Thomas, *op. cit.*, pp. xxix–xxx.

[2] B. Straccha, *op. cit.* L. Goldschmidt, *Universalgeschichte des Handelsrechts*, 1891 edn.

[3] L. F. Bourquelot, *Etudes sur les Foires de Champagne*. Memoires présentés . . . a l'Academie des Inscriptions et Belles-lettres de l'institut Imperial de France. 1me serie, t. V, 1865.

[4] Quoted by R. G. Marsden, *Select Pleas in the Admiralty Court*, Selden Soc., II, p. lxxvi.

already recognised in the Middle Ages, seemed capable of growth. It would not have been difficult for courts merchant such as were found abroad to have been formed under the ægis of the prerogative justice, as the Commissioners of Assurance were founded in 1601. But in the seventeenth century, just as the customs of the Law Merchant were being systematised in England, and their importance had reached an unparalleled height, the destruction of the Council's judicial powers by the Long Parliament left merchant customs without this, their one contact with the law.

No doubt this helped to bring the problem of the future of Law Merchant to a head, and two possibilities began clearly to be recognised. It seemed clear that either some legal recognition must be given to merchant courts in which the customary Law Merchant could be administered and enforced, or else the triumphant Common Law courts must themselves adopt some means to give sanction to claims put forward under the customs of the Law Merchant. The merchants would certainly have favoured the introduction of merchant tribunals which would have led in opposite directions the Common Law and the Law Merchant. The Italian consuls' courts, as described by Straccha, were on the whole their ideal. Bacon, in his speech introducing the bill which established in 1601 the Commissioners of Assurance, expressed merchant opinion when he argued that " our Courts have not the knowledge of their Terms, neither can they tell what to say upon their Causes, which be secret in their Science, proceeding out of their experience." [1] Malynes prided himself greatly on his share in the institution of these same Commissioners. [2] Molloy welcomed the legislation whereby in 1663 an attempt was made to give their powers some effect, [3] while Cary, whose interests were far more insular than theirs, added his support to the continental idea of

[1] Sir S. D'Ewes, *Parliamentary Journal*, 1682, p. 669.
[2] *Op. cit.*, pp. 146–7.
[3] *Op. cit.*, pp. 247–8.

Courts of Merchants . . . for the speedy deciding all differences relating to Sea Affairs, which are better ended by those who understand them, than they are in Westminster-Hall.[1]

On the other hand, though the precedents of Common Law could find no place for them, the common lawyers, with their customary vigour, were anxious to find some way at this, the height of their power, to draw merchant cases into their courts. Whilst at first they could find no method but the clumsy fiction of an " assumpsit " they soon began to take a bolder line, and are found making use of the maxim, " The Law Merchant is part of the laws of this Realm." [2]

Throughout most of the seventeenth century it was clear perhaps that there would be some conclusion, but when or what was still obscure. Side by side with the mounting use of the Common Law courts in merchant cases, stood the inactive Commissioners of Assurance, while the great bulk of mercantile legal business was still carried out by customary arbitration without any legal sanction. It was not till the very end of the century that a decisive step was taken, and when it was, it was done in so unspectacular a manner that its importance then and later was scarcely recognised. By a statute of 9 and 10 William II, c. 15, it was laid down that, for the convenience of trade, arbitration awards could be made a rule of any of the King's courts of record, and appeals could be made to these courts for the enforcement of a judgment or for setting it aside should it be proved to be partial or illegal.[3] Thus for the first time the merchant custom was granted a real place in the Common Law. Until that time, though there were many indications,

---

[1] J. Cary, *Essay on the State of England in Relation to its Trade, its Poor and its Taxes,* Bristol, 1695, p. 27.

[2] W. Holdsworth, *History of English Law,* Vol. V, 145.

[3] In the fifteenth century a somewhat similar procedure was common in the Mayor's Court (cf. Thomas, *op. cit.,* p. xxix), and such cases could also be brought before the Court of Exchequer, but at this period little resort was made to the Court for this purpose, probably on account of the slowness and complexity of its procedure.

no definite assurance of the future could be given. Quite without the intention of its framers, this statute marks an important stage in the reception of the Law Merchant into the law of the land.

The legal uncertainty of the whole seventeenth century is reflected in the treatment by its writers of the relations between the law and the customary *Lex Mercatoria*, with its equitable and international background. Malynes contented himself with defining his *Lex Mercatoria* as " Customary Law . . . and not a Law established by the Soueraigntie of any Prince, either in the first foundation or by continuance of time," though he maintained that knowledge of it " is of so great consequence that without it all Temporall Lawes are not compleat," [1] while Marius, too practical to waste time upon so academic a matter, in his treatment of the business of exchange ignored the law courts altogether. " As for Attachments," he wrote in his Preface, " and some few other cases on Bils of Exchange, I have purposely omitted, lest I should give occasion to any turbulent spirit to make contest where none need. The right dealing Merchant doth not care how little he hath to do in the Common Law or things of that nature." [2]

None of them can hide, however, from subsequent observers the fact that the law of England, despite certain unexpected scruples of Holt,[3] and an occasional reversion by Chancery to mediæval conceptions of usury, was at the beginning of a great reception. The Law Merchant in its non-national and customary development, and in its social need, was breaking a way into the Common Law. It was not, it is true, an altogether steady progress. There were points on which Common Law and the merchant customs were definitely at variance. At the end of the century there was a flicker of opposition from the common lawyers

[1] G. Malynes, *op. cit.*, " Epistle to the Reader."

[2] J. Marius, *op. cit.*, 2nd edition, 1655, " To the Reader."

[3] Clerke *v.* Martin, 1702. Eng. Repts., 92, p. 6. See Holdsworth's explanation of his attitude on the negotiability of promissory notes, *op. cit.*, VIII, 171 *seq.*

against " Lombard St." which " attempted . . . to give
laws to " Westminster Hall," [1] and in return there was a
sharp though temporary intensification of the merchants'
claims for courts of their own.   Sir Josiah Child laid down a
series of suggestions for a merchants' court more strictly mercantile and summary than any in Europe where the Civil Law
stood behind them [2] ; Alexander Justice follows up every
case he reports with laments on the restrictions which the
law of the land imposed on trade.[3]

The reception of the Law Merchant which to the end of
the seventeenth century might still seem not quite certain
became in the eighteenth century inevitable.   It is this
certainty which is the clearest distinction of the eighteenth
century from its predecessor.   Merchants and lawyers both
recognised it.   Though the eighteenth-century merchant
writers might quote with some approval the plans for merchant courts proposed in the seventeenth century, they show
how far men's minds had departed from them.   Malachy
Postlethwayt, writing in 1751, paid lip service to these
ideas, but was nevertheless inclined to see in the Common
Law a movement favourable to the merchants' needs and
to the " fundamental principles and maxims of reason whereupon those peculiar laws and customs ought to be
grounded." [4]   Even Weskett, who as late as 1780 drew up
a scheme for merchant judges,[5] and was in consequence
reproved by Park for giving " another proof of the weakness
and fallibility of the human mind " [6] and for panting after
foreign institutions, meant much less in his scheme than

[1] Clerk *v.* Martin, 1702.   Eng. Repts., 92, p. 6.   Cf. W. Holdsworth,
VIII, 172.

[2] Sir Josiah Child, *A Discourse about Trade*, 1690, pp. 112 *seq.*

[3] [A. Justice], *A General Treatise of the Dominion and Laws of the Sea*,
1705, pp. 422, etc.

[4] *Op. cit.*, s.v. Bill of Exchange.

[5] J. Weskett, *Digest of the Theory, Laws and Practice of Insurance*, 1781,
p. 149.   The only exception appears to be Thomas Mortimer who, in his
Elements of Commerce, Politics and Finances (London, 1772), expresses
the greatest hostility to the Common Law.

[6] Sir J. A. Park, *A System of the Law of Marine Insurances*, 1787,
p. xxxviii.

the seventeenth-century writers had done. He speaks elsewhere in his learned work on Insurance, of the English
law, as taking from the civil and maritime laws what it
considers equitable.

The whole being corrected, altered, and amended, by acts of
parliament and common usage ; so that out of this composition
a body of jurisprudence is extracted, which owes its authority
only to its reception here by consent of the crown and people.[1]

It is clear that he really assumes a complete reception of
this customary law.

The eighteenth century, then, saw the completion of the
reception set on foot by its predecessor. There was no
change in the means by which this came about ; no break
in the systematisation of customs which was the essential
condition of it. The growth of purely practical literature
to meet the purely practical needs of merchant readers
served to mould together, as in a corpus, the traditions and
writings of the preceding century. Beawes' *Lex Mercatoria
Rediviva*,[2] Malachy Postlethwayt's *Universal Dictionary of
Trade and Commerce*,[3] Rolt,[4] Mortimer [5] and others are a
mine of acknowledged and (sometimes) unacknowledged
verbal borrowings from Marius and Roberts, Malynes and
Molloy. Moreover, new foreign influences of a systematising
kind can also be traced. The theory of international law
was growing steadily, and though the Admiralty Courts
had lost nearly all direct touch with trade, the international
problems of the great sea-wars kept them in touch with
the study of international law on the Continent. Indeed,

---

[1] p. 10.
[2] 1st edn., 1752. The author states that this work is based on that of
the two Savarys, but it is greatly changed to suit a later period and a
different place. It continued to be printed and enlarged after its author's
death.
[3] 1st edn., 1751. Originally based on Savary's *Dictionnaire*, this compilation always contained much extra material and by the time of the
enlarged 4th edn., 1774, the original material was quite swamped.
[4] R. Rolt, *A New Dictionary of Trade and Commerce*, London, 1756.
[5] T. Mortimer, *Elements of Commerce, Politics and Finances*, London,
1772.

under the leadership of Stowell the Admiralty Court had its
" short St. Martin's summer," [1] and gave in the development of Prize Jurisdiction, the last gift of the old Civil
Law to the legal organisation of England.   To serve its
needs it had brought together in the Library of the College
of Advocates at Doctors' Commons, editions of the Sea
Laws and Commercial Codes and a fine collection [2] of the
works of foreign jurisconsults, and of political theorists—
" these most excellent persons " as Molloy had said, " Who
joyned Policy to Law." [3]   Weskett relied on it greatly for the
long list of authorities appended to his work.   The interest
in international law, and the recognition of its underlying
principles was moreover at that time general.   The " réponse
sans réplique " to the Prussian king won its authors note
throughout English society [4]; the training of a statesman
was held to require a knowledge of the works of Puffendorf
and Burlamaqui ; Blackstone deplored the neglect by the
gentry of a common law become too complex for the amateur,
while

A fashion has prevailed, especially of late, to transport the growing hopes of this island to foreign universities, in Switzerland,
Germany, and Holland ; which, though infinitely inferior to our
own in every other consideration, have been looked upon as
better nurseries of the civil or (which is nearly the same) of their
own municipal law.[5]

At the same time a more popular type of foreign influence
was exerted by the introduction of the French literature for
merchants, Savary's *Parfait Négociant*,[6] his son's *Diction-*

[1] Maitland, *Roman Canon Law in the Church of England*, p. 97, 1898.
[2] Auction Catalogue of the Library of the College of Advocates, 1861.
[3] Molloy, *op. cit.*, Introduction, p. 6.
[4] John Holliday, *Life of Mansfield*, 1797. Cf. Sir E. Satow, *The Silesian Loan and Frederick the Great*, Oxford, 1915. For its text, see R. G. Marsden, *Law and Custom of the Sea*, Vol. II, pp. 348–74.
[5] *Commentaries*, 1844, ed. I, 4–5.
[6] 1st edn., 1675 ; for him see : A. Trouillier, *Jacques Savary*, Tijdshrift van Rechtgeschiedens, 1931, pp. 109 *seq.*, and H. Hauser, ' *Le Parfait Négo-ciant* ' *de Jacques Savary*, Révue d'histoire economique et sociale, 1925, pp. 1–28.

naire,[1] translated and remodelled by Malachy Postlethwayt, Samuel Ricard's *Négoce d'Amsterdam*, his *Traité Général du Commerce* [2] and many others. From them was gained, among much miscellaneous information, some knowledge of the new codifications of commercial law on the Continent which completed the reception of the Law Merchant into national law and which were to influence the eighteenth-century development of England as earlier compilations had affected her growth in the seventeenth century. Most important among these were the French Ordinances of Exchange of 1673 and of Marine Law and Insurance of 1681. There are several partial collections of these codes made in English translation during the eighteenth century. The earliest big collection of the new sea laws is to be found in N. Magens, *Treatise on Insurances*, 1755, a translation and enlargement of his earlier work in German published at Hamburg in 1753. The French Marine Ordinances are to be found in translation as early as 1705 in A. Justice, *A General Treatise of the Dominion and Laws of the Sea* . . . 1705. In 1760 was published the great Commentary of Valin on the Ordinance of 1681,[3] and it obtained rapid recognition in England, as did the works of Emérigon twenty and twenty-three years later.[4] This knowledge was gained purely for practical purposes. Nothing is more mistaken than to dismiss the compilations of such eighteenth-century writers as Weskett, Postlethwayt and Beawes as of no practical importance and " little more than an index to foreign ordinances and usages."

[1] *Dictionnaire Universel de Commerce, d'histoire naturelle, d'arts et métiers*, Paris, 1723–30.

[2] [A. Justice], *A General Treatise of Monies and Exchanges*, 1707, was based on a translation of this work.

[3] R. J. Valin, *Commentaire sur l'Ordonnance de la Marine du mois d'août* 1681, La Rochelle, 1760.

[4] B. M. Emérigon, *Nouveau Commentaire sur l'Ordonnance de la Marine du Mois août* 1681, Marseilles, 1780. *Traité des Assurances et des Contrats à la Grosse*, Marseilles, 1783. The greatest collection of the Laws of Exchange, J. G. Siegelius, *Corpus Juris Cambialis*, 1742, later continued by Uhlius, does not, on the other hand, appear to have been used in England, probably because it was almost all in German.

" I may be permitted to say without offence," said Weskett, " that in whatever court maritime and *commercial disputes* and litigations are brought for adjudication, those who are to plead or to adjudge in such courts, cannot be too well acquainted with the *maritime laws* of weight and authority that have been promulgated in all wise and civilised nations." [1]

While Postlethwayt, who prided himself on the completeness of his information on exchange, gave in his dictionary the clauses of the ordinances of France, Hamburg, Frankfort on Maine, Augsburg, Amsterdam, Leipzig and Bologna, as well as a number of cases which had occurred in Scotland, all valuable he considered, inasmuch as

They are supported by the authority of those, who are allowed to have wrote the best on the subject, according to the established customs of the principal trading nations in Europe.

Such illustrations, he pointed out, make clear that

besides the laws and usages which are peculiar to particular nations and great trading cities in regard to matters of this nature, there are fundamental principles and maxims of reason, whereupon those peculiar laws and customs ought to be grounded. [2]

It is against such a theoretical background as this that we must see the work in commercial law of Holt at the beginning of the eighteenth century, and still more of Mansfield in its latter half, when they began the definite move towards complete incorporation.   Mansfield has been judged by his contemporary enemies and his subsequent admirers as an alien and revolutionary influence working on English conditions. [3]   But when he drew from all sources material

---

[1] J. Weskett, *op. cit.*, p. 97.

[2] M. Postlethwayt, *op. cit.*, Bill of Exchange.

[3] Lord Campbell, *Lives of the Chief Justices of England*, II, 394, remembered the time when it was the custom at Westminster Hall to sneer at Mansfield as one who had tried " to introduce into the Common Law some ' equitable doctrines ' which had been rejected."   He attributes this to a reaction against his long supremacy, led by Eldon and Kenyon, his personal enemies.

His political opponents accused him of a preference for the Civil over the Common Law, on account of his Scots origin. *Letters of Junius*, ed. C. W. Everett, 1927, p. 178.

for a stabilisation of commercial law, he was doing nothing revolutionary except to organise and to bring into the law itself the knowledge and viewpoint of enlightened merchant opinion. His use of foreign examples, his quotation of the works of jurisconsults, his use of portions of the Civil Law, and finally, the tendency to stress, where necessary, equity rather than precedent, for which his political enemies blamed him, was definitely in accordance with the tone of his age, and it was not unduly in advance of it. Moreover, just as he commanded the comparative material of the latest mercantile custom, so he shared the changing attitude of his time towards law. There was the world of difference between his deft intermixture of equity and tradition, his admiration of Blackstone as the man who made Coke readable, and the hard rationalism of a young man who was at that time attending Blackstone's lectures, Jeremy Bentham. Yet, (though it would have appeared inconceivable to the latter), both Mansfield and Blackstone represented a link between Bentham's ruthless use of reason and the old law, which had become so formal in its dependence on precedent, for they deliberately set themselves to complete the recognition by it, on the grounds both of utility and reason, of a great part of the new *Jus Gentium* of their time, the usages of commerce.

The means whereby this development could be achieved had also become clearer in the eighteenth century. That Mansfield should have been able, between 1756 to 1788, to lay on a firm basis the commercial law of the future, is proof how far by that time the courts had already adapted themselves to the pressure of need and the theory it engendered. This is true in the two chief aspects of the growing Law Merchant. In the law both of insurance and of bills of exchange and similar credit instruments, the basis had been laid by the end of the seventeenth century, though for the merchants of the time it seemed narrow enough, for the work of the eighteenth century. Bitter as was Sir Josiah Child's complaint of the merchant at law " where after great

Expences of Time and Money, it is well if we can make our own Council (being common Lawyers) understand one half of our Case, we being amongst them as in a Foreign Country,''[1] by the end of the century it was clear that the Law Merchant and the Common Law were inevitably drawing together. This can be seen from a series of statutes; in 1698 the regulation of the position of inland bills of exchange[2]; in 1704 the recognition of the negotiability of promissory notes[3]; the Acts of 1710 and 1734 aimed unsuccessfully at gaming policies,[4] and the more ambitious one of 1746 against both wages and reinsurance[5]; all these laid upon the common courts inevitable duties of interpretation. The direction of the development was shown, moreover, by the provisions in the Act of 1720 incorporating the two new bubble insurance companies, the Royal Exchange Assurance and the London Assurance, whereby it was laid down that causes arising in the course of their business should be tried at Westminster Hall.[6] More important than all other statutory measures, however, was the recognition in 9 & 10 William III, c. 15 of arbitration awards, already mentioned. In consequence of this statute, Blackstone noted '' it is now become a considerable part of the business of the superior courts, to set aside such awards when partially or illegally made; or to enforce their execution, when legal . . .''[7] There was no surer way in which to bring into the body of the Common Law the customs of merchants which it was willing to recognise.

In the dictionaries of commerce and the merchant handbooks of all kinds can be seen how this incorporation was steadily going on. Among the quotations of foreign codes, of general customs, and of previous commentators, can now be seen a growing mass of English statutes and common law cases and the maxims which had by now become current

[1] Sir Josiah Child, *op. cit.*, p. 113.
[2] 9 Wm. III, c. 17.   [3] 3 & 4 Anne, c. 9.
[4] 9 Anne, c. 6 and 7 Geo. II, c. 8.
[5] 19 Geo. II, c. 37.   [6] 6 Geo. I, c. 18.
[7] Blackstone, *Commentaries*, iii, 16.

in the common law courts. Such cases and maxims, as Postlethwayt pointed out,

being maturely considered, will enable a thinking man to make a good judgment upon any other occurrences that relate to this important topic.

Their very voluminousness seemed to him valuable as covering more of " that infinite variety of transactions among mankind." Moreover,

Where cases are so faithfully and equitably reported as in England, a man of sense, though not bred to the law . . . may himself form a good judgment in most cases whether he is in the wrong or the right in going to law.

Statute Law appeared to him, indeed, less desirable, were it not that the judges could bring it by interpretation into line with the general trend of the law, for

in matters of law 'tis more for the advantage of the subject that Westminster Hall should, in this respect, controul St. Stephen's Chapel, than the latter the former ; for otherwise the statutes which do not always quadrate with the sense and spirit of the Law, would subvert a great part of it, and render all reported cases useless to posterity.[1]

The merchant thought, in the days of the growth of recognition of his law, as much of tradition as the common lawyer himself. In this way international custom was merging into national law. The general and the particular, the national and the international, were by this means hardening out, the one into a positive law, the other into a supplementary custom, and, so far advanced was the process, that even the consolidating work of Mansfield, invaluable as it was, aroused complaints among their number that, unlike his predecessors, he gave out "not the known settled principles of law, but general rules of equity." [2]

It was the same point of view as that of the eighteenth-century lawyers, who, speaking both of policy of insurance

---

[1] M. Postlethwayt, *op. cit.*, Bill of Exchange.
[2] J. Weskett, *op. cit.*, p. xvi.

and bill of exchange (instruments of a strong legal similarity), upheld, in the old words, " the *intent* of the agreement, the usage of merchants," but also " above all . . . judicial determinations which are the strongest evidence of the received Law of Merchants." [1]

[1] FitzGerald *v*. Pole, House of Lords, March, 1754, Eng. Repts., 2, p. 297.

II

The City of London and Politics

BIBLIOGRAPHICAL NOTE

CHAPTER 3

This chapter, though professing to be only a pioneering survey, has stood the test of time marvellously well. There has been a certain amount of subsequent work, but it has supplemented rather than corrected Dame Lucy's findings. Nicholas Rogers has written a thesis on metropolitan politics from 1733 to 1763, and has published a number of articles on his theme, the most relevant here being 'Resistance to Oligarchy: the City Opposition to Walpole and his Successors, 1725-47', in *London in the Age of Reform*, ed. J. Stevenson (Oxford, 1977). Paul Langford has published a book on *The Excise Crisis* (Oxford, 1975) and Ian Doolittle an article on 'The City Elections Act (1725)', *E.H.R.*, xcvii (1982). Finally, Dame Lucy's own essay on William Beckford in *The History of Parliament: the House of Commons 1754-1790*, eds. Sir Lewis Namier and J. Brooke (London, 1964), should not be forgotten. A distillation of information culled from a variety of out-of-the-way sources, it is a *tour de force*.

CHAPTER 4

There are two main aspects of Dame Lucy's lecture, the 'high politics' of ministerial manoeuvring and the relations between Government and the City financiers. Since 1960 neither subject has fared particularly well. Until very recently political historians steered clear of the period; perhaps they were intimidated by Namier's forbidding presence. However J.C.D. Clark's *The Dynamics of Change* (Cambridge, 1982) helps to fill the gap, and there is important work in hand. The 'City' aspect has been almost wholly neglected, though P.G.M. Dickson's *The Financial Revolution in England ... 1688-1756* (London, 1967) is an expert general guide to public finance up to 1756. Where Dame Lucy's lecture has been significantly supplemented is in relation to the role of public opinion, and here Paul Langford's 'William Pitt and Public Opinion, 1757', *E.H.R.*, lxxxix (1974), and Marie Peters's *Pitt and Popularity* (London, 1980) should be consulted.

CHAPTER 5

Not long after Dame Lucy delivered her lecture, George Rudé published his well-known *Wilkes and Liberty* (Oxford, 1961). Rudé collected a good deal of interesting information on the London 'mob' and on voting patterns in the City, Westminster and Middlesex, but nothing he wrote affected the validity of Dame Lucy's expert analysis of the political aspects of the subject. The relations between the Wilkites and the 'old guard' in the City, and indeed the relations between one 'Wilkite' and another, were exceedingly complex, and Dame Lucy's treatment of them remains unchallenged. The Wilkite phenomenon, quite apart from Wilkes himself, continues to attract attention of course, but few scholarly works have appeared since Rudé. Essays by John Brewer, particularly in *Party Ideology and Popular Politics* (Cambridge, 1976), and by Paul Langford in *London in the Age of Reform*, ed. J. Stevenson (Oxford, 1977), are honourable exceptions; they add to, rather than subtract from, Dame Lucy's work.

Alderman William Beckford
(Guildhall Library, London)

3

THE CITY OF LONDON IN EIGHTEENTH-CENTURY POLITICS

A STUDY of the part which the City of London played in the politics of the eighteenth century involves the examination of two distinct but interrelated topics. The first is limited and specific : the nature and influence of the City in what was then a comparatively new sense, that of its 'monied interest'. The second is wider and more nebulous : the nature of the political opinion and political influence of the City of London in its older sense of a civic entity.[1] Though the borderline between the two is necessarily often more than a little blurred, they involve two very different issues : — the study of the first is a matter of the mechanics of government ; that of the second is, in general, a study of the organization and inspiration of opposition. Though the first will be touched on in this article, its chief purpose is to indicate, however tentatively, the main considerations affecting the second.

The 'City' in the modern use of the term, the 'monied interest', was composed throughout this period of a small but growing number of persons closely and habitually concerned with that machinery for creating and mobilizing credit which had been taking shape since the late seventeenth century. Its organization was developing throughout the eighteenth century, particularly in time of war. Its institutional centre was to an increasing extent the Bank of England, assisted to a lesser degree by the other members of what contemporaries called the 'three great monied companies', the

[1] The phrase 'the City' was used in both senses by contemporaries throughout the century, and the context alone can indicate which is meant.

East India Company (with its own issue of short-term securities) and the South Sea Company, since its recovery from the crash of 1720 almost wholly a financial as distinct from a commercial organization.[1]   With these were associated to some extent the two insurance companies formed in 1720, the Royal Exchange Assurance Corporation and the London Assurance Corporation.[2]   Around this institutional centre there clustered the individual operators working on embryonic markets in stocks and shares, in insurance and in dealings in certain raw materials, a nexus of activities already foreshadowing the organization of a future when London was to become the money market of the world,[3] and already the opportunities it opened up to enterprising individuals were so promising as to lead the most vigorous and successful of the London merchants away from purely commercial activities towards those which were primarily financial.   The purposes for which capital and credit were mobilized were much more restricted then than now, and were more limited than they had been before the Bubble Act of 1720.[4]   They were, at least till the last quarter of the century, almost entirely restricted to the needs of overseas trade and public finance, and the second, particularly in time of war, bulked very large.   Indeed the fortunes of the richest of the monied men would seem at this time to have been largely made by satisfying the credit needs of the State; in subscriptions to Government loans, in Government remittances and in

[1] For this, see J. Clapham, *The Bank of England ; a History* (Cambridge, 1944), vol. i ; L. S. Sutherland, *The East India Company in Eighteenth Century Politics* (Oxford, 1952), chap. ii ; and 'Samson Gideon and the Reduction of Interest, 1749–50', below, pp. 399-413.

[2] The two Assurance Corporations were included, though in a lesser degree, with the three greater companies in arrangements for subscriptions to Government loans.   The most able financier of the first half of the century, Samson Gideon, addressing the Treasury on the means of raising the loan in 1757, speaks of the importance of 'securing the five Companies' (Chatsworth MSS. 512.3).

[3] The history of the origins of the Stock Exchange is still an uncharted field.   On the growth of marine insurance, see C. Wright and C. E. Fayle, *A History of Lloyd's* (1928).

[4] 6 Geo. I, c. 18.   See A. B. DuBois, *The English Business Company after the Bubble Act 1720–1800* (New York, 1938), pp. 1-41.

financing Government contracts.   It was this fact that gave
the monied interest its significance in politics.[1]

Though the rise of an embryonic money market was
making it possible for the State to mobilize to its own use
the resources of the monied individual, there was as yet none
of the impersonality of the modern public subscription.   The
method of raising loans was still so undeveloped and the
number of credit-worthy lenders so small that — although
shares in Government loans passed freely from hand to hand
and market prices were regularly quoted — the actual subscription to loans was normally undertaken as the result of
personal negotiations between the more important of the
monied men and the Directors of the monied companies on
the one hand and the Treasury on the other.   Thus each
Treasury in turn took pains to forge its personal links with
the monied interest in the City, and the relations between
them became very close.   Moreover, in the intricate game of
eighteenth-century political management the Treasury would
often make it clear not only that they would tend to confine
financial advantages to their friends in the City, but that they
would give preference to those friends who were also members of parliament and could thus provide a vote on the Government's side in the House of Commons.   In consequence
the chief monied men in the City, unless they were disquali-
fied by religion [2] or nationality,[3] found it worth while to buy
expensive borough seats (they might, of course, have done so
in any case if they were seeking to use their wealth to move
into the ranks of the landed gentry) to qualify for the reception of financial favours from the Government.   And the
men who made up the nucleus of the monied interest, both
within and outside the House, remained throughout the century in close alliance with the Government of the day.

The influence of such men on the Governments with

[1] Sir Lewis Namier first analysed this situation in *The Structure of Politics
at the Accession of George III* (1929), i. 56 *seq.*
[2] As was Samson Gideon, the great Jewish financier.
[3] As was Sir Joshua Vanneck, of Dutch birth.   See L. B. Namier, *op. cit.*,
i. 70.

which they were in alliance was considerable, both in purely financial matters [1] and on other issues related to them. The combined opposition of the monied interest prevented the reduction of the interest on the National Debt, though Walpole was known to favour it, in 1737,[2] and Pelham only succeeded in carrying out his conversion operation of 1749–50 after making liberal compensations to the main institutions involved.[3] Not only were the terms of Government loans bargained for in advance between the Treasury and their leaders,[4] but their advice on the finance of war was taken on occasion in connexion with peace negotiations,[5] and those of them who sat in the House were often employed as experts on a variety of commercial issues. Their importance as a political force can, however, easily be over-emphasized. Eighteenth-century politicians sometimes gave credence to a myth not unlike that of the 'bankers' ramp' of the twentieth century, and maintained that ministries could be overthrown or rendered impotent by the 'loss of the City' engineered by political opponents. But their only illustration of a ministry 'losing the City' to opponents (and this a confused and inconclusive one) dated back to 1710–11.[6] Though it was some-

[1] Namier, *op. cit.*, pp. 56 *seq.*, and L. S. Sutherland, 'Samson Gideon: Eighteenth Century Jewish Financier', *Transactions of the Jewish Historical Society of England*, xvii. 79 *seq*. See below, pp. 387-98.

[2] The best contemporary evidence for this abortive attempt is the diary of the first earl of Egmont *Historical Manuscripts Commission, Diary of the firs Earl of Egmont*, ii. 380 *seq.*, and correspondence in the *Carlisle MSS., Hist. MSS. Comm.*, pp. 182 *seq.*

[3] L. S. Sutherland, 'Samson Gideon and the Reduction of Interest', *loc. cit.*

[4] This is shown by L. B. Namier, *op. cit.*, i. 68 *seq.*, for 1759, and L. S. Sutherland for other occasions in the two articles quoted above.

[5] For instance, W. Coxe, *Memoirs of the Administration of the Rt. Hon. Henry Pelham* (1829), ii. 318, H. Pelham to Newcastle, 23 Sept.–4 Oct. 1748. 'I have made the best inquiry I can, amongst all the men of business in the city, and I can assure you, they are all of opinion, that peace is absolutely necessary.' On 1 Oct. 1762 the duke of Cumberland consulted Newcastle, recently out of office, on the financial prospects if the peace negotiations fell through. Newcastle consulted a City friend, Thomas Walpole, son-in-law and partner of Sir Joshua Vanneck, who replied that, given a Minister they trusted, 'he thought the money might be had, taking advantage of the present general dislike to the terms of Peace' (Brit. Mus., Add. MSS. 32944, f. 36).

[6] The part played by the monied interest led by the Bank in the fall of Godolphin in 1710 (see J. Clapham, *The Bank of England ; a History*, i. 73 *seq.*,

times claimed that the attempt to oust the Pelhams in 1746 was defeated by the determination of the monied interest to refuse supplies to an alternative administration,[1] this does not seem to be supported by facts; the difficulties which the Devonshire-Pitt administration found in raising supplies in 1757 [2] were not due to political causes; and the hopes of the duke of Newcastle, when dismissed from office in 1762, that his successors would be unable to obtain credit, were disappointed.[3]   In fact, the City, in the sense of its monied interest, was throughout the period a broken reed for the purposes of party politics, for the good reasons that the prosperity of all its members depended on their being on terms with the Government of the day, and that, even if it might have paid them to hold out for a short time, they were much too competitive among themselves to do so.   As early as 1711 Daniel Defoe had argued that it was not the maxim 'They that have the Money must have the Management' which was true, but 'They that have the Management will have the Money'.[4]

So much for the City in the modern sense of the word. In its older sense the City was a great urban centre, by far the greatest in the British Isles, with a population within its ancient boundaries of about 150,000, and a dependent popu-

and C. Buck and G. Davies, 'Letters on Godolphin's dismissal in 1710', *Huntington Library Quarterly*, 1940, pp. 225 *seq.*) and the financial difficulties in Harley's Ministry (see 'Memoirs of the Harley Family, especially of Robert Harley, first Earl of Oxford, by Edward Harley, Auditor of the Exchequer', *Hist. MSS. Comm., Report on Portland MSS.*, v. 650 *seq.*) remains an obscure incident.   Eighteenth-century politicians bore it in mind.   In 1762 Newcastle deplored the threat of the governor of the Bank of England to retire in disgust at the Bute Ministry.   'Besides his successor would probably not be so good a friend as he is, and the Bank might fall into bad hands as it did when Sir G. Heathcote was overpowered by Sir James Bateman and John Ward in my Lord Oxford's time' (Add. MSS. 32940, f. 373, Newcastle to Hardwicke, 16 July 1762).

[1] H. Fox to Ilchester, 13 Feb. 1746, quoted in Ilchester, *Henry Fox, First Lord Holland* (1920), i. 125.   But see W. Coxe, *op. cit.*, i. 289.

[2] Add MSS. 32870, ff. 437 *seq.*

[3] *Ibid.* 32944, ff. 22 *seq.* (Substance of a conversation with the duke of Cumberland, Oct. 1762), and Add MSS. 32940, ff. 302b-3 (Newcastle to J. West, 9 July 1762).

[4] *Eleven opinions about Mr. H[arle]y ; with Observations*, 1711, p. 43.

lation of about 700,000.[1]   It had a proud and ancient corporation from which many of its residents were excluded but
which nevertheless comprised some 12,000–15,000 freemen
by birth, apprenticeship or redemption[2] (some 8000 of
whom were also liverymen of the City Companies) and a
vigorous corporate spirit which expressed the attitude of its
'middling men', as contemporaries called them, the class of
small merchants, tradesmen and master craftsmen.   It was
they who dominated its Common Council, elected its four
members of parliament and, both in the Common Hall and
Common Council, played a great part in the election of City
officers, from the Mayor downwards.[3]   And if the richest men
in the City, its 'monied interest', were supporters of the
Governments of the day, the City in this wider sense was
almost always in opposition to them.   If the state of City
opinion be examined for the sixty-two years between the rise
of Walpole in 1720 and the fall of Lord North in 1782, in
the records of the Common Council,[4] in the utterances of the
City members, in pamphlet and press and the comments of
contemporaries, it becomes clear that the City abandoned its
anti-ministerialism only on occasions when there was some
special explanation of the fact, and that the occasions were
comparatively few.   Such exceptions were the years 1747–54,
when Henry Pelham had set himself to placate the City, as
he was placating all the opponents of his Broad-bottomed
Administration;[5] the years 1756–61, when William Pitt was
carrying on his two war ministries on principles with which
the City was deeply concerned; to them may perhaps be
added the first months of the Chatham administration, when
the name of the late Great Commoner still exercised its spell.[6]

[1] For the problem of the population of London, see M. D. George, *London
Life in the Eighteenth Century* (1930), pp. 21-9.
[2] S. and B. Webb, *English Local Government . . . The Manor and the
Borough* (1908), ii. 574 *seq.*   [3] *Ibid.*
[4] The Journals preserved in the Guildhall Records Office.   See also vol. 8
of the Common Hall Books. 1751–88.
[5] Sutherland, 'Samson Gideon and the Reduction of Interest', *loc. cit.*
[6] The first Rockingham Administration, despite its active support of certain
trading interests (Sutherland, 'Edmund Burke and the First Rockingham
Ministry', *E.H.R.*, xlvii, 40 *seq.*; below, 299-325.), never succeeded in winning

But these years are, at the most, no more than eleven out of a total of sixty-two. For the rest of the time there was suspicion and antagonism, flaring from time to time, in the excitements of political life, into violent hostility.

The question arises, what was the reason for this remarkable consistency in opposition, a consistency which survived changes of kings and administrations and bore so little relation to the ruling persons or forces of the day? There are several possible explanations. Two of them are at bottom based on economic considerations. The first possible explanation is that the attitude was the outcome of friction and conflict within the City itself. In eighteenth-century London there was, partly as a heritage of seventeenth-century strife and even earlier traditions, and partly as a result of contemporary tendencies, a good deal of that latent hostility between the richest citizens and the lesser men which is familiar (as the struggle between 'Magnati' and 'Popolani') to students of the independent communes of Europe. The antagonism was social, economic and political in its origin and showed itself in friction within the City constitution (for instance, in disputes between the Court of Aldermen and the Court of Common Council)[1] and a tendency to seek emancipation from oligarchic leadership and control (for instance, in the choice of the four City members of parliament and sometimes of the chief City officers).[2] The fact that many of these rich citizens were supporters of the Government was in itself likely to lead the lesser men to array themselves with the Opposition,[3] and there were two special reasons

a good press in the City, even the repeal of the Stamp Act being generally attributed to Pitt (*e.g. Public Advertiser*, 1765, *passim*).

[1] The internal friction in the City and its connexion with national politics has been carefully analysed by A. J. Henderson, *London and the National Government, 1721–42* (Duke University Press, 1945).

[2] Instances of the latter are the election of Deputy James Hodges, as Clerk of the City in 1757 (for the controversy surrounding this, see *The Test*, 23 April 1757, pp. 134 *seq.*, and *The Contest*, 28 May 1757, pp. 165 *seq.*).

[3] The aldermen, though popularly elected, were elected by wards, the characters of which varied considerably; they held office for life and it was widely held that a fortune of not less than £30,000 was a necessary qualification. In consequence, though there were always some 'popular' aldermen among

which strengthened this trend. Firstly, in 1725, in his
London Election Act, Walpole had ranged the Government
on the side of the oligarchic faction in the City by giving the
sanction of law to the traditional power of 'Aldermanic Veto'
over the Common Council, and though Pelham repealed the
relevant clause of the Act twenty-one years later, much
bitterness had been engendered in the meantime.[1] Secondly,
those outside the 'monied interest' were bitterly jealous of
the advantages made available to the monied men by the
method of taking up subscriptions to Government loans
already referred to, and they clamoured loudly for an 'open'
subscription in which they could all join, a demand which
the Treasury seldom thought it prudent to satisfy.[2] Thus it
felt of most ministers, as was said of Walpole (however
unjustly), that 'he is hated by the city of London, because he
never did anything for the trading part of it, nor aimed at any
interest of theirs, but a corrupt influence over the directors
and governors of the great monied companies.'[3] But this
internal friction, though no doubt an important contributory
factor to the City's attitude in national politics, does not seem
of itself sufficient to explain the vigour of its anti-ministerialism. Nor does it explain why this anti-ministerialism
was abandoned in special circumstances.

A second economic explanation might lie in the interest
of the City in maritime and colonial war. The commercial
classes of the eighteenth century were exceedingly bellicose
in their sentiments, provided that the wars they were fighting were sea-wars and the aim of them was the retention or
gain of colonial territory, for in such wars they saw prospects of private commercial gain as well as hopes of national

them, the majority tended to express the views of the monied interest, though
few of them at any one time played a prominent or active part in this interest.
When feeling ran very strong in the City, as in the later years of Walpole, or
during Wilkes's predominance in the City, they tended to bow to it in the long
run, but only after a considerable time-lag and always with a strong minority
holding out.

[1] Henderson, *op. cit.*, pp. 74 *seq.*
[2] Sutherland, 'Samson Gideon and the Reduction of Interest', *loc. cit.*
[3] *Some Materials towards Memoirs of the Reign of King George II by John
Lord Hervey*, ed. R. Sedgwick (1931), i. 138.

glory.[1] Indeed there is some truth in Burke's bitter description of the merchants in 1775 as beginning 'to snuff the cadaverous *haut gout* of lucrative war'.[2] They were also, however, the first to be struck in their pockets as well as their pride when such wars went badly, so that the events of the period in time of war, or in the years leading up to war, or (in the reign of George III) the years of conflict with the American colonies, gave ample opportunity for friction between the Governments and the body of commercial and trading opinion finding expression in the City. But this explanation, too, though it may account for the timing of most of the biggest outbursts of anti-ministerialism, is insufficient in itself to explain the whole movement, and fails to make clear why it was maintained in years of peace. Nor do either of these economic explanations account for the forms in which this feeling found expression.

If these two explanations are dropped the conclusion remains that the key to this tendency in the City must be sought in causes less obvious but perhaps even deeper-seated. These causes are best elucidated by considering the relations of the City with the other Opposition interests in national politics, bearing in mind at the same time the stamp set on the activities of the City by its own traditions and experience. If the parliamentary Oppositions of the eighteenth century are examined the first thing that becomes clear is that (oddly enough, at first sight, in an age when ministries made majorities and not majorities ministries) they always sought to bolster themselves up and embarrass their enemies in power by attracting the support of bodies of opinion outside the House. As Burke, one of the most experienced Opposition leaders of the century, remarked, 'we know that all opposition is absolutely crippled if it can obtain no kind of support without doors'.[3] They sought this

---

[1] R. Pares, *War and Trade in the West Indies, 1739–1763* (Oxford, 1936), pp. 56–64.

[2] FitzWilliam and R. Bourke, *The Correspondence of the Rt. Hon. Edmund Burke* (1844), ii. 50.

[3] *Ibid.* ii 51-2.

support in general from two classes, the country gentry, who influenced and were influenced by those independent country gentlemen in the House whose role Sir Lewis Namier has so brilliantly analysed in his Romanes Lecture,[1] and in the body of organized commercial and trading opinion in the City of London. And, when they were successful in gaining this support, they did so by calling to their aid political assumptions and prejudices which were accepted by gentry and merchants alike without question — and which were indeed accepted by everyone except the small ring of persons directly concerned with the day-to-day questions of political power — the seventeenth-century suspicion of the Executive and the desire to limit the scope of its activities. For some forty-five years after the Hanoverian Succession every Opposition, whatever its nature and its real end, pinned its faith on rallying the support of these two powerful extra-parliamentary forces by 'out-whigging the whigs'. They produced a programme which expressed an archaic, academic whiggism, by incorporating the demand for a Place or Pensions Bill, the return to triennial parliaments and the reduction of the standing army.[2] And even in the reign of George III when Opposition found new and sometimes more realistic war-cries, the old ones had not lost their charm.

Moreover, though everyone with inside knowledge of politics knew that no group or party intended to implement these doubtful political principles, the fact that they were so widely accepted made them embarrassing to Governments. These even went so far on occasion (particularly just before a general election) as to let measures incorporating them through the House of Commons, to be quashed in the safety of the Lords, knowing, as it was said in 1731, that to vote

[1] L. B. Namier, *Monarchy and the Party System* (Oxford, 1952). See also his 'Country Gentlemen in Parliament 1750–1785', *History Today*, Oct. 1954, pp. 676–688. Both are reprinted in *Personalities and Powers* (1955).
[2] Extremists sometimes demanded annual parliaments and the total abolition of the standing army, but in the first half of the century they were rare and somewhat eccentric.

against such measures 'would put a great many gentlemen under difficulties' so that they 'must have left them or have hurt their own interest very much in the places they serve for'[1]— an argument which also throws some light on the passing of Dunning's famous Resolution of 1780.[2]

The counties and the City filled somewhat different rôles in the system of Opposition parties. Opinion expressed in the counties was intended to impress the country gentlemen in the House, and was dispersed and loosely organized. That stirred up in the City was much easier to organize and mobilize. City leaders were expert, from long experience of organizing commercial agitation affecting both London and the 'outports', in the art of bringing pressure to bear on authority from without. Petitions, instructions from the Common Council to the City representatives, pamphlets and press campaigns were rapidly planned there, while whenever political excitement ran high the London crowd could be relied on to emerge and give the added support of their clamour to the Opposition cause.

Both these extra-parliamentary allies presented Opposition leaders with some problems, but they were different ones. The country gentry might get out of hand, as from the point of view of the Opposition parties they did at the time of the County Associations. The duke of Newcastle warned his colleagues in Opposition in 1767, 'I know the

---

[1] *Hist. MSS. Comm., Carlisle MSS.*, p. 82. Hon. C. Howard to [Lord Carlisle]. The Pensions Bills of 1730, 1731 and 1732 were handled in this way. The Place Bills of 1734 and 1739 were thrown out by the House of Commons only by small majorities, the first by 39 and the second by 16 votes. The ministers tried to avoid speaking on them.

[2] 'That the influence of the Crown has increased, is increasing and ought to be diminished.' 6 April 1780 (*Parliamentary Register*, xvii. 453). It was passed by a majority of 18 votes in a full House against the Ministry, despite the fact that the North Administration was normally strong in the House at this time ; but it had no consequences. The general election which took place later in the year had not yet been decided on, but it was clear it could not be long delayed. Lord Shelburne told the Common Council of London in reply to a congratulatory letter on the Resolution : 'It is universally acknowledged that the approaching Election has a considerable influence on the members who now support the petitions of the people', and added that the county members 'are understood to have voted for the most part uniformly on the same side'. Guildhall Records Office. Journal of the Common Council, 68, f. 49.

nature and the pulse of our country gentlemen. They are now as well and as quiet as possible ; set them in motion and nobody can tell what may arise.'[1] But this problem was only an extension of the general one of handling the independent gentry in the Commons. But the City, though it could be rallied to the Opposition cause, always had to be handled as a separate entity, following (as the country gentry never did) some specifically City leader who was thought of as one of themselves, and it was a force which approached politics in a manner from outside. It was, indeed, this sense of separatism, of standing outside the dominant social and political system of the time, that gave the City in Opposition its peculiar flavour, and it was this sentiment (which lay at the root of the attitude which the nineteenth century was to call Radicalism) which really explains the persistency of the City's tendency to political opposition. Socially the attitude expressed itself in some resentment against and suspicion of the aristocracy and landed classes, with their easy arrogance and assumption of superiority, and in a somewhat self-conscious and self-righteous pride in their bourgeois virtues and bourgeois traditions — this finds its echo in literature and in drama intended largely for their consumption.[2] Politically, there is evidence of a feeling that they and their interests lay outside the framework of a political system dominated by and organized for the interests of the aristocracy and landed classes, and an irritation because they, with their stake in the prosperity of the country and their contribution to it, were apt to be in the position of outsiders having to bring pressure to bear on the political machine.

[1] Add. MSS. 32980, f. 355, Newcastle to Richmond, 20 March 1767. The occasion was a suggestion by Richmond that the Grand Jury of Sussex should thank the county members for their vote on the reduction of the Land Tax in which the Government was defeated. He remarked, '. . . I am not for opening a correspondence between the Grand Jury and their members. Every man may start a disagreeable thing in a Grand Jury, who can do no hurt in the County. It may put it in the head of some lively geniuses to give instructions, or, at any time, to observe upon the votes and behaviour of their members, which would not be pleasant.' *Ibid*. f. 354.

[2] The writings of Daniel Defoe are early expressions of this attitude. The so-called 'bourgeois' drama of the period shows its influence very strongly.

It is true that arguments have been adduced which would seem to run counter to such an explanation. It is pointed out that there was an easy and constant transit from the merchant classes into those of the landed gentry, and that, not only were commercial questions one of the major concerns of eighteenth-century parliaments, but also that a very considerable number of merchants sat in the House of Commons.[1] But it is important to bear in mind the cleavage between the rich merchant and financial classes and the lesser men. Most of the latter lived lives entirely circumscribed by their urban traditions; a seat in parliament was quite outside their ambitions, and they neither considered that their richer fellow-citizens who obtained seats in the House represented them nor that they represented the commercial interests with which they were concerned. The author of *The Remembrancer*, for instance, in 1748 complains bitterly of the prominent citizens who are to be seen cringing at levées and seeking seats in the House of Commons 'and instead of assisting as they ought to preserve and enlarge the traffic of the kingdom, assisting to traffic it away for the sake of a lucrative share in some contract, some remittance or some other dirty consideration of a like nature'; and he urges that a line should be drawn 'between the m[inisteria]l posse of stock-jobbers, contractors, remitters . . . etc., and the fair and upright exporter' and that one should 'confine the reputable title of *merchant* to the latter and admit of his verdict only in commercial matters'.[2]

This combination of participation in the general political assumptions and activities of the nation and of peculiar local separatism and self-consciousness can be traced throughout the history of the City's political activities during the century. It is possible also to trace the way in which the City's self-consciousness became stronger and more articulate under the pressure of events and with the passing of time; and as it grew, so too did the scope and effectiveness of City influence

[1] For the merchants in the House, see Namier, *Structure of Politics*, i. 56 *seq.*
[2] *The Remembrancer*, 3–10 Sept. 1748, quoted in the *Gentleman's Magazine* (1748), pp. 411-12.

in and over the parliamentary Oppositions with which they were in alliance. A brief (and necessarily imperfect) analysis of those stages in the City Opposition, corresponding also to stages in the history of eighteenth-century parliamentary Opposition, will illustrate this development. The same three periods correspond roughly with those of the personal predominance of three of that curious succession of leaders on which the City's political influence so strikingly depended.

The first period runs roughly from 1720 to 1754, that in which united parliamentary Oppositions, composed of combinations of discontented whigs and broken tories (grouping themselves for some years round the prince of Wales), fought what was on the whole a losing battle against the great whig governing connexion built up by Robert Walpole and continued by Henry Pelham — a losing battle, though Walpole himself was overthrown during its course. At this time the City's leader was a stout, high-principled merchant and ship-insurer of no more than moderate wealth, Sir John Barnard,[1] who represented the City in parliament for nearly forty years. During his prime he was a constant and effective speaker, hardly ever missed a debate [2] and never compromised a principle. He was an inveterate enemy of the financial interests,[3] was responsible for the Act for preventing 'the infamous practice of stock-jobbing',[4] 'which, if it had been effective, would have prevented the rise of the Stock Exchange altogether, and though he never compromised his independence, he seems to have believed implicitly that the purpose of the Opposition which hounded Walpole from power was to carry out those whiggish measures to which it paid lip-service. Under this leader the commercial interests of the City were kept well to the fore, and one of the biggest of the

---

[1] 1685–1764, b. Reading, son of a wine-merchant, M.P. for London 1722–61, knighted 1732, sheriff 1735, Lord Mayor 1737: *Memoirs of the late Sir John Barnard, Knight* (1776); *Reasons offered to the Consideration of the worthy citizens of London for continuing the present Lord Mayor . . . for another year*, 1738.

[2] *Reasons offered to the Consideration of the worthy citizens of London for continuing the present Lord Mayor . . . for another year*, 1738.

[3] See Sutherland, 'Samson Gideon and the Reduction of Interest', *loc. cit.*

[4] 7 Geo. II, c. 8.

Opposition drives, that against the Excise Bill of 1733, arose on a question primarily of commercial importance, but the remoteness of the City from the day-to-day realities of politics and its political naïveté made it little more than an adjunct to any Opposition leader who chose to play on its academic 'whiggism' and its sense of grievance and isolation. The oratory of William Pulteney,[1] for instance, greatly attracted City support and, on the fall of Walpole in 1742, it was widely believed that sweeping constitutional changes would follow. A contemporary describes the ferment of excitement on this occasion, in which the City warmly joined.

Among those who thought themselves most moderate, no two men agreed upon what was necessary ; — some thinking that all security lay in a good place bill . . . some in a pension bill. Some in triennial parliaments . . . some [were] for annual parliaments . . . some for a reduction of the Civil List . . . some for the sale of all employments . . . some for taking the disposition of them out of the Crown . . . some for allowing them to subsist but to be given only to those who were not in Parliament, that is, among themselves . . . some for making the army independent ; others for no regular troops at all.[2]

When it became apparent that, in fact, nothing was to be done, the disillusionment in the City knew no bounds. For years Pulteney appears in City oratory as the great betrayer, whose example must be a warning to those who put their trust in politicians.[3]

During this time, though their detachment from the day-to-day preoccupations of politics was marked, there was still little overt expression of their political and social sense of separateness. There is, however, a good deal of indirect evidence of social and political malaise quite apart from their response to the demands of Oppositions upon them. It is usually disguised, in contemporary references, under the

[1] William Pulteney, earl of Bath, 1684–1764.
[2] *Faction Detected by the Evidence of Facts* [Lord Perceval, later earl of Egmont] (1743), pp. 69-70.
[3] *E.g.* [Richard Glover] *Memoirs of a Celebrated Literary and Political Character* (1813), pp. 1-7.

title of City Jacobitism ; but the more this alleged Jacobitism is examined, the more it appears to be nothing other than a vague and unorganized dislike of the authorities. Horace Walpole said of the 'popular' Alderman Blakiston that he had 'risen to be an alderman of London on the merit of that succedaneum to money, Jacobitism'.[1]   But the sober Lord Waldegrave was nearer the mark when he told George II in 1758 'that as to Jacobitism, it was indeed at a low ebb ; but there was a mutinous spirit in the lower class of people . . .'.[2]

The next period, however, brought some major changes. This second period may be taken to cover that strange interlude in English political history when, in the war years between 1756 and 1761, William Pitt, the Great Commoner, broke through the chains of government by connexion and forced himself, on equal terms, on the group who had been ruling the country for the last forty years. He maintained himself in this precarious position by the general recognition of his essentiality to win the war and by his popularity not only with the country gentry in parliament but with public opinion outside the House. It has sometimes been claimed for the Great Commoner that he was the first eighteenth-century politician to realize the value of the support of public opinion. This is not true, but he was the first to try to continue using in power the support of outside forces hitherto thought to be available only to Opposition.[3]   In consequence in this period the City suddenly found itself in alliance with Government instead of opposing it, and though, after Pitt's coalition with Newcastle in 1757, the City leaders continued as suspicious of his allies as ever — at one time Newcastle accused Pitt of 'letting the mob loose' on them [4] — they adopted

[1] Horace Walpole, *Memoirs of the Last Ten Years of the Reign of George II* (1822), i. 31.

[2] James, Earl Waldegrave, *Memoirs from 1754 to 1758* (1821), p. 130.

[3] In December 1761 the *Gentleman's Magazine*, p. 579, giving extracts from *Charges against the Late Minister with remarks extracted from a variety of Letters*, including the statement 'An opposition to government will always please and gain the people of England, who are great levellers', adds the note that this has not been true for the last four years.

[4] Newcastle to Hardwicke, 27 March 1758, quoted in P. C. Yorke, *Life and Correspondence of Philip Yorke Earl of Hardwicke* (Cambridge 1913), iii. 44.

with enthusiasm the rôle of representatives of the nation supporting the actions of a great national leader. The means by which this support was applied to Administration were the same as those by which it had been given to leaders of the Opposition. It was, as before, under the guidance of a City leader, no longer Sir John Barnard, who was not only nearing the end of his career, but had lost some of his popularity by coming to terms with the Pelham Administration, but a new man, Alderman William Beckford,[1] a rich Jamaica sugar-planter. The new leader was very different from the old : Barnard was first and foremost a merchant and citizen ; Beckford had some interests in and connexions with the City,[2] but also much in common with the landed classes, had sat for Shaftesbury before he became member for London, and he began to foster his interest in the City (taking up his freedom in 1752, and becoming an alderman in the same year) only two years before offering himself as a parliamentary candidate. Active for some time in Opposition politics,[3] he obviously saw the chance of strengthening his political position by having the support of the City behind him, and after he had become the devoted supporter of Pitt he made no secret of the fact that he meant to use his power in the City to further the cause of his patron in national politics.

The propaganda and leadership of Beckford and the personal magnetism of Pitt produced, paradoxically, two conflicting results in the City during these years. In the first place, the City gained greatly in its sense of importance and

[1] 1709–70, born in Jamaica, where his family had great estates and his father was governor ; M.P. for Shaftesbury 1747–54, London 1754–70 ; Lord Mayor 1761 and 1769. A statue was erected to him in Guildhall for his speech when delivering a petition to the king in 1770.

[2] He was described as a West-India merchant, but his trading interests seem to have been restricted to handling the produce of his own estates. In *The Gazetteer and London Daily Advertiser*, 25 April 1754, 'A Liveryman' asks 'If one of your candidates is not Member of a Club of Planters, where merchants are judged unworthy of admittance ?' Beckford claimed that his 'family were citizens, and some of them had borne the highest offices for a century past'. (Speech when elected Lord Mayor in 1762, *Public Advertiser*, 30 Sept. 1762.)

[3] See, *e.g.*, *The Diary of the late George Bubb Dodington* (ed. H. P. Wyndham, 1784), p. 100, and pp. 235-6 ; Namier, 'Country Gentlemen in Parliament' *loc. cit.*, pp. 683 *seq.*

the articulateness of its traditions and outlook. A speech by Beckford in the House in 1761 expresses the attitude of those he was leading. Having referred to the 'sense of the people', he proceeded to define it.

The sense of the people, Sir, is a great matter. I don't mean the mob ; neither the top nor the bottom, the scum is perhaps as mean as the dregs, and as to your nobility, about 1200 men of quality, what are they to the body of the nation ? Why, Sir, they are subalterns, I say, Sir, . . . they receive more from the public than they pay to it. If you were to cast up all their accounts and fairly state the ballance, they would turn out debtors to the public for more than a third of their income. When I talk of the sense of the people I mean the middling people of England, the manufacturer, the yeoman, the merchant, the country gentleman, they who bear all the heat of the day. . . . They have a right, Sir, to interfere in the condition and conduct of the nation which makes them easy or uneasy who feel most of it, and, Sir, the people of England, taken in this limitation are a good-natured, well-intentioned and very sensible people who know better perhaps than any other nation under the sun whether they are well governed or not.[1]

Odd though these words must have sounded in the mouth of a wealthy slave-owner, they reflect accurately the social and political outlook of his followers, views middle-class, commercial, anti-aristocratic and clearly likely to prove difficult for Opposition groups trying to use them for their own purposes in the game of politics.

But if the strengthening of this feeling was one result of the experience of these years, there was another that was rather different. As a result of the example set by Beckford and soon followed by others, the City was brought more closely into day-to-day politics, since the leaders it trusted were themselves, as John Barnard had never been, the agents of political groups.

Both these effects were to become increasingly apparent in the third period under consideration, which was not slow in coming, for Pitt's position was essentially temporary, the

[1] Add. MSS. 38334, ff. 29 *seq.* [13 Nov. 1761].

product of war and crisis, and with his resignation and the return of peace this curious interlude was over. But it left behind it a City opinion more self-conscious, more closely engaged in national politics, in a state of frustration at the loss of its recent importance ; and this at a time when post-war dislocation, bad harvests, political instability and the impact of a variety of national problems were to exacerbate all social and political problems. It is not surprising that the City was so deeply affected by the excitements surrounding the case of John Wilkes and General Warrants, nor that in 1763 a popular pamphleteer claimed that the constitution represented interests once predominant but now so no longer and that the merchant classes should enjoy a greater share in representation.[1]

The period 1762 to 1782 is that of the climax both of the eighteenth-century development of City self-consciousness and of its influence on national politics. The years which saw the rise of the whig Opposition *par excellence*, the years in which the whig interpretation of history was born, were those in which extra-parliamentary pressure on politics became open and organized, first in the City and then later, and for a limited period but with great effect, in the counties. In these years the parliamentary Opposition groups were forced to trim their sails and adjust their courses to meet the demands made on them by supporters whom they had hitherto been able to control and had been apt to have to stimulate, but whom less than ever they could afford to lose.

After the first confused eight years of George III's reign, two main Opposition groups emerged, that which followed Chatham, and of which Lord Shelburne and, later, Pitt the younger were the outstanding figures, and that which was built up round the person of the marquess of Rockingham, of whom Burke and, later, Charles Fox were the most active members. They were at one in their violent opposition to the king and his ministers, but united in nothing else. They

[1] *Political Disquisitions, proper for Public Consideration in the Present State of Affairs in a Letter to a Noble Duke* (1763).

were in active competition with each other in their attempts to capture the support of the extra-parliamentary forces on which Opposition traditionally depended. During the later years of the American War, they competed for the support of the counties, where the gentry were driven to unparalleled independence and activity by the expense and misfortunes of the war. Between 1768 and 1772,[1] and more sporadically up to 1775,[2] competition for influence in the City played a considerable part in their plans.

This competition would in itself have been likely to increase the concern of the City with the day-to-day business of politics but to detract from its position as a semi-independent political force, for the aim was to employ the machinery of City government for the needs of one or other of the groups active in national politics. The Chatham-Shelburne group had the initial advantage of the support in the City of William Beckford, who still had the most crowded years of his City career before him (he died in 1770, having completed a highly popular second term of office as Lord Mayor). Later, they had the support of certain close followers of Lord Shelburne in the City, Alderman James Townsend[3] and Alderman Richard Oliver.[4] The Rockingham group,

---

[1] Evidence of this activity is to be found in the *Burke Correspondence*, i. 228 *seq.*, and the Burke and Rockingham MSS., Sheffield ; Portland MSS., Nottingham University ; *The Correspondence of William Pitt, Earl of Chatham*, ed. W. S. Taylor and J. H. Pringle (1839) ; and the Lansdowne MSS. at Bowood. At the general election of 1768 Barlow Trecothick, a successful candidate, was called in a City squib (*City Races* [1768]) 'Lord Rockingham's wall-eyed horse Mercator'.

[2] *Burke Correspondence*, ii. 55. E. Burke to Rockingham, 23 Aug., 1775. 'Lord John [Cavendish] has given your lordship an account of the scheme we talked over, for reviving the importance of the City of London, by separating the sound from the rotten contract-hunting part of the mercantile interest, uniting it with the corporation, and joining both to your lordship.'

[3] 1737–87. Son of Chauncy Townsend, a prominent London merchant ; M.P. West Looe 1767–74, Calne 1782–7. Took up freedom of City by patrimony in 1769, alderman 1769. Lord Mayor 1772. In close touch with Shelburne at least from 1760. (W. P. Courtney, 'James Townsend, M.P.', *Notes and Queries*, 11th Series, v. 2–4.)

[4] 1734 ?–84. Born Antigua, brought up in London by his uncle, a West-India merchant ; M.P. for the City 1770–80, alderman from 1770 ; committed to Tower by the House of Commons 1771. (*Notes and Queries*, 8th Series, iv. 217.)

however, tried to build themselves up a rival force, using as their chief City supporter Alderman Barlow Trecothick, member for the City and in 1770 Lord Mayor (who had been their agent in organizing the commercial agitation for the repeal of the Stamp Act in 1766).[1] They also had some hopes of using in the same way William Baker, son of Sir William Baker who had in his time been a prominent City supporter of the duke of Newcastle.[2] These tactics of Opposition led, as was inevitable, to comparable activity by the Government, who were able to give indirect assistance in the traditional way to the declining oligarchic influences in the City. Hence in the election of members for the City in 1768 and in elections for City offices for the next few years there was an obscure triangular struggle in process between groups who hoped to use the City as a political weapon, or at least to prevent their opponents from doing so.

This struggle was, however, interrupted almost before it began and suddenly cut across, by a startling revival of City independence in the political field. There emerged in 1768 the strangest of all the City leaders of the century, John Wilkes.[3] With his meteoric rise to power the City appeared once more as a powerful but external force in politics, as independent as in Sir John Barnard's day, but much more formidable and incalculable.

The sudden appearance of this cynical and able demagogue, whose cause had been fostered by Opposition leaders in the past, but who had not occurred to them as a possible rival for the control of the City, struck contemporaries, as it does posterity, with astonishment. Benjamin Franklin, who was in London in 1768, thought it inexplicable.

'Tis a really extraordinary event to see an outlaw and exile of bad personal character, not worth a farthing, come over from France, set himself up for candidate for the capital of the Kingdom,

[1] For him, see Namier, *ibid.*, 270, and L. S. Sutherland, 'Edmund Burke and the First Rockingham Ministry', *loc. cit.*; W. P. Courtney, 'Barlow Trecothick', *Notes and Queries*, 11th Series, iii. 330-2.
[2] Namier, *England in the Age of the American Revolution* (1930), pp. 280-1.
[3] H. Bleackley, *Life of John Wilkes* (1917).

miss his election only by being too late in his application and immediately carrying it for the principal county. The mob, spirited up by numbers of different ballads sung or roared in every street, requiring gentlemen and ladies of all ranks as they passed in their carriages to shout for 'Wilkes and Liberty', marking the same words on all their coaches with chalk, and No. 45 on every door; which extends a vast way along the roads into the country. I went last week to Winchester, and observed that for fifteen miles out of town there was scarce a door or window-shutter next the road unmarked.[1]

Posterity has found it no easier to explain. It has some-times been assumed that his power rested essentially on his influence over the London mob. He certainly had remark-able success in whipping them up at a time when there were various causes for unrest — a fact which in the end con-tributed considerably to the collapse of the movement with which his name was associated. But examination of the stages of his career in the City suggests that his real political strength lay elsewhere. It lay in just those classes of lesser mer-chants and tradesmen on whose support Oppositions always depended, and he was thus directly competitive with the City leaders who were working to obtain the support of this class for the rival parliamentary Opposition groups. He was indeed assisted in his rise by their jealousy of each other. Though Beckford at first opposed him secretly,[2] he soon de-cided it was wiser to appear to back him; but when, in 1771, after Beckford's death his successors Townsend and Oliver quarrelled with Wilkes, Rockingham and Burke thought on the whole they would rather see Wilkes victorious than their political rivals. Rockingham thought Wilkes might be 'per-haps not so dangerous as the others would be . . . and *probably Wilkes single* would be easier to manage than a whole *pandae-*

---

[1] *Memoirs*, quoted in W. P. Treloar, *Wilkes and the City* (1917), p. 56.
[2] Camden to Beckford, 28 March 1768. 'I give you joy of your success in London and hope Middlesex will follow the example of your City and send Wilkes to Jewry (?) which they say is to be his next excursion' If he fails there, I presume he will retreat into that strong fortress the King's Bench Prison' (Hamilton MSS., National Library of Scotland. I am indebted to Miss H. Allen for a transcript of this letter).

monium'.[1] It was an inept judgment, for it soon became apparent that Wilkes, in the strength of his popularity, could break through the webs of connexion which they were weaving, and, though his personal popularity depended on his remaining in active opposition to Government,[2] he could deal on equal terms with the parliamentary Opposition groups.

There seems to be no explanation of the phenomenon of his rise and the hold he gained on this type of follower but the fact that he appealed powerfully to forces in the City which resented subordination to Opposition as well as to Government, that he voiced their hostility to the aristocracy as well as to the Crown and the Executive and (a strong point in view of the personal nature of his power) that he appealed to them in his own person as the victim of the forces which they resented. Perhaps the best example of the attitude of his main City supporters — men of some substance and education — is the rich but misfit and plebeian parson Horne Tooke,[3] who played so big a part in his rise and was so bitterly disillusioned by its results.

Wilkes, strong in this support and backed by the funds of the Bill of Rights Society which his City friends founded, was soon not only driving the rival Opposition groups out of the City [4] but putting them at a grave disadvantage in national politics by forcing on them constitutional programmes which they had no desire to embrace. These programmes were not revolutionary, for his supporters were not revolutionaries; they clung to the idea of shorter parliaments and of traditional

[1] Rockingham to Burke [Jan. or Feb. 1771], Fitzwilliam MSS., Sheffield.

[2] This remained true even after the days of his great popularity were over. As late as 1784 John Robinson said : 'Mr. Wilkes's support of any government is very uncertain, because the safety of his situation depends on his watching as he calls it all administrations and having no apparent connexion with any, but taking the side of all popular questions'. *Parliamentary Papers of John Robinson, 1774–1784*, ed. W. T. Laprade (1922), p. 68.

[3] A. Stephens, *Memoirs of John Horne Tooke* (1813).

[4] Burke, *Correspondence*, ii. 111. 'It was but a few months after Lord Shelburne had told me, gratis (for nothing led to it), that the people (always meaning the common people of London) were never in the wrong, that he and all his friends were driven with scorn out of that city.'

methods of controlling the power of the Crown, but they
added two new demands : an attack on the rotten boroughs
as the centre of aristocratic as well as of royal power, and the
proposal to bind their representatives to carry out their
wishes by enforcing pledges on them at the time of their
election, a proposal very unwelcome to all parliamentary
parties.[1] How successful they were is shown by the fact that
they forced Chatham to subscribe to triennial parliaments
after he had explicitly expressed his disapproval of them ; [2]
and that they drove Burke not only to try to distract attention
from those parts of their programme he thought most dangerous by developing other parts which his friends found
less unattractive, but also to lay down as a maxim for preserving the 'true country interest' that they should not support candidates nominated by 'a mere club of Tradesmen'.[3]
And most Opposition members would probably have agreed
with his indignation at the 'infinite mischief' done 'by the
violence, rashness and often wickedness' of that 'rotten sub-
division of a faction amongst ourselves . . . the Bill of Rights
people'.[4]

These years mark the climax of the influence of London
on the political life of the country during the century, and its
traces are to be found in the programmes of parliamentary
Opposition and in the attitude of the country gentry when,
during the American War, they followed the City's example
and set up their own short-lived but spectacular extra-parliamentary organizations.[5] But it must be admitted that the
climax was a short-lived one and that in the City, as in the

[1] Burke dated the driving from the City of 'all the honest part of the opposition' to 'all this professing, promising and testing'. (Burke, *Correspondence*,
ii. 110).

[2] On 1 June 1770 he had refused to agree to the Common Council's demand
that he should support triennial parliaments (Chatham, *Correspondence*, iii. 464),
but by 1 May 1771, with much uncertainty and disquiet, he announced in the
Lords his conversion.

[3] E. Burke to Portland [28 April 1770], Portland MSS., Nottingham
University.

[4] E. Burke to R. Shackleton, 15 Aug. 1770, Burke, *Correspondence*, i. 229.

[5] The best account of these Associations is G. S. Veitch, *Genesis of Parliamentary Reform* (1913). The primacy of the City movement is shown by H.
Butterfield, *George III, Lord North and the People, 1779–80* (1949).

counties, both the organization and the zeal for exerting pressure on politics disappeared as rapidly as they arose, leaving little obvious trace behind them. In both cases the explanation seems to lie in the limited nature of the aspirations of those supporting the movement, the dependence of these aspirations on the circumstances of the moment, and the unwillingness or inability of most men to realize that the issues they were raising had far wider implications. When something of the nature of what Burke was to call 'the portentous comet of the Rights of Man' appeared to them, the merchant and tradesman of the City, like the country gentleman, stopped abashed.

The check in the City came earlier than in the country as a whole, though even there it did not long outlive the exasperation of the American War. The withering away of the turmoils of the years of Wilkes's City dominance was partly due, no doubt, to the fact that Wilkes himself (never, as he said, a Wilkite) made his peace after 1779 with vested interests and retired to sedate ease in the most lucrative position the City had to offer, that of its chamberlain. But even before he did so the support he could count on was beginning to decline: he lost his following in the Common Council and his supporters became progressively limited to what George III had called 'a small though desperate part of the Livery'.[1] And when, in 1780, the London mob burst its bounds in the Gordon Riots, and this without any stimulation from those who normally expected to exploit it, Joseph Brasbridge spoke for many when he said: 'from that moment, though previously contaminated with the mania infected by Wilkes, the political mountebank of the day, I shut my ears against the voice of popular clamour'.[2]

But, though the City's fervour was thus summarily checked, the forces underlying it were not changed. In the turmoils which surrounded the political activities of Sir

---

[1] *Correspondence of George III*, ii. 256. The king to North, 26 June 1771. The king ante-dated the development.
[2] Quoted by J. P. de Castro, *The Gordon Riots* (1926), p. 147.

Francis Burdett [1] at the turn of the century, their continued vitality can be traced. And, when the great Reform agitation of the eighteen-thirties came on, one can see, in the organization and activities of the radical London master-tailor Francis Place,[2] the unmistakable mark of eighteenth-century City experience and traditions, with its long history of co-operation with parliamentary Oppositions but also its characteristics of isolation and separatism.

[1] M. W. Patterson, *Sir Francis Burdett and his Times, 1770–1844* (1931).
[2] Graham Wallas, *Life of Francis Place, 1771–1854* (1918).

THE CITY OF LONDON AND
THE DEVONSHIRE-PITT ADMINISTRATION, 1756-7

THE Devonshire–Pitt administration, certain aspects of which are discussed in this lecture, was a very short-lived, confused, and ineffective one. It came into existence after the administration of the Duke of Newcastle had been forced in November 1756 by the defection of their leader in the House of Commons, Henry Fox, to bow to the storm of indignation aroused by the early failures of British arms in what was to be the Seven Years' War. Its titular leader was the inexperienced Duke of Devonshire, who assumed the position of First Lord of the Treasury as a temporary measure to oblige the king; its driving power was expected to be the dynamic William Pitt, whose negligible personal following in the House of Commons was offset by the force of his personality and by a popularity 'without doors' which forced him upon an unwilling king. It began to dissolve in April 1757 when the king somewhat precipitately judged it possible to dismiss him from office. The Devonshire administration ended in June 1757 when the great war coalition ministry of that year took its place.

Few periods of the political history of the eighteenth century are better documented than these months. Nevertheless historians, very understandably, have tended to pass rapidly over this transient administration to concentrate on that which succeeded it. But though this ministry achieved little, it is of interest in showing something of the interrelation of public opinion and politics in the mid-eighteenth century, it illustrates the place of the City of London in expressing this opinion, and it illuminates sharply in particular some of the conflicts of views on public finance which affected the City's approach to political matters. It is because the City of London tended to reflect with peculiar intensity the sentiments of what may be called the political nation at this time, and that on certain issues it possessed strongly held views of its own, that I have chosen the title of my lecture, and it is on this aspect of a curious political episode that I shall concentrate.

To make it comprehensible, however, it is necessary both to place it against its background and to indicate something of its complexity.

The achievement of Henry Pelham, that often underrated mid-eighteenth century minister, in the years following the defeat of the Jacobite Rebellion of 1745 and the end of the War of the Austrian Succession, had been to build up a broadly based administration and to damp down the fires of political conflict which had raged so furiously at the end of Robert Walpole's administration and brought about his overthrow in 1742. Though the Tories remained in the wilderness, he not only found a place in his administration for most of the able and ambitious politicians who might be tempted to erect their banners as leaders of the 'rebel Whigs', but (helped by circumstances) he took pains to eliminate, so far as possible, the sources of discontent among those sections of the public where followers for such leaders might be found. Nowhere had hostility to the administration burned more fiercely than in the City of London, and nowhere did Pelham take more pains to remove the causes of their discontents. Thus he not only repealed that part of Walpole's Act of 1725 which confirmed the traditional veto of the Court of Aldermen over the Common Council (an issue which had entangled the Government with social and constitutional conflict within the City),[1] but he sought to eliminate the grievances of the ordinary trading and commercial classes of the City about the conduct of government credit operations and contracts, the arrangements of which, particularly in time of war, were held to give undue financial advantages to the small group of men and institutions known to contemporaries as the 'monied interest'.[2] Though the needs of government finance made it impracticable to go more than a small way to meet these critics, he carried out his Treasury operations with such tact as not only to disarm for the time a hostility which had become traditional and embarrassing, but to win the personal support of the established leader of this anti-ministerial opinion in the City, and a man whose views on finance were particularly

[1] A. J. Henderson, *London and the National Government, 1721–1742*, Duke University Press, N. Carolina, 1945.

[2] L. S. Sutherland, 'The City of London in Eighteenth-Century Politics', *Essays Presented to Sir Lewis Namier*, ed. R. Pares and A. J. P. Taylor, London, 1956; and 'Samson Gideon and the Reduction of Interest, 1749–50', *Econ. Hist. Rev.* xvi, 1946, 15–29. See above, pp. 41-66 and below, pp. 399-413.

respected by it, old Sir John Barnard, for thirty-nine years M.P., for the City and by far the most influential man in it.[1] Pelham's success was no doubt facilitated by the intense disappointment and sense of betrayal felt in the City when the fall of Walpole led to none of the constitutional and political changes which the City, like many others, had been led by Opposition politicians to expect—a disappointment for which they held Walpole's opponent William Pulteney primarily responsible; it was also helped by the reaction to the Jacobite rising, but Pelham's exertions were at least one of the factors which enabled the Duke of Newcastle to boast, as early as the General Election of 1747, 'We scarce meet with any opposition, and those places where friends to the Government were never chosen before, are now foremost in their demonstrations of duty and loyalty to the King, as the County of Middlesex, Westminster and even the City of London.'[2]

The peace which Pelham created did not, however, long survive his death in 1754, and this for a variety of reasons, of which the incompetence of his successor the Duke of Newcastle was only one. In the first place developments within the royal family began to give encouragement to personal faction. The king was growing old; the influence of his son the Duke of Cumberland, commander-in-chief of his armies, was increasing; and the approaching majority of the Prince of Wales, the future George III, brought once again into being something of a 'reversionary court' at Leicester House. Soon this situation was reflected in the attitude of politicians; it was seen that while Newcastle and his friends could count on the support (even if grudging) of the king, Henry Fox had for some time been strengthening his personal position by adherence to a party supporting the Duke of Cumberland; while William Pitt (the loser at this time in the struggle for power, and dismissed from office in November 1755 for his opposition to the administration's policy) had tended since the summer of that year to court the 'reversionary interest' at Leicester House. In the second place, this situation was ripe for exploitation because of difficulties concerning the leadership of the House of Commons, left vacant by Pelham's death. It is significant of the forces which lay behind eighteenth-century politics that all the stable ministries of the period had a commoner in a central position in them, usually

[1] Sir John Barnard (c. 1685–1764), Merchant and Insurer. M.P. for the City of London, 1722–61.

[2] Newcastle to Cumberland, 3 July 1747. Brit. Mus. Add. MS. 32712, f. 24*v*.

at the Treasury. This was necessary because the eighteenth-century House of Commons, with its strong tendency towards what was called 'independency', required weight in those who led them. In the months following Pelham's death it became apparent that there were only two men in the administration who combined the requisite qualifications with the desire to take on the arduous duties of leading minister in the House of Commons, Henry Fox and William Pitt, who soon became bitter rivals.[1] Both were ambitious; neither was near the centre of gravity of the dominant connexion; to neither was Newcastle willing to give the status which they considered their due; while in the case of Pitt, the king himself was not prepared to receive him. How great was the part played by the problem of leadership in the House of Commons in the downfall of the New-castle administration, and thus in the rise of its short-lived suc-cessor, is shown by the reflections of Lord Chancellor Hardwicke after the crisis of 1756–7 was over. 'It cannot be disguised', he wrote to the Duke of Newcastle, 'that the avowal and appear-ance of the same sole power in your Grace, in the House of Commons, is not to be expected. All sorts of persons there have concurred in battering down that notion, and the precedents of my Lord Godolphin's and my Lord Sunderland's time have been overruled by the long habits of seeing Sir Robert Walpole and Mr. Pelham there, which go as far back as the memory of most people now sitting there . . . reaches.'[2]

But the third reason for the recommencement of political strife, and that which bears most closely on what we are consider-ing, was the approach of war and the issues which war was bound to raise, for it was these issues that gained for William Pitt his great reputation 'without doors' and brought the Devonshire–Pitt administration into being. When saying this, however, it is necessary neither to ante-date Pitt's reputation nor to exaggerate its importance. It was only in the five months leading up to his entry into power on the crest of a wave of popular support that the influence of this public opinion became a decisive factor in determining the conduct of politicians; and it was not until about the same time that anyone could have been certain that Pitt would be its hero. Even the approach of war

[1] William Murray, created 1756 Baron (1776 Earl) Mansfield on his eleva-tion to the Bench as Chief Justice, had many of the qualifications, but he preferred the pursuit of the law.

[2] Hardwicke to Newcastle, 29 October 1757. Brit. Mus. Add. MS. 32875, f. 316*v*.

and the chance it gave him to display his formidable eloquence on issues always attractive to the public opinion of the day, did not lead at once either to Pitt's acceptance as a leader by those hostile to administration or to the growth of a strong opposition inside or without the House. He declaimed against European alliances, the alleged subordination of English interests to those of Hanover, the introduction of foreign mercenaries (made necessary by the threat of a French invasion), and against the extravagance of war-like policies which would increase the national debt—all issues to which both the country gentry and commercial interests of London were apt to be quick to respond; he also strongly supported proposals put forward for the establishment of a national militia which, its supporters claimed, would render the presence of mercenaries unnecessary, and even in time perhaps achieve a traditional aspiration by removing the need for a standing army altogether.

But he gained little support either in the House of Commons[1] or the City,[2] apart from the Tories, and even among the Tories who supported him there was little personal enthusiasm for him, while there were some who hoped that Fox might yet stand forth as their leader. An illustration of this attitude is to be found in a man who was soon to become Pitt's devoted follower and the chief organizer of his popularity in the City, William Beckford,[3] West Indian planter, Tory country gentleman and City leader. In 1755 (when he was already an alderman, M.P. for the City, and was serving his turn as sheriff as a prelude to the mayoralty, though his political influence there was still in its early stages) he was doing all that he could to organize an opposition to the administration. In the course of this he played a big part in the foundation and control of that weekly periodical the *Monitor or British Freeholder*[4] which was to give such staunch support to Pitt

[1] J. West to Newcastle, 13 November 1755. Brit. Mus. Add. MS. 32860, f. 471. Describes to him the division on 13 November in the debate on the Address on assisting Hanover, when after a tremendous Opposition speech from Pitt the Government won by 311–105. Seventy-six of the Opposition votes were given by Tories 'so that the great men could avail themselves of no more than 30'.

[2] On 2 March 1756 the Common Council of the City voted a loyal address, and a meeting of principal merchants followed suit, without a hint of opposition to government policy. *Public Advertiser*, 3 April 1756.

[3] William Beckford (1709–70) M.P. for Shaftesbury, 1747–54; London, 1754–70. Alderman and twice Lord Mayor of London.

[4] The *Monitor* was founded by his younger brother and close political ally Richard Beckford, and William was no doubt deeply involved in the venture.

and to play a considerable part in the moulding of public opinion. But until after the end of 1755 it was on Fox not Pitt that he pinned his hopes;[1] even after Pitt had come into office he still praised Fox alone of the former ministers;[2] and it was not until 6 November 1756, five days before the Duke of Newcastle handed in his resignation, that he wrote pledging his support 'as one of your private soldiers without commission' to the leader whom he was to follow loyally for the rest of his life and whom he had now come to see (in his grandiloquent language) as 'the instrument of our deliverance'.[3]

What radically changed the situation and gave Pitt his chance was the misfortunes which followed fast on the declaration of war, in particular the loss of Minorca and the failure of Admiral Byng to relieve it. It was a naval reverse of the kind which has always shaken English public opinion to its base, though one whose strategic importance can be easily exaggerated. The violence of the public reaction to this defeat was shown by the unrelenting ferocity with which popular opinion pursued the unfortunate Byng to an execution later recognized to have been grossly unjust. That this indignation should extend to the ministers directly or indirectly responsible was inevitable, and Henry Fox was not spared.[4] On the other hand Pitt, by virtue

Richard, however, died in 1756, when the paper was carried on, as it said, by 'many gentlemen of the same station and principles with himself'. Comparison of its pages with William Beckford's pronouncements at this time, suggests that he had a strong influence over its policy.

[1] Horace Walpole remarked of a debate on 23 January 1756 that Pitt 'paid great court to Beckford, who, till now, had appeared to prefer Mr. Fox'. H. Walpole, *Memoires of the Last Ten Years of the Reign of George II*, London, 1822, ii. 3.

[2] H. Digby to Lord Digby, 7 December 1756. Hist. MSS. Com. viii, pt. I. Section I, 222*b*, reporting Beckford's speech on the Address said 'Mr. Beckford declared his satisfaction, as well as that of all the people he was connected with, in the late change of administration, spoke offensively of the late Ministers, and said their names stunk in the nostrils of the people, but distinguished Mr. Fox from the rest. . . .'

[3] *Correspondence of William, Earl of Chatham*, ed. W. S. Taylor and J. H. Pringle, London, 1840, i. 185–6.

[4] Fox himself wrote on 31 July, 'The rage of people, and of considerate people, for the loss of Minorca increases hourly. I have not more than my share of blame. . . . But when Parliament meets, the scene of action will be the H. of Commons, and I, being the only figure of a minister there, shall of course draw all the odium on me.' Printed in Ilchester, *Henry Fox, First Lord Holland, his Family and Relations*, London, 1920, i. 335. Fox was extensively attacked in the political caricatures of the time. *British Museum Catalogue* (cf. p. 73 , n. 3 below).

of his personality and the part he had taken in opposition in the previous session of Parliament, was the obvious person to whom an outraged public might turn. (It should be noted that Parliament was in recess from before the receipt of the news of Byng's failure until after the resignation of Newcastle; the rise of Pitt's popularity therefore, depended on what he had said and done before, and not during this crisis of opinion.)

Despite the fact that the House was not sitting, the public indignation soon found means of expressing itself. Even before it was known that Byng's expedition had failed, Newcastle was informed that the City was 'extremely displeased with the leaving Minorca exposed'.[1] After Byng's failure became known, his agents told him of widespread discontent, not only in the City but throughout the country.[2] In the City and in Westminster a host of ballads, broadsheets, caricatures, and other ephemera sprang to life, many of them attacking the ministers as well as Byng.[3] Such periodicals as the *Monitor*, and such papers as the *London Evening Post* (closely associated with it), became violent in their vituperation, and their views were echoed by the monthly magazines and by papers which did not normally adopt an active political line. Horace Walpole, after a visit to town wrote that 'the streets swarm so with lampoons, that I began to fancy myself a minister's son again'.[4] More serious, when the August assizes were held in the counties, Addresses to the Crown and Instructions to their Representatives demanding inquiries and punishment (7 Instructions and 4 Addresses during the month) came from their Grand Juries. London and a few of the big cities followed their example.[5] At a meeting of the Common

[1] *Diary of the late George Bubb Dodington*, ed. H. P. Wyndham (1784 edition), p. 382.

[2] Newcastle to Hardwicke, 2 September 1756. Brit. Mus. Add. MS. 35416, f. 1. Some of this discontent, however, would seem to have arisen from other causes, in particular the high price of corn after disastrous harvests. There were later in the year widespread corn riots in Sheffield, Shropshire, Derbyshire, and among the Cumberland miners.

[3] For the outburst of caricatures see *British Museum Catalogue of Prints and Drawings, Div. I, Political and Personal Satires*, iii, pt. ii, ed. F. G. Stephens and E. Hawkins. Cf. M. D. George, *English Political Caricature to 1792, a Study of Opinion and Propaganda*, Oxford, 1959, i. 101-7.

[4] H. Walpole to G. Montagu, 12 July 1756. *The Letters of Horace Walpole, fourth Earl of Oxford*, ed. Mrs. Paget Toynbee, Oxford, 1903, iii. 438.

[5] Buckinghamshire, Bedfordshire, Herefordshire, Suffolk, Shropshire, Huntingdonshire, and Norfolk instructed their representatives. Dorset, Norfolk, Somerset, and the County Palatine of Chester addressed the Crown. An address was also set on foot in Surrey, but failed (see p. 77 below). London,

Council of the City, summoned by popular demand on 19 August to address the Crown, feeling in favour of such an address was overwhelming. Sir John Barnard who, loyal to his friends in administration, sought to check those who had so long followed his lead, was powerless to do so. 'It was impossible', he said, 'to stem the impetuosity and madness of people' and 'The warmest friends of the King and Administration were carried away by violence or acquiesced through fear.'[1] In October the quarter sessions brought further representations from counties, four of which moreover summoned special meetings to vote them,[2] and more cities and boroughs (including again London) voiced their protests.[3] At the beginning, no more was asked than the punishment of Byng and of those responsible for the national misfortunes; by the end all the constitutional issues of popular anti-ministerialism which public discontent was apt to bring forth, and which had been developed so fully at the time of Walpole's fall were advanced—shorter parliaments, pension and place bills, and a militia to replace the standing army. By October, not only was the Duke of Newcastle reduced to a state of the utmost depression, but the stout old Sir John Barnard, from what he could see in the City, felt that Newcastle had no option but to resign since 'matters were brought to such a crisis and the national ferment wrought up to such a heighth that it was impossible for your Grace to stand it'.[4] And finally it was Henry Fox, when his fear triumphed over his ambition, who touched off the crisis by announcing on 13 October[5] his intention of resigning from office,

Bristol (in two separate addresses), and Chester addressed the Crown in August. At the beginning of September Leominster instructed its representatives, and a little later in the month Maidstone followed suit.

[1] J. West to Newcastle, 20 August 1756. Brit. Mus. Add. MS. 32866, ff. 496–7. Barnard had advised the Lord Mayor against calling the Court. Ibid., f. 448. It was suggested that the Government's friends in the City might organize a counter-address from the London merchants, but this was generally considered unwise. When the Address was presented neither Sir John Barnard 'nor any of those who are called *Whig Aldermen*' attended. Ibid., f. 492.

[2] The County Palatine of Lancaster, Somerset, and Essex instructed their representatives at the Quarter Sessions. Meetings were held in Devonshire (7 October), Lincolnshire (12 October), Yorkshire (18 October), and Brecon (20 November).

[3] Exeter, York, and Lincoln addressed the Crown in October, Southwark, Nottingham, Lichfield, and Bath in November, and Salisbury in December. London instructed its representatives on 28 October. Southwark's address was belated, being undertaken owing to the failure of the Surrey Address.

[4] J. West to Newcastle, 23 October 1756. Brit. Mus. Add. MS. 32868, f. 390

[5] Fox was not only afraid of Pitt in the House and of the popular clamour, but of being used as a scapegoat by Newcastle.

thereby refusing to face in the House when it reassembled the consequences of the popular outcry.

The Newcastle administration thus fell before an upsurge of public indignation. It was, in consequence one of the three, and only three, administrations of the eighteenth century which were driven from power while they enjoyed the full support of the Crown. The resignation of Newcastle may be compared, thus, in some respects with the fall of Walpole in 1742, and that of Lord North in 1782. But there were differences important in themselves and which significantly affected the course of the administration which succeeded him. While both the other ministers fell after some years of the strain of unsuccessful war, Newcastle resigned when the war had barely begun. While the discontent which led to the fall of the others was so deep-seated and widespread that it had permeated the House of Commons, so that they were faced with imminent defeat there, Newcastle on the other hand had when he resigned a substantial majority in the House—Lord Granville said he was 'the first minister that ever quitted with a majority in Parliament of 150',[1] and he retained his majority, had he cared to use it, throughout the life of the succeeding administration. As he told the king there was a lack not of 'numbers' but of 'hands and tongues in the House of Commons'.[2] Finally while the public outcry against the other two ministers was overwhelming, it is doubtful whether that facing Newcastle was either so deep-seated or, at any rate outside of the City, so spontaneous as to make a withdrawal inevitable. His fall was due in fact to a collapse of leadership in the House of Commons brought about by personal weakness and corporate disunity in the face of public clamour.

That the popular indignation was real and strong when the news was first received was, as I have tried to show, indisputable. But there is also no doubt that it was fostered and turned against the administration by its political opponents. A prominent feature of the campaign of lampoons was, for instance, the 'caricatura cards' which were invented by Colonel George Townshend[3] (an ingenious and highly individualist supporter of Pitt)

[1] Newcastle to Hardwicke, 4 January 1757. Brit. Mus. Add. MS. 32870, f. 24*v*.

[2] Newcastle to Hardwicke, 2 September 1756. Ibid. 35416, ff. 2–2*v*. The king had said he could not imagine that 'in this Parliament, we shall lose so many, as not to leave us a very considerable majority'.

[3] The Hon. George Townshend (1724–1807), later 1st Marquis Townshend, M.P. for Norfolk. Walpole, *Memoires*, ii. 68. Though Walpole states that these cards were invented during the agitation against Byng, his *Letters*, iii. 403

who himself produced much the best of them. Over 10,000 copies of a pamphlet entitled *Appeal to the People of England* were said to have been distributed free in the London and Westminster public-houses.[1] When 100 ballad singers paraded through Westminster singing 'To the block with Newcastle and the yard-arm with Byng',[2] someone must have paid them to do so. Even the obloquy directed against Sir John Barnard after he had opposed the City Address appears to have had some connexion with the obscure struggle that had begun between Beckford and him for the leadership of the popular forces in the City, for the *Monitor*, Beckford's organ, not only delivered a vicious attack on him (it had so far treated him with every air of deference) but asked its readers

Would not . . . that capital ship, *the Sir John*, if thoroughly examined by a skilful master in politicks, be found most confoundedly eaten by ministerial worms, and perhaps be reported so rotten and crasy (sic) as not to be ᵗrusted on any future service?[3]

Nor must the Addresses and Instructions from counties and boroughs be taken entirely at their face value. Considerable pains were taken to evoke them. At the end of July both the *Monitor* and the *London Evening Post*[4] exhorted the Grand Juries at the assizes to send in Addresses and Instructions precisely of the kind that began to be passed. About a month later, George Townshend caused something of a political scandal by writing personally to every corporation in the country exhorting them to petition the House of Commons in support of his Militia Bill, in view of 'the situation of this country'.[5] In most of the eleven counties which sent in their representations during August the

show that Townshend had already begun to produce small political caricatures before 4 March 1756 when he was pressing his Militia Bill. Walpole reported that 'he adorns the shutters, walls, and napkins of every tavern in Pall Mall with caricatures of the Duke [of Cumberland], and Sir George Lyttelton, the Duke of Newcastle and Mr. Fox'.

[1] *Whitehall Evening Post*, 9–12 October 1756.

[2] T. Potter to G. Grenville, 11 September 1756. *The Grenville Papers*, ed. W. J. Smith, London, 1852, i. 173.

[3] The *Monitor*, no. 57, 28 August 1756, ii. 52.

[4] *The London Evening Post* on 24–27 July 1756; the *Monitor* on 31 July 1756, no. 52, i. 499–500.

[5] Brit. Mus. Add. MS. 32866, f. 375. Compare Hardwicke to Newcastle, 26 August 1756. Brit. Mus. Add. MS. 32867, f. 73: 'Every body is alarmed at Mr. Townshend's conduct in taking upon him to instruct all the boroughs in England, and to sollicit petitions to Parliament, by circular letters in his own name. 'Tis I believe entirely new and unprecedented.'

Grand Juries were said to be Tories[1] and not necessarily representative of county opinion. In Surrey, the only county in which the Address was circulated round the county for signatures as an indication of the support it enjoyed, the project failed completely.[2] Still further, the number of counties and boroughs taking part during this first month was not large, and there were conspicuous omissions. And even among those who supported the movement the depth of their feeling was sometimes suspect. As Thomas Potter warned Pitt, sending him the good news of the Buckinghamshire and Bedfordshire Instructions, 'many a man has mistaken means for the end, and Patriotism which is not very deeply rooted has often exhausted itself in an angry speech'.[3]

It was, moreover, generally agreed that it was advantageous to administration that the protests had come in so long before the reassembly of Parliament.[4] By the beginning of September reports suggested that the wave of popular exasperation was dying down, and even in the City things were quieter.[5] It would seem to have been the obvious signs of weakness and growing disintegration in the administration that led to the revived protests of October and the mounting tide of hostile opinion during that and the succeeding month. By the end of October when the great county of Yorkshire[6] and the City of London[7] had instructed their representatives in terms which recalled the last assaults upon Walpole, a retreat (at any rate temporarily) had become inevitable, but it is difficult to believe that it was not the internal weakness of the administration which had allowed it to become so.

[1] e.g. in Huntingdonshire. Hardwicke to Newcastle, 26 August 1756. Brit. Mus. Add. MS. 32867, f. 72v. Horace Walpole spoke of 'the instructions which they [the Tories] had instructed their constituents to send them'. *Memoires*, ii. 132.

[2] Newcastle to Hardwicke, letters of 2 and 18 September 1756. Brit. Mus. Add. MS. 35416, ff. 1v–2, and 37. In the second Newcastle mentioned that Speaker Onslow had refused to present the Address 'and it is in such discredit, now, throughout the county, that there are very few hands to it; most of the considerable Tories have refused to sign it; and I hear from my nephew Onslow, that they can scarce get any body to present it'. It was not in fact presented.

[3] T. Potter to [W. Pitt], 15 August 1756. P.R.O. 30/8/53, f. 48.

[4] H. Walpole to H. Mann, 19 September 1756. Walpole, *Letters*, iii. 455. 'The rage of addresses did not go far: at present everything is quiet.'

[5] Joseph Watkins to Newcastle, 2 September 1756. Brit. Mus. Add. MS. 32867, ff. 209–10.

[6] Printed in the *Public Advertiser*, 27 October 1756.

[7] Ibid. 30 October 1756.

Nevertheless, the fall of the Newcastle administration was largely due to popular clamour, and this clamour determined the character of the administration which succeeded it. For not only did it force Pitt upon the Crown, but it limited his actions, and above all made it impracticable for him, even if he so wished, to come to terms with those who were being driven from power. Pitt was left in no doubt by the press and the letters he received that he was expected to satisfy, when in office, not only the hopes which he himself had raised when he was in opposition, but the aspirations in which his supporters had been so greatly deceived when Pulteney abandoned the popular cause after the fall of Walpole, and, as the *Monitor* portentously put it:

Should there come a time, when the prime advocates for the people, the heads of the opposition to those measures, which have brought dishonour to the Crown, and ruin to the nation . . . may be invited to the helm of state; let them not forget the rock, upon which so many before them have split. If they also should veer about, and without blushing become the accomplices of the very criminals they had avowed to bring to justice; and only made use of popularity, to be wafted into a situation, where they may with impunity rivet that yoke, which they stood engaged to . . . break in pieces; let them remember, that the *Monitor* will not fail to tell them in plain English of their doings.[1]

At the meeting where Pitt and his little group of relations and personal supporters drew up their plans for his assumption of the office to which the king was reluctantly forced to call him, they invited a representative of the City to be present. He was one Richard Glover, commonly known as 'Leonidas' Glover, after his political poem of that name, who had taken a prominent part in the City in the agitation against Walpole twelve years before. They indicated to him what might be called their pledges —the dismissal of 'unpopular and undeserving men', the establishment of a militia, the repatriation of the mercenaries, and, in particular, a parliamentary inquiry into the misconduct of their predecessors. He, on his side, put down in writing the principles on which he considered that Pitt must stand. In addition to the points which they had made, he urged that Pitt ought 'to make a reserve, absolutely not to involve the nation with the continent, in case he should at any time disapprove of such a measure', and that he should insist on the removal of all 'efficient members of the last administration'. He also went much farther. It was essential that Pitt should not give up any of these points to the king. 'In the present calamitous crisis', he wrote, 'it is

[1] The *Monitor*, No. 68, 13 November 1756, ii. 162.

indispensably necessary, not only that the King should not be master; but that he should know and feel, he is not and ought not to be so.' If Pitt acted on these lines he would be 'universally applauded without doors', and 'if it be alleged, that Mr. Pitt should pay some deference to the Houses of Parliament, the creatures of the late administration, it is answered, No. He should think of no other support, as Minister, in so dangerous a time, but the rectitude of his measures and intentions; if Parliament will not support these, that Parliament may become a victim of public despair, and he have this satisfaction, at least, of being the single man spared by an enraged and ruined nation.'[1] It is not surprising that the reception of this revolutionary advice by the politicians to whom it was directed was markedly evasive, but it reflects fairly accurately what was being said among the popular politicians of the City, and when Newcastle lamented that Pitt was flinging himself upon 'the People and the Tories',[2] such men were what he meant by 'the People'.

But, just as Newcastle's administration fell not only because of popular disfavour, but because of weaknesses which arose from the more normal workings of eighteenth-century politics, so too the Devonshire–Pitt administration was in no sense purely the product of popular forces. Nor, since whatever the city orators and the press might say, the situation was in no sense revolutionary, could the administration act as if it were. It was, in the first place, a composite body. Pitt and his small band of friends held some of the key posts in it, Pitt as Secretary of State, Lord Temple as First Lord of the Admiralty, and Henry Legge as a Chancellor of the Exchequer who was intended to be far more powerful than was the Chancellor when Newcastle held the Treasury. But the First Lord of the Treasury was the Duke of Devonshire; no attempt was made to interfere with the military authority of the Duke of Cumberland and Lord Barrington continued as Secretary at War, while, to satisfy the king, Lord Holderness retained the position of Secretary of State for the Northern Department, despite the fact that he had incurred great unpopularity over an incident involving the discipline of the

[1] Our account of this meeting comes from a single and admittedly somewhat unreliable source, Richard Glover's *Memoirs of a Celebrated Literary and Political Character*, London 1813. The main lines of his account and of his written document are probably fairly accurate, though he greatly over-estimates his own importance. He says that the meeting took place on a Saturday about the end of October. If so, it seems likely to have been on 30 October.

[2] Newcastle to Hardwicke, 11 December 1756. Brit. Mus. Add. MS. 32869, f. 323*v*.

Hanoverian mercenaries in the country.[1] All these ministers were entirely independent of Pitt, were extremely critical of him, and maintained a much closer contact with Newcastle or Fox than with their new colleagues. In the second place, as the new ministry began to set to work, there were no signs that Pitt and his colleagues were gaining ground either in the closet or the House of Commons. The king remained implacably suspicious, and was looking round for alternative men to serve him from the beginning.[2] The Duke of Cumberland was hostile,[3] and though Lord Bute for Leicester House spoke eloquently of favours in the future,[4] he had little to offer in the present. In the House of Commons, it is true, the Tories, under the lead of Beckford and Sir John Philipps, now came to support Pitt, but he made few converts elsewhere; all the political world recognized the basic instability of the administration, and it could not be ignored that its very existence depended on the abstention of the followers of Newcastle and Fox from challenging it to a division.[5] And in the third place it was not merely Pitt's dependence on their goodwill, but the facts of the situation which

[1] Much heat had been generated over the case of a Hanoverian soldier at Maidstone who had been arrested for an alleged petty theft, and was handed over, on the order of the Secretary of State, to his military authorities for trial in accordance with the terms of the agreement for the employment of these troops. Pitt found this one of his most embarrassing problems.

[2] He found Lord Temple more personally distasteful than Pitt (he told the Duke of Devonshire that he 'could not bear the sight of him'. Hardwicke to Newcastle, 3 April 1757. Brit. Mus. Add. MS. 32870, f. 359), but both of them had annoyed him on several important topics, including their attempt to persuade him to prevent the execution of Byng.

[3] One of the reasons for the precipitate dismissal of Pitt and Temple before a substitute ministry was in sight was that Cumberland, setting out to command the forces in Germany, did not wish to leave his father with these ministers. See Holderness's statement to the Prussian ambassador Michell, *Politische Correspondenz Friedrichs des Grossen*, Berlin, 1883, xiv. 502.

[4] On 2 March 1757 Bute, congratulating Pitt on his courage in bringing forward the vote for an army of observation to aid the King of Prussia, said he was sure that, even had the result not been propitious he would have been buoyed up by the 'countenance of *him* who is some day to reap the fruits of my friend's unwearied endeavours for the public safety'. *Chatham Correspondence*, i. 224.

[5] In February 1757 Lord Waldegrave told the king that though Newcastle was 'no longer a minister, it was very apparent a great majority in both houses of parliament still considered him as their chief, and were ready to act under his direction. That some of these might possibly be attached to him by a principle of gratitude; but the greater number were his followers, because they had reason to expect that he would soon be in a condition to reward their services.' Waldegrave, *Memoirs from 1754 to 1758*, London, 1821, pp. 95–96.

rendered most of the measures he had thundered for in opposition impracticable or irrelevant now that he was in power.

No responsible minister could deny the essentiality of a second front in Europe, or ignore the king's interest in his Hanoverian possessions; Pitt had accepted these facts to some extent when he accepted office. The foreign mercenaries might be sent away (they were indeed urgently required abroad) but if adequate reinforcements were to be sent to America some of them must be kept for some months longer.[1] The Militia Bill was of little practical importance, its real popularity was uncertain and it required drastic pruning;[2] and even the most naïve of the supporters of the new administration had to recognize the danger of forcing their parliamentary enemies to combine against them by proceeding actively with the inquiry into the conduct of the late ministers which had been one of the main planks in their popular programme.[3] Thus the Militia Bill was proceeded with very slowly and was much amended. No definite action was taken to bring on the inquiry until after Pitt's dismissal from office, and then (ironically enough) it was those whom the inquiry threatened who forced the pace, being by this time anxious to return to power but unwilling to do so until they were cleared from its charges. Even a few guerrilla attacks on the late administration by such individuals as Beckford[4] and Charles Townshend[5] were not only unsuccessful but were disapproved by their own colleagues. Nor was it possible to offset these disappointments by an early reverse of the country's fortunes in war. Even the great Coalition Ministry of 1757 brought no dramatic victories until late in 1758.

In short, it soon became clear that popular aspirations were

[1] Pitt was anxious that there should be provision for them in the Estimates for two months only (Barrington to Newcastle, 21 December 1756. Brit. Mus. Add. MS. 32869, f. 387) though he recognized that they must stay longer.

[2] For the course of this Bill see *Debates and Proceedings of the British House of Commons*, xix. 202.

[3] The ex-Lord Chancellor Hardwicke early called on Pitt and made it clear that Newcastle's friends would not combine with Fox in any opposition to the Ministry, unless forced by 'enquiries and censures'. Hardwicke to Newcastle, 6 December 1756. Brit. Mus. Add. MS. 32869, f. 254. For the attitude among the ministry's own supporters see T. Potter to Temple [December 1756], P.R.O. 30/8/53, ff. 95 seq.

[4] On 24 January 1757 Beckford accused Newcastle of encouraging smuggling while he was at the Treasury. *Memoirs and Correspondence of George, Lord Lyttelton*, ed. R. Phillimore, London, 1845, ii. 585–6.

[5] On 7 February 1757 Charles Townshend abused Newcastle, in attacking a contract held by Alderman Sir William Baker. Walpole, *Memoires*, ii. 133.

destined to fail no less in 1757 than they had in 1742, and that those who put their faith in Pitt and his so-called 'popular' administration were to suffer the same disappointment as those who had put their faith in Pulteney some twelve years earlier. The question arises why was the result so different? Why did Pulteney remain in the popular mythology of the City for the next thirty years as the great betrayer, while the popularity of Pitt rose to such heights there that there was widespread dismay when he was dismissed, and when, two months later, he made his coalition with the very men whom he had so bitterly attacked he was able to do so without an appreciable· damage to his reputation?[1]

If this question could be answered comprehensively, we should have the basis for the understanding of much of the City's role in the politics of the time; but the reasons and feelings under- lying public opinion are always both too complex and too inarticulate for precise analysis, and nowhere more than at the point at which principles and aspirations merge with questions of personality. There are, nevertheless, various specific reasons which can be given which do something to explain this pheno- menon. A big part in preserving and augmenting Pitt's popularity was undoubtedly played by the king's impatience in dismissing him so precipitately, for this made it possible to argue that he would have achieved various ends had he not been thwarted by those in high places. Paradoxically also, he was helped by the collapse of his own health (that curious partly psychological collapse which was to afflict him again in 1766–7 when once again he seemed to have the ball at his feet); for, though this ill health greatly limited his activities (he had only six audiences with the king during his four months of office and only attended the House of Commons fifteen times),[2] it saved him from the necessity of advancing unpopular measures, and disarmed criti- cism of the absence of any rapid improvements in the situation of the country abroad. As Horace Walpole said:

Pitt had acted during his short reign with a haughty reserve, that, if it had kept off dependents and attachments, at least had left him all the air of patriot privacy; and having luckily, from the King's dislike of him, and from the shortness of the time, been dipt but in few un- gracious businesses, he came back to the mob scarce 'shorn of his beams'.[3]

[1] It was not achieved, however, without some heart-burning and hard work on the part of such supporters as William Beckford.
[2] Michell to Frederick, 1 April 1757, *Politische Correspondenz Friedrichs des Grossen*, op. cit. xiv. 502.   [3] *Memoires*, ii. 202.

There were, however, at least two other factors which also played a considerable part in preserving and increasing his popularity—the publicity he received and the financial operations of his administration. The question of publicity may be considered first. It had been part of the general ineptitude of the Newcastle administration that they made no attempt to counter the violent campaign in press, pamphlet, and broadsheet that had been opened against them, though they recognized its effectiveness particularly in the City.[1] On 6 November the *Monitor* had been able to boast that no one had taken the field against it.[2] But on the very day on which the boast was printed, it ceased to be true, for on that day appeared the first number of a scurrilous but well-written paper called the *Test* which was produced under the auspices of Henry Fox, and which was directed wholly against Pitt and his administration.[3] It was promptly answered by Pitt's supporters in a paper called the *Contest*;[4] other publications followed on both sides,[5] and soon a pamphlet war was raging so violently that Horace Walpole wrote they 'make me recollect *Fogs* and *Craftsmen* as harmless libels'.[6] Attack is always easier than defence in popular publications, and Pitt's anomalous position was peculiarly difficult to justify; moreover the *Test* was much more ably written than were its opponents. Nevertheless the very virulence of its attack—what a contemporary called 'its bear-garden and Billingsgate language'[7]—redounded to Pitt's advantage by rallying sympathy to him, and it was Fox not Pitt who suffered from the campaign. It is indeed from this episode that Fox's

[1] Hardwicke had recommended that the attacks on the administration should be answered in short papers in some of the newspapers as 'these short diurnal libels do more harm than the larger pamphlets, because they spread more amongst the common people'. Hardwicke to Newcastle, 29 August 1756. Brit. Mus. Add. MS. 32867, f. 146. But nothing was done. A pamphlet was, however, written by D. Mallet in defence of the administration over the loss of Minorca, entitled *Conduct of the Ministry Examined*.

[2] No. 67, ii. 146.

[3] It was written by various hands, but chiefly it was believed by Arthur Murphy and Dr. Philip Francis, father of Sir Philip Francis to whom the *Letters of Junius* are generally attributed. It may be noted that the invective of the *Test* has much resemblance to that later applied with such effect by *Junius*.   [4] Generally attributed to Arthur Ruffhead.

[5] e.g. *The Constitution* (pro-Fox) and *The Aequipoise, or the Constitution Ballanced* (pro-Pitt).

[6] Letter to Sir Horace Mann, 6 January 1757. *Letters*, iv. 26.

[7] John Roberts to Newcastle, 28 December 1757. Brit. Mus. Add. MS. 32869, f. 406*v*.

acute unpopularity in the City, which was to cause him no slight anxiety in the future, seems to date, while the attack succeeded only in making Pitt's supporters close their ranks, and in consolidating the popular picture of him which they were seeking to advance.

This pamphlet war and the stir it created coincided with the second factor tending to the increase of Pitt's popularity in the City, the Government's financial measures—the only serious attempt they made to realize the popular expectations from them. Though these measures were in fact the responsibility of Legge as Chancellor of the Exchequer and there is no evidence that Pitt concerned himself with them in any way, Legge was associated so closely in the public mind with his leader—the *Test* unkindly called him Pitt's Sancho Panza—that the leader's reputation gained as much from them as did that of the follower.

The previous administration had resigned before the plans were completed for the raising of supplies in the coming year, though it was known that a substantial loan would have to be raised to meet the expenses of war.[1] Newcastle at the Treasury, with the assistance of his able secretary, James West,[2] had continued Pelham's practice of consulting Sir John Barnard on the raising of the supplies and of placating the commercial interests which he represented, but he had also followed Pelham's example in buttressing his schemes by a close association with the 'monied interest' which Sir John and his supporters so greatly suspected. Legge, though he had been Chancellor of the Exchequer under Newcastle, appears to have had little to do with this aspect of the Treasury's work; he had a new and totally inexperienced Secretary of the Treasury[3] who had none of West's close contacts with the financiers; but still more, the views of the administration's supporters in the City made any collaboration with the 'monied interest' in the raising of supplies well nigh impossible for him. The *Monitor* was expressing their views when it called on all good men 'to discourage those harpies, called money-jobbers, who, under the pretence of assisting government, become the plunderers of it'.[4] Hence, though it was often claimed for the administration that they were, through their popularity

[1] They had been sounding City opinion on the subject as early as September 1756 and by October had made some progress, but nothing had been settled. The change in administration meant that the raising of the supplies was left considerably later than usual.

[2] James West (*c.* 1704–72) at this time M.P. for St. Albans.

[3] Samuel Martin (1714–88) at this time M.P. for Camelford.

[4] No. 2, i. 14. This was laid down as one of its maxims for a patriot party.

in the City, peculiarly well placed to raise the supplies, they could in fact only do so if they were successful in applying quite unorthodox measures.

This was what Legge tried to do. He was hampered rather than assisted by a flood of projects and suggestions which made their appearance in the press and in the post bags of ministers as soon as the new ministry was formed. He gained, however, a powerful if somewhat unexpected ally in Sir John Barnard. Sir John had remained loyal to his former friends and unreconciled to Pitt whom he had called 'the most overbearing man in Parliament that he had ever known';[1] nor can he have viewed with favour the rise of Beckford's star in the City firmament. But he evidently could not refuse the opportunity of trying out the schemes he had long favoured, unhampered for once by the caution of the Treasury and the rival influence of the 'monied interest', and it would seem that he early placed his services at Legge's disposal. The financial principles he had advocated for many years were based on two main assumptions. The first was the danger of doing anything which would increase the burden of the national debt; the second was the desirability of raising loans by an 'open' subscription, whereby any individual could subscribe in books laid open for the purpose, as against the 'closed' subscription, favoured by eighteenth-century Treasuries as more reliable, whereby negotiations were carried out with a small group of monied individuals and institutions, to whom allocations were given for division among their clients. Other, subordinate, views to which he adhered were an old-fashioned preference for loans to be managed by the Exchequer rather than the Bank of England (part of his dislike of the 'monied interest'), and a liking for a lottery with tickets in small denominations, as a supplement to larger loans, so as to give the man of modest means a further opportunity to participate. In most of these views he was warmly supported by the main body of the citizens of London, and in all he was opposed by the 'monied interest'.

All these ideas (except, ultimately, the proposal to manage the loan without recourse to the Bank)[2] were incorporated in

[1] J. West to Newcastle, 23 October 1756. Brit. Mus. Add. MS. 32868, f. 390.

[2] This would seem to be what is meant by an entry in the *Public Advertiser* of 25 March 1757, where it is stated that there was likely to be 'a change in the Annuity Scheme for a Number of Years certain; instead of having Exchequer orders, 'tis said, they will be transferable at the Bank'.

the propositions which Legge brought forward as his budget scheme, and a further element of unorthodoxy was added as well. On 21 January 1757 he laid before the Committee of Ways and Means, a plan for the raising of a lottery for £1,050,000 in one guinea tickets;[1] after considerable delay, he followed this on 11 March[2] with a proposal to raise £2½ million by the issue of annuities. The details of both these projects were unorthodox and indeed without exact parallel in English financial practice. The issue of supplementary lotteries was not indeed uncommon (Newcastle had issued one, also under Barnard's influence, in 1756) but that put forward by Legge and based on a scheme advanced by an ingenious Jewish projector, one Jacob Henriques,[3] differed markedly from any hitherto employed. In the lotteries hitherto offered to the public the element of chance played a comparatively small part. All who bought tickets obtained the right to an annuity, but at a lower rate of interest than that normally current; in compensation they had the chance of winning one of the fairly numerous money prizes. Henriques's scheme was, on the other hand, that of a modern lottery; half the proceeds were to be paid out in prizes, but those who failed to win one obtained nothing at all.

The proposals for the issue of annuities were equally unorthodox, and had the obvious disadvantage of being exceedingly complicated. Subscribers were offered the alternatives of obtaining either annuities for fixed terms of years, or annuities for fixed terms of years which could be transferred to survivors. Both the interest earned and the number of years for which it could be enjoyed were graded according to the age of the subscriber or his nominee, five categories being provided. Though the limited actuarial knowledge of the period made it extremely difficult to estimate the real rate of interest at which the Government would be borrowing under this scheme, it was thought to work out at about 3½ per cent. Subscribers were given good time in which to make their first deposit, the closing date being fixed for 14 April.

The advantages of these proposals to the Treasury, if they were successful, were that the money would be raised, as Sir John Barnard wished, without permanent increase to the

[1] 30 Geo. II, c. 5.
[2] It passed the House on 14 March 1757.
[3] Horace Walpole (*Memoires*, ii. 132) called him 'a visionary Jew, who long pestered the public with his reveries'. He was said, as inventor, to be getting 1d. per ticket (*London Chronicle*, 27–29 January 1757, i. 98). When the scheme failed he complained to the *London Chronicle* (7–9 April 1757, i. 98) that this was due to modifications in his original scheme.

national debt, and that it would be raised at a very moderate rate of interest. The advantage to the public was supposed to be that everyone who so wished could be a subscriber. The disadvantage of the proposals on the other hand was a decisive one, that they were extremely unlikely to succeed. So far as the lottery was concerned even its friends urged subscribers to take it up rather as a patriotic duty than as a profitable speculation. Legge himself was praised in the Press for his patriotism in announcing that he would subscribe 1,000 guineas to it,[1] and John Calcraft, a shrewd if hostile critic, reported six weeks after it opened 'Legge's silly lottery fills . . . so slowly that there are not 40,000 tickets yet subscribed for, though all placemen have been harassed into the subscription'.[2] Three months after it had opened it was believed to have raised no more than £60,000.[3]

The annuities fared no better. The complexity of the scheme and the rates at which it was offered made it unattractive, and the 'monied interest', without whose help a sum of this magnitude could not be raised on the money market of the day, seem to have made it clear that they would not support it even before the scheme came before the House. In the House it was coldly received. Henry Fox said he 'wished the scheme might be effectual and hoped the gentleman's support in it (for which he had the greatest respect) [i.e. Sir John Barnard] had given him assurance that it would'.[4] Legge himself introduced it with the faintest praise that a Chancellor can ever have given the financial proposition he laid before the House. He said

that he had heard from 100 persons and received anonymous letters that his scheme would not do. Some had affectedly misunderstood the scheme others ignorantly, but that if it did not succeed he did not think the Earth would gape and swallow him up, but that he should come to Parliament with some other proposition, if this was not full in a month.[5]

With this inauspicious beginning it was not surprising that on 14 April when the books closed only £313,000 was found to have been subscribed of the £2½ million required. Even before the resolution was through the House Newcastle's City friends had warned him 'You may depend on it that the money will not be

---

[1] *Public Advertiser*, 3 February 1757.

[2] J. Calcraft to Lord Loudoun, 4 March 1757. Brit. Mus. Add. MS. 17493, f. 49.

[3] By 3 August 1757 it had apparently risen to 'near £300,000'. S. Gideon to Devonshire, Chatsworth MSS. 512. 4.

[4] J. West to Newcastle, 11 March 1757. Brit. Mus. Add. MS. 32870, f. 259v.   [5] Ibid., f. 259.

raised, and the Season advances',[1] but there are no signs that Legge and his financial advisers had any alternative scheme in mind, or that they could have advanced one without a complete reversal of their financial policy. On the day on which the books were shut, Sir John Barnard, it is true, went down to Garraway's Coffee House and tried to obtain support for a modified form of the scheme, apparently hastily thought out,[2] and for ten days or so there seemed to be some chance that he would try to bring a revised scheme before the House.[3] But by this time Legge had resigned, following Pitt and Temple from office on 8 April, and despite these last-minute efforts, and a plea for them from Legge to Devonshire,[4] the cause was a lost one.

When Legge resigned, the unfortunate Duke of Devonshire who was quite unversed in such matters, was left with the urgent problem of raising supplies which were already late, in a year when big campaigns had to be undertaken, and in a situation where it was vital for another reason that no time should be lost. For a new ministry had to be formed and those whose assistance was required were not prepared to take office until this controversial issue was out of the way.[5] Fortunately for him, however, if the Treasury had been inactive, the leaders of the 'monied interest' had not. The day after the books closed two of them, Sir Joshua Vanneck and John Gore, M.P., old supporters of Newcastle's at the Treasury, waited on him with proposals to raise the sum required by the traditional means of a 'closed' subscription.[6] Within a few days Samson Gideon, the great Jewish financier, and other prominent men were in touch with him,[7] and in less than a fortnight, despite the opposition of Sir John Barnard and the outcries of the popular press, arrangements were completed for a loan by closed subscription of £3 million at 3 per cent., with what was known as a 'douceur', a life annuity of £1. 2s. 6d. per cent. to the subscribers.[8]

[1] J. Watkins to Newcastle, 17 March 1757. Brit. Mus. Add. MS. 32870, f. 305.   [2] J. West to Newcastle, 15 April 1757. Ibid., ff. 437–8.

[3] Appendix A, nos. xvi et seq., below.   [4] Appendix A, no. xxvi below.

[5] Paper laid before the king by Lord Waldegrave on 9 March 1757. Brit. Mus. Add. MS. 32870, f. 250.

[6] J. West to Newcastle, 15 April 1757; see n. 2 above.

[7] Appendix A, nos. ii and iii below. West had reported to Newcastle on 15 April that Gideon had said 'he should not go unless sent for', but within a few days he was at the centre of activities, spurred on no doubt by his ambition for a peerage—see L. S. Sutherland, 'Samson Gideon: Eighteenth Century Jewish Financier', *Transactions of the Jewish Historical Society of England*, xvii, pp. 79–90. See below, pp. 387-98.   [8] 30 Geo. III, c. 19.

In its financial policy, therefore, the Devonshire–Pitt administration failed as completely in furthering the aspirations of its supporters as it did in other spheres. Nevertheless its failure was of the kind which the popular forces in the City could easily understand and which could be turned to advantage. It could be, and was, argued that, just as in their other activities, their intentions had been good, but that they had been defeated by vested interests, in this case by a conspiracy among those to which public opinion in the City was peculiarly hostile, the financiers of the 'monied interest'. During the weeks when the loans were under discussion and well after the supplies had been raised, the subject was the staple of Press controversy. The *Contest* for Pitt assured its readers that 'It is indisputable that the present method of raising the supplies constitutes a most shining part of the present administration, and will reflect honour to their memories, to the latest posterity'.[1] The *Test* for Fox, on the other hand, twitted them with the failure of their subscription to fill, and an imaginary Tory up from Oxford is made to lament 'The game is up, and I find that after all their promises they mean nothing. I thought they would have had interest in the city, and I imagined the supplies could be raised by them alone. But their popularity is not so great as we flattered ourselves. . ..'[2] To this the *Contest* retorted that an open subscription could not be expected to fill as quickly as 'when the whole quota is furnished by a few wealthy proprietaries', and that any unnecessary delay that was occurring was due to 'the emissaries of a despairing party' who 'run about to propagate the slowness of the subscription in order to discourage subscribers'.[3] After Legge's resignation, the *Test* blamed him for leaving the country's finances in chaos, after squandering his time on 'idle visionary projects';[4] while the *Contest* assailed the closed subscription taken up after his scheme had failed as a reversion to the custom

---

[1] No. 20, 2 April 1757. Cf. no. 19, 26 March 1757.

[2] 26 March 1757. On 12 February it had attacked the lottery, and on 12 March had attacked the administration's financial policy more generally. 'They have attempted to give us a convincing proof of their great ministerial advantages by opening a voluntary subscription, that we might perceive how readily all England would concur to support the ministers of the people: accordingly there is now subscribed about sixty thousand pounds at the bank. A mighty atchievement truly . . .! Thus is the business of our king and country almost totally at a stand; . . . and the remaining supplies, never before left to so late a day, are again adjourned. . . .'

[3] See n. 1 above.

[4] 14 May 1757.

of beggaring posterity by the payment of 'exhorbitant premiums to Jewish cormorants, who were wantonly called the moneyed-interest, and who, by an iniquitous combination, could either raise or sink the publick credit at their own mercenary will'.[1]

Some three months after Pitt and Legge had been given the freedom of the City on their loss of office—and it is significant that it was Legge, not Lord Temple (a more important political figure) whose name the City joined with that of Pitt[2]—the Grocers' Company feasted them. Among the toasts was one 'to the downfall of monopolizers and infamous stockjobbing'.[3] The financial projects of 1757, unsuccessful though they were, played a considerable part in consolidating Pitt's popularity in the City, a popularity which was to grow steadily through the great coalition ministry and which he was never altogether to lose. As time went on this popularity was to be enhanced by Pitt's great services as a war minister and by the pre-eminence which his personality won him; and his personality, more than expectation of constitutional reform from him, became its basis. But this was for the future. During the few uneasy months of the Devonshire–Pitt administration, it was not his exploits which won the favour of the rank and file of the citizens of London, and their constitutional expectations from him (still fresh in their minds) were doomed to disappointment. Their support of him depended on a feeling—which they were never altogether to lose and which had in it elements of truth—that he was in some manner akin to them, since he stood with them against the big battalions of the political and financial world.

The financial policy of the Devonshire–Pitt administration reflected the views of the City opinion hostile to the 'monied interest'. There remain to be considered, as pendents to this study two matters concerning, on the other hand, the 'monied interest' whom they opposed. The first concerns the allegation, often made by contemporaries, that the 'monied interest' by their control over the means of raising supplies could and did make and unmake administrations. This allegation I have examined elsewhere, and I have suggested that it was groundless.[4] 1757 is one of the occasions on which such allegations were

---

[1] 7 May 1757.

[2] On 12 April 1757 J. Watkins wrote to Newcastle that he found in the City 'nobody so much regretted as Mr. Legge'. Brit. Mus. Add. MS. 32870, f. 409.

[3] *London Chronicle*, 4–6 August 1757, ii. 127.

[4] 'The City of London in Eighteenth Century Politics', loc. cit., pp. 52–53. See above, pp. 44-5.

made. On this occasion it would certainly seem that the 'monied interest' as a whole was hostile to Legge's propositions and that their hostility made it certain that these would fail. They may even have banded together to boycott them (though of this there is no direct evidence), and they certainly joined forces to offer alternative propositions and to advance them as soon as they saw a chance of their being accepted. But there is no evidence that they did so for reasons other than those of business profit and it seems clear that they were not acting in collusion with the political opponents of the administration. Close though their relations had been with Newcastle in the past and as they were to be in the future, his agent James West seems neither to have been in their confidence nor to have encouraged them, while the sole interest of the Duke of Newcastle himself in the transaction was his anxiety that the supplies should be safely raised before he returned to office.

The second matter concerning the 'monied interest' on which some light is thrown during this administration is the operation of the closed subscription. Since the Duke of Devonshire, after Legge's resignation, had to handle the raising of supplies in person, a good deal of material about the closed subscription by which they were raised, has been preserved among his papers. Moreover, since he was entirely inexperienced, the financiers who were working with him, including the great Jewish financier Samson Gideon, found it necessary to give him in writing advice on how to run it. No comparable information about the operation of the system has so far come to light.[1] Some of it is published in appendices to this lecture. Here I mention only a few salient points that arise from it. One is the view taken by the financiers of their great enemy Sir John Barnard; they are said to consider him a man 'whose abilities in points of credit they rank no higher than a schoolmaster who can teach boys to cast sums but not teach a man where to gett credit for them'.[2] They draw a contrast between the open subscription beloved of their opponents and the closed subscription which they advocated.

An open subscription or what is called so is of no other use than that of tying up the hands of the Government by Parliamentary Resolutions and publick advertisement and at the same time leaving the People at liberty to accept or reject the proposals at pleasure. . . .

---

[1] I am indebted to his grace the Duke of Devonshire for permission to use this material, and to the late Sir Lewis Namier for drawing my attention to it.

[2] Chatsworth MS. 512. 23. Abstract printed below, Appendix A, no. xx.

To choose such a subscription was to

... hazard the supplies through the caprice of an unknown multitude and refuse an absolute bargain with a number of people of worth and honour most of them proprietors in the large companies, men of knowledge and ability to raise and maintain the price of their new purchase to the advantage of the old funds and benefit of 70 millions of property.[1]

There is also, among the duke's papers, a statement for the Treasury to make on the occasion of the acceptance of their offer, which may well derive from one of them.

The method for raising the supplies proposed by Sir John Bernard having failed, the season of the year for commencing all military operations being advanced, the Treasury apprehensive least a second attempt of the like nature or like method should be proposed and fail, were under no small concern. It therefore gave them great satisfaction to have proposals made to them by a considerable number of eminent merchants and large proprietors of the old Funds. . . . .[2]

Several lists showing the allocation of scrip to subscribers survive in these manuscripts.[3] There were five big subscribers—popularly known as 'the mighty Five': Sir Joshua Vanneck, who got £500,000—some at least of it probably for the Dutch subscribers for whom he normally acted; John Gore, who got £200,000; Samson Gideon who got £100,000; Joseph Salvador, who got £150,000 for a list of Jewish subscribers; a fifth big list of £340,000 subdivided among a number of City men was probably that of Nicholas Linwood.[4] There were a considerable number of bankers, government contractors, and other businessmen who got between £10,000 and £50,000 apiece for themselves and their clients. The Directors of the Bank of England got £200,000 between them; the South Sea Company £150,000 and the East India Company, under protest, had to content itself with £100,000. The two insurance companies got £50,000 each and the London Hospital (of which the Duke of Devonshire was President, and John Gore one of the vice-Presidents) £20,000. There were a number of smaller allocations including a few to peers and M.P.s who had no obvious contact with the City, and small sums were provided for the editors of certain papers, including the official *Gazette*. Finally £55,000 was put

[1] Chatsworth MSS. 512 O.A.
[2] Ibid. 512 O.
[3] See Appendix B.
[4] His application was made through Henry Fox. See Appendix A, nos. i and ix.

aside for the officials of the Treasury in what was called 'the Treasury list as marked by Mr. Fane'.[1] Apart from the fact that room had to be found for those who had already subscribed to Legge's abortive scheme, no list could have been more typical of the closed subscription in which the Treasuries of the day put their trust than that which followed the financial experiments of the Devonshire–Pitt administration.

[1] One of the Chief Clerks at the Treasury.

APPENDIX A

Selection of Letters and Schemes from the papers of the 4th Duke of Devonshire
(Chatsworth MSS.)

EXCEPT where otherwise stated the documents are transcribed in full.
The use of capitals has been modernized; abbreviations have been expanded, and punctuation added or amended where it is necessary for
the understanding of the text.

I

330. 197. Extract. *Henry Fox to the Duke of Devonshire.* 15 April 1757.

Written on the day when Vanneck, Gore and others made their proposals.
Touchet seems to have got £30,000 and Linwood £20,000. (See Appendix
B.)

'I am desired by Mr. Touchet and Mr. Linwood, two very honest
men and very eminent merchants to speak to your Grace, with their
offer to subscribe largely to whatever bargain your Grace may have made
for raising the money with Messrs. Vanneck and Gore, etc. I don't think
they will be so coming to any scheme of Sir John Barnard's. I have likewise application from several others. If your Grace should make the
bargain for 3 per Cent. with 1 and ⅛ Life Annuity, or even with only 1
per Cent. Life Annuity (paying interest for the whole term subscribed
from the time of paying half of it) I can answer for £500,000, and desire
to have so much for the above-mentioned persons etc. in whatever bargain you may make.'

II

512. 3. *Copy in a clerk's hand. Undated.* [*Ante 20 April 1757*]

This document is a letter written in the third person, the names of the
writer and recipient being represented only by initials. The writer, who
calls himself 'Mr. G', was Samson Gideon; the recipient 'Mr. D' would seem
to be a thin disguise for the Duke of Devonshire, for the contents make it
clear that it was addressed to the minister responsible for raising the loan,
we know (see p. 105 below) that the duke handled the loan himself, and the
duke has completed Gideon's name in his own hand. Gideon had told James
West that he would not take any part 'unless sent for' (see p. 88, n. 7 above),
and may well have been anxious that this correspondence should not be
known.

Mr. G[ideon]'s compliments—is confined to his bed; not permitted
to go abroad, would otherwise have waited upon Mr. D—.

Mr. G has great reasons to be of opinion that the article, Number 2
—will be very essential as well as beneficial to the Publick.

The article No. 8 will be likewise of consequence, and a saving to the
Publick, as shall be explained at sight.

Mr. D— is desired not to let the Distributors have too large sums, as they will clash with each other, and be attended with other inconveniencies.

Mr. D— is desired not to let the Dispersers, (if possible) know the powers granted to each other.

The Dispersers to return their lists—Wednesday next [20 April 1757], as perhaps it may be needful to have a meeting on the day following.

That the Cashiers of the Bank be impowered to take in subscriptions in the room of those that shall be defaulters, upon the day following, to compleat the sum of £—.

That no time should be lost in securing the first payment between the 25th and 29th inst.

That the hint given to Mr. D— will raise a large sum, which may be made use of for some time, will be esteemed a great oeconomy, and render honour to the proposer.

That Mr. D— may be informed of the state of that affair as soon as Mr. G— can go abroad, and it will not be material to be known before.

That Mr. D— will consider that serving the five companies [the Bank, South Sea Company, East India Company, and the two Insurance Companies] will be obliging above 100 people, which should be known to be by Mr. D—'s directions.

Mr. G— has desired Alderman Gossling [Francis Gosling, banker, of Fleet St.] to make his payment upon £100,000 the first day, upon any terms that Mr. D— shall fix upon; and does not confine his contribution to the terms of the Proposal.

III

512. 2. *Copy in a clerk's hand: undated.*

Endorsed in the Duke of Devonshire's hand '(Mr. G's proposals)'. These proposals were evidently those referred to in and forwarded with the preceding letter. Comparison of the proposals with the terms of 30 Geo. II, c. 19 shows that many but not all of the suggestions were adopted.

Proposed, that the Right Honourable the Lords Commissioners of his Majesty's Treasury, be impowered to raise any sum or sums, not exceeding the sum of £— for the courant service etc.; at such times, and by such methods as their Lordships shall think proper, upon the following terms and conditions—vizt.

1st. Either by granting the contributors transferrable annuities at the Bank, bearing an interest after the rate of £3 per cent. per annum (free of stamp duty)—attended with an annuity for life of £1. 2. 6. per cent. or upon so much of £— as shall be subscribed as aforesaid:—or otherwise the subscribers shall be at liberty to make choice of annuities bearing an interest after the rate of £3½ per cent. to be ingrafted and blended with the £1,500,000 annuities raised at £3½ per cent. for the service of the year 1756, subject to the same clauses in every respect, and attended with an annuity for life after the rate of £1. 2. 6. per cent. as hereafter.

2nd. The subscribers to make choice of either of the above proposals at the time of subscribing, or on or before the day of the second payment.

3rd. That in case the subscribers or any of them shall not on or before the — of — declare in which of the aforesaid schemes they intend their several contributions, then and in such cases the said contributors can be credited with annuities at £3 per cent. per annum till redeemed, attended with an annuity of £1. 2s. 6d. per cent. for life.

4th. That £15 per cent. be paid at the time of subscribing, and that the second payment be only £10 per cent. The remaining payments to be made upon the same days and in the same proportions as were proposed for the late intended Tontine.

5th. That interest do commence upon both the annuities at and after the 5th July, and the first six months paid on the 5th day of January 1758.

6th. That the nominees be returned on or before the 24 day of December next.

7th. That such of the life annuities as shall not be fixed by returning nominee or nominees on or before the 24th day of December as aforesaid may, at any time after, claim such annuities by returning nominee or nominees, which annuities shall commence at and from the 5th day of January, or at and from the fifth day of July next ensuing the day of returning such nominees to the Exchequer—and having the same endorsed upon the respective receipt or receipts of the Bank of such annuities for life, as shall be claimed after the 24th day of December 1757.

8th. That no allowance be made to those who shall make any advanced payments before the days of the general payments, but upon compleating the payments the subscriptions to be made transferrable stock.

IV

512. 28. Abstract. *A. Edmonstone to* —. Monday 3 o'clock [probably 18 April 1757]

The writer was Archibald, later (1774) Sir Archibald Edmonstone, Bt. of Dumbartonshire. He made the first payment on £5,000 stock. E 401/2598 1.

Begs that his unnamed correspondent should approach the Duke of Devonshire for £10,000 for him in the 'subscription on foot . . . somewhat more advantagious than the old Funds . . . as the whole is in the Grace's disposal'.

512. 12. Abstract. *Martins, Stone and Blackwell to the Duke of Devonshire*. Lombard Street, 19 April 1757.

John and Joseph Martin, Richard Stone and Ebenezer Blackwell were prominent London bankers. Joseph Martin made the first payment on £50,000. (E. 401/2598.)

As large numbers of gentlemen had approached them 'and gentlemen that were always great supporters of the mony credit of this nation' they ask for at least £300,000 stock, which 'will be not near £10,000' a head.

VI

512. 11. Abstract. *Robert Snow & Co. to the Duke of Devonshire*. Temple Bar, 19 April 1757.

A well-known firm of London bankers. Snow made the first payment on £40,000. (E. 401/2598.)

'As it is confidently reported that a proposal has been made and accepted' they ask to be permitted to subscribe £40,000 for 'ourselves and our friends, over and above twenty thousand pounds standing in our names in their late subscription at the Bank', assuming that this will stand. They are not applying through 'any other person'.

VII

512. 9. *Copy in a clerk's hand, except for the concluding sentence and signature.*

The list of subscribers put forward by Joseph Salvador, the prominent Jewish financier. Those on his list were largely Jewish subscribers. Appendix B shows that the first item applied to subscribers from abroad. The undertaking by the presenter of the list to make himself responsible for the first payments on all sums allocated to those on his list, illustrates one of the chief advantages of the 'closed subscription' to the Treasury. E. 401/2598 suggests that, like other would-be subscribers, those on this list were cut.

A List for £200,000 in a Loan for the Service of the Government to be raised in Annuitys of 3 per cent. with 1⅛ per cent. Annuity on Lives annexed thereto for the payments of which I render myself answerable.

Joseph Salvador for himself and friends	£82,000
Hon. Baron Diegode Aguilar	10,000
Henry Isaacs Esq. for himself and friends	25,000
Joseph Fowke Esq.	4,500
Levy Salomons for himself and friends	15,000
Ruben Salomons for ditto	15,000
Andrew Harrison Esq.	5,000
Michael Lejay	5,000
John Deschamps	5,000

Isaac Jesurun Alvares	5,000
Isaac Fernandes Nunes	3,000
Mrs. Zipora Serra	3,000
Mrs. Leah Delmonte	3,000
Joseph de Pinto	2,000
Moses de Paiba	2,000
Joseph de Chaves	2,000
Anthony Chamier	5,000
Benjamin Lindo	3,500
Levy Norden	5,000

£200,000

London the 19th April 1757.

I render myself answerable for the above.

Joseph Salvador.

VIII

360. 6. Abstract. *Lord Conyngham to the Duke of Devonshire.* 19 April 1757.

Henry, First Viscount Conyngham [Irish peerage] got £20,000 [Appendix B.] asks to be put down for £50,000 'for I have some relations and friends to oblige'.

IX

330. 198. Extract. *Henry Fox to the Duke of Devonshire.* 19 April 1757.

Compare no. I above. William Mabbott got £30,000. See Appendix B.

'You'll see by the inclosed List [not found] how ill I have obeyed your Grace's commands, but indeed I have endeavoured it. I shall say that it is full, and I dare beleive I might have a List of as many more to trouble you with from applications this day in the House of Commons, and yet an impartial friend of mine, a calculator, does not think it a very good bargain. Mr Mabbot, a Member of Parliament and very rich man desired more, but I have put him down for £40,000, I have Calcraft, who has a great many commissions, down for 20 only; I have not put Mr Touchet down for all he asks and yet your Grace sees what it amounts to.'

X

512. 15. Abstract. *Caesar Hawkins to the Duke of Devonshire.* 'Palmal, April 20th 1757.'

Hawkins was a prominent London surgeon, at this time second Serjeant Surgeon in the Royal Household. He made the first payment on £5,000 stock. (E. 401/2598.)

Asks to be put down for £10,000.

XI

512. 13. Abstract. *Edward, Lord Digby to the Duke of Devonshire.* 20 April 1757.

Lord Digby made the first payment on £10,000 stock. (E. 401/2598.)

'One of my brothers having been for some time very desirous of purchasing an annuity for himself' he asks to be allowed to subscribe £20,000, as his brother is abroad. 'P.S. if it is so near full that I can't have 20,000£ I should be glad of 10,000.'

XII

512. 14. Abstract. *William Belchier to the Duke of Devonshire.* Lombard St., 20 April 1757.

A London banker in the house of Ironside and Belchier. E. 401/2598 shows that he made the first payment on £38,000.

He states that when he waited on the Duke to ask to be put down for £100,000 subscription 'you was pleased to say your lists were so full that you could not pretend to assure me of any such sum'. He points out that 'I had for myself and friends the last year subscribed upwards of that sum purely to assist Government, although attended with an apparent loss'. He hopes that as 'a banker and ever an assistant to serve Government' he will be given £50,000 for himself, his partners and friends, 'being informed that sum hath been by you alloted to some bankers'.

XIII

512. 16. *Alderman Sir William Baker to the Duke of Devonshire.* 21 April 1757.

Sir William Baker was M.P. for Plympton Erle, Government contractor and prominent merchant, had been chairman of the East India Company, a political supporter of the Duke of Newcastle.

My Lord Duke
Your Grace will pardon the interruption I give you, knowing, as you do, my motives.
As people are very solicitous to become subscribers to the new loan, it will give an opportunity to have the payments accelerated, and the interest postponed more than otherwise would have been adviseable. The postponing the commencement of the interest will be a saving to the publick. The compleating the payments soon, will furnish matter of argument in favour of the scheme; will put the publick into possession of the money; and by lengthening the time between the present borrowing and what must be next session of parliament, will give the funds more room to rise against that time.

If the commencement of the life annuities be put to a distant period it will be no prejudice to the subscribers, but a saving to the publick. The value of the life annuities being part of the consideration, whatever that value may be computed at is equal to so much money without interest till the commencement of the annuities; the having a reasonable length of time for the subscribers to sell their life annuities before their commencement will give a better chance of mending the market.

The making a demand now on the Parliament for three millions, whereas by the late ineffectual scheme only two and an half were asked, seems to be subject to objection; but I think may in some measure be answered by the present appearance of the sale of lottery tickets, which were estimated to furnish five hundred thousand pounds; if the whole of them are thrown out of the question then three millions are but equal to the first intended borrowing, and though there are some sold yet the number is so few as to justifye the not taking them into the estimate; and if more should be sold than are likely whatever they produce may be in abatement of the vote of credit with which the sessions will close, and prevent paying interest for so much.

To give your Grace an apology would make more necessary, so I only add my desire to be believed, My Lord Duke

etc.
Wm. Baker.

XIV

512. 20. *Sir Joshua Vanneck to the Duke of Devonshire.* Putney, 22 April 1757.

Sir Joshua Vanneck, a rich and able merchant of Dutch origin, was considered the chief originator of the present scheme and his list was far the largest accepted. He and his partner Daniel Olivier did a great business in the funds on behalf of foreign investors. The details of his list are not preserved, but he was allocated £500,000, the first payment on all of which was made by others, since neither his name nor that of Olivier appear in E. 401/2598.

My Lord

Your Grace's service having been my first object in the great business now depending, I have laid all other considerations aside to comply with your Grace's desire, and am now closing my list for £500/m which I will have the honour to transmit to your Grace between this and Monday. I hope the unexpected disappointment of my friends will not loose me their confidence, which I value no less on account of the use it may be for the publicq service, than on account of my personal vanity.

The sooner your Grace closes his list, the sooner your Grace will be rid of the importunity of those who now apply to do their own, and not your Grace's business. I heartily wish their expectations may be answered. If they are gainers they'll be found again another year, and a less chance could not be given them than the present scheme afords, the succes of which every thinking man in the nation must look upon as the effect of the high confidence your Grace so deservedly possesses, and it is no unconfortable reflection that under your Grace's Administration England raises at less than 3⅝ per cent. double the sum which France at this very time is obliged to raise at 5¾ per cent.

I hope your Grace will take effectual care that an end be made of all other proposals in the House, which might otherwise, notwithstanding the present eagerness of the people, make your own precarious.

I fear your Grace may still be brought under some difficulty as to the accessory conditions of this loan, which if many are consulted upon it, I find they will differ in opinion. I am not fond of making myself busy, but as most of my friends have not inquired after terms and have fixed their confidence in those I should stipulate for them, I think I owe them my attention in that respect; wherefore I take the liberty to inclose my thoughts on the subject [not found], which your Grace comparing with those of others, I am confident you will fix on the most reasonable between the Gouvernment and the lenders, not carrying matters to[o] near, for fear of hurting the credit of the new loan.

As the confidence your Grace has been pleased to shew me upon this occasion may create jealousys and reflections, I hope you will occasionally allow your Grace's approbation of my conduct if it has deserved it, and espacialy in a certain place, where though I have no favours to ask I am ambitious of preserving the good opinion I flatter myself I have hitherto injoyed.

I have the honour to be

etc.
Joshua Vanneck.

XV

512. 17. [Abstract]. *Sir William Baker to the Duke of Devonshire.* Winchester Street, 22 April 1757.

The list to which Baker refers in this letter has not been found, but it would seem to be that marked D in Appendix B. i. E. 401/2598 shows that Baker himself made no first payment in this loan, and confirms his statement that he was not personally concerned in it.

He encloses the names of ten persons with sums attached 'amounting in the whole to fifty thousand pounds, the sum you permitted me to recommend'. He is sure that all of them would accept less favourable terms, if these were decided on, and though he himself has 'no concern or interest whatever in this sum now proposed, I will be answerable for the like sum to any other method that shall be offered from the Treasury'.

XVI

512. 3A *Samson Gideon to the Duke of Devonshire. n.d.* [22 April 1757]

The correspondence now begins to concentrate on the attempts being made by Sir John Barnard to introduce a revision of his former scheme, and on methods of thwarting him.

My Lord

The inclosed [not found] is handed about at Garraways and suppose will *else where*. All imaginable pains is taken to increase clamour and if you do not put an end to such unfair and ungentlemanlike proceedings by bringing on the affair Monday [i.e. in the House in Committee of Ways and Means; it was postponed till Wednesday 27 April], every body that has been refused will join.

Pray suffer no answer to be given *or shew the reasons* to demonstrat the false reasoning and calculations, if you do, every day will produce a new scheme.

There are no terms to be kept with those that can, or dare, treat your Grace's polite mesages with appeals to the publick, before they hear the subject debated in its proper place.

Pray order the ages from the Exchequer or as many as can be had there *can be no argument without them*. The clerks will find them in the books wherein they entered the names and discriptions of the nomenees first returned.

Stocks rise as people are satisfied the subscribers will do, as set forth in the reasons delivered your Grace this morning [not found].

Every step answers to what foretold and *if delayed* shall not be surprised at what must follow.

The inclosed [see below] just received from Garraways. The person named who is an understraper to Sir J: should be sent to. *Satisfied* and he will drop the affair, or otherwise acquainted that such proceedings are unbecoming a person that has and is every day solliciting favours.

Your Grace's devoted servant

S. G.

Excuse my haste as no delay should [be] given to the conveyance of the inclosed.

XVII

512. 19. Enclosure with the above. Extract. [*Name cut out*] *to Samson Gideon.* 22 April 1757.

John Thornton was an important banker with interests in Russia, and a friend of Sir John Barnard.

'This place seems at present to bee nothing butt hurry occasioned by scheme against scheem. A subscription is taken inn by the agents of Mr. Thornton for 4 per cent. per annum for 20 years. Large summes have been sett down. I really doe not think it right butt people have been disapointed and make this hurry. I thought it prudent that you should be aprized of it. Inclosed is the scheem given out [not found]. Stocks have risen this day. . . .'

XVIII

512. 18. Extract. *John Edwards to the Duke of Devonshire.* Old Jewry, London, the 22 Aprill 1757. two o'clock.

Edwards was a Director of the South Sea Company and a big dealer in the funds.

'On my returne to the City I found my information of Sir John Barnard's acquiescing in your scheme for raiseing the supplies to be contradicted, and that he was determined to support a new scheme of his own and is now takeing in subscriptions for that purpose. . . .'

XIX

512. 7. Abstract. *Joseph Salvador to the Duke of Devonshire*. Lime St. 22 April [1757].

Writes that he finds 'that spleen and animosity which govern this nation att present have raised a formidable opposition to your Graces measures'. He and his friends will 'concur in any measures your Grace may think proper'. 'I am att any hour or time att your Grace's command and determined to assist as far as my power extends in any thing your Grace may want.' He appends a comparison of the cost of Sir John Barnard's new plan and that which the Duke's advisers had got him to accept.

XX

512. 23. Abstract. *John Hyde to the Duke of Devonshire*. Charterhouse Square, Saturday past 12. 23 April 1757.

Hyde was Governor of the London Assurance Company. Though Devonshire put him down in his list of late entrants for no more than £5,000 (see Appendix B. ii) he is shown in E. 401/2598 as making the first payment on £18,700 stock. Possibly the balance may represent his contribution to Legge's abortive loan.

Acknowledges a letter of 22 April. 'At my return into the City I found many talking of and running to subscribe to Sir John Barnard's new plan—so that the present contest wears the face of who shall have the reputation and benefit of lending cheapest.

If the Publick is well served no matter by whom—lett Sir John or Sir Joshua etc. wear the feather. But lett the Publick be well served. The contest between the Bank and South Sea before the memorable year 1720 was so farr like this that the dispute in the House was—who offers to serve the Publick cheapest. The event was mischeivous. Besides in general one wishes to avoid opposition.

In the present can a fitt expedient be found? I can think of but one and its fitness must depend upon your judgement of engagements made and their complaisance or peevishness in snatching after the bone. . . .

Suppose £300,000 subscribed to the 1st plan, if the nation take still 3 millions it may save borrowing upon the Aids of next year—Would your Grace think proper to send to Sir John and tell him that having the publick at heart as well as he, you had thought it prudent and in your station requisite to take some measures about the intended loan to which he would not be a stranger, that he having been since active in another plan you should be glad to know if he had thougnt of or would think ot and propose any expedient to prevent these clashing in the House—I doubt if he has turned his thoughts that way—if not he will I make no doubt admitt that some regard is to be paid to the labours of your Lordship as well as to his own'. The compromise he proposes is that Sir John and his 'freinds or subscribers (which he pleases to call them)' undertake to provide £1,000,000 'and the other 2 millions you will answer for upon the terms you had agreed and think far from unreasonable to be provided by those whose plans you had accepted'. Pointing out that there is a day or two in which to think this proposal over, he adds that the chief difficulty is the doubt 'whether some Gentlemen who expect they have setled a list with you are not so averse to Sir John (whose abilities in points of credit they rank no higher than a schoolmaster who can teach boys to cast sums but not teach a man where to gett credit for them). I doubt they would call it giving too much way to his projects and would rather push things to an opposition than see such a compromise'. For himself he claims no merit 'and whether you fix something or nothing shall not make the least alteration with me. Only do me the favour to order a note to be sealed ready for me—which I will send for next Tuesday morning about nine—the figures 500 or 5,000 or 50,000. Any sum or a blank paper will be sufficient direction'.

XXI

512. 22. Abstract. *John Payne to the Duke of Devonshire*. Lothbury, 23 April 1757, nine o'clock.

Payne was chairman of the East India Company.

He encloses the list of the Directors of the East India Company [not found] subscribers to the loan 'to the amount of £100,000, being the sum you was so good as to offer them by me, on Thursday last [21 April]'. Thanking him for it he adds 'Had it been your Grace's pleasure to have extend[ed] the same to the East India Company so far as to have put their Directors on the same foot with those of another Company, not superiour to them in point of publick utility' they would have been glad, but he realizes it 'was the effect of a multiplicity of applications, that we were not further indulged'.

XXII

512. 24. Abstract. *Sir Thomas Drury to the Duke of Devonshire*. Dean St., Soho. 23 April 1757.

Sir Thomas Drury, bt. of Overstone, Northants. E. 401/2598 shows that he made the first payment on £10,000 stock.

Asks to be permitted to subscribe £10,000 to the loan.

XXIII

512. 21. Abstract. *Edward Lloyd to the Duke of Devonshire.* 'Nottin Hill near Kensington', Saturday, 23 April 1757.

His name does not appear in the Duke's lists (Appendix B) nor in E. 401/2598.

He would not have troubled the Duke with this application 'was I not informed, that it ought to be made to yourself, and not to either of your secretaries, whom your Grace does not authorise to receive any from persons inclineable to become contributors'. Asks for £5,000 if he is not too late. 'Mr. Gideon will acquaint your Grace who I am, and that I was a constant subscriber to all the loans raised for supporting the late war'.

XXIV

512. 25. Abstract. *Lord William Manners to the Duke of Devonshire.* 24 April 1757.

Manners is shown in E. 401/2598 as making the first payment on £6,000 stock.

He has received some money 'since I came from Newmarket' and would like to subscribe £10,000 to the loan.

XXV

512. 5. [Name erased] *to unnamed correspondent* [endorsed 'Letter to Mr Gideon']. 24 April 1757.

Roger Harenc is shown in E. 401/2598 as making the first payment on £3,000 stock.

Sir

As I have not had the honor of seeing you in the City, you may be ignorant how strangely we are infected with Subscriptions. It perhaps will not be disagreeable to you to be informed of the particulars of the last, which I shall relate with the utmost candor and impartiality.

Mr. Thornton employed three persons in Jonathan's and Garraways whilst he stood in the highways to catch the unwary. He prudently thought that the stockjobbers could be inveigled best by their own party; they were very industrious in executing their charges for they refused no body. I saw many subscribe for several thousands each who were not worth as many pence. They brought as many of their own friends as they could meet with who were immediately admitted; indeed the ceremony was short for whatever they asked for was granted without any enquiry into their birth, character or behavior, nor written demand was required and I have not the least doubt that if any accident should happen that fell the Stocks one per cent. not a fifth would be complied with. Yet these are the persons that are to direct the Treasury, and represent the moneyed interest of this Kingdom. They trust that if the other party should be disapointed and their Scheme take place they will be able to sell the sum they have subscribed at a small premium to persons that are better prepared to make the first payment than they are If there should be no premium they refuse the Subscription and no character is lost. I do not pretend that this is the case with all but I am confident it is with many. I need not mention to you the fatal consequences that would attend this, you are better qualified than any other to judge of it. I have the honor to be, etc.

[Name erased]

Mr. Harenc has wrote to the Duke of Devonshire desiring some of the subscription, having no acquaintance with any of the gentlemen concerned. I should be obliged to you if you had an oportunity to say he is worthy; as he has taken this step at my instigation I hope he will not be disapointed.

XXVI

257. 28. Extract. *H. B. Legge to the Duke of Devonshire.* Downing St. 24 April [1757].

Legge, though now out of office, still interested himself in Sir John Barnard's attempt to develop further the plans they had both adopted. His belief that Barnard had a sound List and would, on the basis of it challenge the new proposition in the House proved unfounded.

'Sir John Barnard I hear has added to his cheaper plan for raising the money the only thing wanted to give it the preference, which is certainty; having procured Lists of undoubted persons for £3,000,000 and upwards. I give you this notice that you may if possible join in this plan, as it will not be possible for me to support the worse proposal to the private benefit of those who have defeated the first scheme against the person with whom the first scheme was concerted. Or in other terms, to join the common enemies against myself and my fellow sufferers. I believe your Grace will see this thing pretty much in the same light that I do and if Sir John B. makes his Lists good, join with him, especially as there is this further good in what he has accomplished that in effect it amounts to an open Subscription, for if one set of contractors can be sett up against another upon cheaper terms, the transaction is as public as an auction and has at the same time all the certainty attending it of a shut-subscription. I write in a great hurry but would not neglect giving you this intelligence as soon as it came to my knowledge.'

XXVII

512. 26. Abstract. *Edward Wortley Montagu, Junior, to the Duke of Devonshire.* 'at the Lobby of the House of Commons' Friday, 29 April [1757].

Wortley Montagu's name does not appear on any of the lists.

He asks for '5 or 10,000 pounds in the new subscription'.

XXVIII

512. 27. Abstract. *Lord Granby to the Duke of Devonshire.* Albemarle St. 'Friday morning' [29 April 1757].

Delafont's name appears in E. 401/2598 as making the first payment on £4,000.

A friend has requested him to ask that Mr. John Delafont's name be put down for £4,000.

APPENDIX B

Schedules of Subscribers to the Loan of £3,000,000 raised in 1757 (30 Geo. II, c. 19)

Among the papers of the Duke of Devonshire at Chatsworth there are two schedules of subscribers, 512. 8 and 512. 10.

(i) The first is a fair copy, with some additions in the duke's hand, of the allocations made to subscribers to this loan up to a total of £2,894,600. This total includes a block sum for the subscribers to the abortive loan for £2,500,000 introduced by Henry Legge. The schedule is arranged in three columns. Column I gives the names of those to whom allocations are made. In most cases the sums allocated to them are inserted against their names in Column II. The entries are divided into sections marked A, B, C, D, and E, the totals of which are added up and transferred to Column III. In Column III are also entered sums against the names of certain institutions and persons for whom there are no entries in Column II, and the sum of £313,100 is inserted to cover the subscribers to the former loan. The totals in Column III are added up, a few other names are added and one subtracted and a total of £2,894,600 is arrived at.

The sections marked by the letters A, B, C, D, and E would appear to represent the 'lists' submitted by the monied men with whom each list was negotiated, and in the case of the South Sea Company the breakdown of the sum allocated to a financial institution. Thus B certainly represents the list submitted by Joseph Salvador (see pp. 97-8 above) and C the breakdown of the South Sea Company's allocation. D would seem to be the list submitted by Sir William Baker (see p. 101 above). A would seem to be the list sent in by Henry Fox on behalf of Nicholas Linwood, Samuel Touchet, William Mabbott and others (see pp. 94 and 98 above). E may possibly be the list of John Edwards.

The sums which are entered in Column III direct would seem to comprise

(*a*) some 'lists' the details of which were either not yet known or omitted for other reasons, e.g. the sum of £500,000 inserted against the name of Sir Joshua Vanneck (see p. 100 above);

(*b*) the block allocations to financial institutions (other than the South Sea Company) to which it would seem the same applied;

(*c*) big individual contributions, e.g. that of Samson Gideon (see p. 95 above) by those who were concerned in the negotiation of the loans;

(*d*) the allocations to a number of persons, mostly bankers and merchants, but some of them M.P.s, Peers and others who have put in to the Treasury for themselves or their friends and clients, but who are on the whole dealers on a moderate scale. They habitually made up the greater part of what was known as the 'Treasury List'.

In the case of this loan we have also, among the Exchequer Papers at the Public Record Office (E. 401/2598), a list compiled at the Bank and handed over to the Auditor of the Exchequer on 29 December 1757 when the payments had been completed. This was required by the terms of the Act. It is stated to contain the names of the 'Subscribers towards raising three millions for

Service of the Year 1747', but it is in fact a list of all those who made the first payments on the subscriptions which had been completed. Except, therefore, where the first payment was made by the clients of those submitting lists (e.g. in the case of Sir Joshua Vanneck) or in the case of the institutions which always subdivided their block allocations, there is a very close correlation between it and the Chatsworth list. As Mrs. Carter of the London School of Economics has pointed out to me, however, there is very little correlation between the lists of those who made the first payments and those who, having made the last payment, registered their names in the Stock Ledgers at the Bank as proprietors of the paid up stock. In fact it is clear that few of those who subscribed did so primarily for purposes of investment, and very active dealings in the receipts for the early payments, i.e. in 'scrip' known on the contemporary market as 'Light' and 'Heavy Horse' must have gone on before the last payments were made. The situation was complicated by the fact that, though no discount was given (see Gideon's advice, p. 96 above) for those who made payments in advance of the last dates fixed for so doing, fully paid up stock could be registered and dealt in at any time after 5 July 1757, the date from which interest on it began to be computed. Mrs. Carter has found entries in the ledgers as early as 6 July 1757, and transfers on 8 July, though the date by which the last payment had to be made was 22 December. Dealings during the second half of 1757 must therefore have been going on both in scrip, of which we have no record, and in stock which was early paid up, and of which the Bank ledgers bear the record.

The first schedule in the Chatsworth MSS. (512. 8) is here reproduced in full.

Subscribers.	£	£	£
Sir Joshua Vanneck Bt.			500,000
Richard Linwood Esq.		20,000	
M. Claremont Esq.		20,000	
Edmund Turner Esq.		10,000	
Mark Jenkinson Esq.		10,000	
R. Burton Esq.		10,000	
Robert Barnes Esq.		10,000	
John Calcraft Esq.		20,000	
Mrs. Anne Moore		5,000	
Mrs. Susannah Knipe		5,000	
John Ayliffe Esq.		5,000	
David Roberts Esq.		5,000	
John Chapman Esq.		5,000	
Mr. Richard Hotham		5,000	
Mr. John Trotter		5,000	
Mr. William Caister		5,000	
Rev. Mr. John Knipe		5,000	
Mr. Fraser Honeywood	10,000		
Mr. Richard Fuller	10,000		
Mr. Richard Cope	5,000		
Mr. John Rogers	5,000		
Mr. Burkitt Fenn	5,000		
Mr. Stamper Bland	5,000		
Mr. Richard Cowley	5,000		
Mr. Edwin Martin	5,000	50,000	
Mr. Griffin Ransom		40,000	
Mr. Giles Rooke		10,000	
Mr. John Rooke		5,000	
Mr. Stephen Guion		5,000	
Samuel Touchet Esq.		30,000	

	£	£
William Mabbot Esq.	30,000	
	40,000 ?	
John Taylor Esq.	20,000	
William Stukeley Esq.	5,000	
	A	
		340,000
Mr. Gore	. .	200,000
Joseph Salvador for himself and friends abroad . . .	44,500	
Hon. Baron de Aguilar	10,000	
Henry Isaacs Esq.	10,000	
Levy Salomons for himself and friends . . .	10,000	
Ruben Salomons ditto . . .	10,000	
Joseph Fowke Esq.	3,000	
Andrew Harrison Esq.	5,000	
Micael Lejay for himself and friends	5,000	
John Deschamps	5,000	
Isaac Jesurun Alvares	4,000	
Isaac Fernandes Nunes	2,000	
Isaac Mendes da Costa	1,000	
Mrs. Zipora Serra	3,000	
Mrs. Ester Delmonte	2,000	
Anthony Chamier for himself and friends . . .	5,000	
Benjamin Lindo	3,500	
Levy Norden	5,000	
Christopher Perry of Fetter Lane for himself and friends	5,000	
Mrs. Rebecca Mendes da Costa	3,000	
Mrs. Rachael Salvador	1,000	
Joseph Caracoza	2,000	
Jacob Dias	2,000	
Joseph Treves	2,000	
Isaac Garcia	1,000	
Joseph da Pinto	2,000	
Moses da Paiba	2,000	
Joseph de Chaves	2,000	
	B	
		150,000
Mr. Gideon	. .	100,000
Bank	. .	200,000
John Bristow Esq.	10,000	
Lewis Way Esq.	5,000	
Richard Baker Esq.	5,000	
Thomas Le Blanc Esq.	5,000	
Peter Burrell Esq.	5,000	
Thomas Coventrye Esq.	5,000	
Samuel Craghead Esq.	5,000	
John Edwards Esq.	5,000	
William Fauquier Esq.	5,000	
Francis Gashry Esq.	5,000	
Joseph Gulston, Jr. Esq.	5,000	
Richard Hall Esq.	5,000	
Josiah Hardy Esq.	5,000	
Tilman Henckell Esq.	5,000	
Richard Jackson Esq.	5,000	
Thomas Lane Esq.	5,000	
Nicholas Linwood Esq.	5,000	
Sydenham Malthus Esq.	5,000	
Nathaniel Paice Esq.	5,000	
Richard Salway Esq.	5,000	
John Smith Esq.	5,000	
Walter Vane Esq.	5,000	

		£	£
John Warde Esq.		5,000	
		120,000	
John Wenham Esq. late Director of the South Sea Company		5,000	
Thomas Sewell Esq.	Counsel	4,000	
George North Esq.	Sollicitor	2,500	
George Wolley Esq.	Cashier	1,500	
James Gossling	Deputy Cashier	1,500	
Peter Burrell	Chief Clerk	500	
Claude Crespigny Esq.	Secretary	2,500	
Martin Eelking	} Clerks to d°	500	
Robert Hassall	. . . . .	500	
John Read Esq.	Accountant General . . .	2,500	
Robert Mountague	Deputy do	1,500	
John Gyles	Clerk of the Transfers . . .	1,500	
Cornelius Drew	. . . . . .	500	
William Nevinson	. . . . . .	500	
William Fothergill	. . . . . .	500	
William Gyles	. . . . . .	500	
Thomas Smalwood	Supervisors	500	
Samuel Bull	. . . . . .	500	
Adam Anderson	. . . . . .	500	
Thomas Pitt	. . . . . .	500	
Benjamin Webb	. . . . . .	500	
Richard Wheler	. . . . . .	500	
		C	150,000
East India	. . . . .		100,000
2 Insurance Offices £50,000 each . .	. . . . .		100,000
Martins & Co.	. . . . .		50,000
Messrs. Colebrooke . . .	. . . . .		50,000
Messrs. Snow & Co. . . .	. . . . .		30,000
Mr. George Amyand . . .	. . . . .		40,000
Mr. C. Amyand	. . . . .		20,000
Lord Conyngham . . .	. . . . .		20,000
Mr. Nesbitt	. . . . .		20,000
Mr. Samuel Smith . . .	. . . . .		10,000
Mr. Belchier	. . . . .		30,000
Dr. Edward Wilmot . . .	. . . . .		20,000
Mr. Hume	. . . . .		40,000
Mr. Fonnereau	. . . . .		30,000
Hermanus Berens of Chapel Court .	. . . .	5,000	
Robert Pocklington Esq. of — .	. . . .	5,000	
William Braund of Copthall Court	. . . .	5,000	
Samuel Blythe of Basinghall St.	. . . .	5,000	
Edward Grosse of Threadneedle St.	. . . .	5,000	
John Berens of Copthall Court .	. . . .	5,000	
James Carter of Devonshire St.	. . . .	5,000	
John Shipston of Threadneedle St.	. . . .	5,000	
Charles Cutts of Salisbury Court	. . . .	5,000	
David Peloquin of Bristow	. . . .	5,000	
		D	50,000
Mr. F. Gossling	. . . .		30,000
Francis Craiesteyn Esq. . .	. . . .	2,500	
Mr. George Kruger . . .	. . . .	2,500	
Mr. Peter Puget . . .	. . . .	2,500	
Mr. Abraham Demetrius . .	. . . .	2,500	
Mr. Timothy Nucella . .	. . . .	2,500	
Mr. William Wynch . .	. . . .	2,500	

	£	£
Mr. John Hale	2,500	
Mr. Philip Hale	2,500	
Mrs. Anna Gomes Serra	2,500	
George Eckersall Esq.	2,000	
Robert Ferguson Esq.	2,000	
Mrs. Rebecca Mendes, widow	2,000	
Thomas Edward Freeman Esq.	1,500	
Theodore Jacobsen Esq.	1,500	
Mr. Lewis Vanden Emden	1,500	
Mr. Isaac Lindo, Jr.	1,500	
Mrs. Jane Edwards	1,500	
Edmund Byron Esq.	1,000	
Francis Freeman Esq.	1,000	
Edward Hooper Esq.	1,000	
John Manship Esq.	1,000	
Mr. Abraham Henckell	1,000	
Mr. James Mathias	1,000	
Mr. William Reynolds of Hackney	1,000	
Richard Jackson, Jr. Esq.	500	
Mr. Henry Henricks	500	
John Edwards (Old Jewry)	6,000	
	E	50,000
Mr. Muilman		50,000
London Hospital		20,000
Mr. Boehm		20,000
Mr. Savage Mostyn		10,000
Mr. Bristow		50,000
Mr. Thornton		60,000
Mr. Burrell		10,000
Mr. Edmonston		5,000
Mr. Hitch Young		30,000
Mr. Chauncey		10,000
Mr. Cooke		5,000
Old Subscribers		313,100
		2,913,100
Sir Thomas Drury		10,000
Mr. Arundel		2,000
Sir Francis Dashwood		5,000
Sir Edward Deering		2,000
		2,932,100
Deduct Thornton		60,000
		2,872,100
John Probyn Esq.		1,500
Col. Lee		1,000
Simon Luttrell Esq.		5,000
Sambrooke Freeman Esq.		3,000
Mr. Brassey, Member of Parliament		10,000
John Olmius Esq.		2,000
		2,894,600

(ii) The second schedule (512. 10) is a rough list of late applications, some of which are ticked and some of which have notes—presumably of proposed allocations—added in the Duke's hand. Many of these names do not occur in E. 401/2598, possibly because they came in too late for inclusion. The first two columns below are transcribed from the schedule. The third is added to show its correlation with E. 401/2598.

Subsequent applications   [E. 401/2598.]

	£		£	
Mr. Ross	10,000		—	
Mr. John Paget	20,000✓		—	
Mr. Roger Harenc	20,000		3,000	See p. 106 above.
Lord Digby £20,000 or	10,000		10,000	See p. 99 above.
Mr. Lock, Member for Grimsby	20,000	8 or 10	5,000	
Messrs. Vere, Glyn and Hallifax	20,000✓		Joseph Vere, a partner, 1,000	
Mr. John Gisborne, Junior	5,000		—	
Mr. Gashry	30,000			
Mr. Caesar Hawkins	10,000	5	5,000	See p. 98 above.
Mr. Hardinge	10,000	say [illegible]	1,000	
Sir William Robinson, Bart.	50,000✓		3,000	
Mr. A. Prado, Low Layton	20,000✓		—	
Sherwood & Gardiner	50,000✓		? Jeremiah Gardiner 500	
Lord Falmouth £25,000 or	20,000✓		Viscount Folkestone 5,000	
Willis & Reade	10,000✓		—	
Mr. Watkin	10,000—		? Joseph Watkins 3,000	
Mr. Child £30,000 or	20,000		R. Cliffe, his partner, 10,000	
Solomon Gompertz	3,000			
Mr. Thomas Martyn	10,000		10,000	
Mr. Evan Thomas (Lord Hyde)	1,000		1,000	
Mr. Adolphus	5,000✓		—	
Mr. Nash and friends	30,000✓		—	
Mr. John Ward	5,000✓		—	
Lord Granby for Mr. John Delafont	4,000		J. Delafont 4,000 See p. 107 above	
Hitch the Bookseller	2,500	Old Subscription ✓	—	
Woodfall the Bookseller	1,000	do. ✓	—	
Mr. Tyzer	2,500	do. ✓	—	
Sir John Elwill for Mr. William Haydon of Guilford	10,000✓		W. Haydon 1,000	
Mr. Ellis for Mr. Tucker	10,000		J. Tucker 5,000	
do for himself	10,000		Welbore Ellis 5,000	
Mr. Gulston	5,000		Joseph Gulston, Jr. 5,000	
Mr. Fanshaw	3,000	200	S. Fanshaw 2,000	
Sir H. Bellandine	5,000		2,000	
Mr. Nugent	8,000			
Mr. Owen, Printer of the *Gazette*	2,000✓		Cornelis Owen 500	
Treasury List as marked by Mr. Fane	55,000—		See pp. 92-3 above.	
Mr. Sawyer	7,000		? A. Sawyer 2,000	
Mr. P. Crespigny	20,000		5,000	
Mr. Richard Oswald	60,000✓		—	
Mr. Chauncey Townshend	20,000—		5,000	
Mr. Thomas Townshend	5,000		? 5,000	
Mr. George Harrison	5,000			
Mr. Henry Talbot	10,000		—	
Mr. Nathaniel Newnham, Junior, besides the £4,000 in the India List	6,000		—	
Mr. Randal of the Pay Office	2,000✓		G. Randall 300	
Sir F. Dashwood	5,000	See the other Paper	5,000	
Sir Edward Deering	2,000	do.	1,000	
Hyde	5,000		? John Hyde See p. 104 above.	
Way	5,000		—	

Henry Pelham (1695?-1754) (William Hoare, 1751[?])
(National Portrait Gallery)

THE CITY OF LONDON AND THE OPPOSITION TO GOVERNMENT, 1768-1774. A STUDY IN THE RISE OF METROPOLITAN RADICALISM

IT is with feelings of gratitude, but also of the liveliest apprehension, that I stand before you today. I am fully aware how great an honour it is to speak to such an audience on such an occasion. The fame of the historian whom this lecture commemorates and the distinction of my predecessors make me very uneasy about my own powers of maintaining adequately so high and reputable a tradition. Consideration of the lectures only of those of my predecessors to whom I am personally indebted for friendship and encouragement over many years— Sir Lewis Namier, mentor of all eighteenth-century historians, and Professor Edwards whose advice no scholar seeks in vain— brings home to me not merely the limitations of my own powers, but also the narrowness of the subject on which I shall be speaking. For while they treated of the growth of great institutions, or the vast movements of peoples and nations, I shall be speaking of a few short years in the history of one city, and the heroes of my tale (so far as I have any) are an almost forgotten Lord Mayor and an only half-remembered demagogue. My only excuse for offering such a subject is that the city of which I shall be speaking is one famous and well known to all of us, and that I believe that what happened in it during these years, and to its Lord Mayor and its demagogue, was of more than local and temporary importance.

In the Guildhall of the City of London, slightly scarred by the mischances of war, there stands a statue erected by the Corporation in 1772 to commemorate Alderman William Beckford, twice Lord Mayor and for sixteen years member of parliament for the City, who had died during his second mayoralty in 1770.[1] It depicts him life-size, in an oratorical attitude, and it bears as inscription the words which he was supposed to have addressed a few weeks before his death to his sovereign George III, when presenting a Remonstrance from the City of London arising out of the famous Middlesex Election dispute.[2] After assuring the King of the City's loyalty and its affliction under royal displeasure, he is there said to have continued:

Permit me, Sir, to observe that whoever has already dared, or shall hereafter endeavour, by false insinuations and suggestions, to alienate your Majesty's affections from your loyal subjects in general, and from the City of London in particular, is an enemy to your Majesty's person and family, a violator of the public peace, and a betrayer of our happy Constitution, as it was established at the Glorious Revolution.[3]

[1] William Beckford b. in Jamaica 1709, d. 21 June 1770. M.P. for Shaftesbury 1747–54 and London 1754–70. Lord Mayor 1762–3 and 1769–70. The statue, voted in 1770, was declared by his fellow-citizens, when displayed to them, to be an excellent likeness (*London Chronicle*, 11–13 June 1772, xxxi, 562).

[2] The Remonstrance was presented on 23 May 1770.

[3] The words engraved on the statue were those published in the Press. John Horne (Horne Tooke) claimed, probably correctly, to have written them up for the Press, and also to have suggested that the Lord Mayor should address the King. Much later he gave his support to the rumour that no such speech had been made. W. P. Treloar, who examined the matter in his *Wilkes and the City*, 1917, pp. 98–100, was convinced that 'Beckford made no rejoinder . . . or merely muttered a few indistinct words, and the speech was concocted afterwards.' The contemporary evidence is, however, quite clear. Richard Rigby wrote to the duke of Bedford on the same day, having just come from court, describing the incident and giving the gist of the words, adding 'This is the first attempt ever made to hold a colloquy with the King by any subject, and is indecent to the highest degree' (J. Russell, *The Correspondence of John, Fourth Duke of Bedford*, 1846, iii, 413–14). James Townsend, present as sheriff, wrote to Chatham, also on 23 May, that the Lord Mayor's speech 'greatly disconcerted the Court. He has promised to recollect what he said, and I fancy the substance will appear in the papers tomorrow' (W. S. Taylor and J. H. Pringle, *The Correspondence of William Pitt, Earl of Chatham*, 1839, iii, 458). Beckford replying to Chatham's congratulations said that he spoke 'the language of truth, and with that humility and submission which becomes a subject speaking to his lawful king' (*Chatham Correspondence*, iii, 463).

The satisfaction of the City with the boldness of these words, and their belief in their value to posterity, was shared by others outside their walls. It was echoed by the great William Pitt, Lord Chatham (whose political follower Beckford was) who wrote in congratulation:

The spirit of Old England spoke that never-to-be-forgotten day ... *true Lord Mayor of London*; that is *first* magistrate of the *first* City in the World! I mean to tell you only a plain truth, when I say, Your Lordship's mayoralty will be revered till the constitution is destroyed and forgotten.[1]

Time has dealt less kindly with Beckford and his mayoralty than either his followers in the City or his leader in parliament expected. William Beckford was a man of some note in his day, and a very unusual figure among the sober ranks of the mercantile Lord Mayors of his time. He was the richest absentee West Indian sugar-planter of his generation, owning vast estates and many slaves in Jamaica (a somewhat embarrassing possession for a spokesman for English freedom),[2] was a big landowner also in Wiltshire,[3] where he exercised some political influence, had been since 1756 the devoted henchman of William Pitt[4] and—a vigorous, loquacious and by no means unintelligent man—he was a prominent figure in parliamentary and City life. Nevertheless, his personal fame, such as it was, has been swallowed up in the notoriety of his son, the eccentric

---

[1] *Chatham Correspondence*, iii, 462.

[2] A rhyme was printed in the *Public Advertiser* on 18 November 1769:
> 'For B[eck]f[ro]d he was chosen May'r
> A wight of high renown.
> To see a slave he could not bear,
> —Unless it were his own.'

[3] He had purchased the estate of Fonthill, at Fonthill Giffard, Wilts., and greatly enlarged and beautified the house.

[4] When he entered the House he supported the country party in opposition and was known as a Tory. After the death of the prince of Wales he gave his allegiance first to the duke of Bedford and then to Henry Fox, but when Pitt's abilities as a war leader became evident he attached himself enthusiastically and permanently to this new leader.

author of *Vathek*,[1] while his reputation in the City has been eclipsed by that of the picturesque demagogue John Wilkes, who may be considered his political successor there. Nor does the speech itself, or the occasion on which it was delivered, convey much to the posterity for which it has been preserved. It is a commentary on the fact that no age finds it easy to judge what about itself will be significant to the future that those wishing to honour Beckford should do so by commemorating an incident, in itself but a nine days' wonder but charged with the memories of past conflicts, while ignoring others of far greater interest in connection with the events of the time and the struggles of the future. Only a few weeks earlier, also in connection with the Middlesex dispute, the Lord Mayor had propounded to the Livery in Common Hall assembled what he called his 'Political Creed'—that 'the number of little paltry rotten boroughs', the placemen and pensioners in the House of Commons, and the corruption of electors and elected alike were ruining the state, and that to cure these evils there should be not only fewer pensioners and placemen (an old cry) but better public accounts and 'a more equal representation of the people'.[2]

For the importance of the career of Beckford as a leader in the City, and of his last mayoralty in particular, is to be sought in their relation to that ill-defined surge of opinion which we call eighteenth-century Radicalism, a movement interesting in itself, and of importance in relation to the nineteenth-century movement which succeeded it. The outburst of popular opinion which found expression during the Revolutionary Wars in the Corresponding Societies, and that earlier movement organized into the County Associations during the latter years of the American War of Independence, have received a good deal of attention from historians interested in the history of the Radical movement. The earlier crisis of 1769–70, associated with John Wilkes and the Middlesex Election, and in which Beckford

[1] William Beckford, junior (1759–1844).
[2] *London Chronicle*, 6–8 March 1770, xxvii, 225.

was concerned, has aroused far less comment though Professor Butterfield has noted its significance[1] and it finds a place in Dr. Maccoby's comprehensive work.[2] Nevertheless, this earlier movement prepared the way for both the later outbursts of popular activity, and was accompanied by a remarkable ferment of opinion within the City and its surroundings—what we may call the metropolitan area—which left its mark upon the future.

It is the contention which I wish to advance today that a study of eighteenth-century Radicalism can best begin with an examination of what was actually going on in and around London at this time; that the origins of these events can be traced, in the City of London at least, as far back as 1756; and that the fact that they took place in the metropolis and found as yet little reflection in the country as a whole is the result of a circumstance of some importance: that in the metropolitan area, and at this time in the metropolitan area alone, there existed the predisposing conditions for the development of Radicalism as a political force—an organization adapted to political intervention and a sizeable body of persons, some of them at least with some education and independence of mind, who felt themselves ill-served by and were in consequence critical of their social and political environment.

All movements of public opinion are in their early stages ill-defined and inarticulate, and their characteristics are in consequence hard to isolate. These difficulties of identification are increased in the case of the eighteenth-century Radical movement by the fact that the organization of expressions of extra-parliamentary opinion had long been one of the recognized weapons of eighteenth-century political warfare; and that petitions and instructions to representatives and thanks to representatives both from the counties and the City of London were

[1] W. Butterfield, *George III, Lord North, and the People, 1779–80*, 1949, pp. 181 seq.

[2] S. Maccoby, *English Radicalism 1762–1785, the Origins*, 1955.

part of the stock-in-trade of parliamentary Oppositions of the period. It is not therefore safe to assume that such manifestations necessarily represent in themselves a movement of spontaneous popular opinion. We can be sure that such a movement is in being only when it can be shown that the initiative in organizing such manifestations has passed from the political groups in parliament to groups of persons outside the House. When, in addition, those taking part in such manifestations begin to display an increasingly critical attitude to existing institutions, and their political programmes to reflect this attitude, we can consider that something which may reasonably be called Radicalism has come into existence. This is, I think, precisely what we can see beginning to happen in the City of London in the last years of the reign of George II, gaining momentum in the first eight years of the new reign, and breaking into full expression in the metropolitan area in the general election of 1768 and the Middlesex Election dispute which succeeded it.

The City of London had a long tradition of corporate solidarity and also a long tradition of political activity in which this solidarity expressed itself. This is not to say, of course, that there were not differences of opinion among its inhabitants, and often active conflict within it. One of the most permanent of these divisions was one based on some sort of class conflict between a City aristocracy of wealth and office and the main body of what contemporaries called the 'middling' class of their fellow-citizens. But it is, nevertheless, justifiable to speak throughout the century of the political opinion of the City since, in times of stress, the climate of political thinking there was determined not by the prosperous aldermen, the directors of the great joint-stock companies, the rich merchants and the thriving financiers of the London money market, nor by those whom they could carry with them (though in quiet and uncontentious times their influence was considerable). It was determined on the contrary by the lesser merchants, the tradesmen, the master-craftsmen and the host of minor intermediaries who formed the majority in the popular organs of City government and who thronged the meetings and clubs where political opinion was formulated. And while the more prominent citizens tended for a number of reasons to give their political support to the Government of the day, the 'middling' citizens tended almost always in times of political controversy to find themselves in alliance with the parties in opposition.[1] It is paradoxical, but true to state, that throughout the first half of the eighteenth century there was no body of men more ready to be swayed by the catchwords of the old 'country' party as advanced by the opposition groups in parliament than these inhabitants of the nation's greatest city. Demands for the repeal of the Septennial Act, for place and pension bills and for the reduction of the standing army—all measures directed at the power of the Crown which the seventeenth-century constitutional struggles had taught Englishmen to suspect—were applauded as enthusiastically by the citizen in Common Council or Common Hall or in his tavern or coffee-house, as by any country squire on his grand jury or at the race-meeting. But the citizen can no more be called a Radical because he held these views than can the country squire. It was only when the City began to some extent to dissociate itself from the politics of Opposition as well as those of Government, to feel resentment at its place in a political system dominated by interests in many ways alien to it, that it can begin to be considered a focus of Radicalism as distinct from a centre of traditional anti-ministerialism.

The first clear signs of such a development seem to appear, like so many changes, as a result of war, and to have been the outcome of one of the rare occasions on which City opinion was ardently in support of, and not in opposition to, the Government. Between 1756 and 1768 its growth can be traced in three

[1] I have treated this subject more fully in my 'The City of London in Eighteenth-century Politics', in *Essays Presented to Sir Lewis Namier*, ed. R. Pares and A. J. P. Taylor, 1956. See above, pp. 41-66.

stages. In the first, during the great war ministry of William Pitt, when his unique personal supremacy depended on the support of public opinion as much outside as within the House, the City's sense of its political significance as a body was stimulated by the court which was paid to it and by its share in the exhilaration of victory. In the second stage, during the dissensions accompanying the peace settlement and the confusion following the break-up of the political system of the old reign, the City was again in opposition, and again acting in support of the opposition groups in parliament; but on such matters as its agitation against the peace terms, and its turbulent adherence to the cause of John Wilkes over the North Briton case and the issue of General Warrants, it displayed a degree of independence of action greater than it had shown on issues of national importance before. But the third stage, that between 1764 and 1768, was perhaps the most important of all, though during these years there was no issue in national politics which called the City into corporate action. For these were years of bad harvests, high cost of living and industrial changes in the metropolitan area which caused a good deal of hardship and discontent and led to great and persistent labour unrest.[1] From 1764 onwards a strong undercurrent of economic malaise and social unrest is discernible beneath the surface of the life of the

[1] The price of wheat reached a peak in the very bad year 1767, but was high (by comparison with the five years ending 1763) in the period 1764–8 inclusive, and the numbers of cattle and sheep brought to Smithfield market were also significantly lower in most of these years (T. S. Ashton, *An Economic History of England: The 18th Century*, 1955, Tables I and VII, pp. 239 and 245). The first serious outburst of labour unrest in London was the riot in 1765 of the Spitalfield silk-weavers, automatically protected from French competition during the war. It was followed in the ensuing years by others, more or less serious, among the coal-heavers, sailors, weavers, tailors, hatters, and even (in 1771) by the cabinet-makers against the importation of foreign furniture by abuse of diplomatic privilege. An official return made in 1772 to the City of the number of death sentences passed at the Old Bailey showed an increase from fourteen in 1760 to ninety-one in 1770 (*London Chronicle*, 3–5 November 1772, xxxii, 440).

metropolis, and though until 1768 no major issue arose to transfer this discontent to the political field, there were already indications that such a transfer was imminent.

The development of these years can also be traced through the career as a City leader of William Beckford, for his entry into City politics in 1754 roughly coincided with it, and his actions did a good deal to further it. Before Beckford's time the political leaders to whom the City paid allegiance were themselves citizens first and foremost, and had risen to prominence through active participation in City government. Beckford, when he first stood for the City, was a man of some note and experience in parliamentary opposition but he had only two years before taken his freedom by redemption and been elected alderman,[1] and these steps were taken in preparation for his candidature.[2] He was the first politician of some experience outside the City to see its value as a backing for his personal power and the causes he wished to further, and, at first in self-interest, then with real zest, he worked his way through the offices of the City Corporation and increasingly identified himself with his constituents to consolidate his power. As Pitt's supporter he played the chief part in forging the links between the City and the great war minister;[3] as Lord Mayor in 1762–3 he led their opposition to the peace[4] and in and after his mayoralty he encouraged their

[1] He became a freeman of the Ironmongers' Company, and was alderman for Billingsgate Ward.

[2] He was supported by the Tory interest in the City, in particular it would seem by Alderman William Benn, a notable City politician of the time. After his election he thanked the electors for the trust they placed in him despite 'the short time I have had the honour of being known to you, and the prejudices that have been injuriously raised against me' (*Public Advertiser*, 8 May 1754).

[3] There is considerable evidence of this in the printed *Chatham Correspondence* and in the unpublished Pitt MSS. in the Public Record Office.

[4] He opposed the Preliminaries of the Peace of Paris in the House in November 1762 and in 1763 when the Court of Aldermen, not daring to summon the Common Council, voted an address, refused to accompany them to present it (Court of Aldermen, Repertory Book 167, pp. 280 seq.; Brit. Mus. Add. MS. 32948, f. 269: T. Walpole to Newcastle, 12 May 1763).

support of John Wilkes, though there was even then no love lost between the two men.[1] And in his speeches and his actions he reflected the growing self-consciousness and dissatisfaction of his constituents, and in doing so he began to earn the reputation of something of a demagogue in the House of Commons.[2] As early as 1761 he had extolled the 'middling classes of England' against 'Your Nobility, about 200£ men of quality' who 'receive more from the Public than they pay to it'.[3] In 1767 when he voted against a reduction in the land tax he did so, he claimed, because 'relief ought to be given to the poor man in preference to the opulent land-holder',[4] and in 1768 he voted, as he said, 'on principle' against the Nullum Tempus Act,[5] forced on the Government to secure landowners against the dormant claims of the Crown. In the light of this attitude, too, may be judged his tentative criticism of the existing political order. At his election in 1761 (though only seven years before he had spent great sums himself in borough elections) he told the City electors that 'our Constitution is deficient only in one point, and that is, that little, pitiful boroughs send members to parliament

[1] Wilkes attacked Beckford savagely in the *North Briton*, though when writing to Lord Temple, who thought well of Beckford, he tried to blame the hostility shown on Charles Churchill (W. J. Smith, *The Grenville Papers*, 1852, ii, 59). Reports made to the Secretary of State on Wilkes's movements reported on 8 November 1763 a visit of Wilkes to the Lord Mayor Beckford at his house (ibid., ii, 158), and on 19 December 1763 Beckford wrote him a friendly letter promising assistance (Brit. Mus. Add. MS. 30867, f. 242). On 17 February 1764 Beckford spoke and voted in the House against General Warrants (Parliamentary MS. Diary of James Harris).

[2] He was called 'The scavenger to throw dirt upon government' (MS. Parliamentary Diary of James Harris, 16 November 1763) and 'the Dr. Lucas of the English House of Commons' (Hist. MS. Com. Emly MSS., 8th Rept., Pt. 1, Sect. 1, 190 b, 7 March 1765).

[3] Brit. Mus. Add. MS. 38334, ff. 29 seq. Apparently an attempt at a verbatim report of Beckford's speech on the Address on 13 November 1761.

[4] So he claimed in 1768 (*Public Advertiser*, 22 March 1768). As he was at this time still a supporter of the Administration set up by Chatham there may well, however, be other reasons.

[5] H. Cavendish, *Debates of the House of Commons during the Thirteenth Parliament of Great Britain*, 1841, i, 241.

equal to great cities, and it is contrary to the maxim, that power should follow property';[1] and in 1768 he introduced a bill (repudiated energetically by Opposition and Government supporters alike) to impose an oath against bribery on parliamentary candidates at elections.[2] And, when he was preparing to fight a contested election for his City seat in the general election of that year, he claimed credit from his constituents for what he had said and done. If the situation in the metropolis and the attitude of the City leaders be taken into account, it seems indeed fairly clear that even had there been no re-emergence of John Wilkes, and no Middlesex Election to bring matters to a head, there would have been a recrudescence after 1768 of political activity in the City in alliance with the opposition groups in parliament, and that the City's share in this alliance would have been far from passive. As it was, the nature of the forces released by these new factors was quickly apparent. When in 1769 the ebullient Parson John Horne declared that 'Boroughs are, indeed, the deadly part of our Constitution';[3] when Beckford in 1770, during his second mayoralty, invited the opposition leaders to dine at Mansion House with the intention of springing on them a pledge to a programme of parliamentary reform;[4] and when these leaders, on their way to the dinner (having evaded the pledge), 'remarked that a great part of the populace had tickets in their hats on which was the following in-

[1] *London Evening Post*, 4–7 April 1761, quoted *Memoirs of William Beckford*, 1859, i, 33.

[2] J. Brooke, *The Chatham Administration, 1766–1768*, 1956, p. 337, n. 4. Sir Roger Newdigate welcomed the proposal as likely to reduce competition for seats from 'Nabobs' and other monied rivals of the landed interests. Cf. H. Walpole, *Memoirs of the Reign of King George III*, ed. D. Le Marchant, 1845, iii, 157–60.

[3] He expanded this statement with the condition 'if they are to be the instruments of forcing through those barriers which the Wisdom of our Ancestors has placed between the hereditary and elective legislators of England' (*Public Advertiser*, 8 September 1769).

[4] A. Stephens, *Memoirs of John Horne Tooke*, 1813, i, 387–8. Horne's account of this incident is supported by a letter from Chatham (*Chatham Correspondence*, iii, 431, n. 1).

scription: "Annual Parliaments. Equal Representation. Place and Pension Bill'";[1] no one could doubt that a fully developed Radical movement within the City had come into existence.

It was, however, the almost unheralded, and quite uninvited, return of John Wilkes during the 1768 general election from exile in France (into which he had fled from justice four years before), and the renewal of his old claim to popularity during the excitement of a contested City election, which brought these forces into the open. His subsequent election for Middlesex, the muddle of his arrest, his sentence to imprisonment for his former offences, and his long contest from behind his prison walls with the Ministry and the majority of the House of Commons, brought about a surge of popular feeling under the pressure of which latent suspicions and hostilities became overt, and strange and unsuspected forces were suddenly released.

The impact of John Wilkes and his grievances on the political life of the nation in this, his second period of political activity, forms an odd interlude in the history of George III's reign. Historians have noted the constitutional precedents created by the Middlesex Election dispute, but have not found it easy to determine the importance of the episode in the politics of the time. It is, I think, only possible to do so with any accuracy if it is recognized, firstly, that the forces released by the excitement of his cause were those already taking shape within the metropolitan area, and that the ferment which prevailed there had only a transient effect outside its bounds; and, secondly, that the activities resulting from the ferment within the metropolitan area had little to do with Wilkes as a person or as a political leader, and arose only indirectly out of his grievances. To make clear why these propositions are correct it is necessary to analyse the character and career at this time of Wilkes himself, and the nature of the sentiments which he called forth, and the situation which was created within the metropolis by the outburst of these feelings.

[1] *London Chronicle*, 24–27 March 1770, xxvii, 296.

John Wilkes was said to have observed some years later of one of his followers, 'He was a Wilkite, . . . I never was',[1] and a recognition of the truth of this admission is the first step to an understanding of his career and what was going on at this time. To many of the issues which most deeply concerned the more thoughtful and intelligent of his followers Wilkes himself was profoundly indifferent, and the fervent loyalty of his less sophisticated followers also raised in him no more than a cynical acceptance. The qualities which brought him success as a demagogical political leader were: a strikingly original, if disreputable, personality, a great deal of assurance, a skill in exploiting the resources of the Press unparalleled up to that time (unlike most demagogues Wilkes was a poor public speaker),[2] and considerable success in those arts of political management which have in more recent times been associated with the office of a 'political boss'. His methods were those of inspired opportunism; his ends simple and purely personal. The gamble of his return from France in defiance of the law and his creditors was largely an enforced one, for his debts in France were too heavy for him to be able to remain there. His intention in this return was to make use of his old popularity and the excitement of a general election to raise, as a supporter frankly said, 'a storm . . . under which you may get into port'.[3] The port he was making for was a seat in the House of Commons with the

[1] He was alleged to have said this to George III of Serjeant John Glynn. The story was widely reported, see H. Bleackley, *Life of John Wilkes*, 1917, p. 376.

[2] He had a weak voice and was unable to sway large assemblies, e.g. the large and contentious meeting at Westminister Hall on 31 October 1770, at which Wilkes completely lost control of proceedings. He himself referred to his 'weak and bad voice' (*London Chronicle*, 8–10 November 1770, xxviii, 456).

[3] Brit. Mus. Add. MS. 30869, f. 175: H. Cotes to J. Wilkes, 15 December 1767. Some time before 16 June 1767 Wilkes had suggested to his friends that he might stand for the City (ibid., f. 131: Heaton Wilkes to J. Wilkes, 16 June 1769). They were uniformly discouraging. He nevertheless persisted, and on 6 October 1767 a letter from him to Arthur Beardmore, a City politician, was printed in the *St. James's Chronicle*. Cotes thought Westminster more hopeful.

protection this would bring him from his creditors, and the improved bargaining power with an unfriendly Administration which the status might be expected to carry with it. After his failure in the City, and the check to his success at Middlesex, the extraordinary outburst of feeling which he evoked opened up an alternative course for him as soon as he should have served his prison sentence. From early in 1769 when (with still more than a year's sentence to run) he was elected an alderman of the City[1] in his absence, he set himself deliberately to the conquest of the City's corporate machine, seeing in it, no doubt, a new sphere of political power and a possible source of revenue when the financial bounty of his followers should be exhausted.[2] And so great was the popular support which he called forth that the very City leaders whom he was working to supplant, including Beckford himself, had to assist his rise in order to preserve their own popularity.[3] Though as time went on during this struggle he was obliged, in competition with those who had been his friends and became his rivals, to advance some programme of reform, in the years when metropolitan Radicalism was taking shape under the pressure of the forces his cause had released, he displayed not the slightest interest in its manifestations, and, indeed, deprecated any widening of the issue raised

[1] He was on 2 January 1769 elected alderman of the ward of Farringdon Without. His eligibility for election was challenged, but legal action was not taken, and after his release from prison he was sworn in. The question is fully treated in Treloar, op. cit., pp. 70 seq.

[2] As early as 1770 it seems clear that he was trying to get profitable jobs in the City for friends and relatives in the proceeds of which he might share (*Public Advertiser*, 27 May 1771 seq.). In 1779, after a three years' struggle, he achieved the climax of his personal ambition, the highly lucrative position of City Chamberlain.

[3] Camden congratulated Beckford on Wilkes's failure to be elected for the City (Letter of 28 March 1768 in the Hamilton MSS.), though during the election Beckford and the other popular candidate Barlow Trecothick had treated Wilkes 'with much civility' (Walpole, *Memoirs of the Reign of King George III*, op. cit., iii, 185) and supported Wilkes's candidature for Middlesex, and for election as alderman.

by the Middlesex Election[1] as likely to distract attention from his own grievances and person.

If then the Radicalism of these years owed nothing to Wilkes but was the outcome of the feelings aroused by his cause, it is necessary both to try to analyse the nature of this feeling and to determine how and by whom it was bent to Radical ends. Though every effort was made by propaganda in the Press to suggest that the personal popularity of Wilkes was strong throughout the kingdom, an examination of the evidence soon makes it clear that there was nothing in the nature of a vigorous and lasting Wilkite movement outside the metropolitan area. All the parliamentary opposition parties were both slow and reluctant to take up his cause against Administration (well-suited though it obviously was for opposition purposes), and when they did, they sought to isolate the cause of the electors of Middlesex from that of their chosen representative.[2] And that they were not merely politicians out of touch with public opinion but reflected the views of the politically active classes as a whole was shown clearly by the events of the petitioning movement of 1769–70.[3] It is true that in some parts of the country, and particularly in the commercial cities and great seaports and in some of the industrialized areas, there were signs of a sympathetic response to the clamorous exaltations of the metropolis, a response due no doubt to some similarities in their general conditions and attitude of mind;[4] but even here it was

[1] *Public Advertiser*, 22 May 1771. H. Cotes in a letter to John Horne said that the breach between Horne and Wilkes really began over the Middlesex petition of 1769, which Wilkes had wished to be confined entirely to the rights of the electors of that county.

[2] Edmund Burke wrote to his friend Charles O'Hara on 9 June 1768: 'The plan of our party was . . . not to provoke Administration into any violent measure upon this subject . . . besides we had not the least desire of taking up that gentleman's cause as personally favourable to him' (printed R. J. S. Hoffman, *Edmund Burke, New York Agent*, Philadelphia, 1956, p. 434).   [3] See below, pp. 138-46.

[4] The response in different parts of the country varied greatly and can only be understood in relation to local conditions. One of the most interesting

for the most part evanescent and it found at this time no organization to give it permanent force. And even the presence of the demagogue himself when he made a triumphal tour through the provinces after his release from prison did not succeed in giving the movement the vitality it was to show some years later.

The Wilkite movement was thus essentially, as the later Radical movements were not, a product of the metropolis. Here the personal devotion which he evoked was of a curious kind, impervious to disillusionment and discreditable revelations, and unaffected by the leader's unconcealed contempt for his followers. Edmund Burke, marvelling at his 'imprudence' and the fact that it did nothing to discredit him in the eyes of his fellows, remarked acutely that 'it may perhaps be . . . some unusual and eccentric kind of wisdom'.[1] The devotion of the rank and file of these followers seems to have been compounded of appreciation of a personality so foreign to their own, sympathy for him as the victim (so they believed) of persecution by the

accounts in the Press was a letter in the *London Chronicle*, 10–12 May 1770, xxvii, 452, from one signing himself 'Viator' whose business, he said, took him much about the kingdom. 'There is scarce an inn, shop, or private house, into which I enter, but the pleasure of conversation, and the regular despatch of business, are hindered by discourse and altercations about Wilkes, Grievances and Middlesex Election.' He adds that he was in Worcestershire when Wilkes was released from prison and that in some places he passed through on 17 and 18 April no business could be done, that Worcester itself was a scene of confusion, but that in Kidderminster the 'Vicar of the Parish, the Bailiff of the Borough, the Master-weavers and principal inhabitants' had managed to prevent riotous behaviour by 'journeymen-weavers, their apprentices and others of the vulgar.' In Bristol there was in 1769 a considerable body of discontent, described by Richard Champion in his MS. Letter Book (in the possession of Miss P. Rawlins, of Denbigh, N. Wales) as having 'a great and formidable appearance, and a real strength'. The local friends of Wilkes 'took advantage of the times to head' it but behaved 'with such a wildness of popularity and so little attention to common sense' that they 'frightened away many worthy men'. At Plymouth there were riotous rejoicings when the news was received in June 1769 that John Sawbridge and James Townsend had been elected sheriffs. The crowd changed the name of H.M. ship *Barrington* to *Liberty*, and burned jack-boots and an effigy of Bute. They were said to be led by an 'eminent attorney' (*Gentleman's Magazine*, 1769, p. 361).

[1] E. Burke to C. O'Hara, 19 November 1773 (Hoffman, op. cit., p. 551).

great whose privileges they resented, and a delighted admiration of the insolence and imperturbability with which he defied and put out of countenance these persecutors. It would seem as if inarticulate resentment and dissatisfaction which had been piling up within the metropolitan area for years had suddenly found an outlet and a solace in identification with him and his cause. So new a phenomenon was this popular feeling that it has sometimes been suggested that it derived its strength from the emergence into political awareness of classes hitherto submerged, of the unorganized and ill-paid manual workers of the metropolis, and its wretched and degraded underworld. But, though the labour unrest of the recent years reached a climax about the time of the Middlesex Election and its accompanying disorders, there seems good reason to believe that it had little direct connection with the Wilkite manifestations,[1] and the support of such allies would, in any case, have checked rather than assisted Wilkes's rise to power.

It is clear indeed that the backbone of Wilkes's support in the metropolis was precisely the same classes as that of the earlier popular leaders, what we should call its lower middle classes. In the City's Corporation it was the Common Hall, composed of the liverymen of the City Companies, which was always the bulwark of his power, and his voting strength there depended largely on the liverymen of the numerous lesser companies, for which the livery fines were low and many of which still retained to a considerable degree their old craft associa-

---

[1] See G. F. E. Rudé, 'Wilkes and Liberty, 1768–69', *Guildhall Miscellany*, July 1957 and 'The London "Mob" of the Eighteenth Century' *Historical Journal* ii, i (1956), pp. 1–18. There was much unrest among the merchant seamen in the Thames-side just at the time of the riots accompanying Wilkes's election for Middlesex, but even his enemies made no attempt to suggest he did anything to exacerbate these disorders. Rockingham, reporting to the duke of Newcastle on 10 May 1768 the dispersal of the mob which had collected outside the House of Lords, said that the Justices returning reported that the crowds were 'much diminished but . . . that they [*sic*] were still some who cried Wilkes and Liberty and some who cried that bread and beer were too dear and that it was as well to be hanged as starved' (Brit. Mus. Add. MS. 32990, f. 36v).

tions.[1] And outside the City, in other parts of the metropolis, the position was very similar. In Westminster, for instance, a list of twenty of his most active supporters drawn up in 1770 included the names of three apothecaries, two carpenters, a well-to-do poulterer, a stable-keeper, an engraver, a bookseller, an upholsterer, a coachmaker, and a working jeweller—as well as a baronet, two parsons (one of whom was respectable), a barrister and a solicitor.[2]

But though the classes on which Wilkes's power ultimately rested were the same as those who supported his predecessors, the very strength of the feeling he elicited made fundamental changes in the movement which was coming into being. In the first place his influence extended over a wider area than that of any of his predecessors. London had long outgrown its ancient city boundaries and the city of Westminster, the borough of Southwark, much of the county of Middlesex and even some of the county of Surrey were already becoming for all practical purposes part of the same great urban centre. But this expansion of the City had so far been reflected only very partially in a unity of political actions and ideas.[3] The strength of the City leaders of the past had depended on their control over the corporate organization of the ancient City, and they had only occasionally concerned themselves with stimulating the political opinion of the surrounding areas and never with giving it a permanent organization. Now, with all these areas united in a community of feeling, co-ordinated action could be planned and was in fact carried out. Not only were their corporate activities now synchronized, but a network of interrelated clubs and societies was created, through which enthusiasm could be main-

[1] J. R. Kellett, 'The Breakdown of Gild and Corporation Control over the Handicraft and Retail Trade in London', *Economic History Review*, April 1958, pp. 381 seq.

[2] List of the signatories to the Westminster Remonstrance, with their occupations, inserted by 'Sly-boots' in the *Public Advertiser*, 7 April 1770.

[3] L. B. Namier, *Structure of Politics at the Accession of George III*, 2nd ed., 1957, pp. 65 seq.

tained and the views of the various parts of the metropolis kept in line.[1] The famous Radical Quadrilateral, or even the Quintuple Alliance, of the future was thus foreshadowed. Wilkes has a claim to be considered at the same time the last of the old City leaders, whose strength rested on their control over the Corporation, and the first of the new metropolitan popular leaders who relied on less tangible but more wide-flung support.

In the second place, and partly because the area over which his influence extended was thus enlarged, the cause of Wilkes attracted to him a type of supporter whose alliance earlier leaders had never enjoyed. These were the men, all of some education and some of considerable standing, who formed the nucleus of the Society of Supporters of the Bill of Rights, a society founded early in 1769 to buy off Wilkes's creditors, but which became in these earlier years the mainspring of the movement's policy. Few of these men were freemen of the City; but most of them had strong interests in the metropolitan area, and the greater number of them pursued their careers there. They were a highly diversified group of men, but they were all for one reason or another dissatisfied with the existing order; with few exceptions they were rather young, and a high proportion of them belonged to the rising professional classes (they tended to be the less prosperous and well-established members of the less socially regarded of these classes) for which, like the ordinary merchant and trading classes of the City, the existing

---

[1] Wilkes was an honorary member of a wide variety of convivial clubs, most of which had some political significance. The most important of the societies primarily political in their purpose were, besides the Supporters of the Bill of Rights, who met at the London Tavern, the Sons of Freedom who met at Appleby's tavern in Westminster, the Society which met at the Standard Tavern, Lincoln's Inn Fields, and the long-established Society of the Antigallicans whose annual meeting was said in 1771 to be 'the most numerous meeting of the year of the Middlesex Freeholders' (*Public Advertiser*, 25 April 1771). The annual May Feast at Southwark was also this year used for political ends (ibid., 29 May 1771).

political and social system made little provision.[1] And though, at first at any rate, most of them were warmly attached to the cause of Wilkes as a person, they were basically more concerned with the wider issues to which the Middlesex Election dispute gave rise. The most prominent among them were the able but erratic and misfit Parson John Horne (later to be known as Horne Tooke),[2] and two new and idealistic members of parliament, James Townsend[3] and John Sawbridge,[4] both of families with City antecedents, though they themselves had not hitherto interested themselves in its affairs. They were all in their thirties,

[1] In the earlier years of the Society several country gentlemen were members, Sir Francis Blake Delaval, Bt., of Seaton Delaval, Northumberland, 1754–68 M.P. for Andover, Sir Robert Bernard, Bt., of Brampton, Hunts., who was returned by the popular interest for Westminster in 1770 and held the seat till 1774, a young Welsh gentleman Robert Jones of Fonmor Castle, nr. Cardiff, and Hill Street, Berkeley Square, 'a gentleman of good character, but not esteemed to be a man of very extensive literature and knowledge' (Brit. Mus. Add. MS. 35632, f. 49: John Vernon to 2nd Lord Hardwicke, 12 June 1769), and Lord Mountmorres, the younger brother of the patriotic Irish peer Lord Charlemont. They each seem to have had different private reasons for their allegiance, to have been concerned chiefly with the activities in Westminster, and to have detached themselves from the movement after the split within the Society in 1771. Another highly individualistic supporter, and one who remained personally attached to Wilkes throughout, was old Dr. Thomas Wilson, Prebendary of Westminster, an ardent admirer of the republican historian Mrs. Catherine Macaulay, sister of John Sawbridge. Among the legal supporters were Serjeant John Glynn, M.P. for Middlesex 1768–79, Wilkes's counsel, two young barristers William Adair and Robert Morris, a Welshman; the attorneys Charles Martin and John Reynolds (the latter Wilkes's attorney), George Bellas, Proctor of the Admiralty Court, Arthur Beardmore and John Boddington. Sir Joseph Mawbey, Bt., brewer and distiller, M.P. for Southwark 1761–74, represented the older type of popular leader.

[2] 1736–1812. For him see A. Stephens, *Memoirs of John Horne Tooke*, 2 vols., 1813.

[3] 1737–87. Son of Chauncy Townsend, merchant and contractor. M.P. for West Looe 1767–74 and for Calne 1782–7. Took up his freedom by patrimony 1769, alderman 1769, sheriff 1769–70, Lord Mayor 1772–3 (see W. P. Courtney, 'James Townsend, M.P.', *Notes and Queries*, 11th Series, v, 2–4).

[4] c. 1732–95. M.P. for Hythe 1768–74, for London 1774–95. Took up his freedom by redemption in 1769. Alderman 1769, sheriff 1769–70, Lord Mayor 1775–6.

were all to be prominent in Radical agitation for many years to come, and it was to a considerable degree through their influence that the fervour of the Wilkites was, in these early years, harnessed to Radical ends.

It might, however, be asked how it was that, with a leader like Wilkes himself indifferent or even hostile to the raising of such issues, they were able to bring about this result. The answer lies in the fact that until his release from prison in April 1770, Wilkes was not in a position to exercise leadership over the forces he had raised. The easy discipline of the King's Bench prison in which he was confined permitted him, it is true, to keep himself in the public eye and to fight his battle with the House of Commons, but he could neither take part in the corporate activities of the City, nor exercise a preponderant influence over the day-to-day activities of his supporters in the rest of the metropolis until he was able to be present in person. In the City it was in consequence William Beckford who, until his sudden death in June 1770, reaped the fruits of Wilkes's popularity, and between Beckford and these new and ardent recruits the links both of personal friendship and similarity of ideas were strong. In particular, both Townsend and Sawbridge adhered in parliament to the Chatham group of which Beckford was an old supporter.[1] And when in the summer of 1769 Beckford persuaded both of them to take up the freedom of the City, and arranged for them not only to be elected aldermen but also sheriffs for the year,[2] and when in November he himself was for the second time chosen Lord Mayor,[3] the control of the popular forces both in the City and in the metropolis as a whole was placed firmly in their united and friendly hands.

[1] In 1771 Townsend called Beckford 'my intimate confidential friend' (*London Chronicle*, 10–12 October 1771, xxx, 360).

[2] John Horne in a letter signed 'Roberto' in *The Gazetteer*, 25 September 1771, described Beckford's initiative in this matter.

[3] Beckford's nomination was organized by James Townsend. Beckford wrote to Shelburne, 24 October 1769, 'Our friend Townsend has, by his encouragement, brought this about '(Bowood MSS.). When his name was put

Since the alliance between Beckford and Wilkes was purely one of convenience—Beckford never joined the Supporters of the Bill of Rights and even in the two months between Wilkes's release from prison and Beckford's death it began to wear thin—Beckford had every reason to stress rather the general issues arising out of the demagogue's cause than his personal grievances. Moreover the main issue which could be extracted from the Middlesex Election dispute, the threat to the rights of the electors from what might be considered a corrupt House of Commons, fitted in well with the tentative ideas about electoral and parliamentary reform which he had already been advancing. Thus the sympathies of the new recruits and the ideas of the old City leader were easily assimilated. In consequence it was during the short period between the rise of the Wilkite movement and the struggle of Wilkes himself to assume control of it, that the main contributions were made by the metropolis to the development of eighteenth-century Radicalism. In this period something in the nature of a programme of parliamentary reform was adumbrated; an attempt was made to set on foot a nation-wide agitation in support of their views, and (less important, but equally significant of the forces at work in the metropolis) a plot was laid to force a pledge of support for a reform programme on the leaders of the opposition groups in parliament.

The first of these contributions was that of the most permanent importance. It would seem to have been Beckford who took the lead here. The first step was taken at the beginning of 1769 when the metropolitan constituencies decided to send instructions to their representatives protesting against the actions of the House against Wilkes, and advancing other grievances. Both Middlesex and Westminster adopted and published their

forward with that of Trecothick, the hostile majority in the Court of aldermen, believing his protestations that he would not stand, elected him in order to force on another election. When Beckford permitted the Livery to persuade him to change his mind, they considered this a disreputable trick.

instructions before the City did, but it was the City's instructions, in the preparation of which Beckford was actively concerned, which first raised the issue of electoral and parliamentary reform.[1] The City representatives were instructed to work for shorter parliaments and a place and pension bill (both echoes of the old Oppositions with which Beckford was familiar) and for the imposition of the oath against bribery at elections which Beckford had demanded in his abortive bill at the end of the last parliament. (A further proposal advanced that voting might be by ballot is of more uncertain origin, and does not occur again.) Further, throughout the rest of 1769 Beckford began to dwell in his speeches in the House on the 'little paltry boroughs' he had complained of as early as 1761, and on the undue influence which they gave to the aristocracy and to other borough-owners.[2] And by 1770 he had produced the three-fold programme of reform—shorter parliaments, a place and pension bill and the more equal representation of the people, which he tried to force on the unwilling parliamentary Opposition, and which obtained widespread support in the metropolis. It was a programme based on the assumption that representation and property were closely related, and it was in no sense a demand for popular sovereignty, but it was (largely for this reason) one which was to remain acceptable to most English reformers for many years to come.

More immediately striking, however, though of less long-term significance, were the attempts in these years to extend the movement inside the metropolis to the nation as a whole.

[1] The Middlesex freeholders met to agree on instructions to their representatives on 12 January; those of Westminster on 25 January. The City instructions were agreed on 10 February 1769. For Beckford's part in this, see *Public Advertiser*, 11 February 1769.

[2] On 29 February 1769 he stated, 'The fact is, a number of great men are got together to parcel out every thing, without regard to the people' (Cavendish *Debates*, i, 150). On 1 March 1769 he stated, 'We should cut off the small paltry boroughs' (ibid., i, 281) and the next day he spoke of M.P.s whose seats were obtained by 'bribing some paltry borough' (ibid., i, 304).

The course of these attempts illustrates so well both the strength and the limitations of this Radical movement of the metropolis in relation to the country as a whole, that it is worth going into it in some detail. A first attempt made by the City on its own at the time of the publication of its instructions to its representatives was an almost complete failure.[1] Even in the commercial centres where it was accustomed to stimulate common action on commercial issues, it ran into unexpected difficulties, and in the counties its contacts were too slight to bring forth a response.[2] A second attempt in the summer of 1769 was made under more auspicious circumstances, and met with more success. It did so because it was undertaken in collaboration with the opposition groups in parliament. As soon as the House of Commons had resolved on 15 April 1769 that, Wilkes being incapable of sitting, Colonel Luttrell, the rival candidate, be declared elected in his stead, a meeting of Middlesex Freeholders was summoned, at which James Townsend announced 'the necessity of seeking out some new remedy for a new grievance'.[3] Shortly afterwards a deputation of the Livery of the City asked for a Common Hall for the same purpose;[4] and it

[1] The *London Chronicle*, 2–4 February 1769, xxv, 114, reported that Essex was said to be considering instructions and that Bristol 'and the capital places in the kingdom, are impatiently waiting the sense of the City of London' to draw up their instructions. In all between 31 January and 9 February the paper reported four cities—Norwich, Exeter, London, Bristol—and six counties—Devon, Middlesex, Essex, Wiltshire, Hampshire and Berkshire—as awaiting the London lead. Copies of the London instructions were sent by post to all parts of the kingdom 'with a view to animate other Counties and Boroughs to follow the example' (*London Chronicle*, 9–11 February 1769, xxv, 144). Bristol sent instructions. For their reaction see W. R, Savadge, 'The West Country and American Mainland Colonies 1703–1783, with special reference to the Merchants of Bristol', unpublished thesis, Oxford University.

[2] Its chief effect was to stimulate a crop of loyal addresses to the Crown, organized by the supporters of Administration. They were duly printed in the *London Gazette* between the beginning of February until the end of May 1769.   [3] *London Chronicle*, 15–18 April 1769, xxv, 366.

[4] The calling of a Common Hall was first demanded on 27 April 1769, the day on which the Middlesex petition was passed, but owing to obstruction the petition from London was not presented until 5 July 1769.

soon became known that the 'new remedy' proposed by both Middlesex and the City was the presentation of petitions to the Crown, which would not only demand redress of various grievances, but (a definitely unorthodox departure) would also protest to the King against the actions of the House of Commons. Early in May it was rumoured that 'a petition of a very extraordinary kind is actually preparing, to be sent through every county in England in order to be signed by such freeholders . . . as may approve of its contents'.[1]

Before any petition was formally adopted, however, on the last day of the parliamentary session a dinner was held at the Thatched House Tavern, attended by the House of Commons members of all the opposition groups, at which it was agreed to take common action during the recess to stir up expressions of public opinion throughout the country in protest against the Middlesex Resolution.[2] All those metropolitan leaders who were also members of parliament were present; the toast of 'the City of London, not forgetting the Livery thereof'[3] was drunk, and though no statement was made about the means to be employed to voice the country's protest, it was obviously generally accepted that petitions to the Crown as proposed in Middlesex and London should be pressed on all counties and some of the larger boroughs, and that the leaders of metropolitan opinion and the parliamentary opposition groups should work alongside each other in the campaign.[4] There are even some signs of a definite 'deal' between the two groups of allies. All sections of the parliamentary Opposition shared, together with their dislike of Wilkes, a suspicion of the Radicalism of the metropolis.

[1] *London Chronicle*, 11–13 May 1769, xxv, 456. There was a precedent. The petition of the City to the Crown against the Cider Tax in 1764 was said in the House to be 'the first instance of a petition to the King against Parliament' (MS. Parliamentary Diary of James Harris, 16 March 1764).

[2] The dinner was held on 9 May 1769. A list of the seventy-two members of the Opposition in the House of Commons present is included in the *Chatham Correspondence*, iii, 359–60, n. 1.

[3] *London Chronicle*, 11–13 May 1769, xxv, 450.

[4] There was no formal agreement on the steps to be taken.

They were, in consequence, anxious to confine the petitions to the issue of the Middlesex Election alone.[1] It may therefore be of some significance that a circumstantial account appeared in the Press a few days before the Thatched House dinner of a meeting between George Grenville and William Dowdeswell, the leaders of the two main opposition groups in the House of Commons, with some persons in the City,[2] to discuss possible modifications in the terms of the Middlesex Petition; and it may also be noted that, though the petitions of Middlesex and the City ultimately came out in their original form, those from other parts of the metropolis, which were drawn up later, followed the pattern set by the rest of the country and confined themselves to the Middlesex issue.[3]

The popular leaders of the metropolis had thus succeeded in reaching an agreement with the parliamentary Opposition to work for a nation-wide expression of public opinion, and had imposed on them their own plan of action—though they may have done so at the cost of narrowing the issues on which the support of the nation was to be sought. In the implementing of the plan they also took an active part. In the county of Surrey[4] as well as throughout the metropolitan area it was they who

[1] The marquess of Rockingham suspected the followers of Grenville and Chatham of a desire to introduce radical matters into the petition. He wrote to Burke about the proposed Buckinghamshire petition expressing gloomy suspicions of the attitude of Lord Temple and his supporters. 'Lord Temple will try to include all the matters mentioned in the City and Livery Petition, he will do it politically as a compliment to them and I even should scarce be surprized if annual or triennial Parliaments were recommended' (Fitz-William MSS. (Sheffield): Rockingham to E. Burke, 17 July 1769). But in fact Temple and Grenville fully accepted the desirability of confining the petition 'to the principal point, and to express themselves upon that with vigour and decency' (ibid.: T. Whately to E. Burke, 23 August 1769).

[2] *London Chronicle*, 4–6 May 1769, xxv, 430.

[3] The Westminster Petition was, however, the first to call for the dissolution of parliament, a point on which they were later followed by the Yorkshire Petition.

[4] See p. 143 below. An account of the popular activities in Surrey at this time was published by Sir Joseph Mawbey under the title of 'Surriensis' in the *Gentleman's Magazine*, 1788, pp. 1052–53.

made the running; they were also able to exert some influence over the commercial centres with which they were in contact, and individuals among them could help in stimulating opinion in counties further afield. It was reported in August that 'many of them are dispersed in different parts of the country endeavouring to stir up meetings of the freeholders . . .',[1] and Serjeant John Glynn in Cornwall and Exeter,[2] Beckford in Wiltshire and Somerset,[3] John Sawbridge in Kent,[4] and possibly one or two others elsewhere were active and prominent in this work.[5]

These activities mark, however, the extent of what they could do to further the progress of the campaign. The appeal was primarily to the counties, and by the very nature of the case, the chief part in arousing support in the counties had to be taken by the political leaders whom they trusted, and it is significant that almost without exception the influence exerted

[1] Brit. Mus. Add. MS. 35632, f. 51; John Vernon to the 2nd Lord Hardwicke, 16 August 1769.

[2] He was a freeholder in Cornwall and was Recorder of Exeter. At the Cornish meeting of Freeholders at Bodmin on 6 October 1769 he spoke an hour. At Exeter at a meeting at Guildhall in the same month he attended as Recorder and made an excellent speech (Wilkes MSS., Brit. Mus. Add. MS. 30870, f. 213: [unsigned] Exeter, 24 October 1769).

[3] Beckford attended the Wiltshire meeting at Devizes on 16 August 1769 with Lord Temple who was visiting him, and spoke. The duke of Grafton considered the petition largely the work of 'our old friends Popham and Beckford' (*Autobiography and Political Correspondence of Augustus Henry, third Duke of Grafton*, ed. W. R. Anson, 1898, p. 239). He was unable to attend the meeting at Wells in October to pass the petition from Somerset, but he sent a letter giving 'my sentiments freely and a copy of the chief grievance', which he authorized his correspondent to make public if necessary (Bowood MSS.: W. Beckford to Shelburne, 24 October 1769).

[4] In Kent a petition was, after a good deal of difficulty, stirred up despite the opposition of the gentry. John Sawbridge was among those active in furthering it. *Chatham Correspondence*, iii, 365: J. Calcraft to Chatham, 25 November 1769. Walpole, *Memoirs*, iii, 393: 'Sawbridge and Calcraft obtained . . . a petition from the county of Kent, though all the magistrates shrunk from it, two gentlemen only appearing there and they dissenting.'

[5] Horace Walpole reported that Sir Joseph Mawbey and Calcraft, assisted by Sir Robert Bernard, also took the lead in obtaining the Essex petition (ibid., iii, 400) without the support of the gentry.

by individual metropolitan leaders in the counties arose from the fact that they were property owners there. More general efforts to exercise influence from the metropolis over the course of events were unsuccessful. An attempt by the Supporters of the Bill of Rights by circularizing the counties to encourage the setting up of permanent local organizations to correspond with, was very coldly received;[1] and the intervention of John Horne, Sir Robert Bernard and others in the borough of Bedford to defeat the mayor favoured by the duke of Bedford,[2] did not (as it was confidently hoped) prove the beginning of a movement of revolt by boroughs against their patrons,[3] and would have been highly unpopular with their parliamentary allies if it had.

When the campaign had once been agreed on therefore the Radical forces in the metropolis could hope to play only a minor part in its course. Their influence was further weakened, moreover, by the open suspicion with which they were regarded by at least one section of the parliamentary Opposition and by large sections of public opinion throughout the country. While that part of the Opposition which followed the lead of Chatham and the Grenvilles were prepared to work amicably with them,

[1] The Supporters of the Bill of Rights at a meeting on 31 May agreed to despatch a circular 'invoking the friends of Liberty throughout the whole British Empire to concur in promoting the Constitutional Purposes for which this Society was established'. Two complementary letters were sent out. Copies, dated 20 July, are reproduced in the *London Chronicle*, 17–20 February 1770, xxvii, 174–5. Dowdeswell, who received a copy, decided not to reply (Dowdeswell MSS. Clements Library, Ann Arbor, Michigan: W. Dowdeswell to E. Burke, 10 August 1769). Walpole reported that it received little response (*Memoirs*, iii, 372).

[2] For this incident see *Public Advertiser*, 6 September 1769, seq.

[3] A good deal of propaganda was put out in the Press to encourage it, and an unsuccessful attempt was made to repeat the operation against the duke of Grafton at Thetford (*Public Advertiser*, 20 September 1769). On 11 October the same paper reported that such was the feeling throughout the Corporations of the kingdom that at their annual elections of officers they 'seem determined to make choice of those gentlemen only whose conduct has proved them to be steady friends to their Country'—an obvious piece of propaganda quite unrelated to fact.

this was by no means the case with the party supporting the marquess of Rockingham. The marquess himself for a long time resisted the proposal to promote a petition in his own county of Yorkshire, and did so largely because of his dislike of the metropolis and its motives. ' I *must say*', he wrote, 'that the thing which weighs most against adopting the mode of petitioning the King is, *where* the example was first set.'[1] And the course of the campaign showed that this suspicion was so widely shared by those whose signatures were being sought, that in many parts of the country the support of the metropolis was a hindrance rather than a help in the agitation. William Dowdeswell, the leader of the Rockinghams in the House of Commons, lamented from Worcestershire that 'Wilkes's character . . . and the advantage which he necessarily must receive from the restitution made to the Public of its rights . . . have checkt this proceeding in most places', and he added 'The injudicious list of grievances, which filled the first petitions, [i.e. those of Middlesex and London] still more disinclined the sober part of the People to signing petitions. . . .'[2] While in Surrey the highly respectable Sir Anthony Abdy, battling in vain against the incursion of metropolitan organizers into the county, protested at 'the wild and warm proceedings of Messrs. Horne, Bellas etc. and others of the London Tavern, the generality of whose opinions and ideas I cannot agree or subscribe to'.[3]

The campaign as a whole had only a limited success. Only eighteen out of the forty English counties[4] and over a dozen of

[1] FitzWilliam MSS. (Sheffield): Rockingham to E. Burke, 1, 3 September 1769.
[2] Dowdeswell MSS. (Clements Library, Ann Arbor, Michigan): W. Dowdeswell to E. Burke, 5 September 1769.
[3] FitzWilliam MSS. (Sheffield): Sir Anthony Abdy to Sir George Colebrooke (copy), 1 July 1769.
[4] Middlesex, Surrey, Devonshire, Cornwall, Wiltshire, Somersetshire, Gloucestershire, Buckinghamshire, Yorkshire, Essex, Worcestershire, Derbyshire, Cumberland, Herefordshire, Kent, Dorset, Northumberland, Durham.

the larger boroughs[1] finally presented petitions, and these often took months to procure despite strenuous efforts on the part of those promoting them. Whether from suspicion of metropolitan Radicalism, or dislike of Wilkes or for other reasons there was little sign that the country gentry as a whole were anxious to make a protest even on the limited issue of the Middlesex Resolution. It was probably true that in most counties there were enough of what Rockingham called the 'young men' and 'the warm spirits'[2] to get a petition through a county meeting if they were given a lead by those whom they were accustormed to follow. It was also true that here and there they took the initiative without such a lead, or, as in Yorkshire itself, forced their leaders into action. In consequence in most counties where members of the parliamentary Opposition were influential petitions were set on foot. But when it came to circulating the petitions for signature the organizers often found a good deal of unwillingness to sign. 'It is amazing', complained Dowdeswell, 'how in most places people of rank and fortune shrink from this measure; and with what deference all others below them wait for their leaders.'[3] And if there were unwillingness among the gentry, there was ignorance among the freeholders. There were indeed some signs of independent approval of the movement among the more substantial class of freeholder. John Robinson, suspiciously watching the progress of the Yorkshire petition from the neighbouring county of Westmorland, wrote, 'It gives me concern to find that the Quakers

[1] It is not always easy to be certain which of the petitions discussed in the boroughs were actually delivered, particularly in the case of those which came late in the movement, when the arrangements for publicity were uncertain. The following seem, however, certainly to have been presented: Westminster, Southwark, Canterbury, Exeter, Bristol, Liverpool, Berwick-on-Tweed, Worcester, Durham, Newcastle-upon-Tyne, Coventry, Wells and Hereford. The official *Gazette*, which so carefully included all the earlier loyal addresses, ignored the petitions completely.

[2] FitzWilliam MSS. (Sheffield): Rockingham to E. Burke, 1–3 September 1769.

[3] Dowdeswell MSS.: W. Dowdeswell to E. Burke, 5 September 1769.

and Dissenters are so infatuated . . . as to sign and support it',[1] and the notably independent freeholders of Kent, and apparently those of Essex,[2] supported petitions against the wishes of most of the local gentry. But in general the situation seems to have been much as Lord Temple described it in Buckinghamshire where he 'found the freeholders in general totally ignorant of the question, and but very little affected with it'.[3] The duke of Richmond also gave an admirable account of the position in an out-of-the-way county, that of Sussex, when explaining why, despite his personal sympathies, he did not organize a petition there. 'You will naturally say then, well why do not the effects appear? The reason is that from the distant situation of Sussex from London, . . . from the weight of Government on account of the many dependants which so many Seaports occasion, from many of the leading men being in place or attached to Court; from the long habit in which the Duke of Newcastle had brought the Whigs of approving all the measures of the old Court, the attachment of the Torys to the new Court, and from the natural indolence of men who do not feel the immediate effects of oppression. From all these causes, there was a supineness, that of itself would not stir, tho' they must and do see that things are not right. I could plainly see that there was discontent enough, if it was encouraged to do the business of a Petition, but I must have stirred it up, and in so doing I should have appear'd factious.'[4]

Nor was the response of the boroughs, even the more important ones, much more encouraging. Even in Bristol, though a petition was set going with enthusiasm, it hung fire so much that at one time doubts were felt whether it would ever be

[1] Brit. Mus. Add. MS. 38206, f. 149. J. Robinson to C. Jenkinson, 3 November 1769.

[2] See above.

[3] FitzWilliam MSS. (Sheffield): E. Burke to Rockingham, 9 September 1769.

[4] Rockingham MSS. (Sheffield): Richmond to E. Burke, 2 September 1769.

presented,[1] and at Liverpool a petition from a body of freemen was immediately offset by a counter-petition from the Corporation. In view of the conflicting interests among those sponsoring the petitions, and the evidence of widespread indifference and even dislike of the measure among those who were approached, it is not surprising that Administration, at first alarmed at the prospect of an outburst of public feeling on a nation-wide scale, ended by ignoring it altogether, nor that the movement petered out.

With the dying away of the agitations of these years, the bid which the Radical forces of the metropolis had made to enlist the country in their cause was virtually over. Beckford's attempts in 1770 to pledge the leaders of the Opposition to his programme of reform were easily evaded and were thus of comparatively little significance,[2] and the Remonstrances of the same year, in the course of which he won his posthumous statue from his fellow-citizens, called forth little response outside the metropolis. And with his death and the violent internal dissensions which accompanied the succession of Wilkes to power, the breach between the metropolis and the rest of the country was further widened. When in 1771 the Lord Mayor, Brass Crosby, was committed to the Tower by the House of Commons during the dispute between the City and the House over the printing of the Commons' Debates, the incident aroused in the country as a whole, as Edmund Burke mournfully observed,[3] little general comment or even surprise.

[1] Add. MS. 30870, f. 190: J. Green (of Wine Street, Bristol) to J. Wilkes, 16 September 1769.

[2] See p. 136 above. Besides the attempt to pledge the Opposition leaders into a programme of reform, they also tried to trick Chatham into pledging his support of triennial parliaments (*Chatham Correspondence*, iii, 464 n. 1). He rejected the idea, though on 1 May 1771 he declared himself converted to it.

[3] He wrote to Charles O'Hara, 2 April 1711 (printed Hoffman, op. cit., p. 488): 'The people of the City have habituated themselves to *play* with violent measures. A Mayor of London sent to the Tower in his year of office, would at any other time have been a very dangerous symptom. It is now no indifferent one; but not what it would have been formerly.'

Nevertheless, the events of these years had a real importance in the history of eighteenth-century England. It was not without cause that Christopher Wyvill, leader of the famous Yorkshire Association ten years later, printed as the introduction to his political papers the proceedings in Yorkshire in 1769–70,[1] and in the metropolis itself forces had been set at work which did not again die down. Moreover the sketch of a programme of parliamentary reform had been drawn up which was to serve as the basis of the ideas of the majority of reformers for many years to come, and which might also serve as a starting-point for more revolutionary proposals. In 1771 when Wilkes and his friends felt obliged to advance proposals for reform they adopted Beckford's propositions *en bloc*,[2] but five years later, when Wilkes made his speech on reform in the new parliament in which he was permitted to sit, Beckford's 'more equal representation of the people' had developed into the principle 'that every free agent in this kingdom should . . . be represented in parliament'.[3] And even when Wilkes spoke, Major Cartwright's famous pamphlet *Take Your Choice*, in which he advocated universal suffrage, was being shown round in manuscript in preparation for publication.[4]

[1] C. Wyvill, *Political Papers, chiefly respecting the Attempt of the County of York and other Considerable Districts, . . . to effect a Reformation of the Parliament of Great-Britain*, n.d., York, i, xi seq.

[2] The Bill of Rights Society first adopted this programme at a meeting on 11 June 1771 (*Public Advertiser*, 13 June 1771).

[3] *Parliamentary History*, xviii, 1295.

[4] F. D. Cartwright, *The Life and Correspondence of Major Cartwright*, 1826, i, 95.

III
The East India Company
and Politics

BIBLIOGRAPHICAL NOTE

CHAPTER 6

Material used in this chapter reappeared in an expanded form in chapter ii, 'The Moneyed Company', of *The East India Company in Eighteenth-century Politics* (Oxford, 1952).

CHAPTER 7

For more recent general treatments of the Peace of Paris, which do not modify the conclusions reached in this article, see Z.E. Rashid, *The Peace of Paris, 1763* (Liverpool, 1951) and R. Hyam, 'Imperial Interests and the Peace of Paris (1763)' in R. Hyam and G. Martin, *Reappraisals in British Imperial History* (London, 1975), pp. 21-43.

CHAPTER 8

Dame Lucy added an appendix on 'Lord Shelburne's financial concern in the East Indian crisis of 1769' to chapter vii of her *The East India Company in Eighteenth-century Politics* (Oxford, 1952). Some additional material can be found in J.N.M. Maclean, *Reward is Secondary* (London, 1963), pp. 219-35.

CHAPTER 9

The recent collection of essays on Macartney, published by the Ulster Historical Foundation, *Macartney of Lisanoure 1737-1806: Essays in Biography*, edited by Peter Roebuck (Belfast, 1983), contains a contribution on 'India 1780-6' by T.G. Fraser. Dr Fraser discusses Macartney's appointment on pp. 158-65. There is a valuable assessment of Macartney's Indian governorship in J.R. Phillips, 'The Development of British Authority in Southern India: the Nawab of Arcot, the East India Company, and the British Government, 1775-85' (Dalhousie University Ph.D. thesis, 1983).

CHAPTER 11

This article on the political background to this famous case was followed in *E.H.R.*, lxxv (1960), pp. 223-38, by an interesting reassessment of the case's legal implications by J.D.M. Derrett, 'Nandakumar's Forgery'. The role of the 'banians' and other Indians who collaborated closely with the Europeans, on which this article throws much light, has subsequently attracted considerable attention; see for instance, P.J. Marshall, 'Masters and Banians in Eighteenth-century Calcutta', in *The Age of Partnership: Europeans in Asia before Dominion* (Honolulu, 1979), pp. 191-213.

It is now generally agreed that the proper spelling should be Nandakumar.

CHAPTER 12

The obscurity, which this article discusses, about the powers given by Hastings to Macleane, has been in some degree lifted by the identification of an item in the Hastings collection in the British Library as 'Copy of my Instructions to Graham and McLeane' (Add. MS. 29204, ff. 279-82; see also J.N.M. Maclean, *Reward is Secondary* [London, 1963], p. 528).

Warren Hastings (1732-1818) (Sir Thomas Lawrence, 1786)
(National Portrait Gallery)

THE EAST INDIA COMPANY IN
EIGHTEENTH-CENTURY POLITICS

P ROFESSOR L. B. NAMIER, in considering the earlier years of the reign
of George III, has drawn attention to the need for work in the
further elucidation of the part played in their politics by the East
India Company.[2] The need exists to a greater or less extent throughout
a great part of the century. For Professor Namier was going behind the
great question of the significance in the development of British imperialism
of the expansion of territorial control in India after the Seven Years War
and the high issues raised in the greatest *cause célèbre* of eighteenth-century
England, the trial of Warren Hastings; he was drawing attention to the
way in which a large financial, trading and territorial corporation, itself
undergoing great administrative and political strain, could be affected by
and itself affect the intricate workings of politics at Westminster, and the
unending struggle of the governments of the day to maintain the 'connexion' on which their survival depended.

His interest in this problem is an illustration of the difference of
outlook between the modern historian and his predecessors. To the latter,
the circumstances immediately surrounding an event, though they might
be of high interest, were in the last resort no more than incidental to the
great evolutionary trend in which they believed, a trend which under the
heroic influence of great forces and ideas was leading the men who thought
they controlled these events to ends greater and more distant than they
knew. When historians actuated by this belief explained an event by the
statement that the 'time was ripe for it' or that 'public opinion demanded.
it', they were giving an explanation which for them was more valid than
a wealth of detail about the circumstances surrounding it. To the modern
historian however, bereft of this underlying belief in purposive progress,
these high-sounding phrases mean very little. To him every specific act has
a specific cause and, though among these causes may be a variety of social
forces including those powerful forces which we call ideas, he is inclined
to see these forces as conflicting and diverse, given coherence by the
practical decisions of individuals, rather than all-pervasive and purposive.
Hence what were to his predecessors the incidental circumstances surrounding an event are to him precisely the factors which give it unique
significance. It is from the details which occasion events alone, from

[1] A paper delivered at the Anglo-French Historical Conference, Paris, on
26 September 1946.

[2] L. B. Namier, *Structure of Politics at the Accession of George III* (1929); II,
352, n. I.

knowing as closely as possible 'how the wheels went round', that he can build up the much more intricate and detailed system of historical causation towards which, amongst the ruins of past assumptions, he is feeling his way. It may be said that the unity which the work of nineteenth-century historians obtained from its dependence on certain accepted convictions can only be found in the work of contemporary historians through their preoccupation with certain common problems. One of the problems which preoccupy many of them and which inspires much of the most interesting of contemporary work is the problem of the nature and significance of political power in relation to the society in which it is exercised. The study of what political power consists, in various societies, the means by which it is gained, maintained and lost, and how it adapts itself to changing social conditions; these are central points for much of the best of modern historical work, and it is as a historian in this tradition that Professor Namier was speaking.

The change in the approach of the historian resulting from the change in his outlook has necessarily brought about some revaluation of all historical periods. For some it has had a peculiarly vivifying effect. One of these is the eighteenth century in England. To the nineteenth-century historian the politics of this age with its negative conception of the functions of government and its absence of the pressure of political ideas, sandwiched as it was between the turbulence of political ideas of the seventeenth century and the great achievements of the nineteenth, were apt to seem hardly more than an arid waste. The twentieth-century historian, on the contrary, turning on it his interest in the varied forms and workings of political power, finds its politics full of interest. It is true that for at least three-quarters of its course the governments of the day found the obtaining and retaining of power in itself a full-time occupation, and that even when a more vigorous *use* of power began to be imposed on them by the pressure of circumstances, the change found little reflection in general principles; but it is also true that the limited ends at which they aimed were, for long stretches of time, achieved with very fair success and that those who achieved them were facing a difficult problem, the nature of which we at the present time can perhaps understand more fully than our predecessors. The nineteenth-century historian tended to accept the robust nineteenth-century assumptions that a people got the government they deserved, and that if national life showed vigour and enterprise a people could expect to achieve almost automatically a government which reflected these qualities and ensured them of their opportunity to develop. We are less convinced that the world is so beneficently planned. And if one regards the political scene at the death of Queen Anne with a mind free from the preconception that the present British constitution was pre-ordained, one can readily understand the views of those contemporaries, both English and foreign, who believed that the English system of government as it emerged from the convulsions of the preceding century was entirely unworkable and that the struggles of a factious and irresponsible parliament, torn by dissensions still fresh and bitter in men's minds, and a Crown nominally responsible for administration but morally weakened and stripped of all its most effective administrative machinery, must result either in anarchy or a reversion to some form of despotism. That nothing of the kind happened, but that on the contrary it gave place to a stable if inert political system based on a certain balance of forces out of which the flexible yet powerful governmental system of the future ultimately arose, was due in part no doubt to the good sense and absence of rancour of the English landed and commercial classes in a society both prosperous and expansionist. It was also due to the skill shown by a few men, in particular Robert Walpole and his successor Henry Pelham, in all that appertained to the consolidation and manipulation of political power under the curious conditions of the time. Those arts of the 'political boss' which have alienated students of the careers of these politicians were precisely those which played so great a part in ensuring the survival of the bases of the constitution and which underlay the whole structure of eighteenth-century prosperity.

The political and constitutional development of eighteenth-century England after the Hanoverian Succession falls roughly into three periods. The first covers those years of order and stability to achieve which (and their own political survival) Walpole ingeniously built up and Pelham painfully maintained their intricate political machine. It ended formally with the partial breakdown of that machine when George III was able to dismiss the Duke of Newcastle and the remaining friends of the old connexion in 1762, though its end was inevitable as soon as Pelham died. The second period covers the years of uncertainty and of jockeying for power when the machine creaked dismally beneath the inexpert hands of George III and a succession of weak or half-hearted ministers called in to assist him. It was, however, a period which, though it revived memories of the great factions of the past, did not revive the chaos of those past factions because, though the machine creaked, it never completely broke down. Lord North's administration might not be a strong one, but it survived for twelve years, six of which were difficult years of war. The third period begins with the rise of the younger Pitt in 1784 and his gradual imposition on the politics of his time of a system and order comparable to that which Walpole had earlier achieved. In this period the machine was working again, was reinforced by a more impressive administrative structure, and its workings began to be affected by more positive ideas as to the *use* to which political power should be put. Cut across though this development was by the Napoleonic and Revolutionary War, the first war to impose on the country something of the moral and physical strain of modern warfare, this period prepared the way for the great legislative and administrative activity which characterized the nineteenth century.

It is against the background of these three periods that we must consider the relations of the government and the East India Company in the eighteenth century. They are of interest for two main reasons. First, in a study of eighteenth-century government, because the problem of political relations with a great corporation was for eighteenth-century politicians rather an unusual one; in the eighteenth century the normal type of what we should now call a 'pressure-group' was the loose and informal association of individuals bound together by a common interest; it was only in the financial field that they had to deal with powerful and formally organized interests in the 'three Monied Companies' as contemporaries called them, the Bank of England, the South Sea Company and, from one important point of view, the East India Company. Secondly, it was of interest because of the remarkable developments of the East India Company itself.

The East India Company was one of the few survivors of the trading and territorial monopoly companies characteristic of the late sixteenth and early seventeenth centuries.[1] It first came into existence in a makeshift sort of way in 1599–1600 as a by-product of a slump in the trade of the Levant Company, and followed in a modified manner the example of the Portuguese and Dutch in their use of the new route to the old riches of the East. It owed its continuance partly to the success of its earliest voyages, partly to its gradual adoption of the new joint stock organization which enabled it to conserve the wealth it gained, but still more to the way in which a wealthy organization of that type on the rising London money-market became associated with and ultimately essential to government finance. Though it ploughed a hazardous way through the tempests of seventeenth-century politics, the value of the revenue that could be extorted from it forced government after government to protect it against the rivalry of its individualist opponents anxious to break down its monopoly trading rights to the East; and it emerged [2] into the smoother waters of Walpole's England rich, well organized by the standards of the time, deeply and painfully experienced in the technique of political intrigue both with monarchy and with parliament, its strength in the political field consisting in its financial usefulness to the government, its weakness in the fact that its charter was revocable by parliament (and indeed required periodic renewal) and that strong commercial hostility to it was always potentially existent.

In the eighteenth century its history [3] follows with some modifications

[1] W. R. Scott, *The Constitution and Finance of English, Scottish and Irish Joint-Stock Companies to* 1720 (Cambridge, 1912), II, 89 seq. for the origins of the Company. Its history, 1635–76, is copiously documented in the ten-volume *Calendar of the Court Minutes etc. of the East India Company,* 1635–76, ed. E. B. Sainsbury (Oxford, 1907–35), and in the *Calendar of State Papers Colonial, East Indies,* 1513–1634.

[2] Technically the United Company of 1708 was a new creation, deriving less from the 'old' than the 'new' Company which after the Glorious Revolution had hoped to replace it. In fact the leaders of the 'old' Company rapidly succeeded in dominating it.

[3] The chief sources for the history of the Company during this period are its administrative and trading records preserved at the India Office; its stock records preserved in the Bank of England Record Office; the MSS. of Warren Hastings (British Museum), Clive (in the possession of Lord Powis); the Newcastle and Jenkinson MSS. (British Museum) and the Robinson MSS. (partly in the British Museum and partly in the possession of Lord Abergavenny); and the mass of evidence before Parliamentary Commissions, of newspapers and pamphlets. In addition, there is a wealth of less concentrated contemporary material both in manuscript and print.

the divisions I have suggested for national politics. In the first of these it enjoyed the fruits of its past successes and took full advantage of the calm and prosperity of the period. Its trade was more prosperous than at any other period of its history, its internal organization was developed into an orderly and oligarchic control by the twenty-four prominent London merchants who at any one time made up its Court of Directors, backed by a sound executive machine built up by a succession of competent secretaries. In the rapidly evolving stock exchange of London its stock enjoyed what would now be considered a gilt-edged reputation and was sought after by the *rentier* classes of the rich European countries as well as of England, while its short-term bonds played as important a part in the money-market as the government's paper itself. This was in fact its great period as a monied Company, and as such, as will be explained at more length later, it inevitably held a respectable and even a prominent position in the political system which Walpole built up.

Underlying these satisfactory and apparently stable conditions, however, were certain features which were neither stable nor satisfactory, and this period of equilibrium came to an end before that of the governmental arrangements within which it took its place. The origin of this instability lay in India. The English Company had been loath to follow the example of its predecessors in undertaking territorial responsibilities in India and indeed was in their earlier days in no position to do so. With the collapse of the Mogul power, however, and as a result of their own growing interests, they were obliged before the end of the seventeenth century to admit that the age of 'fenceless factories' was past and to follow the Dutch example in building up areas of security round their factories and of drawing revenues from these territories to cover the costs involved.[1] With the rise of the power of the French Company and the growing disintegration of what they called the 'country powers' they were increasingly caught up during the first half of the century in the web of Indian native states diplomacy until the period of annexation which Clive inaugurated just after the Seven Years War became almost inevitable. The results for the Company from the point of view with which we are now concerned were threefold.

In the first place, the growth of Anglo-French rivalry in India inevitably made the concern of the Company the concern of the government in each country. In consequence, on the English side, both in the War of the Austrian Succession and the Seven Years War, the armed forces of the English Company were reinforced by Royal forces both military and naval. It became clear that in the colonial rivalry of the period too much prestige and even power depended on the success of the Company for the government to disinterest itself in its fortunes in India. Though governments were slow to face this fact except under stress of war, recognition of it was gradually forced upon them. In the succeeding years even the weakest of governments began to show anxiety whenever the Company's

[1] W. W. Hunter, *History of British India*, 2 vols. (1899); *Cambridge History of British India*, ed. H. H. Dodwell (Cambridge, 1929), I, 101 seq.

uneasy relations with the country rulers gave reason to believe that a
hostile European power might take advantage of them.

In the second place, the growing intricacy of Company affairs in India,
and the new temptations to which their servants there were put, led to
a serious failure in their Indian administration. The illegitimate wealth
which certain of their servants amassed (particularly after Clive, their
victorious general, had set his dazzling example) meant not only that the
Company lost its power to control them in India, but that when the
directors tried to make examples of offenders the culprits transferred the
scene of battle from India to England and to the heart of the Company's
organization. The meetings of the Courts of Proprietors, which had been
so decorous and well controlled by the directors, became in the course
of a few years turbulent and faction-ridden assemblies, packed with
members who owed their qualifications to collusion between big stock-
holders, while the elections of directors, hitherto scarcely more than the
formal endorsement of the House List drawn up by the directors themselves, became pitched battles between rival lists of candidates in which
every device of corruption, influence and management can be seen at work.
As a result the Court of Directors also became unstable in membership and
policy and divided between sharply contending factions.[1]

And thirdly, the financial position of the Company, the very basis of its
political power, was affected, first by exaggerated ideas of its wealth which
irresistibly tempted harassed governments to its spoliation and then by the
inevitable reaction which, reinforced by confusion and dishonesty, led it
very near to bankruptcy. The great boom in East India Stock which
followed Clive's annexation of the *Diwani* of Bengal in 1765 not only
stimulated the speculators of all the financially advanced countries of
Europe (the Company's stock-books record the progressive change in the
character of its stock-holders) but tempted Lord Chatham's government
of 1766–7, struggling with the financial aftermath of the Seven Years War,
to break the alliance of Company and government which had held for
over fifty years and to launch an attack on it,[2] much as seventeenth-century
governments had done before. Once again, as in the late seventeenth
century, the Company became involved in the factions and intrigues of
intricate national politics. The result, as so often before, was a compromise.
The government, which began by threatening the Company's whole
territorial revenue and even its survival, agreed to content itself with an
annual levy of £400,000 upon it. What seemed at first no more than an
isolated financial expedient, however, with many parallels in the past,
turned out under the force of events to be the beginning of a new relation
of government and Company. The boom of 1766–7 was followed by the
crashes of 1769 and 1772, the latter the first international crisis to originate

[1] There is a good deal of material bearing on this subject in J. Malcolm, *Life of
Robert, Lord Clive*, 3 vols. (1836); and J. Forrest, *The Life of Lord Clive* (Oxford,
1918).
[2] See my 'Lord Shelburne and East India Company Politics, 1766–9', *E.H.R.*
(1934), XLIX, 450. See below, pp. 177-213.

on the London market, and successive governments found themselves, in order to insure their own revenue, forced increasingly to intervene in the Company's affairs. Thus we have the statutory limitation of their dividend [1] and the more ambitious attempts of Lord North's Regulating Act of 1773. These interventions caused, and their form was in part the result of, highly complicated relationships between factions in the Company and various parliamentary groups. Already, however, the intervention which began from so simple a motive began to take on a more intricate character. The problem of security of the Indian possessions could not be ignored; Commissions of Enquiry [2] set up to investigate what was wrong began to bring to light the facts of a complex situation, and so, even before the advent of the stable ministry of William Pitt, one can see, beneath the flurry and noise of partisan warfare, the way in which the concern of governments was being led to shift from the comparatively simple questions of finance to those of Company administration and even to those of social justice. Already, even in this period of weak and harried governments, far-seeing and hard-working young men of business, as career politicians were then called, men like John Robinson (North's secretary), Charles Jenkinson (afterwards first Lord Liverpool) and Henry Dundas (who was to play so great a part in the next period), were beginning to work up the Indian question, to draw up schemes for reforming the Company and to digest the mass of material brought before the New Commissions, still unversed in the difficult art of sifting the mountains of irrelevant and often disingenuous evidence presented to them. Without this background of knowledge and experience the great changes in the relations of Company and government which occurred in the third period of the century would have been impossible. And at the same time as problems of administration were being explored the revelations of the more deplorable aspects of the breakdown of Company rule in India were stimulating a different type of interest among a different class of people. The problems of social justice involved began to awaken the concern of the growing humanitarianism of the age. The feeling of indignation that began to stir among the professional and commercial classes of the cities and certain of the country gentry was sharpened no doubt by old hostility to the Company and by a new exasperation at the ostentatious wealth of a few returned 'nabobs' enriched by the fruits of their dubious practices. This feeling was, moreover, inevitably harnessed to the wheels of party warfare; but despite these considerations there was real force behind it. Party and personal interests were, for instance, certainly among the variety of motives that made Edmund Burke take the lead in precipitating the Warren Hastings impeachment, but when once he was embarked on his course his first partisan motives were swept away in a torrent of fury at the injustices and cynicism of Company rule in India as it was now unfolding before the

---

[1] 7 Geo. III, c. 49.
[2] The great parliamentary investigations of the period were the Select and Secret Committees of 1772 and the Select and Secret Committees of 1781.

eyes of observers, a righteous fury that has made his speeches a landmark in the history of English relations with subject peoples.

Both these facts, the growing impossibility for the government to dissociate itself from problems of Company administration both in England and in India and the growing feeling of indignation among an influential public increasingly sensitive to such questions, made it inevitable that East Indian concerns should feature prominently in the period of increased government activity and awareness of government responsibilities which began with the rise to power of the younger Pitt. Indeed, circumstances made Pitt's East India Act of 1784 almost the first of his Ministry's preoccupations, and it is hardly an exaggeration to say that the activities of the official Board of Control set up under that act formed the spear-head of the movement towards the more positive view of the functions of government which was to characterize the nineteenth century.

These then were the three stages of the relations of state and Company during the eighteenth century. Each of them is full of points of interest for the student of the growth and complexities of political power. To the last of them Professor Philips has recently devoted his study of the Company 1784–1834;[1] the middle period is at once the most intricate and the most fruitful of study, but it is far beyond the scope of this paper. The first period, however, with its simple yet highly significant lines of development is also of high interest both in itself and as the background for the later periods. It is to the problems of this period that the remainder of this paper will be devoted. This is the period in which the Company's political role remained primarily that of a monied company within the political system which Walpole had built up.

The political system which Walpole had built up was founded on four bases; the confidence of the Crown, the solidarity of interest of a knot of important Whig families who often inaccurately described themselves as the Revolutionary families, a co-ordinated use of public and private patronage managed with economy to achieve directly or indirectly the requisite parliamentary majorities, and the support of a strong financial interest in the City of London. The use of the power thus gained was, as I have said, almost entirely negative. As David Hume said in one of his essays, 'We are...to look upon all the vast apparatus of our government as having ultimately no other object or purpose but the distribution of justice or the support of the twelve Judges'.[2] In fact to maintain the machinery of law and order at home, to keep up, however inefficiently, the strength of the armed forces so that they would not prove wholly inadequate to the demands upon them of the balance of power in Europe and the pressure for expansion in the areas of colonial conflict, and to be able to lay hands on financial resources sufficient for these purposes; these may be said to sum up the public obligations of a government of the time, and it was with these limited public obligations in mind (as well as

---

[1] C. H. Philips, *The East India Company* 1784–1834 (Manchester, 1940).
[2] David Hume, 'Essay on The Origin of Government' in *Essays, Moral, Political and Literary*, ed. T. H. Green and T. H. Gross, 1, 113–14.

a wide variety of private obligations to individuals) that the machine was carefully built up. In this machine the East India Company had its place and quite an important one.

In the first place, even in this period there was always a small body of members of parliament with strong East Indian interests. Of the twenty-four directors a few always sat in the House, attracted thither, like other prominent merchants,[1] by the prospect of government contracts and other suitable rewards. The Company's stock-books also show a number of other M.P.'s as large holders of stock and thus likely to react with the directors on matters concerning the Company. It was not, however, until the returned 'nabobs' began to seek seats in the House that an East India group of any significance appeared in parliament, and in the first half of the century it never rivalled the powerful West India group or the more loosely related group of persons with interests, direct or indirect, in the American trade. The government did not, however, disdain the support of any interest, and the adherence of East India directors had a certain special advantage in that it broadened the scope of ministerial patronage. The Company exercised a wide range of patronage. As the opposition paper *The Craftsman* pointed out, they had in their bestowal 'several governments more valuable than any in the King's gift',[2] and they appointed to a great number of minor positions both at home and abroad. This patronage was not yet as widely sought as it became when the fame of the 'nabobs'' wealth made a writership or a commission in the East Indies the goal of the younger sons of England and the more senior posts a haven for the ruined jackals of great men trying to recoup their own and their patrons' fortunes. Still, ministers active in seeking out spoils for their lesser supporters were already exploiting their connexions with the Company's directors in favour of their protégés.

In the second place, the East India Company, with its wide commercial connexions, was clearly an important element in the City of London, not only when it came to parliamentary elections but in the elections to the City government in which, in view of the unique importance of City opinion, the government of the day often found it wise to concern themselves. For this purpose, the machine which the directors had built up for their support in the Company's Courts of Proprietors or at the annual elections of directors was valuable. This machine was based on the mobilization of what the City called the directors' 'Household troops', which included a much wider range than the Company's servants resident in England. They included the Blackwell Hall Factors, wholesale dealers in cloth whose woollens the Company bought for export; the packers and dyers who prepared these goods for shipment; the private bankers and brokers whose bullion it bought; the diamond merchants whom it licensed to export coral and bullion to the Indies and to bring back precious stones on their own account or on that of foreign merchants; and, most important

[1] For the advantages of a seat in the House of Commons to a prominent merchant see L. B. Namier, op cit. 1, 56 seq.
[2] *The Craftsman*, 31 March 1727.

of all because most numerous and highly organized, they included the body known as the East Indian Shipping Interest,[1] the part-owners of the great ships hired to the Company, the commanders and officers of these ships and the shipbuilders, ships' chandlers, warehousemen, etc., connected with them. Contemporaries felt no doubt that the government expected these household troops to be deployed in their support in City elections when circumstances made this necessary.

Third, and by far its highest importance, however, was the role which the Company played in the system of public finance. I have indicated that in the seventeenth century the Company survived the assaults of its enemies largely because of its value to the government as a source of revenue. Before the days of full parliamentary control, the contributions forced from the Company were made to the Crown in a variety of more or less informal ways; when parliamentary control of finance became complete and as the funded debt developed, the contributions exacted from the Company, like those exacted from other Corporations (e.g. the Bank of England), took the form of funded loans at a fixed rate of interest, extorted under threat of termination of their charter and usually rewarded by a renewal of the charter for a term of years. In the eighteenth century loans from the big corporations proved insufficient to meet the heavy expenses of a succession of big wars, and, with the growth of the London money-market, subscriptions by the monied public began to supplement the loans from the three monied companies that had so far made up the national funded debt. By 1749 only 27% of the 4% annuities were made up of loans from these Corporations. But, despite this development, the three monied companies continued to stand at the centre of the system of public credit. Their opposition to a reduction in the rate of interest prevented Walpole from undertaking it in 1737, and it was only by winning them over by careful negotiations that Pelham was able in 1749–50 to carry out a similar operation, thereby inaugurating the famous 3% Consols.[2] Their representatives were present at all meetings at which the terms of loans were discussed, and individual directors banded together to take up a considerable proportion of the subscriptions. In this way the East India Company remained intimately concerned with the government's long-term credit system. It was also of importance in the short-term credit arrangements. Though the Bank of England by this time held the predominant position in the handling of the government's short-term credit needs,[3] the Treasury found it necessary also to keep in close touch with the East India Company on such matters on account of the high importance on the short-term market of the Company's own short-term contract debts or bonds.

The strength and weakness of their position was shown on the only two occasions during these years on which specifically East India affairs became

---

[1] See my *London Merchant, 1695–1774* (Oxford, 1933), chap. IV.

[2] See my 'Samson Gideon and the Reduction of Interest, 1749–50', *Econ. Hist. Review* (1946), XVI, no. 1. See below, pp. 399-413.

[3] Sir John Clapham, *The Bank of England: A History* (Cambridge, 1944), vol. I.

a parliamentary issue. The first was in 1730 when opposition to Walpole was mounting and the opposition groups (knowing that the question of renewing the Company's charter, due to expire in 1733, would soon come forward, if it were not indeed already under discussion) staged a full-scale attack on the Company.[1] They based their case on a carefully concerted petition from merchants of London, Bristol and Liverpool demanding the abolition of the Company and its replacement by a 'regulated' Company, all members of which would trade independently on th ir own capital.[2] The strength of the Company's position is shown by the ease with which the government defeated the motion, the petition being rejected by 223 votes to 138, and by the comparatively slight fall in the price at which the Company's stock was quoted during the debates.[3] Its weakness was shown in the same debate by the care the government took not to put the Company too much at its ease. An attempt by the Company to argue that a statute of Anne's reign[4] had by implication granted it a perpetual monopoly of its trade was treated as firmly as it would have been by William III or the Stuarts, and in fact the Company only obtained a renewal of its charter until 1766 (with the customary three years' grace if it were terminated) in return for a reduction of the interest on their existing loan to the State and the contribution of a further sum of £200,000.[5]

My second illustration dates from 1758–9 when, Pelham being dead and the problems of the Seven Years War having submitted the government to heavy strain, the old system was a good deal weakened. It was indeed only kept in existence by an unwilling coalition with the elder Pitt, who owed much of his strength to the support of members of the opposition both in the City and the country. It was under these conditions that one, Alderman Blakiston, a leading member of the City opposition, tried to force a breach

[1] The attack followed an unsuccessful assault on the 'court party' in control of the South Sea Company (Boyer, *Political State*, xxxix, 208 seq.).

[2] *Journals of the House of Commons*, 26 February 1729/30. A considerable part of the debate is extensively reported in the Diary of Viscount Percival, afterwards first Earl of Egmont (Hist. MSS. Commission Reports, *MSS. of the Earl of Egmont*, 1, 65 seq.).

[3] The debate took place, evidently on short notice, on 26 February 1730. The first reference I have found to the attack on the Company in the London Press was in the *Whitehall Evening Post*, 21–24 February: 'there is handed about here a scheme for a free and open trade to the East Indies'. Nearly two hundred London merchants had, however, signed one of the petitions and the collection of the signatures must have taken some time. On 5 February East India Stock had fallen from 181 to 179¼ and it did not reach 180 again until the danger was over. The lowest it touched was 176 on 24 February. The slightness of the fall suggests that Boyer's scepticism about the success of the attack was widely shared, despite a fairly vigorous outburst of pamphleteering against the Company.

[4] 10 Anne, c. 28.

[5] On 3 March 1730 the directors informed the proprietors that all danger seemed to be over and asked for sanction to accept a proposal shortly to be made by the government 'which may be advantageous both to the Publick and the Company' (India Office, East India Company Court Book, LIII, 432). Two days later the bargain was completed (ibid. p. 435).

in the monopoly of the Company's tea sales.[1] In its weakened position the Treasury was at first inclined to press the Company to make some concessions,[2] but when this attempt failed and Blakiston got the matter raised in the House the Chancellor of the Exchequer and other members supported the Company, and the great Pitt himself, though his own friends took part in the attack, remained silent.[3] The alliance was still too useful to both sides to allow it to break down.

In these ways and for these reasons the East India Company was worked into the machinery of government in the first half of the eighteenth century with results that contributed to the stability of both State and Company. From the point of view of the government, a big vested interest was harnessed to the support of their political machine. From the point of view of the Company, their security in the exercise of their privileged rights was assured and, so long as the government remained strong and stable, the association of the parliamentary opposition groups with the cause of their opponents was of little significance to them. The breakdown and chaos of conflicting interests of the succeeding period and the gradual emergence of the control by the state of the Company's complex affairs was to change the picture fundamentally in the next forty years, but the marks of this period could be seen on the organization of the Company throughout its whole history, as they could and can be seen on the political system in which it played its part.

[1] India Office, East India Company Court Book, LXVIII, 63–5 and 329.
[2] British Museum, Add. MS. 32889, f. 384. Newcastle's Memorandum for the King, 6 and 8 April 1759.
[3] Ibid. f. 416.

THE EAST INDIA COMPANY AND THE PEACE
OF PARIS

THE preliminaries of the peace which ended the Seven Years'
War were signed at Fontainebleau on 3 November 1762, and
the definitive treaty on 10 February 1763. As Professor Pares
says, it was a settlement ' which secured the original objects of
the war and satisfied the reasonable ambitions of all Englishmen
but those who lived by war or war-mongering ',[1] and neither the
preliminaries nor the peace encountered serious opposition when
debated in the House. ✦ Nevertheless the terms of both, and
particularly the preliminaries, were subjected to violent criticism
(attributable, it is true, largely to the unpopularity of Lord Bute
and his administration) which would certainly have had serious
parliamentary repercussions if the opposition had been organized
and their case a little stronger.[2]

The criticism centred for the most part on questions concerning the West Indies, the Newfoundland fisheries and the compensation to be extorted from Spain for the return of Havana,
captured when the negotiations were far advanced. The provisions concerning the settlement in the East Indies, however,
also aroused some feeling which had its effect on the general
political situation, and still more on the internal politics of the
East India Company. The split between Lord Clive and Lawrence
Sulivan which lay behind most of the misfortunes of the Company
in the succeeding years arose out of divisions within the Company
due to this issue. They arose in connexion with the terms agreed
with France in the preliminary treaty.

In general the differences between the preliminary and
definitive treaty were slight,[3] but the clauses concerning the

---

[1] R. Pares, *War and Trade in the West Indies* (Oxford, 1936), p. 610.

[2] *Ibid.* pp. 606 *seqq.* See also L. B. Namier, *England in the Age of the American
Revolution* (London, 1930), pp. 417 *seqq.*

[3] At the beginning of the negotiations between the two Courts it was assumed
that the preliminaries would be much less detailed than the definitive treaty, but
during the course of discussions the British government changed their mind and
urged that as much as possible should be incorporated in the preliminaries so as to
hasten on the signing of the definitive treaty. The chief authorities for the course
of the negotiations are : (a) S.P. 78/254–6 in the Public Record Office, containing
copies of the official correspondence 1762–3 between the earl of Egremont, secretary
of state, and the duke of Bedford, minister plenipotentiary in Paris ; (b) Volumes 168

settlement in the East Indies are an exception to this rule, as may be seen by a comparison of their terms :[1]

PRELIMINARY TREATY	DEFINITIVE TREATY
ARTICLE X	ARTICLE XI

'Dans les Indes-Orientales, la Grande Bretagne restituera à la France les différens Comptoirs qu'avoit cette Couronne sur la côte de Coromandel, ainsi que sur celle de Malabar, aussi bien que dans le Bengale, au commencement des hostilités entre les deux Compagnies en 1749, dans l'état où ils sont aujourd'hui ; à condition que Sa Majesté Très Chrétienne renonce aux acquisitions qu'elle a faites sur la côte de Coromandel depuis ce même commencement d'hostilités entre les deux Compagnies en 1749. Sa Majesté Très Chrétienne restituera de son côté tout ce qu'elle pourra avoir conquis sur la Grande Bretagne aux Indes-Orientales pendant la présente guerre ; et elle s'engage aussi à ne point ériger de fortifications et à n'entretenir aucunes troupes dans le Bengale.'

'Dans les Indes-Orientales, la Grande Bretagne restituera à la France dans l'Etat òu ils sont aujourd'hui les differens Comptoirs que cette Couronne possédoit, tout sur la Côte de Coromandel et d'Orixa, que sur celle de Malabar, ainsi que dans le Bengale, au Commencement de l'Année 1749. Et sa Majesté Très Chrétienne renonce à toute Prétension aux Acquisitions qu'elle avoid faites sur la Côte de Coromandel et d'Orixa, depuis le commencement de l'Année 1749. Sa Majesté Très Chrétienne restituera de son Coté tout ce qu'elle pourroit avoir conquis sur la Grande Bretagne dans les Indes-Orientales pendant la présente Guerre, et fera restituer nommément Nattal et Tapanoully dans l'Isle de Sumatra ; Elle s'engaga de plus à ne point ériger de Fortifications et à ne point entretenir de Troupes dans aucune Partie des Etats du Subah de Bengale. Et afin de conserver la Paix future sur la Côte de Coromandel et d'Orixa, les Anglois et les François reconnoitront Mahomet Ally Khan pour Légitime Nabob du Carnate, et Salabat Jing pour Légitime Subah du Décan ; et les deux Parties renonceront à toutes Demande ou Prétension de Satisfaction qu'elles pourroient former à la charge l'une de l'autre, ou à celle de leurs Alliés Indiens pour les Déprédations ou Dégats commis, soit d'un Coté soit de l'autre pendant la Guerre.

(A declaration by the British plenipotentiary as to the boundaries of Bengal was appended to the Treaty.)

The terms obtained in the definitive treaty fell somewhat short of those which the English Company at first demanded, but they were conceded by all concerned with its affairs to be ' very advantageous to the East India Company '.[2] The article on the East Indies contained in the preliminary treaty was held, on the other hand, to be far from satisfactory, even by those who

to 169 among the manuscripts of the earl of Egremont preserved at Petworth (their owner, Lord Leconfield, kindly permitted me to have them examined ; I am grateful to Miss K. M. E. Murray of Girton College, Cambridge, for inspecting them for me). These are also copies of the official correspondence, but there are some variations between the contents of these volumes and those in the P.R.O. ; (c) The published *Correspondence of the Duke of Bedford*, edited by Lord John Russell (London, 1842), vol. iii.

[1] G. F. von Martens, *Recueil de Traités*, vol. i.

[2] R. Clive, *Letter to the Proprietors of East India Stock* (London, 1764).

supported the preliminary terms in general. Lawrence Sulivan, the acknowledged leader of the Company at that time, voted with the government in support of the preliminaries ; Clive, its great and successful general, who was soon to challenge his supremacy, divided against him. It is true that Sulivan was in general a strong supporter of Administration,[1] while Clive at that time gave his allegiance to the Newcastle group which had recently been thrown from power,[2] but their votes were inevitably held to reflect their views on the clauses of the agreement bearing on the East Indian settlement.

The East Indian article in the definitive treaty differed from that in the preliminaries, partly in the greater precision of its definition and elaboration of its detail, but also in two points of substance : (1) in the date at which possession of ' comptoirs ' by the French justified their restoration under the terms of the treaty ; (2) in the recognition of Mohammed Ali and Salabat Jang as rulers in the Carnatic and Deccan respectively, included in the definitive but not in the preliminary treaty. At the time the negotiations began in 1762 the relations between Clive and Sulivan were those nominally of friendship, but really of armed neutrality. Sulivan's rise to power in the Company in 1758 had won the approval of Clive [3] and most of the Company's servants in India and, though the misdeeds of the Company's servants in Bengal had led to a sharp breach between those controlling the Company's fortunes and a band of ex-servants returned from Bengal, Sulivan had taken great pains not to alienate Clive, the greatest and most powerful of them. The means he had employed were partly those of favour but partly of blackmail. He had made high professions of friendship to Clive, and readily conceded to him wide facilities in patronage, and consulted him frequently, but he had taken care to remind him that the Company had not yet taken official cognizance of, still less approved, the large ' jagir ' or annual rent which Clive had accepted from the ruler of Bengal as a reward in his military services.[4] These

---

[1] The East India Company direction was always necessarily in close touch with the government of the day. Sulivan was, however, in addition a close personal supporter of Lord Shelburne, then entering politics as the protégé of Henry Fox. As early as September 1761 Shelburne was concerning himself, and interesting Lord Bute, in Sulivan's entry to parliament (Lansdowne MSS. at Bowood : Correspondence Sulivan and Shelburne 1761 and Lady Shelburne's Diary. I am indebted to the Marchioness of Lansdowne for permission to make use of these documents).

[2] L. B. Namier, *Structure of Politics at the Accession of George III* (London, 1929), ii. 352 *seqq.*

[3] Letters quoted G. W. Forrest, *The Life of Lord Clive* (London, 1918), ii. 118–19.

[4] The ' jagir ' was the rent (some £27,000 per annum) attached to an office of honour granted by the Nawab to Clive at the head of his army. In fact the grant involved the Company in paying a rent for lands in their possession which would otherwise have been due to the Nawab, and they saw serious inconveniences in the arrangements and indicated in a Bengal General Letter, 13 March 1761, that its

tactics were successful for more than two years. In February 1763, however, the uneasy truce broke down and Clive, defying the threat to his jagir, went into open and violent opposition to Sulivan within the Company. His biographers have assumed that the reason for this change was some fundamental disagreement between the two men over the terms of the peace, and the accusations flung about during the contest which followed have given them some grounds for doing so. Since Clive stated that he approved of the definitive treaty and disapproved of the preliminaries, they have not unreasonably concluded that the explanation must lie in the divergencies between the two documents.

They have not, however, been successful in elucidating what the cause of the disagreement was. It has been suggested that Clive wanted a ' Carthaginian ' peace, while Sulivan held more moderate views,[1] but if the preliminaries were not ' Carthaginian ' neither was the final treaty. Clive himself, in his *Letter to the Proprietors of East India Stock*, criticizes (though mildly) the recognition of the Indian princes, and this has been seized on as the cause of the conflict between the two men ; [2] but this is not tenable, since this clause appears, not in the preliminaries to which Clive objected, but in the final settlement which he approved, and in any case is hardly an issue of major importance.

The truth seems to be that the circumstances of their disagreements were much less clear-cut. It is certain that both Clive and Sulivan, and indeed the Company as a whole, wanted more than they got in either the definitive treaty or the preliminaries ; it is equally certain that there was no difference of opinion as to what they should ask for. They wanted the total exclusion of the French from Bengal and the qualifying date for the restoration of the ' comptoirs ' taken from the French during the war to be fixed no later than the end of 1744, so as to exclude from French possession in the future the gains which Dupleix had made at the expense of the country powers in the Carnatic. Sulivan and the Company also wanted (and Clive did not at that time object to it) the formal recognition of Mohamed Ali and Salabat Jang. The first of these demands was tacitly modified as the negotiations proceeded ; the last was ignored in the preliminaries but obtained in the final treaty ; the second, which was a point of real substance, was the cause of most of the difficulties between the Administration and the Company and of ill-feeling

legality was still under consideration (India Office, *Bengal Despatches*, ii. 238). Clive was given hints by Sulivan and others that it might be challenged. (Clive to Amyatt, quoted by J. Malcolm, *The Life of Robert Lord Clive* (London, 1836), ii. 220). Throughout 1762 Clive was kept in constant anxiety about its fate and stated explicitly that fear of precipitating an attack on it prevented his joining the discontented ex-servants.

[1] A. Mervyn Davies, *Clive of Plassey* (London, 1939), pp. 337 *seqq.*

[2] J. Malcolm, *op. cit.* ii. 208 *seqq.*, and G. W. Forrest, *op. cit.* ii. 193 *seqq.*

within the Company. When the preliminaries were being negotiated the English government refused to put forward a date earlier
than the ' commencement of hostilities between the two Companies' in 1749, but in the definitive treaty they forced the
unwilling French to agree to move that date back to ' the commencement of 1749 ' thereby excluding Dupleix's most recent
gains and going a considerable distance towards meeting the
Company's claims. Behind these changes lay a great deal of pressure and personal recrimination but also some adroit diplomacy.

Neither Clive nor Sulivan were directly responsible for the
negotiations on the Company's behalf. Clive held no official
position in the Company and Sulivan, though admittedly the
ruling spirit in the court of directors, was at the moment in the
same position, since he had chosen that year to be out of the
direction ' by rotation '.[1] Clive, however, played some unofficial
part in the negotiation, and Sulivan a very active one, as he was
in close touch with Administration on the one hand, and on the
other with the court of directors through his supporters there, in
particular the deputy chairman John Dorrien, a close personal
follower.[2] With the chairman, Thomas Rous, a weak man of
limited ability, he was on less close terms.

The Company did not itself take part in the discussions with
the French ; the negotiations were carried out by the two governments as part of the general peace settlement. This was the
first time that the government undertook the responsibilities of
negotiating a general East Indian settlement,[3] and in theory at

[1] By the Company's by-laws no director could serve more than four consecutive
years. The intention was no doubt to prevent the control of the Company by a
small oligarchy, but it was not achieved, since directors habitually stood down for
one year and then stood for re-election. Sulivan stood down a year earlier than necessary, possibly so that he and Dorrien might not be out of the direction at the same
time. Clive, always suspicious of Sulivan's motives, believed he did it to avoid the
unpopularity of negotiating the peace settlement. In the draft for a speech found
among Clive's papers (for the access to which I am indebted to Lord Powis) (Powis
MSS., Box I, 15) an entry runs, ' Mr. Sulivan called upon to declare what were his
motives for quitting the Direction the year before it was his turn and whether it was
not to throw off from his own shoulders all the inconveniences which might arise from
settling the Dutch Disputes and from the making of a Peace '. Whatever the explanation, the results must have been unsatisfactory to him, as he was left in a poor
strategic position for guiding the directors in an intricate negotiation.

[2] Clive said (Powis MSS., *loc. cit.*), ' All the world knows the connection between
Sulivan and Mr. Dorrien and that the latter took no step without the advice of Sulivan,
and of consequence that Mr. Sulivan knew from Dorrien everything that passed with
the Committee [i.e. the Secret Committee appointed for the negotiations] when he
was not present and consulted '.

[3] In the negotiations which Pitt had begun with the French in 1761 it had been
agreed to allow the two Companies to negotiate directly with each other through
commissaries (*Grenville Papers*, ed. W. J. Smith, London, 1852, i, 379). In settling
the differences between the Dutch and English Companies which arose in 1762 the
same method was adopted though, since the ill-feeling threatened Anglo-Dutch relations, there was a good deal of consultation with the government (India Office : Home
Miscellaneous, vol. 96 *passim*).

least they took up the attitude that they were conferring a favour on the Company by acting on their behalf. When the Company proved intransigent they threatened, not to over-ride it, but to leave it to try to get what terms it could by direct negotiations, though one may doubt, in view of the important national issues at stake, whether the threat would have been carried out.

The negotiations with the French, broken off in 1761, were formally re-opened as early as March 1762, though it was not until September that the duke of Bedford was sent to Paris with powers to treat, and the duc de Nivernois came to London on a similar mission. The East Indian settlement does not seem to have come up for systematic consideration until June, when Lord Egremont, the secretary of state, and his under-secretary Robert Wood consulted the chairman (Thomas Rous), the deputy chairman (John Dorrien), and Lawrence Sulivan informally.[1] These last submitted a copy of the letter which Sulivan as chairman had sent to Pitt on 27 July 1761 in a similar connexion,[2] and indicated that in general it still expressed their views, which they expanded in further documents. Their claims included the exclusion of the French from Bengal, the return of ' comptoirs ' elsewhere only if in French possession prior to 1745, and the recognition of the present rulers of the Carnatic and Deccan. The minister appears to have indicated at once his doubts whether these claims were viable and soon sought to shift the negotiation to the official plane by asking the directors to appoint a secret committee with which the Administration might deal while the negotiations were in progress.[3] A committee was accordingly set up on 21 July [4] and, after consulting Sulivan, Abraham Hume (another prominent ex-director) and Clive,[5] they put forward terms which differed in no essential respect from those already put forward informally. Sulivan, it is true, tried to get the committee (and when he failed

---

[1] This and much of our information about the negotiations between the Administration and the Company is due to a curious account clearly based on inside information and partly a résumé of semi-official correspondence of which we have no other trace, published in a *North Briton Extraordinary*, 1765, an abridgement of which may be found in the *London Magazine*, April 1765. It was evidently intended as a justification of Thomas Rous, chairman of the Company in 1762, and was to have been published by Wilkes in April 1763 at the time of the contested election of directors. Press rivals (*The Auditor*, 25 April 1763) asserted that Wilkes had been bought off by Clive, as it contained matter discreditable to him, but this is not the case. Where it can be checked the account is very reliable. Thomas Wood (traveller and author of *The Ruins of Palmyra*) carried out most of the negotiations with the Company, and was in close touch with the French minister plenipotentiary then in London, the duc de Nivernois. The latter described him as ' homme d'esprit, et de bon esprit, avec qui je suis fort lié . . . C'est lui qui a conduit toute cette affaire des Indes vis-à-vis la compagnie anglaise '. (*Oeuvres Posthumes du Duc de Nivernois* (Paris. 1807) ii. 157.)

[2] Powis MSS., quoted by Forrest, *op. cit.* ii. 189–90.

[3] *North Briton Extraordinary.*

[4] India Office: East India Company Court Book 71, p. 98.

[5] *North Briton Extraordinary.*

Dorrien pressed the same point on the directors) to propose some concessions to the French with regard to the status of Masulipatam which might make the Company's other demands more palatable.[1] The proposal was, however, heavily defeated ; the chairman left the Company's proposals with Egremont on 4 September.[2]

So far there was no difference of opinion as to what the Company wanted except for Sulivan's rather half-hearted suggestion of minor concessions. Clive, though he later expressed some annoyance that the minister had consulted Sulivan rather than him,[3] fully approved the terms, and indeed claimed that they were largely based on his suggestions, and he wrote a memorandum to Lord Bute in support of them.[4]

The ministry, however, could hardly be expected to be satisfied with the Company's attitude. The instructions dated 4 September with which the duke of Bedford left for Paris must, it is true, have been drawn up before the Company's views had been obtained, but it is most improbable that their general tenor was unknown, and when they were received no attempt was made to incorporate any of the points made by the Company in the instructions. In these instructions Bedford was empowered to agree to the restoration of the pre-war French possessions on the Coromandel coast, while demanding the exclusion of the French from Bengal except for the enjoyment of trading rights on the Ganges.[5] The article might be couched in general terms in the preliminaries, since it could be elaborated in the definitive treaty. After a few weeks' negotiation, when a temporary hitch in the discussions occurred (partly as a result of excessive French demands, but more because the receipt of the news of the conquest of Havana made it necessary for the British Administration to reconsider their terms) the agreement later incorporated in the preliminaries was well on the way.[6]

The Company had in the meantime been curtly told that their terms were inadmissible as leaving no room for negotiation, and that the minister was disappointed in his expectation of having from them ' a confidential communication of their real expectations '.[7] The result was a deadlock. After lengthy

[1] India Office : East India Company Court Book 71, p. 141.

[2] A copy of this document exists in the Powis MSS., ' Sentiments of the Secret Committee concerning terms of a Treaty with France '.

[3] Powis MSS. In his draft of a speech Clive complains that he was ' not called upon to give my opinion about a peace for India for months after Mr. Sulivan had been acquainted with it by the ministry although he was no more a director than myself '.

[4] Powis MSS., quoted by Forrest, *op. cit.* ii. 192–3, and Malcolm, *op. cit.* ii. 206–7. Bute acknowledged it civilly but non-committally.

[5] P.R.O. S.P. 78/253, 4 September 1762 ; Egremont MSS., vol. 168, fo. 1.

[6] P.R.O. S.P. 78/253, Bedford to Egremont, 21 September 1762, and *North Briton Extraordinary*.

[7] Letter from Robert Wood to the Company, 11 September 1762. Referred to in the *North Briton Extraordinary*. On 16 September the chairman waited on Egremont

debates the directors agreed by a narrow majority on 24 September to offer the compromise on the status of Masulipatam which Sulivan had earlier urged on them, but their offer, left with Lord Egremont on 29 September,[1] remained unacknowledged until 16 October,[2] when they were informed that it was unacceptable.   By this time, however, the hitch in the Anglo-French talks was coming to an end, and since the ministry was extremely anxious for the preliminary agreement to be signed before parliament met in November,[3] steps were necessary to break down the Company's resistance.   The ministers were already working on the *Contre-projet* sent to the duke of Bedford on 26 October. On 20 October accordingly Wood re-opened negotiations with them on Egremont's behalf.   He did so by a mixture of rush tactics, of which we have full particulars, and (it would seem) of hints of future compromise the nature of which we can only deduce.

He began in a minatory manner by complaining again of the unco-operative attitude of the Company, and by pointing out the difficulties they would encounter if they were left to negotiate a separate agreement.   The government was not, he made plain, prepared to hold up the general agreement for the convenience of the Company.   He went on to explain, however, that Egremont was prepared to give them a last chance to come in if they would offer reasonable concessions.   A reply must be given by noon on the 22nd.   Faced with this ultimatum, the secret committee met on the 21st, and on the 22nd tried some further bargaining with Egremont out of which they obtained ostensibly nothing but an extension of time for their deliberations to the following day and an official draft which they were required to accept or amend. This draft did not differ materially from the clause which was to appear in the preliminaries.   The restoration of the ' comptoirs ' was, however, to include all in French possession ' before the present war '.   The secret committee, gloomily abandoning the points for which the Company had been holding out, accepted the draft with no more than verbal amendments.   Among the latter was the alteration of the phrase ' before the present war ' to ' at the commencement of the present war between the two Companies in India, viz. in 1749 '.   This was accepted, but next day Wood summoned the chairman in haste and, pointing out that hostilities between the Companies preceded any declaration of war, got him

with success and on 22 September reported to the directors (India Office : East India Company Court Book 71, p. 158) that the government found their terms unsatisfactory as giving the ministry no latitude in making concessions.

[1] *North Briton Extraordinary*.   The ' Further Sentiments of the Secret Committee ', 29 September in the Powis MSS. is no doubt the document left with the secretary of state.   [2] *Ibid.*

[3] The meeting of parliament was eventually postponed from 11 to 25 November to give time for the completion of the preliminaries.

to agree on his own responsibility to a change in the wording so that it might run ' before the commencement of hostilities between the two Companies in 1749 '.[1] Two days later Egremont forwarded the draft to Bedford, saying that agreement to it had been extracted from the Company with some difficulty,[2] and on 3 November Bedford reported that the French had accepted it, together with the rest of the terms, without query.[3]

It could not be expected that the East India Company as a whole would feel any satisfaction at this sudden abandonment of their position by the secret committee, the steps towards and the explanation of which were understood by very few. Feeling against the government had already been rising among the directors and proprietors, as the parliamentary opposition had been quick to note. As early as 1 October the duke of Newcastle notes that

> ' I am told from very good hands, that, notwithstanding what has been given out by the Ministry that the E. I. Company are satisfied, the contrary of it is true ; Mr. Sullivan [sic] and the Deputy Chairman Mr. Dorient [sic] as creatures of my Lord Bute pretend to be so, but the Chairman Mr. Rouse and the Company in general are very far from being pleased.'[4]

Clive, who appears to have been fully informed of the situation up to the end of September but to have been taken by surprise by the rapid developments in the latter part of October gave shortly afterwards a clear, if hostile and not altogether accurate, account of the transaction to a correspondent.

> ' In September after Mr. Sulivan, Mr. Hume and myself had given the Committee the meeting to consult of these matters, the Court of Directors gave their ultimatum to Lord Egremont which was founded principally upon my advice and memorial ; the period of the Pronunciation [sic] was fix't to the year 1744 and the French were to be totally excluded Bengal, and the Committee persevered in their opinion till the middle of October in spight of all the threats of the Ministry to leave the Company to act and negotiate for themselves. At last poor Rous was sent for and after having been scolded and sworn at by Mr. Wood (Lord Egremont's Secretary) and then by his Lordship himself, the articles were consented to be altered as they now stand in the Preliminaries. I wish Sulivan has not been some way accessory to this timid and unpardonable step, being known to be under Ministerial influence.'[5]

There can be little doubt that Sulivan was fully aware of what was happening, but there is also no reason to doubt that he

[1] Our authority throughout is the *North Briton Extraordinary*.
[2] P.R.O. S.P. 78/253, Egremont to Bedford, 26 October 1762 ; Egremont MSS. vol. 168, fo. 263.
[3] P.R.O. S.P. 78/254, Bedford to Egremont, 3 November 1762 ; Egremont MSS. 168, fo. 287.   [4] Brit. Mus. Add. MS. 32944, fo. 30 v. Notes of conversation.
[5] Powis MSS., Box III ; Clive to Palk, 15 December 1762.

deplored it ; there is also some reason to believe that, as he later claimed, he saw that it was useless further to oppose the preliminaries, and that the best hope for the Company lay in getting a modification of the terms in the definitive treaty. The ministry in their anxiety would stop at nothing to get the preliminaries signed before parliament met, so that the House might be presented with a *fait accompli*. It seems probable that, to achieve their end, they did not rely solely on threats, but also on hints to the Company's representatives that, once the preliminaries had been signed, adjustments to meet their points might be made in the definitive treaty. It is significant that the secret committee, in accepting the article in the preliminaries, put in a plea for modifications ' either in the preliminaries or in the definitive treaty,[1] and the complete change in the attitude of the Administration to the Company's demands as soon as the preliminaries were signed seems explicable in no other way.

The preliminaries were signed on 3 November ; on the 8th Wood forwarded details of the East Indian article to the Company, and warned them that if modifications were to be asked for in the definitive treaty, they must be formulated at once.[2] The Company promptly replied with the demand that the date conditioning the return of French comptoirs be changed to ' the commencement of 1749 ' [3] and in the course of November and December put forward a number of suggestions of less importance, all of which were now sympathetically received by the Administration, and all of which appeared in the definitive treaty. The only quarters in which they were not well received were among the French negotiators, who claimed with some justice that the introduction of new matter and the alteration of the terms agreed in the preliminaries was unjustifiable ; [4] and by the duke of Bedford, who had to try to get the French to accept them, and who evidently failed to disguise from his opponents that he was ' scandalisé de l'article des Indes '.[5] When, on 15 November, Egremont wrote to him enclosing a copy of the Company's letter of 9 November, and suggesting disingenuously that the proposed amendments were purely verbal,[6] Bedford was not convinced, and expressed considerable unwillingness to re-open the question with the French, whom he understood already to be unhappy about the East Indian article. [7] (In the French draft ' projet ' for the

---

[1] *North Briton Extraordinary.*

[2] India Office. Reports of Committee of Correspondence, vol. viii, documents included in reports of 3 and 8 December 1767.   [3] *Bedford Correspondence*, iii. 163–5.

[4] P.R.O. S.P. 78/255.   French observations on the English ' projet ' for the definitive treaty, 24 December 1762.   Cf. Nivernois, *Oeuvres Posthumes*, ii. 196.

[5] Nivernois, *op. cit.* ii. 179, duc de Praslin to duc de Nivernois, 26 December 1762.

[6] P.R.O. 78/254 ; Egremont MSS., vol. 268, fo. 309.

[7] P.R.O. 78/254.   Bedford to Egremont, 27 November 1762 ; Egremont MSS., vol. 268, fo. 353.

definitive treaty which he forwarded to his government they raised questions about the meaning of certain geographical definitions used in the article in the preliminaries.[1]) On 24 December he reported that he ' despaired of accomplishing ' [2] the terms now being pressed. By 2 January the situation of the preceding October seemed to be arising again ; the signing of the treaty was being held up by disagreements between the Powers on the East India issue. Bedford reported ' I find among all sorts of people as well of this country as of other Nations an uneasiness and anxiety at the *Retardement* caused by the unexpected disputes between our two courts in relation to the East Indies in bringing the great work of Peace to a happy conclusion '.[3]

Negotiations were in process to smooth out these differences not only in Paris but in London, where they were taken up with Nivernois in December,[4] and, as a letter from Egremont on 23 December shows, an attempt was made to play off the acceptance by the British of a geographical definition satisfactory to the French against the more drastic demands they were themselves putting forward.[5] Nevertheless, so little progress was made that on 22 January, Bedford was empowered to withdraw the change of date and to accept a decision favourable to the French on the boundary of Bengal if this should be necessary to obtain agreement.[6]

In the meantime, however, an odd chance changed the course of the British negotiators. A Jewish merchant in Paris, Isaac da Pinto, who happened to have inside information of the affairs of the French East India Company and of the attitude of the French government, got in touch with Bedford.[7] It is not altogether clear what he told him, but it was sufficient to earn da Pinto a lavish reward from the English Company some years later,[8] and to change Bedford's tactics radically. Presumably da Pinto gave him, besides more detailed information about the issues at stake, good reason to believe that the French negotiators would not stand out if he pushed his claim. As a result, he put forward his demands in full, and was able to report on 10 February that the treaty was signed and the British claims in the East Indies had been accepted in full.[9]

[1] P.R.O. 78/254, sent by the duke of Bedford as an enclosure to his letter of 2 December 1762 ; Egremont MSS., vol. 268, fo. 368.

[2] *Bedford Correspondence*, iii. 181.

[3] P.R.O. 78/256 ; Bedford to Egremont, 2 January 1763 ; Egremont MSS., vol. 169, fo. 29.

[4] Nivernois, *Oeuvres Posthumes*, ii. 157, duc de Nivernois to duc de Praslin, 10 December 1762.   [5] P.R.O. 78/255 ; Egremont MSS., vol. 168, fo. 569.

[6] Egremont MSS., vol. 169, fo. 112 *seqq.*

[7] *Bedford Correspondence*, iii. 184.

[8] India Office : Reports of the Committee of Correspondence, vol. viii, 3 and 8 December 1767.   [9] *Bedford Correspondence*, iii. 193–4.

In this way the eminently satisfactory terms of the definitive treaty were reached, and it might have been hoped that all parties in the Company as well as the government would have been satisfied. Unfortunately, however, the indignation which had been aroused over the preliminaries had not only stirred up Clive but had alienated Rous, the chairman of the Company, from Sulivan and the group he controlled there. Rous had, apparently, been much blamed for his handling of the negotiations which led up to the preliminaries, and it was commonly, but quite unjustly, believed, as is shown by the extract from Clive's correspondence quoted above,[1] that the last-minute change in wording to which he had agreed on 24 October was a grave mistake. All parties agreed that he was a feeble man of mediocre abilities, but he seems to have had reason to complain that his more powerful colleagues in the Company had done little to clear him of unjust aspersions. Whatever the cause, however, by the end of November he and a band of supporters had declared themselves openly in opposition to Sulivan, and had joined with the malcontents from Bengal in preparing to contest the election of directors in the following March. Clive did not immediately join them, still withheld by the caution which Sulivan had taken pains to foster in him. 'I must acknowledge', he wrote, 'that in my heart I am a well-wisher for the cause of Rous, although, considering the great stake I have in India it is probable I shall remain neuter. Sulivan might have attached me to his interest if he had pleased but he . . . never has reposed that confidence in me which my services to the Company entitled me to.'[2] Caution was not, however, a quality likely to withhold Clive indefinitely. The offensive was more to his taste, and as the feeling within the Company rose to its height as the election of directors drew near, his decision to remain neutral was abandoned. On 17 February 1763 he announced his adherence to Rous's party; on the two following days he canvassed the City in person, and on the 23rd he announced his intention of standing for the direction.[3] The great civil war in the Company had broken out. It had broken out, as the above analysis shows, as a result of the dissensions within the Company arising out of the peace negotiations; it did not, however, originate in any serious conflict of opinion on the terms of the peace settlement between the two chief contestants.

[1] See above, p.173.   [2] Malcolm, *op. cit.* ii. 197.
[3] Bute MSS., Sulivan to Lord Shelburne, 24 February 1763. (I am indebted to the Marquess of Bute for permission to make use of this document.)

LORD SHELBURNE AND EAST INDIA
COMPANY POLITICS 1766-9

OF all the ministers of the first twenty years of the reign of George III Shelburne remains the most mysterious. Foremost among the obscurities of his public career stand his relations with that abstraction called by his contemporaries ' the City '. Two stages may be traced in his relations with that important entity. In the second and more spectacular stage, a period roughly covering the seventies, he stands in the tradition of the elder Pitt, the last and greatest of the ' rebel Whigs ' who had learned the art of opposition under George II, for like them in their day he was in close touch with what we may call the ' radical ' opinion of the anti-ministerial sections of the city. Hence the part he and his immediate followers played in the politics of Wilkite London. But in the first stage, the period from 1763 to 1769, he stood in the tradition of Henry Fox, with whom he had gained his first experience of politics. It was a tradition altogether different from that followed by Chatham ; city connexions not with the radicals but with the monied interest, as represented in Shelburne's case by the East India Company. To understand the career of Shelburne it is therefore necessary to examine his activities in East India affairs in the years when it first became apparent that they would assume a vast importance in English politics. Such an examination is also important for the understanding of the politics of the period, for it throws some light on a complex political situation. During these years two more or less closed systems of politics, that of the Company and that of parliament, were interacting.

The years 1763–9, and particularly those from 1766 on, when the Chatham ministry, with Shelburne among them, were active in East Indian affairs, form a period in the history of the Company. They are important as the years in which the Company experienced the glories and dangers of success, through the triumph of Clive. The victories and the wealth which the conquerors had tapped changed, even by the conception of them, the nature of the East India Company. Their glamour, translated into the prosaic terms of Change Alley, turned East India stock from a sober security comparable to the funds into a gambling venture. By 1767, with stock above 270 and a court of proprietors organized and clamouring for higher dividends to check any fall in price, the country was justified in fearing another Bubble.

A second reason for the importance of these years to the Company was that they saw the growth not merely of faction in the Company but of solid party. It began in 1757 on questions of policy, when the parties headed by Rous and Sulivan arose and a ' proprietary ' list of directors went out in opposition to the directors' ' house ' list.[1] It hardened into battle when that over-mighty subject, Clive,[2] returned from India, and he and Laurence Sulivan, the leader of the directors, once friends now rivals, stood face to face. This was the period in which they fought out, amid the ebb and flow of many other issues, the personal hatred and the divergence of views they stood for : Clive for the extension of territorial power ; Sulivan, for the time at least, for the peaceful progress of trade.[3]

If in this period we see already the stock turned from its steady commercial position and party flourishing in the Company, both characteristics noted by Burke in 1783, the last great characteristic of a later period also becomes apparent. In 1763, for the first time since the struggle of the Old and New Companies, government and opposition openly and in a body took part in East Indian affairs. For the first time the great Whig lords in opposition, Rockingham, Lord John Cavendish, Portland, and others, took up their voting qualifications and went down to India House to vote for the proprietary list of directors.[4] For the first time and indeed the only time in so crude a form, a

---

[1] A pamphlet, *Reflections on the Present State of our East Indian Affairs with many interesting anecdotes never before made public. By a gentleman long resident in India* (London, 1764, Guildhall, Tr. 298, 1), gives an account of the ' list '. ' Amongst the candidates there is generally one, who, by dint of drudgery and application to the business of the India house . . . has rendered himself necessary in the direction. This person takes upon him to form a list of such directors for the ensuing year as are agreeable to him, copies of which are usually delivered out beforehand to his own friends, but to others they are distributed at the door of the house when the proprietors assemble to vote. If the proprietor receiving this list dislikes any one or more names, he scratches such out and inserting others, delivers it in as his list. If as last year there be several lists, he takes that of his friend. When all are delivered in, the different lists are scrutinized, and the majority declared.'

[2] Clive had resigned from the Company's service, but became a great stock-holder. His share in the General Letter of the majority of the council of Bengal (quoted J. Malcolm, *The Life of Robert, Lord Clive*, 1836, ii. 129 *seq.*) naturally irritated the directors, and it was soon clear that friction would arise. That it did not arise sooner was due to the caution inspired in Clive by the vulnerability of his *jaghire, op. cit.* ii. ch. xii.

[3] Sulivan already expressed this view in 1761. See his letter to Pitt in 27 July 1761, quoted G. Forrest, *Life of Lord Clive*, 1918, ii. 189.

[4] Obtained a few days before the election from agents of the Clive faction, such as Sir Francis Gosling, &c. (Ledger P. fo. 108, &c.) ; for this reference see *infra*, p. 180, n. 2).

minister, Henry Fox, used his funds through the officials of his department to buy votes for the house list of candidates.[1]

The election of directors in 1763 was, it is true, a special case and remained for some time unparalleled. The East India Company, with the other monied companies, had been for years a bulwark of the administration in the city. Now Clive, who had opposed the administration on the proposed East Indian clauses in the Peace of Paris, and had joined the parliamentary opposition, was trying to capture the direction of the Company at the head of a large party among the proprietors. This was reason enough for Henry Fox's unusually active intervention and for Clive's subsequent defeat. When Clive, finding his *jaghire* threatened by his triumphant enemies, turned round and made his peace with the government, the incident was over.[2] The government continued in the following years of party warfare to intervene in East Indian elections but only in the indirect way that had become customary in city affairs.[3] There occurred no clear-cut issue between government and opposition again until 1766–7. It was only then, when Chatham's 'tesselated pavement' ministry deliberately attacked the Company in an attempt to wrest from them the profits of Clive's territorial conquests, that a similar antithesis of ministry and opposition is seen, though this time complicated by divisions both in government and opposition. From that date until the power of the Company was finally destroyed, there was no time when East Indian questions were not to the fore in party politics.

There are three points which must be elucidated in an examination of the years 1766–9. The first is the political situation in the Company during these troubled years; the second is the very tangled skein of politics within the Chatham ministry itself during its attacks on and negotiations with the Company; politics complicated by the presence of Chatham, ill and grandiloquent and incapable of action, Charles Townshend in the last and most reckless stage of his reckless career, and Shelburne, capable and acute but also secretive and a difficult man with

[1] Cf. *infra*, p. 181.

[2] Evidence of Clive's activities in the Brit. Mus. Add. MSS. is quoted by L. B. Namier, *Structure of Politics at the Accession of George III*, 1929, ii. 352 *seqq.* This evidence shows that the ministry was not in 1763 solidly against him, for he was corresponding with Grenville, the rising minister, at the time when Fox was exerting the strength of the Pay Office against him. This facilitated his *volte face*.

[3] The intervention of the ministry is best seen in the correspondence of Joseph Salvador with C. Jenkinson (at that time Grenville's man of business). Particularly significant of the normal technique of government intervention is the letter of 8 April 1764 (Brit. Mus. Add. MS. 38202, fo. 224): 'Our returns seem to foretell a Majority. yet we are not rightly acquainted with the State of your friends. we have no advices from the Post Office Custom house nor excise. we now come near and should be able to determine our fate to a man.'

whom to work. The third point is the part played by Shelburne in both the first and the second, for they cannot be kept apart. For elucidating these questions there are two peculiarly valuable sources of information besides the ordinary ; the Court Books of the East India Company,[1] and the Transfer Books and Stock Ledgers of the Company preserved at the Bank of England Record Office.[2] The latter are of inestimable value to the student of Company politics, since, through the institution characteristic of the Company, the 'split vote ', can be traced the personnel of its faction and many of its connexions with national politics.

I

Since 1698 the vote for the election of directors had rested on a £500 stock qualification, and one vote was the most that the greatest proprietor could have. A means of evading this enforced equality was, however, early found.[3] It was apparent that a large holding of stock could be temporarily turned into a number of £500 shares and votes could thus be created. From the beginning this was a recognized abuse. But a glance at the transfer books before 1763 shows that the abuse had not yet become systematic. At the most the large proprietor transferred a number of £500 shares to various dependents, tradesmen, relatives, or colleagues a few days before the election in return for some security, such as a promissory note. After the election they were returned to him. In the first half of the century, moreover, quite as much electioneering seems to have been done by influence and the votes of men connected with the directors, such as the shipping interest, who permanently held voting qualifications, as by the more troublesome and costly method of splitting. Even after the party quarrels sprang up in 1757 there was not much change. But from 1763 all the organization of the London money market was to be turned to the purpose of East Indian campaigning.

[1] Preserved at the India Office. Quoted as India Office Ct. Bk.

[2] The Bank took these over in 1860. For the seventeenth and eighteenth centuries there are 89 folio transfer books, running from 1676 to 1802 ; 33 ledgers of stock (quoted here as Ledger) running from 1706 to 1807 ; 27 books of sales by attorney, and one volume of powers of attorney (1770), kept as a specimen. There are the following odd volumes : Journal to Ledger A. 1709–18, Calls on stock. Interest Journals (1) 1675–81, (2) 1681–4. Stock Journal of subscription issue of 1657. 1657–69. Subscription Journals to £800,000 additional stock at £155 for £100 capital stock, 2 vols. Dividend Books. 1709–12 (destroyed 1932). Alphabetical List of Stock-holders with sums of stock held in 1709.

I am greatly indebted to the Governor and Directors of the Bank for permission to use these documents, and to the Librarian and officials of the Record Office for their courtesy and help while I was doing so.

[3] A by-law was passed against this abuse in 1703 (no. 21). Accusations of splitting were made against Sir Josiah Child in a pamphlet *A Brief Abstract of the Great Oppressions and Injuries which the Late Managers of the East-India-Company have acted* . . . (c. 1698). Bodleian Fol. θ 658 (19).

In these years when splitting was organized as a system several classes emerge to serve the purposes of the leaders of Company faction. First stand the great managers who organized the whole for the party leaders. They were bankers or other men of business administering great funds, partly their own, partly those placed at their disposal by, or borrowed on behalf of, the patrons they served. The chief manager of the Sulivan party splits was from the beginning Thomas Lane, Director of the South Sea Company.[1] Clive's interests were managed by a group : John Walsh, Luke Scrafton,[2] and his brother Richard Clive, who jointly administered his estate ; the banking firm of Cliffe, Walpole, and Clarke ;[3] and that of the Goslings into whose partnership George Clive was introduced in 1763.[4] The other big organization at the time was that run by Henry Fox, at first in March 1763 on behalf of administration, afterwards in the interest of the private profit he drew from the unsettled funds of his office.[5] His interests were managed in 1763, until their quarrel, by John Calcraft,[6] then by two of the Pay Office officials, John Powell and Charles Bembridge. Two other important organizations within this period were the more temporary ones of the returned Company servants in 1766 under John Harman,[7] a Dutch merchant, and that built up for the directors after 1767 by the banker Sir George Colebrooke.[8]

To be a great monied man was not, however, enough. The money had, at the right moment, to be embodied in the form of East India stock. When a party entered the field suddenly, as did that of Fox in 1763, this was of vital importance.[9] Even

---

[1] He had wide East India interests.

[2] For John Walsh see J. M. Holzmann, *The Nabobs in England*, New York, 1926, p. 166. Scrafton was a director, and in 1769 was one of the Commissioners sent out to India who were lost in the *Aurora*.

[3] See F. G. Hilton Price, *Handbook of London Bankers*, 1890–1, p. 172. Thomas Walpole, cousin to Horace, was the leading partner.

[4] Francis Gosling, Robert Gosling, and George Clive. Price, *op. cit.* p. 70, has no reference to the presence of Clive in the firm before 1764. The *Universal Director* of 1763, however, already gives his name.

[5] For his Pay Office funds see Lord Ilchester, *Henry Fox, First Lord Holland*, 1920, ii. 271–2. In March 1763 not only did Fox and all his personal followers buy in voting qualifications from Sulivan's agents, chiefly from Thomas Lane, but so did Lord Shelburne, his ally (Ledger P. 1761–4, fo. 620).

[6] Formerly of the Pay Office, then Deputy Commissary-General. He handed over the balance of his stock account to Powell in September 1763. The two latter were eventually involved in disaster through their connexion with Fox. They were dismissed, and Powell committed suicide in 1783 (*Gentleman's Magazine*, June 1783, p. 539).

[7] Of Gurnell, Hoare, and Harman.   [8] Lesingham, Binns, and Colebrooke.

[9] Most of the stock split on Fox's behalf in 1763 was bought and transferred straight to the voters just before the election. Some was borrowed from jobbers and split directly, e.g. William Fisher (for whom see p. 182) split £3500 which he was later repaid by Powell. Powell collected splits after the election to the amount of £14,000 stock. Fox never held much of his stock in his own hands until in June, July, and October 1767 (Ledger, 1767–9, fo. 424) he was paid in £36,500 by his agents, principally by John Powell and Fisher and Younger.

when a party was well organized, moreover, no banker or other agent could afford to have an undue proportion of his resources permanently tied up in East India stock.   Here a second class came in, the great stock-holder, like Sir Mathew Fetherstonehaugh,[1] who always put his holding of £15,000 to £16,500 at the service of the Clive faction at need, though he played no part in its distribution.   Still more important here were the great jobbers who were willing, no doubt for a consideration, to be of service to any group with whom they had connexions.   Most prominent among them at this period were John Harman mentioned above, the stockbroker Elias de la Fontaine,[2] of whom more will be said, and William Fisher, of the firm of Fisher and Younger, a stockbroker of Change Alley, a great ' bull ' of 1766–7, whose assistance was invaluable to the interest first of Sulivan and later of Sir George Colebrooke.   These great jobbers usually themselves played a big part in the distribution and re-collection of their stocks, and co-operated closely with the chief managers. Indeed, when issues which concerned themselves arose, as in 1766, they were to show they could organize a group of their own.

Still farther down the scale were the small jobbers and brokers and lesser agents who could perhaps contribute some stock themselves, or to whom stock could be transferred in a block for them to distribute to trustworthy acquaintances.   These men might be merchants or officials, like William Cholwich of the Six Clerks' Office, or even sailors like Lord Howe, or Irish gentlemen, like Clotworthy Upton.[3]   By the side of these professionals in the growing business of splitting there still existed the old-fashioned splitter who split his own moderate holdings among his connexions and received it back himself.   Lowest of all were those to whom the stock was split, a miscellaneous body that in time had a nucleus of permanency.   Under some centralized control the transactions of all these agents and principals make a perfect network of transfers, only to be disentangled by following the cross-references in the ledgers.

This machinery of splitting, which grew up so suddenly and indicates the interactions of the Company with both politics and finance, was a cumbrous mechanism, and all sides were nervous of the Frankenstein they had created.   Walsh complained to Clive in 1765, while promising to split £20,000 for him, that it was ' troublesome and dangerous ',[4] and both parties would have welcomed its disappearance, though neither could neglect it while its use lay open to the other.   Nevertheless, one must be careful

---

[1] Of Up-park, Sussex, M.P. for Morpeth and Portsmouth.
[2] Of de la Fontaine and Brymer, Lombard Street.
[3] Later Lord Templetown, a friend of the Hollands.   Ilchester, *op. cit*. ii. 286.
[4] Malcolm, *op. cit*. ii. 212 n.

not to over-estimate the extent to which it was put into action. Between 1763 and 1769 there were only six full-dress campaigns ; the elections of directors in 1763, 1764, 1765, and 1769 (under the regulations newly in force the splitting took place in October 1768), the ballot for Clive's appointment to India (April 1764), and for the increase of the dividends in 1766. There were many other controversial issues on which some votes were split or where only the less exacting forms of party pressure were used.[1] Moreover, even on important occasions not every group was in action. Clive did not use his splitting strength between 1765 and 1768 ; Sulivan did not employ his own agents during the same period, though he co-operated with the agents of the returned Company's servants. On the other hand, it was not until 1767 that the forces organized by Sir George Colebrooke, so important in the last years of this period, came into being at all.

It was hoped that the act of parliament of 1767 restricting the vote to those who had held stock for six months would kill the splitting system. It did nothing of the sort. It only meant that the splits for the elections in April occurred in the preceding October. It did, however, increase the risks entailed, for the stock was long out of the owners' hands, credit was thus lengthened, and disaster might overtake the holder. There can be little doubt that the crash of India stock in 1769 was intensified by the increased use of long credit now introduced into this speculative political business, and that the embarrassments of that year led to the financial panic of 1772.

This was the machinery of Company warfare in 1766, when the news that Clive had taken over the *Diwani* of Bengal arrived, and when the Chatham ministry came in, with Shelburne as secretary of state. The political situation within the Company was then as follows. Clive had, before he left the country, captured half the direction for the Rous party, which he virtually commanded, by the aid of a great splitting campaign, the help of the government, and the real belief of independent proprietors that he was the best man to deal with the alarming situation created by the Massacre of Patna. The hold of his faction was assured by a successful effort in the election of directors in the following year. Sulivan, himself defeated, was left in an unquestionable minority. The position remained, nevertheless, unstable. Clive's very proper enforcement of the Company's prohibition of

---

[1] The administration thought that the vote in the General Court, 6 May 1767, for a rise in the dividends was the result of scandalous splitting, and the house of commons ordered a list of transfers between 9 April and 7 May 1767 to be given them (*Journal of the House of Commons*, xxxi. 348). Copies exist in Brit. Mus. Add. MS. 18464, fos. 367ᵛ *seq.* Actually, the measure was influenced only to a minor degree by splitting : there was no extensive preliminary campaign, though a certain amount of hasty splitting.

presents, and his firm handling of the mutiny of officers in April 1766, began from 1766 to bring back discontented Company servants under the same threat of prosecution which had, in its time, made Clive himself so dangerous an enemy to the direction. Chief among these were the Johnstones [1] and, from 1767, Sir Robert Fletcher.

The danger of their forming an alliance with the Sulivan party was obvious, and the more probable since Sulivan was already closely allied with another malcontent, Henry Vansittart, late Governor of Bengal. It was Clive's spectacular actions, however, which brought East Indian affairs to a sudden crisis. On 30 March 1766 cypher letters from Clive notified the chairman of the steps he had practically decided to take. Significant of the effect which this decision would have in England was the second cypher letter he enclosed for his agent :—

Whatever Money I may have in the public Funds, or anywhere else, and as much as can be borrowed in my name, I desire may be, without loss of a minute, invested in East India stock.

Before the public dispatches arrived stock could be bought at 165¼, shortly after at 175 and 179, and soon at 190.[2] The great boom had begun.

As stocks rose unbounded hopes began to be formed. The obvious demand was for an increase in the dividend not only to its pre-war level but far above. The knowledge that the directors thought it premature and dangerous did not discourage the optimists, the great holders of stock, and the speculators. The directors' feeble attempt to ward them off only whetted their ardour, and the opposition groups under Sulivan were quick to see their chance. A coalition of malcontents was formed ; organization began on a large scale. In September rival papers, the *East India Observer* and the *East India Examiner*, began to appear canvassing the opposing causes ; [3] a great splitting campaign

---

[1] There were, altogether, four brothers, John, George, William, and Gideon. Holzmann, *op. cit.* p. 148. For prosecutions by the Company, see India Office Ct. Bk. 75 *passim*.

[2] Forrest, *op. cit.* ii. 258–9. He tries to exonerate Clive from this accusation of using his inside information on the stock market, but it seems impossible to do so ; see the full account in *Reports of the House of Commons*, vol. iii. *Third Report of the Committee of 1773*, pp. 313 *seqq.* The suggestion he makes that Clive ordered the stock to be bought for election purposes is untenable, since the Clive interest did not split for any election after 1765 until that of 1769 ; moreover, in view of the distance, Clive had to leave all such business in the hands of his English advisers. On the contrary, his attornies admitted to buying up £12,000 stock (the ledgers show it was not in his name) before the price of stock rose.

[3] The *Examiner* was the opposition paper ; the *Observer* the directors' one, in which Luke Scrafton was believed to be concerned. See *A Letter to the Proprietors of East India Stock from Mr. H. Vansittart*, London, 1767. Nos. 1–7 of the *Observer* and Nos. 1–11 of the *Examiner* reprinted together exist in the Bodleian, apparently all that was printed. The India Office and the British Museum possess complete sets of the *Observer* but not all the *Examiner*.

began, in which the stock-jobbers (including Lord Holland) and the returned servants took the lead ; jobbers like Fisher, probably themselves interested, played a great part, and the chief Amsterdam dealers, such as the Cliffords,[1] lent their resources on the Dutch markets. As a result, on 26 September, in spite of the Directors' opposition, the dividend was raised to 10 per cent.,[2] and measures favourable to the accused servants were pushed through. This was the first step in the financial recklessness that finally brought the Company to downfall.

It was about this point that Chatham's government intervened. It was the first intervention of administration in the problems of East Indian government ; but it must be noted that, although it entailed a parliamentary inquiry, it had less in common with the investigations and reforms of the next twenty years than with those exactions which had always been levied on the Company at the renewal of its charter. It is difficult to attribute any sense of the responsibilities of an empire to Chatham and his government, nor had they the spur which drove on North in 1772, the fear of the bankruptcy of the Company. They were out first and foremost to obtain, and, if possible, to justify a division of the spoils. George III said, with his accustomed frankness, that it was ' the only safe method of extracting this Country out of its lamentable situation owing to the load of Debt it labours under ',[3] and Chatham, saying the same thing in his more grandiloquent style, hoped for ' the *redemption* of a nation, within reach of being saved at once by a kind of gift from heaven '.[4]

The idea of such a source of spoil rose then as the excitement of the East India proprietors rose. Even in May, while still out of power, Chatham murmured that the conquests were ' too vast '.[5] In the city in particular, but also among the country gentry, the Company had always been unpopular, both as a monopoly in an age when the individual entrepreneur was gaining the day, and as one of the three monied companies associated with government finance. William Beckford, Chatham's chief city supporter, had always been a strong opponent of this, as of other companies, and had declaimed in his character of leader of the city ' radicals ' against the ' intolerable monopoly of the East India Company '.[6]

---

[1] Only one Dutch firm split its stock personally. This was the firm of Clifford, who, through their agent Pieter Clifford, of Lime St., London, split £10,500 stock on 23 September 1766 (Ledger Q. 1765–7, fo. 166). There is only one precedent for this in the period. In March 1763 Adriaan Hope of Amsterdam split £11,000 through his agent, Sir George Amyand, in co-operation with Thomas Lane (Ledger P. 1761–4, fos. 332–5). [2] Ct. Bk. 75, fos. 196–7.

[3] *Correspondence of King George III*, ed. J. Fortescue, 1927, i. 424.

[4] *Autobiography . . . of Augustus Henry, Third Duke of Grafton*, ed. W. R. Anson, 1898, p. 110.

[5] Malcolm, *op. cit.* iii. 189.

[6] *Parliamentary History*, xiv. 1212, in debate of 25 February 1752.

Now even before the Rockingham ministry fell he was flaming against the new wealth of the Company,[1] and when the Chatham ministry succeeded men remembered uneasily speeches to which they had paid little attention and began to wonder if they represented the intentions of the ministry.[2]   That the opportunity of easing public burdens was exceedingly tempting even opposition admitted, and the ministry's intentions soon became apparent. In August they informed the directors that their affairs were likely to come before parliament.

Chatham's proposal to intervene in the Company's affairs was, therefore, acceptable to all members of the ministry and to the king himself.   But while they might agree on the end, it was by no means certain that they would agree on the means.   Two definite groups, indeed, soon appeared within the ministry on this point.   In the one stood Chatham, Grafton, and Shelburne.   The attitude of Chatham was simple in principle but hard to determine in detail.   In principle he was for challenging directly the Company's right to the revenue of their new conquests.[3]   Six years later he said that he held

that there is in substantial justice a mixed right to the territorial revenues between the State and the Company as joint captors ; the State equitably entitled to the larger share as largest contributor in the acquisition by fleets and men.[4]

This view has much to recommend it, but it was certainly not his opinion in 1767, when he wrote explicitly of the right to the revenue that it ' cannot (upon any colourable pretence) be in the Company '.[5]   Consequently he put forward two propositions ; first, ' That the East India Company was instituted for the purposes of trade ', and secondly, ' That the acquisitions . . . were made in consequence of actual and extensive operations of war and succours stipulated '.[6]   He intended, however, that some concessions should be made to the Company when their right should have been disproved.   What they would have been it is impossible to say, for, as he grew increasingly ill and incapable of facing detail, he proclaimed the louder that he would make no plan, would let the matter ' find its way through the house ', and informed his colleagues that ' the ways to ulterior and final proceedings upon this transcendent object ' (for so he always alluded to the East India affair) ' will open themselves naturally

[1] Brit. Mus. Add. MS. 38205, fo. 81 (James Cresset)—C. Jenkinson, 25 August 1766.
[2] *Grenville Papers*, ed. W. J. Smith, 1852, iii. 323.
[3] For the peculiar difficulties involved, see Forrest, *op. cit.* ii. 177–8.
[4] B. Williams, *Life of William Pitt, Earl of Chatham*, 1915, ii. 233.
[5] *Grafton Autobiography*, p. 112.
[6] *Life of William, Earl of Shelburne*, by Lord Fitzmaurice, 1876, ii. 25.   (Probably to be dated *c.* 14 February 1767, in reply to a demand for instructions from Beckford.)

and obviously enough '.[1]   In this line of policy he was loyally followed by Grafton, though with a little dismay as time went on, and supported in the house of commons by Beckford, whose hatred of the East India Company was thought to echo that of his leader, but may well have carried him farther.   Shelburne, Chatham's ablest supporter, was with him in general principle, but considered the question, as events were to show, in a more practical light.   Even before Chatham's collapse he had been suggesting, and it would seem tentatively attempting, less sledge-hammer methods of intervention.

On the other hand, there was a strong case against this whole method of attack.   If it were a question of legal right, there was force in Grenville's suggestion that its proper place of determination was the law courts ; only the staunchest Chathamites could persuade themselves that the legal position was at all clear, and many frankly based their claims on expediency alone.   There was truth in Burke's gibe that this was ' the first instance of dragging to the bar men with whom the public meant to treat '.[2]   In the second place, such a direct attack would provide an excellent ground for the action of opposition, as they were quick to see, since it could be interpreted as a threat to private property and the validity of charters.   And in the third place, as Charles Townshend acutely pointed out, the threat was no more than bluff.   As he wrote to Chatham :

' Perhaps I may have thought, more than others of sounder judgment than mine, that the only way of making the issue adequate was to make it amicable ' ; it was ' from a sincere, though it should be thought an extreme, sense of the endless difficulties accompanying every idea of substituting the public in the place of the Company in the collecting, investing and remitting the revenue '.[3]

Townshend was throughout in favour of proceeding by negotiation with the Company, and he was supported by Conway.

Thus Charles Townshend and Conway formed from the beginning a group in the ministry unfavourable to the means, though not to the end, of the ministry's policy.   This was as unfortunate as it was to be expected, since they both had close connexions with opposition groups and formed, in any case, the weak link in the ministry.

Moreover, personal friction added to the difficulties.   Chatham and Charles Townshend were impossible colleagues, and their hostility, particularly on the Indian question, was so acute that

---

[1] *Correspondence of William Pitt, Earl of Chatham*, ed. W. S. Taylor and J. H. Pringle, 1838, iii. 189.

[2] *Memoirs of the Reign of King George III*, by Horace Walpole, ed. D. Le Marchant, 1845, ii. 407.

[3] *Chatham Corr.*, iii. 156.   Letter of 4 January 1767 ; for Conway see *Corr. Geo. III*, i. 458.

it seemed as if the ministry must founder on it before it met
parliament.   Even in September the Company papers were playing
on it,[1] and that acute observer, Charles Jenkinson, wrote in
November : ' A quarrel which has arisen between Lord Chatham
and Mr. C. Townshend on Indian affairs will be brought to its
issue.   I am persuaded . . . the Government is drawing to a
conclusion.' [2] Its continued existence and what success it achieved
in East Indian affairs (short-sighted as such success might later
seem to be) may fairly be attributed to the withdrawal of
Chatham through illness on the one hand and the emergence of
Shelburne on the other.

Shelburne's importance in this ministry has tended, then and
later, to be under-estimated.   He was a young man of little experience, and, as he himself said, ' it has . . . been my fate
through life always to fall in with clever but unpopular connections ',[3] and the absence of Chatham left him without real support
in the ministry.   But he had very considerable capacity and,
in the only two things in which the ministry had an active policy,
American affairs and the East India question, he played an energetic part.

So far as East Indian affairs were concerned, those who knew
their inner workings expected this from the start.   To them it
was Shelburne as much as Chatham who came into power in
1766.[4]   For Shelburne was the one member of the ministry who
already possessed an ' interest ' in East Indian politics.   Chatham's
' radical ' city interests were here powerless.   Since the days of
his political apprenticeship under Henry Fox in 1763, Shelburne
had been concerned in the factions of the Company.   He had
first supported Sulivan in 1763, and after his quarrel with Fox,
he continued the alliance in the election of 1764.   He had fostered
this interest for the reasons which made any ambitious eighteenth-
century politician keep up a connexion in the city, and the close
relations between him and Sulivan remained a fixed point in
East Indian politics till 1769.   In 1766 Sulivan was frequently
in his house, and he sat in parliament in his interest.[5]   It was the
knowledge that ' Shelburne, Barré and the enemies of the present
direction ' [6] were in power that drove Walsh to seek out Chatham
and take steps to ensure that no personal attacks would be made
on Clive and his *jaghire*.   Now that Shelburne was in power it
was in the interest of both sides to make use of this connexion.

[1] *East India Examiner*, no. 2, 10 September 1766.
[2] Brit. Mus. Add. MS. 38205, fo. 106.   Letter to Sir James Lowther.
[3] Fitzmaurice, *op. cit.* i. 17.
[4] *Historical MSS. Commission*, lxxiv, *Palk MSS.*, p. 30.   Col. John Call—R. Palk,
19 March 1767.
[5] Fitzmaurice, *op. cit.* i. 311 and 391.   The seat was actually Dunning's.
[6] Malcolm, *op. cit.* iii. 191.

Sulivan to facilitate his return to power in the Company, Shelburne to bring about a settlement favourable to the government. This alliance is clear from the first number of the *East Indian Examiner* in September 1766.

If Shelburne was the only member of the ministry with an East Indian connexion, Charles Townshend, however, as chancellor of the Exchequer and a most prominent member of administration, had no difficulty in finding one, though in his case for purely temporary reasons. He found it in the opposite camp, among the directors of the Company, with whom he entered into quite unofficial negotiations. As early as September the East Indian opposition paper spoke of him as in close connexion with the directors. By October he was asserting publicly that it was absurd to threaten extreme measures against them.[1] By the first half of 1767 he seems to have been in fairly close personal relationship with the ambitious banker, Sir George Colebrooke, whom they were bringing into the direction to strengthen their party.[2]

We have thus not only the spectacle of an administration split in two, but the far more extraordinary spectacle of the East India Company meeting the government's attack on its property not by opposition but by a competition between the two parties within it which should offer terms most acceptable to the administration. They were only checked by the suspicion of the main body of proprietors, and the use their opponents could make of it.

The situation in the Company is, however, easily explainable. In the first place, on the directors' side Clive's interest, usually a very important element in their strength, was neutral in the struggle, although his political patron, Grenville, was in strong opposition. Clive's *jaghire* was a hostage too valuable to risk in opposition to any stable government. Hence, though Clive himself was still in India, his agent Walsh hastened to assure Chatham of his goodwill and neutrality,[3] and his great forces remained motionless during the period. Among the directors there were others with political connexions in opposition, but their interest in this crisis was obvious. It lay in establishing a connexion with the more moderate elements of the administration to counterbalance the threats of the more extreme party.

The opposition in the Company was led by Sulivan, who had round him the nucleus of his old party, but it now contained the most diverse elements. As a pamphleteer noted, ' Mr. Sulivan

---

[1] *Grenville Papers*, iii. 334.

[2] Walpole, *Mems.*, iii. 26. The editor quotes (apparently from MSS.) Sir George Colebrooke's memoirs, which suggest intimacy between them by 10 May 1767, and in March Townshend had taken out a voting qualification from an agent of Colebrooke who was splitting £6000 for Colebrooke and Fisher, his agent (Ledger 1767–9, fo. 861).

[3] Malcolm, *op. cit.* iii. 191 *seq.* For Chatham's support of Clive's interest, see Shelburne's letter, Publ. Rec. Off. G.D. 8/56.

was at that time the leader of a party, combined of various interests ; and his language was accommodated to the views of those by whom he was supported '.[1] These varied interests, stock-jobbers, and big proprietors of stock, Company's servants afraid of prosecution, or like Vansittart,[2] in desperate need of reappointment to situations in India, produced a curiously composite policy. On the whole two interests predominated in it, interests by no means always compatible ; to raise the price of stock through increases in the dividend (the rise of 1766 being checked by political uncertainty) ; and to make terms with the government and thus bring Sulivan back to power. This was the easier since Sulivan had already opposed the expansionist views of Clive as harmful to trade. Hence they tried to combine, with what success will be seen, the offer of favourable terms to the ministry with a policy of inflation and increase of dividend, which the ministry could scarcely be expected equally to approve. Thus both parties in the Company had their connexions with one or other of the two groups in the ministry.

Both parties had also, however, some connexion with one or other of the two big sections of the parliamentary opposition. The Grenville-Bedford section of the opposition were connected with the direction through Clive and such lesser men as Robert Jones, the close follower of Sandwich.[3] They remained in close touch with the directors even when the latter were negotiating with the government, and their opposition in the house strengthened the hands of the directors in their negotiation. In elections of directors their influence was exerted strongly on the side of their allies, and even when Clive quarrelled with the directors after his return to England in 1767 and resented the growing influence of Sir George Colebrooke,[4] he knew he had no alternative to supporting them in the perennial struggle against his foe, Sulivan.

Sulivan's party, on the other side, had certain connexions with the other group in opposition, the Rockingham party. This was to some extent the result of accident ; certain members of Sulivan's group had formed political alliances with the Rockinghams before the East Indian affairs were a party question. Sulivan himself had no relations with them, but his friend and supporter, George Dempster, had close ones.[5] Moreover, Sulivan's party was strongly

[1] *A Second Letter to the Committee of Twenty-Five Proprietors of India Stock*, London, 24 January 1773 (*India Office Tract*, 50).

[2] *Hist. MSS. Comm.* lxxiv, *Palk MSS.*, p. 127.   [3] Namier, *Structure*, ii. 352.

[4] Clive, in 1767, expressed disgust with ' Rous and Saunders for unfitness and Colebroke and Cust for their Politicks ' and wished to ' purge the Direction of them ' (Forrest, *Clive*, ii. 352).

[5] Dempster was already a supporter of Sulivan in 1764 (India Office Ct. Bk. 73, fo. 48), and joined the Rockinghams in parliament in 1765 (Fitzmaurice, *op. cit.* i. 335–6).

affected by considerations of stock-jobbing and the leaders themselves speculated heavily.   In so doing they worked in co-operation
with a group of speculators who were active supporters of the
Rockingham party.   The most prominent of these was Lord
Verney and his agent, William Burke, the close companion of
Edmund.[1]   Thus Sulivan's party, except when they were negotiating with the administration, were on many issues strongly supported by the Rockinghams, as for instance in their opposition
to the limitation of the dividend by act in 1767.   It was on this
occasion that the duke of Richmond in particular began a connexion that led to a preoccupation in Company politics lasting
for more than ten years.[2]   On the other hand, on personal issues,
or when they were negotiating with the ministry, Rockingham
and Newcastle were dubious or definitely disapproving.[3]

It may be seen, therefore, as has already been said, that the
whole course of negotiations between government and Company
forms an extraordinary game of cross-purposes, and that it is
best understood if we remember that two more or less closed
systems of politics were interacting, and that each side was trying
to make use of the other.   When Sulivan's party insisted on trying
to force up the dividend in May 1767, Shelburne opposed them
rigidly, and when Newcastle complained of Sulivan's negotiations
in March, he was told : ' If any reasonable plan should be proposed . . ., neither ministerial nor opposition interest will avail
anything with the Majority, who never did, nor ever will, regard
anything but self and immediate advantages '.[4]

II

The complexities of party alignment in both parliament and
Company are reflected in the course of the negotiation.   It falls
into three stages.   The first is that in which Chatham still retained
some grip on the ministry which bore his name.   It ended at
the beginning of March.   During this period the field was set and
Chatham's simple policy of force was tried and failed.

After the intimation given to the Company in August that
their affairs would probably come under consideration, nothing
could be done officially until parliament opened in November.
All the political world was, nevertheless, active.   Walsh saw
Chatham at Bath ; [5] the directors were in touch with Townshend,[6]

---

[1] Shown by the prominence of the names of the group in demanding ballots, &c.,
in Ct. Bks.

[2] For his activity on this question in the Lords, see Brit. Mus. Add. MS. 32982,
fos. 391, 398.

[3] E.g. Brit. Mus. Add. MS. 32980, fo. 321.

[4] *Ibid.* fo. 310.   [5] Malcolm, *op. cit.* iii. 190–1.

[6] This is implied in Townshend's letter to Chatham of 1 January 1767 (*Chatham
Corr.*, iii. 149 *seq.*), also in letters of Beckford and Shelburne (*ibid.* iii. 176 and 182).

and the party of jobbers and company's servants forming under Sulivan already showed both sides of their future policy. They first forced the increased dividend through the General Court,[1] quite possibly against the better judgement of Sulivan himself, for his patron Shelburne wrote that not only the directors but the ' honestest ' proprietors were against it.[2] They then tried to cement their alliance with that section of the administration to which Shelburne belonged by obtaining from the General Court an abnegation of the purely territorial gains of the Company. The attempt was well timed, and, if successful, would greatly have strengthened Chatham's hands. Shelburne was certainly in touch with the movement ;[3] Chatham was probably not, for his contact with the Sulivan party seems to have been through Shelburne alone, and their correspondence at this time contains no reference to the affair. If they expected the attempt to succeed, however, they were disappointed, for the directors succeeded in having it defeated, not without difficulty, in the General Court of 14 November.[4]

As a result of these conflicting activities, Parliament opened uneasily. The debate on the motion for an inquiry into the state of the East India Company did not lessen the uneasiness, for, though opposition was not yet at its full strength, it was clear that the opposition were to act together on this question and that the ministry would probably not. The very person who opened the question in the house of commons made this clear, for it was neither Conway nor Townshend, the two leaders, but Chatham's city supporter, William Beckford. After this motion was passed nothing was done before the Christmas recess except to pass a further motion of Beckford's for papers for the inquiry. Even this was not done, however, without friction in the cabinet, and while Chatham had retired again to Bath angrily demanding full parliamentary inquiry,[5] Townshend remained in London to work with the directors of the Company to forestall it by obtaining permission from the General Court to enter into negotiations with and offer terms to the ministry. The first move in the Company had been that of the Sulivan party in the General Court in November ; the second was that of the directors in December. They succeeded where their opponents failed, and on 31 December they were empowered to open negotiations with the ministry ' upon such points relative to . . . the affairs of this Company as

---

[1] India Office Ct. Bk. 75, fos. 196–7.   [2] *Chatham Corr.*, iii. 93 (5 October 1766).
[3] Fitzmaurice, *op. cit.* ii. 17.
[4] India Office Ct. Bk. 75, fos. 270 *seq.* This General Court was demanded by nine prominent supporters of Sulivan's group (fos. 240–1): Isaac Panchaud, John Townson, Charlton Palmer, James Johnson, George Dempster, John Whiteside, Solomon Ashley, John Scott, and Duncan Clerk.
[5] *Grafton Autobiog.*, p. 110.   Chatham—Grafton, 7 December 1766.

shall seem to them most requisite and conducive to the Extending our Commerce, Security and Possessions, and perpetuating the prosperity of the Company '.[1] Charles Townshend looked on it as a personal triumph.

The likelihood of terms from the Company only served, however, to bring out more clearly the antagonisms of the ministry. When Townshend saw in the Company's resolutions the hope of an ' amicable and happy issue ',[2] Chatham suggested acidly that the adjective ' adequate ' should be added, and defined adequate as ' assuming or deciding the question of right, and . . . considering consequently whatever portion of the revenue shall be left to the Company as indulgence . . .'[3] Such terms (which would, indeed, have been complete surrender) he had, he said, no expectation of seeing. Since terms were to be offered, however, he was obliged to admit that they must await them ; so the parliamentary inquiry was postponed with many laments on the stupidity of ' enervating the principle of the Parliamentary inquiry, totally contrary to my notions '.[4] His sentiments were shared by his supporters in London and their relations with Townshend and Conway became very strained. When the directors' proposals of 6 February came before the cabinet (on 14 February) a breach between the two parties was only averted by referring them back for further explanation.[5] Thus the decision was postponed until these explanations drawn up by the directors on 20 February were received by Grafton.

Before that date, however, a worse blow had fallen and the ministry was thrown into confusion by the collapse of Chatham. Grafton and Beckford had for some time been imploring him to return to London. On 16 February, on his way thither he succumbed to a violent attack of gout. From that date, though his condition was not realized, his serious nervous illness must be dated.[6] He refused absolutely to consider details, refused to see Grafton, to consider the Company's proposals, to give any guidance to parliament when the question should come before it. It seems clear that the neurasthenic horror of business and responsibility which was so marked when he finally came to London in March had already overcome him.

The receipt of the directors' explanation brought to a head the antagonisms of the cabinet. Already by the 16th they were common property. Newcastle reported as from Onslow that ' *Govr*. Beckford went into the City abusing all the Directors ;

[1] India Office Ct. Bk. 75, fos. 336–7.   [2] *Chatham Corr.*, iii. 156.
[3] *Ibid.* p. 158.   [4] *Ibid.* p. 199.
[5] *Ibid.* p. 204. Grafton—Chatham, 15 February 1767.
[6] This seems a valid conclusion to draw from his correspondence with Grafton and Shelburne.

that nothing could be done with them etc. ; And that Sir George Colebrooke said, Stock would fall 20 per cent. upon it '.[1]

When he saw the terms Grafton assumed that they were quite unacceptable and turned his attention to the next step. ' Resolutions ', he wrote to Chatham, ' must be well weighed and worded so as to carry the effect that administration aims at ',[2] and Shelburne very tactfully echoed his advice, reminding Chatham that to leave the matter ' pretty largely to parliament must naturally startle such of the King's servants whose minds went to a composition '.[3]   But they obtained no help from Chatham, and on 3 March the battle was fought out in the cabinet. The majority decided to reject the proposals, the minority supported them, and the king threw in his voice with the majority. This seems to have been the cabinet which Horace Walpole mentions as breaking up in disorder, after which Conway and Townshend would attend no further meetings.[4]

The result was complete confusion. Though the matter was due in parliament on the 6th, no one knew how it was to be handled,[5] and the majority which had refused the proposals tried to hide the fact, so that their differences might not be published.   Still worse, the return of Chatham to London only increased the confusion, for, except for an abortive attempt to supplant Townshend by Lord North,[6] he was sunk in inertia.   Though he visited the king on 13 March, he seems to have played no part in public affairs after 5 March, and it soon became only too apparent that he was quite unfit for business.

It was not surprising, therefore, that when Beckford moved his long-deferred motion for the printing of the papers accumulated under the provisions of his motion of 10 December, and including the proposals of the Company, the ministry showed itself in a pitiable light.   Townshend opposed the motion as premature, and while the chief speakers were silent as to the rejection of the propositions, the lesser speakers let out the secret.[7] As a result, the opposition, who had recently won a ' snap ' victory in defeating the 4s. land tax, were inspired to stronger action than they had intended.   The followers of Grenville, with their close East Indian connexions, suggested that it might be possible to hamper the ministry in its present state of disunion, by getting

[1] Brit. Mus. Add. MS. 32980, fo. 110.   Newcastle—Rockingham, 16 February 1767.
[2] *Chatham Corr.*, iii. 217.   Letter of 22 February 1767.
[3] *Ibid.* iii. 221.   Letter of 25 February 1767.
[4] For date see *Hist. MSS. Comm.* ix., *Stopford-Sackville MSS.*   Lord George Sackville to General Irwin, p. 27.   Walpole, *Memoirs*, shows that Chatham was not there (ii. 428), although he had arrived in town.   *Ibid.* for the attitude of Conway and Townshend.
[5] Brit. Mus. Add. MS. 32980, fos. 207–8.   Rockingham—Newcastle, 5 March 1767.
[6] *Corr. George III*, i. 459–60, and *Grafton Autobiog.*, pp. 122–3.
[7] Walpole, *Memoirs*, ii. 430, and Brit. Mus. Add. MS. 32980, fo. 215.   West's report to Newcastle, 6 March 1767.

a petition from the East India Company against printing their papers on the ground of damage to trade.[1] This plan received favour from the Rockinghams and was rapidly and secretly put into effect.[2] On 9 March Robert Jones presented a petition from the directors ; and so well had the opposition mustered their forces and so unprepared were the ministry that their motion to adjourn was only won by 33 votes.[3] This experience was unpleasant for a divided ministry recently defeated on the land tax. Two days later, after hearing the chairman of the Company, they withdrew in a debate in which almost every one, the opposition noted, ' denied any design of force '.[4] The denial showed that Chatham's simple plan for forcing the Company to come to the aid of government finance failed, and with it the first stage of the negotiations ended ignominiously for the ministry.

The next stage of East India negotiations had, however, already begun. In this Shelburne took the initiative. That he had done so was not clearly seen by the opposition. They saw Townshend's flank turned by a skilful move, and they believed in consequence that Chatham as an ' invisible minister ' was still controlling affairs. There is, however, as little ground for this belief as for the longer-lasting myth of the invisible control of Bute. Chatham took no part in the policy, which was indeed a reversal of that which he had been pursuing. On the other hand, it followed logically from one already suggested by Shelburne.

The period of negotiation which Shelburne inaugurated seems to last from March to May. It began by a daring stroke which, while it did not succeed, at least opened up the possibility of success in the future. It is characteristic of Shelburne's position that it began in the East India Company. The attempt of the Sulivan party in November 1766 to push a motion through the General Court as a basis of negotiation with the ministry has already been noticed. In January Sulivan worked out another, apparently more detailed proposal which he discussed with Shelburne and asked him to communicate to Chatham. Shelburne did so, with the remark that Sulivan had thought he could get the proprietors to agree to it and ' he seems to think the same still, but is not so sanguine '.[5] Chatham, however, paid no attention to it,[6] and nothing was done. Now that the negotiation had broken

---

[1] Brit. Mus. Add. MS. 32980, fos. 220 *seq.* Rockingham—Newcastle, 7 March 1767. The form of action was certainly suggested by the Grenville group. It is not clear that the idea was. It is possible Dowdeswell originated it. The Rockinghams were certainly very active in pursuing the measure.

[2] Brit. Mus. Add. MS. *ibid.* and fos. 230, 244, all 8 March. Newcastle's ' whips ' to supporters.

[3] *Ibid.* fo. 246. Portland—Newcastle, 9 March 1767.

[4] *Ibid.* fo. 262. West's report to Newcastle. Endorsed 11 March 1767.

[5] *Chatham Corr.*, iii. 184. Letter of 1 February 1767.

[6] *Ibid.* pp. 189–90. Letter to Shelburne, 3 February 1767.

down and all was in confusion the time seemed ripe to revive the proposition. This is what Sulivan proposed to do, and this was the scheme to which Shelburne gave his support, and all his part of the ministry their assistance.

Had all gone well the directors had intended to have their proposals passed in the quarterly General Court of 13 March, but since they knew the ministry had rejected them, the position might be thought to have changed. Emboldened by the success of their petition, however, the directors decided to push farther, and resolved to have the terms passed by the General Court and offered straight to the house of commons in defiance of the ministry. This General Court, in consequence, acquired a new importance. Hitherto, although the election of directors was only a month off, there had been little activity in the Company. Sir George Colebrooke, who was entering the direction for the first time, may have been preparing his ground, but on the whole the absence of splitting suggests that the Sulivan party had decided, as in the preceding year, that there was little to be gained by seriously contesting the election. Now on 10 March, however, there was a sudden activity in splitting, clearly connected with the new political issue, and the issue itself soon became of importance in Company politics as a ' ballon d'essai ' for the election. The political element in this splitting was marked. On the one side, for instance, Shelburne's friend and follower, the lawyer Dunning, split his stock,[1] while on the other Charles Townshend took up his voting qualification from one Henderson who was acting as agent for Colebrooke.[2] The next day West fluttered the duke of Newcastle by the information that he had received ' an unusual summons ' to the General Court on the 13th.[3] On the eventful day he reported the proceedings of the Court.

Sir James Hodges (after all the proposals & explanations . . . had been read) moved that the Court of Directors of the E.I. Company do lay the same before the H. of Commons as the Basis of an Accomodation and was seconded by Sir Geo. Colebroke. This motion was much opposed by Mr. Sullivan (*sic*) and Mr. Dempster, as a letting the Government into a Partnership with the Company would soon end in the absolute dependency & ruin of the latter.[4]

Sulivan then offered to draw up a less exceptionable plan and the meeting adjourned.

An unprinted letter from Shelburne in the Chatham Manuscripts explains the inner history of this move.[5] Writing on

---

[1] He split his £1000 stock on 10 March. (Ledger 1767–9, fo. 251.)

[2] See *supra*, p. 189, n. 2.

[3] Brit. Mus. Add. MS. 32980, fo. 272. Endorsed 11 March 1767.

[4] *Ibid*. fo. 280. Endorsed 13 March 1767.

[5] Publ. Rec. Off. G.D. 8/56. Dated only Saturday morning, but internal evidence makes its attribution to 15 March perfectly clear.

15 March, after failing to gain admission to Chatham, he tells him of the happenings in the Company. After outlining the events leading up to the General Court of the 13th (though with an assumption of detachment from them which is scarcely supported by the evidence of political splitting in the *Ledger*), he reports that Sulivan has consulted him on a new plan which he hopes he can carry, since he found ' his own weight considerably greater than he had ever imagined and that the Directors on the contrary certainly saw themselves very weak '. Shelburne adds : ' I have myself very good reason to believe that he has a considerable Majority for any reasonable Purpose if he manages wisely '. The question to be considered, Shelburne suggests (though it would seem he had himself answered it already), is, whether they should encourage him to pursue this plan. He writes :

I am at a loss however whether it's safe or rather Proper, for his Integrity and Prudence is undoubted, to give him advice. On the one hand the Situation of the House of Commons, too bad to be describ'd, appears to make what passes in the City very material ; on the other I easily conceive, that it were to be wish'd the genuine Sense of the Proprietors could be had, but this the Proceeding of the Opposers of Government and the Imprudence of these Directors meeting them so entirely, makes impossible as far [as] they have weight.

It seems unlikely that he received an answer, but the plan went forward. Its effect was electrical. It took back the initiative in East Indian affairs from Charles Townshend to the opposing camp. Newcastle wrote to Rockingham two days later :

I suppose you know that Charles Townshend is outrageous at what Lord Chatham is doing with the East India Company ; where his creature Sulivan is to offer some better Proposals tomorrow at the General Court to be laid before the Parliament ; And all this is done without the knowledge of the Chancellor of the Exchequer. Sulivan, who is the person employed in all this is a Creature of Lord Chatham's, an Enemy to Lord Clive and to all the present Directors.[1]

Rockingham, characteristically both more cautious and more accurate, wrote the same day : ' I think, by what I hear, that he is set on by *Part* of the Administration who wish for a *Loophole* but probably it will fail.' [2]

The prophecy was correct. Sulivan produced his plan which combined a scheme for dividing the territorial from the trading revenue to please Government with a dividend of 14 per cent. to please his followers.[3] The directors, too cautious to try to get it thrown out directly, moved that it should be referred to their consideration. Sulivan's party, on the other hand, moved that

---

[1] Brit. Mus. Add. MS. 32980, fos. 300^v–301. Letter of 15 March 1767.
  Ibid. fo. 296. Letter to Newcastle.   [3] India Office Ct. Bk. 75, fos. 443 *seq.*

it should be referred to a committee of directors and proprietors. In a ballot of 19 March this was defeated by 452 to 264,[1] and it was generally agreed that the defeat meant the loss of the scheme. Rockingham remarked that it ' happens extremely appropos (*sic*) and will be a very unpleasant hearing for the Gt. Man '.[2] The directors in due course turned down the plan, and, though Sulivan's supporters demanded another ballot on it, which coincided with that for the new directors on 9 April, its interest to the public was over. It remained as an election issue in the Company, however, and much use was made in propaganda of the allegation that Chatham and the ministry had approved it.[3] This accounts for Horace Walpole's assertion that the opposition were encouraged to renewed activity in the House ' by a point that had scarcely been contested with them ; this was the re-election of most of the late board of Indian directors. The duke of Bedford was carried to the India House to vote—his son had not been dead three weeks.' [4]

The interlude had, however, served the purpose of getting the ministry out of its *impasse* and of opening up the possibility of further negotiations. No fewer than twelve proposals were sent in to the directors after Sulivan had offered his,[5] and the directors themselves in the interest of their electioneering had to get out a counter-proposal to Sulivan's. Hence, before the election of 9 April they drew up a new set of proposals which owed a good deal to the Sulivan scheme they had rejected. As soon as the new directors were established, it was understood that these new offers would be made to the ministry. Thus the two sides of the administration were able to come together again, and both succeeded in saving their faces, for on the one side, the negotiation was now fully recognized, and on the other the parliamentary inquiry, so long postponed, was opened by Beckford on 20 March.[6]

The importance of the inquiry is chiefly that it was the precursor of the much more important inquiries of the next twenty years. Though the opposition contested it hotly at all its stages, its importance was clearly only subordinate to that of the

[1] India Office Ct. Bk. 75, fo. 452.

[2] Brit. Mus. Add. MS. 32980, fo. 344.   Letter to Newcastle, 19 March 1767.

[3] *Gentleman's Magazine*, March 1767, p. 101.

[4] *Letters of Horace Walpole*, ed. Mrs. P. Toynbee, 1903–5, vii. 102.   The duke of Newcastle had been nervous as to the result, as is shown by Sir M. Fetherstonehaugh's letter of 9 April (Brit. Mus. Add. MS. 32981, fo. 77).

[5] India Office Ct. Bk. 75, fo. 472 *seq.*, and Committee of Correspondence Memoranda, vol. xxiii (no pagination).

[6] *Journals of the House of Commons*, xxxi. 25.   The original motion for a committee was one ' to enquire into the state and condition of the East India Company *together with the conduct of all or any persons concerned in the direction or administration of the said Company* '.   The words italicized were finally omitted, on an amendment by Conway (Flood—Charlemont, quoted *Chatham Corr.*, iii. 144–5 n.).

negotiations. Like the later inquiries it was exceedingly general in nature. It sought rather to show the corruption and lack of discipline of the Company's servants, and the unsuitability of the Company's situation for that reason, than to prove any one point. From the scanty information we have of its proceedings it would appear that a wide range of evidence was covered, but its essential unimportance is shown by the fact that, when the new negotiations were approaching fruition, the inquiry faded away. Even at the adjournment of April the ministry had positively denied that they would use force towards the Company, ' a language very different,' as Sackville remarked,' from that which Mr. Beckford . . . open'd this affair with and which was held by the Ministers when they rejected the proposals of the Court of Directors as inadmissible '.[1]

The negotiations were much more serious. By 2 May they were so far complete as to be satisfactory both to ministers and directors and had only to be passed by the General Court and presented to the House of Commons. At this point, however, a new and acute difficulty suddenly arose. The second stage of the negotiations ended abruptly with a new outbreak of faction in the Company, followed by a recurrence of the former disunity in the ministry. The result was a third stage of negotiations marked by a renewed trust in parliamentary action, a curious revolution of alliances between ministry and Company, and an important change in the propositions which were laid before and accepted by Parliament.

The difficulty arose, as might have been expected, on the question of raising the dividend. The proposals put forward by the directors after their defeat of Sulivan's scheme had to contain, for the purposes of Company electioneering, a reference to an increase of dividends.[2] All parties within the Company continued to ignore the dangerous magnitude of its contract debts. It was proposed that, as soon as they were paid off, the dividend would begin to rise gradually to a maximum of 16 per cent., and the chairman stated in the General Court that he expected the debts to be paid off by September.[3] This would make possible a rise in the next half-yearly dividend, and it was generally believed it would be raised to $12\frac{1}{2}$ per cent. When the terms to be offered to the ministry were considered in detail, however, a less optimistic spirit prevailed, and it was proposed as a provision for repayment that a loan of £500,000 should be raised. The difficulty arose when, on 30 April, the ministers suggested and the

---

[1] *Hist. MSS. Comm.* ix., *Stopford-Sackville MSS.*, p. 27.
[2] The terms are summarized in *Gentleman's Magazine*, March 1767, p. 101.
[3] *Letter to a Minister on the Subject of the East India Dividend*, London, 1767 (Brit. Mus. 102, i. 51, and *India Office Tract*, 688).

Court of Directors agreed to a change in the terms which threatened the expectation of increased dividends. The ministry were averse to public borrowing by the Company. With this provision dropped, the agreement would entail an indefinite postponement of the rise in dividend.

This decision was very alarming to the speculators of Sulivan's party, and they promptly took action. On 15 May the Jew J. P. Fatio split £16,000 to supporters of their cause,[1] and a marked activity in splitting began. On the same day Dempster and other prominent members of the party asked for papers, and the Directors ordered that the propositions and the government's amendments should be printed.[2] The Sulivan party had decided that at the next General Court they would press for a rise in dividend. The ministry saw the danger and tried to avert it. They intimated that they did not wish their side of the negotiations to be printed, and they informed the chairman that they would consider an increase in the dividend before the completion of the negotiations to be a breach of faith.[3] The policy of their step was doubtful, for though the directors supported them strong feeling was aroused in the General Court against this intervention, and the Sulivan party determined to brave directors and ministry alike. It does not seem that they had on this occasion the support of any members of the ministry (certainly not of their usual supporter, Shelburne) nor of the Grenville part of the opposition, though the Verney party among the Rockinghams were actively concerned with them.[4] Their strength on this issue was nevertheless considerable, for the interests of so many proprietors seemed to be on their side, a fact which compensated for absence of time to organize a splitting campaign comparable to that of September 1766. Besides there was disunion among the directors ; Clive's supporters thought, as he himself did later, that the directors were belittling his successes when they urged economy and caution.[5]

All these mixed motives and the new excitement aroused by the intervention of the ministry made the General Court of 6 May, in which the directors had hoped to pass their propositions, a sweeping victory, on the contrary, for the Sulivan opposition. The dividend was raised to 12½ per cent. and (as usual on the occasion of such triumphs) prosecutions against former servants were

---

[1] Ledger, 1767–9, fo. 235.　　　[2] India Office Ct. Bk. 76, fo. 33.

[3] There was controversy as to the exact form of the communication.

[4] On 12 May William Burke, with Sulivan and others, demanded a General Court (India Office Ct. Bk. 76, fos. 54–5), and in the House ' Dempster and W. Burke . . . ventured to avow their own share of the criminality ' (Walpole, *Memoirs*, iii. 22).

[5] *Letter to the Proprietors of East India Stock: Containing a brief relation of the Negotiations with Government*, London, 1769 (*India Office Tracts*, 50, 202, 378, and Brit. Mus. T. 796(2); cf. Malcolm, *op. cit.* iii. 216–17).

stopped.[1] All the directors could do was to register a protest in their court.

The ministry and indeed the house of commons as a body were infuriated by this act of ' impertinence ' by the Company. The following day the house asked for papers, and a parliamentary inquiry of a new sort seemed about to begin.[2] Grafton told the directors, who disclaimed all responsibility for the General Court, that the matter now rested with the house of commons, ' whose attention to this great affair has been too often turned aside by fallacious appearances of accommodation '.[3] The Sulivan party could expect no help from their accustomed friends. Shelburne may have wavered for a moment,[4] but he soon adopted the most rigid attitude. For the first time he is attacked by the pamphlets of the Company opposition, and it would seem to have been at this time that he put down his own ideas of a satisfactory settlement, differing considerably from those of Sulivan, which he had approved in general terms two months before. Now he thought a 10 per cent. dividend should be fixed by Parliament, ' as a particular set of proprietors may be led away by the hopes of present profit '.[5] On the 8th a bill was introduced to prevent the Company raising its dividend without the consent of parliament for the space of a year.[6]

It was then that the full rashness of their precipitate action became apparent to the opposition in the East India Company. This bill would lose them all they had hoped to gain. They determined to petition against it ; they held General Courts of such violence and disorder that their only result was the introduction of another bill, long overdue, to prevent the abuse of splitting.[7] They also took more practical measures. How far Sulivan had hitherto personally approved of their action it is impossible to say. His name did not appear among those pushing it. Now, however, he personally led an attempt to escape from their position by his former tactics of offering the government better terms than had the directors. On 8 May, the very day on which the bill was introduced, a proposition was made in the Court of Directors that the government should be offered the more advantageous terms of the fixed sum of £400,000 a year, instead of a share in the profits (thus returning to Sulivan's earlier suggestion of separating the Company's and nation's shares), in return for the

---

[1] India Office Ct. Bk. 76, fos. 39 *seq.*

[2] *Journals of the House of Commons*, xxxi. 344.

[3] India Office Ct. Bk. 76, fo. 67.

[4] Brit. Mus. Add. MS. 32981, fo. 359. West reported to Newcastle on 11 May 1767 that Barré, Shelburne's mouthpiece in the Commons, had not committed himself at that date to 10 per cent. rather than 12½ per cent. though he supported the dividend bill.

[5] Fitzmaurice, *op. cit.* ii. 19–20.　　　　[6] Geo. III, c. 48.　　　　[7] 7 Geo. III, c. 49.

omission of all reference to the dividend. When this had no
success, Sulivan and eight others demanded a General Court to
discuss it. Accordingly one was called for 18 May.[1] Their activities, moreover, as it soon became clear, were not limited to the
Company. Three days before the General Court met, Bradshaw,
the invaluable secretary of Grafton, warned him :

I am assured from good authority, that the leaders of the last general
court have fallen upon a new plan for carrying their point, and hope to
bribe parliament into an allowance of their increasing their dividend, by
an immediate offer of a large specific sum instead of a moiety of the
surplus. I think it my duty to apprize Your Grace of this intention, lest,
when the offer is made, or the view of it held out, any attempt should be
made to conceal from your Grace the real motive.[2]

The warning meant, as the last line would suggest, that the danger
lay not only in the attitude of the opposition but of a section of
the ministry. Under new conditions the old division within its
ranks reappeared. Townshend and Conway were still insecure
in their allegiance, Townshend never more so. Though he had
agreed to the dividend bill, his ' champagne speech ' the same
night showed his instability and his ' sovereign contempt ' for
Grafton and Shelburne. He was not, therefore, at all unwilling
to play them the trick they had played him, and when the Sulivan
party began to make higher offers in return for freedom to raise
their dividend, it was not this time Shelburne who listened to
them but Townshend, who had before opposed them. Contemporaries speak of meetings between him, the leaders of the Sulivan
party, and the opposition leaders at the St. Albans' Tavern, where
he was generally believed to have pledged himself to opposition
to the dividend bill in return for specific improvements in the
Company's terms.[3] Whatever may have been the nature of the
agreement, the results were soon plain in the house of commons
and the Company. Townshend and Conway were again acting
in conflict with the policy of the rest of the ministry, and
the Sulivan party in the Company were again forcing the directors
to offer the government better terms than they had intended.

The Sulivan party carried out their side of the bargain. In the
General Court of 18 May, one of the stormiest in the history of
the Company, they passed the minor proposals of the directors,
but substituted for the major ones a proposition to grant £400,000
a year and two minor concessions to the nation. No reference was
made in the proposition to the dividend, but a petition was voted
against the dividend bill.[4] To these terms the directors had

[1] India Office Ct. Bk. 76, fos. 54 *seq.*   [2] *Grafton Autobiog.*, p. 180.
[3] *A Letter to the Proprietor of East India Stock*, 1769.
[4] India Office Ct. Bk. 76, fos. 65 *seq.*, account of this General Court; fos. 85–8,
the petition containing the terms offered to government.

unwillingly to agree, and the propositions were handed in and accepted by the house of commons as the definite agreement with the Company. This agreement was to bind the ministry and the Company for two years.

The other side of the bargain was, however, less successfully carried out. The sacrifices made by the Sulivan party were in vain, for the dividend bill was passed in spite of them. Townshend, Conway, and the opposition opposed it at every step, but the rest of the ministry stood firm and they had no success. Conditions were less favourable for such opposition than they had been when Chatham's inquiry was opposed in March, for any eighteenth-century government gained in prestige by the mere fact of continuing in existence, and Charles Townshend was by this time a good deal discredited. Of the last debate on the measure Jenkinson wrote :

On Tuesday last (May 26) we had a long Debate whether the Dividend of the East India Proprietors should be 10 or 12½ per Cent. . . . The Duke of Grafton thought it right to support Mr. Dyson, who had declared that by his Bill he meant it should be but 10 ; we thought ourselves bound to support him likewise, and though Townshend, Conway, Grenville and Dowdeswell with their respective parties were all against us we beat them by 152–86. Townshend carried of (*sic*) with him only Touchet, and Conway only his two nephews and Frek (?) Harris. This is looked upon as the most extraordinary event that ever happened in the House of Commons, and has convinced the World that the personal influence of these Gentlemen who assert to be Leaders is in fact nothing ; and they are sufficiently humbled by it.[1]

When this had failed them the only hope lay in the lords. Here the opposition considered itself to be particularly strong, and both sides of it co-operated in active measures against the dividend bill.[2] In the house both Richmond and Mansfield waged a vigorous campaign, and in the Company, though nothing was to be hoped from the court of directors, Rockingham himself proposed to ' some of the directors and proprietors ' [3] the stratagem of combining with their petition against the bill an offer to restrain their own dividend to 12½ per cent. until the agreement with the government expired. Once again, however, they failed and, though thirty-seven peers dissented, the bill was passed.

In this extraordinary way the East Indian agreement was finally made. It owed its origin to government need and Chatham's love of direct measures. Its course was determined by Shelburne's

---

[1] Brit. Mus. Add. MS. 38205, fos. 174–5 (Liverpool papers), C. Jenkinson—Sir James Lowther, 2 June 1767.

[2] Brit. Mus. Add. MS. 32982, fos. 148 *seq.*

[3] *Ibid.* fo. 302. Rockingham—Newcastle, 11 June 1767. For Rockingham's active interest in the Company, see also Newcastle—Rockingham, same date, fos. 303 *seqq.*

East Indian connexions, and its final form conditioned by the attempt of a faction in the Company to which Shelburne would offer no terms, although they were his connexions, but with which Charles Townshend was willing to treat. It is not to be wondered that the agreement was bitterly attacked later, for its intentions were simply those of gain. But in the progress of the negotiation other issues had arisen, and the government had been driven to two measures of a quite different kind which it had certainly not envisaged : the limitation of the dividend, though in the first place only for a year, and the regulation of voting qualifications in an attempt to check split-voting. The age of intervention was perceptibly approaching, for the issues which the legislators had to face in 1772 and 1783–4 were already becoming clear.

Of the further dealings of the ministry, of the renewal of the dividend act and the extension of the agreement, nothing need be said here, for Shelburne's part in them was not apparent. In spite of his active part both in the American policy and the East Indian policy of the government, he was all the time drawing away from his colleagues. The continued absence of Chatham meant that the nature of the ministry began to change and Grafton began to look to other and new connexions where Shelburne was unpopular. Though he was not dismissed from office until October 1768, he had taken no part in the business of the ministry for over a year before. Hence he seems to have taken no open part in these further East Indian affairs. This did not mean, however, that he had severed his connexions with the Company. There was as yet no permanent breach between himself and Sulivan. This did not come until 1769, when, with Shelburne in opposition and Sulivan at last again in power in the Company, the latter was forced to go over to the government. On 6 November 1769 Burke reported : ' Sullivan [*sic*] has gone over to the Court . . . How he has arranged with Lord Shelburne with whom he was generally supposed in connexion, I know not '.[1]

This breach was still, however, in the future, and in 1768 the Sulivan party had never been more active in Company politics, for they saw the hope of a return to power in 1769. Various circumstances seemed to favour them. There was disunion among the directors. Sir George Colebrooke, the rising power in the Company, though he opposed them in the election, had coquetted with them as a means of obtaining the chair in 1768.[2] He had

---

[1] *Correspondence of the Right Honourable Edmund Burke*, ed. Earl Fitzwilliam and R. Bourke, 1844, i. 211–12.

[2] *To the Proprietors of East India Stock*, 12 April 1768. Broadsheet. (*India Office Tract*, 688.) Compare *A Second Letter to the Committee of Twenty-Five Proprietors of India Stock*, 24 January 1773 (*India Office Tract*, 50).

also, it would appear, entered into some kind of relations with them in national politics, for Shelburne's under-secretary, Lauchlin Macleane, began to sit for one of his boroughs in 1768. Further, the shipping interest had quarrelled with the directors,[1] and at the last moment Sulivan won a measure of support from North's government by promising to support a prolongation of the agreement of 1767 between the Company and nation.[2] All this justified a great splitting campaign, and September and October 1768 saw splitting which rivalled or even surpassed that of the campaigns of 1764 and 1766. Thomas Lane was once again dealing with Sulivan's business, and a new agent, the broker Elias de la Fontaine, took a great part as his coadjutor. On the other side there was equal activity, and Clive, Crabb Boulton, Colebrooke, and Robert Jones borrowed £130,000 from Fox's holdings and £50,000 from Sir Matthew Fetherstonehaugh.[3] Sulivan's friends scarcely expected his success,[4] despite all his efforts, but when the ballot was taken, out of twenty-four directors, fourteen were from his list (five were common to both) and he himself was returned.

So in 1769 the long period in the wilderness ended for the party. Sulivan was in power, and Vansittart went out to India as supervisor ; but an ironic fate pursued them. Vansittart's ship never reached India, and the spectacular crash in East India Stock caught Sulivan with his election commitments still on him. That was why he and the others left their patron Shelburne that year and sought the shelter of alliance with the North ministry.

III

The sudden collapse of Shelburne's East India interests in 1769 leads directly to consideration of Shelburne himself, as it brought forth significant evidence which otherwise would never have come to light. Shelburne is in the curious position of a man universally suspected, but against whom few specific charges of dishonesty

---

[1] India Office Ct. Bk. 76, fos. 647 *seq.*, 23 March 1768, and Ct. Bk. 77, fos. 77 *seq.*, 17 June 1768.

[2] *Letter to the Proprietors*, 1769. ' Mr. Sulivan by his last compliance will gain the support of Government, and probably obtain a seat in the Direction.' Cf. Malcolm, *op. cit.* iii. 245.

[3] *In the Memoranda of the Committee of Correspondence of the Court of Directors* (India Office), vol. 24, there are copies of two bonds in the hand of the secretary of the Company borrowing this money. £25,000 coming from John Powell, Fox's agent, was to be in the form of stock and to be transferred to their manager, William Fisher, to split. £10,000 of Fetherstonehaugh's money was to be in stock, half of which was to be transferred to John Durand, the ship's husband, half to John Barnard, packer.

[4] *Hist. MSS. Comm.* lxxiv, *Palk MSS.*, p. 91. ' Mr. Sulivan would not be dissuaded from trying his luck once more : the list of Proprietors will be published in a few days, and then, if I mistake not, he will see clearly that, with all the split votes the Dutch could furnish, he has not the least chance.'

have been made. Throughout his political activities in the period under review there is certainly no ground for such a charge. In his correspondence there are, on the other hand, enough minor instances of disingenuousness—often quite unnecessary—to explain why he became the object of distrust. The circumstantial evidence of 1769 about his East India concerns seems to give still further explanation of contemporary suspicion.

It is his whole connexion with the Company that raises the question, was it merely the result of a political alliance between him and the Sulivan party in the Company on certain important issues,[1] or was it closer and more personal ? Is there any reason to think that his connexion was so close that he helped the Sulivan party in their election campaigns by splitting stock for them, or had he an even more carefully hidden interest in the Company through jobbing in its stock ? There is some circumstantial evidence which suggests that he may have done both.

There is no doubt that he gave up his East Indian connexions entirely in 1769. After that date he might have a policy in East India affairs, but he was never associated with a party in the Company. He himself said eleven years later that when the Company's affairs took ' a very corrupt turn I scrupulously shut my door against them '.[2] There are, however, two reasons, both more concrete and convincing, which may be advanced to explain the abrupt end of these connexions in 1769. Not only had he been deserted by Sulivan, but this desertion was preceded by heavy financial loss which he himself estimates at nearly £40,000, in the same crash of East India stock which caused Sulivan to take refuge with the government.

The main problem is to account for this financial disaster. Sulivan's misfortunes seem simple to explain. He does not appear to have been jobbing in East Indian stock. All his resources were employed in splitting for the 1769 election. His loss, therefore, arose entirely from heavy political obligations which the fall in the price of stock made it hard for him to meet. The loans that he and his allies had made for splitting had been received in two forms ; when received in the form of stock, repayment presented no difficulties, but when the loans were made in money to buy in stock the position was very different. Hence Sulivan and Vansittart, as the former admitted, were ' pledged and engaged mutually for large sums ' to avoid loss by the sale of stock ' in these hours of panic ', and, since the fall was not merely momentary, and Vansittart died with his affairs in confusion, Sulivan's position became very serious.[3]

---

[1] His biographer, Lord Fitzmaurice, thought that it was.
[2] Fitzmaurice, *op. cit.* i. 318. In a letter to Lady Ossory, 20 October 1780.
[3] *Hist. MSS. Comm.* lxxiv, *Palk MSS.*, pp. 126 *seq.* and 188 *seq.*

The reasons for Shelburne's loss are not so easy to understand. They are bound up with the failure of his late under-secretary and personal follower, Lauchlin Macleane, who was, like Sulivan, thereby driven to desert him for the government. Macleane, his enemies said, ' becoming once a bull at the rencounters [*sic*] of the East India gamblers was so hard-pursued by the bears that he has thought proper ever since . . . to bow the knee to administration '.[1] Shelburne himself refers to his loss as if it arose from pure good nature. When applying privately to Hastings in 1774 for aid in recovering some of his losses from Macleane,

' I dare presume so far ', he wrote, ' upon yours as well as Mr. Impey's good opinion, that however my Understanding may suffer in your Judgement, from your knowledge of this Transaction, you will not think the worse of my Heart in lending my Hand as I hop'd to save a drowning Friend, where I could possibly have no other Interest.' [2]

And in some notes written for his heirs he says : ' It may serve as a warning to my own family to be told that I have lost near £40,000 by being bond for other men . . . and all the return I had was treachery and a great deal of unjust public abuse '. Lady Shelburne's diary adds the information that the bonds were in favour of Lauchlin Macleane to cover his losses in East India stock in 1769.[3] The ' treachery ' was no doubt the defection of the latter ; the ' public abuse ' is understandable. His account of the transaction may be true, for Lauchlin Macleane obtained great sums from many sources in the course of his career ; but it must be admitted that he usually obtained them from men who had some concern in his tortuous business affairs, and moreover, for a statesman to give bonds to the amount of nearly £40,000 for debts incurred in dealing in stock to a man who is known as his political dependent, his close personal follower, and who has been recently his under-secretary at a time when that situation implied a close connexion with the minister, is an action which lays itself open to uncharitable constructions. These constructions would not be shaken by anything we know of the reputation of Macleane.

Some particulars of these bonds, drawn up to the amount of £30,000, can be discovered in the records of the Courts of Exchequer and Chancery. On 12 May Shelburne drew up three bonds in favour of Macleane totalling £15,000, and on 24 May three more to the same amount. The first were used to satisfy a debt to Isaac and John Francis Panchaud, well-known English bankers

[1] *London Magazine*, February 1771, pp. 74 *seq.*
[2] Brit. Mus. Add. MS. 29124, fo. 366 (Hastings papers). He seems to have had no success though seven years later he thanked Hastings for his kind intentions communicated to him (S.) through Impey (Add. MS. 29149, fos. 380 *seq.*).
[3] Fitzmaurice, *op. cit.* ii. 332 n.

in Paris.[1]   The second satisfied a debt to Lord Verney,[2] Burke's
patron.   For neither does Shelburne appear to have had any
security, though in July 1769 he took over from Macleane what
was apparently his sole asset (and one already encumbered) an
eighth share of a plantation in Grenada.   This he transferred to
Verney in December 1770 as security for his still unpaid debt.[3]

It is unfortunate that the dates at which Macleane had contracted these debts for East India stock do not appear, for they
might have thrown light upon their nature.   In both cases
the demands may have arisen either from stock-jobbing claims
brought forward when creditor and debtor found it hard to meet
their ' differences ' at the disastrous May rescounter, or from an
attempt by embarrassed creditors to get security for money lent
to Macleane to finance ' splitting ' operations for the Company
election.   The activities both of the creditors and of Macleane
would support either of the above hypotheses.

The Panchauds were certainly jobbers in East India stock and
were badly hit by the fall of prices in May.   They had to transfer
Shelburne's bonds at once to an urgent creditor,[4] Thomas Tierney,
and in July they became bankrupt.[5]   In 1766, moreover, Isaac
Panchaud and Macleane had common jobbing interests in
Amsterdam, for they went there together and the latter wrote to
Wilkes : ' We are so deeply interested in what caused our Journey
hither, E. I. Stock, that we must give our whole Attention to it
'till after the Rescounter or quarterly day of settling Accounts '.[6]
On the other hand, Isaac Panchaud was also one of the leaders of
Sulivan's party in the General Court.[7]   His name occurs prominently in controversial demands for ballots or the summoning of
General Courts, and he had in September 1766 split £30,000 stock
in the interest of the party in close connexion with John Harman,
and, it seems likely, with William Burke, Lord Verney's agent,
and with Lauchlin Macleane himself.   While £15,000 of this was
returned to John Harman and the rest was transferred to various
individuals, including William Burke and Macleane,[8] and though
he never personally split large sums again, it would be most un-
safe to assume that he took no further part in the financing of
East Indian splitting in the controversial year ahead.   Indeed,

[1] Publ. Rec. Off. Exchequer Bills, London and Middlesex, 12 Geo. III, E. 112,
1904.   The case can be followed through till 1773, when a settlement was apparently
reached.

[2] Publ. Rec. Off. Chancery Bills, C. 12. 554/26.

[3] The evidence of this case does not support Dilke's hypothesis that the Burkes
were partners of Macleane in his Grenada lands (C. W. Dilke, *Papers of a Critic*, 1875,
ii. 336).

[4] This emerges from the Panchaud case.   [5] Walpole, *Letters*, vii. 299.

[6] Brit. Mus. Add. MS. 30869, fo. 51, 5 July 1766, Wilkes MSS.

[7] India Office Ct. Bk. 75 *passim*, and Brit. Mus. Add. MS. 38205, fos. 79–81.

[8] Ledger Q. 1765–7, fos. 121, 567 and 656.

it is improbable that, in the existing state of East India organization, a banker with such jobbing issues at stake, should not have contributed towards the splitting operations of the party to which he looked for his financial salvation. Hence Macleane's debt to him might arise equally well in jobbing operations, or in the course of supporting the party in which they were jointly interested.

Lord Verney stood in much the same position as the Panchauds. He certainly lost heavily at the May rescounters, and seems to have been jobbing heavily in association with the Burkes. Edmund Burke was unwilling to think of East Indian affairs after the disaster of his friends in them, disaster in which, incidentally, he was probably himself concerned.[1] It was said at the time that Verney had lost £27,000 on ' one bargain ',[2] but he was also, partly for the same reason, an ardent East Indian politician and a strong supporter of Sulivan's. His name and that of William Burke's are as prominent as that of Panchaud, and as time went on, a certain desperation is evident in the measures he supported.[3] He had, therefore, good reasons for supporting the Sulivan party in the election. That he did so is strongly suggested by the fact that he was able to set against the losses incurred by the Burkes in ' differences ' in July 1769 a debt of £17,000 due to him by de la Fontaine, one of the chief distributing agents of the Sulivan campaign.

If both Macleane's creditors were concerned at the same time in East Indian jobbing and in party politics, so too was Macleane himself. Macleane was not a very reputable under-secretary for a secretary of state. His usefulness was his possession of the arts of the ' Jackal '.[4] An early career in America was followed by an attempt to float himself to fortune on the friendship of John Wilkes. Later he was to win considerable notoriety as the agent of Warren Hastings and of the Nabob of Arcot. In 1766 he was on good terms with the Rockingham administration apparently through Fitzherbert and his friends the Burkes, but by August he had made himself sufficiently familiar with Shelburne for the latter, on assuming office, to make him his under-secretary.

[1] Burke, *Corr.*, i. 211. Cf. Dilke, *op. cit.* ii. 338 *seq.* To Dilke's evidence as to Burke's share in the jobbing of his family must now be added that of the Verney papers (*Verney Letters of the Eighteenth Century*, ed. Lady Verney, 1930, ii. 277) that he and Richard Burke owed Verney £25,000 in 1769. On the other hand, Dilke appears to be wrong in believing that Verney and W. Burke were finally ruined in 1769. It seems more probable that the final disaster was in 1773. *The Memoirs of William Hickey*, ed. A. Spencer, 1913, pp. 284–5, are supported by the signs of stress in Verney's affairs of that year, and the date of William Burke's departure for India.

[2] Dilke, *op. cit.* ii. 338.

[3] He may have evolved the scheme for keeping up the price of stock by ' pegging ' it proposed to the Company in 1769 (India Office Ct. Bk. 79, fos. 99–100). A broadsheet was also published.

[4] For his career see L. B. Namier, *England in the Age of the American Revolution*, 1930, p. 316 n.

While he held this position the negotiations with the East India Company made the markets very speculative and Macleane is soon found jobbing heavily in East India stock. He is also found identifying himself in the politics of the Company with the Sulivan party which his patron supported, and it was at that time he first came to know Sulivan personally. Some of his jobbing operations came out in two lawsuits brought after his failure. In a case brought by his former patron in America, the Hon. Robert Monckton, against Macleane's brokers, de la Fontaine and Brymer, it came out that Macleane had large dealings with the brokers in, after, and before July 1767. Since 1767 he had always been to some extent in their debt. On 25 July 1769 he admitted to owing them £25,555 13s. 2d. for ' differences ' of which, however, all but about £6000 was later paid.[1] In another case brought by an Amsterdam broker, Gerrit Blaauw, who had carried on business for him on the Dutch market, the resort of so many of the East India speculators of the time, it appears that Macleane had been dealing with him in and since 1767, ' buying, selling and prolonging great quantities of East India stock '. In this he sometimes gained very considerable sums. In the May rescounter of 1768, however, he bought £45,000 stock for prolongation to the August rescounter. It was prolonged at each rescounter until that of February 1769 when he sold £20,000 of it at a profit. The remaining £25,000, however, he unluckily prolonged again to the fatal May rescounter and sold at a heavy loss. He was left owing Blaauw £4124 2s. 1d.

These stock-jobbing ventures of Shelburne's under-secretary were not undertaken for himself alone. He also acted as agent for other men whose situations disposed them to use a ' cover '. Monckton had bought £10,000 through him from Hope of Amsterdam for the rescounter of August 1768. He was also managing the affairs of Sir John Hort, bart.[2] It is extremely likely, as Dilke suggests, that he was the man referred to by *The Repository or Treasury of Politics and Literature for 1770* (i. 236) when it complains of members of parliament who combined in their speculations, and left their agent as a scapegoat to pay 2s. 6d. in the pound.[3] This would help to explain the great scale of his operations.

Macleane, however, besides being an active jobber on the

[1] Publ. Rec. Off. Exchequer Bills, London and Middlesex, 10 Geo. III, E. 112/1410. Mentioned in *Gentleman's Magazine*, 1824 (ii.), December, p. 488. Dilke, *op. cit.* ii. 338 *seq.*

[2] This emerges in the Gerrit Blaauw case.

[3] Dilke, *op. cit.* ii. 45 n. Sulivan—Hastings (Brit. Mus. Add. MS. 29133, fo. 535ʳ), praising Macleane for trying to pay his creditors, supports this. Macleane was again connected with a jobbing syndicate in 1772. *Reports from Committees of the House of Commons*, iv. 394 *seq.* *Eighth Report from the Committee of Secrecy on the State of the East India Company.*

English and Dutch market in the most speculative years of India
stock, was very closely connected with the leaders of the Sulivan
party in the East India Company. Though his name does not
occur among those demanding ballots and general courts for
the party's purposes until he and his patron were safely out of
office, he was always one of their scrutineers at elections,[1] and in
his business affairs his connexion with their leaders was of the
closest. One of the most prominent of them, John Stewart, was
a close business associate and friend, with whom he was sharing
a house in 1766 ;[2] and when he went to India to mend his ruined
fortunes, another, John Townson of Gray's Inn, was left to
manage his affairs. With Sulivan himself he had a friendly
connexion. When he deserted Shelburne for the government,
his promotion, which was rapid and lucrative, was Sulivan's
especial care. Observers remarked that his succession of places
probably arose from ' a strong sense of some peculiar obligation '.[3]
They were, however, probably wrong. It represented rather the
extent of his indebtedness to Sulivan. In the serious losses which
Sulivan had incurred in the campaign of 1768–9 Macleane was
one of his few debtors, and clearly to a considerable sum, and
Sulivan hoped much and gained something from his appointment
in India.[4] His debt to Sulivan under such circumstances, and
his close connexion with the leaders of the party, suggest that
Macleane's difficulties may well have been connected with splitting
activities as well as with stock-jobbing.

If this is so, what conclusion can be reached as to the origin
of Shelburne's bonds of nearly £40,000 ? There can be no doubt
of the closeness of his connexion with Macleane during these
years. His creditors pleaded ' The well-known Friendship which
subsisted between him the said William Earl of Shelburne and the
said Lauchlin Macleane ; who was closely connected with him
and had Acted in the public Character or Station of Secretary to
him '.[5] It is certainly difficult to believe that, dealing with such

[1] E.g. on 13 April 1768 with Isaac Panchaud, John Stewart, Charles Fergusson,
and Richard Burke (India Office Ct. Bk. 77, fo. 1).

[2] For his close associations with Macleane see Brit. Mus. Add. MS., Wilkes MSS.
passim. He appears also to be the agent whom Shelburne sent to Corsica in 1768
(Fitzmaurice, *op. cit.* ii. 123 and 141) and to have conveyed in 1760 a message from
Choiseul to Pitt (Publ. Rec. Off. GD. 8, 60). He was left in a bad financial position
on the death of Macleane (Brit. Mus. Add. MS. 29153, fo. 478).

[3] John Galt, *Life and Works of Benjamin West, Esq. . . . subsequent to his Arrival
in this Country,* 1820, p. 60.

[4] *Hist. MSS. Comm., Palk MSS.,* p. 188. £9070 is here mentioned as the aggregate of debts due from Macleane, Shelburne, Verney, and Mrs. Forest. Macleane's
debt is spoken of as ' very large '. For Sulivan's efforts to get Macleane a profitable
job, and the results, see *ibid.* pp. 189, 302. Also Hastings papers, e.g. Brit. Mus.
Add. MS. 29133, fos. 534–6. Macleane died owing him, he alleged, £15,000 (Brit.
Mus. Add. MS. 29153, fo. 478).

[5] In the Panchaud case.

a man, he had no concern in the transactions for which he pledged himself for so vast a sum, though it is also quite possible that he was cheated by him.   There is a little evidence which appears to bear on the subject.   On the one side it suggests that Shelburne was concerned in the Sulivan election campaign of that year. It is stated in Malcolm's *Clive*, a work remarkably accurate and well-informed on these details, that Shelburne was ' said to have split £100,000 for the Sulivan party in 1769 '.[1]   Shelburne, who had supported Fox in his splitting in 1763, and who admits an ' interest ' in the campaign of 1764, himself said that before the corrupt turn in the Company affairs which led him to close his door against them he ' interfered a good deal . . . in the affairs of the Company ', though ' it was always my maxim to avoid all personal canvassing '.[2]   If this were the case, his natural agent for the purpose was Macleane, and Shelburne may well have suffered, like Sulivan, by pledging himself to large sums in support of his agent when the latter was pressed by anxious creditors who had provided money for the campaign.   The thoroughly unsound financial position of Macleane, which became fully apparent by July, would be enough to explain both Shelburne's heavy loss and his subsequent indignation.

On the other hand, however, there is a contemporary reference which might suggest that Shelburne himself was concerned in Macleane's stock-jobbing losses.   Charles Lloyd, Grenville's private secretary, writing on 1 June with details of the stock-jobbing crisis which was about to reach its head in a failure of the broker de la Fontaine involving Macleane, Lord Verney, and the Burkes, says : ' Lauchlin Macleane I hear is absolutely ruined ; Lord Shelburne is very deep '.[3]   If this statement were well founded, the fact that Shelburne had already given bonds for £30,000 to support Macleane on the stock-market would suggest that Macleane stood in relation to Shelburne much as the Burkes stood in relation to Lord Verney ;   that, while he had great personal interests involved, he was also acting as an agent or ' cover ' for his patron, as we know he was doing for others.   If this were so, it would give some grounds for the ' unjust public abuse ' of which Shelburne complained, for even in opposition a statesman does not gain by a reputation for stock-jobbing, and, moreover, since Macleane had been jobbing on his own account and that of others since at least 1767, it seems unlikely that his activities on his patron's behalf began only on their resignation from office in October 1768.   It seems, indeed, by no means impossible that Shelburne, like many of his contemporaries, was a ' jobbing

[1] Malcolm, *op. cit.* iii. 245.   The comments appear to be derived from a narrative of Strachey's in the papers of Lord Clive in the possession of Lord Powis.
[2] Fitzmaurice, *op. cit.* i. 318.   [3] Dilke, *op. cit.* ii. 338.

minister '.[1]   In the mid-eighteenth century they were not uncommon.   Henry Fox, Shelburne's first political mentor, was one
almost openly, and had Shelburne been, like Chatham, rigidly
averse to such transactions, he would scarcely have had such
a man as Macleane in office under him.   If he were a jobbing
minister, however, it is at least just to say that his policy was
not subordinated to his jobbing.   The men with whom Macleane
worked most closely were those who struggled the most desperately for a higher dividend in 1767, against which Shelburne
showed himself adamant.

To sum up, it may be said that in the crash of East India stock
prices in 1769 there were two chief classes of sufferers : the jobbers
who were ' bulling ' the market, and the financiers of the East
India splitting campaign.   One person often combined both these
activities, as did the broker de la Fontaine,[2] Vansittart, and
probably Lord Verney, and his position was grave indeed.   Though
it is unlikely that the interlocking and carefully hidden finances
of the jobbers and embarrassed East India leaders will ever be
fully known, it seems quite possible that Shelburne, acting through
Lauchlin Macleane, was involved in both these unfortunate enterprises.   He may indeed have been lucky to escape with his loss
of ' nearly £40,000 '.

Whether this were so, or not, appearances were certainly
against him.   Neither when in office nor out was the reputation
of such connexions desirable for a statesman who sought to
follow in the footsteps of the elder Pitt.   The events of 1769 must
have made this clear to Shelburne, both in his financial loss, in
the scandals which were subsequently laid bare in the law courts,
and in the desertion of his embarrassed followers and allies.
In 1769 he gave up for ever his close association with the East
India Company.   In 1773 he could speak with disgust of government and opposition as men who had competed who could best
defend the guilty directors,[3] and among these directors had been
Sulivan.   Hasting's tentative advances to him received unrespon-
sive though polite replies.   Shelburne had given up the connexions
he had formed under the influence of Henry Fox.   From henceforth, in opposition, he turned his attention increasingly to that
force which had made much of the power of his newer model,
Chatham, the force of what was later called ' city radicalism '.

---

[1] Shelburne was popularly accused of stock-jobbing while in power in 1783.   These
accusations were thought, however, to be disproved (*Edinburgh Review*, xxv. 212,
June 1815).

[2] De la Fontaine was given, at the end of 1769, the position of Barrack-Master
of the Savoy ' for his secret services in the Ally ' (*Letters of Junius*, ed. C. W. Everett,
1927, p. 303).   It is possible that he owed this place to Sulivan, who had recently
gone over to government.

[3] Fitzmaurice, *op. cit.* ii. 269.

LORD MACARTNEY'S APPOINTMENT AS GOVERNOR OF MADRAS, 1780: THE TREASURY IN EAST INDIA COMPANY ELECTIONS

THE election of Lord Macartney[1] to the governorship of the Presidency of Fort St George or Madras in December 1780 is of interest for several reasons. To begin with it was the first time that the East India Company elected to one of its major positions a man who had held responsible office in other spheres, but who had had no experience as a servant of the company. Lord North's Regulating Act of 1773 had nominated three such persons to the Council of Bengal, one of whom, General Clavering, was intended to succeed to the governor-generalship; but this was an arrangement imposed on the company from without.

Secondly, the election is of importance in the career of Lord Macartney himself, a man now chiefly remembered as the leader of the first official mission to Pekin in 1792–4, but who had a career of varied service to the Crown at home and abroad, and who was at this time, at the age of forty-three, well-known in political and social circles. He was a lively, self-confident and personable young Irishman, of a good ascendancy family, and like many such, impecunious as well as ambitious. Horace Walpole paid tribute to his social gifts, 'He is extremely good-humoured, equal, conversable on all subjects unaffected and perfectly agreeable in great or small companies',[2] though in his *Memoirs* he allowed him (perhaps rather unfairly) 'no extraordinary talents'.[3] His first attachment was to Henry Fox, Lord Holland, who employed him as a sort of travelling tutor to his sons Stephen and Charles James while they were in Europe.[4] It is an indication of his tact that he retained the friendship of the sons as well as the father. It was through Lord Holland that he obtained his first official job, that of envoy to the Court of Russia in 1764–7, when England was trying to negotiate a commercial treaty with Catherine the Great. In this he was less than successful,[5] but his career as a government supporter had begun, and he strengthened his ties by marrying in 1768 the second and favourite daughter of Lord Bute. He supported administration in both the English and

---

1. (1737–1806). Knighted 1764: created Baron (Irish) 1776: Viscount (Irish) 1792: Earl (Irish) 1794: Baron (G.B.) 1796.

2. Horace Walpole to Lady Ossory, 4 Dec. 1775. *Horace Walpole's Correspondence with the Countess of Upper Ossory*, ed. W. S. Lewis and A. Dayle Wallace, i (1965), 280.

3. *Memoirs of the Reign of George III*, iii (1894), 174.

4. Ilchester, *Henry Fox, First Lord Holland*, ii (1920, pp. 462–8).

5. W. F. Reddaway, 'Macartney in Russia 1765–7', *Cambridge Hist. J.*, iii (1931); Michael Roberts, *Macartney in Russia. The English Historical Review Supplement*, no. 7 (1974).

Irish house of commons, served as secretary to the Lord Lieutenant of Ireland, and finally as Governor of Grenada. He was raised to the Irish peerage while holding the last of these posts, and had enjoyed an Irish pension of £1,500 a year for some years.[1] Nevertheless, he also had good friends among the Opposition, and took pains to keep them. These included the Foxes, the Burkes (with whom he had been intimate since the 1760s – though in 1780 politics were temporarily to divide them), the earl and countess of Upper Ossory, and through them Horace Walpole, and a number of others.

At the beginning of 1780 he was available in London and place-hunting, since he had been taken prisoner-of-war when the French occupied Grenada, and had lost both his position and his prospects. Released on exchange, he turned up at Lord Bute's house in November 1779, where Horace Walpole noted that 'he is shrunk and has a soupçon of black that was not wont to reside in his complexion'.[2] He was also notoriously penniless. As he told his confidante Lady Ossory, he had a private income of £2,400 p.a. (of which £1,500 came from his Irish pension) and had gone to Grenada with debts which he admitted to total £12,000. As he expected his governorship to bring him in at least £4,200 a year, he had hoped to clear this debt while in office;[3] but with this hope gone a profitable job was essential and he considered that Lord North's Administration owed him one.

What drew his attention to the possibility of succeeding Sir Thomas Rumbold as Governor of Madras is not clear. Though he later had strong support from the administration in his candidature, and North was certainly anxious to find a job for him, the initiative does not seem to have come from them. His first biographer John Barrow, who knew him well, thought that, though it was generally believed that he owed the appointment to ministerial influence, this was not the case, adding that Lord North had been heard to say that 'it would be idle to give themselves any trouble about Macartney, as it was utterly impossible he should ever succeed to an Indian appointment'.[4] He admits that Macartney in an address to the Proprietors stated that he had the countenance of Ministers (and well before that he certainly had their full support) but points out that in the same address he stated that some of his warmest friends were members of the Opposition. More to the point is Macartney's letter of application to the Court of Directors of 9 October. In this he claims that he would not have ventured to apply 'had not several of my friends, men of high character and large property, perfectly

1. *Calendar of Home Office Papers, 1766–1769*, p. 548: *1770–1772*, p. 637.
2. Horace Walpole to Lady Ossory 14 Nov. 1779 *op. cit.*, ii. 135–6.
3. Macartney to Lady Ossory 19 Aug. 1780, Fitzpatrick MSS. National Library of Ireland, Dublin 8012 (IV), quoted in Horace Walpole's *Correspondence*, ii. 219, n. 25.
4. J. Barrow, *Some Account of the Public Life . . . Of the Earl of Macartney* (London, 1807) i. 78.

versed and deeply interested in Indian concerns, expressed a strong opinion that the situation on the Coromandel Coast would probably require at this particular Juncture the appointment of one totally unconnected with any of the contending interests there, and absolutely free from local passion or prepossession'[1] and that he was the man for the job. There seems little doubt that he owed his adoption as candidate in the first instance to a group of company politicians.

For the third point of interest about Macartney's candidature is that it came at a time when government and company were facing a series of problems at home and abroad, and when intricate negotiations were in process to solve at least the most immediate of them.[2] This was the danger of no less than a complete collapse of the system of control of the company's affairs through influence, which the Treasury, through the hard work of its Secretary John Robinson (assisted by Lord Sandwich at the admiralty and in a lesser degree by other departments), had succeeded in keeping going ever since the settlement of the Regulating Act in 1773. Over the large Court of Proprietors, or General Court (composed of all holders of stock of the nominal value of £1,000 or more and which voted on demand by secret ballot) their hold had always been precarious, but they had normally preserved their control over the Court of Directors (the company's rulers except when the Court of Proprietors intervened). At the beginning of 1780, however, this too was threatened, for the administration . . . had to face the intensely controversial issue of negotiating a new Charter for the Company and of replacing the Regulating Act by new legislation, and this at a time when they were so much burdened by the problems of an unsuccessful war, that they had little energy left for battle on other fronts. To make things worse, Laurence Sulivan the most skilful East India politician and the patron of Warren Hastings, whom they had obstinately kept off the Direction since 1773, had succeeded in forcing his way back on to it against their will in 1778, and was building up a group in opposition to them there. Nor was this central problem by any means the only one which harassed the government and the company. In Bengal government and directors alike were on record as disapproving of Warren Hastings as governor-general, though they had failed to dismiss him, and as supporting his opponent Philip Francis, though they did not in fact intend to nominate him as Hastings's successor. Agents for both of these men had been at work in England bombarding both government and directors on their patron's behalf. The situation with regard to Madras was even more unsatisfactory. After the scandal of Governor Pigot's death in 1776 during the *coup* against him, all company servants concerned in the affair were

1. P.R.O. of Northern Ireland: Macartney MSS. D.O.D. 572/19/48.
2. For the general situation see L. S. Sutherland, *The East India Company in Eighteenth Century Politics* (Oxford, 1952), pp. 329–50.

recalled for investigation, and they had been in England for some time with little progress being made either in proceeding against them or in reinstating them. Among them was the notorious Paul Benfield, the chief creditor of the Nawab of Arcot, and there was also in England the equally unscrupulous if less obviously disreputable John Macpherson, who had been dismissed by Pigot before the *coup* for his activities at the Nawab of Arcot's Court, and who was now operating on his own account in both national and company politics in close connection with Benfield, and simultaneously as an unofficial agent of the Nawab of Arcot and Warren Hastings.[1] Supporters of the Nawab on the one side, and of his enemy the Raja of Tanjore on the other were active in parliament, the company and the press; and the position was still farther complicated by the fact that the misdeeds of Pigot's successor as governor of Madras, Sir Thomas Rumbold, were already becoming known, and that in any case he was expected soon to be returning to England.

Most of these problems were far beyond immediate solution by either the government or the company. The political crisis between them was, however, solved just before the annual election of directors in April, by a secret negotiation carried out behind the backs of powerful interests both in Administration and the Company. The chief credit for bringing it about lies undoubtedly with John Macpherson, and was due not only to his great ingenuity and plausibility in negotiation, but to the close links between his friend and collaborator James Macpherson[2] (North's ablest political pamphleteer) and John Robinson. For some months John Macpherson had been working to bring Sulivan and Robinson together so as to reconcile the Ministry to Hastings. All attempts had failed until it became apparent that unless active steps were taken administration would lose control of the next direction. At this point they suddenly caved in. Just before the annual election of directors in April a meeting took place between Lord North, Lord Sandwich and John Robinson on the one side and Laurence Sulivan and the Macphersons on the other, to which the government's chief supporters in the company were later called in. As a result a treaty of alliance between Sulivan and some of his followers and the government supporters in the company was made.[3]

The results were striking for all concerned. Administration preserved a shaky control over the company, and finally succeeded in pushing through the negotiations for a new charter and a modified (and far from satisfactory) amendment of the Regulating Act.

1. For the East Indian activities of the Macphersons at this time see the unpublished Edinburgh Ph.D. thesis of James N. M. Maclean: 'The Early Political Careers of James 'Fingal' Macpherson (1736–1796) and Sir John Macpherson, Bt. (1744–1821)', 1967.
2. Often known as 'Fingal' as the translator (or author) of Ossian.
3. Sutherland, pp. 347–8.

Laurence Sulivan, after seven years in the wilderness, was once more where he longed to be, at the head of the company's business. The government dropped its hostility to Warren Hastings as governor-general and began a support of him which lasted till the end of the North administration. Those who had engineered the agreement also gained. John Macpherson, despite the dubious circumstances in which he had left India[1] found himself in due course elected to the Council of Bengal; Paul Benfield, after a rougher passage thanks to outraged public opinion led by Edmund Burke,[2] was permitted to return to Madras to resume his business with the Nawab. And by August Lord Macartney had appeared as a candidate for the governorship of Madras, strongly backed by administration and its followers in the direction, including Laurence Sulivan.

The evidence supporting the view that Macartney owed his prospects to the revolution in the relation of administration and company is circumstantial, but in total strong. When he had first raised his claims to the then chairman of the directors in March, he received no answer to the three letters he sent in, and was not surprised at this silence since he recognized the difficult situation of the company.[3] Well into April there were members of administration who were pressing for Philip Francis to be given the reversion of this job, as compensation for his disappointments in Bengal. After the reconciliation between the government and Laurence Sulivan, both Sulivan and Macpherson made their opposition to this proposal clear and it was dropped.[4] An alternative scheme was then floated to set up a commission to assume the governor's powers – as late as the first week of July, Macpherson mentioned the proposition to Hastings as a possibility, though he also spoke of the possibility of a new governor.[5] As early as 21 July a press rumour said that Macartney was beginning to canvas for the appointment.[6] His papers make it clear that before 14 August he was doing so, and that he had the backing of administration. On 25 and 26 August he drafted stock

1. Gone into at length in the *Third Report of the Select Committee on the Administration of Justice in Bengal. Reports from Committees of the House of Commons*, v. 631 ff.

2. He led the case (unsuccessfully) against his reinstatement in the General Court of 17 Jan. 1781. India Office Library. East India Company Court Book, B/96, pp. 536 ff.

3. Macartney to G. Staunton. Quoted in H. H. Robbins *Our First Ambassador to China* (1908), p. 119.

4. John Macpherson to Warren Hastings 28 Apr. 1780, B.M. Add. MS. 29145, fos. 61–62.

5. John Macpherson to Warren Hastings, 6 July 1780, B.M. Add. MS. 29145, fos. 299–300. Sir Abraham Hume, prominent in East Indian affairs, wrote to Macartney from Auckland Castle on 25 Aug. 1780 'Before I left the neighbourhood of London, I understood that a Commission to settle the affairs of that Presidency was talkt of, and that Mr. Cuming intended offering himself to go as one of the Members of it, but as that is probably laid aside, I shall write to him again immediately on your Lordship's subject.' P.R.O. Northern Ireland, Macartney MSS. D.O.D. 572/19/12.

6. *The London Courant*, 21 July 1780. On 1 Aug. 1780 John Woodhouse wrote to Hastings (B.M. Add. MS 29145, fo. 327) with a list of alleged candidates, including Macartney.

letters to send out to individual directors and proprietors.[1] Laurence
Sulivan and the friends of Warren Hastings were also among his
supporters.[2] To what was this sudden change in his fortunes due?
Edmund Burke was convinced that his candidature was associated with the campaign for the reinstatement of Paul Benfield, and
for that reason (despite old friendship) he could not support him.
Modern scholars have believed him to be mistaken.[3] But there is
ample evidence of the connection between Macartney and Benfield at
this time though naturally it was kept very quiet. Not only did
Macartney go out to Madras pledged to assist Benfield in every way,[4]
but Benfield had lent him £6,000 towards his travelling expenses,
and when Benfield finally won his permission to return to Madras in
the following January (shortly after Macartney had sailed) Macartney's friends were among his supporters in the General Court.[5]
Thomas Allen wrote to Macartney, 'We were hard run with Benfield
and must have been beat, but for very particular and good Management'. He added, 'I know but little of him in Truth doe not much
Approve his Connexions'.[6] So far as the Macphersons were concerned, no correspondence between either of them and Macartney
seems to have survived before December of this year,[7] but by that
time he was obviously on very friendly terms with John Macpherson, a friendship which persisted for some years after both were in
India – 'cor unum via una' Macartney wrote to him in 1781.[8] Both
of them appear in the comparatively short list he drew up of friends
who had helped in his election and for whom patronage was due.[9]
Finally, in 1782, when Macartney had withdrawn his confidence
from Benfield, the latter burst out to a colleague 'that Lord M. was
an ingrate! a scoundrel! Oh! the villain that he had borrowed

1. W. Falkener to Macartney 14 Aug. 1780, P.R.O. Northern Ireland, Macartney
MSS. and D.O.D. 572/19/13 and D.O.D. 572/19/14.

2. L. Sulivan to Warren Hastings 1 Jan. 1781, 'Lord Macartney has had and shall
have my warm support', B.M. Add. MS. 29147, fo. 44.

3. *Correspondence of Edmund Burke*, ed. T. W. Copeland, vol. iv, ed. J. Woods (1963),
p. 323. It also would seem that Burke was backing Claud Russell, who had married one
of Lord Pigott's natural daughters, for the position.

4. Macartney–J. Robinson 26 Oct. 1781 Misc. bundle, Deccan College, Poona. I am
indebted to Mr J. Gurney, St Antony's College, Oxford, for this reference. Cf. C. C.
Davis (ed.), *the Private Correspondence of Lord Macartney, Governor of Madras, 1781–85*
(1950). Correspondence with John Macpherson, *passim*. North's letter of introduction
of Benfield to Macartney, 31 Jan. 1781 suggests that he did know they were already
acquainted (Deccan College, Poona, d. 1013c. Information provided by Mr J. Gurney)
J. Robinson's letter of 1 Feb. 1781 (P.R.O. Northern Ireland, Macartney MSS. D.O.D.
572/19/70) shows him to have been better informed.

5. Macartney to Thomas Coutts & Co. 8 Aug. 1782. National Archives of India.
Cleveland Public Library, microfilm roll 80, no. 42. Also in B.M. Add. MS. 22462,
fo. 18. Information from Mr J. Gurney.

6. 6 Feb. 1781 P.R.O. Northern Ireland, Macartney MSS. D.O.D. 572/19/73.

7. John Macpherson to Macartney 27 Dec. 1780. Printed in *Correspondence of Lord
Macartney*, ed. C. C. Davis, p. 68.   8. *Ibid.* p. 7.

9. Both their names are recorded in a list in a small notebook Macartney drew up for
this purpose. (Macartney MSS. Deccan College.)

£6,000 from him to carry him from England – that Mr. Robinson would hear nothing of him till he (Benfield) and Fingal [James Macpherson] had pledged themselves for him —!' Macartney justified himself in respect of the loan, which he had offered to repay in India, but made no comment on the other allegation.[1]

The reasons why Macpherson and Benfield should press him as a candidate are easy to see, and are apparent from the whole tenor of their later relations with him. They thought he would be a respectable figure-head, and not only under obligations to them but, through his ignorance of Indian affairs and his lack of connections in Madras, easily swayed by them. Laurence Sulivan, as his letters to Hastings show, was actuated by similar motives, though in his case he hoped that the new governor would show due deference to the governor-general. As it happened both were wrong. Macartney was a proud man, and basically an honest one. There is no doubt that his original purpose in seeking to go to India was to make his fortune and that he did not mean to stay there any longer than was necessary for this end; but he was not prepared to blacken his reputation in the process. Nor was he prepared to be treated *de haut en bas* by Hastings. Moreover, as his campaign went on he came genuinely to believe that he could serve his country in India. In October he wrote to Lady Ossory:

In truth I am so deeply engaged in Indian affairs, that I grow an enthusiast on the subject. A voyage to Asia is become a sort of passion, and I am determined to go there in some capacity or other if any can be found suitable to the situations in which I have already served. . . . The East Indies are an object of immense magnitude and are still Ours, but if they continue to be administered as they have been, God knows how long we shall keep them.[2]

His governorship (like most of his achievements) was composed more of failure than success, but whatever the circumstances of his election to it, it marked a definite step forward in the provision of disinterested administration in British India.

Macartney's method of campaigning was in one way unusual. Appointments were normally made by the Court of Directors, though they could be challenged and brought before the Court of Proprietors. At least two of the senior servants from Madras, one of whom would have normally hoped to succeed to the governorship, had made formal application to the directors many months before. Macartney did not make his until 9 October, when his canvas of the proprietors had been proceeding apace for about two months, a

1. Memorandum, Fort St George, 22 Apr. 1782 [by J. C. Hippisley] India Office Library, microfilms. Macartney MSS. Roll 1543. For this and the preceding reference I am also indebted to Mr J. Gurney.
2. Macartney to Lady Ossory, 13 Oct. 1780. Fitzpatrick MSS. National Library of Ireland, Dublin MS. 8012 (iv).

breach of 'established usage' much disapproved of by his com-
petitors.[1] His approach was nevertheless realistic. There was
widespread dislike in the company to the intervention of an outsider
with government support;[2] even the sympathy of all the directors
was not to be counted on,[3] and the opposition party among the
proprietors was strong and organized; and in fact Macartney and his
allies had to meet the challenge of two General Courts before his
success was assured. Had the company opposition not been thrown
into disarray by the unsuitability of all the Madras servants implica-
ted in the recent disorder, had he and his allies not mounted a powerful support from the press,[4] and had he himself not campaigned
vigorously and created an excellent impression by his speeches in
the General Courts, it is very doubtful whether he would have won
the day, whatever his official support.

For the fourth point of interest which arises in connection with
this incident is the evidence it provides of the methods used by
administration in influencing company elections at this period, and
the limits of the powers they could exert. Macartney's papers are
unfortunately widely scattered, but it happens that almost all which
concern his election are preserved in the Public Record Office of
Northern Ireland in Belfast.[5] No comparable documentation has so
far come to light. The occasion is not perhaps an ideal one for
illustrating the administration's activities in company elections. In
the first place the campaign took place in the midst of the 'snap'
general election of 1780, so that prominent government managers
such as John Robinson and Charles Jenkinson, normally active in
Indian conflicts, were heavily engaged elsewhere. In the second
place, so complete was the confusion of his opponents that the
forces which administration were prepared to put at his disposal
were not in the event required. The first General Court where an

1. John Call (printed copy of the case he presented to the Directors 30 Oct. 1780,
reminding them of his earlier application), P.R.O. Northern Ireland, Macartney MSS.
D.O.D. 572/19/46 and Claude Russell letter to the Court of Directors, 23 Sept. 1780
(*ibid*. D.O.D. 572/19/36).

2. See letters from Francis Sykes to Warren Hastings, *e.g.* 5 Jan. 1781, B.M.Add.
MS. 29147, fo. 12ᵛ.

3. Richard Barwell writing to Hastings 15 Sept. 1780 (B.M. Add. MS. 29145, fo.
521ᵛ) did not speak for all the directors, but no doubt represented the views of some of
them. 'The pursuit of my Lord Macartney I have reason to think is not agreeable to the
Directors yet they dare not tell him their real sentiments and by hiding them . . . it
will be too late when his Canvass is compleated and they have acquiesced I am satisfied
on a supposition the Proprietor [*sic*.] will negative his application.' Barwell thought they
probably would.

4. Particularly in the *Public Advertiser* a paper much favoured by John Macpherson.

5. The only other correspondence from Macartney relevant to this issue are letters
to Lady Ossory in the Fitzpatrick MSS. in the National Library of Ireland and part of a
letter to Sir George Staunton dated 18 Sept. 1780 in the Osborn Collection, Yale
University Library (I am indebted to Dr Osborn for a copy of it). It is the original of a
letter quoted in *Memoir of the late Sir George Staunton, Bart.* (privately printed) 1823,
pp. 254–5.

attempt was made on 23 November 1780 to block his nomination was only moderately attended.[1] At the second, when his appointment was confirmed on 21 December 1780, there was a large attendance and speeches were made on both sides, but a division was not attempted.[2]

The material on the election in the Macartney MSS. falls under three main headings. The first is a certain amount of correspondence from canvassers and those who were canvassed. Some of it is from Macartney's personal friends, some from members of administration and East Indian politicians. There are also copies of circulars from Macartney himself. Of more importance is the material which bears on the constituency for which he was canvassing. This consists of what was called 'the printed list of proprietors'.[3] Though there must have been numbers of these lists about on this and other occasions, it is the only one so far known. It is not the official list of the proprietors of East India Stock, drawn up by the company's officers to check votes at elections.[4] It is not strictly accurate (those using it added in manuscript names that had been omitted); it does not include the names of proprietors resident outside the British Isles, though these were entitled to vote, and, unlike the official lists, it is not arranged strictly alphabetically. Entries for residents in what it calls 'The City of London etc Westminster and Suburbs' are broken down into 133 small topographical units in alphabetical order, from 'Admiralty' to 'Whitehall', with an extra heading at the end for 'Persons without any Residence specified' (chiefly army and navy officers). Within each unit the names of proprietors are placed in alphabetical order and the number of votes each can exercise is marked against him. The names of proprietors in the rest of England and Wales are entered alphabetically under the counties in which they reside. There are entries for Scotland (9 proprietors), Ireland (7) and Alderney (1).

This is clearly a list intended for canvassing purposes, and a product of private enterprise. We know something about earlier lists of a similar kind, and can, indeed, date their origin. On 12 January 1765 John Walsh wrote to Lord Clive 'I enclose you a list of proprietors which they have printed in a new manner; foreigners and trustees are omitted'. He adds 'The amount of the stock in the list is fifteen hundred and odd thousand pounds, not half the Company's capital'. A little later he mentions that Laurence Sulivan

1. India Office Library. East India Company Court Book B96, pp. 398–9. The division was 79 to 60.

2. *Ibid.* p. 471 and Press reports, *e.g. St James's Chronicle*, 19–21 Dec. 1780.

3. Northern Ireland P.R.O. D 2225/4/60. There is a preface showing it was primarily intended for use in the annual election of directors, and at the end there is a list of the directors and a summary of the votes in London, Westminster and suburbs.

4. There is a printed copy of this official list for 1773 in the British Museum (B.M. 8022.b.33). The India Office Library also has a copy in vol. 404 of its *Tracts*, where there are also some later lists.

was 'printing off lists of Proprietors in small pocket books with broad margins for the use of his canvassers. . . . We have followed his example.'[1]

The 1780 list contains 1,040 names – a reduction in numbers from 1765 less than might have been expected, since the voting qualification had been raised from £500 to £1,000 stock in 1773, and the old abuse of 'splitting' stock for voting purposes had been abolished.[2] Of the 1,040 voters 765 lived in the area described as 'the City of London etc Westminster and Suburbs' and 112 more lived in Essex (17), Middlesex (56) and Surrey (39) which were largely in the Metropolitan area. Only in Hampshire (15) and Kent (22) was there any other concentration of voters. If the residents in Essex, Middlesex and Surrey are added to those in the London area, only 163 voters are left in the rest of the British Isles. The great majority of voters held no more than £1,000 stock which was the qualification for a single vote. There were only 14 Persons who held the £10,000 or more which qualified them for the exercise of four votes (all but one resident in the London area and nearly all with close East Indian affiliations).[3] Twenty-three (also most of them in the Metropolitan area and with East Indian affiliations) held £6,000–£10,000, qualifying them for three votes. About 80[4] held £3,000–£6,000, qualifying them for two votes. The distribution of votes lends colour to Burke's claim (no doubt exaggerated) that the chief purpose of holding East India stock at this time was the political one of being able to dispose of a vote at India House.[5] The size of the constituency and the elaborate arrangements for canvassing it effectively emphasize the fact that in East Indian, as in National, elections much depended on the effort and personality of the candidate himself. In 1774 when Sir Thomas Rumbold first stood for the governorship of Madras, with full backing from the administration and the majority of the directors,

1. Powis MSS. (India Office Library), 12 Jan. and 14 Feb. 1765. See Sutherland, *East India Company in Eighteenth Century Politics*, pp. 132–3.

2. The 1765 list was, however, drawn up when most of the collusive 'split' votes had been returned to their owners. Sutherland, *op. cit.*, p. 132, n. 4.

3. They were James Alexander (Ireland), formerly serving in Madras and Bengal: Charles Boone, M.P., formerly Governor of Bombay: John Courtoy (of Oxenden Street, London): Lionel Darell, junior, (later M.P.) formerly serving in Bengal, East India Director: Josias Dupré, formerly Governor of Madras: Welbore Ellis, M.P., Secretary of State for America: Robert Gregory, M.P., East India director and formerly a free merchant in Bengal: Edwin Lascelles, M.P., of the well-known sugar family. Though not active in its business he had connections (see p.226): Henry Lyell, long a large proprietor: John Pardoe, prominent supporter of Lord Sandwich in company politics: Brigadier-General Richard Smith, formerly in the company's army, prominent creditor of the Nawab of Arcot, and at this time leader of the opposition in the company: Francis Sykes, formerly a prominent Company Servant in Bengal: James Walto (of Throgmorton Street).

4. The document is occasionally smudged, and this figure may be a little out.

5. Ninth Report of the Select Committee appointed to take into Consideration the State of the Administration of Justice in Bengal . . . (Reprinted in Bohn ed. of the *Works of Edmund Burke*, iv. 6–7.

and without Macartney's disadvantage of being an outsider, he was defeated, though narrowly, by Lord Pigot. Experts attributed his defeat to his failure to make enough personal effort to win over voters.[1] Macartney made no such error.

Even more valuable is the material available to show what influence Administration could exert if it so wished, and how they did so. It consists of a series of lists, and two letters accompanying them, together with a few rough lists made out by Macartney on the strength of information from friends (Lady Ossory for instance produced the names of thirteen persons from whom she hoped – not in all cases accurately – for support).[2] The first group of lists are six in number, identical in format and written in the same clerkly hand. They seem to have accompanied a letter from Anthony Todd, secretary of the General Post Office. The part played by the post office in national and city elections is well-known.[3] It is not surprising to find it also active in East Indian elections, and this the more since Anthony Todd was a brother-in-law of John Robinson. He wrote to Macartney on 6 September:

'The Dissolution of Parliament has made it so busy a Time here, that I have hardly kept my Word with Your Lordship respecting the Lists inclosed, some persons in which you may be so secure of already as to make it not at all necessary to apply to them, and there may perhaps be some few more in the General Printed List of Proprietors besides, whom upon a Pinch one might speak to or make interest with, but many that I so allude to I daresay Mr. Robinson will secure.'[4]

His own list contains ten names of those who can be counted on 'to oblige Mr. Todd' and twelve more 'which Mr. Todd can very well ask'.[5] There are also four short lists originating with individuals – 'Mr. Lascelles List' ('9 sure and 10 at least not likely to be against you') 'Mr. Gompertz List' (eleven names) 'Mr. Boehm's List' (nine names), 'Mr. Robert Nixon and Mr. Portis's List' (seventeen), and one from 'Mr. Burt, Egham Surrey' (eleven names)[6] in a different hand. There are occasional overlaps, but the names of some fifty persons said to be either prepared or likely to give support are listed. Also included is a longer list headed 'Ordnance List, if Lord Sandwich & Government approve'.[7] The reference to the approbation of Lord Sandwich as well as government is significant, confirming as it does the interest he was known to foster in East Indian elections.[8] It contains forty-four names, many of them also appearing

1. Sutherland *op. cit.* p. 289.

2. P.R.O. Northern Ireland, D.O.D. 572/20/6/3–/6–/8.

3. K. Ellis, *The Post Office in the Eighteenth Century. A Study in Administrative History* (1958).   4. P.R.O. Northern Ireland D.O.D. 572/19/21.

5. *Ibid.* D.O.D. 572/20/6/4.   6. *Ibid.*, D.O.D. 572/20/6/1 –/5 –/7 –/1.

7. *Ibid.*, D.O.D. 572/20/6/4.

8. Sandwich was a keen supporter of Macartney (see his letter of 3 December 1780. *Ibid.*, D.O.D. 572/7/65.)

on other lists. It would seem that these lists provided by the post office were intended to assist Macartney in his canvas; apart from the twelve persons whom 'Mr. Todd can well ask' there is no suggestion of any initiative being taken by the post office itself.

The second group of documents is of a different kind. They come from the Treasury and consist of a letter from William Brummell, private secretary to the first lord, acting as an understudy for John Robinson – the first evidence we have that he was accustomed to enact this role in the Treasury's East Indian activities. He wrote on 30 September:

'Upon looking over my Indian Papers I do not find any one of the several States of Canvasses in which I have had any Concern – The Inclosed List I have therefore made from Memory, but I am sure I have omitted several of those who usually support Government in their India Contests. The Memorandums [sic] opposite the Names in the Inclosed List merely suggest the Lines of Interest which may influence Them, or serve to mark the Connections of Office – Those Names to which is affixed *Government* are usually applied to directly from the *Treasury* – There are a few before whom I have made *Crosses* to denote that they are intimate Friends of my own, and whom I can personally as well as officially apply. – If this Short State can in any Shape serve as a key to Your Lordship's Information, or be in the least degree usefull to You, I shall be very happy. . . .[1]

The list referred to [2] consists of 259 names arranged in alphabetical order, each with an entry against it showing one or more channels of approach. 158 of the 259 names have the word 'Government' (or occasionally 'Government–Treasury') written against them showing that they were 'usually applied to directly from the Treasury', 40 of these are also marked by the cross which indicates that they are Brummell's personal friends. Forty-two out of the 158 have, however, also an alternative channel of approach, either another government department or a prominent individual, 101 of the 259 do not bear the entry 'Government or Government–Treasury' against them. They have instead the names of one or more influential individuals. Only one of these names stands out as a big patron. It is, as might be expected, that of Lord Sandwich whose entry, twenty-three voters, is the biggest after that of the Treasury itself. Macartney's correspondence shows that he won Sandwich's personal support.[3] It seems clear that Macartney was not expected to canvass those on the list whom the Treasury normally applied to, but to concern himself with the others.

1. *Ibid.* D.O.D. 572/19/38.
2. *Ibid.* D.O.D. 572/20/6/10.
3. Two out of 23 are marked both 'Government' and 'Lord Sandwich'. In 3 cases the name of Sir George Wombwell, the Director who was the most prominent East India supporter is added to his own. Otherwise, approach through Lord Sandwich alone is proposed.

That Brummell's list of regular Treasury supporters is a reasonably reliable one is supported by some corroborative evidence. On 6 June 1781 John Robinson wrote to Charles Jenkinson that in preparation for a controversial General Court, he had sent personal letters to 12 persons and circular letters to 150 others.[1] This corresponds closely to the 154 on Brummell's list. Moreover, there is preserved among the Burke MSS. at the Northamptonshire Record Office a list in a clerk's hand endorsed by Burke 'India Proprietors applied to by the late Treasury.'[2] We do not know how it came into his hands. Internal evidence shows it to date from 1781 or 1782. It contains more names than Brummell's, 176 as against 154, and the names of ten Peers, all government supporters are appended. It omits some names Brummell had included, but includes some which Brummell had put down as under the influence of other departments or of individuals; reading through the two lists it is easy to identify the hard core of the government supporters in East Indian elections. Its strength lay primarily in a combination of prominent men in the city and of minor office-holders.

An analysis of its personnel would no doubt be of interest; what is significant for the purpose of this study is the fact that in contests at India House where as many as 800 votes might be cast on occasion, hardly more than 150 voters were in receipt of the direct Treasury 'whip', and the whip itself was used only when it became urgently necessary.

1. B.M. Add. MS. 38216, fo. 192. Quoted Sutherland, p. 276.
2. Northamptonshire Record Society, A.XXIX 43.

A LETTER FROM JOHN STEWART, SECRETARY
AND JUDGE ADVOCATE OF BENGAL, 1773

A MONG the papers of the second Marquess of Rockingham, statesman and patron of Edmund Burke, which have been deposited by Lord FitzWilliam in the Sheffield Public Library[1], there is a lively account of his impressions of Bengal written by one John Stewart, dated 7 March 1773. The account gives evidence of an alert and somewhat journalistic intelligence rather than of any depth of insight or knowledge, but it is a good illustration of the impact of the country on an educated Briton of his day, and contains two features of special interest—its writer was closely associated with Warren Hastings in his first years as Governor of Bengal; and, since Stewart was intimate with Edmund Burke[2], the latter is likely to have read this letter at a time when his contacts with and interest in Bengal were still very limited.

John Stewart was a Scottish adventurer, a relative it would seem of Archibald Stewart, wine merchant of York Buildings, Buckingham Street, the Jacobite Provost of Edinburgh in 1745, and his son another John Stewart[3], who was active in the affairs of the East India Company in the 1760's and early 1770's as the 'jackal' of Sir George Colebrooke, one of the leading figures in the Court of Directors[4]. In 1771, through the influence of Colebrooke, Stewart was appointed Judge Advocate of Bengal with the reversion to the Secretaryship[5], and went out with a personal recommendation to Hastings, whom he accompanied to Bengal. He owed his appointment to Sir George Colebrooke, and

1. I am indebted to the Earl FitzWilliam and the Trustees of the Wentworth-Woodhouse estate for permission to make use of and print this document.

2. See letters in the FitzWilliam MSS. (Sheffield).

3. The first trace so far found of him is in 1761 when his address was York Buildings (Royal Society of Arts, Subscription Book). There were at least four men named John Stewart or Stuart at this time concerned in East India affairs, and their identification presents considerable difficulty.

4. See L. S. Sutherland, *The East India Company in Eighteenth Century Politics.* Oxford, 1952, *passim.*

5. East India Company Court Book 79, p. 323.

had been strongly recommended for employment by Lord Rockingham[6], urged on by Edmund Burke, who had known him for some years and who had a high opinion of him. His reason for seeking employment in India, was the financial straits to which he had been reduced since 1769 by the collapse of the fortunes of Lauchlin Macleane (an adventurer of much more note who also sought refuge in India[7]), with whom he had been intimately associated.

His qualifications to hold offices and to supersede experienced Company servants[8] were not obvious. He had received, as he claimed 'a liberal education', had travelled in America, France and Italy[9], is believed to have written various pamphlets on East India affairs in 1767[10], certainly wrote in the newspapers against the Grafton Administration in 1769[11], and in 1768 was sent by the Secretary of State Lord Shelburne on a confidential mission to Corsica, on which he wrote an interesting report published in Lord FitzMaurice's *Life of Lord Shelburne*[12]. On the other hand his private life was scandalous[13], he had seen the inside of a debtor's prison[14], and he had failed to make his way in the world. Hastings, however, spoke well of his work[15] (though he later stated "I never placed any confidence in John Stewart")[16] and he was personally well-liked. After his early death a friend wrote, I never think of his wit and sociality without regret"[17].

6. Rockingham had supported his unsuccessful application to go out as Secretary to the Commission of Three Supervisors sent out to India in 1769, whose ship was lost on the way out (FitzWilliam MSS. (Sheffield) J. Stewart to E. Burke, 24 September 1769), and also his attempt to be elected Secretary of the Society for the Encouragement of Arts, Manufactures and Commerce in 1770. (Royal Society of Arts. Loose Archives A6/72.)

7. Sutherland, *op. cit.*

8. Hastings had protested mildly against this, *e.g.*, Letter to L. Sulivan, 10 February 1770. Quoted G. R. Gleig, *Memoirs of the Life of the Right Hon. Warren Hastings*, 1841, 1, 187-8.

9. See his memorandum to the Society for the Encouragement of Arts, Manufactures and Commerce.

10. See the volume numbered 189 in the pamphlet collection in the London Library, St. James's Square.

11. FitzWilliam MSS. (Sheffield) letter referred to in n. 6 above.

12. ii, 123 *seq.*

13. See the scurrilous *Memoirs of Mrs. Anne Bailey containing a narrative of her various adventures in life*. Printed for the author, 1771.

14. In 1765. Publ. Rec. Off. King's Bench Prisons Commitment Books. Prisons 4/vol. 3, p. 434.

15. Letter quoted by Gleig, *op. cit.*, i, 189. "I am much pleased with Mr. Stuart. He is a sensible man and appears to possess a good temper."

16. *Ibid*, Add. MS. 29129, f. 24. W. Hastings to S. Pechell, 23 February 1782.

17. *Ibid*. Add. MS. 29143, f. 82. J. MacPherson to W. Hastings, 13 February 1779.

His career in India was destined to be a short one. On the arrival of General Clavering, Colonel Monson and Philip Francis he fell a victim to their partizan reforming zeal. He was dismissed from his offices in 1775[18], and after an unsuccessful attempt to get the Supreme Court to intervene on his behalf[19]; he sailed for England, determined to demand redress from the Court of Directors. Arriving there in September or October 1776, he was in time to play a part in the curious incident of the resignation of Warren Hastings offered by Hastings's agent Lauchlin Macleane[20], and to benefit by the private clauses of the agreement which accompanied it, to reinstate Hastings's friends. It was not, however, till 1777 that he was promised in lieu of his former positions that of a member of the Bengal Board of Trade, and some months later that he sailed for India[21]. Nor did he reach his destination for he died of tuberculosis in 1778 on the voyage leaving a penniless newly-married wife[22] and an illegitimate son, who later entered the Company's military service. While in England he was elected a Fellow of the Royal Society and published in the *Philosophical Transactions* of 1777 'An account of the Kingdom of Thibet, in a letter from John Stewart, F.R.S., to Sir John Pringle, Bart. F.R.S.', incorporating the report of his friend George Bogle, whom Warren Hastings had sent on a mission in the hope of opening up intercourse with that unknown land[23]. Stewart's account made some impression, being translated into French and Italian.

FitzWilliam MSS. (Sheffield) R77-10-6[24].

Calcutta, Bengal.

7th March 1773.

My Lord,

By the opportunity of Captain Hamilton's return to England I present my most humble respects to your Lordship from Bengal taking advantage of permission which your Lordship was pleased to grant me when I had the honour to wait on you to take leave before I came away.

18. Hastings reported what had happened to Lord North on 20 November 1775 (Brit. Mus. Add. MS. 29127, f. 234).
19. Vansittart MSS., Bisham Abbey. George Vansittart's European Letter Book iii, 121-4. G. Vansittart to J. Graham, 25 November 1775.
20. Stewart gave verbal testimony in support of Macleane's assertion that he was authorised to resign on Hastings's behalf.
21. Brit. Mus. Add. MS. 29138, ff. 424 *seq.* J. Stewart to W. Hastings, 23 May 1777.
22. Johanna Maria Murray d. of William Murray of Jamaica. See her letters to Hastings. Brit. Mus. Add. MS. 29143, f. 303, and Add. MS. 29147, f. 306.
23. See India Office Library Orme MSS. O.V. 71.4, and Home Miscellaneous, Vol. 118.
24. The punctuation and spelling of the original have been preserved, but contractions have been expanded and the use of capitals adjusted to modern usage.

I wish I had any thing to communicate worthy your Lordships notice. Occurrences at present are few, and I feel myself from my situation rather restrained from such speculations and observations on the state of things here as might be acceptable to your Lordship. I may be permitted however to say that I have found Bengal on a near view to be an object even exceeding in importance what I had conceived it to be at a distance. Under whatever name it is held I foresee that it may be always made one of the brightest jewells in the British Crown and I am confident, one of the most easy to be secured.

It is almost impossible in imagination to exceed the real beauty, fertility, and convenience for trade which this country exhibits, and even for the salubrity of its climate; if the last year was a fair specimen I know none equal to it. By the returns made to me of the burials in Calcutta of Whites of our Communion including soldiers, sailors, women and children etc. etc. there were only 170 died, and I am confident the whole number of that body of people cannot be less than 7 or 8000 in the place, for in the article of women I include all the Mestizes[25] etc. that live with the white men, and their children of course go in the list. Of near 230 Company's civil servants in Bengal only 2 died[26].

The heats here begin about the latter end of this month and continue till June. The mercury in the thermometer rises to a great height in that time, but the weather much more tolerable than I have felt it in North America during their summer months. In June last I had it often at 106 in my tent on a tour up the country with the Governor[27] and we were all in health and spirits at the time. While the rains continue it is pleasant and healthy. In about October and till the latter end of November when the rains first begin to take off, it is sickly and disagreeable enough, but in December the north wind from the high mountains of Napal and Thibet covered with eternal snows, set in, and make I believe the pleasantest climate in the universe for 3 compleat months. We all get into cloths and shauls and sleep under 2 or 3 blankets. The air is clear and sharp, the sun shining always out and not one drop of rain. In this time we eat, drink and take all sorts of exercise as in Europe. Indeed almost all the year round you have garden stuff of every kind in the greatest abundance, a thing

25. Women of mixed race. A term originally used of inhabitants of Goa born of a Portuguese father and Indian mother.

26. Stewart was unusually lucky in his experience during this year. The mortality was often considerably higher.

27. Stewart accompanied Warren Hastings in his tour upcountry to Murshidabad etc. which began on 3 June and lasted for two and a half months.

unknown in the rest of India, and you have beef, mutton, veal as in London and some excellent fish such as what we call a manga[28] fish which is the most delicious of all fish that swims.

I had imagined the country to be exceeding low from the annual overflowing of the lands, but I found it almost every where finely elevated above the common bed of the waters. Indeed in the summer when the Ganges comes down it fills it to the top of its banks and spreads creeks canals and communications every where. The whole country is then alive and commodities of all sorts are transported 1000 miles at almost the same expence that it would cost you to bring them from Dorking to London. I have calculated that at the price of grain last season in some of the distant provinces a man might live for 3 rupees per annum, but if you gave him 4 he could live like a prince[29]. A rupee is about 2/4 sterling.

Perhaps your Lordship would not dislike I should attempt giving you some notion of this city of Calcutta. You will then imagine a large river very much resembling the Thames at London, but broader and much more deep and rapid. Along its banks bending into a large arch, the town stretches itself for near 4 English miles and runs back about one in breadth. The quarter inhabited by the English is the lowest on the river and is laid off in regular and wide streets with spacious and showy houses, such as in appearance eclipse, (not to speak of London) almost any thing in Paris or Italy. I say in appearance for they will not bear an examination, they are all of brick plaistered over and whitewashed, but all attempt some order of architecture and you see nothing but portico's, columnades, galleries, etc. etc. some few in good taste, several tolerable, and many more wretchedly bad. However the approach to the town in front of the Esplanade of the new Fort[30], presents you at a distant (*sic*) with an appearance more of a city of antient Greece or Asia (according to my notions) than any thing I ever beheld. The other quarters of the town are a mixture of miserable huts and old Moorish and Indian kelhats[31] and seraglios where they (*sic*) inhabitants mew themselves up with their women and servants unvisited by Europeans or indeed by one another.

28. Mango fish.
29. This would seem to be an exaggeration even in remote districts. At Kasimbazar in 1739 the pay of a coolie was 2 rupees a month. S. Bhattacharya, *The East India Company and the Economy of Bengal from 1704 to 1740*, 1954, p. 204-5.
30. The new fort which Clive had begun to build for the defence of Calcutta and which was now nearing completion. The Esplanade was the official centre of the city.
31. Kalhat[ti], a collection of huts (?).

I know of no rule by which to compute the inhabitants of a place, but when I observe the extent of the town the numbers of people that appear stufled (*sic*) into one hut, and the eternal croud which fills the streets and bazars I should not hesitate to say that there are to a third or a fourth near as many inhabitants in Calcutta as in London["][32].

The city of Moorshedabad the residence of the Nabob[33] is still larger than Calcutta and was formerly much more inhabited, it is now falling off every day. I went there with Mr. Hastings on business of no insignificant importance[34] and had then an opportunity of observing very near, the manners, forms and intrigues of an Asiatic Court. The splendour however of that of Moorshedabad is almost gone. We put the finishing stroke to it. I own I felt a degree of compassion and remorse when I saw so many great families sinking into indigence, and proud Musselman Lords excluded from honours, profits and employments and obliged to bend to the ground before a parcel of *Fringuis*[35] from t'other end of the world, whom a few years ago they hardly regarded as on a level with their dogs. When I considered however the treatment these same Mahometans bestowed upon the Hindoes (*sic*) the original inhabitants I got over my remorse.

I cannot conceive how any person at Home can entertain a doubt of our being able to hold this country, when we see how long the Mahometans have kept it, so inferiour to us either in policy or the art of war, and more detested I believe by the natives. The number

32. The population of London at this time was estimated at about 700,000; opinions varied greatly as to that of Calcutta.

33. The Nawab of Bengal, at this time the minor Mubarakud-Daulah.

34. Hastings said of his visit there, "This period was employed in settling the collections and the government of the districts dependent on Moorshedabad ......in reducing the Nabob's stipend from thirty-two lacs to sixteen......in reducing his pension list, and other expences; in forming, recommending and executing a new arrangement of his household; and in framing a new system for conducting the business of the Dewannee, or revenue" (quoted Gleig, *op cit.*, 1, 261). These changes were the result of the Company's decision to "stand forth as Dewan" of Bengal.

35. Feringis, Frangis or Franks, Arab term originally used to denote the inhabitants of Western Europe. The hard lot of the nobility at the Nawab's Court was recognised in the official report. "Some hundreds of persons of the ancient nobility of the country, excluded under our government from almost all employments, civil or military, had ever since the revolution depended on the bounty of the Nabob. It is not that the distribution was always made with judgement and impartiality......but when the question was to cut off the greatest part, it could not fail to be accompanied with circumstances of real distress. The President [Hastings] declares that even with some of the highest rank he could not avoid discovering under all the pride of Eastern manners, the manifest marks of penury and want." (General Letter, Secret Department, 10 November 1772, quoted M. E. Monckton Jones, *Warren Hastings in Bengal 1772-1774*, Oxford, 1918, pp. 191-2.)

of Musselman bear not the smallest proportion to the Hindoos. The differences of their manners are strongly marked. The Musselmans are active, proud, despotic, liberal, cruel, and the most easy and polite in their address of any people I have ever met with. The French are clowns to them. The Hindoos are gentle, indolent, submissive, covetous, and rather awkward and reserved in their address. I feel a great veneration for the antient Rajahs of the country. We look upon them very unjustly as meer (*sic*) officers of Government in their quality of Zamindars[36], but they are in fact the true nobility of the country, and the people feel them as such. They are what our feudal Lords were and have their retainers about them in the same manner, keeping up much of the state and dignity of that character. Your Lordship may judge of what consequence a man may become who enjoys, as many of them does (*sic*), an estate of, to the amount of 40, or 50,000 pounds sterling per annum, in a country and of a religion that allows him to eat nothing but rice. How many mouths may he not feed ?

Your Lordship will naturally expect that I should say something of the state of defence of this country, particularly against a European enemy. First I must observe that if our Ministry are any thing watchful I think it impossible the French should ever be able to send a great force here, without our having a greater at their heels, but supposing they were, they can only come on this coast in a certain season. The landing is almost impracticable but in the river and the entry is the most difficult navigation in the world. We could at all times take up the buoys. If they could even push up, they would meet a post called Brunswick which commands the river absolutely lately erected by Colonel Campbell[37] that would be exceedingly difficult to force. If they disembarked their troops below it on either side, they would meet a country intersected with creeks and nullas where they might be continually harassed and opposed at every pass. If after all they arrive at Calcutta they would find a morsel in the new Fort which they could not digest. According to my notions, it ought to be, if properly garrisoned, impregnable to any thing that can attack it in this country[38]. If one was to reckon by what it cost, it should be stronger

36. The Zamindars, originally officers of government of the Mughal Empire, but became with the passing of time more in the nature of hereditary landowners, contained in their number many descendants of the pre-Mughal aristocracy. The nature of the Zamindar's position was to lead to much dispute in England. Stewart's opinion, though expressed differently from that which Philip Francis later advanced was not dissimilar from it.

37. Colonel Archibald Campbell, formerly of Bombay, the Chief Engineer.

38. Hastings, unlike Philip Francis, always maintained that Bengal was, "incapable of attack by sea", though he feared attack from land in alliance with an Indian ally.

than Luxembourg, Lisle and Bergen op Zoom put together", but it is in fact a noble, commodious and strong fortification and as far as it has been finished by Campbell executed in a masterly manner. Little is wanting to compleat it. Both the body of the place and the outworks are in the best stile, the casemates airy and convenient, the ditches wide and clear, and there is a peculiar advantage attached to them, that you   may fill them and drain them twice every day, if you   chuse. Campbell's sluices are capital works.

While we suppose you an European enemy employed before Fort William, our force would be collecting; and having possession of all the provinces we have the revenues of course. There is now on this establishment about 28,000 men. We had lately a Review here of about 6 battalions with 16 pieces of cannon and I assure your Lordship they would have made a figure in Hyde Park. I mean as to the seapoys. They are well composed and well disciplined. The Europeans are well as to the last but if you won't allow us good men from Home we cannot make them here⁴⁰.

The   only Country Power from   which   we have any thing   to apprehend is the Mahrattas, and we are only open to them, and that in a small degree, by one way   I mean from the south west, and even there they have to penetrate through Midnapore, a province of small account before they could do us hurt. To the west we have the Beerboon Mountains⁴¹, the Soan⁴², the Carumnassa⁴³ and the Ganges to defend us and to the northward we are fenced in from all enemies by the frozen Tartar Wall, part I believe of the southern Caucasus⁴⁴, which stretches all along to the westward⁴⁵ as far as Assam and China. I have been very inquisitive about Assam since I came here without being able to obtain much information⁴⁶. I suspect however a communication with China that way would not be difficult, nor the distance   be found so great as the maps lay down. The river   of

39. The expense of the new fort had greatly exceeded expectations.

40. The Company had had to withdraw its Recruiting Bills of 1770 and 1771. Sutherland, *op. cit.*, p. 218.

41. The Birbhum Mountains, about 150 miles north west of Calcutta.

42. The river Son, a right-bank tributary of the Ganges.

43. The river Karamnasa, a smaller and more westerly right-bank tributary of the Ganges.

44. The Himalayas had been so described since Pliny and Strabo, though James Rennell's map has the name 'Himmaleh Mts.' at the eastern end of the range.

45. Stewart meant not 'westward' but 'eastward'.

46. For the contacts between Assam and Bengal at this time *see* S. K. Bhuyan, *Anglo-Assamese Relations* 1771-1826, Gauhati, Assam, 1949, pp. 67 *seq.*

Barrampoota" which we take hardly any notice of at Home is certainly one of the largest in the world. It is greater than the Ganges. We know nothing of it but that it enters our provinces from the east and pouring down an amazing flood of waters on the skirts of our territories, disembogues itself into the sea, near the mouth of the great Ganges by Sundeep".

We are now in all appearance ready to get into hostilities with the Mahrattas, about the Province of Corah[49] of which they have obtained a free grant from the Mogol, much as we obtained that of Bengal. That is to say after we had thrashed him, stript him and tyed his hands, with this difference that we only got a grant of what we had already, and would have kept without it, and the Mahrattas, of what they never had, nor will not now get. We defend these provinces with their own revenues and the Vizir Souja Dowla's money[50] who has called us in, and I believe the Mahrattas will think seriously before they enter into an offensive war with us or attack our own territories[51].

It is now about a year and a half since Shaw Allum the Great Mogol, tired out with waiting for our assistance to replace him on the throne of Delhi,[52] quitted to Korah Province and threw himself upon the Mohrattas (*sic*). They did carry him to Delhi and put him on the throne, but he soon found he was only their lieutenant. He quarrelled with them they fought, and in a pitched battle about 3 months ago which lasted from morn till night, he was defeated altho his two Seapoy battalions trained up under our officers (who were withdrawn afterwards) retreated in good order in the face of the whole Mahratta army of 50 thousand men[53]. I mention the Mogols condition

47. The river Brahmaputra.

48. The Island of Sandwip.

49. Kora. After the Mughal Emperor, Shah Alam, had put himself under the protection of the Marathas at Delhi in 1771, they persuaded him to cede to them the Provinces of Kora and Allahabad, assigned to the Emperor by Clive. The Company were not prepared to allow the transfer to take place.

50. Shuja-ud-daula, Vazir of Oudh. The Bengal Government were pledged to support him against the Marathas, in return for a fixed payment for the use of Company troops. In the following August, Hastings handed over these provinces to Oudh in return for a considerable sum, got the payment for the Company troops raised, but agreed to assist the Vazir in his plan of conquering the Rohillas.

51. Though minor brushes occurred, Stewart was correct in this assumption.

52. Ever since 1761 the intention to bring about his return to Delhi had been expressed by the Bengal Government, but steps had not been taken to implement the intention.

53. On 17 December, 1772. Stewart does not mention that the French mercenary troops under Rene Madec were the heroes of the day. J. Sarkar, *Fall of the Mughal Empire*, 2nd edn. Calcutta, 1952, iii, 48 *seq.*

at present that your Lordship may be better able to form an idea of the consideration which his ambassador Major Morrison[54] has a right to expect. He is gone Home to treat with his Majesty for a surrender to him of all which the Company now hold in India. By my notions it is little less than treason for any subject to accept of such a commission. We would not recognize him in that quality here, we are impatient to hear how he will be received at Home.

Your Lordship is undoubtedly acquainted with Mr. Hastings being at present Governor of Bengal, he was moved from Madrass. I came here with him, and have been happy enough to conciliate his intimate friendship and favour. I was appointed by my friend Sir G. Colebrooke[55] Judge Advocate with the reversion to the Secretaryship. I am now in possession of both and before I succeeded to the latter I lived with Mr. H. and acted as his private secretary. My appointments would allow me to lay up a good deal of money in any country but this, but the unavoidable expences are so great that I am afraid I shall not effect it, nor raise a Nabobs fortune soon unless I can strike out some concerns in the country to bring in a yearly profit, and I have some prospects that way.

I observe the cry is now up against the India Company and that she is marked out to be baited in Parliament[56]. I imagine she may be sweated but I am confident there are enough of good men in both Houses to prevent her from being sacrifized (*sic*) altogether either to ministerial power or popular clamour. I am too new here and of too little consequence to apprehend that my name will be bandied about in public, but I dare say Mr. Hastings will be mentioned and I am anxious that it be treated with the respect it deserves[57]. I dare say your Lordship is no stranger to the character he bears and to the general estimation in which he stands both with the Company and the world at large. I should be glad if I had leisure and permission to submit an account of his management here at the head of a great State

54. Major John R. Morrison, late of the Company's forces was sent to Calcutta by the Emperor to demand his tribute (which the Bengal Government refused to pay since he had put himself in the hands of their enemies). When disappointed he sailed for Europe in a foreign ship to put the Emperor's case before the King. Hastings was uneasy lest he should be received in England, but unnecessarily (letter to Sir G. Colebrooke of 14 January 1773 printed Gleig, *op. cit.*, i, 275 *seq.*).

55. In 1772-73 Chairman of the East India Company.

56. The enquiries preceding Lord North's Indian legislation of 1773.

57. Hastings's reputation stood on the contrary so high at this time that he was appointed first Governor General under the Regulating Act, Rockingham and his friends in Opposition protesting, however, on general grounds.

(as I may call Bengal) to your Lordship's judgement and knowledge in public affairs; perhaps I may obtain both and I am persuaded your Lordship will receive my attempt favourably. Indeed I acknowledge I have a design to introduce Mr. H. to your correspondence[58]. I have even hinted it to him. He seemed flattered with the notion, but is backward for fear it should appear intruding upon you. The high respect I entertain for your Lordship's rank and qualifications, and pardon my expression the warm friendship I bear to your person, would ever prevent me from introducing to your acquaintance a person unworthy of it, but I am positive you would look upon Mr. H. as an acquisition. His name your Lordship will observe is not such as you meet commonly in the list of India Governors and let me assure you, he possesses sentiments worthy of his name and both in education and manners as well as in talents is fit to fill any station with credit. His absence from England has kept him from entering much into our factions at Home, but with a true independent spirit he values good men of either side and has a peculiar respect for that set of men with whom your Lordship is particularly connected and with the party of which I may say your Lordship is the head.

I would not have taken up your Lordship's attention on this subject did I not mean as I have said before to introduce, some time or other Mr. Hastings to you. In a private capacity I am sure you will think him a valuable acquaintance and in a public light, I look upon it that in the line of public affairs which your Lordship is pleased to adopt, you will consider a Governor of Bengal as no loose card in the pack.

When I look over this desultory and uncorrect (*sic*) epistle I hardly know how to appologize (*sic*) for my presumption in addressing it to your Lordship. I sat down only to write a few lines conveying my respects and wishes for your health and prosperity. I have indeed been unlucky in some curiosities particularly in 2 Napal birds which by so good an opportunity as that of Hamilton I thought to have sent to your Lordship. They died in coming down. I must endeavour to make the loss up next year. While I remain in India I trust your Lordship will honour me with your commands of any sort where I can be of service to you. The Rockingham is gone down the river. I had no time while the public Despatches were on hand to write my own letters. I send them now express after the ship and I hope this will serve as my excuse for not transcribing and correcting this blotted peice (*sic*).

58. Hastings was a notoriously bad correspondent and did not follow this up.

I am happy to learn by Hamilton that Lady Rockingham has recovered her health so compleately[59] (*sic*).

With my most respectful compliments to your Lordship, allow me the honour to subscribe myself

My Lord Marquis
Your Lordships most obedient and
most humble servant
John Stewart.

59. Lady Rockingham had been seriously ill in 1771.

NEW EVIDENCE ON THE NANDAKUMA TRIAL

THE trial, condemnation and execution for forgery in Calcutta in 1775 of the Brahman Raja Nandakuma Bahadur (known to his English contemporaries as Nundcomar) [1] is one of the *causes célèbres* of the eighteenth century. That the accused, a man of sinister reputation, was guilty of the crime for which he suffered, hardly anyone doubted at the time and most writers have accepted since; on the trial itself opinions have varied, but most recent writers have concluded that (given contemporary conditions) it would seem to have been reasonably conducted; [2] but it was felt widely even at the time that the exaction of the death penalty was harsh, and it has always been generally admitted that the circumstances of the trial were such as to arouse suspicions of disavowed political forces at work, however much opinion may have varied as to the validity of the suspicions. Since the persons on whom these suspicions became focused were Warren Hastings, the first governor-general of Bengal and Sir Elijah Impey, Chief Justice of the supreme court recently set up to provide an independent judicature in Bengal, and since the fate of Nandakuma was entangled in the disputes between the governor-general and the majority of his council, partisanship has always played its part in invigorating the controversy to which the trial gave rise.

The case against Hastings and Impey was first put by their bitter personal and political enemies in its most extreme form and, though it was rejected in the debate on Impey's impeachment, [3] it inspired a still more formidable accuser in the person of the great

---

[1] An attempt has been made throughout this article to employ a modern form of Indian names as used in recent historical works; and where the eighteenth-century English .terms are transcribed, suggested modern renderings are included in the footnotes, though sometimes these are doubtful. I am indebted to Professor Habibullah, of Dacca University, Pakistan, and Mr. C. C. Davies, Reader in Indian History at Oxford, for assistance in this part of the work for which I have no qualifications.

[2] There were, by modern standards, some irregularities in the evidence allowed, and the judges themselves (owing to the weakness of counsel) took an active part in examining witnesses. That the jury, chosen from among the English inhabitants of Calcutta was not free of prejudice is probable in view of the heated atmosphere in which the trial took place.

[3] A full account of the proceedings with accompanying documents was published by Stockdale in 1788. (*The Speech of Sir Elijah Impey . . . together with copies of the several documents. . . .*)

publicist Macaulay.[1] To make the issue comprehensible an outline
of the circumstances of the trial is necessary. In the violent
dissensions which broke out on the Bengal council at the end of
1774 between General Clavering, Colonel Monson and Philip
Francis, ' the New Gentlemen ' on the one side and Warren Hastings
and Richard Barwell, the two old Company servants on the other,
the newcomers soon found individuals (a few Englishmen and a
number of Indians) who were prepared to seek their favour by
lodging accusations of corruption and misconduct against the
former régime over which Hastings had presided.   The methods of
Company rule, and the activities of the Company's servants in
seeking their fortunes, made such accusations easy to advance
against any Company servant who had been some years in India,
and they nearly always had some element of truth in them.   On the
other hand those who, through ambition or spite, advanced such
accusations were notoriously indifferent to truth, so that perjury
and even forgery were commonplaces on such occasions.

The newcomers, inexperienced and blinded by party spirit, were
ill equipped to sift the allegations brought before them, and they
had the good or ill fortune to attract to their cause Nandakuma, one
of the most ambitious and unprincipled of the Indians connected
with the Government of Bengal, who, after a lifetime of battle for
power, first under the Nawabs of Bengal and then under their
English successors, now saw the chance to turn their coming to his
advantage.   In addition to his experience, ability and absence of
scruple he had the advantage of having been in close touch with
Hastings's administration since 1772, when, on the Company's
orders, he had been employed in the investigations into the misdeeds
of his old rival Muhammad Reza Khan, Naib Subah of Bengal, and
he had at this time enjoyed considerable influence and power,
though no love had ever been lost between him and Hastings, and
he knew his position to be precarious.[2]   The rise to favour of such
a man with a majority of council anxious to discredit their opponents
was bound to mean the presentation of a mass of complaints and
accusations against the governor, the Company servants under him
and (equally important) their Indian clientèle, and to herald drastic
changes not only in the English administration but among the
Indian holders of places, farms and contracts.

The work was begun in 1774, and at the beginning of 1775 the
governor-general forbade Nandakuma his house,[3] but it was not

[1] T. B. Macaulay, *Critical and Historical Essays ; Warren Hastings.*
[2] There is no adequate account of the career of this remarkable man, though much
material for it (usually discreditable) is to be found among the sources for the period.
[3] Nandakuma's account of this is given in his own written statement presented
to council on 11 March 1775 printed in the *Eleventh Report of the Select Committee of
1782 : Reports from Committees*, vi. 706.   See also Hastings's evidence in the conspiracy
trial, *State Trials*, xx. 1179 *seq.*

till 11 March 1775 that the first written accusations were laid before council and battle was joined. Hastings refused to answer the allegations in council and the matter was referred by both sides to the authorities in England. But since no reply could be received for eighteen months, the campaign was carried on in Bengal without interruption. The governor, faced by a hostile majority, had the choice of resigning forthwith, of submitting to become a cypher in his own administration (awaiting helplessly the flow of accusations which would come in as those in search of places, or seeking to retain those they had, tried to win the favour of what they would consider the rising party), or of fighting to maintain his prestige and thus to hold his position until a decision arrived from England. Hastings was nothing if not a fighter and, though he sometimes talked of resignation, it was the third of these lines which he chose.

At first the Majority carried all before them, but a chance for the governor to retrieve the initiative came on 19 April 1775 when one Kamal-ud-din,[1] an Indian farmer of revenue appointed under his Government, came and confessed (for reasons that have never become altogether clear)[2] that he had made false accusations against Hastings and others under pressure from Nandakuma and an English free merchant Joseph Fowke who had thrown in his lot with the Majority.[3] Hastings at once brought the matter before the supreme court, which, after a hearing on 20 April, pronounced that a case lay for a charge of conspiracy by Hastings, Barwell, George Vansittart (member of the board of trade), Krishna Kantu Nandi[4] (Hastings's ' banyan ') and Ganga Govind Singh[5] (Diwan to the Calcutta committee) against Nandakuma, his son-in-law Radha Charan[6], Joseph Fowke and Francis his son.[7] On 24 April

[1] Known to the English as Commaul-ul-dien, or other variants.

[2] He was in considerable financial difficulties and for some time had been pulled between Nandakuma and Indian supporters of the Hastings party. The previous December Fowke had already got some damaging statements out of him which he had later disclaimed. (See evidence in the forgery and conspiracy trials, *State Trials*, xx. 1179 &c.)

[3] Joseph Fowke, 1716–1806. Went to India as writer 1736. Rose to third on council in Madras 1752 and returned to England with a moderate fortune. M. 1753 Elizabeth, d. of J. Walsh governor of Fort St. George and sister of Clive's close friend John Walsh, M.P. Having gambled away his fortune returned to India 1771, as a free merchant and engaged in the diamond trade. He had quarrelled with Hastings and, as his brother-in-law had recommended him to Philip Francis, he threw in his lot at once with the Majority, whom he sought out on their arrival to lodge his complaints with them.

[4] Known to the English as Cantoo Baboo.

[5] Known to the English as Gunga Govind.

[6] The English called him Radachurn. He was said by Vansittart to be ' banyan ' to Joseph Fowke. (Vansittart MSS., European letter-book iii. 103, letter to R. Palk, 3 August 1775.)

[7] The evidence against Francis Fowke was considered slight and he was not held to bail. He was included among the accused in Hastings's proceedings, but not in those of Barwell or Vansittart.

Hastings, Barwell and Vansittart announced their intention to proceed against them.[1]

The significance attributed to this move in the party battle is shown by the reaction of the Majority who, considering Nandakuma, as they said, ' a victim of State policy ' were indiscreet enough to pay him a formal visit as ' a public demonstration of our opinion that he was innocent '. A further incident on 2 May, when one Gholam Hussein, said to be in Nandakuma's employ, was imprisoned for trying to suborn Kamal-ud-din's ' munshi '[2] shows how hotly the case would have been contested had not a more dramatic development deflected attention from it.[3] But on 6 May Mohan Prasad,[4] executor of a rich Hindu banker, Bolaki Das,[5] lodged an accusation against Nandakuma (against whom civil proceedings had previously been attempted) alleging that at some time before the end of 1769 he had forged a bond to defraud the estate of the deceased, a bond to which the seals of three witnesses (one of them the Kamal-ud-din already involved in the conspiracy charges) were fraudulently attached. Two judges of the supreme court committed him to gaol for trial at the forthcoming assizes, and here, despite efforts by his patrons to get him bail, he stayed till his trial which began on 8 June, at which, after his witnesses had created a most unfavourable impression under cross-examination, he was found guilty on 16 June. He was condemned to death and, despite some efforts to obtain a respite, he was hanged on 5 August before a great crowd who till the end could scarcely believe that so influential a man would be executed, or that the blood of a Brahman would be shed.

To Macaulay, as to Hastings's and Impey's enemies, these facts spoke for themselves. Declaring that no-one, ' idiots and biographers excepted ', could doubt their guilt, he maintained that Hastings and Impey were guilty of the judicial murder of Nandakuma in order to close his mouth. This dramatic conclusion was never generally accepted, but it was not till Sir James Stephen wrote his *Story of Nuncomar and the Impeachment of Sir Elijah Impey* in 1885 that a serious attempt was made to refute it in detail.[6] Stephen, using his legal gifts to unravel the confusing account in the *State Trials*,[7] examined the evidence then available and came to the conclusion that both Impey and Hastings were entirely innocent.

The case against Impey was the easier to deal with. Not only has no direct evidence of his collusion with the governor-general

---

[1] See p. 254 below.   [2] Writer or secretary.   [3] See below, p. 256.
[4] Called by the English Mohan Persaud.   [5] Called by the English Boolaky Doss.
[6] Elijah Impey, son of the Chief Justice, wrote *Memoirs of Sir Elijah Impey* (1846) in defence of his father which, though confused and unsatisfactory, contained a good deal of material.
[7] The report in the *State Trials* (vol. xx) is a far from satisfactory record. Among other weaknesses it fails to make clear by whom the various witnesses were called.

ever come to light, but he acted throughout the trial in agreement
with his colleagues [1] (by no means all his loyal friends or those of
Hastings), and Nandakuma's counsel later paid tribute to his conduct
of the trial.[2] In dealing with the case against Hastings Stephen's
lawyer's approach was less useful. Since, if Hastings took any part
in the business at all, it was one which could hardly be expected to
appear in legal or other public records, Stephen had to content
himself with pointing out how hard it would be to prevent evidence
of any intervention leaking out over so many years, and with
arguing that Hastings had little to gain from such a conspiracy since
Nandakuma's accusations were already on record. His chief
contribution to the defence lay, however, in his attempt to show
that the curious felicity in the timing of the accusation, from the
governor-general's point of view, was purely accidental, and that
the accusation (long meditated) was made at the time it was because,
for reasons of legal routine, it could not have arisen earlier.[3]

Stephen's attempt to defend Hastings was violently attacked by
Henry Beveridge with more zeal and ingenuity than balance of
judgment in *The Trial of Maharaja Nanda Kumar*, . . . (Calcutta,
1886). More sober successors have agreed with part of what
Stephen argued but have thought that he went too far. This would
certainly seem to be the case. It is idle to argue that Hastings had
little to gain from the disgrace and punishment of Nandakuma, even
if there were at that stage no great gain in shutting his mouth. The
gain was the re-establishment of prestige among the Indian population and the checking of the flow of accusations from all sources.
John Stewart, Secretary of Bengal and a member of his ' family ',
makes this clear when he says, comparing those coming forward

[1] Justice Chambers expressed doubts on a point of law, but he did nothing during
the trial to dissociate himself from his brethren.

[2] In the debate on Impey's impeachment (*Parl. Hist.* xxvii. 443 *seq.* and *The Speech
of Sir Elijah Impey* Part III, appendix 1. 104 *seq.*). Impey's own account of his actions is
perhaps best put in a letter to Governor G. Johnstone, August 1778 preserved in his
manuscripts and reproduced by Stephen, *op. cit.* i. 255. For views on this letter see
Brit. Mus. Add. MS. 29143, fo. 79: John Macpherson to W. Hastings, 13 February 1779.

[3] Stephen (*op. cit* i. 90 *seq.*) hinges his argument on the date at which the relevant
documents were released by the civil court where they were held in connection with
earlier civil litigation. He argues that their release (which had been requested as early
as March 1774) was demanded to make possible the opening of a criminal prosecution,
and adduces in support of this contention the evidence of Thomas Farrer, Nandakuma's
counsel in the forgery trial, when Impey's impeachment was under consideration.
Farrer then said that James Driver, an attorney, had informed him in November 1774
that criminal proceedings were under consideration and that the documents had
' accordingly ' been asked for. (*Speech of Sir Elijah Impey*, Part III, Appendix 1. p. 105-6).
H. Beveridge, who in an article in *The Calcutta Review*, lxvi, had published an account
of the trial strongly antagonistic to Hastings, sought to refute Stephen in *The Trial
of Maharaja Nanda Kumar ; a Narration of a Judicial Murder* (Calcutta, 1886). He placed
no reliance on Farrer's evidence and believed the date of the release of the documents
to be of little relevance, since he argued that they were required for further civil and
not for criminal proceedings. Material in the Vansittart papers seems to confirm in
broad terms Stephen's interpretation of the events. (See p. 263 below.)

with accusations to the *delatores* of Nero's reign : ' I do not .. really believe the *Delatores* will come out very thick till they see how Nundcomar's ears hang in his head, that is to say, if he is not hung up head and tail and ears and all before the other [the conspiracy charge] is decided.' [1]   And, while earlier Hastings had lamented that all his Indian supporters were deserting him,[2] when the trial was over his friends told each other with satisfaction that he was ' in high credit '.[3] Nor is it easy to believe that the timing of the forgery charge was entirely fortuitous, and the writers who know most of Indian administration are the first to point this out.   It is from them that there comes a modified interpretation of the course of events.   As Mr. Woodruff says, agreeing with Mr. Penderel Moon,[4]

> Such a man would have in progress a dozen disputes and in-
> trigues in none of which would his conduct bear examination;
> some-one—no doubt a friend of Hastings, but Hastings need have
> said no word to him—someone stirred up the embers of a dying
> quarrel . . . [Nundcomar] was hanged for forgery according to the
> law of England, but the bazaars of Calcutta—to whom forgery was
> just as serious as accepting a few ounces of meat beyond the ration
> —the bazaars knew very well that Nundcomar was hanged for
> telling tales against the Governor-General.[5]

Some such explanation of the course of events seems extremely likely, and it is supported by what little circumstantial evidence there is.   Mohan Prasad, who brought the charge, was a follower of Hastings, high in his favour ; [6] the chief witness for the prosecu-tion was the same Kamal-ud-din whose timely complaints brought about the conspiracy charges, and both were in close touch with the most active Indian supporters of the Hastings party.   Hastings's most recent biographer, Dr. Keith Feiling, has in consequence accepted it as the basis for his treatment of the subject,[7] though he believes that, whatever Hastings's supporters did, he himself had no hand in it.   In reaching this conclusion he lays stress on Hastings's own statement made upon oath, when, in answer to the question, ' Did you directly or indirectly countenance or for-ward the prosecution ', he replied, ' I never did.   I have been on

[1] Brit. Mus. Add. MS. 29127, fo. 204: note by J. Stewart attached to the end of a letter from Hastings to Lauchlin Macleane and John Graham, 20 May 1775.   (Quoted in part by K. Feiling, *Warren Hastings*, 1955, p. 148.)

[2] *Ibid.* fo. 192ᵛ. W. Hastings to John Graham, 3 April 1775.

[3] Vansittart MSS., private letter-book, ii. 49-50: notes of letters from G. Vansittart to Thomas Graham and to John Dacres, 14 July 1775.

[4] P. Moon, *Warren Hastings and British India* (1947), pp. 162-5.

[5] P. Woodruff, *The Men who Ruled India ; the Founders* (1953), p. 126.

[6] Nandakuma had complained about this in the representation which was presented to the council on 11 March 1775 (*Eleventh Report of the Select Committee of 1782 ; Reports from Committees*, vi. 706).

[7] *Op. cit.* p. 150 *seq.*

my guard. I have carefully avoided every circumstance which might appear to be an interference in that prosecution.'[1]

The chief weakness of this explanation so far (as of all other theories about the origins of the trial) has been that it is unsupported by any direct evidence. The discovery of additional material bearing on the question is therefore of some importance. This material has been found among the private papers of George Vansittart, Hastings's most trusted friend and subordinate at this time, which are preserved at Bisham Abbey, Berkshire.[2] These papers comprise, in addition to trading accounts and travel diaries, several letter-books containing copies or abstracts of his letters to England or to friends in India and a thin paper-bound folio labelled 'Indian Journal 1775'.

George Vansittart, at that time thirty-two years of age, was the younger brother of Governor Henry Vansittart, whom Hastings had loyally served in his youth, and in all whose family he felt a deep interest. George, a promising Company servant and, like most of his family, an excellent linguist, had a good knowledge of the languages and people of Bengal gained while serving in the provinces. He had held the chiefships of Patna and Midnapur and had reached council. Displaced by the reorganization imposed by the Regulating Act of 1773 he had thought of retiring to Burdwan, but decided to accept a seat at the board of trade in Calcutta to be with the governor-general and to help him as 'I may on many occasions be of use to him in the management of the business, as he will have more upon his hands than he will himself be able to attend to'.[3] Since these papers show the assistance he gave to have consisted largely in helping to maintain relations with the Indian farmers, contractors and office-holders on whom the administration of Bengal depended, they are particularly valuable in connection with the subject under examination.

As Dr. Feiling has said :

All experience in Bengal showed that, though British officers took decisions and moved the pieces, without an Indian following they were helpless. Society was set in a complex frame of land revenue, embarrassed by sub-tenures and masked titles, ruled by an aristocracy of Moslem land-owners and Hindu bureaucrats and Armenian money-lenders, each living by the profits of office and retailing government patronage. And over all this a few score young Britons, wholly dependent on Indians for the intricacies of

[1] Evidence given in his prosecution of Nandakuma, &c., for conspiracy (*State Trials*, xx. 1181).

[2] The house which Vansittart bought to retire to. I am much indebted to Mrs. Paget, Bisham Abbey, for putting this material at my disposal and permitting me to make use of it.

[3] Vansittart MSS., European letter-book, iii. 48 (G. Vansittart to R. Palk, 30 November 1774).

the revenue and tolerable administration of justice, not to speak of channels for the private trading whereby nine out of ten of them must live.[1]

A good deal of light on the history of Bengal in the troubled years following 1756 will be thrown when more is known of the small but powerful and unscrupulous group of such men upon whom Government depended and who enriched themselves in its shadow. The management of relations with them, always important, took on a new significance when friction broke out between the new councillors and the governor-general; for whichever party enjoyed the allegiance of these men were the true rulers of Bengal. On the other hand, this allegiance would be forthcoming for whichever of the two parties was believed to be likely to triumph in the end.

Always well informed of what concerned their English rulers, these men were skilled in reading the political portents which meant so much to them. But the confused portents of 1775 could be interpreted in different ways. In consequence it soon became clear that the Indians whose fortunes depended on Government favour or who might hope to gain that favour, fell into three classes. The first class comprised those so closely associated with Hastings and the old régime that they had little to hope from the new order. To these may be added the open enemies of Nandakuma. The second class was made up of those who, on the contrary, threw in their lot with Nandakuma and the new-comers. The third was the considerable band who hoped to play out time without irrevocably committing themselves to either side, a manoeuvre not too difficult for those who did not hold important offices but much less easy for those in conspicuous positions. And if these facts became apparent, it also became clear that if the governor-general was to keep any grip on the situation, both to preserve his prestige and to avert attack, the only weapon he had to set against the immediate power which the Majority could wield was the greater skill and experience possessed by himself and his supporters in managing these Indian auxiliaries. It is one of the chief values of the Vansittart papers that they show, in part at least,[2] how this was done, and how much care and intelligence was put into it.

These papers show that each class was handled differently. So far as Nandakuma and other declared enemies were concerned, all that could be done was to collect the best information of their activities and to forestall their intentions whenever possible. Vansittart set up an excellent intelligence service and few moves by the Majority or their allies passed unnoticed. His papers show that

[1] *Op. cit.* p. 138.
[2] They give very little evidence of the activities of Hastings's ' banyan ' Krishna Kantu Nandi and none of those of either Hastings or Barwell.

chief among his agents in this work was one Sadar-ud-din,[1] formerly
'banyan' of John Graham at Burdwan [2] and now nominally at
least attached to Barwell, a man whose importance has not hitherto
been fully apparent. 'I get more from him than anybody.' [3] Vansittart told John Graham. When the Majority were working up
their first case against Hastings, in (as they believed) deep secrecy,
Vansittart was able to piece together the whole story and claimed,
'I believe you may depend upon all this information being pretty
exact. The particulars have been regularly brought to me by
Sudder-ul-deen from M[ahomed] R[eza] C[awn] himself.' [4] And
again when the Burdwan charges [5] were taking shape, 'This
intelligence is from Contoo, Sudder-ul-deen and Gunga Govind.
Bussunt Roy [6] and my Dinagepoor [7] friend Ram Chunder [8] are
among the attendants of Nundcomar and Goring,[9] but give intelligence of what passes to Sudder-ul-deen.' [10]

With the waverers a different policy was necessary. Those who
were not immediately at risk had to be persuaded that a 'connexion
with Mr. Hastings would have as much weight as . . . connexion
with the Majority in the minds of all those who have no immediate
cause of hope or fear '.[11] With those who had much to lose a
flexible line was adopted, as may be seen from Vansittart's handling
of Muhammad Reza Khan who, though he ultimately came down
on the side of the Hastings's enemies, tried for some time to keep
both ways open. Vansittart advised him to comply with the
demands made on him by the Majority so far as was necessary to
avoid ' drawing upon himself the immediate enmity of people who
had the power in their hands '.[12] He even urged him ' not to

[1] Known to the English as Sudder-ul-deen. He had at one time been a servant
of Nandakuma, and was believed to have once been his accomplice in forgery (Beveridge, *op. cit.* p. 241). Beveridge suggests that he may be the Sadar-al-Hak Khan
later appointed by Hastings as supreme magistrate at Murshidabad who, he believes,
died in 1780. This seems to be incorrect, as Sadar-ud-din was one of a cabal of banyans
said to be 'presecuting' Ganga Govind Singh in Calcutta in 1785 (Brit. Mus. Add.
MS. 29168, fo. 276: G. N. Thompson to W. Hastings, 26 April 1785).

[2] John Graham, appointed writer 1759, rose to be Resident at Burdwan and Midnapur, member of council of Murshidabad and in 1772 of the committee of circuit;
he left for England at the beginning of 1775 under heavy attack (with others) by the
Majority for corrupt practices in Burdwan. He was one of Hastings's agents in England but had to retire to Lisbon on grounds of health and died in 1776 of tuberculosis.

[3] Vansittart MSS., European letter-book, iii. 112 (G. Vansittart to J. Graham,
4 August 1775).

[4] *Ibid.* p. 66 (G. Vansittart to J. Graham, 23 February 1775).

[5] *Eleventh Report of the Select Committee of 1782. Reports from Committees,* vi. 733 *seq.*

[6] Basant Rai.   [7] Dinajpur.   [8] Ram Chandra.

[9] Charles Goring, a Company servant who threw in his lot with the Majority, and
later became Francis's agent.

[10] Vansittart MSS. *loc. cit.* pp. 69 (G. Vansittart to J. Graham, 23 February 1775).

[11] *Ibid.* private letter-book, ii. 72 (G. Vansittart to T. Motte, 3 October 1775).

[12] *Ibid.* European letter-book, iii. 64 (G. Vansittart to J. Graham, 23 February
1775). In a letter of 25 March 1775 to the same he said that Nandakuma was 'trying
to get his Jagheer [jagir] resumed which is his only support '. (*Ibid.* p. 72.)

hesitate about condemning the measures of the late administration ',[1] but he tried to ensure that he took no step without prior consultation and he hoped at least to keep him from damaging personal accusations. As he said on 20 May : ' My opinion is that he is heartily afraid of our new Furies ; that he seeks his safety by connecting himself with Mr. Goring ; and that he would submit to almost anything to please them except being instrumental in the producing of accusations against his old friends.'[2] With Muhammad Reza Khan he was ultimately unsuccessful ; with others (as for instance with the ' unspeakable ' Raja Naba Krishna,[3] formerly Clive's ' banyan ') he seems to have had more success, and it is surprising how much useful information was supplied and goodwill expressed (no doubt as a kind of re-insurance) by those who might have appeared to have more to gain from the hostile faction.

The problem of relations with the governor's own followers was no easier. As time went on many of them were losing their jobs, some of them were in fear of proceedings against them in the Kachahri courts.[4] All that could be done in their case was to mitigate their hardships and hold out hopes for the future. All possible steps were taken. Emissaries such as Sadar-ud-din tried to rally drooping spirits.[5] Friends in the Company service were urged to do all they could to help them.[6] In some cases financial aid was forthcoming.[7] But what is particularly significant for the question in hand is, that in addition to these makeshifts, there was an important new type of defence which could be offered to them, the protection of the independent supreme court against arbitrary proceedings by the executive and its agents English and Indian.

The difficulties which were likely to be caused in the collection of revenue by the interposition of an independent court administering English law was one of the chief dangers which Hastings and others foresaw when the court was set up. It was later the occasion of the great clash between Hastings and Impey in 1779–80 out of which arose the Judicature Act of 1781. The judges were not, at

---

[1] Reported to John Graham in his letter, 25 March 1775 (see above p. 249 n. 12).

[2] *Ibid.* p. 99 (G. Vansittart to J. Graham, 20 May 1775).

[3] Known to the English as Nobkissen, one of the few Indians in touch with the Government who knew English. He rose from humble beginnings to be Clive's ' banyan ', and he played an active and unscrupulous part in politics for many years. At this time he held no employment.

[4] The ' Cutcherry ' or local revenue courts.

[5] Vansittart MSS., European letter-book, iii. 69 (G. Vansittart to J. Graham, 23 February 1775).

[6] *Ibid.* private letter-book, ii. 46 (G. Vansittart to E. Baber, 2 May 1775). About one Shanker Dutt (known as Sunkerdutt): ' I hope you will make a point of befriending him because he has behaved very well, and it is particularly necessary at this time to shew favour to those who do.'

[7] See below p. 251.

any rate at the outset, unduly doctrinaire.   Vansittart said of them :
' The Judges have a difficult part to act.   They are unwilling to
interfere in the demands on the Farmers, lest they should interrupt
the Collections, at the same time that their duty obliges them to
prevent any notorious acts of injustice.' [1]   But there was in fact a
real incompatibility between the system of law' they represented
and the administrative methods then employed (perhaps necessarily)
by the Government of Bengal.   It was an ironical result of the
faction into which this administration was plunged that Hastings
and his supporters were soon found praising the supreme court as
the salvation of the country, for doing precisely what they had
feared it would do.[2]   When the Majority tried to prevent one of
Hastings's friends, John Graham, chief of Burdwan, from leaving
the country until investigations into alleged misdeeds there could
be completed, the supreme court over-ruled their order,[3] and
Vansittart can soon be seen using this unfamiliar weapon in the
interest of Hastings's Indian supporters.   As early as 25 March
1775 he reports : ' I am obliged to assist Birgekishvur with money
to defray his expenses in Calcutta, for he dares not trust himself at
present out of the protection of the Supreme Court.' [4]   Later such
references become increasingly common.   In August he wrote to
Motte at Benares, ' Let not Ramnarayn [5] be alarmed.   The supreme
court is an effectual security that Joarymull [6] will not dare either
directly or indirectly to exercise authority over him.' [7]

It should be noted that in no case is there any evidence of
collusion between Hastings's party and the court, but, on the other
hand, great ingenuity was shown in bringing this weapon into play.
When one of the judges, the obstinate and tiresome Le Maistre, went
on tour, Vansittart wrote to a friend Edward Baber on the council
at Murshidabad :

> Mr. Le Maistre is set out on a visit up the Country. . . . He
> will stay some days at Moorshedabad.   He has the power of

[1] Vansittart MSS., European letter-book, iii. 114 (G. Vansittart to J. Graham,
4 August 1775).

[2] Brit. Mus. Add. MS. 29127, fo. 203 (W. Hastings to L. Macleane and J. Graham,
20 May 1775): ' What a blessing is the Supreme Court to me and to the whole country!
Without such a protection I declare I would not have staid two months after the
assembly of the new Council.'

[3] Vansittart MSS., European letter-book, iii. 56 (G. Vansittart to R. Palk, 11
January 1775).   It should be noted, however, that when John Stewart, secretary of
Bengal, and a friend of Hastings, tried to get the supreme court to intervene to reverse
his dismissal, the court refused, Impey giving the casting vote against it.   (Vansittart
MSS., European letter-book, iii. 124: letter to John Graham, 25 November 1775).

[4] Bajna Kishor Rai, late Diwan of Burdwan, displaced by the Majority.   (*Ibid.*
p. 76.   Letter to John Graham, 25 March 1775.   See also private letter-book, ii. 86,
writing to T. Pierce, 2 January 1776: ' Sudder-ul-deen has purchased for Chundergose
[Chandra Ghose] a house in Calcutta, which will give him a more certain claim to the
interference of the Supreme Court if he wishes to be released from his confinement and
to come to Calcutta.')   [5] Ramnarain.   [6] Johury Mull.

[7] *Ibid.* private letter-book, ii. 55–6 (G. Vansittart to J. Motte at Benares, 17 August
1775).

exercising a judicial authority at Moorshedabad the same as in Calcutta. . . . It would be an excellent opportunity for any persons who have been injured by Mr. Goring or Mr. James Grant[1] or their Muttaseddies[2] to apply for justice. It would be well that intimations were given of this circumstance to the Begum, Yeitabar Aly Cawn[3] and the Mohurrirs[4] of the Treasury, but they should be careful not to make any frivolous complaints. Mr. Le Maistre's station and rank should be made as publick as possible that proper respect may be paid to him. This must be managed by you and Martin and Aldersey, but it would be bad that Martin should appear in it and still worse that you should. . . .[5]

Sometimes the plans for obtaining the protection of the court were Machiavellian. On 15 August 1775 Vansittart, expressing a desire to help Dulal Rai,[6] formerly farmer of the Rajshahi revenues, but displaced by the Majority, wrote to Baber :

> I wish him to come to Calcutta, but would not have it appear to be done with your consent. Might not he present a petition to your Board and request leave to proceed to Calcutta to lay his case before the Council? Might not you refuse but at the same time send his petition to the Council, inform them that he seems determined to come, and desire to know if you shall detain him by force? If they say yes and you in consequence do detain him, he may then obtain a *Habeas Corpus* and prosecute for false imprisonment as well as for the injustice he has suffered.[7]

It is against this background that the Nandakuma case must be considered, and it is clear that, however it originated, it was bound to be considered a test whether or not the supreme court could take vigorous action against an influential man who had protection in high places. And in consequence neither Hastings's group nor their opponents could be indifferent to its result. That the Majority, far from standing aside, angered the court by what it considered improper pressure, is well-known. The Vansittart papers do something to show the activities of the Hastings group. The letter-books contribute something, since Vansittart gave accounts of the trial, its origin and sequel to friends in England including John Graham who (having so recently left the country) knew the background well. But these letters were written in self-justification, as were those of all the parties to the dispute. More valuable therefore is the 'Indian Journal' which begins on 20 April 1775, the day when the judges declared that a case for conspiracy lay (and the first entry in the journal shows that this date was no accident)

---

[1] Like Goring, one of the few Company servants who had embraced the cause of the Majority.

[2] Muttasaddi, clerk.   [3] Etebar Ali Khan. See p. 258.   [4] *i.e.* Writers.

[5] Vansittart MSS., private letter-book, ii. 59 (G. Vansittart to E. Baber, 23 August 1775).   [6] Called by the English Dullul Roy.

[7] Vansittart MSS., private letter-book, ii. 53 (G. Vansittart to E. Baber, 15 August 1775).

and ends on 5 November of the same year. It is entered up fully until about the middle of June (in fact until shortly after Nandakuma's condemnation). After that date the entries become erratic and from September, when Vansittart was beginning to turn his eyes to England, they begin to peter out. The document is clearly intended solely for private use. Its entries consist of jottings in Vansittart's own hand in a highly abbreviated form, so that its purpose must have been that of an *aide-mémoire*, not the production of a record comprehensible to others than the writer. Its main contents are brief notes of interviews with Indians, giving their names and the gist of their conversation. A few striking events are noted, sometimes apparently inserted later. Hardly any of the interviews are on normal Government business ; most of them deal with the collection of evidence to rebut charges against Hastings, himself and others ; with information about the fate of Indian supporters ; with attempts to collect evidence of corrupt practices on the part of their enemies ; [1] and (taking up more space than any other topic) the Nandakuma trial and the conspiracy trials which overlapped with it. The whole document is of considerable interest, but for the purpose in hand only the entries bearing directly on these trials need be considered. They are here reproduced in full.[2] The entries are so compressed and the case for and against Nandakuma so complicated that their significance in detail can hardly be recognized without reference to the published report of the trial and the careful analysis of it made by Stephen.

N.B.   20 April [1775]
    I intend to keep this journal because Mr. Fowke mentioned to me today at Sir Elijah's that he doubted not similar accusations would be retorted.[3]
Saturday 22 April [1775] M[orning]
    6. Juggutchund [4] calls on me. Tells me that the General,[5] Monson and Francis went yesterday afternoon to see Nundcomar. . . .

[1] Hastings through Krishna Kantu Nandi and others collected allegations that Francis (and possibly Monson) took presents, which he hoped to be able to bring before the supreme court but ' it is no easy matter to meet with a Bengally who will venture to stand forth against an all-powerful Majority ' (Vansittart MSS., European letter-book, iii. 116–18: G. Vansittart to J. Graham, 5 September 1775). The matter is also mentioned in an earlier letter of 16 May 1775 (*ibid.* pp. 94–9).

[2] Abbreviations have been expended, the spelling of names retained. The writing is cramped and transcription, particularly of proper names, sometimes difficult.

[3] At the hearing before the judges in which they found that a case lay for conspiracy against Nandakuma, Fowke, &c. Fowke meant accusations of procuring evidence from Indians by improper means. He seems to have shown during the proceedings the violent temper for which he was noted.

[4] Jagat Chand, Nandakuma's son-in-law and an employee of his son Raja Guru Das [known as Gourdass], whom the Majority had appointed Diwan to the Household at Murshidabad. He had quarrelled with Nandakuma who complained on 11 March 1775 that though he had ' educated ' Jagat Chand from childhood and patronized him, Jagat Chand had come to Calcutta without permission and was plotting against him with his ' inveterate enemy ' Mohan Prasad and was received by Hastings (*Reports from Committees*, vi. 700).   [5] General Clavering.

8. Gungagovind [1] calls on me.—Tells me that a great noise is made about the town of Nundcomar's power and favour and the inability of the Court of Justice to hurt him in consequence of the Majority's visit to him last night. . . .

11. Cummaul-ul-dien [2] calls on me. I asked him a number of questions as per separate paper [3] to which he replied distinctly and with the strongest professions that all he had sworn to was strictly true. I told him to be particularly cautious that he never deviated in the least from truth. Cossynant [4] was present all the time, and my Moonshy the latter part of the time. He went about 1.0, Sir John D'Oyly [5] too came.

A[fternoon]

6. Called on Mr. Hastings at Belvidere—supped at Barwell's.
Sunday [23 April 1775] A[fternoon]

7. . . . Sudder-ul-deen [6] also comes. He says that Cummul-ul-dien did actually tell him in December that Mr. Fowke had told him he should be punished if he did not give the account.[7] Gunga-govind says the same and denies the conversation which is mentioned to have past between him and Cummaul-ul-dien—Sudder-ul-deen says that Cummaul-ul-dien did actually tell him on Tuesday evening that Mr. Fowke had made him give the Ferd.[8] They go at 9.

[Monday] 24 [April 1775]

9. Went to Sir Elijah Impey's. Fowke, Nundcomar and Radachurn [9] bound over.

[Tuesday] 25 [April 1775]

At 6 a[fternoon] saw Sudder-ul-deen. Moohunpersaud [10] desires to wait on me tomorrow morning. I gave him permission.

[Wednesday] 26 [April 1775]

8. Sudder-ul-deen and Moohunpersaud. Moohunpersaud tells me of his intention to prosecute on the business of Boolakydoss.[11]

[1] Ganga Govind Singh, Diwan to the Calcutta committee, shortly to be dismissed by the Majority. (See p. 243 above.)

[2] Kamal-ud-din (see p. 243 above).

[3] Queries concerning his allegations against Nandakuma, Fowke, &c. The paper has apparently not survived but was sent to R. Palk (Vansittart MSS., European letter-book iii. 83, G. Vansittart to R. Palk, 13 May 1775). Hastings had examined him previously and asked Vansittart's assistance in arriving at the truth (Feiling, *op. cit.* p. 147).

[4] Kashi Nath ' A principal merchant of Calcutta and a man of considerable rank ' (*Reports from Committees*, v. 22).

[5] The Company's assistant Persian translator. He earned the disfavour of the Majority by pleading incapacity to interpret at the Nandakuma trial.

[6] Sadar-ud-din (see p. 249 above).

[7] An earlier allegation and retractation made by Kamal-ud-din (*State Trials*, xx. 1176 *seq.*). Ganga Govind Singh was one of those he accused.

[8] ' Fard ' or account. For the dispute whether or not he had given Fowke this document as well as an ' arzi ' or petition, see *State Trials*, xx. 1147 *seq.*

[9] Rhadha Charan (see p. 243 above).

[10] Mohan Prasad (see p. 244 above).

[11] Bolaki Das, the rich Hindu ' Shroff ' or banker whose estate Nandakuma was alleged to have defrauded. This is the first reference bearing on the forgery trial.

I told him he knows best—that the Court of Judicature makes very strict justice and his success will depend upon his right. He intimates to me that he is at a loss for a Counsellour that he had interviewed Mr. Farrer but cannot confide in him as he was Security for Nundcomar.[1] I recommend Mr. Durham [2] to him. He shewed me a bond which he said Nundcomar had forged and another Persian paper of which he wanted translations. I told him he had better ask Mr. Durham about them than me, that I could not give him any information. He goes at 9 and so does Sudder-ul-deen.

Sunday 30 [April 1775] M[orning] 6.

Nubkisshun [3] calls on me . . . Nubkisshun says that after the death of Boolakydoss, Puddumdoss [4] who was his executor came to him and complaining that Boolakydoss by his will had left him very little proposed that he (Puddumdoss) should make out a bond in his (Nubkisshun's) name, that the amount should be plain [?] and they should share it between them—that upon his refusing he went and made the like proposal to Nundcomar—that hence arose Boolakydoss's bond to Nundcomar for 129,000 rupees [5] that the seal was put by Puddumdoss and that there is no signing to the bond —that afterwards Puddumdoss complained to him that Nundcomar had taken a bond from him and would not give him any part of the money and asked him what he should do—that he (Nubkisshun) replied that the robber was robbed and he knew not what remedy he could have.[6]

A[fternoon] 7.

Sudder-ul-deen calls on me and tells me as follows . . . Roop-narayn Chundry [7] has advised Sudder-ul-deen to make friends with Nundcomar. . . . He [Sudder-ul-deen] sent word to Cummaul-ul-dien by Meer Shereef [8] of Nundcomar sending Gullam Hossein [9] to tamper with his Moonshy and offering 200 rs and 60 a month.

[1] Thomas Farrer, the only fully-qualified barrister then at the Calcutta bar, stood bail not for Nandakuma but for Joseph Fowke in the conspiracy charges; in the forgery trial he acted as Nandakuma's counsel. This entry would seem to solve one of the difficulties Beveridge felt (*op. cit.* pp. 99 *seq.*) in accepting Farrer's evidence that Mohan Prasad had been in touch with him at an earlier date about criminal proceedings against Nandakuma (*Letter of Sir Elijah Impey*, Part III, Appendix 1. pp. 105 *seq.*), though it does not prove that they were in touch before 1775.

[2] Hercules Durham, retained as attorney to the Government of Bengal. This entry shows the inaccuracy of Beveridge's suggestion (*op. cit.* pp. 190 *seq.*) that Durham was acting in any sense as the Company's employee and Joseph Price's gossip (*A Letter to Edmund Burke, Esq. on the latter part of the late Report of the Select Committee . . . 1782*, pp. 64–7) that the case was stirred up by lawyers looking for a chance for professional gain.

[3] Raja Naba Krishna (see p. 250 above).

[4] Padma Das, the close friend of Bolaki Das, who with Mohan Prasad had held his power of attorney and was left in charge of his business after his death. Padma Das himself had since died.

[5] This was the sum under dispute in the civil proceedings. In the forgery trial it was narrowed down to 48,021 rupees. (*State Trials*, xx. 1014.)

[6] The Chief Justice in his summing up (*loc. cit.* p. 1065) indicated that he believed Padma Das (deceased) had been a party to the forgery.

[7] Rup Narain Chandra, employed by the Rani of Burdwan, and a supporter of the Majority.   [8] Mir Sharif.   [9] Gholam Hussein (see p. 244 above).

Intelligence has been given to him by Moulavy Mahomed Saanjut.[1]

[Tuesday] 2 [May 1775]

Gullam Hossein imprisoned for tampering with Cummaul-ul-dien's Moonshy.[2]

[Wednesday] 4 [May 1775] M[orning] 10.

Cummaul-ul-dien comes and acquaints me of the circumstances of Gullam Hossein endeavouring to bribe his Moonshy Cadur Novauz[3] to forswear himself.

10. Sudder-ul-deen comes 'Moonhunpersaud has given a petition to Mr. Durham—Juggutchund says the forged bond of Boolakydoss was written by Munnoshir Moonshy[4] and that Nandakuma himself wrote Govan Shâd.[5] Roopnarayn has repeated his message to him and sent him word that Keenga Mohrcund[6] has made some complaints against Nundcomar. Let Abdoolla[7] produce some letters of Munnoshir Moonshy. Let Moulavy Saanjut be taken notice of.'

[Saturday] 6 [May 1775] M[orning] 8.

Sudder-ul-deen . . . 'Durham sent for Juggutchund. Juggutchund when I shewed him that writing told me it was Munnoshir Moonshy.[8] I could not compare it with the Bond because Mr. Durham has the Bond.'

A[fternoon] 9.

Nundcomar imprisoned on an accusation of forgery.

[Monday] 8 [May 1775] M[orning] 8.

Sudder-ul-deen comes 'Mr. Fowke was 3 hours yesterday with Nundcomar in the gaol. Nundcomar reports that he will be bailed. . . .'

[Tuesday] 9 [May 1775] M[orning] 6.

Nubkisshun comes—'Nundcomar sent to him yesterday to put him in mind (*vide* 25 April)[9] and to tell him now was his time to serve him. He replied he could not take a false oath. Cheitun

[1] Moulvi Muhammad Sanjur (?).

[2] This incident was referred to by Vansittart as one of the measures 'proving to the native inhabitants of Calcutta that there is a power established which is capable of distributing Justice notwithstanding the opposition of the Council' and so emboldening Nandakuma's accuser to stand forth. (Vansittart MSS., European letter-book, iii. 84: G. Vansittart to R. Palk, 13 May 1775.)

[3] Kadar Nowaz.

[4] Manahar Munshi.

[5] Govah Shud, *i.e.* 'witnessed'.

[6] I have not been able to identify the name Keenga. Mohrcund is Muhr-Kan (a seal-cutter).

[7] Abdulla.

[8] It was pointed out during the trial that the 'munshi' who wrote the bond in dispute had not been traced. This and the entry for 4 May represent attempts by the prosecution to bring the munshi forward. Manahar Munshi, formerly in Nandakuma's pay, denied that the writing was his, and the defence tried to prove that Mohan Prasad attempted to bribe him (*State Trials*, xx. 1046-9). Durham said his attention was drawn to Manahar by his sarkar (servant) three days before the commitment.

[9] Reference untraceable.

Naut,[1] Jeidub-Choby,[2] Yar Mahomed [3] and Perminand Muccarjea [4] are four false witnesses in Nundcomar's pay.[5] He will produce them on his trial—he will not lose cast by being in the gaol, nor even be obliged to do penance, for instance Kisshanchurn Tacur [6] and Panachoo Tacur.[7] The old Radshay [8] Bramin had a hint from Nundcomar.' [9]

[Wednesday] 10 [May 1775] M[orning] 8.

Gungagovind comes . . . 'Nundcomar says he will send a Vackeel [10] to England.

10. Cantoo comes . . . 'Keenga Mohrcund cut 3 publick seals which Nandakuma has got.'

[Thursday] 11 [May 1775] M[orning] 8.

Juggutchund comes. 'Nundcomar sent me word that he had turned out the Begum etc., and that I should see what more he would do. He is now tutoring Jeidub Choby, Cheitun Naut and Yar Mahomed to bear witness for him ; see what witness they gave before Mr. Rous.[11] The two former bore witness in Nundcomar's trial in my brothers' [12] time for intriguing with the French. I am apprehensive of being forcibly sent to Moorshedabad.' N.B. Nundcomar alludes to the resolution of the Council on Tuesday the 9th for suspending Munny Begum [13] and give the charge of the nabob to Goordoss.

I go to the Governor's.

10. Cumaul-ul-dien comes . . . Says Mahomed Sadur Mohrcund [14] at Hoogly has made a great many seals for Nundcomar.

11. Sudder-ul-deen comes 'Nundcomar is preparing Cheitun Naut, Jeidub Choby and Yar Mahomed to bear witness for him, also one Permanind, a relation of his. Three instances of C. J. and Y. hearing false witness (vid. separate paper).[15] Two evidences

---

[1] Chaitanya Nath.   [2] Jai Deb Chaubé.

[3] Yar Muhammad. These three men gave evidence purporting to show that they were present when the bond was signed, and sought to prove the existence and subsequent death of a witness of whom no one else seemed to have knowledge.

[4] Perminand Mukherji.

[5] Vansittart had mentioned on 10 April the first two as 'two of Nundcomar's retained swearers' (Vansittart MSS., European letter-book iii, p. 79: G. Vansittart to J. Graham, 10 April 1775). Later (*ibid.* p. 110: G. Vansittart to J. Graham, 4 August 1775) he said, when describing the rout of Nandakuma's witnesses at the trial, 'Even his veterans Yar Mahomed, Cheitun Naut and Jeidub Choby could not stand their ground, although the two last have been employed on such services for full fifteen years'.

[6] Krishna Chandra Thakur.   [7] Panchu Thakur.   [8] Rajshahi.

[9] Attempts to obtain bail for Nandakuma were partly based on the grounds of his religion, but these were disallowed by the court, after consultation with pandits.

[10] Envoy or agent.

[11] A reference to earlier civil proceedings in the Kachahri court presided over by William Boughton Rouse (see entry for 26 May below). Yar Muhammad was pressed on this during the forgery trial. (*State Trials,* xx. 1014–15.)

[12] This would seem to refer to Vansittart's brother, Governor Henry Vansittart, not to Jagat Chand's. (*Third Report, Select Committee of 1772 : Reports from Committees,* iii. 368 *seq.*)

[13] Munni Begum.   [14] Muhammad Sadar Muhr-kan.   [15] Not found.

against Ramchurn swore they had been bribed by Nundcomar—In Mr. Verelst's [1] time when Nubkisshun was accused 14 blank covers (sealed) were seized in Nundcomar's house '—Nundcomar caused a false letter to be put into a cover under Ramchurn's seal. . . .[2]

A[fternoon] 8.

I give Memorandum to Durham.

[Saturday] 13 [May 1775] M[orning] 7.

Juggutchund brings me a letter from Eitabar Aly Cawn [3] to him . . . ' Pudmundoss, Moohunpersaud and Nundcomar jointly forged the bonds in Nundcomar's Balakana. . . .' [4]

[Tuesday] 16 [May 1775] M[orning] 9.

Sudder-ul-deen comes. ' I hear that Moohunpersaud offered some English gentleman 30,000 rs. if he could carry his point against Nundcomar and that he gave 500 rs. to one of the witnesses, and that these circumstances have been acknowledged to the General.'

[Thursday] 18 [May 1775] M[orning] 9.

Sudder-ul-deen. ' Moohunpersaud denies the truth of what is mentioned on the 16th. Nubkisshun has been mentioning to me his fear of suffering from the new Gentlemen if he appears against Nundcomar,[5] and also his unwillingness from religious considerations to get a Bramin hanged.[6] Nubkisshun says Nundcomar has been preparing two false witnesses to swear they saw his jewels in Boolakydoss's house, to swear they saw Boolakydoss sign the bond, and to swear he (*sic*) knew Cummaul and that he is dead, and to be brought from Burdwan to personate the 3rd witness to the bond. These witnesses write Zebanbundees [7] before Mr. Gerard [8] and they are attended by a Writer and a Banyan.'

[Wednesday] 24 [May 1775] M[orning] 11.

Sudder-ul-deen brings a copy of what he knows in Cummaul-ul-dien's complaint. ' It is reported the General has threatened vengeance against any man at all concerned in the prosecution of Nundcomar. Goring has got all the papers.'

[Thursday] 25 [May 1775] M[orning] 9.

Cummaul-ul-deen. ' I have brought down Mahomed Sadur Mohrcund [9] who cut many seals for Nundcomar in my house in

---

[1] Governor of Bengal, 1767–9.

[2] This story was widespread. It is found in the history Sair al Matakharin (trans. Raymond), quoted Beveridge, *op. cit.* p. 361.

[3] Etebar Ali Khan. A friend at the court at Murshidabad (see above p. 252).

[4] House or mansion.

[5] Later Naba Krishna, anxious to retain the favour of the Majority (though professing it would not be safe for him to back them openly), gave an account of the trial, which implied that his only part in it was to petition on behalf of Nandakuma (India Office, Francis MS. 7, fos. 127 *seq.*: translation of letter from Naba Krishna to H. Strachey 23 March 1776, sent via Francis).

[6] In his evidence at the trial he refused a direct answer to a question, stating ' The prisoner is a Bramin . . . it is not a trifling matter; the life of a Bramin is at stake ', but he succeeded nevertheless in making his final answer damaging to the defendant (*State Trials*, xx. 962 f.).   [7] Zabanbandi, *i.e.* personal statement.

[8] Robert Jarret, Nandakuma's attorney.   [9] Muhammad Sadar Muhr-Kan.

Calcutta. Mohamed Wasit Mohrcund [1] is coming. Nundcomar wrote for my seal to put it to an Arzee to the Nabob. It was sent from Hoogly just after Meer Jaffer's restoration. Sheik Hosain Aly Consamann [2] (who is now here) put it up in a piece of cloth.[3]

[Friday] 26 [May 1775] M[orning] 7.

Nubkisshun comes ' Birgekishvur Roy [4] lately came to me from Nundcomar and told me there was no harm in taking a false oath for the preservation of a Bramin. Dodysan,[5] Muccurjea [6] and Radocant Tishbaughir [7] were present. Pudmundoss sent frequent messages to me by Buttachurge [8] who is now present. Eight witnesses proposed by Nundcomar and Mr. Gerard [Jarret] bought like birds.'

8. Sudder-ul-deen ' Radachurn and Neta Sing [9] desired Dullol Sing [10] to swear that Moohunpersaud paid 15,000 rs. to Rous; he says Nundcomar paid him 7,000 '.

[Saturday] 27 [May 1775] M[orning] 11.

Sudder-ul-deen brings me a paper of observations concerning Boolakydoss's bonds and teeps [11] to Nundcomar.

[Sunday] 28 [May 1775] M[orning] 11.

Sudder-ul-deen. '. . . Moonshy Nusseer-ul-deen [12] with Nundcomar.'

[Saturday] 3 June [1775] M[orning] 11.

Moonshy Sudder-ul-deen. ' Myrza Mahdy [13] was concerned with the Mohrcund in the accusation against Cummaul-ul-dien.

[Sunday] 4 [June 1775] M[orning] 7.

Nubkisshun. 'Boolakydoss's being allowed to remain in Calcutta—recovery of his money from the Company—conversations with Pudmundoss. Radacant acquainted with every thing.'

[Wednesday] 7 [June 1775] M[orning] 9.

Sudder-ul-deen. 'Cauzy Abdoolla [14] has brought down a man from Hoogly (a Fucheer) [15] to swear that Cummaul-ul-deen had confessed to him he had taken a false oath. Keenga Mohrcund would confess if he was not afraid of being punished himself.'

[1] Muhammad Wasit Muhr-Kan.
[2] Sheik Hussein Ali the Khansaman (household steward).
[3] This was an essential part of Kamal-ud-din's evidence as to how Nandakuma gained possession of his seal. He stuck to the story and the defence apparently admitted a letter in which Nandakuma acknowledged the receipt of the seal, though at the court's suggestion the admission was withdrawn as damaging (*State Trials*, xx. 936-7) but see Farrer, in 1788 (*Letter of Sir Elijah Impey* Part III, Appendix 4, p. 161). The attempts (which were ultimately unsuccessful) to get evidence about seal-cutting are reflected in evidence about ' Mahomet Wassen ' (*State Trials*, xx. 963).
[4] Bajna Kishor Rai. He had evidently made his peace with Nandakuma. (See entry for 17 June below.)
[5] Debi San.   [6] Mukherji.   [7] Radha Kant Tejbahadur.
[8] Battacharya.   [9] Neta Singh.   [10] Dulal Singh.
[11] *I.e.* thumb impressions, used in the same way as seals. This would seem to refer to papers thus signed.   [12] Nasir-ud-din.
[13] Mirza Mahdi, a dependent of Nandakuma, in July appointed Faujdar of Hoogly.
[14] Kazi Abdulla.   [15] A fakir, or religious mendicant.

[Thursday] 8 [June 1755] M[orning] 9.

Sudder-ul-deen. 'Mahomed Pusinan [1] found last night under the Musnud [2] of Myrza Mahdy a blank paper with Cummaul-ul-dien's seal upon it. He has given notice to Cummaul-ul-dien. Meerza Amany [3] has been employed by Myrza Mahdy to accuse his brother Sheek Hosain Aly the Consamann of Cummaul-ul-dien of having taken a false oath.'

[Saturday] 10 [June 1775]

N.B. Yesterday morning [4] came on the trial of Nundcomar for the forgery of a bond for 48,000 rs. in the name of Boolakydoss.

[Tuesday] 13 [June 1775] M[orning] 6.

Nubkisshun came 'fresh messages from Nundcomar'.

[Friday] 16 [June 1775]

At 5 this morning the Jury brought in Nundcomar guilty of forgery.

[Saturday] 17 [June 1775] M[orning] 9.

Lolloo [5] says Birgekishvur has been to Petroos [6] telling him that Nundcomar had promised he should be Diwan of Burdwan or Dacca and required him to take a false oath in the conspiracy business.

10. Gungagovind. Nundcomar is conveying away his effects to Soocden Mullic [7] and Muddundutt.[8]

[Wednesday] 21 [June 1775] M[orning] 8.

Juggutchund . . . 'Nundcomar complains of Radachurn, of his bringing about the connection with Mr. Fowke, of his persuading him to lend money to Coll. Thornton,[9] etc., etc., not very safe men.'

[Tuesday] 27 [June 1775] M[orning] 7.

Juggutchund. 'Nundcomar blames old Fowke. Brothers have made application to principal people to petition.' [10]

[Wednesday] 28 [June 1775] 7.

Nubkisshun and Sudder-ul-deen . . . 'Principal people will not petition. Muddundutt thinks of doing it at the head of a party of low people.'

---

[1] Unidentified.   [2] Masnad, cushion.   [3] Mirza Amani.

[4] The case formally opened on 8 June, but proceedings began on the 9th.

[5] Lala Doman Singh (?).

[6] Khwasa Petruse (known to the English as Coja Petruse), the well-known Armenian banker.

[7] Shukr-ud-din Malik (?).

[8] Madan Dutt. By English law Nandakuma's goods would be forfeited to the Crown on conviction, but the forfeiture was not exacted. (Beveridge, *op. cit.* pp. 364–5; *Speech of Sir Elijah Impey*, pp. 82–3.)

[9] In the Company's military service and a supporter of the Majority. He stood bail for Nandakuma (with Captain Weller, Clavering's A.D.C.) on the conspiracy charges (*State Trials*, xx. 1093).

[10] Farrer, Nandakuma's counsel, in his evidence on Impey's impeachment, refers to a proposed petition in the name of Sumbonat Roy (Sambh Nath Rai), Nandakuma's brother (but he added—'it was the first time I ever heard that Nuncomar had a brother'), which he advised against (*Speech of Sir Elijah Impey*, Part III, Appendix 3. p. 153–4). He was in fact Nandakuma's cousin (Beveridge, *op. cit.* p. 297).

11. Ramruttun.[1] 'Ramchunder Seyn[2] carried an Arzee this morning to be signed by Gocul Gosaul in favour of Nundcomar—intended to be signed by the principal inhabitants of Calcutta in behalf of Nundcomar.   Gocul[3] refused.'

N.B.   Sentence was passed on Nundcomar on Saturday the 24th. He was condemned to be hanged.

12. Received a note from Sudder-ul-deen—contents of the Arzee ' that Nundcomar was a man of high rank, had held great offices under the Nabob, was a friend always to the English, did good to numbers, harm to none—requesting he might either be tried by the laws of the Bramins or be reprieved.   It is addressed to the Judges.'

N.B.   A great many Bramins assembled yesterday in behalf of Nundcomar—collected by Ramchunder Seyn.

[Tuesday] 4 July [1775]

Radachurn takes an affidavit before the Chief Justice that he was not acquainted with the contents of the paper to which he had before sworn and which was produced in Court the 28th.[4]

[Monday] 10 [July 1775] A[fternoon] 2.

Conspirators not Guilty at the Governor's indictment.[5]

[Tuesday] 11 [July 1775] M[orning] 8.

Gungagovind, lamenting the acquittal.

[Saturday] 15 [July 1775]

Conspirators (Nundcomar and Fowke) brought in Guilty on Barwell's indictment.[6]

---

[1] Ram Ratan.

[2] Ram Chandra Sen, a supporter of Nandakuma who had been appointed Diwan to the Calcutta committee in succession to Ganga Govind Singh.   Farrer also refers to this second petition, and says those to whom it was shown did not wish to sign it (*ibid.*).   Vansittart said in a letter to John Graham of 4 August 1775 (Vansittart MSS., European letter-book, iii. 109): ' Ramchunder Seyn and Rada Churn, supported by the Majority have been taking much pains to prevail upon the principal Hindoos of Calcutta to present a petition to the Judges requesting that his life may be spared on account of his cast but they have not succeeded.   They could only get it signed by Monson's and Francis's Banyans and their immediate connexions and by a parcel of indigent people most of whom are in quest of employments.   Elliott will furnish you with a list of them and some account of their situations and characters.'

[3] Gokol Gosaul (or ? Gokol Gosain).

[4] In connexion with the conspiracy charges.   For affidavit see *State Trials*, xx. 1142.

[5] The conspiracy charges were not seriously pressed, now that Nandakuma was out of the way.   The varying verdicts in the prosecutions by Hastings and Barwell have not been explained (Stephen, *op. cit.* i. 204).   Vansittart elsewhere (Vansittart MSS., European letter-book, iii. 102: G. Vansittart to R. Palk, 3 August 1775) suggests that Fowke had complained that his son was included in the indictment in this case, and so his evidence could not be called, and ' I think this consideration had weight with the jury '.

[6] *Ibid.* p. 102.   Vansittart attributed the verdict in this case on the other hand to the fact that Francis, son of Joseph Fowke was excluded from the indictment and was therefore able to give evidence and was thought to have made the matter worse.   He confirmed the fact referred to in Stephen, *op. cit.* i. 203–4, that Barwell asked that the penalty should be light.   The delay in holding the conspiracy trials, interpreted sometimes in a sinister sense, is stated by Vansittart but not admitted by Impey to be due to the fact that Joseph Fowke had been ill, so that the trials were postponed.

[Monday] 17 [July 1775] A[fternoon] 7.

My indictment withdrawn.[1]

N.B. The Assizes began on Saturday the 2nd of June. The Grand Jury were dismissed on Friday the 14th of July and the Petty Jury on Thursday the 18th. On the 14th an address was presented to Sir Elijah Impey by the Grand Jury—on the 18th by the Free Merchants—on the 19th by the Armenians.[2]

[Thursday] 20 [July 1775].

About the 20th a petition was presented to Sir Elijah Impey by Soocden Mullic and others to spare the life of the Bramin Nundcomar. N.B. This petition has been collected with great labour by Radachurn and Ramchunder. The principal people refused to sign it.

[Tuesday] 1 [August 1775] M[orning] 7.

Nubkisshun and Moonshy Sudder-ul-deen. Nubkisshun says that Neelmunny Tacur,[3] brother of Dirjnarayn,[4] Muttasuddy of Colonel Monson came to him on Friday (the 28th) and told him that 2 or 3 gentlemen had desired him to write an address to be tried by the Shaster laws [5] and even forcibly to oppose the execution of Nundcomar, as had been done at Madras.[6] He says also that the General has assured Nundcomar that he shall not be hanged. . . .

[Saturday] 5 [August 1775] M[orning] 9.

Sudder-ul-deen shows me a letter from Moorshedabad mentioning that Kishvar Cawn is set out with a *Soorathaul* [7] which

---

[1] Vansittart explains this (*ibid.* p. 102 and pp. 110–11: letter to J. Graham, 4 August 1775) partly by his desire not to waste the judges' time, partly by a belief that ' when Mr. Fowke made Cummaul-ul-dien sign the paper of bribes I do not suppose that he thought it to be false ' and partly, perhaps more significantly, because ' Besides I thought it possible that Cummaul-ul-dien, without any intention of deviating from the truth, might nevertheless by repeated cross-examination and the mistakes of interpreting be harassed into some contradictions which, though immaterial, might be laid hold of as arguments against his veracity both on the Conspiracy trial and on that of the Forgery '.

[2] An address of thanks was presented later by over 200 prominent Hindus (see *Speech of Sir Elijah Impey* Part I, Appendix 12, pp. 45-51). Vansittart wrote (*loc. cit.* p. 111) to J. Graham on 4 August: ' I believe the principal Hindoo inhabitants too are inclined to present an address and at the same time to require that the English Law may not interfere with them in matters of religion, but, as Nundcomar is a Brahmin, they cannot decently present it before his execution, lest they should deem to solicit his death.' Naba Krishna, Krishna Kantu Nandi and other Indian supporters of the Hastings group were among the signatories.

[3] Nilmoni Thakur.   [4] Dhiraj Narain.

[5] Vansittart (*loc. cit.* p. 109) wrote: ' they have since been trying but still without success to procure a petition from the principal Hindoos in a more indirect manner. They have recommended to them to request they may be judged by the Laws of the Shaster [the 'Shastra, or holy Hindu laws] and not by those of England, and represented that if they neglect to do it on this occasion they will in future be liable to punishment for acting according to the tenets of their religion.' No such petition seems to have been presented, though the point was incorporated in the address of the Hindus to the judges (see n. 2 above).

[6] This was so widely believed in Calcutta that Clavering thought it necessary to swear an affidavit denying it.

[7] Surat-i-hal, a representation. This was too late to be the document from the Nabob which was apparently presented to the judges, since Nandakuma had been executed on the 5th (*Speech of Sir Elijah Impey* Part III Appendix 3, pp. 133-4).

Goordoss has got signed by the Nabob etc., in favour of Nundcomar. Radachurn wrote to him to get it down and said the General desired it and would send it home, and that it would ruin Mr. Hastings.

[Thursday] 10 [August 1775] M[orning].

Juggutchund. 'Nundcomar sent for me on Friday, he committed Goordoss to my care, told Danoo Samant [1] to tell Goordoss, complained of Radachurn absenting himself, said the new Gentlemen were the cause of his death.[2] I am told he had prepared an account of 11 crores and 40 lacks and directed that Goordoss, Radachurn etc. should prove it.'

[Wednesday] 16 [August 1775] M[orning] 9.

Sudder-ul-deen. 'Kishvar Cawn says Mr. Farrer wants more money under plea of securing the effects—Mr. Fowke wants to borrow money from Radachurn—52,000 rs. have been already expended. Radachurn has embezzled a part. . . .'

[Thursday] 17 [August 1775] M[orning] 8.

Juggutchund. 'Neta Sing will go with Mr. Fowke to Moorshedabad to take measures with him to induce Gordoss to interest himself for Radachurn. Radachurn expended 80,000 rs. of Nundcomar's.'

N.B. On the 14th the Gentlemen introduced Nundcomar's petition in the Proceedings as worthy the attention of the Company etc.—On the 16th Mr. Hastings moved that a copy should be sent to the Judges, of whom it was in abuse. The Majority then declared it a libel and ordered it should be burnt and erased.[3]

From these brief jottings a number of points of interest emerge. The most important from the standpoint of this study are those which concern the origin of the trial and the part played in it by the Hastings group. As to its origin they seem to confirm Stephen's view that criminal proceedings had been under consideration for some time. Mohan Prasad's reference at his interview on 26 April to an earlier contact with Farrer on this topic lends some support to Farrer's evidence at the time of Impey's attempted impeachment that criminal proceedings were under consideration in November 1774.[4] Moreover, Vansittart had mentioned in a letter of 23 February, 'Mohan Persaud I am told has commenced a prosecution against Nundcomar—Juggut Chund is arrived from Moorshedabad and Nundcomar is a little frightened '.[5] Nevertheless they also do

---

[1] Danu Samant.

[2] This was the day before Nandakuma's execution. Compare the words of his letter to Francis of 31 July 1775, five days earlier (quoted Stephen, *op. cit.* i. 234-5). ' As I entirely rely on your worship's endeavour to do me all the good you can, I shall not, according to the opinion of the Hindoos, accuse you in the day of judgment of neglecting to assist me in the extremity I am now in.'

[3] For this see *Speech of Sir Elijah Impey*, pp. 149 *seq.*   [4] See above p. 245, n. 3.

[5] Vansittart MSS., European letter-book, iii. 70: G. Vansittart to J. Graham, 23 February 1775; quoted Feiling, *op. cit.* p. 143.

much to confirm the opinion of those who believe that the case, arising from an old dispute, was brought to a head by Hastings's Indian friends for political reasons.   No definite steps would seem to have been taken and Mohan Prasad had not even selected his counsel, until the day after Hastings and the others concerned had made public their intention to prosecute on the conspiracy charges. It is true that, as Stephen claimed, proceedings could not have begun earlier, for the documents required, including the bond which was alleged to be forged, had only recently been released by the civil court which held them ; [1] but it had been known that they would be produced and at about what date, and Stephen's assumption that the criminal prosecution was only held up by absence of the necessary documents is clearly incorrect.   On 25 April, however, Sadar-ud-din, the chief Indian intermediary for the Hastings group, makes an appointment for Mohan Prasad and himself to call on Vansittart, and the following day Mohan Prasad unfolds his intentions and asks Vansittart's advice about them.   Beveridge's accusation that a plot had been concerted between Hastings and Mohan Prasad some time earlier in the year and that a month to six weeks was needed to suborn witnesses before proceedings were undertaken seems totally without foundation.[2]   But whether on 26 April the initiative rested with Mohan Prasad, with Sadar-ud-din (already active in connection with the conspiracy charges) or with others of the group it is not possible to say.   However this may be, the persons concerned, the timing of the approach and the need felt to get Vansittart's backing, seems to make the conclusion inescapable that political considerations played a big part in the decision to proceed forthwith.

Vansittart also played his part in bringing the case into the courts.   The entry describing the interview (which lasted an hour) is as full as most in the journal, but it leaves much unsaid.   Nevertheless it is clear that he gave his general approval to the plan, and he advised Mohan Prasad on the choice of his counsel.   It is hard to believe that, had he been discouraging, the action would have been proceeded with, at any rate at that time.   Indeed, in view of his relations with Sadar-ud-din and his skill in using the courts as a weapon, one is bound to consider the possibility whether he had not himself inspired the approach.   But the tenor of the entries in the journal seems to rule this out.   It would seem that he had not so far troubled himself to find out the details of the dispute (it was only after the decision had been taken that he obtained from Indian informants with claims to inside knowledge their accounts of the

---

[1] Evidence given during the trial put the date of the release of the documents at about 27 April.   The journal shows that they were in Mohan Prasad's hands on 26 April and probably on 25 April, when the appointment with Vansittart was made.

[2] Beveridge, *op. cit.* p. 104.

rights of the case), he did not commit himself as to the justice of Mohan Prasad's claims and he refused to examine the material the latter had brought in support of them. And if Vansittart was not behind the move it is still less likely that Hastings was. Indeed it seems quite probable that Vansittart did not consult Hastings before giving his support. It is true that between the time when Sadar-ud-din made the appointment at 6.0 p.m. on 26 April and the interview (which was at 8.0 a.m. next day) [1] he had time to discuss the matter with the governor if he so wished. But it would seem more likely that he would have seen Mohan Prasad himself before asking for a decision, if he thought one necessary, and his papers give ample evidence that he took important steps in Indian affairs on his own responsibility.

Even after the interview had taken place Vansittart did not at once take active steps in the matter. Though he interviewed Indian callers on 27 and 29 April, it was on other subjects, and though on 30 April he notes Naba Krishna's account of how the forgery was committed, he saw Sadar-ud-din on that and the next three days without the matter apparently coming under discussion. It was not till after 4 May, when Sadar-ud-din let him know that Mohan Prasad had actually submitted his petition to his counsel and that the die was cast, that the journal shows Vansittart beginning to take action. From that time on, however, the subject looms large and he is soon hard at work collecting from Indians evidence of a type likely to be useful to the prosecution and information about the line which the defence is going to take.

The entries show who were the Indians most active in furthering the prosecution. They were Mohan Prasad (whom Vansittart for for obvious reasons did not see again, but with whom Sadar-ud-din kept in touch), Kamal-ud-din (the chief witness for the prosecution), Jagat Chand (Nandakuma's hostile son-in-law) Sadar-ud-din (the active intermediary) and Raja Naba Krishna. All of these were men who had long and chequered relations with Nandakuma. Two of them, Mohan Prasad and Jagat Chand, he considered his bitter enemies ; a third, Kamal-ud-din, after much twisting and turning had come down on his enemies' side ; all the first four were strong supporters of the Hastings group. Personal enmity, and fear for their own futures, as well as loyalty to their patrons must have actuated them. Naba Krishna's position was different. He was neither committed to the governor-general's cause nor was he at this time an open enemy of Nandakuma (though he had in the past ample cause for hostility). Nandakuma seems indeed at this time to have believed that he could count on his support. But Naba Krishna was in fact the most dangerous of all his foes, and betrayed

---

[1] Presumably Sadar-ud-din gave him some idea what the interview would be about.

him both in the evidence he gave in court [1] and by passing on his confidences to Vansittart.

The evidence collected by these men was carefully noted in Vansittart's journal. Some of it, no doubt, was inserted solely for information and some of it was probably unsolicited, but the impression which is conveyed is that Vansittart was organizing the production of this information and was doing so for the practical purpose of assisting the prosecution. That considerable material was passed on to the counsel for the prosecution seems to be indicated by the entries of 9–11 May. On the 9th Naba Krishna called with an account of four false witnesses on whom he said (and correctly so far as three of them were concerned) Nandakuma intended to base his defence. On the 11th at 8.0 Jagat Chand called and spoke of three of these witnesses, with illustration of their past misdeeds. At 10.0 a.m. came Kamal-ud-din with an account of a seal-cutter alleged to have cut false seals for Nandakuma. That evening Vansittart notes that he handed over a memorandum to Mohan Prasad's counsel, Hercules Durham. And if it is not at all clear that Hastings was concerned in the origin of the case, his intimate relations with Vansittart make it inconceivable that he remained in ignorance of what was going on ; still further, in the course of the crowded activities of 11 May which preceded the production of Vansittart's memorandum there occurs the significant entry ' I saw the Governor '.[2]

It is not easy to judge how far these activities in fact affected the course of the trial. In the event the prosecution relied very little on the attempt to discredit Nandakuma and his witnesses, though the latter discredited themselves. This may have been due to the incompetence of the prosecution (to which the Chief Justice referred during the trial) [3] or to the quite understandable difficulty in persuading witnesses to testify (of which there is also evidence), but it may also have been due to the difficulty in obtaining from bazaar talk evidence which would stand up in a court of law. It is noteworthy that at the trial the only attempt to discredit a witness for the defence depended on obtaining official records from the council, and these the Majority refused to make available,[4] and that attempts

---

[1] In addition to ambiguous answers to questions (see p. 258 n. 6 above) he made a very bad impression when, overhearing a question which Nandakuma wished his Counsel to ask him, he said ' Rajah Nundcomar had better not ask me that question '. The court warned the jury not to be prejudiced by this incident. In view of Naba Krishna's character and experience it is hard to believe this remark was that of a naïve witness, or that the effect was not a calculated one.

[2] From his correspondence it is clear that Vansittart was in constant personal touch with the governor. In his journal he only twice notes meetings with him, on this occasion and on 22 April, when the decision to prosecute on the conspiracy charges was under discussion. These entries may be taken as indicating interviews concerned with the business treated in the journal.

[3] *Speech of Sir Elijah Impey*, Part III, Appendix 2. p. 129.

[4] *State Trials*, xx. 1057–59.

on the part of the defence to discredit the prosecution witnesses met with no success. It may well be that the most useful outcome of the efforts of Vansittart and his Indian informers lay in the information which they provided about the case that the defence was going to put up. By 18 May Sadar-ud-din had got from Naba Krishna a full and in the main accurate account of the line which the defence in fact adopted when the trial opened some three weeks later. There is a further point of some significance. Without the backing obtained from the supporters of the governor-general the prosecution would probably not have got under way; if it had, as Mr. Penderel Moon has pointed out it would ' certainly had come to nothing in the end. Nuncomar, as soon as things looked dangerous, would have settled the civil suit and with the plaintiff's collusion squared the prosecution witnesses.' [1] There are some indications in the evidence of Ram Nath of attempts at such a settlement. When approached with suggestions for a settlement Mohan Prasad was reported to have said ' I have told a great many English gentlemen of it ; I cannot desist '.[2] Vansittart's part in stiffening the prosecution must have been considerable.

The journal also adds to our knowledge of the way in which the defence was built up. The activities of the Majority during the trial are well-known, and rumours brought in from the bazaars add little reliable evidence about them, but light is thrown on Nandakuma's own efforts to organize his defence, a subject upon which little or no information has hitherto been available. It strongly confirms the conclusions which the court reached as to the credibility of his witnesses, and it also shows (when taken in conjunction with the report of the trial) that he was quite as successful in obtaining information about the activities of those furthering the prosecution, as they were in discovering his intentions.

What information the Vansittart MSS. provide of the petitions and counter-petitions which followed Nandakuma's condemnation, and of the progress of the conspiracy charges which came on at the same time, comes as much from the letter-books as the journal, and this is indicated above in the footnotes to the journal. Though they throw no light on the rejection by the Majority of Nandakuma's last appeal, for which posterity has harshly judged them,[3] they show that Nandakuma's English patrons did at least do what they could, through their ' banyans ' and Indian supporters, to stir up public opinion in favour of a respite. That these attempts failed miserably was due partly no doubt, as they alleged, to the tendency of partisans to flock to the conquering side, but the failure seems to have also represented real public opinion among not only the English but the Indian population. Vansittart was an interested witness, but he was also a shrewd and usually realistic observer of Indian opinion, and

[1] *Op. cit.* p. 163.   [2] *State Trials*, xx. 1039-40.   [3] Stephen, *op. cit.* i. 234 *seq.*

he was probably right when he wrote the day before Nandakuma's execution,

> I imagine he will quietly receive his fate. It is so universally wished for that neither the influence of power nor the prejudice of religion can persuade the principal Hindoos to take any measure to prevent it. A report prevailed about the town that he had purchased 200 false witnesses to make attacks upon all his enemies in case he had been acquitted.[1]

The story is not a pleasant one, but neither was the political situation that gave rise to it. Hastings spoke truly, it would seem, when he said, ' I have carefully avoided every circumstance which might appear to be an interference in that prosecution ', but, even if we assume that the decision to prosecute was taken without his sanction, he spoke with an economy of truth. On the other hand his opponents could not honestly have said as much. Nandakuma fought his last battle to the end by the only means he knew and, when it was lost, died with dignity. The proximate cause of his death was that for the first time he found himself before a court independent of the executive, and that he was caught up in the wheels of a judicial system whence neither bribery nor influence could extract him. But the real cause was a much less worthy one : he found himself before the court in the first instance largely because of the part he had taken in the internecine war among those who were ruling Bengal, a part which threatened Europeans and Indians alike, and the full penalty was exacted because the bitterness of this warfare made clemency impossible.[2]

---

[1] Vansittart MSS., European letter-book, iii. 110: G. Vansittart to J. Graham, 4 August 1775.

[2] Impey said at his trial (*Speech of Sir Elijah Impey*, p. 94) that if the council or the majority of it had made application for a respite, he would have given it, but in view of the strained relations between the Majority and the court at this time it seems very unlikely. More accurate would seem to be his statement in his letter to Governor G. Johnstone, 18 August 1778 (quoted Stephen, *op. cit.* i. 257–8) that the granting of a respite was impossible since ' No explanation could have made the natives . . . understand that the escape from justice, if the sentence had not been carried into execution, had not been occasioned by the artifice of the prisoner, unless, indeed, it had been attributed to corruption or timidity in the judges, or a controlling power in the Governor-General or Council '.

THE RESIGNATION ON BEHALF OF
WARREN HASTINGS, 1776:
GEORGE VANSITTART'S EVIDENCE

ON 18 October 1777 despatches were received in Calcutta informing Warren Hastings the Governor-General and his Council, General Clavering, Richard Barwell and Philip Francis, that the Governor's agent Lauchlin Macleane had handed in his principal's resignation to the Court of Directors of the East India Company, that it had been accepted, and that a new member of Council had been appointed in his place. It had already been laid down that General Clavering should be his successor in the Chair. That Clavering made a violent and indecent attempt to seize the Chair at once, and that Hastings disavowed his agent's action and refused to resign is well-known. What has never been clear, however, is how far Hastings could properly justify his action on the ground that his agent exceeded his authority in proferring this resignation.

This is not a problem that can readily be solved. In the first place the instructions given to Macleane and to his fellow-agent John Graham (who was out of the country on account of illness and took no part in the negotiations) have not come to light ; and, though they were often referred to in the recriminations, which followed; it is not clear precisely what they were or how they were expressed. Historians have been, moreover, confused by the error of Gleig, Hastings's first biographer, who believed that these instructions were to be found in a letter of 27 March 1775, and that, in consequence they were countermanded by a further letter of 19 May (1). This contention is manifestly incorrect. In the first place both these letters were written after the agents had sailed for England, and Hastings himself makes it clear that the instructions were given them before they left Calcutta, which they did about the middle of January (2). In the second place these two letters contain no instructions as to how the agents were to act on their arrival in England : they are concerned with the actions which Hastings might take in certain conditions, without awaiting the result of their negotiations. In the letter of 27 March he informs them "of a resolution which I have formed to leave this place and return to England on the first ship of the next season, if the first advices from England contain a disapprobation of the treaty of Benaris, or of the Rohilla War, and mark an evident disinclination to me" (3). In the second of 18 May he informs

---

(1) G. R. Gleig *Memoirs of the Life of the Right Hon. Warren Hastings*, 3 vols, 1841.

(2) They left Calcutta shortly after 13 January, and proceeded to England via Madras.

(3) Gleig *op. cit.*, i 521 Hastings wrote separately to each of his agents, and preserved a copy addressed to Graham in his letter-book Brit. Mus. Add MS 29 127 f 190 v.

them in a postscript "I now retract the resolution communicated to you separately in my letters of the 27th March. Whatever advices the first packet may bring, I am now resolved to see the issue of my appeal. . . . ."(4) The instructions they took with them were something quite different. Hastings, in the official letter to the Court of Directors of 15 August 1777, in which he justifies his decision not to resign, states "I am in possession of two papers which were presented to those Gentlemen at the time of their departure from Bengal ; one of these comprizes four short propositions, which I required as the condition of my being confirmed in this Government. The other paper contained an explanation of one of these" (5).

Even were these two papers to come to light, however, they are not likely in themselves to solve the problem, for it was admitted that they were inconclusive with respect to Macleane's precise powers. When the Court of Directors received on 11 October 1776 Macleane's notice of his resignation on Hastings's behalf, they took the precaution of asking to see his credentials (6). Macleane, pointing out that these were combined with confidential material, asked that they might be examined by a small Committee, and his request was granted(7). In the Committee he was asked, as he himself wrote to Hastings "Have you no instrument, saying, I, Warren Hastings, authorize you etc." To this he replied "No ; I believe neither Mr. Hastings nor any of those who were present, thought it a matter of so much formality ; if certain things were not obtained, I was ordered to signify Mr. Hastings's wish to be relieved ; if they were obtained, I was ordered not to make this signification (8)". In these circumstances the Committee decided to take supporting evidence from George Vansittart, recently returned from Bengal where he had been a member of the Board of Trade and Hastings's closest associate (9), and who had been present when the agents received their instructions ; and from John Stewart, late Secretary and Judge-Advocate of Bengal, a member of Hastings's "family", to whom the proceedings had been reported the following day. Their evidence was held to confirm Macleane's statements, and on 23 October the Directors accepted the proferred resignation (10).

There seems, indeed little doubt that Macleane was acting in good faith and in the spirit of his instructions, even though their wording might leave a loophole for escape. In the letters which Hastings wrote immediately after the receipt of the news he virtually admitted as much. He wrote to Francis Sykes for instance on 30 June 1777 "I believe and think it obvious, that I gave them [his agents] an unlimited discretion to act for me as they thought best,

---

(4) *Ibid.,* i 532-3 Brit. Mus. Add. MS. 29 127 f 200 v.

(5) *Ninth Report of the Select Committee on . . . the East Indies* 1783 Appendix 113. Letter from Hastings to the Board of Directors, 15 August 1777. Printed in *Reports from Committees of the House of Commons* vi 390.

(6) India Office Library. East India Company Court Book 85 pp. 353 and 368.

(7) *Ibid.,* p. 368.

(8) Gleig *op. cit.,* ii 88.

(9) He was a younger brother of Hastings's early patron Governor Henry Vansittart.

(10) East India Company Court Book 85, p. 376.

for my confidence in them was, as it ought to have been unbounded (11)''. But as time went on he began to change his attitude. Already in his letter to the Directors of 13 August 1777 this begins to become apparent (12), and by 20 November 1777 he could write to Dunning "I could find no traces either among my private papers or in my memory of any authority given him [Macleane] to use my name for so desperate a purpose" (13). By 1780 he considered all who had taken part in it as his betrayers.

Before this line was fully developed, however, he advanced an alternative one. According to this he admitted tacitly that he had authorized his agents to act but argued that they should have seen by his further correspondence, both with them and with the Company, that his intentions had changed. In this contention his letter of 19 May, on which Gleig laid such stress, played its part, for he appeals to "all the letters I have written to Colonel Macleane and my other friends since his departure, and to my letters to the Court of Directors, which all call out for a decision, either by my dismission or confirmation, and all vow that I will not resign" (14). But what he does not appear to have realized is that all the letters to which he refers and which were received in England before the resignation, referred not to his agents' proceedings, but to his own actions and intentions while awaiting the results of their mission, and that therefore they had no direct relevance to the point at issue. Only in one, his letter to Macleane of 14 July 1776 which (as he himself realized) came too late to affect the resignation, does he appear to link together these two issues. In this, it is true, he seems to suggest that the ultimate decision would be taken, if it came to a question of resignation, not in England on his behalf but by himself in India (15).

It would seem certain, therefore, that when the agents left Bengal they honestly believed that they were empowered to hand in Hastings's resignation unless certain conditions were obtained. It would also seem certain that, though the rise of his own fighting spirit and changing conditions including in India the death of Colonel Monson, which gave him a majority in Council (16), and in England the refusal of the Court of Proprietors in the ballot which followed the Court of 15 May 1776 to recall him at the Directors' request (17)—had modified Hastings's views—no new instructions had been given to his agents

---

(11) Quoted Gleig *op. cit.*, ii 155. He added, "But I never could mean, at least I think not, that when they had committed me to a public contest, and had engaged a whole people in my support, that they should make me quit the field, and decide the victory against myself."

(12) Printed in Appendix 113 to the Ninth Report of the Select Committee of 1783 (see n. 5).

(13) Brit. Mus. Add. MS. 29 128 f 152.

(14) Gleig *op. cit.*, ii 154.

(15) Brit. Mus. Add. MS. 29 127 f 251. "Though ruin or death should attend it, I will wait the event, and if I must fall I will not be the instrument of my own defeat by anticipating it, unless my friends at Home shall all join in advising it, and I shall be at the same time convinced of the propriety of a retreat."

(16) In September 1776.

(17) The circumstances are described in L. S. Sutherland *The East India Company in Eighteenth Century Politics*, Oxford 1952, pp. 301 seq.

which would lead them to doubt their authority. His emissaries were the victims of a failure of communication partly inevitable at such a distance but a good deal the fault of Hastings himself.

In a situation so fraught with confusion and misunderstanding any evidence from those concerned is of value, and it is therefore of interest that there should have come to light among the papers of George Vansittart preserved at Bisham Abbey, Berkshire (18) a copy of a letter written by him to Hastings on 15 November 1780. It was called forth by an attack made by Hastings on his good faith on this occasion. Though much of the letter is taken up with an attempt to minimize the extent of the support he gave to Macleane, it also contains his account of the interview when the agents received their instructions, and provides information about the instructions themselves which is not available elsewhere. It makes clear that one of the conditions Hastings was insisting on was either the recall of one of his enemies on the Council (he does not seem to have minded which) or the addition of a friend of his own to this body. Other letters among the Vansittart papers show that Vansittart himself was the friend most favoured for this position (19). The letter does not appear among Hastings's papers in the British Museum, since for some reason Hastings does not seem to have received it (20).

Vansittart MSS.   Private Letter Book 1772-1789, pp. 38-42(21).
        Warren Hastings Esq., Calcutta.

London 15 November 1780.

O[riginal] per Chapman.
D[uplicate] per Hinchinbrook.

DEAR HASTINGS,

I have addressed you in my usual style because I do not consider a few rash and intemperate words however unhandsome as sufficient to obliterate the remembrance of an intimate friendship of near 20 years standing. You will judge that I have seen your letter to Mr. Sulivan dated in January last, in which after denying your having empowered Mr. Macleane to resign on your behalf you add, "If Mr. Van Sittart has asserted it, he is false ; if he has sworn it, he is perjured(22)". Had any one informed me that you had made an assertion, which I thought or knew to deviate from fact, I would most certainly have written to you for an explanation, and till I had received such an explanation I would not for a moment have supposed a possibility that Mr. Hastings could be perjured or Mr. Hastings could be false. Surely you should have observed the same delicacy towards me. If you had not thought it generally due from one gentleman to another, yet I might have expected it from the very strict confidence which had so long subsisted

---

(18) I am grateful to Mrs. Paget of Bisham for permission to examine and make use of this document.
        (19) Vansittart M.S.S. Bisham Abbey.   European Letter Book III, pp. 49-61.
        (20) See n. 41.

between us, and which I was so little conscious of having done anything to interrupt that within these few days I did not hesitate to avow it both to a leading man among the Proprietors and to one of the Directors who mentioned this intimacy as their only objection to my succeeding to the vacancy in the Supreme Council (23).

The reason which induced you to make use of these terms is a supposition 'of my having born testimony to the Court of Directors that you had empowered Mr. Macleane to resign on your behalf. The motives for this resignation have long ago been explained to you. I will only say that Mr. Macleane came to Mr. Palk's (24) at Haldon (25) where General Caillaud (26), Mr. Pechell (27) and myself were at that time on a visit ; that he gave us an account of the determination of Lord North concerning you (28) (which by the bye was afterwards confirmed by Elliott) (29) and of his negotiations with him ; that he signified his resolution of resigning on your behalf if we did not disapprove it ; and that in consideration of the circumstances he represented to us we all agreed in opinion that the proposed resignation was an expedient measure and most conducive to your advantage. Nothing could have turned out more fortunate (30) than this has done, but at any rate I conclude you cannot have taken offence on this account as you retain the same confidence as before in Pechell and Caillaud who equally with me assented to it.

As to my testimony (31) it was merely to this effect, "that when you gave your instructions to Macleane on his departure from Bengal you told him you would not remain a nominal Governor without any real power but were resolved to quit your station unless by the removal of Clavering, Francis or Monson or by the addition of some friend of your's to the Council the

---

(21) The following transcript preserves the spelling and punctuation of the original (except for the insertion of full stops where these were clearly intended but omitted) ; modern practice has been adopted in the use of capitals, and contractions have been expanded.

(22) Brit. Mus. Add. MS. 29128, f. 212. 6 January 1780. Vansittart's quotation has a slight verbal difference from the original.

(23) Vansittart unsuccessfully applied for the position of member of the Supreme Council in Bengal in 1780. Hastings's friends supported the successful candidate John MacPherson, see Brit. Mus. Add. MS. 29147, ff. 24-28, S. Pechell to W. Hastings, 8 January 1781, and elsewhere.

(24) Robert Palk, M.P., formerly Governor of Madras, brother-in-law to the late Governor Henry Vansittart.

(25) Haldon Hall in Devon. Macleane went down there to discuss the proposed resignation at the beginning of September 1776. For the negotiation see L. S. Sutherland, *op. cit.,* pp. 312-3.

(26) General John Caillaud, retired from service in India, brother-in-law to Samuel Pechell.

(27) Samuel Pechell, Master in Chancery, a staunch supporter of Hastings at India House.

(28) North was determined to remove Hastings by Act of Parliament next session, Sutherland, *op. cit.,* pp. 310-11.

(29) Alexander Elliot, son of Sir Gilbert Elliot, M.P., a close friend of Hastings over on leave from India. He was well-informed about this affair through William Eden, who was about to marry his sister, *Ibid.,* p. 311, n. 1.

authority was given you as well as the name, and that you authorized him to declare this resolution wherever he thought proper". The words of the Committee's report the 23rd of October 1776 are "that from the purport of Mr. Hastings's instructions contained in a paper in his own handwriting given to Mr. Macleane and produced by him to them Mr. Hastings declares that he will not continue in the Government of Bengal unless certain conditions therein specified can be obtained, of which they see no possibility. And Mr. George Vansittart has declared to them that he was present when these instructions were given to Mr. Macleane and when Mr. Hastings empowered Mr. Macleane to declare his resignation to this Court. Mr. Stewart has likewise confirmed to them that Mr. Hastings declared to him that he had given directions to the above purpose to Mr. Macleane (32). So stands the report as recorded in the proceedings of the Court of Directors ; but the testimonies at length as delivered to the Committee are not to be found, and in the original proceedings of the Court of Directors the words *and when Mr. Hastings empowered Mr. Macleane* are interlined(33). I am perfectly satisfied that the words actually used by me were to the purport I have mentioned. Mr. Becher (34) thinks so too, and says that many alterations were made before they could fix upon the wording of the report. In confirmation of this I well remember, and so does Mr. Becher, that he expressed himself at the time not perfectly satisfied with Macleane's authority(35), which would hardly have been the case had Stewart and I positively testified that you had empowered Macleane to declare your *resignation* to the Court of Directors. That my testimony was as I have mentioned I think I can safely trust my memory although the distance of time is now very considerable ; but of this I am quite positive that when it was delivered to the gentlemen deputed from the Directors I had a perfect recollection of the words you used to Macleane and that I reported them literally without attempting to alter or explain them. They were merely a confirmation I believe of your written instructions to him and little more than was implied in some of your publick letters.

Conceiving as I did that your resignation was the measure most advisable for your benefit, in which your best friends (Palk, Pechell, Caillaud, Elliott) entirely co-incided, what might not you have justly said to me had I refused, when called upon by your Agent, to have reported a conversation which he thought necessary to enable him to carry that measure into execution ?—As a further proof that, although I wished Macleane to be able to satisfy the Directors of his authority, I did not mean to support it by asserting more than the precise fact I well remember to have told him that if the Directors asked my opinion whether you would resign were you present to determine for yourself, I should be obliged to say that I thought you would not without the

---

(30) The result was certainly fortunate for Hastings, if it prevented his removal by Act of Parliament, but in this context Vansittart probably meant to write "unfortunate".

(31) Before the Committee set up by the Court of Directors to advise them on Macleane's credentials. See p. 2, ns. 4 and 5.

(32) See n. 10.

(33) This is so.

previous approbation of the Proprietors but yould deem yourself in honour bound to stay after the support they had given you(36) But as that support did not and could not amount to the point of giving you a majority in Council I imagined you would be well pleased with Macleane's resignation for you. This was the language I held to everybody who inquired of me and it was my real opinion.

In your letter to the Court of Directors wherein you disavow Macleane's authority to resign on your behalf you speak I believe of the above-mentioned instructions being superseded by a subsequent letter(37) to him, in which you declared that you would not be driven to a resignation by the attacks of the Majority but would bear with every indignity they could put upon you till the disputes between you were decided in England. Doubtless you best know your own meaning, but I confess I considered Lord North's determination to remove you by Act of Parliament as a full decision in favour of your Opponents, and consequently as entitling Macleane to make use of his former instructions. If you ask why I imagined Macleane's resignation would be agreeable to you, the constant tenour of your declarations how much you were disgusted with your situation whilst a determined Majority were thwarting you in every measure you planned and continually harassing you with unmerited attacks upon your character, and the strong injunctions you laid upon your Agents not to let your name be made use of for the purposes of party in opposition to Lord North (38) were I think sufficient grounds for such an imagination ; but if I was mistaken (as every one must sometimes be) it was surely very inconsistent with that candour, which used to form a part of Mr. Hastings's character, to suppose in consequence that I could merit the injurious terms in which you have expressed yourself. Nothing could warrant them but an idea that I had sacrificed truth and betrayed your interest for sinister views of my own, and how such an idea could be entertained by you is to me utterly inconceivable. Every part of my conduct in India and particularly the line I pursued after the avowal of Clavering etc. (39) must surely have rendered it wonderfully improbable ; and since my return to England, whether you have been in favour with the ruling people or out of favour (40), I have constantly professed the greatest esteem for you and been always ready to contribute

---

(34) Richard Becher, a Director of the Company and Company servant returned from India, was a member of the Committee. Macleane reported the part Becher played on it.

(35) Gleig, *op. cit.*, p. 88.

(36) At the Court of Proprietors of 15 May and the ballot following it when the Proprietors defeated the attempt of the Directors, urged on by the Ministry to recall Hastings. See n. 17 above.

(37) Hastings's letter to the Directors of 15 August 1777. See n. 5 above. He had not alluded here to any one particular letter to his agents. Vansittart would seem to be alluding to that of 18 May—see p. 2 above.

(38) Hastings himself admitted this fact. See Gleig, ii, 155. Letter to F. Sykes of 30 June 1777.

(39) Illustrated in the Vansittart MSS., Bisham Abbey, *passim*.

(40) Since early in 1780 Hastings's party in the Company had the support of Administration, which had hitherto been hostile. (Sutherland, *op. cit.*, p. 346).

every assistance in my power to your support. I have considered our friendship as unalterable and looked with much pleasure to the time of our meeting again whether in India or in England. On what footing we are to be in future must depend upon you. I shall write no more till I receive your answer (which I hope to do as expeditiously as possible) but I will still join with your other friends in supporting your cause wherever occasion requires. I wish our former intimacy to be renewed, and I can overlook the harsh terms you have used (I assure you most unjustly used) but I confess with Mr. Hastings a mere acquaintance would rather give me pain than pleasure. If therefore on reflection you can still have an idea that I could merit such terms or be induced by any other motive than a regard for your welfare to approve of Macleane's resignation, I lament the loss of a once valued friend and with much regret (though with the consolation of reflecting that it is without the smallest fault of mine) I bid you adieu for ever (41).

I have long been and should be happy always to remain
dear Hastings
Your very sincere and affectionate friend.

---

(41) This letter apparently never reached Hastings, who continued implacable. After S. Pechell wrote to intercede for Vansittart on 8 January 1781 (Brit. Mus. Add. MS. 29147, ff. 24-28) Hastings apparently wrote him a letter but spoke harshly of him on 23 February 1782 to Pechell (Brit. Mus. Add. MS. 29129, f. 24) and it was not till late in 1783 that he realized that Vansittart had sent an explanation which he had not received. He then wrote warmly to him on 1 November 1783 (*Ibid.* ff. 205 *seq.*), apologising for "the expressions which I used in my letter to Mr. Sulivan".

IV
Edmund Burke

BIBLIOGRAPHICAL NOTE

The definitive edition of *The Correspondence of Edmund Burke*, general editor T.W. Copeland (Cambridge and Chicago), contains a number of very valuable introductions to individual volumes, including Dame Lucy's contribution to volume 2 (1960).

CHAPTER 14

On the politics of the Rockingham party in general see F. O'Gorman, *The Rise of Party in England* (London, 1975); P. Langford, *The First Rockingham Administration, 1765-66* (Oxford, 1973); P.D.G. Thomas, *British Politics and the Stamp Act Crisis* (Oxford, 1975).

CHAPTER 15

The death of John Woods in 1983 leaves this as the definitive work on the subject.

Edmund Burke (1729-97) (After James Barry, 1774)
(National Portrait Gallery)

EDMUND BURKE AND RELATIONS BETWEEN MEMBERS OF PARLIAMENT AND THEIR CONSTITUENTS

On 3rd November 1774, Edmund Burke at the close of the Poll which won him his memorable success in the contested election for Bristol, made a speech thanking those who had supported him and promising to serve his new constituents faithfully. He had been in the House of Commons since 1766 and was to sit there till 1794; this was the only occasion in his long parliamentary career in which he had to fight a contested election, and the only time he represented a constituency numbering more than 300 persons and with any claim to independence. He assured them that he believed "it ought to be the happiness and glory of a representative to live in the strictest union, the closest correspondence and the most unreserved communication with his constituents." But he went on, in famous words still quoted with approval today in a greatly changed political world, to warn them that, if Government were no more than "a matter of will upon any side" their will should be superior to his, but that

> "Government and legislation are matters of reason and judgment, and not of inclination; and what sort of reason is that, in which the determination precedes the discussion; in which one set of men deliberate and another decide; and where those who form the conclusion are perhaps three hundred miles distant from those who hear the arguments?"

He summed up in the great phrase: "Your representative owes you, not his industry only, but his judgment; and he betrays instead of serving you, if he sacrifices it to your opinion." And he concluded:

> "Parliament is not a congress of ambassadors from different and hostile interests; which interests each must maintain, as agent and advocate, against other agents and advocates; but parliament is a *deliberative* assembly of *one* nation, with *one* interest, that of the whole. . . . You choose a member indeed; but when you have

chosen him, he is not a member for Bristol, but he is a member
of *Parliament.*"[1]

Burke, as he made clear to his audience, was stating his case against the
contemporary movement for issuing instructions to representatives.

It has long been recognized that in making this statement he was enun-
ciating no new constitutional principle. He was clothing in his own rhetoric
the generally accepted views of almost all reputable eighteenth-century politicians. As Mr. Emden has pointed out in *The People and the Constitution,*[2] such diverse seventeenth-century authorities as Coke and Algernon
Sydney, and, in the first half of the eighteenth century, successive editions
of popular books of reference, such as Chamberlayne's *Magnae Britanniae
Notitia,* had made the same point. Moreover, that oracle of eighteenth-century constitutionalism, Speaker Onslow, had made a balanced and authori-
tative statement on precisely the issue later raised by Burke:

> "Every member, as soon as he is chosen, becomes a representa-
> tive of the whole body of the Commons, without any distinction
> of the place from which he is sent to parliament. Instructions
> therefore from particular constituents to their own members are
> or can be only for information, advice and recommendation
> (which they have a perfect right to offer, if done decently; and
> which ought to be respectfully received and well-considered);
> but are not absolutely binding upon votes, and actions, and con-
> science in Parliament."[3]

Eighteenth-century Members of Parliament in adopting this position saw
themselves as protecting not only the authority of Parliament in its corporate capacity, but also one aspect of what they prized equally, their own
personal "independency."

The Corporation of Bristol, like the City of London and other commercial centres, frequently requested their representatives to take up matters
of concern to them, both in the House and with departments of State. In

---

[1] Bohn Edition Works i. 446-7.
[2] C. S. Emden. *The People and the Constitution,* 2nd edn., 1956, pp. 23ff. Dr. W.
Ferguson of Edinburgh University has kindly pointed out to me a very different tradition in the Scottish counties, where, particularly in the earlier years of the eighteenth
century, representatives were not only frequently given instructions by their electors,
but were pledged at their election (e.g., in Sterlingshire in 1727) to obey "instructions
. . . transmitted from time to time by my Constituents . . . relative to the interest of
North Britain in General and the Shire of Sterling in particular the same being subscribed by a plurality or Quorum appointed by them." (Scottish Register House G.D.
22/3/798.) A committee was often set up to handle such instructions (e.g., in Midlothian
in 1774. Ibid. Records of the Sheriff Court of Midlothian, Freeholders' Minutes, vol. 3,
pp. 9-10).
[3] Attributed to Speaker Onslow in a note in J. Hatsell *Precedents and Proceedings in
the House of Commons* ii. (1781) 55.

so doing they were conforming to a tradition going back to the boroughs of the middle ages. Though Burke was often to find such business tiresome, and though even where issues of this kind were in question there was the possibility of a clash of opinions between electors and representatives (as he was to discover in connection with the Irish trade) it was not to instructions of this kind that he took exception. It was to instructions demanding of representatives their support of a prescribed line in matters of national and constitutional interest that he objected—and, as Burke well knew, Bristol had from time to time also issued instructions of the type to its representatives, the last time no longer than two years before.[4]

Evidence of the employment of instructions to representatives as a means of expressing public opinion on national issues can be found spasmodically as early as the beginning of the seventeenth century. Later, during the Exclusion Crisis of 1679-81, Shaftesbury, that arch-propagandist, made extensive use of them in his struggle against the Crown. In the fierce party conflicts of Anne's reign, their use is found alongside other methods of bringing pressure to bear on governments from 'without doors,' though for the most part addresses and petitions were more commonly used.[5] Rather surprisingly the issue of such instructions became peculiarly prominent as a means of expressing public opinion in the quieter days of the first two Hanoverians. Hence the need which began to be felt to examine their constitutional validity.

It might on the face of it seem strange that this particular form of expression of extra-parliamentary opinion should be widely employed in a period when the parliamentary system had become so unrepresentative, when electorates were for the most part small and irrationally based, and when even in the counties and open boroughs elections were largely fought, if at all, on local and personal rather than national issues. In part the explanation is simple: such instructions were not the result of spontaneous action by the constituents; they were carefully planned by the representatives themselves.[6] They came to be, in fact, one of the main weapons of politicians in opposition striving to embarrass their opponents in power. The politicians made use of them because they agreed with Burke himself that "we know that all opposition is absolutely crippled if it has no sort of

[4] Urging them to support Alderman John Sawbridge's motion for shorter parliaments. *London Chronicle*, 22-25 Feb. 1772.

[5] I am indebted to Professor G. Holmes and Dr. W. A. Speck for information about the practice in Queen Anne's reign.

[6] Horace Walpole, *Memoires of the Last Ten Years of the Reign of George the Second* ii., 132, speaks of the Tories in 1757 and "the instructions which they had instructed their representatives to send them." Embarrassment to members usually arose only when those sitting for the same constituency represented different interests, e.g., at Bristol and in the City of London.

support without doors." They could not make use of them, however, except by calling on and making use of some already existent public opinion and presuppositions. In consequence, campaigns of instructions to representatives were associated with issues on which a number of people 'without doors' could be expected to feel strongly—Walpole's relations with Spain and the waging of the war against her;[7] the loss of Minorca by the Newcastle administration in 1756;[8] the Excise Bill of 1733 (which not only affected important commercial interests, but awoke through the word 'excise' sinister seventeenth-century echoes); the Jewish Naturalization Act of 1753,[9] against which commercial jealousies were reinforced by religious anti-Semitism. But they always incorporated in addition the set of political principles (or shibboleths), which lay at the base of what has been called the 'Country' tradition, the hatred and fear of the executive. Dr. Holmes has recently shown, through the party turmoils of Queen Anne's reign, the power of this tradition in cutting through all party barriers.[10] Its vitality continued into the Hanoverian period, and it continued to find expression in forms born of past conflicts—opposition to standing armies and foreign entanglements, demands for place and pension bills, and a request for shorter Parliaments. Every campaign of instructions to representatives contained demands for some or all of these measures, a programme for political reform one could say, but one looking much more to the past than to the present.

Since the eighteenth-century opposition politicians made use of public opinion in this way, it is obvious to us (if not to them) that they were bringing nearer the time when this public opinion would express itself without awaiting their guidance. But in the England of the first two Georges such a possibility seemed remote. The agitations which the politicians roused died down with the political situations which created them. The only partial exception lay in the metropolis, with its centre in the City of London. The support of the City was essential for any campaign of Instructions on account of its long tradition of political activity, the strength of the 'Country' tradition among its middling citizens, is preponderant commercial and financial importance, its vicinity to the political capital, and the influence it could wield over other commercial centres.[11] Its own firm confidence in what a

---

[7] A volume was published in 1741, *Great Britain's Memorial containing a Collection of Instructions* . . .

[8] See L. S. Sutherland. *The City of London and the Devonshire-Pitt Administration 1756-7.* Raleigh Lecture of the British Academy, 1960. Above, pp. 67-113.

[9] See T. W. Perry. *Public Opinion, Propaganda and Politics in Eighteenth Century England, a Study of the Jew Bill of 1753.* Harvard University Press, 1962.

[10] G. Holmes. *British Politics in the Age of Anne* (1967), pp. 116 seq.

[11] L. S. Sutherland. 'The City of London in Eighteenth Century Politics,' *Essays presented to Sir Lewis Namier*, ed. R. Pares and A. J. P. Taylor (1956). Above, pp. 41-66.

seventeenth-century Londoner called "London's power . . . and the irre-
sistible influence of her actions over all the nation for many hundreds of
years"[12] made it peculiarly independent of political leaders from without;
but even in London the danger of a break-away was not serious in the first
half of the century. A city pamphlet of 1739 shows both the limitation of
popular participation in such campaigns at this time and also the possibilities of a changed situation in the future:

> "You have, Gentlemen,"—its author wrote, addressing the Liv-
> erymen of the City—, "All the Reason in the world to applaud
> yourselves in the Choice of your Representatives in Parliament. . . .
> But some have . . . found fault with the Constitution of Britain,
> in that Powers vested in our Representatives are too independent
> of the People. The only Remedy to prevent the Abuse of these
> powers, which the People can apply, is, by their giving their Rep-
> resentatives Instructions how to behave on all Points of National
> Concern. But we are sensible how difficult it is for small Cor-
> porations to know, in complicated Points, what is their real In-
> terest. Thus they are at a loss what Instructions they are to give
> their Representatives who are left at Liberty to act as they
> please . . ."

The solution to this problem lay, in the writer's opinion, with the City of
London as leader of the Nation:

> You need only fix it as a Rule to give Instructions to your Rep-
> resentatives upon these Great Points, whenever they shall occur,
> and make these Instructions public to the world. This would be a
> Direction to all the Nation . . . . It is true that at present Represen-
> tatives are under no obligation to regard the Instructions of their
> Constituents, but such a conduct in you would make the meanest
> of the People Judge how far their Members have acted consist-
> ently with the Interests of the People. . . .[13]

It was in the earlier years of George III's reign that the situation began
to change, and the change came in the metropolis with the growth of City
Radicalism, that curious outbreak of popular opinion associated with the
name of John Wilkes. To the old demands of the 'Country' tradition the
Radicals added a new one for 'the more equal representations of the people,' a demand which led directly to the pressure for the reform of the fran-
chise and the parliamentary reforms of the nineteenth century; and the
Radical forces in the City and the metropolis made an effort both to exercise the influence which the City believed itself to exercise over the coun-

---

[12] W. Gough. *Londinum Triumphans or an Historical Account of the Grand Influence
the Actions of the City of London have had upon the Affairs of the Nation for many
ages past*, 1682.
[13] *The Conduct of the Liverymen Justified*, 1739.

try, and to do so not under the leadership of parliamentary groups but on
their own initiative. These were the years of Burke's political apprenticeship, and it was against this background that he made his statement to his
constituents in 1774.

In the new situation during these years, a new type of campaign of instructions to representatives began to develop. The first took place at the
beginning of 1769 when Middlesex, Westminster and the City instructed
their representatives to protest against Wilkes's expulsion from Parliament,
to press for redress of other grievances, and to urge the old 'Country' tradition demands for reform. Alderman Beckford, an old leader of the popular forces in the City—though one who was beginning to feel the challenge
of Wilkes, played a big part in stimulating the movement. Since he was
himself one of the representatives instructed, it might seem at first sight that
the move was not unlike others in the past; but, though there were two
parliamentary groups in opposition, both anxious to show that they had
support 'without doors' (the Chatham-Shelburne group with which Beckford himself had affiliations, and the Rockingham group to which Burke
belonged), his move was concerted with neither, and was devised, in part
at least, to bring pressure to bear on both.[14]

A few weeks later, in a debate in the House of Commons on the payment of the Civil List debts, he took the opportunity to assert his belief
that members were bound to obey the instructions of their constituents.[15]
The result was the first extended debate on this constitutional issue. The
Government's line was obvious and traditional, Jeremiah Dyson, something of a constitutional expert, speaking for them:

> I will offer a few words on the subject of instructions to mem-
> bers of parliament. I conceive there is, and ever has been, the
> most essential difference between deputies appointed to act ac-
> cording to the orders of those who send them, and representatives
> of the people who are chosen to act and judge for them. Which
> of the two is the Constitution of Parliament?

There could be only one answer:

> Has the constitution provided any means of collecting the sense
> of the constituents? Who, Sir, authorized the recent violent meet-
> ing at Guildhall to represent the Livery of London? Are members
> of this House to follow the instructions of any set of men who
> may meet violently together?[16]

---

[14] L. S. Sutherland. *The City of London and the Opposition to Government, 1768-1774.*
Creighton Lecture, 1958. See above, pp. 115-47.
[15] Debate of 1 March 1769. J. Wright. *Sir H. Cavendish's Debates of the House of
Commons.* 1841. i. 280.
[16] *Ibid.* i. 285.

Beckford found unqualified support in the House from only one City radical[17] (the other metropolitan members appear to have remained discreetly silent), but it is the reaction of the parliamentary opposition groups which is the most interesting. Isaac Barré, a prominent member of the Chatham-Shelburne group, which always prided itself on its popular connexions, was sympathetic but ambiguous:

> The notion of members receiving instructions from their constituents has been treated by a certain party of the House with great contempt. I do not rise for the sake of encouraging a factious disposition; but when instructions, proceeding from the true voice of the people, come to us in the spirit of the constitution, they are not to be laughed at.[18]

Edmund Burke, spokesman for the Rockingham group, also anxious for extra-parliamentary affiliations, but handicapped by its unusually aristocratic composition, was more downright. Though he agreed emphatically that "when they come to us upon constitutional ground, the sense of the people without doors is to be listened to with great attention, with great care," he pinned his colours to the mast against instructions. "As to the doctrine of instructions to representatives, it is unfounded in reason; if not put down, it will destroy the constitution."[19]

The movement in the City was only at its beginning and in the turbulent years ahead the Radicals pressed their demands by organized petitions, by remonstrances, by instructing their representatives and persuading others to do the same, and, a new development, by trying to force their representatives to comply with their instructions. With this end in view they adopted a new device, suggested it would seem by that formidable Radical lady Mrs. Catherine Macaulay,[20] that of the pledge to be extorted from candidates at the time of their election. In 1771 the Society of the Supporters of the Bill of Rights incorporated in a resolution a scheme inviting all candidates to pledge themselves at the hustings to obey the instructions of their elec-

---

[17] Sir Joseph Mawbey, M.P. for Southwark. He stated that he had the instructions of his constituents, "a body of the most independent electors of the kingdom," with him. *Ibid.* i. 282.

[18] Debate of 1 March 1769. J. Wright. *Sir H. Cavendish's Debates of the House of Commons.* 1841. i. 283.

[19] *Ibid.* i. 287-8.

[20] She had made the proposal in her pamphlet replying to Burke, *Observations on a Pamphlet, Thoughts on the Cause of the Present Discontents.* (1770) Quoted I. R. Christie, *Wilkes, Wyvill and Reform* (1962), p. 43. For her see L. M. Donely. 'The Celebrated Mrs. Macaulay,' *William and Mary Quarterly,* Vol. IV, No. 2. Apr. 1949. It does not seem that Sir Francis Dashwood's *Address to the Gentlemen, Clergy and Freeholders of all the Counties in Great Britain . . .* 1747, in which a pledge of the same kind was proposed, had influenced them in any way. For this pamphlet see B. Kemp, *Sir Francis Dashwood, an Eighteenth Century Independent* (1967), pp. 159-163.

tors, and as an earnest of their good faith, to accept forthwith a programme of instructions.[21] They voted to circulate this resolution to all the constituencies of the United Kingdom so that they might follow the metropolitan example. The resolution was put into effect with success at a by-election in the City in 1773;[22] but it could only be applied on a large scale at a General Election, and the General Election of 1774 was that in which they made a determined attempt to carry it out in the metropolitan area, and to persuade other constituencies to follow their example.

In the early autumn of 1774, the Parliament which had been sitting since 1768 was unexpectedly dissolved about nine months before its term ran out. Preparations for the election were less forward than usual and the City Radicals were particularly hard-hit, as they were in the midst of a battle to obtain the return of John Wilkes as Lord Mayor. Nevertheless, they set vigorously to work. As early as 13 September the *Public Advertiser* reported that the Society of the Supporters of the Bill of Rights had proposed that their Committee of Correspondence should circulate to all Sheriffs and Returning Officers their resolution of 1771, and were also preparing division lists to show how sitting members had voted on recent controversial issues.[23] As soon as the writs were out for the new Parliament, they began to prepare pledges and make out programmes to impose on their own candidates, first for Middlesex, then for the City, Westminster and Southwark, drawn up in almost identical terms. As soon as the City proposals had been adopted, circular letters were sent off with all haste, urging counties and boroughs to follow their example.[24] The Instructions themselves followed the patterns used in earlier campaigns. They contained orders on how to act on the questions of political importance which were the occasion of the agitation. The exclusion of Wilkes as M.P. of Middlesex must be reversed; so too must recent Government policy towards the American colonies. They also contained the traditional 'Country' measures—support for shorter parliaments and for anti-pension bills, together with the recent demand for the "more equal representation of the people." Their most marked originality lay, however, in the pledge to be extorted from candidates, and here they not only insisted on unqualified obedience, but they carried to its logical conclusion the 'Country' tradition of hostility to place or pensions. The pledge imposed on City candidates is worth quoting verbatim:

[21] Christie, *op. cit.* p. 48.
[22] I. R. Christie. 'The Wilkites and the General Election of 1774,' *Guildhall Miscellany*, 1962. The pledge was also taken by the unsuccessful candidate in two by-elections at Worcester, 1773 and 1774. *Ibid.*
[23] *Public Advertiser*, 13 Sept. 1774.
[24] 1-4 Oct. *Middlesex Journal.* Quoted I. R. Christie 'The Wilkites and the General Election of 1774,' *loc. cit.*

> We do also solemnly promise never to accept from the Crown or
> its Ministers, place, pension, contract, title, gratuity or emolu-
> ment of any kind whatsoever; and we do further promise to fol-
> low on all occasions such instructions as our constituents, in
> Common Hall assembled, shall think proper to give us.[25]

The *Public Advertiser* of 5 October 1774, an organ always sympathetic to
the City Radicals, contained a 'puff'—"It is generally supposed that the noble example set by the Freeholders of Middlesex in insisting on a Test from
their candidates will be followed throughout the kingdom." In fact, as Professor Christie has shown,[26] the ambition behind these efforts was completely unrealistic, and the results outside the metropolitan area were negligible. The claims of the City to speak for the nation were rejected even in
the open boroughs and the commercial centres whose links with the City
were strong. A Wilkite who had taken the pledge was returned for Dover,
and two Radicals who had taken the pledge, but were not Wilkites, were returned for Bedford. Otherwise, outside the metropolitan area, so far as we
know, the issue was only seriously raised at Newcastle-on-Tyne, Worcester
and Southampton. At Bristol itself Henry Cruger, Burke's radical colleague-
to-be, offered a pledge, but the offer was not taken up. Only in the Metropolitan area were there real successes. Of the ten seats involved (4 for the
City; 2 for Westminster; 2 for Southwark; 2 for the County of Middlesex)
6 fell to the Radicals; but even here the two pledged candidates were defeated at Westminster, and only one of the two pledged candidates at Southwark was returned. In the City itself, though four Radicals were returned,
one of them (through enmity to Wilkes) had refused to take the pledge.

No great movement therefore swept the country, as distinct from the
Metropolis in the 1774 Election. Nevertheless, when the individual candidate faced the demand on the hustings, it was an awkward moment. It
was one thing to justify one's 'independency' speaking in the House of
Commons. It was quite another before an election crowd whose suffrages
were sought. Where a demand was made and the candidate had no intention of acceding to it, he generally decided to sweep it aside without argument. At Worcester for instance, when Sir Watkin Lewes, a Radical candidate from the City who had already unsuccessfully contested the seat,
tried, as the Press reported, "to introduce certain articles as a test of the
several candidates' political principles of the same purport as those of London and Westminster,"[27] he was "interrupted before he had read them by

---

[25] As printed in the Press, e.g., *The London Chronicle*, 1-4 Oct., 1774.
[26] I. R. Christie. *Wilkes, Wyvill and Reform* (1962) and 'The Wilkites and the General Election of 1774,' *Guildhall Miscellany*, 1962, pp. 155-164, on whom I rely for this account.
[27] *London Chronicle*, Oct. 13-15, 1774. Letter from Worcester.

Mr. Walsh[28] who declared he would not sign any articles at all." Similarly at Southampton, just before the Poll opened, the agent of a candidate, Lord Charles Montague "read over in a loud voice" to the candidates a similar engagement for them to sign. At this Hans Stanley (who had sat for the borough since 1754 and was to continue to do so till his death in 1790) retorted that whoever signed it he would not, and that the only "true thing" in the declaration was "the beginning of it, namely, that the City of London took the lead, for that indeed those who call themselves the City of London take the lead a great deal more than becomes them."[29]

There are on record only two attempts during this election to put a reasoned case against the Instructions to and the pledge from candidates; that of Burke, which was made after his election was over, and that of an unsuccessful candidate for the City of London, William Baker, who tried to read out his case against the demands at the nomination meeting at Guildhall, was howled down, and then published his statement in a letter to the Press. As I shall suggest these two statements were connected and complementary.

A rather odd aspect of Burke's famous statement is why he felt impelled to make it when he did. If the position at Bristol is taken in isolation, it seems hardly necessary. The election was safely over, no one had been asked to sign a pledge, there was no suggestion that instructions should be given either to him or his colleague, and throughout the country as a whole the attempt to obtain them had failed lamentably. But the reason why the issue weighed on Burke's mind is easier to understand when it is realized how much he had been affected by the movement in the metropolis to enforce it. In the first place, his own attempt to stand for Westminster (before he was suddenly called to Bristol)[30] was wrecked by it. In the second place, William Baker, who made his unsuccessful stand for the City against it, was his personal friend, in whose candidature he had been closely concerned.

When the General Election of 1774 came on earlier than was expected, Burke was among those who had made no arrangements for a seat. Lord Verney could no longer offer him a seat at Wendover, and his own finances

[28] John Walsh (1726-95), friend of Lord Clive. Sat for Worcester 1761-1780 at considerable expense.

[29] *London Chronicle*, Oct. 11-13, 1774. Letter from Southampton. Stanley added that at Westminster it was the rule to debate first and sign afterwards, that he did not believe in shorter parliaments and was doubtful about the more equal representation of the people.

[30] The possibility of Burke standing for Westminster had been discussed before 18th September. The possibility of contesting Bristol was first raised round about 1st October but was abandoned; was renewed on 4th October, and discussed by Burke and emissaries from Bristol at Bath on 5th October, once again without success; and finally his nomination was made in his absence on 9th October, when he was in the North for his election to Rockingham's borough of Malton.

were at a low ebb. In this situation he had either to rely on Lord Rockingham for a seat for one of his much-sought-after boroughs, or be adopted
for one of the few big popular constituencies where, to get a well-known
candidate, the leading constituents might meet most of the expenses. Before the possibility of Bristol came up, it had been suggested to Burke by
some of the popular party that he might stand for Westminster.[31] For success the support of the great John Wilkes was necessary, but Burke, acting
for his party in the City, was in fairly close touch with the demagogue
(whatever his personal opinion of him might be),[32] and Wilkes was at first
encouraging about the candidature. But Wilkes never laid much store by
alliance with the Rockinghams, and the hopes soon proved illusory. "The
great Patriot's memory," Burke said bitterly, proved "as treacherous as
everything else about him,"[33] and indeed as soon as it became clear that
all Wilkite candidates were to be asked to take the Pledge, it was obvious
that Burke's prospects were doomed. As soon as Rockingham heard of
the Middlesex pledge—"the declaration which poor Glynn has been drove
into to sign"—he took it as a "proof there could be no chance of your being an adopted candidate."[34] He was quickly proved a sound prophet; on
2 October, two days before the Westminster nomination day, Wilkes let
Burke know indirectly but unequivocally, that if he stood, Wilkes himself
would rise and demand "that he took the pledge."[35] Burke knew what this
meant, but he was not at once prepared to accept defeat. As late as 6 October, the Duke of Portland informed Rockingham that "he is very anxious
. . . if he can be properly supported . . . to expose the folly and the wickedness of the Tests insisted on by Wilkes etc. at a meeting which is summoned
at Westminster tomorrow."[36] But the tide was running too strongly, the
meeting was postponed,[37] and Burke was already looking elsewhere. The
chance of a direct attack by him on the Radicals in their own stronghold
was lost forever.

It is here, however, that the case of William Baker becomes interesting.
Baker was the son of Sir William Baker, Bt., a City magnate who had sup-

[31] Sometime before 18 September Burke was approached by John Churchill, brother
of the late Charles Churchill, the poet, and close friend of Wilkes, on behalf of "the independent interest" (Edmund Burke, *Correspondence*, ed. Copeland. iii. 34). He was evidently given to understand that the offer was made on behalf of Wilkes (Ibid. iii. 32),
though there were early signs that the latter was pursuing other plans.

[32] See Edmund Burke *Correspondence* ii. 107, 192, 483, 490, 492.

[33] *Ibid*. iii. 32.

[34] *Ibid*. iii. 50.

[35] Duke of Portland—William Burke, 2 October 1774. MS. at Sheffield. See *Correspondence* iii. 53. Lord Mountmorres, the candidate now favoured by Wilkes, informed Portland, who was acting as an intermediary on Burke's behalf, of Wilkes's intention.

[36] *Correspondence* iii. 6 October 1774.

[37] The meeting would appear to have been that advertised for the 8th; not the 7th as
Portland thought. It was postponed to the 10th October.

ported first the Duke of Newcastle and then the Rockinghams. The son maintained the connexion, and in 1770-1 when the Rockinghams were trying to exercise some influence in the City, they persuaded him to stand as Sheriff, a candidature in which he was successful. Burke played a considerable part in the negotiations, the two became personal friends, and when the Wilkites, in the course of one of their recurrent vendettas, attacked Baker and his fellow Sheriff in the Press, Burke offered to help him prepare an answer, giving him in two notable letters the lines he thought proper for his defense.[38] Disgusted by his treatment during his year of office, Baker withdrew from City affairs; but in 1774, having failed to find a seat elsewhere, he suddenly decided to try for one of the four City seats and on 30 September wrote to Burke, asking him for help in obtaining the necessary support.[39] Burke at once took the matter up, urging that there was no time to lose. On 2 October, the day before the nomination meeting at Guildhall, Baker decided to stand, and his letter announcing his candidature appeared in the morning papers of the 3rd. It was at just this time that Burke had been warned by Wilkes that a pledge would be exacted from him if he stood for Westminster. Baker knew that one would be asked of him at Guildhall, and he came to the meeting with his case against it prepared. Enough of it penetrated to the reporters through the din of the Wilkite supporters shouting it down[40] to show that this case was more or less identical with that he made more shortly in a letter addressed to the *Worthy Liverymen of the City of London,* which he published in the morning papers of 5 October, and repeated in the morning and evening papers for several days.

A fair copy of this letter, with which the published copies agree in all but insignificant detail, is preserved among his correspondence now in the Hertfordshire Record Office. It is appended herewith; it would seem that he prided himself on it. In style and argument, it is strikingly reminiscent of Burke in a way that none of his other writings are, and this—together with Burke's interest in his candidature, the fact that on an earlier occasion he had been prepared to help Baker in writing for publication, and his own preoccupation with this issue at the time—makes it almost certain that it was at least the product of discussion between them, and very probable that it was, in

---

[38] *Correspondence* ii. 240-243.

[39] M.S. at Sheffield. He wrote: "I go this afternoon to London—with a firm intention if my friend Martin gives me his Sanction, of offering myself for that place. You shall hear my determination when it is finally taken. In the meantime if there are any Interests there which you can arrange in my favour on the supposition of my standing—I shall esteem myself infinitely obliged by your Assistance."

[40] The meeting was fully reported in the morning papers of the 4th October. *The London Chronicle,* 1-4 October, gave the fullest account. *The Public Advertiser,* 4 October, also gave him some space.

part at least, Burke's production.[41] If this is so, it is of interest because Burke's own speech was made after the election was over and to constituents who had not sought to pledge him, and thus dealt with the issue of Instructions in general terms; while Baker had to meet the demand at the hustings and to deal not only with the general question of the validity of Instructions to representatives, but with specific demands made on him by the electors.

Baker begins by putting the case against mandatory instructions in general. His words echo not only the views Burke was a month later to express to the electors of Bristol, but Burke's attitude towards the contingent in politics—"the propriety of Great Reformations in the Laws and Constitution can only be determined by a full Examination of the Time, the Manner and the Circumstances under which they are proposed." While maintaining the member's freedom to decide on all matters of policy, he obviously thinks it only prudent in the circumstances to hedge on those contained in the Instructions offered him. He admits that they "contain matters of the most interesting nature." On one specific issue, however, he is not prepared to compromise. This is the demand that he should pledge himself never to take an office of profit under the Crown. Stating that he is quite prepared to assure them that he will not accept office under the present government to which he has clearly expressed his opposition, he goes on to state his disapproval of any attempt to enforce in sweeping terms the traditional 'Country' hostility to places and pensions:

> The Generality and indefinite Extent of the Engagement for the Exclusion of Placemen and Pensioners must put a Stop to all Parliamentary Business whatsoever, and must fatally discourage all Public Merit, of which Pensions have often been the Honourable Reward:—Unless that Fund of various Knowledge, necessary to Legislation, That Experience in many Departments of Business, which official Practice can alone confer, are to be caught by Intuition, or the Public Treasure can be more properly applied, than to the Reward of great and Eminent Service.

Burke had already, four years earlier in the *Thoughts on the Cause of the Present Discontents,* touched on the problem of a general exclusion of officers of the Crown from the House of Commons and distinguished it from "the disqualification of revenue officers from seats in parliament"

[41] The date of the published letter, 5 October, might at first sight seem to make it difficult to argue that Burke helped in writing it, since he left for Bath for his first meeting with those representing his supporters at Bristol, on 4 October at 4:30 p.m. (having received the letter summoning him thither at 3:00 p.m.). But in fact Baker's letter must have been written not later than the 4th, as it appeared in the morning papers of the 5th, and in the case of a previous letter to the Press he appended the date of publication rather than that of writing.

and the exclusion of the few or inconsiderable. The latter he thought desirable, the former dangerous and difficult. "It is not easy to foresee what the effect would be of disconnecting with parliament the greater part of those who hold civil employments, and of such mighty and important bodies as the military and naval establishments."[42] The remarkable vitality of this 'Country' tradition is made clear not only by the extreme caution with which Burke felt it necessary to approach the question in the *Thoughts* (Sir George Savile, the *beau idéal* of the Rockinghams—and one of those whose approval of the pamphlet was asked—shared fully this tradition), but also by the emphasis placed on the issue in Baker's letter, and the damage which Burke judged two years after the 1774 Election was over that the Radicals had done to his group's popular reputation by raising this issue during its course. In 1776 Wilkes was himself finding difficulties in detaching himself from the effects of a similar pledge he had taken in the City and which now embarrassed him in his candidature for the lucrative position of City Chamberlain. Burke wrote:

> "This wolf is now howling in the snare which he originally laid for honest men. This traitor raised an outcry, among that Mob . . . against all the honest part of the opposition, because they would not join him and his associates in disclaiming the fair Objects of ambition or accommodation, whenever private honour or public principles admitted of them. We were put out of the Question as Patriots; stripped of all support from the Multitude; and the alternative wildly and wickedly put between those who disclaimed all employments, and the mere creatures of the Court."

This, he concluded, was the result of "all their professing, promising and testing."[43] He might equally have applied to the situation his own earlier comment: "I have constantly observed, that the generality of people are fifty years, at least, behind-hand in their politics."[44]

All students of the growth of the British constitution would agree that Burke and Baker were right in their stand against an indirect attempt to return to the principles of the 1701 Place Act. They would agree too in the refusal which those men voiced to the concept of the Member of Parliament as the delegate of his electors, subject to their mandatory instruction. Indeed, the publication of Burke's speech at Bristol may well have played an important part in discouraging demands for mandatory instructions in the

[42] Bohn Edition *Works* i. 367. It is doubtful if he envisaged at this stage an exclusion as complete as that which the Radicals would have achieved if they had been successful in their policy, since the pledge exacted would seem to exclude the acceptance of any office under the Crown, including that of Minister of State.
[43] *Correspondence* iii.
[44] *Thoughts* loc. cit. 311.

1780 election,[45] as it has certainly done in influencing subsequent thought on the subject. Nevertheless, there certainly exists in the contemporary British practice and theory of representation an assumption that a member is in some degree bound by what he has promised his electors at the time of his election. It is widely felt that if he departs from such a promise on a major issue he is under some obligation to ask that this departure be condoned by supporters in his constituency, and possibly even to resign if he is unsuccessful in obtaining their support.

Basing himself on the modern situation, Mr. Emden has suggested that Burke and the eighteenth-century opinion he represented were right in objecting to mandatory instructions given to representatives while they were sitting in the House, but wrong to object to mandatory instructions imposed on candidates at the hustings.[46] This distinction certainly did not exist in the conditions with which Burke was presented. The movement for mandatory instructions to representatives in the late seventeenth and eighteenth centuries was essentially one to force members to vote according to instructions from outside on issues which arose while they were sitting in the House; and the efforts in 1774 to enforce pledges at the time of elections were thought of, as the contents of these pledges plainly show, essentially as a means for achieving this end.

Moreover, the modern situation differs fundamentally from that of the eighteenth century in the development of the party programme, and its product, the party's mandate. The responsibility of the individual member to his electors is now closely related to his position as a member of his party, and a supporter of the programme this party advanced. Both the party programme and the mandate are the outcome, not of the specifics of the 'Country' tradition for ensuring popular control over Government, "remedies," as Burke said, "so famous in speculation, but to which their greatest admirers have never attempted seriously to resort in practice,"[47] but of what was Burke's own specific for the same purpose, the growth of the political party.

When the first Rockingham Administration of 1765-6 went out of office, Burke, by writing his *Short Account of a Late Short Administration*, produced for his group the first justification a ministry had ever made of what it claimed to have achieved while in office. When the second Rockingham Administration came into power in 1782, they were the first administration to make it a condition of accepting office that they should be permitted to

---

[45] *Correspondence* iv. 297. . . . "nor has any one Elector thought proper to propose a Test, or to give an Instruction . . . "
[46] *The People and the Constitution loc. cit.*
[47] *Thoughts* loc. cit. 366. pp. 14-22.

introduce a legislative programme already specified.[48] Burke also believed that a party should take all steps to achieve support 'without doors' and he even went so far as to admit that in a crisis of confidence "the people ought to be excited to a more strict and detailed attention to the conduct of their representatives. Standards for judging more systematically upon their conduct ought to be settled in the meetings of Counties and Corporations;"[49] but neither he nor anyone else had yet thought of the possibility of such a party fighting a general election on a programme announced to the electorate in advance. Nevertheless, this was the logical conclusion of his arguments and of the way events were shaping; and it was with this development that the future relations of parliament and the electorate lay and not in his own words with "all this professing, promising and testing" imposed on individual members.

APPENDIX

To the Worthy Liverymen of the City of London.

Gentlemen,

An Exception having been unjustly taken against me for declining to sign an Engagement, proposed at Guildhall on Monday last, and since published, I have a Right to expect that every Gentleman, who designs to vote at the Ensuing Election, would weigh with Candour and Impartiality those Reasons for my Conduct which collectively you refused to hear.

Freedom of Thought and Freedom of Speech are essential to the Character of a Free Man:— Liberty to discuss, deliberate and decide on every Question which may arise in Parliament, is a necessary Privilege of every Member who sits in that assembly. — The Propriety of great Reformations in the Laws and Constitution can only be determined by a full examination of the Time, the Manner and the Circumstances under which they are proposed. — With what Pretension then to Independence can any Man subscribe an Engagement, which precludes Discussion, shuts his Ears against all Argument, and pledges him irrevocably to support, or to oppose, Measures, of which he knows neither the Time, the Manner, nor the Circumstances? — If the Engagement is revocable, it is nugatory. — If binding, it can never apply to all the various Exigencies which may arise, and may make a Deviation from it, in many instances, necessary. — But the Subscriber has no Alternative; — His Voice and Private Judgement, thus tied

---

[48] R. Pares. *King George III and the Politicians*. Oxford, 1953, pp. 112-120. Pares would seem to underestimate the difference between the conditions insisted on by this administration, and earlier attempts by George Grenville and Chatham to obtain 'conditions' from the Crown.

[49] *Thoughts*, loc. cit. i. 369.

up, are lost to the Public, at a Time, when his Country may stand most in need of the Assistance of Both.

Truths, clear in the Abstract, are not always maintainable in Practice. The Generality and indefinite Extent of the Engagement for the Exclusion of Placement and Pensioners must put a Stop to all Parliamentary Business whatsoever, and must fatally discourage all Public Merit, of which Pensions have often been the Honourable Reward:— Unless that Fund of various Knowledge, necessary to Legislation, That Experience in many Departments of Business, which official Practice can alone confer, are to be caught by Intuition, or the Public Treasure can be more properly applied, than to the Reward of great and eminent Services.

The Engagements, for Shortening the Duration of Parliaments—against Bribery—for procuring a more fair and equal Representation in Parliament —for vindicating the injured Rights of the Freeholders of Middlesex,—and for redressing the various Grievances under which all America labours, contain Matter of the most interesting Nature, to which the Attention of an Honest Parliament cannot too soon be applied. But they are all subject to the same unanswerable Objection, That they impose a solemn Obligation on the Subscriber, not on any account to be departed from, to promote the several Measures to which they refer: From which this strange Solecism will follow — That what is thought right to be done in the present moment, must ever be so, however the Circumstances of the Times may vary.

It is unnecessary to pledge myself not to accept Place, Pension, Contract, Title, Gratuity or Emolument, from the Crown or its Ministers, as I cannot condescend to solicit any thing from a Court to which I have from Principle acted in direct Opposition.

Great Attention is certainly due from a Representative to the Sense of his Constituents, fairly taken, and properly signified:— But, as I must preserve my own Judgement free on all the Subjects which may arise in Parliament, I cannot, with Honour, engage myself indefinitely and beforehand, to the fulfilling of Instructions which I do not know.

As this Refusal arises from a Sense of Duty, which I cannot otherwise discharge with Honesty, I trust it will not prejudice me in your good Opinion and Confidence:— And in this Assurance I continue to solicit your Votes Interest and Poll at the ensuing Election.

I have the honour to be,

Gentlemen, your faithful humble

Servant

Wm. Baker

London October 5th 1774.

Charles, 2nd Marquess of Rockingham (1730-82)
(Studio of Sir Joshua Reynolds)
(National Portrait Gallery)

EDMUND BURKE AND THE FIRST ROCKINGHAM MINISTRY

'THERE never was a season more favourable for any man who chose to enter into the career of public life.'[2] So Burke wrote of the time of his political beginnings, and with justice, as his own experience bears out. The break-down of the predominance of half a century had brought about a time of change within the solid ranks of the great whig connexion to which he belonged, and in which, always against the old traditional background, new men and policies were coming to the fore. It was in the opposition of 1762–5 and the short ministry of 1765–6 that such men as the Townshends, the younger Onslow, Dowdeswell, Meredith, and Burke himself, never before of much prominence, laid the practical foundations of that political theory which Burke was to evolve for his half-comprehending but admiring party, and gave form to the whiggism of the second half of the eighteenth century. Theory and practice grew up closely side by side. Of the former a supporter said, with simple surprise, ' Although everything seemed a kind of new political philosophy, yet it was all to the purpose ',[3] and for the reason that both theory and the actions of the men for whom it was made were being moulded by the difficulties of a new transition from government to opposition.

Nothing is more difficult than to show accurately the ' connexions ' which lay behind the names of whig and tory in the middle of the eighteenth century. Throughout the shifting of the groups, however, there is clear a more or less permanent tenure of power in the hands of the great whig connexions of Pelham and Cavendish, sometimes in alliance with those of Russell and Grenville. Round this nucleus grew up a certain solidarity and the traditions of aristocratic rule characteristic of the age. It is this group that is here called for convenience (by analogy with Disraeli's phrase) the ' High Whigs '. On Newcastle's authority, they

---

[1] Since this was written an article has appeared in the *American Historical Review*, vol. xxxv, p. 735, by W. T. Laprade, 'The Stamp Act in British Politics.' It uses the contemporary press to advantage, but only touches lightly on the questions treated here.

[2] *Burke Corr*. i. 67, Burke to Hely Hutchinson, n.d. (c. May 1765).

[3] *Ibid*. 103, Marriott to Burke, February 1766.

are subdivided into the ' Great Whigs '—the aristocratic leaders—
and the ' Little '[1] or ' Young Whigs ', their followers. In contradiction to the ' High Whigs ' stand the various bands of ' Rebel
Whigs ', who broke off from time to time into the opposition which
long centred in Leicester House. From this first connexion, driven
into opposition in 1762, there grew up gradually the party of the
Rockingham whigs, who, through Burke, claimed the apostolic
succession of the whiggism of the age.[2]

Characteristically, as a man who never originated but always
idealized and intensified the thought which he found about him,
Burke assumed that the course of his career had been inevitable.
' As to myself and the part I have taken in my time', he wrote, ' I
apprehend that there was very little choice.'[3] In the same way, as
on an unavoidable hypothesis, it was on the basis of his experience
in these first years that he developed the official whig theory of the
Thoughts on the Cause of the Present Discontents, and in consequence,
it was on this experience that his party moulded their tactics.

Burke might claim that true political wisdom was ' the progressive sagacity that keeps company with times and occasions
and decides upon things in their existing conditions ',[4] but his own
methods, like his opinions, changed in reality remarkably little.
When he had once grasped the necessity of some form of party connexion for political strength, a necessity already clear in practice
to a series of oppositions, he rather consolidated and elaborated
upon the possibilities of internal solidarity of the great whig family
system as he knew it, than sought any development of the conception. Throughout all his active career he remains the man who
wrote in 1767 to the old duke of Newcastle that he had ' from
inclination and principle a strong attachment to that system of
which your Grace forms so eminent a part'.[5] In the same way for
the practical tactics of this party, for which he worked so loyally,
he had throughout his identification with it only two distinctive
principles. The first, to be applied not only to opposition but to
government, was : ' We know that all opposition is absolutely
crippled if it can obtain no kind of support out of doors ',[6] and his
context shows that he was thinking primarily of the support of
the commercial interests in the city of London. The second was
the significant suggestion, ' I never yet knew an instance of any

---

[1] Brit. Mus. Add. MS. 32967, fo. 69, Newcastle to Rockingham, 19 June 1765.

[2] When I speak of the whigs in opposition, I do not wish to suggest a newly defined
party division between tory government and whig opposition, nor to ignore the Russell
and Grenville connexions, nor the position of Pitt, the greatest of the rebels. I merely
wish to indicate that it was they who, carrying on, though in a changed form, the tradition of the old predominant groups, formed and organized the way of thinking which
was to be accepted as essentially whig.

[3] *Burke Corr.* ii. 277, Burke to Shackleton, 25 May 1776.   [4] *Ibid.* 276.

[5] Brit. Mus. Add. MS. 32985, fo. 284, 30 September 1767.

[6] *Burke Corr.* ii. 51, Burke to Rockingham, 23 August 1775.

general temper in the nation that could not have been tolerably well traced to some particular persons.' [1] The need of party in the sense in which the word was then used, the advantages to this party of a fairly widespread popular support, particularly among the trading interests of the city, where it was most vocal, some understanding of the policies most likely to obtain it, and very considerable experience in the methods whereby its existence, even in a very limited degree, might be given the most spectacular prominence : this was the practical knowledge which Burke won from observation of the first years of whig minority, and from his first taste of power as Rockingham's private secretary and prominent government supporter in the house of commons during the short ministry of 1765–6. It was a practical lesson which he was only able to learn because tactics new to the high whigs were beginning to be used by them as they turned to opposition. It was a lesson which he never learned completely, partly for personal reasons, partly because his party itself never learned it, so that he and they both tried to use rising forces without comprehending their direction.

The key-note of Burke's ideas and of the new whig tactics is struck firmly in his first important work as whig apologist, *The Short Account of a Late Short Administration*. Here Burke stressed as the chief claim to fame of the ministry of 1765–6, the policy of commercial reform which it embodied in the three linked acts—the repeal of the American Stamp Act, the American Duties Act, and the Free Port Act of the West Indies—and the close touch which it kept with a wide range of commercial interests while the policy was being evolved.[2] Though the emphasis was new and for his connexion surprising, it may be taken as a true interpretation of the actions of the Rockingham ministry, which was continually occupied with commercial matters. The trace of commercial interests can be seen even upon those of its measures which were not in themselves in any way commercial.

This emphasis is remarkable and can be attributed neither to party tradition nor to the leaders themselves in the high whig territorial group which had followed Newcastle and now turned to Rockingham. It is only necessary to examine their attitude when in uneasy alliance with Pitt, from 1757 to 1761, to see that the alliance between the high whigs and the bulk of the merchant classes of which Burke boasts, as distinct from the support of Newcastle in the treasury by the aristocracy of finance on which its business rested, was, so far as it existed, a development not dating back before their

---

[1] *Burke Corr.* ii. 49, Burke to Rockingham, 23 August 1775.
[2] *Works*, i. 183 (Bohn ed.) : ' That administration was the first which proposed and encouraged public meetings and free consultations of merchants from all parts of the kingdom ; by which means the truest lights have been received ; great benefits have been already derived to manufactures and commerce, and the most extensive prospects are opened for further improvement.'

opposition and this ministry. This new commercial policy was the result of the first unmethodical attempt at adaptation made by the connexion to general conditions themselves in a state of change.

At the beginning of their period of opposition, the whigs found a marked development taking place in the growth of outside influence on parliament and ministries, under stress of which the Mercantile System was changing from a control of trade in the interests of policy to a control of policy in the interests of organized trade. And the rapid growth of the political influence of the export trading interests which this implied, in particular those concerned in American waters, was closely associated with a greater movement of opinion with its centre in the city of London, popular radicalism. It is not possible to separate the rising clamour of the ' American Trades ' from the ferment, half social and half political, which was leading in the city to the Wilkite disturbances, and the early reform organizations. A particular stage of this development caught the first whig opposition and the Rockingham ministry and moulded its commercial policy.

The whole movement, developing through the century, had become far more immediately serious at this time as a result, on the one hand, of the economic consequences of the Seven Years' war, and on the other of the political conditions caused by Pitt's war ministry. The centre of the commercial changes lay in the three great and closely connected trades in western waters, the West Indian, the North American, and the African trades. The alternating struggles and alliances of these trades obscure to some extent their power and political importance, but everything shows how much, in the eighteenth century, the tide of individualist commercial expansion had set to the West, and how surely these western trades were becoming a formidable political force, and were binding to themselves the interests of the more slowly rising manufacturing classes who depended upon them.[1]

The Seven Years' war, the problems of the peace, and the depression which followed it made both their strength and their anti-ministerialism clearer than had even the excise and ' Jenkins' Ear ' agitations before. All trades were affected by the depression after the speculative boom of the war years, but those concerned with export in American waters suffered the most severely, for here the problems of colonial policy entered in. The result was the gradually rising commercial discontent which the American riots and anti-importation agreements brought to a climax under the Rockingham ministry of 1765–6.

---

[1] The two peaks in the rising line of their political importance were : the agitation against Walpole's Excise Scheme, 1733 (see N. A. Brisco, *The Economic Policy of Robert Walpole*), and the Jenkins' Ear agitation of 1739 (see H. W. V. Temperley, ' The Causes of the War of Jenkins' Ear ', *Roy. Hist. Soc. Trans.*, ser. iii, vol. 3).

The indirect commercial results of these years were equally important and reached an equally critical situation during the Rockingham ministry, for they took the form of a series of changes in the relations of two of the component parts of the great western trade, the West Indians and the merchants trading to North America, which had the greatest effect on the history of the whig commercial alliances. The conflicts between the North American trade and the powerful, because closely interrelated, West Indian interest in England[1] have been stressed in the study of commercial conditions at this time to an extent which has excluded the recognition of the great range of interests which were common to both.[2] By the end of 1766, as will be shown, this interpretation of their relations has become definitely misleading, but even before that year it leaves out of account some important factors. Throughout the war they had been in complete agreement,[3] and the occasional antagonism of their policies only became acute when in the peace of 1762 most of the West Indians opposed territorial expansion in the interests of their sugar monopoly. It became worse when those interested in North America began to attribute their trade depression in part at least to the limitations of the Molasses Act upon the North Americans, and to enforcement of the regulations against smuggling introduced in the West Indian interest. The hostility thus begun continued to grow through 1764–5 ; but the events of 1766 under the Rockingham ministry brought a complete change. In 1764 it could be said that ' island interest ' and ' mainland interest ' were completely antagonistic.[4] In 1766, on the other hand, an observer needed to remind his correspondent that mainland and island interests were not always the same.[5] By the beginning of the war of independence West Indian planters and merchants and American merchants were working side by side.[6] The reasons for this change of attitude lay in economic considerations more fundamental than those responsible for the earlier conflict. Since the West Indies depended upon the mainland for their food-supply, it was the threat of an anti-exportation agreement in 1765 as in 1774 which aroused their alarm.

While these commercial developments were taking place,

[1] L. M. Penson, *The London West India Interest in the Eighteenth Century, ante,* xxxvi. 373.

[2] F. W. Pitman, *The Development of the British West Indies, 1700–63,* Yale Historical Publications, Studies 4 ; G. L. Beer, *British Colonial Policy, 1754–65.*

[3] They had agreed in their pressure for war with Spain, for the expansion of the African trade at the expense of the French, for the growth of the Newfoundland fisheries, and the retention of Canada in order to make this possible.

[4] Governor Bernard, quoted F. W. Pitman, *op. cit.* pp. 322–6.

[5] *Hist. MSS. Comm., IXth Report,* part 3, 24 ; Stopford-Sackville MSS., Sackville to Irwin, 25 April 1766.

[6] ' The evidence delivered on the petition presented by the West India planters and merchants to the House of Commons, as it was introduc'd at the bar, and summ'd up by Mr. Glover (1775).' Bodleian Library, Godw. P. 491(1).

moreover, Pitt's war ministry had strengthened politically the position of those very radical commercial interests to which the trade belonged. From the time of Bolingbroke and Pulteney, who first saw the strategic possibilities of eighteenth-century opposition, it had become clear that there existed this potential anti-ministerialism among the commercial classes in the city, to whom solidity and influence was given by the widely spread interests of the traders to America. That here was the basis of a ' National Opposition ' both tory leaders and rebel whigs recognized. Not, however, till the experiment of Pitt did any leader consider the possibility of retaining these allies when again in power.[1] Coming into office in abnormal circumstances, without the long-established power of Newcastle, Pitt thought he saw valuable reinforcement of his uncertain position in the combined support of the merchants and the independent country gentry which he had recently won.[2] When an alliance with the whigs became essential, Pitt, with the greatest difficulty, even reconciled the more extreme of his supporters to uneasy alliance with the hated whig oligarchy.[3]

When Pitt fell, city opinion, with increased claims to consideration and a dangerous potential leader, could never again be safely ignored. Pitt's ministry had thus opened up a problem. What was the value, not only to an opposition, but to a ministry, of support from general outside opinion and particularly from commercial interests other and wider than those of direct financial importance ? It fell to a great extent to the whigs, in the transition of their first opposition and in the ministry which emphasized their fall rather than restored their strength, to reap what Pitt had sown, and to realize by experience the implications of the situation into which circumstances had led them. Among those to whom the realization was quickest, most fruitful, yet most typical in its reservations and limitations, was a new recruit of 1765, Edmund Burke.

The significance of these changes began to be clear as soon as political affairs began to settle down, after the defeat of the whigs in the struggle over the preliminaries of the peace. On the one side, it was reflected in the problems of the ministry. Though there was

---

[1] Their growing disillusionment within and without the house was particularly emphasized in the case of Pulteney, who was never forgiven in the city for his desertion.

[2] Cf. [R. Glover] *Memoirs of a Literary and Political Character* (1813 ed.), p. 65 *seq.*

[3] R. Glover, *op. cit.* pp. 86, 99, 105 ; Publ. Rec. Off., Chatham MSS., G. D. 8, 19, Beckford to Pitt, 20 September 1757. The uneasiness was shown by such incidents as the attack on Hardwicke and Mansfield in the city in 1758, re-echoed by Beckford in the house, and the opposition to Beckford's election as mayor (C. P. Yorke, *Life of Lord Hardwicke*, iii. 45, and Lord Lyttelton, *Memoirs*, ii. 609; Publ. Rec. Off., Chatham MSS., G. D. 8, 19, Beckford to Pitt, 15 March 1761. C. P. Yorke, *op. cit.* iii. 317).

nothing strikingly new in their commercial policy,[1] they found themselves, as the depression grew, coping with the ever-increasing though vaguely expressed commercial discontent, and their difficulties in the city were increased by social and economic unrest among the mob of the Spitalfield silk weavers. It was largely in view of the ugliness of popular opinion that they welcomed with such enthusiasm an address from London merchants praising the peace,[2] and that such efforts were made by a section of them for reconciliation with Pitt.

The whig minority, however, had much more difficult readjustments to make. In order to organize any form of opposition, they had to consider a course of action in which their leaders had no experience and to which years of office had made them averse. As Hardwicke had said to Newcastle, they were too old easily to go into opposition,[3] most of their links with the financial interests and place-seekers were suddenly snapped, and moreover they relied too much at first on an early return to power to enter readily into the tactics which contemporaries distinguished as a ' system ' of opposition. Fundamentally, moreover, they were facing without realizing it the transition period of the whig point of view from a governmental principle to that theory of opposition which is implicit in the writings of Burke and overt in the expressions of such men as Dunning and Dowdeswell in the second half of the century. The readjustment could not be made immediately and, though some have seen in the barrier which stood between Pitt and the whigs in their common opposition not mere personal interests but a conflict of principle between the old political concept and a new one of organized party opposition,[4] the distinction is scarcely tenable. Organized ' systems ' of opposition were not new ; the rebel whigs had carried to a high pitch the organization of ' faction ', as the high whigs had called it. It was new only to the high whigs themselves. It was they who had in office put upon it the stigma of ' faction ', which barred it to responsible statesmen, and they no less than Pitt were restrained

[1] Even the tightening up of customs regulations in American waters which made Grenville so unpopular, had been begun by Pitt during the war (F. W. Pitman, *op. cit.* p. 318).

[2] *Bedford Corr.* iii. 230, George Grenville to Bedford, 19 May 1763, reports the presentation of the address. ' The effect it has had at this conjuncture for the support of the honour and quiet of the King's government, and for discouraging the spirit that has been raised against it, has more than answered the most sanguine expectations.' Bedford replied, 25 May 1763 (*Grenville Corr.* ii. 58) : ' The address of the Merchants of the City of London gives me great satisfaction, as I think it must to every good subject of His Majesty, as it is a strengthening in the hands of Government, and is but a just tribute to His Majesty.'   [3] C. P. Yorke, *op. cit.* iii. 354, 10 May 1762.

[4] D. A. Winstanley, *Personal and Party Government, 1760–6*. Since this was written Mr. Namier's *England in the Age of the American Revolution* has appeared, in which he makes the same point as I do here with regard to the whigs in opposition in 1757 (pp. 55–8).

by their own conception. Cumberland, the king's uncle and their
sole remaining support at court, Portland, Albemarle, Bessborough
and Devonshire and Hardwicke, agreed with Newcastle that it was
a course that would be below them, the 'Great Whigs', though
conceivably open to the 'Young Men' and 'Little Whigs',[1] their
followers. A combination powerful enough to be immediately
successful was one thing, a long series of parliamentary protests
was quite another.[2] The result of these difficulties was that the
whig transition to opposition was a hesitating one, and that when
the movement began it was in the hands of younger and less
prominent men, and it is significant that some of them, like their
more important but fitful ally Charles Townshend, had known the
tactics of rebel whig opposition. The movement towards opposition had in fact, until 1765, more of the nature of a half-admitted
revolt than of a continuation of the high whig traditions, and the
'violence of the young men' became the burden not only of the
laments of Newcastle, but at times of the indignation of Horace
Walpole,[3] and the shrewd contempt of the old country supporters.[4]
The young men used as their centre their new opposition club at
Wildman's, which the older leaders did not care to attend,[5] and
like other oppositions earlier they quickly gained the support of
the commercial sections of the party, in particular of Newcastle's
old ally, Sir William Baker, who still wielded considerable power
in the city.[6] But if they remained outside the effective control of
the whig families, they also remained without distinctive leaders
until, in the last months of the ministry, the marquis of Rockingham, encouraged by the Cavendishes, showed himself alive to
their hopes and ideas, and at the same time bridged the gap which
threatened to appear between them and the traditional leaders of
the great whig families.

It was inevitable that this new whig opposition should follow
the lines both of tactics and measures laid down earlier by the

[1] Brit. Mus. Add. MS. 32964, fo. 109. Newcastle wrote (25 November 1764): ' As
to being at the Head of such a Sort of Opposition as I am afraid This must be, his Royal
Highness [the duke of Cumberland] thinks it below Him, and was pleased to say that it
was below me *also*, But he will have no objection to The Young Men going on as they
please.'

[2] Hardwicke told Egremont (G. Harris, *Life of Lord Chancellor Hardwicke*, 1847,
iii. 351): 'He [Egremont] knew as well as any body, that in this country, there were
such things as honourable connexions, which some might represent under the odious
name of faction; but might really be only necessary engagements, in order to carry on
and effectuate right and necessary measures.'

[3] H. Walpole, *Corr.* vi. 236, Walpole to Mann, 14 May 1765.

[4] Brit. Mus. Add. MS. 32966, fo. 79, Newcastle to Onslow, 21 March 1765, quotes
the opinion of ' Stag ' Forrester.

[5] *Ibid.* 32965, fo. 127. It was only with the greatest hesitation that Newcastle
agreed to attend a dinner there in the later stages of the opposition, though he
was, of course, nominally a member (*History of the Late Minority* [J. Almon], 1765 List
of Members).

[6] *Ibid.* 32963, fo. 375, Newcastle to Rockingham, 14 November 1764.

rebel whigs, with only such variations as circumstances made necessary, for the essence of such opposition was popularity with important sections of opinion outside the house. In tactics, therefore, they aimed more or less at the course outlined by Charles Townshend in a burst of energetic protest against the supine attitude of the old leaders. Some coalition within the house should be only supplementary to a strong movement outside :

To gain upon the minds of the people, a daily paper, upon the plan of the Prints, should be set up and circulated diligently tho' quietly, and two good pens should be employed to write from materials suggested by men of knowledge and subject to their inspection. Some leading men in each Town through the several Counties, should be admitted to confidence, and be persuaded to give their clubs and districts the tone of conversation directed from hence.

A Committee should be desired to consider and prepare heads of business for the next winter, and in one word the kingdom should be kept warm and the chiefs active and laborious during the recess. Sir W. Baker should be desired to put the City in motion, both as an example to other Counties and as the attack nearest Home.[1]

It was a programme which might have been given by Pulteney earlier or Burke later,[2] but it was the first opposition programme which had been presented to the high whig leaders, and though they received it half-heartedly, the young whigs tried with some consistency to carry it out. By their parliamentary measures, too, they sought every means to gain support from outside and particularly from city opinion.[3] Their shrewdest move was to make themselves the strongest supporters of Wilkes in the house,[4] for, wiser here than Pitt, they realized what Wilkes told Temple, that ' The trials . . . have demonstrated to me where the strength of our cause really lies; for the merchants, as I had ever the honour of submitting to Your Lordship, are firm in the cause of liberty.' [5] Their least successful side, on the other hand, was shown in their failure, especially in 1764, to take up a definite line on the question of the American trade. Correspondence preserved among the Newcastle papers suggests, however, that their failure, at least in 1764, was due more to the divergence between the West Indian and North

---

[1] *Ibid.* 32958, fo. 248, 30 April 1764 (also printed, from copy, in *Hist. MSS. Comm.* xi. 4, *Townshend MSS.*, p. 399).

[2] *Burke Corr.* ii. 49, Burke to Rockingham, 23 August 1775.

[3] As early as January 1764 the opposition club at Wildman's alarmed the government, and opposition dinners became matters of political significance (H. Walpole, *Letters*, v. 439). Prominent members, including Townshend, wrote pamphlets, and in November 1764, Fitzherbert, Sir William Baker, and Almon, the bookseller and friend of Wilkes, tried to negotiate with the far too cautious Horace Walpole about founding a paper (*Grenville Corr.* ii. 457).

[4] Brit. Mus. Add. MS. 30867, fo. 243 (Wilkes Correspondence), Onslow to Wilkes, 19 December 1763 ; *ibid.*, fo. 249 (Wilkes Correspondence), Wilkes to Cotes, 4 January 1764.

[5] *Grenville Corr.* ii. 71, 9 July 1763.

American interests among their supporters, than to a lack of touch with the development of the affairs of American trade.[1] With it, indeed, as its importance grew, their connexion was becoming ever stronger.

Little as we know of Burke's career until he broke his connexion with ' Single Speech ' Hamilton early in 1765, there are facts enough to suggest that at this time he gradually began to appear politically among this younger group of the whigs. A great deal had happened to the ambitious young Irishman since, in 1750, he came to London, and observed that figures were more important than eloquence in the house of commons, and that, his idea of the aristocratic patronage of letters being exaggerated, writers swarmed in London living only on their wits.[2] Although he had taken at least a share in *An Account of the European Settlements in America* in 1757,[3] and was writing the masterly annual summary of events in the *Annual Register*, and though he was acting as private secretary to a rising politician, Burke was still in 1761 a young man who thought ' nothing so charming as writers and to be one ', and who was known to Horace Walpole only as the author of the *Advantages of Natural Society*.[4] But by 1765 his ambition had turned definitely to public life. It may be no coincidence that his obscure breach with Hamilton began in 1764, for Hamilton then became considered a man who notoriously awaited his chance between minority and government,[5] and Burke thought his policy became ' very reproachful to himself and extremely disgustful to me'.[6] Among the recriminations of this quarrel he suggests that Hamilton resented that ' others were inclined to show me more attention than he did ', and though he takes pains to deny having at that time any connexion with a ' Mr. T—— ' (possibly Charles Townshend),[7] his acquaintance with Rockingham dated at least from 1763,[8] and he appears to have been personally known to Wilkes before his exile.[9] Moreover, a well-informed contemporary

[1] An opposition to the American Duties Bill was seriously discussed (Brit. Mus. Add. MS. 32957, fos. 47, 85, 87, 230, and 235) ; Rose Fuller, a prominent West Indian supporter, sent a letter to Newcastle strongly objecting to such a step (*ibid.*, fo. 116), and the idea was finally given up, since unified opposition seemed impossible, Charles Townshend, however, dividing ' in civility to Sir William Baker ' (*ibid.*, fo. 239).

[2] Burke to Smith, quoted by J. Prior, *Life of Burke* (Bohn ed., 1891), p. 33.

[3] The grounds for believing this seem satisfactorily expounded by J. Prior, *op. cit.* p. 52. It is accepted by Burke's recent biographer, B. Newman.

[4] H. Walpole, *Letters*, v. 86, Walpole to George Montagu, 22 July 1761.

[5] *Hist. MSS. Comm. VIIIth Report, Emly MSS.* p. 190 ; *Hist. MSS. Comm. Xth Report*, App. I, *Weston Underwood MSS.* p. 382.

[6] *Burke Corr.* i. 77, Burke to Flood, 18 May 1765.

[7] *Ibid.* i. 74, Burke to Hely Hutchinson, n.d. (*c.* May 1765). Burke was in touch with Charles Townshend about this time (see *Corr.* i. 76, Burke to Flood, 18 May 1765).

[8] Brit. Mus. Add. MS. 35424, fo. 16 (Hardwicke MSS.), Burke to Hardwicke, 20 October 1763.

[9] This is suggested by a reference to Burke in a letter from Wilkes to Fitzherbert, 8 December 1765 (W. P. Treloar, *Wilkes and the City*, p. 46).

states that he obtained his position as private secretary to Rockingham through Fitzherbert, one of the most advanced of the young whigs of Wildman's.[1] At this same time, through the studied impartiality of his review in the *Annual Register*, his predilections began to appear.

In several ways, however, this new opposition, to which Burke was drawn like the other young whigs of his time, had met with unfavourable circumstances. They suffered partly, indeed, because they were unled, but partly for more serious reasons. Their relations with the ' Great Whigs ' were unsatisfactory, without the latter allowing them to come to an open breach.[2] The old leaders looked on with distaste at the policy and alliances into which they were being forced. Hardwicke, in 1763, tried to check their enthusiastic support of Wilkes and his followers in the city. 'These are fellows ', he reminded Newcastle bitterly, ' Who would have hanged Your Grace and me a few years ago, and would do so still had they the power.'[3] Newcastle and Cumberland, even while submitting, agreed that 'We must not be . . . led by Sir William Baker and some warm very well-intentioned young friends'.[4] On the other hand, their secession, which Newcastle always feared,[5] on the model of the rebel whigs before, and to which their relations with Pitt's city supporters, such as Beckford and Calvert, might have led them, was made difficult by the incalculable behaviour of Pitt. To alliance he would not commit himself, and with Pitt's formidable figure in the role which they wished, like their forerunners, to fill before the country and particularly before the restless antiministerialism of the city, the young whigs found their way towards ' popular opposition ' seriously blocked. Had Pitt been a political leader of men, or had Rockingham not stepped in to bring together again the young whigs and the great families, there might never have been the practical crystallization of whig transition to which Burke gave a creed. Both factors, however, combined to leave them no choice but that intermediate political

---

[1] J. Almon, *Anecdotes of the Life of the Rt. Hon. William Pitt, Earl of Chatham*, 7th ed., 1810, i. 423. This was the kind of political information which Almon was in an excellent position to collect, particularly as at this time he had personal relations with Fitzherbert. (*Memoirs of a Late Eminent Bookseller*, 1790, p. 31.)

[2] Newcastle at least recognized that they would be forced to follow the course of the extremists (Brit. Mus. Add. MS. 32964, fo. 257): ' I said our Zealous friends, Sir William Baker etc would certainly make an opposition, and we should have to go with them, or dissolve the Whig party, for aught I know for ever. It is a Sad Dilemma To be brought to by the Behaviour of some of our Pretended Friends.'

[3] G. Harris, *Life of Lord Chancellor Hardwicke*, 1847, iii. 357, Hardwicke to Newcastle, 8 June 1763. Cf. *ibid.* iii. 344, Hardwicke to C. Yorke, 2 May 1763.

[4] Brit. Mus. Add. MS. 32963, fo. 375, Newcastle to Rockingham, 14 Nov. 1764.

[5] *Ibid.* 32965, fo. 26, Newcastle to Rockingham, 3 January 1765. He thought he saw ' a certain spirit of indifference as to persons and all parties ' which suggested a plan ' To set up for Themselves without any Connection with us, or any Concern for us—or the Whig Party '.

position which made of the new whig party the compromise which
was its strength in Burke's theory and its weakness in fact ; though
in their last months of opposition, more or less united under
Rockingham, the position was not yet clear. It is interesting,
however, to note that it was not the young enthusiasts but the
old leader Newcastle who encouraged Rockingham to accept the
offer made through Cumberland,[1] and by making ' the most rash
experiment that ever was made ',[2] to form the first whig ministry
under the new conditions, which gave Burke his chance, but which
came into existence without the support of Pitt, and in the teeth of
the Bedfords, Grenville, and the much-feared though disputable
influence of Bute.

The experiment was as unsuccessful as their most hostile
critics had prophesied. The complexities of opposition were as
nothing to those which they had to face on coming into power.
With uncertain support at court, and a majority of placemen left
over from the last two administrations, which would, as they knew
' last no longer than They find the Administration carries Everything clearly and roundly ',[3] and with the personal infidelities of an
eighteenth-century administration enhanced by new divergencies
of view among themselves, not even the most hopeful could see in
their accession to power a return to the high whig *status quo*. Like
Pitt before them, therefore, their chief hope lay in maintaining
their prestige by the appearance of a widespread national and city
support, and by keeping up contact, not only with the financial
interests but with the wider bodies of opinion for whose favour
they had played during their opposition. In doing so, however, they
were hampered not only by their more conservative members'
suspicion of ' popular ' policies, and by the lack of support from
Pitt, who, as they were unpleasantly reminded by a city address on
their accession,[4] retained his place in the popular affections, but by
the exasperated exigence of their city supporters, whose trade
remained consistently bad. One of them put with brutal frankness
their attitude to politics and party. ' The Nation has lost its good
Humour and unless things are set to rights, it is become a Matter
of great Indifference to the Publick, and will be more so every day,
" who have the places ".' The dangers before the ministry would be
less parliamentary opposition than ' jealousies and disagreements
among yourselves ', and, in ominous terms, ' a loss of publick
Esteem by disappointing their Reasonable Expectations '.[5]

Just because of these difficulties, however, the ministry was of

---

[1] Brit. Mus., Add. MS. 32967, fo. 186, Newcastle to Portland, 1 July 1765.
[2] *Bedford Corr.* iii. 304, Sandwich to Bedford, 3 July 1765.
[3] Brit. Mus. Add. MS. 32969, fo. 392, Newcastle to Albemarle, 15 September 1765.
[4] Burke was at great pains to explain this away as representing only the less considerable sections of city opinion (*Annual Register*, 1765, p. 46).
[5] Brit. Mus. Add. MS. 32967, fo. 226, Colebrooke to Newcastle, 4 July 1765.

great historical importance. The adaptation of whig theory to opposition would never have taken the form it did without this fleeting experience of power, and the attempt it was forced to make to build up a compromise between the exigencies of new demands from without and old social and political conceptions still strong within. Because it had followed without system in the ways of others and played for commercial support, it was put at the mercy of a new commercial strength and organization, and the Rockingham ministry saw within a few months, what it had certainly never foreseen, the most fundamental changes of the century in British trading policy. It also saw the most definite step in the growth of the commercial men's confidence in their own political power, which among other things formed a basis for the widening claim for greater direct share in it. But, since this was rather accidental to than because of the ministry's policy, their practical experience, so far from leading them away from the traditions of the old whig rule, once again consolidated even the extremists among them in it. A disunited opposition it was before 1765, an opposition of compromise it became afterwards.

From the first this compromise was apparent. Though they succeeded, with some adroitness, in freeing themselves from obligations to Wilkes,[1] they knew on the other hand that concessions to the public's ' reasonable expectations ' were essential. A great part of their policy is to be explained as the twofold attempt, firstly, to satisfy these demands by concessions and carefully planned publicity ; and, secondly, to bring pressure to bear for this purpose on the court and the more conservative members of their party, when they fretted under this new commercial emphasis, and tended to complain, like the second Lord Hardwicke, of ' the little weight that was given to my opinion when it interfered with the plan which Lord Rockingham and his friends were previously determined to follow . . . in mercantile affairs'.[2] Their active part, therefore, in the commercial policy which Burke held forth as their chief claim to popular gratitude, consisted chiefly in seeking solutions which would be acceptable both to them and their increasingly clamorous commercial supporters, when the demands of the latter became political issues. As time went on, it consisted also in trying to minimize the conflicting interests which existed within the ranks of their commercial supporters themselves. They played on the other hand scarcely more than a passive part in the inauguration of the commercial policy, which they took up piecemeal as outside

---

[1] *Ibid.* 30877, fo. 51 (Wilkes Correspondence), Horne to Wilkes, 3 January 1766; J. Almon, *The Correspondence of the late John Wilkes*, vol. ii, *passim*; A. Stephens, *The Life of John Horne Tooke*, i. 231, Wilkes to Onslow, 12 December 1765. The delicate negotiation of keeping Wilkes from the scene of political action without driving him into opposition was one in which Burke took an important part.

[2] Quoted, *Rockingham Memoirs*, i. 284.

pressure was brought to bear on them. Neither Burke, as has been rather rashly claimed for him,[1] nor any member of the ministry could be said to have a scheme of commercial reform.

Burke was in any case of far too slight consequence to be a deciding factor in the policy of the party, but though he can claim no credit as a commercial reformer, in the working out of the ministerial policy he rose from obscurity and appeared, not yet as the prophet of the system, but instead, rather surprisingly, as one of its most practical organizers. By the end of the ministry, in spite of his occasional rashness he had become, together with Dowdeswell, the chancellor of the exchequer, the most noted man of his group. It was indeed said in the last months of the ministry that Burke, 'not ... Lord Rockingham's right hand, but ... both his hands', was a metaphysical visionary.[2] But his success in organizing commercial propaganda, in keeping in touch with commercial leaders, in encouraging every sign of public support, for popularity, he remarked, 'is current coin, or it is nothing',[3] show that practical vigour, which, in the most fortunate periods of his political career, was the complement of his speculative genius. It was this which compensated in part for his lack of political finesse and judgement, and won him his place in the Rockingham connexion, more than his much greater intellectual claims.

The evolution of the Rockingham commercial policy, which circumstances made their only consecutive policy, falls into three periods, which correspond also with definite stages in the growth of Burke's influence. Each centres in an aspect of the growing question of the claims of the American Trades.

A general but still vague feeling that something should be done to revive the North American trade was characteristic of commercial opinion in the earlier months of the ministry. The new ministers were quite willing to satisfy these demands which, unless the measures adopted should clash with the interests of the West Indians, appeared uncontroversial. Fortunately, in so far as any one cause of complaint had become general, it was one on which the interests of the two trades were the same, the decline in the smuggling of bullion from the Spanish colonies in Spanish ships to the West Indian Islands. General commercial opinion put this down to the activities of the authorities against them under Grenville's new regulations.[4] The prevalent commercial bullionism of the time laid the greatest importance on it,[5] and it would even

---

[1] B. Williams, *Life of William Pitt, Earl of Chatham*, ii. 183.

[2] Brit. Mus. Add. MS. 22358, fo. 35. Quoted by D. A. Winstanley, *Personal and Party Government*, p. 243. [3] *Burke Corr.* i. 108, Burke to Rockingham, 21 August 1766.

[4] The complaints had really begun well before the war, e.g. Pub. Rec. Off., Col. Off. 137/25, fo. 225. Humble Address of the Council and Assembly of Jamaica, 20 November 1752.

[5] Brit. Mus. Add. MS. 38339, fo. 225. Opinion of J. Salvador, the Jewish financier

seem that some effort at organized agitation had already been used
to crystallize demands into this form.[1] No very active measures,
however, were necessary, as the ministry almost at once set about
providing a remedy, and their deliberations resulted in the treasury
minute of 13 November 1765, which Burke later praised as so notable
a development,[2] and which was received with satisfaction by the
chief bodies of American merchants in the country.[3] From the point
of view of the ministry it was a satisfactory settlement of the
claims upon them. ' It is ', wrote Newcastle, 'as strong an Article
of Impeachment against George Grenville as can be formed ; and
it will show you have been doing something.' [4] There is some irony
in the fact that it did nothing at all ; more than a year before
Grenville, approached by the West Indian merchants, had, though
with the secrecy which relations with Spain made desirable, sent
the same orders for exempting the Spanish ships from smuggling
regulations.[5] Both ministry and merchants were to find that something more was wrong with the situation than ' those fatal orders' of
Mr. Grenville.

Even without this further experience, however, the ministry
began to find that commercial demands were not limited to one
point. Before the end of October Rockingham had discovered that
' to admit the Spanish Bullion into any Part of our Dominions in
America . . . would not quite do our Business'.[6] A very definite
breach in the Navigation Laws was suggested by the words,
which a merchant must certainly have put into Newcastle's mouth,[7]
when he hoped that ' Liberty will also be given to Spanish vessels
to return with certain Commodities . . . or otherwise the Great
Stagnation of our Trade with North America and the Exportation
of our Woollen Manufactures thither will not be put upon the
Foot it was '.[8] At this point, however, the lines of development
of commercial problems were cut across by the sudden develop-

[1] P. R. O., T. 1/443, fo. 53, Memorial of the Merchants and Principal Manufacturers
of Manchester, 5 September, 1765; and fo. 47, Memorial of the Merchants of Liverpool,
August 1765. Some organization was suspected at the time, see Brit. Mus. Add. MS.
33030, fo. 103 *seq*. Questions asked Trecothick when giving evidence in the house,
March 1766.

[2] *Works*, i. 304, ' Observations on a Late Publication '. There is a copy of the minute
in the Newcastle Papers, Brit. Mus. Add. MS. 32971, fo. 394.

[3] P. R. O., T. 1/443, fo. 50, Memorial from the Merchants of Lancaster (docketed,
read 2 December 1765); P. R. O., T. 1/447, fo. 351, Memorial from the Merchants of
Liverpool, November 1765 ; P. R. O., T. 1/451, fo. 83, Letter from the Master of the
Society of Merchants of Bristol, 21 November 1765.

[4] Brit. Mus. Add. MS. 32971, fo. 422.

[5] *Grenville Corr*. ii. 47, Jenkinson to G. Grenville, 30 April 1763. The whole transaction is described by Beeston Long, chairman of the West Indian Association, in his
evidence before the house in 1766. Brit. Mus. Add. MS. 33030, fo. 188.

[6] Brit. Mus. Add. MS. 32971, fo. 13, Newcastle to Rockingham, 22 October 1765.

[7] *Ibid*.

[8] Newcastle was consulting Sir W. Baker at the time (*ibid*., fos. 165 and 173. Newcastle Memorandum, 27 October 1765.)

ment of the great agitation for the repeal of the Stamp Act. If events had been able to develop naturally, there were two further demands which would certainly have been raised ; and had this happened the Rockingham ministry would have had to face at once a great commercial conflict, for they were the demands on which the North American and West Indian interests were at this time fundamentally opposed. The first, the demand by the North American interests for the further reduction of the duty on foreign molasses, though it had already been made, was not at this time raised ; the second—their claim, on the analogy of the Spanish trade, for the legalization of certain forms of smuggling from the other foreign West Indies by the opening of ' free ports ', to which the West Indians were strongly opposed as threatening indirectly the effectiveness of their monopoly—was already being tentatively suggested.[1] The common danger in which the American disturbances placed them, however, interrupted this development, and threw them suddenly into alliance.

The commercial problems of the Rockingham ministry thus did not begin with the Stamp Act disturbances, though the latter completely changed their relative significance. Of Burke very little is known at this time, but he must have had opportunities, as his grip on affairs was growing, to learn lessons of the nature of the forces with which the ministry was in contact. That his influence began growing early is suggested by Lord Charlemont's story that it dated from Newcastle's attempt in the first days of the ministry to oust him in favour of another candidate by denouncing him to Rockingham as a papist and a Jacobite.[2] By the beginning of December he was certainly carrying out most confidential work,[3] and with the opening of parliament a new field was opened to him, for he was given a seat for Wendover, through the interest of Lord Verney.[4]

In the first period of the ministry commercial questions had been in considerable but not disproportionate prominence, and although the demands from without were growing under sympa-

---

[1] The fullest early exposition of the idea came from Lt.-Col. Campbell Dalrymple (Guadeloupe) to Lord Bute, 27 February 1763 (*Corr. of King George III*, i. 44). In P. R. O., T. 1/441, fo. 8, there is a proposal from Hughes, distributor of stamps, Philadelphia, 23 November 1765, on the same lines.

[2] Lord Charlemont, *Memoirs*, ed. F. Hardy (1810), p. 343. Charlemont did not vouch for the truth of the story. Some support is, however, given to it by the fact that Newcastle certainly had a candidate for the position, one Royer (Brit. Mus. Add. MS. 32967, fo. 346), for whom he later found another subordinate place (Brit. Mus. Add. MS. 32969, fo. 438).

[3] The buying off of Wilkes, to prevent his return. See correspondence quoted in W. P. Treloar, *Wilkes and the City*, pp. 46 *seq*.

[4] J. Prior, *Life of Burke* (Bohn ed., 1891), p. 86. His statement is supported by the List of Borough Patronage of Commoners, drawn up by Mr. L. B. Namier, *The Structure of Politics at the Accession of George III*, i. 179. Verney was also in close relations with his, at that time better-known relative, William Burke (*Grenville Corr.* ii. 49 ; *Hist. MSS. Comm., Xth Report*, App. I, *Weston-Underwood MSS.*, p. 403).

thetic treatment, there was no sign of the sudden development which was to follow. The shock to trade from the American Stamp Act disturbances, however, brought to a head tendencies which might have developed much more slowly, and by causing a rapid growth of organization, brought the ministry into relation with a new and formidable extra-parliamentary force. The second period of the ministry, covering, in the months from December to March, the agitation in England for the repeal of the Stamp Act, was its turning-point. The movement among the wide sections of commercial opinion which were affected cut across the course of commercial unrest by diverting and concentrating its needs into one political demand ; after this had been satisfied, it intensified the earlier and more general grievances, because organization and experience had given commercial opinion a confidence and knowledge of its own demands which it had not had before. It had also changed the position, however, for it had made considerable changes in the permanent relations of the West Indian and North American merchant interests.

Though the Stamp Act disturbances in America were known in England by October, and though even earlier the colonial merchants through their correspondents were sending in appeals and denunciations,[1] nothing was done until, a fortnight before the first parliamentary session of the new ministry, the first step was made in London towards a formidable commercial movement. On 4 December a meeting of London merchants trading to North America,[2] with Barlow Trecothick, who was to be the organizer of the movement, in the chair, chose a committee of twenty-eight prominent merchants to manage the business of a national commercial agitation.[3] They began their work with energy, and henceforth there was a new and incalculable factor in the relations of the ministry with the commercial opinion from which they claimed support.

The position of Rockingham and the majority of the ministry in view of this development of this active extra-parliamentary organization was a curious one, for their opponents were [4] right in accusing them of deliberately supporting the agitation. A copy of the circular which the Committee sent out to thirty trading and manufacturing towns was among the Rockingham papers, en-

---

[1] 'Letters of Dennys de Berdt, 1757–1770', ed. A. Mathews. *Publications of the Col. Soc. of Mass.*, vol. xiii, p. 431.

[2] The meeting had been publicly advertised (Brit. Mus. Add. MS. 38339, fo. 166).

[3] A copy of the names and terms of appointment of this committee is kept in the Liverpool papers (Brit. Mus. Add. MS. 38339, fo. 166). They were chosen to 'Consider of the best Method of Application for Procuring the Relief and Encouragement of the North American trade, and to apply to the Outports and to the Manufacturing Citys and Towns for their Concurrence and Assistance'. They extended their powers far beyond the wording of their appointment.

[4] Summary of the debate on the Repeal of the Stamp Act, in *Annual Register*, 1766, p. 37 : ' They represented the petitions as the result of ministerial artifice.'

dorsed by Burke, with enthusiasm ' N.B. This letter concerted
between the Marquis of R. and Mr. Trecothick, the principal
instrument in the happy repeal of the Stamp Act.' [1] A few weeks
later an elated American agent was reporting the complete support
of the ministry,[2] although Dowdeswell had definitely failed to carry
his proposals for repeal in the meeting of the leaders of the connexion before Parliament opened.[3] Later, Burke himself was in
direct communication with the outports on details of the agitation.[4]
These facts accord ill with the generally accepted belief that the
ministry made no effort to meet the situation, and that it was Pitt
who forced the undecided ministry into action which conformed
with public demands. Yet it is true that they did not declare
themselves until well into the new year, and that even then, unlike
Pitt, they compromised by laying heavy stress on the right, if not
the expediency, of colonial taxation.[5] The explanation of this
apparent contradiction would seem to be that with Pitt dangerous,
and commercial opinion becoming organized, as it had not been
since Walpole's excise, they had in reality no alternative but to
support the American claims for repeal. Nevertheless, since the
court and a considerable part of the non-commercial opinion from
which their party was drawn took a purely political view of the
colonists' riots, and were totally out of sympathy with their claims,[6]
they were forced to act indirectly. There is no doubt that their
intention was to force the hand both of the king and the large
section of their party who thought that repeal was shortsighted
cowardice, by alarming them by the ' clamour of the merchants ',[7]
as a whig lord called the expression of commercial opinion, but
that, to make this possible, as they made clear to their merchant
supporters,[8] certain concessions must be made, on the other hand,
to conservative opinion.

Under the skilful control of Trecothick, and with the knowledge
of ministerial support (a condition entirely new to commercial
movements of this kind, which had in the past been bitterly anti-
ministerial), the organization proved the most effective of the
commercial agitations up to this date, and showed at the same
time how widespread were the American trading interests, yet

[1] *Rockingham Memoirs*, i. 319.   [2] 'Letters of D. de Berdt', p. 308.
[3] J. Adolphus, *The History of England from the Accession of George III* (1802), i. 217.
[4] *Burke Corr.* i. 99, Henderson (Glasgow merchant) to Burke, 9 February 1766.
[5] The first decision was reached in a meeting of 17 January (Brit. Mus. Add. MS.
35430, fo. 31) referred to in D. A. Winstanley, *Personal and Party Government, 1760–1766*,
p. 262.
[6] The king made it clear that it was only under pressure of necessity that he agreed
to the repeal on any terms (*Corr. of King George III*, i. 269. Memorandum by the king,
11 February 1766), and at one stage observers thought that the ministry would fall on
the subject (*Letters of the Earl of Chesterfield* (1892 ed.), iii. 1335).
[7] Rockingham, *Memoirs*, i. 284. The expression was the second Lord Hardwicke's.
[8] 'Letters of D. de Berdt', p. 311. Reports conversations with Conway.

how surprisingly easy to bring under centralized control from London. Barlow Trecothick, in an examination before the house, showed this in a frank account of their methods.

> I will give a candid account—we find America in confusion, our property in danger, our Remittances uncertain and the Trade in danger of annihilation—we were called on by the Bristol Merchants—this hastened our meeting for all the Merchants trading to North America. They met, chose a committee, they instructed that committee to write circular Letters to the manufacturing Towns requiring their Support in an application to Parliament, and to use their interest with the Members to make the interest of Great Britain the Basis of their application. . . . Many of the manufacturing Towns sent for the form of a petition which we declined particularly at Bristol—we thought it too indecent and desired them to speak for their own feelings and that none should complain but what were aggrieved.
>
> .   .   .   .
>
> Thirty circular letters sent for petitions to most Towns. In every Answer they were thankful for our Motions and desired copy of Petitions. In general I believe the petitions would have come though Letters had not been sent.[1]

Local bodies were formed in Liverpool, Bristol, Manchester, and Glasgow, with which the central committee kept in touch,[2] and from which at a later stage witnesses were sent to represent their grievances. Twenty-three petitions were received by the house of commons between 17 and 29 January, all expressed in terms of concerted similarity,[3] and even before they came in the first step was gained, for a parliamentary inquiry had been agreed to.

This was a valuable advance, for here there was a further opportunity to show the nature and extent of the movement, and again the ministry and merchants' organizations worked together. Rose Fuller, a West Indian and a strong supporter of the ministry, was made chairman ; witnesses of every type were called together, members of the London committee of merchants, whose powers were expanding as the agitation grew, among them Trecothick, who also sent in written notes ;[4] merchants from Glasgow, Liverpool, Manchester, and Bristol ; manufacturers from Leeds, Bradford, and Manchester. A London goldsmith gave valuable evidence on the bullion trade, a few merchants and agents from America, including Benjamin Franklin, described American conditions, and the chairman of the West Indian Association gave support [5] which showed how much the jealousies between the two trades were, at

---

[1] Brit. Mus. Add. MS. 33030, fo. 101. Cf. 'Letters of D. de Berdt', pp. 307–8, and copy of correspondence between Trecothick and the Mayor of Norwich, 6 to 27 December 1765 (Brit. Mus. Add. MS. 22358, fo. 32 *seq.* Buckingham Corr.).

[2] *Ibid.*, fo. 214 *seq.* Trecothick's notes on the Petition from the merchants of London.

[3] *Journ. of the House of Commons*, xxx. 462 *seqq.*

[4] Brit. Mus. Add. MS. 33030, fo. 214.

[5] *Ibid.*, fo. 188.

least temporarily, overborne by this new common danger.[1] Public fervour was still further aroused by the political issues which the colonists and their supporters in Parliament had introduced into what seemed a commercial subject, and by the great speeches of Pitt who was stirred from his torpor. Only less successful were the first speeches of Burke, worked to a fever of enthusiasm by this the first great issue of his political career.

The result was what they had hoped. Unwillingly and with careful reservations the king and most of their supporters gave way, the repeal was passed, and the Rockingham ministry, though it shared the popular glory with Pitt, had passed successfully through the crisis. Burke shared fully in this success. Not only did he make his successful beginning in the house, but his real power in the party had grown remarkably. His activities in keeping the ministry and the merchants in touch, during this agitation and the parliamentary inquiry which was part of it, were probably the most successful practical work that he ever did in power. So active were he and Dowdeswell in establishing relations with the merchants all over the country that he had already founded his reputation among the general commercial interests. With Rockingham and Dowdeswell alone among the ministers, he received before and on the fall of the ministry addresses of thanks from several towns in terms which justify his boast that the Rockingham administration tried to understand and satisfy the needs of every section of commercial opinion.[2]

The third period of their office was, however, upon them. In the crisis they had triumphed by making the demands of the organized American trades their own, but machinery had been set going which it was beyond their power to control. From the beginning of the inquiry, as is plain from the fragmentary accounts of their evidence,[3] the commercial witnesses tended to wander from the question immediately before them to all the vague complaints that had been only hesitatingly formed in the preceding period. It is even possible that Trecothick and the merchant leaders, in framing their agitation from the beginning in general terms, had deliberately played for this object. In any case, the opportunities for joint action, the success of their organization, and the knowledge that they were carrying the government before them, led them, even before the repeal of the Stamp Act, to demands which

---

[1] The co-operation with the North American interests appears to have been complete among the merchants in the West Indian interest, the only exception being Sir Alexander Grant, but some of the landlords voted against the repeal; see *List of the Minority in the House of Commons who voted against the Bill to Repeal the Stamp Act*. Paris, 1766. (It said that it was printed in 'Paris' to avoid the possibility of unpleasant consequences to printers and publisher.)

[2] *Burke Corr.* i. 104, 12 June 1766, address from the Merchants of Lancaster; Prior, *Life of Edmund Burke* (Bohn ed., 1891), p. 90.

[3] Brit. Mus., Add. MS. 33030, fo. 78 *seqq.*

only increased with the chances of success, and removed all initiative from the Rockingham ministry. When on 21 February, after reporting the resolutions which were to form the repeal of the Stamp Act, the chairman announced that the house wished to continue sitting in committee on American trade affairs,[1] just as public opinion thought the whole matter was satisfactorily ended, the elated merchant leaders knew it had only begun.

> There is yet much to be done [wrote Dennis de Berdt, member of the London Committee, and Agent for Massachusetts], The Admiralty Courts must be restrained, the exorbitant Duty on Molasses Lowerd, and the restraints on Trade removed, and this we hope to effect through the favour of the present ministry who Justly think the Interest of England and her Colonies one.[2]

With the political elements removed the purely commercial ones began to show themselves again in a truer form, but no longer an uncontroversial one. This form was the challenge by the now confident North American merchants to the West Indians, with whom they had just been in alliance, on the two points where their interests clashed most directly, and on which they had been drifting to open conflict before the interruption occurred. The remaining two of the triad of acts [3] which make up the Rockingham commercial policy are the product of this last period. It became plain, however, that the centre of activity did not lie in the ministry, whose internal difficulties were also at their height, as the dislike of the king and court party on the one hand, and the renewed activity of Pitt on the other, undermined their unity and control. It lay in the extra-parliamentary negotiations to which business in the house tended to become merely the sequel, and particularly in the relations of the committee of merchants trading to North America, and the similar committee of the West India merchants. There was considerable truth in Grenville's sneer at ' the overbearing and delegation of administration to a Club of North America merchants at the King's Arms Tavern ',[4] and the ministry could do little more than anxiously await the result.

At first it seemed as if a conflict might be avoided. The West Indians, shaken by the danger of the Stamp Act disturbance and realizing the formidable strength of the organization against them, were prepared to compromise. Rose Fuller wrote, what they would never have admitted before, that the proposed reduction of the duty on foreign molasses from 3*d*. to 1*d*. per gallon might be an

---

[1] *Journ. of the House of Commons*, xxx. 586.
[2] 'Letters of D. de Berdt', p. 314. Cf. p. 315.
[3] (i) Act for Repealing Certain Duties, and Encouraging, Regulating, and Securing the Trade of this Kingdom, and the British Dominions in America; (ii) Act for Opening Certain Ports in Dominica and Jamaica, &c.
[4] Brit. Mus. Add. MS. 32975, fo. 58, J. West to Newcastle, 30 April 1766. Account of Proceedings in the House of Commons.

improvement as a duty 'which will certainly be collected' and 'will also accustom the North American Colonies to obedience ',[1] and only six days after the third reading of the repeal and a fortnight before the house again resolved itself into committee, the two committees had met and come to a compromise.[2] This was reported to the ministry by a joint committee. Greatly relieved, Rockingham reported to the king that there was ' The Greatest Prospect of an Advantageous System of Commerce being Established for the Mutual and General Interest of this Country ', since ' several of the matters which might have occasioned dispute were nearly agreed between them '.[3]

Though it is unlikely that the compromise satisfied all sections of West Indian opinion, which was naturally finding some difficulty in readjusting itself to the sudden change in the relations of the American trades,[4] all would probably have gone well, had the North American merchants pressed no farther. With the two West Indian leaders, Beckford and Fuller, supporting their policy, moreover, the ministry might have maintained unbroken the united commercial support which was becoming increasingly necessary for its prestige as its position grew weaker. Early in April Horace Walpole became convinced that their only hope of maintaining themselves was by recuperation after a hasty prorogation,[5] by May Newcastle was urging the hurrying of the necessary business through the house for the same purpose. Even if this were done, he thought on the last night ' the Thoughts of our principal Friends might be known—the Sense of the City and even in some degree of the country . . . and from thence the possibility or Propriety of going on may be better judged of '.[6] It was just at this crucial point, however, that parliamentary business was held up, the opposition and malcontents given an opportunity which they were quick to take, and the ministry's prestige definitely broken, by the violent breach between the North American and West Indian interests. On 7 April there suddenly came to a head the demand among traders and manufacturers with American interests for the opening of Dominica as a free port for ships from all the foreign West Indies. Concerted petitions stressing particularly the manufacturing needs came from Bristol, Liverpool, Lancaster, and Manchester, to be followed later by a great petition from London.[7] Though it is just possible that the London Committee which was

[1] Brit. Mus. Add. MS. 32975, fo. 147, R. Fuller to Newcastle, enclosure in letter of 10 May 1766.

[2] *Ibid.* 38339, fo. 235 (copy) ; printed in *Gentleman's Magazine*, 1766, p. 228.

[3] *Corr. of King George III*, i. 282, 12 March 1766.

[4] See article in *Gentleman's Magazine*, 1766, p. 228.

[5] H. Walpole, *Memoirs*, ii. 232.

[6] Brit. Mus. Add. MS. 32975, fo. 72, Newcastle to Rockingham, 2 May 1766 (secret). One of his chief reasons was his well-grounded fear of the defection of Grafton.

[7] *Journ. of the House of Commons*, xxx. 708 and 750 (London Petition).

in negotiation with the West Indians had not initiated this movement, it certainly took it up with enthusiasm. The West Indians
in return, under the leadership of Beckford,[1] at once threw themselves into violent opposition, though a small section, among whom
were the Fullers, seem to have maintained their whig alliance.

The administration realized the gravity of the situation, but,
unable to check its supporters, it hastily called a cabinet
meeting to decide on a policy before the matter was brought up
in the house.[2] Their usual disunion on commercial matters was
now accentuated by even more ominous factors. While Rockingham and his group were as ever prepared to support the North
American merchants, with whom Burke and Dowdeswell were
again in close touch, Newcastle hesitated at first in face of West
Indian hostility. Others definitely opposed the suggestion with a
decision which was increased by the news which went round that
Pitt, under the combined influence of irritation with the ministry
and the pressure of his personal friend Beckford, was prepared to
support his old allies the West Indians.[3] Neither Burke nor a
deputation of London merchants,[4] moreover, could change his
attitude.

There is no space here to describe this last and greatest struggle
of the West Indian and North American merchants, which in the
dying days of a now totally discredited ministry was fought out
through rather than by ministry and opposition in the house.
Pitt indeed left the field, deserting his West Indian allies when he
discovered, what he had not before had occasion to realize, the
' ill-success to his popularity ' which a conflict with the great
North American interests brought.[5] The struggle, however, continued, and became more serious to the ministry as they realized
that the opposition, knowing their weakness, was playing for time,[6]
and that despite all their efforts their majority was melting away.
An observer remarked :

Mr. Beckford has treated the House of Commons every day this week,
and I may say until night too, with his evidence relative to the duties, free
port etc. . . . it makes but a ghastly appearance on the part of the directors

[1] P. R. O., Chatham MS. G. D. 8, 19, Beckford to Pitt, 18 April 1766.
[2] Brit. Mus. Add. MS. 32974, fo. 348, Rockingham to Newcastle, 11 April
1766.
[3] *Ibid.*, fo. 350, Newcastle to Rockingham, 11 April 1766 ; P. R. O., Chatham MS.
G. D. 8, 19, Beckford to Pitt, 18 April 1766.
[4] Brit. Mus. Add. MS. 32974, fo. 370, Rockingham to Newcastle, 13 April 1766;
ibid., fo. 389. Newcastle, rough memorandum. ' Ald. Trecothick, Mr. Barclay, Mr.
Hanbury, Merchants that went to Mr. Pitt.' Burke had seen Pitt several days earlier
when reporting the suggestion from Rockingham (*ibid.*, fo. 417).
[5] Pitt's change of attitude was first seen in the debate of 30 April (Brit. Mus. Add.
MS. 32975, fo. 58).
[6] *Ibid.*, fo. 97, West to Newcastle, 7 May 1766. *Ibid.*, fo. 98, Onslow to Newcastle,
7 May 1766.

of the political machine when in a question of such importance as that now before the House . . . only seventy members could be found to attend their dutys.[1]

Such a position could not be allowed to continue, and the ministry through Rose and Stephen Fuller, the West Indians, as well as its usual intermediaries, was trying desperately, since the opposing bodies could come to no compromise, to persuade the West Indians into agreement by the grant of new concessions to their other trade demands. Negotiations of this kind had been going on continually behind the business of opposition,[2] and on 8 May the ministry was rejoiced to hear that, through the ' infinite merit '[3] of Rose and Stephen Fuller, an agreement satisfactory to all shades of West Indian opinion had been reached. That the West Indians had good cause to be satisfied by the compensations which were made them is shown by the rough drafts and final copy of their agreement, preserved among the Newcastle papers.[4] For the ministry the success of this negotiation was the last satisfaction which they obtained, for though opposition at once collapsed, when the West Indian change of front became apparent, and the resolutions embodying their two acts for American trade were passed the same night,[5] it was too late to strengthen their cause. Fully reconciled, however, the North American and West Indian merchants continued to follow up their successes, and, laying down the main lines of the regulations for the new Free Ports,[6] concluded the commercial policy which they had forced into existence, although the ministry gave it their own name.

At this very time the exhausted ministry was falling. In July, with Burke still loyally struggling to keep up, by the example of an address from the North American and West Indian merchants, the claim of his patrons to be the favourites and benefactors of the great merchant classes with their interests in the West,[7] the first Rockingham ministry disappeared.

[1] *Chatham Corr.* ii. 417, Nuthall to Pitt, 8 May 1766.

[2] Brit. Mus. Add. MS. 33030, fo. 247. Notes on Suggested Agreement—names of West Indian witnesses, accompanied, it is stated, by a letter from S. Fuller (Agent for Jamaica) to Dowdeswell, probably that of 30 April (Add. MS. 32975, fo. 62).

[3] *Ibid.*, fos. 110, 112, 114, G. Onslow to Newcastle, 8 May 1766.

[4] *Ibid.* 33030, fo. 243. Agreement of the West Indian Committee (rough copy) docketed house of commons, 8 May 1766. Fo. 245, fair copy, with alterations. (See appendix.) That the West Indians did not consider the compromise in the light of a defeat is suggested by the wording of an invitation to Newcastle to a West Indian dinner 13 June 1766 (*ibid.* 32975, fo. 400).

[5] *Ibid.*, fo. 112, West to Newcastle, 8 May 1766.

[6] Printed. Brit. Mus. 213. i. 5(99), *Regulations for Opening the Island of Dominica as a Free Port*, approved by the Merchants of the West Indian and North American Committees in order to increase the Consumption of our Manufactures and to extend the Trade and Navigation of Great Britain. n.d. I am indebted to Miss H. Allen of Vassar College for this note. These regulations were incorporated in the statute with slight modifications.

[7] *Burke Corr.* i. 107, Burke to Rockingham, 21 August 1766; *Rockingham Memoirs,*

With it went Burke into the long opposition in which his genius was to be formed, but the lines of his career had already been laid. A year before almost unknown, he had, at a time when young and ambitious men were numerous, made a striking success in the house, and won a name in the organization of complicated commercial affairs. Friends thought that ' whatever side he engages on . . . his abilities will be conspicuous ',[1] but he had never the personal enterprise of the free-lance such as Pitt and Townshend.[2] Already his ambitions and enthusiasms were pledged to the first patrons of his political life.

Few contemporaries can have thought that the short ministry which had failed to revive the solidity of half a century's firm whig rule had in any way a permanent influence upon the political development of its time. Yet Burke saw more truly, though not for the reasons which he gave, when he saw in it great significance. In the growth of the influence of outside opinion on parliament, and in the formation of the claims of control and parliamentary reform to which this was inevitably leading up, it played, though involuntarily, a part. Further, this ministry gave its form both in practice and theory to what we consider the whig tradition of the eighteenth century. It was not the principles of the Pelhams, Cavendishes, and Russells, ruling securely as the heirs of the glorious revolution, but those which were forced out by the change from power to opposition, a compound of new needs with old loyalties. They were the principles which Burke conceived as underlying the endless personal friction, the expediencies of long opposition, and the crises of short-lived power among the band of men, for him ' far the best that probably ever were engaged in the public services of this country '.[3]

ii. 9–10. Hardwicke wrote to Rockingham, 24 August 1766 : ' I was much edified by the account in the papers of your reception in Yorkshire, with the Address of the manufacturers etc., and had before read with pleasure the handsome and well-merited compliment to your Lordship by the Committee of Merchants in town upon your dismission from office. You are really beating the late Great Commoner at his own weapons.'

[1] *Hist. MSS. Comm. VIIIth Report, O'Conor MSS.*, p. 483, O'Conor to Curry, 17 November 1766.

[2] Grafton in a letter to Chatham, 17 October 1766 (*Chatham Corr.* iii. 111) gave a shrewd estimate of him. ' I cannot help saying, that I look upon it, that he is a most material man to gain, and one on whom the thoroughest dependence may be given, where an obligation is owned.'

[3] *Burke Corr.* ii. 278, Burke to Shackleton, 25 May 1776.

APPENDIX

I. *Agreement of the West Indian Committee.* Endorsed House of Commons, May 8th. 1766. (Rough Copy.) (Brit. Mus. Add. MS. 33030, fo. 243.)

(Erasures, here enclosed in brackets [ ], occur in the original. Phrases in parentheses ( ) indicate that they are in another hand.)

1. That the 18d Duty on Sugar be taken off and that 1d per Gallon be laid upon Melasses of the British Sugar Colonies imported into North America.
2. That the Time of paying the Excise on bonded Rum be prolonged (to a twelvemonth).
3. That [either] 6d per gallon be [taken off Rum and] (additional duty be) laid upon Brandy, [or that 1s. per Gallon be laid on Brandy and Rum remain as it is].
4. That Relief be given to the Spanish Trade (by a species of Free port in Jamaica for Spanish bottoms to be proposed this year).[1]
5. That the Duty on French Sugars in North America be *settled* (continued) at 5 p.c. (as it now is.)
6. That the Duty on foreign Cotton be taken off.
7. That the Duty on foreign Melasses imported into North America be reduced to 1d. per Gallon.
8. [All other Articles as Administrations think proper.]
9. That all Sugars coming from North America to Great Britain [to be warehoused and reexported] be deemed foreign.
10. (marked). [The free port of Dominica not to be carried into Execution this Year.] (The Freeport at Dominica for Goods of foreign American Growth etc. to be proposed for consideration but not absolutely determined whether to pass it or not this Session.)
11. The Consumption of foreign Sugars not to be permitted in Great Britain but upon the present high Duty.
    That the West India Committee inform the North American Committee of . . . .

II. *Fair Copy of the Above.* (Brit. Mus. Add. MS. 33030, fo. 245). This would appear to be the final form of the agreement. Here the following phrases are omitted :

4. (to be proposed this year)
10. To be proposed for consideration but not absolutely determined whether to pass it this session.

The end. That the West India Committee inform the North American Committee of . . . .

---

[1] The Jamaica free port created is to be distinguished sharply from that of Dominica (dealt with in 10). The Jamaica free port was desired by the West Indians to encourage the Spanish smuggled bullion trade. The Dominica free port was intended (like 6) to get raw cotton and other materials ' In as great a Quantity and as Cheap as possible for the benefit of our own Manufacturers at Manchester where 120,000 persons are employed therein'. The West Indians were afraid of the latter, as they saw in it a means of smuggling foreign sugar through North America. ' It is a fact very remarkable that in some years the Sugars imported from North America to this kingdom as of British Growth, exceeded considerably in Quantity what they Exported from our Colonies.' (Brit. Mus. Add. MS. 33030, fo. 247.)

III. Fo. 247 of the same manuscript consists of rough notes on the agreement point by point. Several have against them in the margin the names of three prominent West Indians, Maitland, Beeston Long, and Thomas Collett. Reference is also made to a letter from Stephen Fuller, agent for Jamaica. The notes attributed to their authority stress the bad position of the West Indian Rum trade. With regard to clause 2 it is said :

> ' The Want of this Regulation hath been most severely felt this Year, for there hath been lying in the Warehouses about 5000 Puncheons of 100 Gallons each at one time for want of a market. . . .'

So that after six months the owners had to sell it at auction to raise the Excise, and lost heavily.

With regard to clause 3

> ' If Rum should continue for many Years in the situation it is in at present, it will ruin the Proprietors of the old Sugar Plantations, and prevent the settlement of our new acquisitions, so far as relates to Sugar and Rum.'

They would have preferred the 6d to be taken off Rum, but this will do.

15

THE EAST INDIA SPECULATIONS
OF WILLIAM BURKE

(WITH JOHN A. WOODS)

I

The speculative activities of William Burke, like the rest of his career, are of interest primarily because of their effects upon the life of his great kinsman, Edmund, with whom he was so long and closely associated. William's own life-story is a depressing one, for it is that of a man of parts and enterprise, though of doubtful judgement and few fixed principles, who wrecked his prospects by a few years of financial folly from the effects of which he was never able to recover; who, after some fruitless struggles, dragged out the rest of his life in increasing disintegration, an exile in Madras, and returned (under an amnesty from his chief creditor)[1] only to die. It is the more distressing because, by the circumstances of his failure, he gravely embarrassed the kinsman to whom he was devoted and whom he was trying to help, and because he was to be a burden on this kinsman for the rest of his life. The only redeeming feature of the story is the unfaltering loyalty which Edmund and his family showed to the luckless failure, and the fact that, as a result of their efforts, he was able at the last to die in their care.

The friendship of Edmund and William was a peculiarly close one; their blood relationship is uncertain. Their fathers, Burke said, 'did sometimes call each other cousins'.[2] They seem to have become friends when Edmund came to London in 1750 to read for the bar when William's father, a Chancery lawyer, stood bondsman for him at the Middle Temple; and he was much at their house. Little though we know of the 'missing years' of Edmund's early manhood, we know that he and William were constantly together and that, after Edmund's marriage, William (who never married) became as much part of the household as Richard, Edmund's younger brother, was to become. And the 'common purse' which at least one later observer noted as characteristic of the close little family group seems already to have been in existence.[3]

---

[1] Mary, Baroness Fermanagh, heiress to Ralph, 2nd Earl Verney.
[2] Deposition by Edmund Burke in Chancery, 26 November 1783. Quoted by Dilke, *Papers of a Critic*, London, 1875, II, 369.
[3] Mrs Vesey referred to it in a letter of 28 May 1777: "They have long made one common purse." Quoted R. Blunt, *Mrs Montagu, Queen of the Blues*, London [1923], II, 23.

At first William might have seemed to have a slight advantage over Edmund. In their earlier years he had the better means; William's education at Westminster and Christ Church, Oxford, had given him contacts not open to a young Irishman from Trinity College, Dublin, who had no connexions with the families of the Ascendancy. And, though Edmund had a striking success in the world of letters when he published his *Philosophical Enquiry into the Origin of our Ideas of the Sublime and Beautiful* in 1757, William, himself quite a successful pamphleteer,[1] was better known in political circles. The Governor of Guadaloupe under whom he served for two years as Secretary and Register of the Island judged him "one of the few comforts in this dissolving climate",[2] though his good-will may have abated later, and Henry Fox in 1763 called him "a very clever fellow, and I believe a very honest one".[3] Moreover, at least since 1762, he enjoyed the advantages of a close friendship with the rich and extravagant Ralph, second Earl Verney,[4] for whom he acted as a kind of man of business; and Verney, though his interest in politics had to take its place with a variety of other activities, maintained his own interest in the House of Commons in which, an Irish peer, he sat himself.[5] As late as 1765 when the Burkes both obtained employment under the Rockingham administration, William's job, as Under-Secretary of State to General Conway, seemed a better one than Edmund's, as private secretary to Lord Rockingham;[6] and it was William, standing down from the first seat offered him by Lord Verney (who, however, provided him with another six months later), who gave Edmund the chance to show the Parliamentary talents which were to be the making of his public life.

Yet that he did so underlines the fact that from the beginning Edmund was the dominating partner in their friendship, a fact which tells us something not only of the personal ascendancy this remarkable man was apt to exert over those who came in touch with him, but also of the character of the lesser man whose life he unintentionally absorbed. To other friends William appeared, before his troubles came on him, lively, rattling and self-confident. Charles O'Hara speaks of "all thy noise, etourderie and abuse".[7] Later he was judged more harshly, though it is doubtful whether contemporaries would have recognized in him the "sinister and

---

[1] In particular *An Account of the European Settlements in America*, 1757, said to have been corrected by Edmund.

[2] Public Record Office, C.O.110/1. Quoted *Correspondence of Edmund Burke*, ed. T. W. Copeland *et al.*, I, 140 n. 1.

[3] Henry Fox to Lord Sandwich, 12 November 1763. Quoted Sir Lewis Namier, *England in the Age of the American Revolution*, 2nd ed. London 1961, p. 186 n.1.

[4] William Burke to Charles O'Hara, 20 November 1762. *Correspondence of Edmund Burke*, I, 154.

[5] Verney appears to have helped the Burkes when their careers were at a moment of crisis. In a list of bonds at Claydon (made in 1784) there is a mention of a bond of 15 March 1765: "Messrs. E. and W. Burke and Jos. Hickey to Lord V. £4,500." Nothing else is known about this bond.

[6] Charles O'Hara to Edmund and William Burke, 30 July 1765: "Edmund you are a little less lucky than Will." *Correspondence of Edmund Burke*, I, 214.

[7] *Ibid.*

disreputable figure" described by Sir Philip Magnus.[1] To the world at large he must have seemed at this early stage much like other vigorous, pushing, youngish men on the fringes of politics, though unlike most of them he was pushing for others as much as (or more than) himself. To Edmund he appeared differently. Edmund was not usually realistic in his judgement of those in whom he had placed his affections, and in later years his panegyrics of William, as also of his own shiftless brother Richard, aroused a good deal of derision; but in the character he drew of William in the early days of their friendship, under the name of Phidippus, he made two points that probably had substance. "You would take Phidippus", he wrote, "for a man confident and assuming; but in reality he has nothing less in his Character. He is timorous and diffident. . . . If you see Phidippus positive and violent, do not think I am wrong in my observation. This violence is only a sort of Clamour in which he would drown his own fears," and he adds, no doubt from his own experience, that he could show "a tenderness even to the feminine".[2]

One of the major obscurities in the career of Edmund Burke is, and is likely to remain, his finances; partly because of the acute personal secretiveness taught him by a scurrilous Press, partly because he himself always knew as little about them as possible, but also because of the speculative disaster which overwhelmed William in 1769 and affected the whole family. It is therefore worth while to try to find out, so far as is possible, the nature of this disaster and of its sequel.

Because of the obscurity in which their affairs were wrapped, it has been customary to speak of the Burke family as if they were penniless adventurers; but while they were certainly poor by the standards obtaining in eighteenth-century politics where Edmund's gifts were leading them, this was not altogether true. William drew an official salary between 1759 and 1763, as Secretary and Register of Guadaloupe and between 1765 and 1767 as Under-Secretary of State, and inherited in 1764 some £3,000 from his father.[3] Edmund drew a salary while he was employed by W. G. Hamilton, but had no official salary as private secretary to Lord Rockingham, though some small payments were apparently made to him.[4] His father, when he died, left an estate of £6,000[5] which Edmund inherited after the death of his brother Garrett in 1765. The major item in it was the Clogher

---

[1] P. Magnus, *Edmund Burke*, London, 1939, p. 9. We do not know the accusations made against him by Bishop Markham in 1771 which called forth Edmund's passionate defence (*Correspondence of Edmund Burke*, II, 250 ff.). Oliver Goldsmith's mock epitaph on him in *Retaliation* is ambiguous, concluding with the words

"Would you ask for his merits? alas! he had none:
What was good was spontaneous his faults were his own."

Laurence Sulivan, who knew him and had no reason to feel friendly towards him, called him, in 1778 when he had recently gone out to Madras, "a flimsey petulant Man, he does not want understanding but I think his judgement below Par. I have never heard his character slur'd, unless it was in Alley [crossed out and 'certain' substituted] Transactions". Bodl. MS. Eng. Hist. C.269, p. 11.

[2] *A Note-Book of Edmund Burke*, ed. H. V. F. Somerset, Cambridge, 1957, pp. 58, 59.

[3] C 12/356/12.

[4] *Correspondence of Edmund Burke*, I, 211. Later Rockingham made loans to Burke, which were cancelled in his will.

estate, valued in 1790 at £3,000[1]. We do not know what he obtained from Dr. Nugent (at one time at least a well-to-do physician) when he married Jane Nugent, nor how much assistance Dr. Nugent gave them during his life, nor what he left them when he died in 1775. Nevertheless these resources could by no means give them what they wanted, financial independence, and it was to acquire this that William seized what seemed to him a magnificent opportunity opened up to him directly by his patron Lord Verney and indirectly by the most unscrupulous adventurer of the time, Lauchlin Macleane, who was to deceive men with far more experience and acumen than either William or Lord Verney could claim. The occasion arose through the wave of speculation in East India stock which followed in 1766 Lord Clive's assumption of the Diwani of Bengal. After three years of frenzied activity, complicated by Government intervention and by faction within the Company, years during which the "bulls" flourished, it ended in a sudden collapse of the price of East India stock in the middle of 1769, as a result of which a whole group of speculators, including Lauchlin Macleane, Lord Verney and William were ruined.[2]

A good deal is known about the losses of those involved. Lauchlin Macleane, whose collapse was the most spectacular, admitted that he owed £90,000 (certainly a gross under-estimate), against which he had assets the value of which was uncertain, but indubitably far below the level of his indebtedness. His creditors, many of whom were influential, for they included Lord Shelburne, his patron, and Laurence Sulivan, a powerful figure in the East India Company of the time, succeeded in obtaining a position for him in India in the hope that he would retrieve his fortunes and meet his liabilities. Though his Indian career was meteoric, he died with the task unfulfilled.[3] Lord Verney's position was on the face of it less grave. He alone of the three speculators with whom we are mainly concerned had the resources to retrieve himself by the exercise of strict economy, if he had been prepared to do so. Already embarrassed, however, by his extravagance in other fields, particularly in electioneering and in his building operations at Claydon,[4] he entirely failed to check his expenditure and he never recovered a stable financial position, dying hopelessly insolvent;[5] William Burke, without the resources of Verney or the connexions and range of operations of Macleane, was involved in the misfortunes of both and suffered more severely than either.

Among those involved in Macleane's downfall was his patron Lord Shelburne who was able to claim (apparently with justice) that he had nothing to gain financially from his client's speculative activities and also (probably with less accuracy) that he had not known what was going on.[6] It has sometimes been assumed

---

[1] Dublin Deed Office, 425/347/277331.
[2] For these episodes see L. S. Sutherland, *The East India Company in Eighteenth-Century Politics*, Oxford, 1952, pp. 134 ff.
[3] *Ibid.* See J. N. M. Maclean, *Reward is Secondary*, London, 1963, for the biography of Macleane.
[4] See Appendix IV.
[5] *Verney Letters of the Eighteenth Century*, ed. Margaret Maria, Lady Verney, London, 1930, II, *passim.*
[6] Sutherland, *op. cit.*, pp. 201–12.

that much the same applied to the relations between William Burke and Lord Verney. John Nicholls, for instance, wrote "Soon after Mr. Edmund Burke became a political character, he, and his cousin William Burke, embarked on a speculation in India stock. They prevailed on many of their friends to join them, among others, on Earl Verney, who fell a victim to this connexion".[1] But this was not the case. Though William was believed to exercise a strong influence over his patron,[2] Verney's own activity in the pursuit of his speculative concerns was too open and sustained for such a plea to be valid; and he himself is not known to have advanced it.[3] Nor does the evidence suggest that the speculative project in which they were jointly embarked originated with William. Though in his later years Verney and his friends became extremely bitter against the Burkes, and against William in particular, it was on the grounds that they could "never fully answer or make an equivalent return for" all Verney had done for them;[4] that William in India, so Verney believed, "makes 12 or 15 per cent of my Money",[5] and, more generally, that it was a good thing "to bring such monsters to Justice and Shame".[6]

In short the charge against them was that of ingratitude for past generosity, not of leading Verney astray or of any abuse of his confidence in the conduct of joint operations. The gravamen of this charge was necessarily against William. So far as Edmund was concerned, he certainly had benefited from Verney's generosity in providing a seat for him in the House of Commons, and their relations had been very friendly, but he took no part in their speculations and seems to have had little grasp of their nature.[7] The accusation of ingratitude against him was based on the allegation that he had in 1769, just before the crash, received £6,000 borrowed by William from Verney to help in the purchase of his country house, Gregories, and that he refused to repay it; but Edmund claimed (apparently correctly) that he had never received this sum.[8] The demand on Edmund was first made formally in 1779, ten years after the debt was contracted, and in 1783 Verney tried to proceed against him at law, but unsuccessfully. It should be noted that Edmund continued to be a political supporter of Verney, even after the unpleasantness which this dispute aroused. He was active for him in 1779, 1784 and 1790, and Lord Fitzwilliam's contribution to the expense of the Buckinghamshire election of 1784 is unlikely to have been given except in conformity with Edmund's wishes.[9]

---

[1] J. Nicholls, *Recollections and Reflections*, London 1820, I, 54–5.

[2] Henry Fox on 12 November 1763 wrote to Lord Sandwich: "He has as great a sway with Lord Verney, as I ever knew one man to have with another." See p. 328 n. 3 above.

[3] Laurence Sulivan who suffered from his relations with Verney certainly did not think he was a sleeping partner in his speculative activities. Describing his own misfortunes in the slump of 1769 he wrote in 1778: "I fell a Victim to (then unknown to me) a sett of desperate Gamblers outside [without] characters Earl Verney at their head and a greater Rascal is not in this country." Bodl. MS. Eng. Hist. C. 269, p. 29.

[4] J. Twinberrow to Verney, 9 Jan. 1789, quoting Elias de la Fontaine, the broker. Claydon MSS.

[5] L. Heslop to J. Forster, 12 March 1790, quoting Verney. Claydon MSS.

[6] S. Rogers to Verney, 11 September 1783. Claydon MSS.

[7] *Correspondence of Edmund Burke*, II, 26–9.

[8] See *Correspondence of Edmund Burke*, II, Appendix.

[9] Accounts of Lord Fitzwilliam, Northamptonshire Record Office.

In William's case the issues were more complex. He too had owed to Verney's generosity his seat in Parliament, and had no doubt received great kindness at his hands. Still more Verney had, with what seems almost absurd generosity, financed most if not all of William's share in their joint speculations in East India stock. The trouble arose, however, from the way in which he exerted this generosity; he did so, as will be shown, by taking William into a partnership, in which William took his share in profits he could never otherwise have aspired to (though it is doubtful how much of these profits were ever realized in cash), but in which he also shared in risks which he could never have run on his own, and which, when disaster came, produced liabilities which he was quite unable to meet.

With the aid of the papers of some of those involved,[1] and evidence produced in a number of cases in Chancery and at the Exchequer which followed the crash of 1769,[2] it is possible to piece together a good deal of the story.

The operations which led to this disastrous result began in June 1766, when the news from Bengal had already led to a rise in the price of East India stock, and when speculators and investors had been steadily buying it up. Some of these had early inside information, including Clive himself, who sent orders in cypher to his attornies to buy in stock, and Henry Fox, Lord Holland, who, on the private advice of John Walsh, one of Clive's attornies, bought a large amount out of his Pay Office balances.[3] It was generally expected that the Directors would declare an increase in the dividend, but this they were unwilling to do for sound reasons commercial and political. Before the Quarterly General Court of 18 June 1766, however, it became known that a proposal was to be made from among the Proprietors to increase the dividend from 6 % to 8 %.[4] It was in preparation for this that a small consortium was formed during the month of June to buy India stock for the rise. The man who claimed to have originated the idea was Robert Orme, author of *The History of the Military Transactions of the British Nation in Indostan* (1763–78), a former company servant and at this time much connected with Clive's supporters in the Company.[5] He was, however, not only a man of moderate means, but one far too cautious for the company in which he found himself, and the lead soon fell into the more daring and skilful hands of Lauchlin Macleane, an Irish-Scots adventurer, who, after a stirring career in America and the West Indies, followed by a stay in Paris, was now seeking to carve out a career for himself in London in

---

[1] The private papers of Lord Shelburne (Bowood MSS), preserved at Bowood. We are indebted to Lord Lansdowne for permission to examine and use them. The papers of Lord Verney at Claydon (Claydon MSS), which we have used with the permission of Sir Harry and Major Verney. The Fitzwilliam and Burke MSS at the Sheffield City Library and the Northamptonshire Record Office: for permission to use these manuscripts we are indebted to Earl Fitzwilliam and the Earl Fitzwilliam Wentworth Estates Company. There is also useful information in the Orme MSS, India Office Library, Commonwealth Relations Office, in Clive's correspondence (Powis MSS, India Office Library) and in Laurence Sulivan's papers in the Bodleian Library.

[2] See Appendix V.

[3] See Sutherland, *op. cit.*, pp. 141 ff., and, for Lord Holland, L. S. Sutherland and J. Binney, "Henry, Fox as Paymaster General of the Forces", *E.H.R.*, lxx (1955); See below, p. 433.

[4] East India Court Book, vol. 75, p. 87. India Office Library, Commonwealth Relations Office.

[5] R. Orme to I. Panchaud, 20 June 1766. Orme MSS, O.V. 222, p. 136. India Office Library.

the lower ranges of politics. From October 1766 until June 1768 he was Under-Secretary of State to Lord Shelburne. The plan was in the first instance to purchase, chiefly in Amsterdam, £30,000 East India stock for delivery at the next August 'rescounters' or quarterly settlement day.[1] One third of this sum was to be held by Isaac Panchaud, a prosperous Anglo-Swiss banker in Paris,[2] who remained associated with the group throughout its activities; another third was to be held jointly by Robert Orme, Lauchlin Macleane, and one John Stuart, long a partner in Macleane's ventures.[3] The remaining third was to be held by Lord Verney.[4] The portion for which Orme, Macleane and Stuart were responsible was raised largely if not wholly on credit.[5]

At this stage of the operations there is no sign that William had a personal interest in the affair, though it is difficult to think that he was not privy to it, not only because he was busy with Verney's affairs at the time, but because of the very close relations which then existed between Macleane and the Burkes. Macleane had been at Trinity with Edmund, had renewed their old acquaintance when he returned from Paris, and in December 1765 had told John Wilkes that he was more often at Edmund's house than his own.[6] References to him in William's correspondence in 1766 show how much William (like many wiser men) was dazzled by him.[7] It would even seem likely that it was William who introduced Macleane to Lord Verney.[8]

The first assumptions of the consortium proved to be unfounded. The Directors successfully opposed the proposal to increase the dividend; but they did so in terms which encouraged the belief that they would soon give way, and, after a slight check, the stock began to rise again. Even before this, the consortium had decided to "stand out for the riscounter",[9] and Macleane left for Amsterdam to superintend their affairs immediately after the General Court.[10] Within a few days the effects

---

[1] *Ibid.*

[2] *Ibid., passim.* For Isaac Panchaud see H. Lüthy, *La banque protestante en France de la Révocation de l'Edit de Nantes à la Révolution*, Paris, 1959-61, II, 421 ff.

[3] For him see J. N. M. Maclean, *op. cit., passim.*

[4] £10,000 East India stock was bought for him at Amsterdam by I Panchaud at 195 (R. Orme to Verney 25 June 1766, Orme MSS, O.V. 222, p. 138). Orme reported: "This will now be thrown into the common stock; the price is high, but it was purchased in expectation of an increase of dividend at the last General Court, the result of which was not then known at Amsterdam." He added that it was expected that the price would be 200 by the rescounters.

[5] R. Orme wrote to I. Panchaud on 1 July 1766 explaining why he could not join in extended operations; he could not borrow for it. (Orme MSS, O.V. 222, p. 139). "But in the joint concern amongst three shares, Macleane Stuart and I are as one share [ånd] are precluded from that advantage, because the total stock purchased will be previously engaged as security for the loan at 140."

[6] L. Macleane to John Wilkes, 24 December 1765. British Museum Add. MS 30, 868 fol. 221.

[7] e.g. he wrote to James Barry, 3 December 1766, that Macleane was "most deserving of your, and every honest man's love and esteem". (*The Works of James Barry*, London, 1809, 1, 76). Macleane joined with the Burkes in supporting Barry in his visit to Rome to pursue his Art.

[8] An intended deed of sale, dated 28 March 1765, between Macleane and Verney for an estate in Dominica is preserved in the Burke deeds in the Fitzwilliam MSS at Sheffield.

[9] R. Orme to I. Panchaud, 20 June 1766. Orme MSS O.V. 222, p. 136 and elsewhere.

[10] *Ibid.*

of his enterprise were seen, and he sent back plans not only to maintain but expand their activities. We do not know the precise nature of his "great Scheme" as its originators called it, but we do know that it involved increasing their commitments and carrying on after the August rescounters at least till the end of the year.[1] We also know that Orme cried off as beyond his means[2] and that Lord Verney "engages with you with as much warmth as you could expect".[3] There is no reason to think that the originators of the 'great Scheme' had as yet any intention of bringing pressure to bear on the Directors if the dividend were not increased, though when, from August onwards, the price ceased to rise, they rapidly turned their attention to doing so.

It looks as if William Burke obtained his first personal interest in these affairs in the early days of the 'great Scheme'. All we know about this beginning is contained in a rambling letter which he wrote on 4 October 1766 to the Burkes's family friend Charles O'Hara. As Edmund had been in Ireland since about the middle of August, some of its half truths may have been intended for him as well as for his friend. He obviously knew of the earlier stages. The Burkes, William wrote, were now "in a condition to second our views of Independency". He explained:

> "You will be glad to know that in this we have no division of our Obligations, all this, Like as the all before we owe to Lord Verneys wonderful goodness and friendship; in one word the necessary rise of value of East India stock was foreseen, before the price rose or an increased dividend was talked of, but as that increase might possibly not be determined on in 3, or 6, or 9 or even 12 Months those who bought on what they call speculation, that is, who agreed to pay such a price for such a quantity at a particular day, ran the risk of loosing if the price at that particular day happened not to answer his Speculation; so that no one could with safety venture on buying with safety but those who could actually lay down their money, and keep their Stock in their possession quietly till the dividend was increased. This Lord Verny could you know easily do and [if] he had chosen to lay out a Million that way no one could have objected to his taking the consequential Benefit of all the money he employed that way, but he considered this an opportunity of making us independent, and actually paid down to his own above £9000 and engaged for above forty more for me. The dividend is come sooner than I expected, and though the accounts are not yet settled, I may within compass say that I have made £12000 at least . . . It is our good fortune you see to have this advantage without even the Imputation of Stock jobbing, or the term of Bull or Bear being applicable to us."[4]

The most creditable part of this letter is its generous assumption that anything gained by its writer was the gain of the whole Burke family. But behind its vagueness, there lay a far from creditable situation, and the letter was no doubt purposely misleading. William's estimate of his gain may be about right if the stock was

---

[1] Our information about it derives solely from Orme's letters in Orme MSS O.V. 222. He wrote to I. Panchaud on 1 July 1766 (Orme MSS O.V. 222, p. 139) "I wrote a line by the last post (fryday [27 June]) to Mr. Macleane advising the receipt of your letter to Lord Verney with the great Scheme". Explaining why he could not take part in it himself he hoped Panchaud would understand "it will be with the utmost regret if I do not hold on with you in the scheme for the year, . . . Should therefore at the riscounters my situation be as it is at present Lord Verney and you will go on between you from that time. Until that time all purchases stand as at present; and it will be very easy at the riscounters to settle what loss or profit will be forthcoming to M:S: and O as proprietors of one third of the adventure".

[2] *Ibid.*

[3] *Ibid.* Orme adds "and indeed I should have been very much surprised if he had not".

[4] *Correspondence of Edmund Burke,* I, 269-70.

bought early in July. His description of the means by which it was made is (probably intentionally) obscure. He distinguishes between purchases for spot cash and for future delivery, which he calls 'speculation'; but makes no reference to the speculative dealings on margin — "in differences" as the eighteenth century called it — in which most of the speculative activities of the London market took place.[1] Yet he is in fact describing a transaction of precisely that nature. He is explaining that Verney gave him the necessary backing to enable him to deal in "differences" in East India stock to a value of £40,000. Since he was calculating on a rise in the price of the stock he was, however much he denied it, undoubtedly a 'bull'.

There are, however, more reprehensible facts behind the account. That he did not apparently consider it discreditable for an Under-Secretary of State (as he was until February 1767) to speculate in the stock of the Company at a time when it was under government investigation, is not perhaps altogether surprising. Though it was rare at this time for major political figures to put themselves in a position in which they could be accused of using inside knowledge for speculative purposes,[2] it was common among the lesser men and officials to do so[3] — though Lord Shelburne tried (quite ineffectively) to check Lauchlin Macleane's speculative activities while the latter was in his service.[4] But even if this consideration is ignored, William was concerned in a transaction which was not condoned by contemporary opinion. The eighteenth-century hostility to 'stock-jobbers' — as speculators were generically termed — was based not only on dislike of their speculative gains, but on the belief that they often adopted dishonest and anti-social means to obtain these gains. At the time he wrote this letter William and his associates had been concerned in precisely such an operation. The rise in the Company's dividend which had come, he said, "sooner than I expected" had come about, not by normal means, but as a result of their own actions. When it became clear that the Directors still hesitated to raise the dividend, partly at least because the Chatham administration were threatening the Company with a Parliamentary enquiry as a prelude to taking part of their new wealth for the State, the price of stock stopped rising. At this the speculators became impatient, and, after failing to move the Directors by a

---

[1] The great bulk of speculative business on the London market took this form. Dealing in options though common on the Amsterdam market was little employed in London. This point will be covered in a forth-coming work by Mr P. Dickson.

[2] Charles Townshend however did so. See below, p. 443.

[3] e.g. Philip Francis at the War Office speculated on the chances of war during the Falkland Islands affair, and though he carefully excised from his autobiographical fragment all references which might have been embarassing, left in the statement ". . . we thought a Spanish War inevitable, and that Chatham must be employed . . . and I lost five hundred pounds in the Stocks". (Quoted J. Parkes & H. Merivale *Memoirs of Sir Philip Francis*, London, 1867, I, 363.)

[4] L. Macleane to Shelburne, 30 Oct. 1766 (Bowood MSS). "I promised your Lordship to have no concerns in Funds of any Species in England, accordingly I gave Orders to sell whatever Stock I had here although at a Loss. And I am not concerned in any Stock in England that has been bought since the 24th September, neither directly nor indirectly." He added that he would wind up his speculative activities in Holland too, though more gradually. It is clear from material in various Exchequer and Chancery cases brought against him, that he did not keep his word.

vehement Press campaign,[1] they decided to force an increase through the Quarterly General Court of 24 September in the teeth of the Directors' opposition, by the use of the new technique for the creation of fictitious votes which had recently been developed in the Company's annual election of Directors. This was the first time the technique had been employed to force on the Directors' decisions on policy, and it provided a most dangerous precedent. The credit or discredit for organizing it rests with Lauchlin Macleane;[2] the stock for the 'splitting' of votes was said by John Walsh (who as Clive's chief advisor was very well-informed on East India matters) to be provided chiefly by "the principal new stock holders . . . Lord Holland, Lord Verney, Lord Coleraine and Panschaud [sic] a French Banker in Partnership with Foley".[3] An alliance was made with the Company opposition led by Laurence Sulivan and with some of the Company's servants threatened with prosecution by the Directors.[4] As a result, ten days before William Burke wrote his letter, the dividend had been forced up to 10%,[5] though public opinion was obviously shocked at the violence of the measure. Macleane admitted that some of their "new-raised forces" had left them at the ballot "either through Idleness or Scruples"[6] and Hope and Company of Amsterdam reported that "the advance in India Stock has not been in proportion to the important Increase of dividend and we fear it will be some Time before it reaches its value, so many partizans for the insufficiency of the Stock to bear it leaving much apprehension of a reduction when the opposite party prevails".[7]

William Burke himself was concerned in these events. Among the fictitious votes created out of stock provided by Panchaud was one in the name of E. Boyd. When the 'split votes' were retransferred after the General Court, Boyd's £500 was not returned to Panchaud, but was transferred on 30 September into the name of William Burke, who had now a voting qualification in the Company. On 2 May 1767, just in time for a similar operation, a £500 voting qualification was

---

[1] In particular a weekly paper called *The East India Examiner* which ran from 1 September to 19 November was published attacking them. Their supporters replied in *The East India Observer*.

[2] This is made clear by Macleane's letter of 27 September 1766 to Lord Holland and by Holland's reply of 6 October (Holland House MSS. B.M. Main series of 1st Lord Holland). It was known that Lord Holland before going abroad left orders that his stock should be used for this purpose (J. Walsh to Clive, 22 November 1766, Powis MSS, India Office Library). These letters make it clear that Macleane was organizing its use.

[3] J. Walsh to Clive, 22 November 1766, Powis MSS, India Office Library. Gabriel, Baron Coleraine (1697–1773), son of Sir George Hanger, Turkey merchant, had been in the East India Company's service in Bengal from 1714 to 1724. In 1754 he inherited large estates from a relative, Anne, Baroness Coleraine. In 1760, when applying to the Duke of Newcastle for a peerage, he claimed "a fortune equal to that or almost any title of nobility whatsoever". (B.M. Add. MS 32, 916, fol. 15).

[4] Sutherland, *op. cit.*, 142 ff. Attempts to help the latter after the dividend was raised were blocked by Holland, who had, he said, given his 100 votes solely to increase the dividend. See n. 2 above.

[5] East India Court Book, vol. 75, pp. 192–3, at the General Court of 24 September 1766.

[6] L. Macleane to Holland, 27 September 1766. See n. 2 above.

[7] Hope and Company to George Clive, 3 October 1766. Powis MSS, India Office Library.

taken out for another member of the Burke family, Edmund's younger brother Richard.[1]

When William took out his voting qualification it was a sign that his East India speculations were not the once-for-all operation his letter might suggest. If they had been William would have realized his gains and Verney would have made them possible without incurring any cost. But about this time, a much more generous, but also more dangerous arrangement seems to have been made between them; for by some time in the first half of 1767 Verney and William are found as joint owners of £29,000 of East India stock. None of this stock was registered in the Company's books in either of their names. In the books of their brokers De la Fontaine and Brymer, the account was in Verney's name, but a note is appended at the end of each surviving account dividing the relevant items equally in the names of Verney and William.[2] With dealers other than their brokers they did business as equal partners. Those they dealt with were accustomed to receive instructions from either or both of them.[3] Since the purchase price of the stock must have been well over £55,000, and William's contribution to it, even if (as seems likely) it included his speculative gains of 1766, must have been small, this seems a startling piece of generosity on Verney's part. It is hard to believe, that had they sold out in the next few years, Verney would have handed over to William half of this big capital sum, but even if the arrangements meant no more than that William enjoyed one half of the dividends (over £1,400 per annum) and had a right to one half of any capital gains, it was a princely gift. India stock, though not without fluctuations, rose during 1767, 1768 and the first part of 1769. It never realized the great hopes of the speculators, but between the beginning of 1767 and the beginning of 1769 it had risen some 24%. At any time during these years they could have sold out at a good profit.

But Verney and William were working with speculators who had no intention of selling out quickly. This is clear from the part they began to play in East India Company politics and from what we know of their operations on the market. In their activities in Company politics they continued to follow closely the lead set by Macleane, though Macleane himself as Under-Secretary to Lord Shelburne until June 1768 tried to keep in the background. William Burke and Isaac Panchaud, with Verney coming in on important occasions, played a vigorous part in the Company's General Courts between the end of 1766 and the summer of 1769. Their aim was undisguised. Up to May 1769 it was to stimulate a rise in the price of the stock, in particular by increases in the Company's dividend. From May to July 1769 it was to check, if they could, the alarming fall in the price of the stock

---

[1] East India Company Stock Ledgers. Bank of England Record Office.
[2] See below p. 342 and Appendix I.
[3] e.g. when dealing with Cazenove and Van Jever (Public Record Office, C12/542/17). De la Fontaine and Brymer were also accustomed to deal either with Verney or William. They had no written instructions, but acted on private conversations "between them or some of them which were then very Frequent" (*ibid.* C12/1627/8).

when the boom broke and they were heading for disaster. To achieve their aim they consolidated the alliance set up in September 1766 with the Company opposition led by Laurence Sulivan. Their most striking intervention was in May 1767 when, in the midst of the Company's negotiation with Administration for the partition of its new revenue, they repeated their exploit of the previous September and forced upon a protesting Court of Directors a further increase of dividend, this time to 12½%. In the stormy General Courts which followed William Burke was one of the most vocal orators.[1]

This time, however, they had over-reached themselves, and the Administration riposted by pushing through Parliament two bills intended to check abuses caused by what their opponents called "a Clan of temporary Stockjobbing Proprietors".[2] The first bill lowered the Company's dividend to 10% for the next twelve months. The second restricted the vote to proprietors who had held their £500 stock voting qualification for at least six months, thus checking for the future such 'snap' campaigns as the speculators had recently mounted, and making much more dangerous the 'splitting' of stock to create votes for the Company's annual election of Directors.

It was at this point that the aims of the Opposition in Parliament, to which Verney and William (but not Macleane) owed allegiance, most closely coincided with those of the speculators. The Opposition had already been attacking the Administration for its threats of forcible intervention into the Company's affairs, and in so doing they formed alliances within the Company. But their allies were not Sulivan and his party, whose proposals were solidly supported by the speculators,[3] for Sulivan, like Macleane, was closely linked with Shelburne and thus with a part at least of the Administration. The determination of the Administration to restrict the dividend aroused the Opposition to still greater activity, and they made a determined attempt to attack the bill both in the Commons and the Lords. Now they and the speculators were speaking with one voice. But it was still not upon the speculators, upon Verney and William Burke and their friends, that the leaders of the Opposition (Newcastle, Rockingham, Grenville and Bedford) chiefly depended in planning their tactics with interests within the Company. Indeed there are clear signs that the speculators were a political embarrassment to them. Charles Yorke said of the Company that he was "a friend to their rights, and not to their passions, or to the selfish views of stock-jobbers",[4] and the Duke of Newcastle noted with concern "I find, there is every where a general dislike to the wildness, and behaviour of the General Court".[5] To the bill restricting the voting qualification, the Opposition raised no objection whatever.

---

[1] East India Company Court Book, vol. 76 *passim*, and, for example, J. West to Newcastle, 6 May 1767, B.M. Add. MS 32, 981, fol. 303, description of the General Court of 6 May 1767 at which the decision to increase the dividend was reached.

[2] J. Walsh to Clive, 26 March 1767, Powis MSS, India Office Library.

[3] East India Company Court Book, vol. 76, pp. 52 ff. General Court of 12 May 1767.

[4] C. Yorke to Newcastle, 9 May 1767, B.M. Add. MS 32, 981, fol. 340.

[5] Newcastle to J. Rigby, 29 May 1767, B.M. Add. MS 32, 982, fol. 168.

The close relationship of the speculators with the Sulivan party in the Company, led the former into activities in its support at each of the annual elections of Directors between 1767 and 1769, though at first without success. In the 1768 election, the new legislation checked the creation of fictitious votes and it was optimistically believed that this abuse had been permanently done away with.[1] But in April 1769 Sulivan and the ex-Governor of Bengal, Henry Vansittart, made a desperate attempt to return to power, and the result was one of the most fiercely contested Company elections of the period, in which, despite the danger of keeping 'split' votes out from the previous August, great numbers of fictitious votes were created on both sides. In these activities the speculators played their full part, and in addition joined in a scheme, originating in the fertile mind of Lauchlin Macleane, to create 200 votes by forming a group of subscribers to borrow stock on the Amsterdam market for the purpose. They promised to return it in July 1769 at 280, a price which the stock never had reached (and never was to reach). The names of Verney, William and Richard Burke, Macleane, Sulivan and Lord Shelburne were among the twenty-three signatories to the undertaking, the whole being guaranteed by Sulivan and Henry Vansittart.[2] The scheme was sufficiently unusual to be noticed by their enemies, the supporters of Clive, one of whom observed: "By all this you see the Dividend is meant to be forced."[3] Even before the elections the dividend was pushed up (after the expiry of the first agreement with the Government) by 1%, a demand for a General Court to achieve this being made on 14 February 1769 by Verney, William Burke and seven other proprietors.[4] When Sulivan and Vansittart were among the successful candidates at the April election they must have felt that their prospects were good indeed.

But in fact, less than a month after this triumph the tide turned against them. The market had already shown signs of nervousness, and the great credit operations for the purchase of stock for 'splitting' had increased the malaise. The price began to slide; when alarming news came in from Madras at the end of the month it fell precipitately. As the settlement day at the opening of the Company's books on 18 July[5] drew near a condition of panic set in, and the three years' boom was over. The speculators did not at once recognize this unwelcome fact and they tried various ways to check it. On 30 May 1769 Verney, William Burke and Panchaud were among those demanding a general court to reassure the market.[6] On

---

[1] J. Walsh to Clive, 15 April 1768, Powis MSS. India Office Library.
[2] There is a good deal of information about this scheme in the Bowood MSS, especially in letters of I. Barré, J. Dunning and L. Macleane to Shelburne, written during June, July and August 1769 and in the Sulivan MSS (Bodl. MS. Engl. Hist. C. 269, p. 23).
[3] J. Walsh to Clive, 27 June 1768. Powis MSS. India Office Library.
[4] East India Company Court Book, vol. 77, p. 469.
[5] There were two systems of settlement day operating on the London market at this time, one dependent on the Amsterdam system of quarterly Rescounters, and another on the "several intermediate Settling Days which depend upon the Shutting and the opening of the Books of the several Stocks". (Verney and William Burke v J. L. André etc. C12/1623/1. Amended bill 9 Feb. 1774). Speculators might work to either system, or a combination of the two.
[6] East India Company Court Book, vol. 78, p. 50. The Court was held on 1 June 1769 (*Ibid.* p. 58). W. Burke was among the speakers at it. (*London Chronicle*, 1–3 June 1769). The Press thought the results satisfactory.

6 July, Verney, William Burke, Macleane and six other proprietors demanded a General Court, at which it was hoped that an ingenious plan for pegging the price of the stock might be pushed through to save the situation. The plan originated with Macleane, and, after others had refused to advance it "Poultney [William Pulteney] and Lord Verney then undertook it". But even they quailed when the moment for acting came, and they "shrunk from a measure which carry'd so Jobbish a complection at this particular period of time".[1] This was their last attempt to exercise pressure on the Company in the interest of their speculations.

We know more of the measures Verney and William took in Company politics, than we do of the speculations in support of which they were acting, until the last disastrous one which brought about their undoing. Nevertheless there is a good deal of information about their joint operations. The £29,000 East India stock which they held in 1767, can be considered under two heads: £20,000 of the stock formed the permanent basis of their speculative activities; the extra £9,000 stock served different purposes. £1,500 of this £9,000 stock was divided into three voting qualifications held in the names of three friends.[2] The other £7,500 stock represented a debt owed them by Lauchlin Macleane, a debt partially repaid in September 1767, when the stock passed out of their possession. The debt was contracted by Macleane for dealings in Amsterdam in "the great Scheme". "My engagements in Holland with Lord Verney" wrote Macleane on 30 October 1766, "Are paid for by a Loan subsisting till next August".[3] An account between Verney and Macleane shows Macleane indebted to him in September 1767 for £7,500 East India stock, valued at £19,950. £14,800 of this debt was however repaid by pledging the stock to Isaac Ximenes of Amsterdam, leaving the debt at £5,150 plus interest. A note on the account shows that half of it was credited to William Burke. The debt was not paid off, and sometime in 1768 Verney and William made a further loan to Macleane. By May 1769 he owed them £13,204 — £6,602 each. In addition he had contracted in 1768 a further debt of £2,300 which was credited to William alone.[4] We do not know what happened to the stock pledged to Ximenes, or what Verney and William did with the £14,800 which was paid over to them.

Their holding of £20,000 stock provided the basis for their speculative operations, which were, for the most part, carried out through the well-known brokers Elias De la Fontaine and William Brymer. It was customary at the time, as a statement by a prominent firm of dealers, Anthony and John Lewis André, makes clear, for speculators who had their funds in East India stock, to pledge their holdings for periods of 6 to 12 months to dealers into whose names the stock

---

[1] I. Barré to Shelburne, 14 July [1769] (Bowood MSS). Macleane had written of the plan with enthusiasm to Shelburne on 29 June 1769 but admitted that it would need "very able and distinguished Persons" to move it. (Bowood MSS). W. Pulteney, M.P. for Cromartyshire, was brother to Governor George Johnstone, and had through him and other members of the Johnstone family strong East India connexions.

[2] James Winch, Patrick Mead and Nathaniel Patrickson. C12/1623/1; Claydon MSS.

[3] L. Macleane to Shelburne, 30 October 1766, Bowood MSS.

[4] Claydon MSS. See Appendix I

was transferred and who provided them in return with cash (often borrowed on the Amsterdam market where interest was low) or other securities.[1] By doing so the speculators kept their stock available for use in the Company's elections if required, and they might also hope to gain by the appreciation of its capital value. The dividends were paid over to them, and the dealers charged 5% interest and took the risk of fluctuations in value, though they were careful to cover themselves against this risk by pledging the stock at a price well below that ruling on the market, and sometimes by other means. John Lewis André deposed that Verney and William were before and during the years 1767 and 1768 "greatly concerned in the borrowing and lending Monies on East India stock and well understood the Management of such Transactions".[2] We know that some time in 1767 (probably in February) De la Fontaine and Brymer arranged such a loan for them on the security of their £20,000 stock with the firm of Sir Joshua Vanneck & Co., who transferred to them in return 47,000 3% Bank Annuities. In February 1768 this loan was wound up and the brokers negotiated another loan on the same security with the firm of André. This time they obtained in all £42,000, £22,500 Bank Annuities and £21,000 in cash. In February 1769 when the loan came up for renewal Verney and Burke pressed for better terms, since the price of the stock had risen, but the Andrés were cautious. They finally agreed to lend £39,100 on the security of £17,000 of the stock, but they added a new proviso. A further £1,000 stock should be deposited with them if the price of stock fell to 240[3] (this proviso was honoured on 1 June 1769) and £1,000 more for each 10% fall in the price of stock thereafter (Verney and William were to default on this when the time came). Verney and William then sold the £3,000 stock on which the Andrés were not prepared to make a loan at the very high price of 279½.[4]

We know a little of their business with De la Fontaine and Brymer, partly from a case against the brokers brought by a jobber John Hobson of Abingdon Street, Westminster, for the discovery of the "Book or Register . . . which they call their Broker's Book";[5] partly from an incomplete account drawn up by these brokers in 1769. The former shows that Hobson, who had some financial links with Lauchlin Macleane, opened a jobbing account with De la Fontaine on the security of £2,000 East India stock, operating between both the dates of the opening of the Company's books in July and October 1768 and January 1769, and the quarterly 'rescounters' of August and November 1768 and February 1769. In disclosing their books in Chancery the brokers followed the custom of the time by

---

[1] J. L. André deposed (C12/1623/1) that "some Merchants were induced to raise money upon Stock either here or in Holland where money is plentiful and the Interest lower". Examples of this are found in C12/1927/15. It is not clear why part of the payments were made in other stock—in both cases here referred to the stock was a very safe one, 3% Bank Annuities. It may have been difficult to raise such large sums in cash.

[2] C12/1623/1.

[3] J. L. André deposed that provisoes of this kind were often made. *Ibid.*

[4] *Ibid.*

[5] Hobson v. De la Fontaine. C12/57/22.

disguising the names of 'principals' while giving those of dealers in full. The disguise is, however, very thin. Hobson's biggest dealings were with 'a principal L V', readily identifiable as Lord Verney, presumably with William Burke as usual having a half interest. Other principals with whom he dealt on a small scale were A and J L A (Anthony and John Lewis André); C U and W B (it seems likely that these initials stand for Clotworthy Upton[1] and William Burke); W B and J P (probably William Burke and John Powell); and Jos H (Joseph Hickey). In July 1768 'L V' contracted to receive £96,000 East India stock at the opening of the Company's books on 14 July at 277, but also to deliver the same quantity of stock at the August rescounter at 275. On this transaction he lost £1,920. On 30 September he contracted to buy £30,000 East India stock at the opening of the Company's books on 11 October at 274¼, but also to deliver the same amount of stock at the November rescounter at 277. On this transaction he gained £825. L. V.'s name does not occur again in the accounts. 'C U & W B' and 'W B & J P' engaged on 8 December 1768 to buy £5,000 and £3,500 stock respectively at 275 and 275½.

The second source of evidence is an undated fragment preserved among Verney's papers at Claydon. It is drawn up by De la Fontaine and its date can be fixed by internal evidence at the beginning of June 1769. The conclusion runs:

> So that to this present there has been a real profit of £904. 18. 6 besides your claim upon Mr. Macleane amounting to £13204 — besides also what may arise from the £17000 India Stock pledged with Messrs. André and the Qualifications of Mr. Winch and the £1000 deposited as a further Security with André.
>
> Mr Will Burke will be indebted to your Lordship about the £6000 and £1072 lately advanced him against which he will be entitled to ½ your claim on Mr. Macleane, as well as what may be coming from the loan with André and the three Qualifications.[2]

By the time this was written the affairs of Verney and William were already gravely compromised by engagements not included in the accounts of their brokers. The brokers' summary shows, however, that Verney and William on their joint account were in credit with their brokers at this critical time.

The transactions which brought Verney and William to ruin were three in number. For two of the three Macleane was directly responsible. The first in time was a loan by Lord Verney to Macleane on the security of bonds from Lord Shelburne. In May 1769, when the price began to slide, Macleane found himself in unexpected, though he hoped temporary, difficulties. Lord Shelburne had apparently offered to lend him money if necessary and on 11 May he asked to take advantage of this offer to the amount of £30, 000, assuring Shelburne that Verney

---

[1] Clotworthy Upton (1721–1785) created Baron Templetown in 1776. He succeeded to the family estates on the death of his brother on 27 September 1768.

[2] D. Wecter, *Edmund Burke and his Kinsmen*, Boulder, Colorado, 1939, p. 40, printed this document from the Claydon MSS. We have not been able to find it in our searches among them. The reference to the "£1000 deposited as a further Security with André" dates it after 1 June 1769. The deposit was made up of two of the three 'Qualifications' which Verney and William owned.

and Panchaud would supply him against the security of his bonds.[1] He already, he said, owed Panchaud (who was getting into difficulties himself) £10,000, and Verney about £8,000, so these debts were deducted from the total and he obtained from them in cash for the bonds no more than £12,000. From Verney he appears to have obtained £7,325.[2] Whether this would have been enough to meet his needs if his assumptions had been correct is uncertain, but the decline in the price of stock sharply increased and before the settlement day on 18 July, a panic set in. It soon became clear that neither Panchaud nor Macleane would be able to meet their speculative liabilities on that date. It also became clear that Macleane was likely to drag down his broker De la Fontaine with him, for he owed him no less than £23,500 for 'differences'.[3] On 13 July, Lord Verney, in a last minute attempt to save De la Fontaine lent him £22,500,[4] but it was too late. De la Fontaine had other bad debts as well, and on 14 July the firm stopped payment.[5] In this way Verney paid out two very large sums at a critical time, against which he could hope for no early repayment.

These failures on the market caused a sensation. Lord Shelburne was warned that "great liberties [are] taken with your name",[6] and inaccurate reports of the way in which Verney and William were involved began to appear as innuendoes in the Press. It was thought desirable by 21 July to contradict at least one of them in the *Public Advertiser*.

In order to prevent any injurious Reports or Conjectures which may arise from a Paragraph in the Daily Gazetteer of Wednesday last, *that a certain Irish Peer had been given up by his Brokers for refusing to pay his Differences*, and a subsequent Report that Lord V——y was the Nobleman alluded to; it is thought necessary to publish the following Note from his Lordship's Brokers, who were wrote to upon this Occasion.

Messrs —— Compliments to Mr ——: They are very sorry to say, that instead of his L—d—p being in any way indebted to them, they are greatly so to his L–d–p for Money advanced to them to pay their late Differences.[7]

Better informed, though still misleading, accounts were circulated privately. Thomas Whately on 2 August 1769 told George Grenville:

I find that on the opening of Mr De la Fontaine's books, the names of the Burkes stand against very large sums. Richard Burke, 29,000*l.* stock, upon which 10,745*l.* is the difference, — Richard Burke and S. Dyer, 13,000*l.* stock upon which 4,870*l.* is the difference, — Richard Burke and William

---

[1] Bowood MSS. A number of cases at Exchequer and in Chancery arose out of this transaction e.g. E112/1632/1904 (Tierney v Shelburne), C12/554/26 (Shelburne v Verney), C12/1625/48 (Verney v Simond and Hankey). Shelburne knew that Macleane was in real difficulties and made the loan with his eyes open. Lady Shelburne noted in her diary on 12 May 1769 "He [Lord Shelburne] told me he was going to stand security for Mr Maclane [sic] for thirty thousand pounds in order to get him quite out of the India business in which he has embarass'd his affairs." Bowood MSS.

[2] C12/1026/18; C12/122/36.

[3] Lauchlin Macleane's account with De la Fontaine & Brymer. Claydon MSS. See Appendix II.

[4] Claydon MSS. See Appendix III and L. Macleane to Shelburne, [June 1769] Bowood MSS, who puts the sum at £22,000.

[5] Brymer and De la Fontaine were not strictly speaking partners; De la Fontaine was a sworn broker and Brymer was not. Though De la Fontaine was completely ruined, Brymer remained in business on his own account.

[6] I. Barré to Shelburne, 14 August 1769. Bowood MSS.

[7] *Public Advertiser*, 21 July 1769.

Burke, 5,000*l*., upon which 1,900*l*. is the difference: but it is said, that Lord Verney having a debt of 17,000*l*., on Mr De la Fontaine for money actually lent him, he sets up that demand against these differences.[1]

Accounts at Claydon show that Whately's figures were incorrect — he underestimated Verney's loan to his brokers; he was right in attributing liabilities to both Richard Burke and Samuel Dyer (for both of whom events make it clear William felt some responsibility) but the sums were exaggerated. Richard Burke's debt totalled £8,844. 7s. 9d. and Dyer's £2,044. 15s. 5d.[2] William Burke does not seem to have owed the brokers anything on his own account at this time.

Insofar therefore as Verney and William found themselves in difficulties at the July settlement, these arose primarily from their association with the disasters of others, and in particular from the resounding collapse of Lauchlin Macleane. These difficulties were increased by their commitment in another of Macleane's schemes, the subscriptions of June 1768 to purchase East India stock for the 1769 Company election. The repayment of this stock at the now ridiculous price of 280 was due on 18 July. It soon became clear that many of the subscribers were in no position to bear their share of the heavy loss which must follow. This loss was finally calculated at £3,140 a head.[3] Among those recognized as unable to meet such a liability out of their own resources were William and Richard Burke. It had been optimistically suggested that Verney would "probably answer for the Burkes",[4] but in fact neither he nor they, nor indeed a number of others, paid anything towards the loss, the greater part of which was left on the two guarantors Sulivan and Vansittart.[5]

But if contemporaries were wrong in detail about the situations of Verney and William in July, they were right in principle. For they were both in the gravest financial difficulties and these difficulties arose from unsuccessful speculation though they had to meet their liabilities at a later date. The greatest single cause of their ruin was neither Macleane's debts to them nor Verney's loan to De la Fontaine, still less their share in the ill-fated subscription (since they defaulted in their obligations in connexion with it) but a large-scale operation they had entered into in Amsterdam with a Dutch dealer Theophilus Cazenove and later with his father-in-law Volkert van Jever, who took over the conduct of the business.[6] In

---

[1] Quoted C. Dilke, *Papers of a Critic*, II, 339–40. C. Lloyd's account to G. Grenville of 1 June 1769 was even less reliable. "Lord Verney has paid 27 thousand on one bargain. The Burkes are likely to be great sufferers." Quoted *ibid.*, II, 338–9. Macleane told Shelburne [undated July 1769] that he found Verney "embarked on this affair deep beyond conception, for Himself, for the Burkes and for his broker, to which last to prevent his Ruin he lent twenty two thousand pounds the very day before the great crush [sic] came". Bowood MSS.

[2] See below p. 348.

[3] I. Barré to Shelburne, 14 August 1769. Bowood MSS.

[4] I. Barré to Shelburne, 19 June 1769. *Ibid.*

[5] Sulivan MSS. Bodl. MS. Eng. Hist. C. 269, p. 23. Macleane had drafted the agreement so loosely that John Dunning's opinion was that it was "too ambiguously pen'd to be of much use, in case the Parties should be inclined to evade it." J. Dunning to Shelburne, 7 July 1769. Bowood MSS.

[6] C12/909/59. Verney and William Burke v Cazenove.

November 1768, Verney and William, believing that prospects in Amsterdam were better than in London, had instructed Cazenove to purchase for them for the February rescounters £20,000 English East India stock at a price not exceeding 274. In December, for reasons we do not know, they changed their minds and instructed him instead to engage for a deal in 'differences' on £100,000 East India stock on the same terms. When Cazenove failed to procure the whole amount in time for the February rescounters, they ordered him to provide it for the May rescounters, which he duly did. But by May the price had begun to slide, and believing, like Macleane, that the fall was temporary, they decided to prolong till the August rescounters. This was a serious mistake, for, before August, the crash in prices at the time of the July settlement had taken place, and they could have sold out only at a crippling loss. Though the rate for prolongation was running very high they made one last desperate fling and prolonged till November; but the price remained obstinately low, and the transaction was wound up at the huge loss, including interest, charges and cost of prolongations, of £53,000, a liability against which Verney had no immediately available assets, and William no assets at all. The £17,000 East India stock pledged to the Andrés, which had stood behind their earlier speculations, had been sold off, unredeemed, in August.

This was the end of the high hopes of their joint speculations, and this the origin, as the records show, of almost the whole of William's indebtedness to Verney. It is true that early in 1769 when he still had reason to believe that he had substantial sums to his credit, and when there was no reason to believe that Macleane's debt to him was insecure, he had borrowed two sums from Verney; the first the £6,000 which the latter tried to extract from Edmund Burke ten years later; the second the sum of £1,072 which William repaid in 1770.[1] It is also true that he felt himself in some degree responsible for the speculative debts left owing to their brokers by Richard Burke and Samuel Dyer; but these, as will be shown, were dealt with in the general settlement of his and Verney's affairs after the crash. An unlimited liability for £53,000 or, as Verney seems to have argued, the 50% of it which was the basis of their partnership, was, however, a disastrous burden for a man by now almost wholly without resources.

II

The arrangements to liquidate the debts arising from these transactions were almost as complicated as the speculation itself. From William's point of view they were dominated by the fact that he was at law a partner with Lord Verney in joint speculation, a partner with an agreed right to fifty per cent of their joint assets, and an unlimited liability for their joint debts. Three distinct settlements were necessary. First Verney and William had to deal with the enormous debt they

---

[1] It appears to have been repaid on 24 May 1770. In Christopher Hargrave's accounts with Lord Verney in the Claydon MSS there is an entry under this date "Received of William Burke Esq for the use of Lord Verney £1138. 15. 0." Compare the accounts in C12/122/36. There is no further reference to the debt in either Court proceedings or in the Claydon MSS.

jointly owed to Volkert Van Jever of Amsterdam.[1] Second, the ruined Lauchlin Macleane owed Verney and William, in partnership and severally, very substantial sums. Third, Macleane, Verney and William were all concerned in the affairs of the brokers De la Fontaine and Brymer who had failed, Macleane as the brokers' greatest debtor, Verney (and probably William as his partner) as an important creditor. In addition others of the Burke family and connexions were involved in a minor way — Richard Burke (acting for others as well as himself, and almost certainly for William)[2] and Samuel Dyer,[3] both indebted to the same brokers for speculative losses.

As has been said, the total debt of Verney and William to Van Jever amounted to some £53,000 by November 1769, when their dealings in Amsterdam came to an end. At first they made some attempt to evade the payment of this large sum. The nature of the debt made it impossible for Van Jever to proceed against them at common law, so he brought a suit in Chancery. In answer to his bill Verney and William argued that both by Dutch and English law their contracts with the Dutch merchant were illegal and therefore null and void.[4] It is doubtful, however, if they hoped much from this plea, for the equity courts acted upon the principle that a statute should not be made an instrument of fraud, and they were apt to be unsympathetic to attempts of this kind to evade liabilities. So after prolonged negotiations[5] they reached an agreement on 20 February 1771 to pay Van Jever £47,000.[6] A decree was made in Chancery recording their liability for this sum, and it was confirmed at Common Law by judgments enrolled in the Court of King's Bench.[7] The £47,000 was to be paid in nine instalments, the first and last

---

[1] Van Jever died on 3 February 1774. Legal proceedings against Verney and Burke were continued by his widow, Quirina Catherine Van Zijpesteijn, and, when she died, by his daughters, Emerentia Helena Van Jever (wife of Jan Frederick Godfrey, Baron Van Freisheim, and afterwards of Ocker Van Schuylenburch) and Margaretta Helena Van Jever (wife of Theophilus Cazenove).

[2] e.g. Charles O'Hara, *Correspondence of Edmund Burke*, II, 29. Writing to O'Hara on 1 June 1769 Richard speaks of his own speculative activities as for "ourselves".

[3] A close friend of the Burkes. *Correspondence of Edmund Burke*, II, 334.

[4] By English law they were illegal under the 1734 Act against 'stock-jobbing' (7 Geo. II c 8). In Dutch law Verney and William apparently depended on an obsolete law prohibiting dealings in English East India Stock in Amsterdam (J.-P. Ricard, *Le Negoce d'Amsterdam*, Rouen, 1723, pp. 62 and 402 ff.). Speculative dealings were not illegal in Holland. See E112/1630/1836.

[5] In December 1770 John and Robert Day were sent to Amsterdam. 'The precise object of the journey is not told, but it appears to have been connected with some financial scandals in that city. "A commission" we are told, "was arranged by Lord V and Mr. B" ' (E. B. Day, *Mr Justice Day of Kerry*, Exeter 1938, p. 60). Robert Day wrote to Robert Fitzgerald in January 1773: 'On the Dutch Commission in which you know I was employed this time two years, those men the [Cliffords] who were the second, and the Hopes who were the first House in Europe, were examined before us and were largely concerned in the whole of that great and important transaction.' *Ibid.*, p. 62. The manuscripts on which *Mr Justice Day of Kerry* is based are deposited in the Royal Irish Academy, but add no further details. The negotiations may also have related to the arrangements for the purchase of East India Stock for splitting. Both John and Robert Day obtained judgments against Verney in the King's Bench, presumably for their expenses.

[6] C12/554/47.

[7] C33/436, fol. 307; K.B. 122/366 Rolls 92 and 93.

of £6,000 and the rest of £5,000. Each annual payment was to be made on the twentieth of December and the whole debt was to be extinguished on 20 December 1779. Four per cent interest was to be paid on the diminishing capital sum. It is clear from the court records that in fact Verney made himself responsible for fulfilling this agreement and that William Burke paid nothing. The first two instalments of £7,566. 13s. 4d.[1] and £6,640 were paid on time; Verney was short by £750 on the third payment,[2] but made good the deficiency and was able to pay the fourth, fifth and sixth instalments.[3] On 20 December 1777, however, he defaulted entirely. At this point he still owed £16,000 of which £5,000 was due with the year's interest of £640 (on which interest would also have to be paid). To meet his obligation Verney assigned timber at Great Baddow in Essex, but this still left outstanding on 1 September 1779 £3,023. 7s. 9d. of the £5,640 and interest.[4] The Van Jever trustees succeeded in having this debt secured upon Verney's estates, but in 1790 £20,300 was still due to them.[5]

The second settlement was that of Macleane's liabilities to Verney and William. It fell into two parts. The first part was his pre-1769 debt which, with interest, totalled by this time £15,338. Of this, as has been shown, some £9,000 was due to William and the rest to Verney.[6] The second part was the further £7,325 which Macleane had obtained from Verney in May 1769.[7] If, as seems likely, this latter sum came out of the £39,100 Verney and William had borrowed from the Andrés on the security of their East India stock, Macleane's liability for this sum was legally divided equally between Verney and William. It is note-worthy that on none of these debts from Macleane did William make any claim, for reasons connected, it would seem, with the third settlement. All the transactions from this time are based on the assumption that monies were owed by Macleane to Verney alone. The first of these debts was taken to be covered as to £15,000 by the three bonds totalling this sum given by Shelburne to Macleane in 1769. From this debt there remained therefore £388 not covered by the settlement, together it would seem with the whole or part of Macleane's new debt of £7,325 which remained to be dealt with.

The third settlement, that with De la Fontaine and Brymer, was a highly complex affair. It was completed in May 1770. It combined a settlement of the brokers' debt to Verney; of debts owed by Macleane to the brokers; of the balance of Macleane's debt to Verney left over from the second settlement; and also a settlement of the speculative losses which Richard Burke and Samuel Dyer owed to De la Fontaine and Brymer. Its basis was the fact that Macleane owed the

---

[1] £6000 and ten months' interest on £47,000; this payment was probably made by borrowing £8,100 from Biddulph and Cocks, K.B. 122/370 Roll 1079.

[2] C12/554/47.

[3] C12/582/36.

[4] *Ibid.*

[5] Account of Verney's debts on 1 November 1790. Claydon MSS.

[6] See p. 340 above and Appendix I.

[7] See p. 343 above.

brokers £23,500[1] for which he gave them a bond, and that Verney's best hope of repayment of the loan he had made the brokers was to take over this bond, since Macleane still had some assets, and his reputation as a financier, though badly shaken, was not yet demolished. The accounts at Claydon show that, against £22,500 of the bond for £23,500, Macleane gave Verney a mortgage on his West Indian estates for £15,407. 1s. 2d., £338 of which was for the remainder of the old debt under the second settlement. The rest was made up of the following items: Verney's final adverse balance of accounts in the books of De la Fontaine and Brymer for professional services, £9,480. 4s. 7d.; the debt owed by Samuel Dyer to them of £2,044. 15s. 5d.; and the value of some securities given by Verney to them totalling £3,544. 1s. 2d. In addition Macleane took over responsibility for Richard Burke's debt to them for £8,844. 7s. 9d. Macleane also threw in his own notes of hand for £2,750 owed to Verney (possibly the balance of the £7,325 which he had borrowed in 1769).[2]

The West Indian estates on which the greater part of this third settlement were based, were lands which Macleane and others had purchased long since in in Grenada and Dominica, and all Macleane's creditors were anxious to get their hands on his share of them.[3] He estimated the value of his share, very optimistically, at £100,000, but there was still £40,000 owing to the original owners. Though his share was heavily mortgaged he still had a claim to three-eighths of the estates, and reacquired a further eighth part from Isaac Panchaud.[4] This reacquired eighth part was kept free from encumbrances and was conveyed to Lord Shelburne

---

[1] See Appendix II.

[2] See Appendix III. There is another account in the Claydon MSS which if taken at its face value would make Macleane's debt to Verney larger, but would seem to include double counting, and was not agreed by Macleane. In 1776 Macleane tried to claim he was not responsible for Richard Burke's debt, but the accounts make it clear that it was part of the settlement. The following rough calculation in the Claydon papers shows how the sums were arrived at:

	31,344	7 9	[£22,500 of Macleanes' bond to De la Fontaine & Brymer. And 8844 7 9. Richard Burke's debts to ditto. See Appendix III.]
less	15,000		[Lord Shelburne's Bonds]
	16,344	7 9	
less	15,407	1 2	[The mortgage on the West India Estates—See Appendix III]
	937	6 7	
plus	2,750		[Macleane's notes of hand]
	3,687	6 7	

[3] Information about these estates can be found in two Chancery cases (Verney v Simond C12/1625/48 and Shelburne v Verney C12/554/26); in correspondence relevant to them at Bowood; in a letter-book of Robert Orme in the India Office Library (O.V. 202); and in accounts and a detailed list of legal charges at Claydon drawn up by — Bray. For Macleane's acquisition of these properties see J. N. M. Maclean, *op. cit.*, pp. 81 ff.

[4] The other encumbrances on the estate were as follows: an annuity of £600 to John Crawford, a mortgage to Simond and Hankey of £6457 8 0; a mortgage to Aaron Franks of £9235; a mortgage to Isaac Ximenes of £8000; a mortgage to Clotworthy Upton of £2250; and one to Laurence Sulivan (taken over from Sir George Colebrooke) of £6000. Since Clotworthy Upton became a proprietor he presumably redeemed a part of these encumbrances. After Macleane's death his widow (Elizabeth, *née* Hewitt) was paid an annuity of £100 on the estate.

as security for the three bonds for £15,000 which Macleane had passed on to Verney in 1769. Under this third settlement Verney's £15,407. 1s. 2d. was also secured by a mortgage on the estates, which were now under the management of Robert Orme and the banking firm of Simond and Hankey on behalf of five proprietors, one of whom was Orme himself. Verney also held, as something in the way of collateral securities, Macleane's bond for £23,500 and Richard Burke's for £8,844. 7s. 9d., but so long as the mortgage held, he could obviously make no use of them.

Since William Burke, if he were deemed to have the liabilities of a partner, had also the rights of one, at least some £9,000 of Macleane's debts (and probably a good deal more) were in the first instance due to him. It would seem that he gave up his claim to his share of these debts on condition that those of Richard Burke and Samuel Dyer were taken over by Verney and that Macleane made himself responsible for their payment.

All these settlements had two weaknesses; they brought in little or no ready money[1] and, in part at least, they depended on Macleane's creditworthiness. In this his creditors were disappointed. Though they had high hopes of his restoring his fortunes in India (hopes that were fortified by his appointment to what seemed a lucrative job there in 1772 and by his subsequent Indian career), he was still hopelessly insolvent in 1778, when he was lost at sea.[2] But though Verney had expected much earlier repayment than he got and though even the interest was greatly in arrears, the securities which he held (other than Macleane's notes of hand) were ultimately sound. In 1772 an attempt was made by Macleane and Shelburne, under pressure from Verney, to repay the £15,000 secured by Shelburne's bonds by handing over to him the unencumbered eighth part of the West Indian estates so that he might sell it. It proved, however, unsaleable, and in 1774 Shelburne repaid him the whole £15,000 with interest. The mortgage on the West Indian estates proved a less satisfactory security. Robert Orme complained in 1771 that, despite the pains they had taken, the affairs of the estates were still 'in a state of great intricacy and distress',[3] and a year later 'Never I believe was such an unfortunate purchase as we are plunged into'.[4] By the gradual sale of the Dominican properties, however, and the development of those in Grenada, they slowly pulled the estate together, though interrupted by the capture of the island by the French during the American War. It was not till 1791 that the proprietors received a dividend. By that time the money they had borrowed for its development had been paid back, and the estates, reduced in extent, were valued at just over

---

[1] In December 1772 Verney obtained from Macleane sums in the form of drafts on Gemmell, the Banker, and of a note of hand, totalling £2984 15 10, part at three months, part at twelve months and part at two years. These were the only monies he received from Macleane himself. Part of this was attributed to the payment of the interest on Lord Shelburne's bonds. Claydon MSS.

[2] See J. N. M. Maclean, unpublished thesis, Bodleian Library, 'Lauchlin Macleane and his connexion with East India Company Politics 1773–1778'.

[3] R. Orme to C. Bunbury, 20 August 1771, Orme MSS O.V. 202, fol. 59.

[4] R. Orme to W. Ridge, 1 July 1772. *Ibid.*, fol. 90v.

£90,000. They were finally sold, apparently in 1810. It is not known when regular interest began to be paid on Verney's mortgage, or when his heirs received the capital due to them.

William's debt to Verney after these settlements were completed was thus £23,500—his half of the debt to Van Jever, and the £6,000 he had borrowed from Verney in March 1769 which Verney was later to claim from Edmund (unless indeed this too was deemed to be cleared in the settlement).[1] No immediate steps were taken to give legal form to his liability to Verney; he continued to sit in the Commons through Verney's influence, and there is no sign of any breach between them. In 1769, when there was some hope that Macleane might go out to India to restore his fortunes, there was also talk of William going out in a minor capacity, but nothing came of it:[2] even before Macleane obtained employment in India in 1772, sinecures had been found for him by the Government. But William had no friends in power and no employment came to him. Until 1774, however, he at least had his seat in Parliament and the protection this gave him from his creditors.

There has been as much misunderstanding about his debts to others as about his debts to Lord Verney. For this C. W. Dilke — as usual ingenious in the discovery of material, but impetuous in interpreting it — is largely to blame. In the *Papers of a Critic* he wrote:

> Judgments were now [by implication the date was 1774] entered up in the King's Bench, and "honest William" had, we fear, to fly the country. In a casual search made for another purpose, we stumbled on five of these sad judgments in one twelvemonth and in one court — against William and Richard for 1,500*l*. — against Richard for 72*l*. 12*s*. 6*d*. — against William for 1,760*l*., 2,677*l*. 10*s*. and 1,616*l*. 13*s*. 4*d*. There may have been dozens, for our notes were taken carelessly, and without a purpose.[3]

Carelessly indeed, since two of the four judgments against William were made a fter his return from his first voyage to India and none of them before he set out on it in 1777; and no mention is made of the fact that in judgments upon penal bonds the real sum owed is half the amount specified in the judgment.

A full list of judgments made against William in all Courts between the years 1774 and 1779 presents a less startling picture than Dilke evidently expected. Putting their number at their highest (for it is possible that one or two of them concerned another William Burke),[4] there were nine of them. They are as follows:

1. John Connor   Common Pleas Easter 1774   46. 7.6.   Index 6540
2. James Christie 17 June 1777   1500. 0.0.   K.B. 122/415
                                                            Roll 1267
3. Edward Astley   King's Bench 17 Jan. 1778 1760. 0.0. Index 9647,
                                                            p. 42.

---

[1] In favour of this suggestion is the negative fact that there is no reference to this debt in the Claydon MSS, or elsewhere, until ten years after it was contracted; but on the other hand there is no positive evidence to support it.

[2] The *Public Advertiser* on 7 August 1769 reported that they heard that William Burke was going to India as private secretary to Henry Vansittart, Chief of the Supervisors sent out by the Company Had it been true the tale would have ended abruptly, for they were lost at sea on the way out.

[3] II, 341.

[4] Nos. 3 and 4 below.

4.	Jacob Wilkinson 5 August 1778	2677.10.0.	K.B. 122/425 Roll 1649
5.	John Powell 24 November 1778	1616.13.4.	K.B. 122/426 Roll 203
6.	John Powell 29 July 1779	1679.10.4.	C.P. 40/3744 Roll 769
7.	John Woodman 13 November 1779	200. 0.0.	E12/48, M20GIII, p. 2
8.	John Robinson 17 November 1779	51.14.0.	Index 9648
9.	Joseph Cowper 23 November 1779	60. 0.0.	K.B. 122/437 Roll 791

All the larger ones, with the possible exception of No. 3 (and this is one of the doubtfully attributed ones) are judgments on penal bonds. The two judgments obtained by John Powell (Nos. 5 and 6), moreover, almost certainly concerned the same sum, for the first was 'satisfied' in Trinity 1779, and the second made in July of the same year was doubly secured by a precisely similar judgment against Edmund. The total of these debts may thus be taken as amounting to about £4,200, and most of the judgments date from 1778-9, after his first return from India and before his second journey thither. The dates may be of some significance. When William went out to India in June 1777 he was not in the East India Company's employ. He went out with their consent, on behalf of the political friends of Governor Pigot to inform him of the action which had been taken in England with regard to his arrest and imprisonment. Haste was necessary, and he went by a most expensive route. No doubt those who sent him paid for the basic costs of travel but we know that Edmund exhausted his resources "to discharge [William's] engagements" before his journey,[1] and the debts here mentioned may well be connected with the preparations for it.[2]

These judgments did not, of course, exhaust the whole of William's indebtedness. We know he owed money elsewhere — for instance the £500 borrowed by Edmund and William from Henry Fox on June 11 1766 and still outstanding in 1780.[3] His debts were also sufficient to make the loss of his seat in Parliament in 1774 a grave embarrassment to him. Verney could no longer afford to provide seats for the Burkes, and William was unsuccessful in a contest for Haslemere, where the Duke of Portland supported him.[4] It was in 1776, after attempts to upset the return had failed, that he began making strenuous attempts to obtain an appointment in India. But when once he obtained employment in India these debts were not sufficient to make his position desperate. By 1792 Richard Burke junior, Edmund Burke's son, who struggled valiantly with his affairs as well as those of his father, could write of these liabilities: "I do not find you have many debts

---

[1] *Correspondence of Edmund Burke*, III, 373.

[2] The judgment for John Powell (Nos 5 and 6) is probably an exception.

[3] Henry Fox's accounts, Bunbury Papers, Bury St Edmunds Record Office. See Sutherland and Binney, *loc. cit.* He also owed money to Christopher Hargrave and, of course, to Edmund.

[4] L. B. Namier and J. Brooke, *History of Parliament, The House of Commons 1754-1790* (1964) II, 156.

remaining in England . . . The whole of what remains will I think come within £2,000."[1] They seem to have all been repaid by the time he finally left India.

What did make his position desperate was the undertaking he had to enter into with Verney before he returned to India in 1780. He gave Verney bonds for £20,000 in settlement of the £23,500 with interest which he owed him as his partner in the Van Jever affair. The bonds were to be paid in instalments — £5,000 on 1 January 1782 and £2,500 each succeeding year (except 1783) until 1 January 1789. He paid none of this money, and it is obvious that unless he had succeeded in making a fortune in India and remitting it to England, he could never have paid more than a fraction of it. In fact, despite all attempts to help him, he failed completely to make a fortune in India.

Verney, as his own financial difficulties became intensified, refused to admit that his former partner could not pay his share, and became obdurate and very bitter against William, and to a lesser degree against the other members of the Burke family. When Richard Burke junior tried to enter into negotiations with him from about 1788 onward to reduce the load to more realistic proportions, Verney remained adamant, though his own friends thought him unwise.[2] After Verney's death his heiress proved more reasonable. She agreed on a composition payment of £5,250 to be paid at once and a further £5,000 after four years if William could afford it.[3] In June 1791 the first of these sums was paid by Richard Burke junior to the Trustees of Lord Verney's estates.[4] When she had William arrested after his final return from India, it seems merely to have been to ascertain whether or not he had the funds to make the second payment. It was established that he had not, he was released, and this was the final outcome of the long dispute.

Though the above analysis of the complex financial relations between Verney and William Burke is difficult to work out, on account of the confusing and incomplete records of it which survive, it seems to square with the evidence. The only exception is a curious document at Claydon in Verney's hand which purports to be a list of debts due to him on 10 September 1784, incorporating simple interest on them at 5%. It is one of several such documents, which do not fully correspond with each other.[5] In this list Verney distinguished those debts which he (optimistically) marks G as "good". There are two entries under the name of William Burke. They run:

---

[1] Letter to William Burke, 17 August 1792, Fitzwilliam MSS at Sheffield.
[2] L. Heslop to J. Foster, 12 March 1790. Claydon MSS.
[3] Claydon MSS and R. Burke Jr. to William Burke, 16 May 1792, Fitzwilliam MSS, Northamptonshire Record Office.
[4] Claydon MSS. "June 1791. By cash received of Mr Richard Burke, being a composition on Mr Burke's Bonds. £5250." An account of Lord Verney's debts on 1 November 1790 records two sums paid "by W. Burke" of £1968 and £1312 10 0 towards discharging mortgages. It seems probable that these payments were from the £5250. The account was clearly prepared for Lady Fermanagh. It is likely that the proceeds of the sale of Edmund's Clogher estate (see pp. 329-30 above) were used to make up part of this sum.
[5] There is another for 1782. In this Macleane's debt is stated as £50,000, while in that of 1784 it is put at £70,000.

William Burke.   G.   about £20,000
       do.   no security excepting Honour about £40,000

This £40,000 is mentioned in no other document at Claydon, and there seems no reason to think that it arose from any transactions other than those here mentioned.[1] Clearly the £20,000 was itself a composition for William's share of the Van Jever indebtedness. William had originally offered bonds for no more than £13,000.[2] Verney must therefore have added up all that he thought William owed him, calculated the interest on it, and deducted £20,000 from the total, in order to decide that William owed him a further £40,000. It is not impossible to see how Verney could have reached this conclusion. With interest William's share of the Van Jever debt would amount to some £39,000, while the £6,000 which Verney was trying to extract from Edmund would with interest have reached £10,650. One of Verneys' friends wrote to him at this time: "Indeed, I am told you charged William (in the account you furnished him with) with the £6,000 in question, between you and Edmund."[3] In 1772, moreover, Verney and William had jointly borrowed £8,100 from Biddulph and Cocks.[4] William's share with interest would amount to £6,500. Hence a total of £56,000 or so is easily reached. And undoubtedly there were other smaller debts that might be included, as well as a share in the sizeable legal expenses in which they were jointly involved.

Such an account would, of course, have been misleading. There is, apart from all else, a great deal of double-counting in it. The loan from Biddulph and Cocks would seem to have been used to pay off part of the Van Jever debt. The £6,000 was also charged to Edmund Burke in the same list. And precisely the same thing is found when other items on the list are scrutinized. Macleane's debt is entered at £70,000, and a note is added "The greater part of Macleane's if not the whole of his debt is well-secured". But Macleane had died penniless, six years earlier, and not only is it impossible to make his debt at any time amount to this sum, but the only part of it still outstanding which was "secured" was the mortgage of £15,407. 1s. 2d. on the West Indian estates. Even with unpaid interest this could not have exceeded £25,000. Moreover the debts of Richard Burke and Samuel Dyer were originally included in Macleane's debt, and here they are also listed separately. There seems little doubt that in drawing up this list, Verney — at all times a most unbusinesslike man, and one now becoming desperate—had lost his contact with reality.

To sum up the situation, therefore, the financial burden under which William was to sink, arose almost wholly from the speculative partnership which his patron had offered him, which, however generous in intention, was an unmitigated disaster to him. That the speculative losses incurred were a disaster to Verney as well there is also no doubt, but there is no reason for assuming that he would have

---

[1] Even higher estimates of William's debt were current among Verney's friends. Sir John Lovett on 6 January 1788 speaks of "a demand that at first was more than £80,000". Claydon MSS.
[2] Claydon MSS.
[3] Michael Bourke to Verney, 27 August 1784. Printed in *Verney Letters of the Eighteenth Century*, II, 284.
[4] See above, p. 347 n. 1.

plunged less recklessly without a partner than with one, since the partner brought no capital with him. Had Verney stopped to think in the euphoria of success, he must have been aware that if they failed, William could be of no assistance to him—as a partner he was a man of straw. No doubt William was foolish to run such risks, but so was Lord Verney. And if he had been most generous in their days of success he proved far less so in their time of failure; making any rehabilitation of William impossible yet gaining no benefit from his obduracy himself. Yet Verney was a kindly man, and there is no sign that when the disaster actually hit them he gave way either to bitterness or recriminations against his partner, and the settlements made in 1770 were both fair and considerate. The question is, what was the cause of his change of attitude and what lay behind the bitterness which made him deaf to all reasonable suggestions of compromise in his last years?

The answer is suggested by the date (1780) at which the legal settlement between Verney and William took place. It lay in the belief, widespread in England at the time, that great fortunes were to be won by the agents of Indian princes. The belief had been fostered by Lauchlin Macleane when a few years earlier he had returned to England as the agent of the Nabob of Arcot, and the lesson of his failure had not yet been learned. In 1780 William was in England as agent of the Raja of Tanjore, and similar hopes were aroused. It was to further these hopes that Verney tried once again to find a seat for William in Parliament, being (as William wrote to the Duke of Portland) "deeply interested in the success of my fortune, which (if I can go out accredited with a seat in Parliament) is certain, easy and considerable".[1] When these hopes failed, the short-lived Rockingham administration, which did nothing for Verney, gave William what looked like a most profitable Indian job, and his expectations must have risen again. William himself in 1785 had hopes of a profit of "not less than £5,000 a year", in addition to his salary of £2,000, and believed that between his salary and an annual remittance of £2,000, the Burkes could hope for £4,000 a year towards paying off his and their debts for two or three years "if I last so long".[2] But even this assumed some composition with Verney, and like all William's Indian dreams, it faded away. It was not easy for an outsider to make a fortune in India. None of the broken men who went out at this time did so — not even the ingenious and indefatigable Macleane — and it was becoming increasingly difficult to achieve this end by irregular means. William had neither the toughness, the acumen nor the experience for success in this world, and by 1785 he was showing all the signs of demoralization.

Nevertheless Verney remained until his death firmly convinced that William was a rich man who could easily have met not only the legal obligations he entered into (which Verney obviously thought very moderate) but much more, and that his failure to do so was due to gross ingratitude. This belief, fed on rumours, was accepted by his friends. In 1783 William was said to have remitted £2,000 to other

[1] Quoted *History of Parliament*, II, 157.
[2] William to Richard Burke Jr., 30 December 1785. P.R.O. Chatham MSS. Quoted D. Wecter, *op. cit.*, pp. 32 and 88.

creditors and to be about to remit much more.[1] Boldero the banker told Luke Heslop, one of Verney's trustees, in 1788 that William had "satisfied all their Demands — but he did not apprehend that he had remitted any more money — he also told me that he did not apprehend he saved much money for he lived at a very great Expence and a very dissipated life".[2] Only Thomas Calvert, lately returned from India in 1790, reported that he "does not think him rich".[3] It was easy for Verney's friends to forget the circumstances of the liability, to ignore Verney's other extravagances, and to believe that his difficulties were all the fault of his former partner.[4] In his obituary in *The Gentleman's Magazine* in April 1791 it was stated "For many years before his death his affairs were in the greatest confusion, owing to some friends, who induced him to speculate in Change-alley", and a footnote was added to the word "friends": "One of these now lives in the greatest splendour in the East Indies, but has not thought it necessary to remit any part of the large debt due from him to his Lordship." Before these words were written Verney's heiress had recognized the fallacy of the belief they expressed, and had accepted the composition which Richard Burke junior had pressed on her predecessor, and two years later William was back in England, broken in health, demoralized by failure and "as much ruined as when he went".[5]

---

[1] S. Rogers to Verney, 3 May 1783. Claydon MSS.
[2] L. Heslop to Verney, undated [1788]. Claydon MSS.
[3] L. Heslop to Verney, 10 March 1790. Claydon MSS.
[4] The list of Verney's debts on 1 November 1790 in the Claydon MSS shows that he owed then some £115,000.
[5] Sir Gilbert to Lady Elliot, 2 May 1793. Countess of Minto, *Life and Letters of Sir Gilbert Elliot first Earl of Minto from* 1751 *to* 1806 (London, 1874) II, 136.

APPENDIX I

Accounts between Macleane and Lord Verney and William Burke 1767–1769
(From Claydon MSS).

	Dr.	
L. Macleane Esq to L. V. and Mr B.		
£7,500 India Stock pledged with Samuel Ximenes of Amsterdam in September 1767 which cost 266 per cent	£19,950	
Advanced on ditto by Samuel Ximenes	14,800	
	5,150	
Interest on £5,150 from 25 September to 25 July 1769 One year ten months at 5 per cent per annum	472	
	5,622	
Amount of Bills drawn by John Motteux Esq on Messrs. I. and J. Panchaud of Paris the 29 March and 1st April 1768 as per his note	7,000	
Charges of circulation from March to November 1768 say 8 months cost 5 per cent	350	7,582
	7,350	
Interest on £7,350 from 25 November to 25 July 8 months at 5 per cent per annum	232	
	13,204	
To L. V. for his half of £13,204		6,602
To William Burke for his ditto ditto		6,602
To ditto for money lent the 12 March 1768	2,300	
Interest on £2300 from 12 March 1768 to the 25 July 1769 being 1 year 4 months	153	
	2,453	2,134
Deduct so much being due to L. Macleane	319	8,736
		15,338

London the 25 July 1769

Signed L. Macleane

The above amount is   £15,338

APPENDIX II

Lauchlin Macleane's account with De la Fontaine & Brymer. 1768–1769 (From Claydon MSS)

Lauchlin Macleane Esq.   His Account Current

Dr

1768		£	s	d
October 11	To balance of account delivered him	5,723	16	9
November 24	,, India setled this day	6,586	17	6
November 25	3 % Consols	1,182	10	
	4 %	187	10	
	To loss on 20 Lottery Ticketts	45		
1769				
February 28	To Balance of India setled this day	230	–	–
April 6	do ——— do	305	–	–
		£14,260	14	3
	To balance brought on	9,842	13	2
April 25	To balance of Bank setled this day	157	10	0
May 25	To balance of India do	13,267	10	0
May 26	Bank do	275		
June	To expenses to Lord Shelburne	13		
		£23,555	13	2

Cr

1768		£	s	d
November 11	By balance of Lottery Ticketts setled this day	97	10	
24	By cash received in Bank Notes	475		
1769				
January 10	By balance of India this day	2,696	17	6
	By his remittance on Solomon Norden	761	3	7
27	By balance of 3 per cents	187	10	
February 28	By cash received of him	200		
	By balance due to D.&B. besides interest and charges	9,842	13	2
		14,260	14	3

London 25 July 1769. I believe the above Account to be right and I approve of it Errors excepted.

Signed L. Macleane.

APPENDIX III

Settlement between Lord Verney, Lauchlin Macleane and De la Fontaine & Brymer 1770
(From the Claydon MSS. This document is written on the back of a copy of the
signed account printed in Appendix I)

De la Fontaine and Brymer by deeds dated the 15 May 1770 assigned to the Earl
of Verney part of L. Macleane's Bond of 25 August 1769 payable to them
of   £23,500
                                                                    22,500
And Richard Burke's debt due to them   8,844. 7. 9.
                                                             _____

                                                            31,344. 7. 9.

The Consideration which the said Earl of Verney paid for the said assignments
of said part of said L. Macleane's Bond and of said Richard Burke's Debt when
all accounts settled and liquidated and mutual Releases dated the 15 May 1770
were executed by his Lordship and De la Fontaine & Brymer, was the Earl's
Ballance of account

                                                             9,480. 4. 7.
Samuel Dyer's ballance of Account current   2,044. 15. 5.
And his Lordships Securities to De la
Fontaine & Brymer for the payment by
installments of   3,544. 1. 2.
                                                             _____

                                                            15,069. 1. 2.

But to enable his Lordship to make a final
settlement of accounts with L. Macleane
and Richard Burke, must be added the
ballance of the said L. Macleane's
Account settled the 25 July 1769 due to
his Lordship and William Burke   338. 0. 0.
                                                             _____

                                                            15,407. 1. 2.

APPENDIX IV

Lord Verney's Financial Position in 1769

Lord Verney had an income from his estates of £10,000 a year or more.[1] His chief property was in the counties of Buckingham and Northampton, but he had lesser interests elsewhere — in London, Essex, Yorkshire and Cornwall.[2] He had married in 1740 Mary Herring, one of the three daughters of a wealthy London merchant, Henry Herring. As a result of his marriage Lord Verney received in all £40,000 and a third interest in some London property.[3] Lady Verney in her own right inherited a third of her father's estate which was invested in £13,202 Bank Stock.[4]

Apart from his disastrous speculation in East India Stock, Lord Verney had other interests, some of which cost him large sums of money. In 1763 he was one of the foundation Directors of the unsuccessful English Linen Company set up at Winchelsea by Act of Parliament (4 Geo. III, c 37). Fortunately this statute gave the adventurers limited liability, so his losses may have been restricted to about £2,000.[5] His interest in Ranelagh Gardens, on the other hand, appears to have been profitable. More important was his involvement in politics: he tried to secure control of three boroughs — Great Bedwyn (until he sold his interest to Lord Bruce in 1766), Wendover and Carmarthen. In addition he was eager to build a vast new house at Claydon, as a rival, it is said, to the splendours which the Grenvilles enjoyed at Stowe. How much he spent on politics is not known. Nor can the full expenditure on Claydon be ascertained, but according to his own evidence in two Chancery cases he allowed his architect and draftsman, Luke Lightfoot, £30,000 between 1757 and 1769 and received a return equivalent to £7,000.[6] As a result of financing these varied interest Verney was heavily in debt before the stock market crash in 1769. The following is a list of his known debts in 1769.

1.	Joan Land	28 June 1763	639	5	0
2.	Samuel Savage	20 August 1766	12000	0	0
3.	Maria Catherine Gell	25 July 1767	9000	0	0
4.	George Grenville	8 September 1767	12000	0	0
5.	Mrs Elizabeth Nugent	28 October 1767	1498	15	0
6.	Jane Joliffe	27 October 1768	6500	0	0
7.	Andrew Stone	December 1768	10000	0	0
8.	Elizabeth Thorp Pyke	9 February 1769	3600	0	0
9.	Mary Gell	10 April 1769	1000	0	0
10.	Elisha Briscoe	3 May 1769	10000	0	0
11.	Peter Halford	15 July 1769	5000	0	0
12.	Sir George Colebroke	19 July 1769	3000	0	0
			74,238	0	0

[1] In 1781 Verney surrendered estates to trustees with a rental of £10,000 and was left with an income of £2,000 a year (E112/1730/4454).

[2] He had an interest in Cornwall in a tin mine and smelting house, both of which became financial liabilities (Alexander Brymer to Verney, 14 February, 1771, Claydon MSS; C12/576/48).

[3] Will of Henry Herring (Prerogative Court of Canterbury, 1752, Bettesworth 251).

[4] C33/451, fol. 320.

[5] Copies of Chancery Proceedings, Colebrooke v Verney, 1767–69, Claydon MSS.

[6] C12/1519/83 and C12/558/29.

Sources

1 Judgment in Exchequer of Pleas, Easter 1779; satisfied Michaelmas 1793.
2 Repaid by borrowing £14,000 from Arthur Jones in 1772 (C12/582/36).
3 K.B. 122/360, Roll 380; satisfied Easter 1793.
4 Judgment in Exchequer of Pleas, Easter 1771; not known when repaid, still outstanding in 1779
   (C12/2116/23).
5 Originally 1998 10   0 (K.B. 122/432, Roll 1116); £500 further repaid in 1773.
6 Joliffe v Verney, 1779 (C12/2405/36)
7 C12/122/36; part repaid in 1774 (C33/451, fol. 320), the rest in 1776 when Verney borrowed
   £10,000 (C12/2116/23).
8 Borrowed by Verney and Joseph Bullock, the debt to be repaid by transfer of £4000 of 3%
   consol bank annuities (repaid by borrowing, C33/451, fol. 320; C33/461, fol. 69).
9 K.B. 122/360 Roll 381; satisfied 1793.
10 Exchequer of Pleas Judgment, Trinity 1778.
11 K.B. 122/373, Roll 1059.
12 K.B. 122/361, Roll 696.

APPENDIX V

Cases in Exchequer and Chancery relating to the East India Speculation

Hobson v De la Fontaine	1769	C12/57/22
Van Jever v Verney	1769	C12/542/17
Verney v Macleane	1769	C12/1026/18
Verney v André	1770	C12/550/34
Monckton v De la Fontaine	1770	E112/1618/1410
Verney v Cazenove	1770	C12/909/59
Shelburne v Tierney	1771	E112/1619/1473
Tierney v Shelburne	1772	E112/1632/1904
Van Jever v Verney	1772	C12/554/47
André v Verney	1773	C12/1623/1; C12/1627/8; C12/1927/15
Verney v Simond	1773	C12/1625/48
Townson v Blaauw	1773	E112/1630/1836
Rutland v Verney	1773	C12/554/17
Shelburne v Verney	1773	C12/554/26
Van Zijpesteijn v Verney	1774	C12/909/60
Van Freisheim v Verney	1775	C12/562/36
Van Schuylenburch v Verney	1780	C12/582/36; C12/585/32
Verney v Hargrave	1782	C12/122/36
Van Schuylenburch v Macnamara	1783	C12/589/30

V

Merchants and Financiers

BIBLIOGRAPHICAL NOTE

The general world of government finance in this period is surveyed by P.G.M. Dickson, *The Financial Revolution in England ... 1688-1756* (London, 19670. Particular aspects of it, including the operations of the Duke of Newcastle, are examined in R. Browning, *The Duke of Newcastle* (Yale, 1975). Above all, see J.E.D. Binney, *British Public Finance and Administration, 1774-92* (Oxford, 1958).

CHAPTER 16

This chapter was the basis of chapter 2 of Dame Lucy's first book, *A London Merchant: 1695-1774* (Oxford, 1933).

CHAPTER 20

See Dame Lucy's biography of Sir George Colebrooke in *The History of Parliament*, eds. Sir Lewis Namier and J. Brooke (London, 1964).

Samson Gideon (artist unknown)

THE ACCOUNTS OF AN EIGHTEENTH-CENTURY MERCHANT: THE PORTUGESE VENTURES OF WILLIAM BRAUND

W HEN Malachy Postlethwayt suggested that a Mercantile College should preserve, as examples of the greatness of their craft, the "accounts of many distinguished and eminent merchants deceased . . . who trod the Royal Exchange with supreme credit and dignity,"[1] he spoke in the height of the commercial pride which was reached in the eighteenth century, before the challenge of industry and an economic interpretation based on its predominance brought its sobering influence to bear on " the great mercantile classes of England." In a wider sense, now that that age with all its vigorous yet obscurely developed commercialism has become perhaps more difficult to estimate in commerce as well as in politics than any of its predecessors, because its similarities to succeeding ages serve to mask its differences, we can echo his wish for the books of a Sir Theodore Janssen, a Sir Peter Delmé, or a Sir Henry Furnese.

In default of the books of these merchant princes, which would show not only the extent of their traffic, but its adaptation to the trend of their time, interest attaches to any consecutive collection of accounts of prominent merchants which chance may have saved from destruction. Worthy illustrations of this type of records, unfortunately so scarce, are the Papers of William Braund, merchant, ship-owner and shipping insurer, Director of the East India Company and of the Sun Fire Office.[2] The papers, which consist almost wholly of accounts, cover, with a few gaps and not with equal thoroughness, the years 1741-1774, when he

---

[1] M. Postlethwayt, *Universal Dictionary of Trade and Commerce* (4th ed., 1774), *s.v.* Mercantile Accountantship.

[2] These papers are in the possession of Champion Russell, Esq., of Stubbers, Essex, to whom I am indebted for their use. William Braund (1695-1774) was the son of a prosperous merchant and citizen of London, who was also of Upminster, Essex. William is first mentioned in Kent's Trade Directory, 1736, as a merchant trading in Rood Lane, Fenchurch Street. Osborn's Directory of 1744 gives his address as Tokenhouse Yard (an office he shared with his brother Samuel, ship's husband). From 1745-53 he was Director of the East India Company, and from 1751-74 Director of the Sun Fire Assurance. He had various changes of business address, but from 1768-73, when he retired from business, his office was in Fenchurch Street. He bought several estates in the vicinity of Upminster, and lived unmarried in a house he had himself built, Hacton.

died in prosperous commercial ease at the age of seventy-eight. They open, then, when he was in his prime, aged forty-five, with his commercial position well established. A man of substance, a member of the " Sun Fire " group of merchants, to which such men as Brice Fisher belonged,[1] of a family of merchants, ships' captains and ships' husbands, his career must have been an illustration of that of many respectable merchants of his time. It has been remarked that the careers of all prominent London merchants of the mid-eighteenth century show a trend from commercial pursuits proper to those of pure finance, as the great credit expansion of the eighteenth century opened new ways before them.[2] Within its limits Braund's career shows the same tendency. Though he never speculated, even in the East India Company, where he formed part of the later redoubtable " shipping interest "—and indeed he tended increasingly in his later days to place his faith in the solid wealth of the land—and though he never grew rich on contracts or on contact with the Treasury and its loans, yet his activities shifted none the less. From the time we first see him until 1756, he divided his activities between underwriting and a wholesale woollen trade, which, at least from 1747, concentrated chiefly on the exportation of woollens to Portugal. He is also beginning some ventures in ship-owning. From 1763 until his death in 1774 he was still partly interested in ship-owning, but otherwise confined his attention to his increased business in underwriting. From 1756 to 1763 the transition between the two stages of his commercial career, his withdrawal from the ranks of the merchants, was taking place under cover of his sudden and extensive venture in the Portuguese bullion trade, which, together with his marine insurance, took up the full force of his energies during the years of the Seven Years' War.

It is his venture in the bullion trade and its direct development out of his woollen exportation to Portugal which will be studied here. It is an episode complete in itself and interesting in several ways. In the first place, it is an illustration of one of the means by which the exporting merchant dominated yet adapted himself to the development of English commerce—that is, through sheer mobility and the poise of a purely intermediary position. For Braund had neither store nor warehouse, nor any stock to put into them, nor did he ever play a part other than a financier's in any of his trading activities at home. In his foreign trade, he bought woollens when he thought fit to send a consignment to Lisbon, had them dyed, packed and despatched by other firms, and received the profits of the transaction in due course.

---

[1] L. B. Namier, " Brice Fisher, M.P.: A Mid-Eighteenth-Century Merchant and his Connexions," in *The English Historical Review*, vol. xlii. 514.

The Braund Papers show continuous business relations between Brice Fisher and Braund.   [2] L. B. Namier, *loc. cit.*

When circumstances suggested to such a man, as they did to Braund in 1756, that a new course of trade would be more profitable, it was no great matter for him to change from exporter to importer, from dealer in woollen goods to dealer in bullion.[1]   In the second place, this episode serves as an individual illustration of one of the obscurest trades of eighteenth-century England.   What William Braund was doing from 1756 to 1763, when he ceased to export woollen goods and began to bring gold to England and to tranship gold to the great banking firm of Cliffords in Amsterdam, was being done continually and in the same way by others, and no doubt often on a bigger scale; collectively they were building up a position for England in the bullion distribution of the world which played its part in the rise of London's money market.

The obscurity in which the bullion trade of the eighteenth century has remained is not due to its lack of importance: it is due partly no doubt to the fact that the period was not, until cut across by the Napoleonic Wars, one of great price movements, partly to the fact that it was by the development of credit rather than the exploitation of new metallic sources that it met its growing commercial needs, but more to the fact that the conditions of the trade and its extent were veiled by a certain secrecy which political causes made desirable.[2]   For, much as conditions had changed, the bullion supplies of the world remained chiefly those which Spain and Portugal controlled in South America, and the function of the trade in precious metals was still their more or less illegal distribution.   While the centre of this distribution had been in the sixteenth century the centralized markets of Antwerp and Genoa, and their place had been taken in the seventeenth century by Amsterdam, in the eighteenth century circumstances were favouring in more ways than one the growing organization of London.[3]   For one thing, the great increase of Portuguese gold which followed the development of the Brazil mines at the end of the seventeenth century began to pass largely through English hands, on account of Portugal's

[1] Such merchants, though ones far nearer the adventurer than Braund ever was, are spoken of by Adam Smith (*Wealth of Nations*, ed. Cannan, vol. i. 115) as " the speculative merchant " whose trade " can be carried on no where but in great towns "; who " enters into every trade when he foresees that it is likely to be more than commonly profitable, and quits it when he foresees that its profits are likely to return to the level of other trades."

[2] The force of this necessity was strongly brought out, for instance in the discussions with regard to the Spanish American bullion in 1764-66.   Compare, for example, B.M. Add. MS. 33030, f. 189 *seq.*: Evidence before the House of Commons of Beeston Long of his interview with Grenville.

[3] The whole organization of the Bank of Amsterdam was, however, so arranged as to give every advantage to the City's great bullion trade.   For a contemporary account see Adam Smith, *Wealth of Nations* (ed. Cannan), vol. i. 443 *seq.*   His information came from Henry Hope, a member of a prominent Amsterdam firm.

commercial dependence on England. By the half-century England was admittedly the importer of the major part of the gold which, however checked, had to flow out of Portugal to pay for her imports. The importance of this factor in the commercial alliance between England and Portugal cannot be over-estimated.[1] For another thing, there developed in the silver trade at the beginning of the eighteenth century a new and more direct supply, in the contraband of the Spanish-American colonies with the foreign West Indies and mainland settlements. This trade, which became very extensive, fell largely into English hands.[2]

In the ordinary course of her trade, then, England was obtaining increased supplies of precious metals, which she required the more as her East Indian trade, and the silver export which it necessitated, were increasing. Her transactions were increased by her importance as a transhipper of gold and silver for other nations. In the Portuguese trade it was said, as Beawes stresses in his *Lex Mercatoria Rediviva*, that shipments of gold were made directly to Italy alone, but to all other nations through England " on account of the convenience of the Exchange and of shipping."[3] In the Spanish South American trade in silver[4] an even more striking development was seen, for here England actually transhipped silver for Spain herself. A financial adviser told the English Government:

"A vast quantity of Bullion hath been sent for many years last past to His Majesty's Dominions in America, not to be laid out there,

[1] Compare *The British Merchant* (ed. C. King, 1721), vol. ii. 24, vol. iii. 19-20, etc. See J.-G. Van Dillen, "Amsterdam Marché Mondial des Métaux Précieux au XVIIᵉ et au XVIIIᵉ Siècle," in *Revue Historique*, July, 1926.

[2] The recent development of this trade was brought out in the discussions from 1764-66 of its place in the provisions of the Navigation Acts (*vide* B.M. Add. MS. 32971, f. 16 v., Memorandum, n.d. [late 1765]: The Advice of Mr. —— to the Ministry). "When the Statute of the 7th and 8th of King William was made Mr. —— doth not believe the practice of the Spaniards bringing Bullion to the said Dominions, to lay out in goods and Manufactures, had then begun. . . . Mr. —— believes, that the Practice of the Spaniards remitting Bullion to Great Britain did not take place till many years after the passing the Act."
Despite the fears of N. Magens (*Universal Merchant*, 1753, 15) that the trade was being lost and passing into French hands, the Bullion Report of 1810 (E. Cannan, *The Paper Pound*) mentions this trade as one of first-class importance.

[3] p. 624.

[4] It centred chiefly in Jamaica. Interesting returns were made by the Bank of England at command of the House of Commons in January, 1766, of the silver imports from the British American Colonies, 1748-65. (B.M. Add. MS. 32971, f. 64 *seq*.)
The following are the total imports for these years: Jamaica, £2,368,484; Other West Indies, £20,826; Havana, £559,110; New York, £171,782; Virginia, £22,750; South Carolina, £23,200; Quebec, £20,000; Not distinguished, £69,504.

but to be sent to Great Britain to make remittances, or on freight only for the use of the Spaniards, with a design to avoid the heavy indultos of 12 and sometimes more per cent on Bullion and other charges remitted to Spain, by which the senders gain as circumstances vary from 8 to 12 or 13 per cent."[1]

The development of the market in London to deal with this increased flow of bullion was considerable. Its central feature was, of course, the rise to predominance of the Bank of England as a buyer of bullion. By 1765 it was stated that into its hands "almost all comes."[2] Some houses of goldsmith bullion merchants, however, kept up an independent position. George Masterman, goldsmith, giving evidence before the House of Commons in 1766, as one of the chief buyers of silver bullion in Lombard Street, stated that as much as £320,000 of American silver passed through his house in the years 1761-65, and maintained that he could not put himself "at the Head" of his trade.[3] The position he describes is not essentially different from that described in 1810 by Goldsmid of Mocatta & Goldsmid, bullion brokers to the Bank of England, except that the private buyers seem to have still had a somewhat more prominent position than they maintained later.[4] His evidence makes it clear that it was customary for the ships' captains, both merchantmen and men-of-war, to take bullion directly either to a goldsmith banker or to the Bank. The Bullion Office, or Warehouse as it was called until the end of the eighteenth century, was said to have existed since almost the Bank's institution "for the purpose of accommodation and safety between merchant and merchant, as a place of deposit."[5] Masterman mentions that "all Captains of Men of War make it a rule to go to the Bank of England," but that merchantmen sometimes preferred to take the bullion to a goldsmith buyer, who kept what he wanted himself, and "carried to the Bank" the rest. This very convenient method for the importer explains why there is only the one entry of each bullion import in the Braund books, an entry with freight deducted, and that

[1] B.M. Add. MS. 32971, f. 16, n.d. (1765): Opinion of Mr. ——.

[2] B.M. Add. MS. 38339, f. 225, Jan. 28, 1766: Joseph Salvador, the Jewish Financier.

[3] T. Mortimer (*The Universal Director*, 1763) mentions a firm, How & Masterman, goldsmiths, of White Hart Court, Gracechurch Street. F. G. Hilton Price (*Handbook of London Bankers*) has found no reference to a Masterman as goldsmith or banker earlier than 1780, when the firm of Mildred, Masterman & Walker, of Lombard Street, is mentioned.

George Masterman's evidence is found in rough notes among the Newcastle Papers (B.M. Add. MS. 33030, f. 148 *seq.*).

[4] *Reports, etc., from Committees of the House of Commons* (1810), vol. iii. 35: Minutes of Evidence before the "Bullion Committee."

[5] *Ibid.* 146: Evidence of J. Humble, Clerk in the Bullion Office of the Bank of England.

there is no trace of any method of handling or disposing of the gold. The methods of a merchant transhipping gold for a correspondent to another foreign centre are illustrated by the Braund accounts. Two transactions were involved. First, the bullion entering from Portugal for this purpose was credited to this correspondent with the other shipments he sent to Braund himself, and was therefore paid for in the usual way. Then, to carry out the commission, Braund bought bullion to the amount specified in foreign coin and shipped it to the recipient as if it were a private venture, receiving in due course from him repayment in bill of exchange.

The buying required some skill and foresight, and was placed by Malachy Postlethwayt among the most skilled branches of the great " art of merchandising," though so wide a knowledge of " the markets where and seasons when it is to be bought cheap and sold . . . dear," as he assumes, was more necessary for a skilled arbitrageur than a simple importer such as William Braund became. Nevertheless, not only were his problems those which required knowledge of the exchanges, and an understanding of the imperfection of the normal arbitrage activities of his time, but they were further complicated by the unstable eighteenth-century bimetallism, and a market in gold disordered by depreciation of the currency and by the prohibition of the export of English coin. Thus during the eight years of Braund's activities the price of gold fluctuated from £3 17s. 0d. to £4 1s. 2d. per standard oz.,[1] and Malachy Postlethwayt in his tables for the calculation of the value of precious metals of all degrees of purity gives figures for silver from the price of 5s. to that of 5s. 6⅞d. per standard oz., and for gold from £3 15s. 6d. to £4 1s. 0d.[2]

The trade which William Braund carried on to Portugal, at first in woollens and then in bullion, was organized according to the manner of his time, and it is significant of that time that the change from one commodity to another was effected without the need of any marked alteration in the methods or channels of his business. Throughout, his trade was carried on through a firm of merchants living in one of the foreign factories in Lisbon, who acted as his agents or factors; as importing agents in the first period of his activities they received his shipments of woollens and distributed them, generally on long credit, to Portuguese tradesmen or merchants; later, as exporting

[1] The causes are analyzed in the Bullion Report of 1810 (E. Cannan, *The Paper Pound*).

[2] *Op. cit., s.v.* Bullion. A distinction must be made at this time between the price of gold in foreign coin, in which Braund dealt almost exclusively, and that of bar gold—the former always tending to be somewhat higher than the latter, on account of the greater demand for it abroad.—Bullion Report of 1810. (E. Cannan, *The Paper Pound*, 4.)

agents, they bought and despatched his gold for him to England. Such agents were rarely Portuguese, for, as contemporaries said, with fine trading scorn, " The Portuguese carry on no active commerce . . . they buy everything from foreigners settled in factories there."[1] In 1741, when Braund's accounts begin, and when his activities, less concentrated than later, included relations with firms in Holland,[2] he appears to have been employing as agent in Lisbon a Dutch firm, Schutte, Buess & Renner. After 1743, however, no transactions with them are recorded in his journal, though old debts are sent by them through his new agents for some years. In his choice of new agents Braund was more orthodox, for he chose a firm in the English factory, Jackson & Carse. Still more characteristic of the commercial habits of the time was the fact that his nephew, Benjamin Branfill, shortly after the connection began, entered the firm as a junior partner. The firm stands finally in Braund's great ledger under the name of Jackson, Branfill & Goddard.[3] The relations between Braund and Jackson, Branfill & Goddard were complicated, but not, it seems probable, uncommon. The Lisbon house cannot be put under the category of either Agent, Commission House, or Branch Firm.[4] The connection was more than the simple one of agent and principal, for there was the close relationship of kin, and an equally close one of credit. In 1758 the firm owed Braund £12,500 on its own account, in addition to a personal debt of his nephew, Benjamin Branfill.[5] Jackson, Branfill & Goddard was not, on the other hand, a branch firm, for Braund had not founded it, and a relationship similar to that with Braund appears also to have existed with a London merchant, Philip Jackson, whose name first appears in 1753, and who was, presumably, a relative of the Jackson of the Portuguese firm.[6] Branch

---

[1] Mercator's *Letter on Portugal and its Commerce*, 1754. Note that this letter is reproduced verbatim under the title *Portugal* by Postlethwayt, *op. cit.*, under the sub-heading, *A Short Account of the Commerce of Portugal as lately given us on a very Interesting Occasion*.

This taunt, never altogether justified, ceased to be true at all after the formation in 1756 by Pombal of the Companies of Brazil and the Alto Doura. V. M. Shillington and A. B. Chapman, *The Commercial Relations of England and Portugal*, 265 seq.

[2] J. Daniel Baur, and Tempelman's widow and Kroeger.

[3] Goddard's name first appears in the accounts in September, 1754.

[4] R. B. Westerfield, *Middlemen in English Business*, 351.

[5] Benjamin Branfill owed his uncle personally, in 1758, £1,561 19s. 11d. The debt of the firm appears in that year to have been written down to half.

[6] Philip Jackson, merchant, of Charterhouse Yard, appears first in Kent's Directory in 1754, and his name continues there until the issue of 1774. He was Director of the South Sea Company and Deputy Governor. He is among the signatories of a petition of Portuguese merchants to the Board of Trade and Plantations, May 15, 1756 (P.R.O., C.O. 388/48, ff. 16 *seq.*).

firms were indeed a common method in the Portuguese trade, as in other kinds of distant commerce, of seeking to evade the very real dangers of careless or fraudulent agents, but it seems probable that many of the well-known names, such as Bristow, Ward & Co., the agents of John Bristow of London; Burrell, Duckett & Hardy, the agents of Burrell & Raymond; and Chase, Wilson & Co., the agents of T. Chase, had a more independent existence than that of branch firms proper. Nor can Jackson, Branfill & Goddard be regarded, finally, as a pure Commission House, for though it carried on " commission business " for Philip Jackson and Braund, and the accounts seem to suggest for another London merchant, Thomas Godfrey, it also carried on its own independent trade, as its bullion ventures were later to show. It is more proper to consider it not only as one of those firms of " the highest credit throughout Europe," whose custom it was "to act mutually in the capacity of factors for each other,"[1] but as one that had close relations with, and possibly even some dependence on, Braund and other English merchants.

Braund's transactions through Jackson, Branfill & Goddard can be examined in four different account books: his great Ledger F, " the grand and principal book of accounts,"[2] covering the years 1758-1765;[3] his Fair Journal, which also begins only in 1758; his Rough Journal, with its daily entries under separate accounts, which runs from 1741-1764 (with, however, an unexplained gap from 1745-1749 inclusive); and his Cash Book, which runs from 1747-1774, thus covering, though not by its nature completely, the later years of the gap in the Journal.[4] Trading relations between the two firms evidently began during the years of this gap, for the first evidence which we have of them is a note in the cash book of a bill of exchange from Jackson & Carse on December 9, 1747. During the remaining two years before the resumption of the Journal there is no evidence of the trade except such receipts of bills of exchange. Their annual totals—

							£	s.	d.
1747 (August to December only)		...	...	470	3	1
1748 ...	...	...	...	...	...	...	1,490	6	10
1749 ...	...	...	...	...	...	...	3,523	1	7

although they cannot, owing to the use of long credit, be held to represent the value of the consignments of woollen goods for the year in which the payment occurs, suggest at least a growing trade.

[1] Postlethwayt, *op. cit., s.v.* Factors.

[2] *Ibid., s.v.* Mercantile Accountantship.

[3] Two Ledgers only have survived, F and G, the latter of which runs from 1765 to Braund's death in 1774.

[4] The cash book has no record of shipments of woollens or of charges. Braund kept, in addition to the journal here used, another journal which brought together his insurance business and other activities. Only one volume of it is extant.

By 1750, however, both sides of the transactions are before us, and, though the Ledger alone could make clear the entire position, we can examine in detail the extent and methods of trade, for Braund clearly supported the current commercial maxim that " in journalizing the waste book lies all the difficulty of account-keeping,"[1] and his Journal is full and methodical. An examination of his trade from 1750 onwards shows that the volume of his exportation for the next five years was, like that of England as a whole, fluctuating but not increasing, and that in its organization as in its extent it had become very systematized. Except in unusual circumstances, every consignment of woollens was entered in two forms, first as a debit to " Voyage to Lisbon," when the " first cost " and " charges " were entered; later, after varying intervals, as a debit to Jackson, Branfill & Goddard, when the " net price " was given, the sum for which they disposed of the goods to Portuguese merchants, less freight, customs and warehouse charges. This method has the convenience of enabling a calculation to be made of the profit or loss of each transaction.

The " first cost " was the price actually paid by Braund for the materials. They consisted of various types of woollens, some cloths and serges, but the greater part woollens and semi-worsteds such as Shalloons, Tammies, Long Ells and in particular " our very great article, Long Bays."[2] He obtained the materials from three of the different sources opened to the merchant buyer by the complicated machinery of the distribution of the woollen trade.[3] Probably the most important among them individually was his packer, Thomas Burfoot, who, like many packers and warehousemen of the time, had evolved from his packing business a very considerable position as a merchant.[4] Burfoot, who had connections with a firm of woollen drapers in Cornhill, Burfoot & Ellis, not only packed all Braund's goods, but supplied him with most of the Long Ells which he required, occasionally undertook some of his dyeing (presumably having it done elsewhere), and was, at least on one occasion, the intermediary through whom he bought his blankets. When Braund gave up the woollens trade, his name is one of the few which is still to be found in the accounts, for he then began to appear as the drawer of numerous bills of exchange on a Portuguese firm in Lisbon.[5] It was the rise of such extra intermediaries which was deplored by mer-

---

[1] Postlethwayt, *op. cit.*, *s.v.* Mercantile Accountantship.

[2] Mercator, *op. cit.*

[3] *Cf.* E. Lipson, *History of the English Woollen and Worsted Industries*; H. Heaton, *The Yorkshire Woollen and Worsted Industries*.

[4] R. B. Westerfield, *Middlemen in English Business*, 312-13.

[5] Thomas Burfoot. He is to be found at the same warehouse in Bucklersbury in the Directories from 1736-76. In 1759 the firm appears as Thomas Burfoot & Son. From 1774-76 as Burfoot & Bristow.

chant and clothier alike, but which really was an essential condition of the mobility and power of the exporting merchant. The second of Braund's sources was also a type, and a very notable one, of London intermediary, the Blackwell Hall factor. From a well-known man among them, Brice Fisher,[1] with whom he had other relations as well, Braund obtained all the broadcloth which he exported. In the same way he purchased his coatings from the well-known firm of London warehousemen and merchants, Samuel and Thomas Fludyer,[2] and for Shalloons he relied chiefly on a very solid and long-established London firm, Jeremiah, John and Robert Royd, who are described in Kent's Directory of 1754 as " Yorkshire Factors," but in T. Mortimer's *Universal Director* of 1763 as " Norwich Warehousemen." His third source was local merchants. His Tammies were obtained chiefly from Thomas Humphreys, who does not appear to have been a London merchant, but whose town I have not been able to discover, and the needs of his great exportation of Long Bays were almost entirely met by one Thomas Ruggles of Bocking, with whom, moreover, he carried on for some years a joint inland trade.[3]

The woollens when bought were undyed, and in the case of the Tammies, unscoured, and, since Braund had no warehouses, were despatched directly to the firms of dyers and packers, whose payment makes up the item of " charges." The proportion of these charges to the " first cost " was often very high, sometimes almost half as much again, and it is noticeable that in almost every case Braund makes in his entries a small but varying addition to their total, presumably the small increment, varying from 5 to 10 per cent., or even more, which, as Postlethwayt notes, merchants were accustomed to add to the prices

[1] Brice Fisher, *vide* note 1, p. 368, above.

[2] Samuel and Thomas Fludyer. This distinguished firm (Thomas was knighted and Samuel was made a baronet, and was in 1761 Lord Mayor of London) is throughout Kent's Directory described as a firm of warehousemen. They traded widely, however, as West India merchants, and were generally designated as such. In fact, Thomas Mortimer in his *Universal Director* of 1763 includes them as West India merchants in a work which is specifically intended to enable " foreigners to avoid dealing with warehousemen who call themselves Merchants, whereas their proper business is to supply the Retailer." (For the Fludyers *cf.* L. B. Namier, *England in the Age of the American Revolution*, 254 n., 281-2.)

[3] The account for trade in company with Thomas Ruggles closes in 1759, and in 1760 there is a note of cash received from his executors. The sums paid to profit and loss on this account show that for the last three years at least this trade was very small.

						£	s.	d.
1757 ...	...	...	...	...	...	30	8	0
1758 ...	...	...	...	...	...	35	9	5
1759 ...	...	...	...	...	...	11	6	9

These sums, together with £500 carried over from the preceding Ledger, were paid by Ruggles in 1759.

of goods sent to their agents, " especially if the goods happen to be well-bought."[1] Braund dealt regularly with three firms of dyers, John Spence, Owen Larton, and Thomas Maryatt, whose place was later taken by Roberts & Kinleside. Thomas Burfoot, the only packer employed, was presumably also the shipper. Since the freights were paid in Lisbon, and deducted from the net price owed by the agents there, the accounts give no information as to their amounts,[2] but they show that the goods were consigned, as was to be expected, on English ships, with only one exception, and that among the ships' names which constantly recur are two in which Braund had an owner's share, as he had later in one of the packet boats which shipped his bullion.

The fluctuation in the bulk of the exports, which was probably occasioned among other things by the slowness and uncertainty with which the agents were able to distribute them, is illustrated by the following table of the annual totals of bales exported, and their cost:

Date.	No. of Bales.	Cost.		
		£	s.	d.
1750	109	7,694	13	1
1751	29	1,836	5	10
1752	81	4,047	19	8
1753	86	5,453	6	6
1754	101	7,127	16	3
1755*	127	8,300	16	10

* An abnormal year.

The remittances in payment for the woollens show none of this irregularity, for the long credit necessary in this trade prevented their having any close relations with the amount of the consignments. The accounts bring out in this connection some important facts with regard to the exchange between England and Portugal. Though the exchange was notoriously and necessarily against Portugal during the greater part of this time, the payments never took the form of bullion until Braund became an importer of precious metals, but always that of bills of exchange, primarily Portuguese trading bills, many drawn by agents on their English correspondents in connection no doubt with the wine

---

[1] Postlethwayt, *op. cit.*, *s.v.* Factors.

[2] An illustration occurs in these accounts of freights from Holland in 1741:

	£	s.	d.
Paid feci [*sic*] of entry of 8 sacks of Estridge Wool (*i.e.*, ostrich down) per Two Brothers	0	4	6
Wharfidge and Lighteridge 16s., Porters Landing 8s. ...	1	4	0
Land waiters 8s., Cartidge 9s. 6d.	0	17	6
Freight and primidge	19	10	0
	21	16	0

(Primage was a customary perquisite of the captain. Commonly 5 per cent. of freight: Beawes, *Lex Mercatoria Rediviva*, 1751, 142.)

trade. This consistent remittance of payments by bill makes clear another point, for they show that there could be a very marked discrepancy between the levels of the London and the Lisbon bill markets. In London the milrea generally stood below gold export point—5s. 6·01d.[1]—a position characteristic of the exchange on a country whence gold is exported as a commodity, while in Lisbon it might, and usually did, stand at the same time from 5s. 6·25d. to 5s. 7d. The explanation lay primarily, no doubt, in the risk created by the prohibition of the export of gold, though the seriousness of this risk varied greatly. It is significant, however, that just the reverse position existed at the end of the eighteenth century between England and Hamburg, and Nathan Rothschild attributed it largely to the fact that, as the exchange tended to be fixed at Hamburg, merchants there bought bills for investment, and—

" sending them to London to get returns: they have, therefore, to take into their calculation the amount of interest on the bills so sent, as well as those received in return, together with two brokerages, and a commission to the London merchant."[2]

It seems probable that this factor of investment played its part in the opposite way in the Lisbon-London exchange.

A comparison of " first costs " and " charges " with " net price " shows the profits of the trade. Taking 1753 as a more or less representative year,[3] we see that Braund gained on an outlay of £5,462 14s. 6d. a profit of £618 10s. 3d., about 10⅓ per cent., a satisfactory return and above Adam Smith's " good, moderate, reasonable profit," for it was more than " double Interest,"[4] though it must be remembered that credit was long, and, as the sequel showed, bad debts common.

It was a moderate, stable, well-ordered trade, and might have gone on unchanged for years, but on November 1, 1755, there came upon it with shattering effects the great Lisbon earthquake, which temporarily paralyzed the commercial activities of the whole of Portugal.

---

[1] So taken from official sources by Shillington and Chapman, *op. cit.*, p. 290 n. *The British Merchant* (ed. 1721), vol. iii. 108, quoted without correction by Postlethwayt, *op. cit.*, *s.v.* Exchange, states that it was under 5s. 6d.

[2] *Reports, etc., from Committees of the House of Commons* (1810), vol. iii. 73-4. Evidence before the Bullion Committee of Mr. ——, to be identified in all probability, as has been suggested (E. Cannan, *The Paper Pound*, xlii.), with Nathan Rothschild.

[3] See Table, below, p. 385.

[4] Adam Smith, *Wealth of Nations* (ed. Cannan), vol. i. 99. He also states that in England " the ordinary profits of stock . . . are supposed to run between six and ten per cent." (vol. i. 293).

It is impossible to isolate the expenses which were incidental to Braund's Portuguese trade from those which he incurred for other purposes. As has been already pointed out, as he had no warehouses, they were not heavy.

It affected Braund both in his own trade and in that of the country. In his own trade he suffered personal losses, both through goods burnt in the customs house, no doubt through ruined customers, and, it would appear, through the shaken credit position of his agents. It is suggestive that he should within three months have closed down his old account with them, and that for the next eight years they were repaying personal debts incurred by them for the most part, if not entirely, before the earthquake. It was clear also that a shock had been given to the woollen trade in general at a time when, in any case, as the next twenty years were to show, it was meeting new and adverse conditions.[1]   At first, it was true, as soon as the immediate dislocation of the earthquake was over, there was a temporary but acute scarcity of and demand for woollen goods. To meet this demand Braund rushed out to his agents (apparently on what he called " the New Account ") in November the largest shipment (eighty-one bales) that he had ever sent, and in January another of considerable size. The profits which he obtained upon them, ranging from 16 to 67 per cent., indicate sufficiently the disorganized condition of trade in Portugal. But Braund was too shrewd not to realize that this was a passing phase. After his shipment of January, 1756, he sent only three bales for the rest of the year. In 1757 he sent only two; from thence onward his activities as a woollen exporter ceased altogether, never to be renewed. Already on February 4, 1756, there is the first entry in the accounts of a remittance from Jackson, Branfill & Goddard in gold bullion; on April 8 there is the first mention of a new and separate account with them, " the exchange account," and from that time on, with no change in the relations between the firms, and with little perceptible reorganization of Braund's resources, the old woollen

---

[1] A petition from the Portugal merchants, among whom was William Braund, was sent in to the Board of Trade and Plantations on May 15, 1756, in which they speak of " their great and heavy losses upon this calamitous occasion (more than many could well bear)." It was signed by sixty-three London merchants, and was supported by a letter from thirteen merchants of Norwich. (P.R.O., C.O. 388/48, ff. 16 *seq.*)

But C. Whitworth's tables (*State of the Trade of Great Britain,* 1776, ii. 28), while they show a very heavy fall in imports from Portugal in 1756, show a large increase in exports to her, and no fall until 1758. Braund's accounts for 1756 would suggest that this increase was largely to meet the losses of the earthquake, and it is possible that, under the spur of the first high prices, the exportation of goods thither was overdone. The depression of 1758 was not permanent, Portugal beginning to share in the general war boom of Europe. The permanent depression did not come until after the peace.

The import of gold bullion from Portugal, which made up the balance, is, of course, not included in these figures, as no record was kept of its entry.

For the other conditions adverse to the trade at this time, see E. Lipson, *The Economic History of England,* vol. iii. 113-4.

export trade merges into a new bullion import one, a merging the more indistinguishable because part of the bullion remittances were in payment for old debts in wool. War-time conditions were soon to help the growing trade, for in May, 1756, England declared war on France, and when in August Frederick the Great invaded Saxony, the Seven Years' War had really begun.

It was thus not the war which tempted Braund to show his adaptability and powers as " a skilful and vigilant merchant,"[1] though, as the rising price of gold followed the needs of war, his ventures expanded greatly. It was firstly the damage done to his woollens trade, and secondly the increased profits in the bullion trade which followed the sudden movement of the exchanges against Portugal, already beneath gold point, after the disaster. That he was not alone in seizing the opportunity is suggested by the occurrence in 1755 of one of the spasmodic attempts made by the Portuguese Government to check the smuggling of bullion out of the country. The increase of gold importation into England, moreover, was considerable enough to upset seriously once again the always unstable English bimetallism. The position of silver in relation to gold during the whole of the obscure development of England towards a virtually monometallic standard was one of under-valuation, which, in any case, tended to leave none but the lighter coins in circulation, but during periods of abnormal drain of silver or abnormal increase of gold a scarcity in the chief internal currency of the country took place. Such was the case during the succeeding years. Even in 1717, when it was decided to lower the value of the guinea, it was only suggested that the English would soon refuse to pay in silver except at a premium, " as they do in Spain," but in 1759 Sir John Barnard stated that the payment of such a premium by the banks was a well-known fact.[2]

[1] Postlethwayt, *op cit.* (*s.v.* The British Mercantile College), says that in the decision to be " particular [merchants] generally, and general [merchants] occasionally . . . consists the judgment, in some measure, of the most skilful and vigilant merchant."

[2] Sir Isaac Newton, " Mint Reports, 1701-25," in *Select Tracts and Documents Illustrative of English Monetary History* (ed. W. A. Shaw). The Spanish premium was said to be generally 6 per cent. Sir John Barnard said in his *Some Thoughts on the Scarcity of Silver Coin: with a Proposal for Remedy thereof* (March, 1759): " It is well known that the Bankers generally give a Premium for silver Coin to supply their Customers." He had already written on the subject in the preceding May. In 1759 the position was aggravated by a heavy fall in the quantity of silver imported from the Spanish South American colonies, the Bank of England returns showing a fall in the imports from Jamaica from £76,900 in 1758 to £23,400 in 1759. The decline was only temporary. (B.M. Add. MS. 32971, f. 64: " An Account of the Bullion Imported and Brought to the Bank from the several Colonies in North America from the Year 1748 to the Year 1765 both inclusive." Drawn up at the command of the House of Commons. *Commons*

The first consignment of gold which Braund received in February, 1756, was not the beginning of a new trade, but a new means of payment for his old—the first occasion on which this method was used in preference to that of bill of exchange—and from that time on until the final closing of his old woollens accounts it continued to be used. The debts owing to him on this old trade can, unfortunately, only be seen in full when the Ledger opens in 1758, almost two years after the woollen trade had ceased to be of importance to him. By that time the distinction between the " old " and " new " accounts (or " woollens," as it begins to be called in contradistinction to " exchange "), first seen at the beginning of 1756, stood for the distinction between a debt owed by the agents personally, the " old " account, and debts which they were, in their capacity as agents, collecting. On the first there was a heavy debt of £12,500, written down to half that sum,[1] on which annual repayments were made through Philip Jackson of London, but of which £681 remained unpaid when the account was finally closed. The method of repayment, and the final loss to Braund, suggest that the firm of Jackson, Branfill & Goddard had been so badly crippled by the earthquake and possibly other misfortunes and mistakes, that they had, like Defoe's *Complete English Tradesman*, been " wise enough as well as honest enough to break betimes,"[2] and were during these years in composition with their creditors, but that the opening of the bullion trade had given them a renewed opportunity for " commission business," and thus a renewed lease of life. On the New Account there was also, in 1758, a heavy debt, £7,613 16s. 6d. The difficulties of collecting this debt are suggested by a note in the Ledger:

" Debts out Standing the first of March 1762.

" 314ψ235. Jono Texeira Macedo, will pay on the arrival of the Rio fleet.

" 995ψ630. Balthasar Pinto de Miranda, to pay when he can Sell his Hides, lately accepted a considerable post in the New Treasury.[3]

Journal, vol. xxx. 500, January 27, 1766.) The Evidence of W. Merle before the Bullion Committee of 1810 (*Reports, etc., from Committees of the House of Commons*, 1810, vol. iii. 54) states that bankers continued giving a premium for silver until the introduction of stamped dollars as currency, and at harvest time or other occasions of great scarcity sometimes did so since that time. The premium was said to be 1¼ per cent.

[1] So it would appear from the not very explicit entries in the Ledger.

[2] Reprint of 1839, 43.

[3] This customer, however, later became bankrupt. Losses also occurred through having to accept payments in kind. In February, 1763, there is the entry, " Loss on my debt of 2659ψ140 of Bernardo Gomez Costa by taking Hydes ... £49 16s. 7d."

" 222ψ640. Jose Devarte Ferreira dead, but are assured his
partner in the Rio will pay all his debts, expected
by the next ffleet."

Nevertheless, all but a small sum, £41 8s. 5d., was paid off by remittances in bullion between 1758 and 1763, remittances which came in
side by side with the new trading imports.

While this repayment went on the trade in bullion gradually grew.
The remittances were for two purposes, for Braund, and for re-export
to Holland; in the first Braund was the principal, in the second the
agent, a new mutual relationship. The imports were distinguished from
the remittances of debts, by the fact that, while 1 per cent. commission
was credited to the agent on the latter,[1] only ⅓ per cent. plus postage
was allowed on the former, the same commission as Braund received
on his re-exports to Holland. Brokerage on the bills of exchange and
freight were paid by Braund himself and deducted from his profits.

In the first two years Braund's ventures were only tentative. The
price of gold was still relatively low, fluctuating about £3 17s. 10½d.
per standard oz., and the effect of the Portuguese dislocation was not
fully reflected in the exchanges until the beginning of 1757. In 1756
there were only four shipments of gold on the Exchange Account,
worth £1,852 8s. 10d., received by Braund, and two bills of exchange
sent out, worth £9 16s. 8d. In 1757 there were again only four, for the
value of £1,400 6s. 9d., though the price of gold had risen by the end
of the year to £3 18s. 3d.; on the other hand, the extreme lowness of
the exchange in England (about 5s. 4½d.) led Braund to much greater
purchases of bills of exchange to further the trade, and ten are entered
in the Ledger, for the value of £2,778 7s. 3d. By 1758, when the
price of gold was hovering between £3 18s. 1½d. and £3 19s. 3d., and
was still rising, the trade was at its height. This period of zenith
lasted from 1758 to 1761. With the needs of a European War, the
price of gold rose to a peak price in June, 1761, of £4 1s. 2d., and even
when the exchanges with Portugal rose above the normal gold export
point, as they began to do during certain months of these years, the
rising price of gold made its continued import into England profitable.

Braund's dealings may be shown by the following figures:

Date.	Value of Bullion Imported.			Value of Bills of Exchange.		
	£	s.	d.	£	s.	d.
1758	11,559	9	1	11,921	18	9
1759	12,164	9	6	11,415	19	7
1760	12,704	9	7	14,725	6	9
1761	12,369	14	9	11,162	0	5
1762	7,152	7	9	3,641	14	8
1763	443	1	6	—		

[1] Postlethwayt, *op. cit.* (*s.v.* Factors), quotes 2 per cent. as the customary
factorage in the Portuguese trade.

The imports were in gold, with the exception of two remittances in silver,[1] and were only on one occasion in bars,[2] being for the rest in Portuguese coins. Where possible they were shipped on one of the four packet boats, in one of which, the *Hanover*, Braund had an owner's share; otherwise they were sent by man-of-war, as no ship could be used for this smuggling trade which had not immunity from search. The advantage of the former was that the freight was charged at only ¼ per cent. of the value of the bullion, while on the latter it was 1 per cent.[3]

The bills of exchange in which payments for the remittances were made were drawn from much more varying sources than those which had before been drawn from Lisbon in payment for the trade in woollens. They suggest both the organization of the London bill market and its growing width. The majority of the bills which are entered in Braund's Ledger are, indeed, as in the earlier case, those drawn by merchants on their correspondents in Lisbon, as, for instance, those of Philip Jackson drawn on Jackson, Branfill & Goddard themselves. Others, however, while still bills of prominent London merchants connected with the Portuguese trade, were clearly not ordinary trade bills. The bills drawn by Thomas Burfoot, the packer, for instance, were far too frequent and regular in their amounts to be the trading bills of a merchant. They are found almost monthly, usually for 1,000 milreis, from 1758 until early in 1762, when two of them were protested for non-payment, and the series abruptly ends. The circumstances clearly point to some arrangement for "accommodation" bills such as the needs of the bullion trade called forth. That the mechanism was not, however, as elastic as it might have been, was shown by the fact that the market was sometimes strained beyond capacity by the demands made upon it in the course of the trade; for instance, in 1737 the influx of Portuguese gold through Falmouth caused serious inconvenience in the internal trade of England, for it engrossed all the bills of exchange from Cornwall to London."[4]

Apart, however, from such developments of the organization of exchange made by London merchants themselves, there are signs of a very real development of the London bill market, both in its national and international aspects. Within England itself it is interesting to see

[1] Silver could be legally exported from Portugal by licence. Mercator, *op. cit.*, says the licence was "rarely or never sollicited." Jackson, Branfill & Goddard, however, obtained one for one of their two silver remittances.

[2] No doubt because the price obtained for coins was higher.

[3] "Carriage" appears to be the word used for the packet boat, "freight" only for man-of-war.

[4] Col. Treas. Books and Papers, 1735-8, 314-5. This is not made clear by Shillington and Chapman, *op. cit.*, 249.

a fair sprinkling of bills on Portuguese correspondents from merchants in such country towns as Exeter, Leeds and Norwich, as, for instance, the Gurneys, no doubt direct dealers in the cloth or wine trades, who worked independently of such London exporters as Braund had been. In drawing by bill of exchange on their correspondents, however, they could not maintain this independence, and the bills were in each case discounted by a London goldsmith banker, such as Coutts or Hoare. This followed logically from the centralization in the hands of such bankers of the internal bill system. In the sphere of international exchange, while Amsterdam was admittedly still the arbiter of the exchanges of Europe, it may be seen how the predominance of English trade to Portugal was bringing to the London bill market bills from all countries of Europe. There are among those sent by Braund to his agents bills drawn on Portuguese merchants in Lisbon or Oporto, foreign or native, by firms in Hamburg, France, Amsterdam, and even Genoa and Leghorn.

If Braund's bills of exchange show the growing position of London as a bill market, his " commission business " in transhipping gold to the Amsterdam firm of bankers, Clifford & Sons, limited though it was, stresses its development as a bullion market. From 1758 to 1761 he shipped to them in men-of-war, either Dutch or English, £3,831 3s. 11d. in five shipments. Since only one of them was in silver, he was not taking part in the process whereby gold was driving out silver from the English market. The gold was exported in the form of foreign coins, and payment was made for them by bill of exchange from Amsterdam, after deduction of his commission, freight, brokerage and postage, all of which Braund charged to the account of Jackson, Branfill & Goddard themselves. It was a very minor part of his activities, and the sums handled were small, but it had value as an illustration of the working of a notable English commerce.

By the end of 1761, though the price of gold had reached its height, and the exchange was only slightly higher than the year before, both the shipments of gold and the number of bills of exchange entered began a small falling off. It is possible that the negotiations for peace and the anxiety which existed for it in England began to suggest a cautious hesitance as to the continued rise in the price of gold. After the peak price in 1761, indeed, it fell fairly steadily, and throughout 1762 did not again reach £4. Still more important to Braund were conditions in Portugal itself. By the later part of 1761 it had become clear that there was danger of an invasion by Spain. By December, 1761, when the English ambassador left Madrid a rupture was certain, and although the invasion which followed was finally defeated by

English forces, the position was not reassuring for merchants during the earlier months of the year. There was an abrupt fall in the rate of the exchange between November 13 and February 4, from 5s. 6½d. to 5s. 5d. Then, when by June the position seemed more secure, the needs of a British army in Portugal had brought the exchange rate up to 5s. 7d. Braund's activities, a little checked by the dangers of the first part of the year, were finally stopped by the rise of the exchange of the latter part. The import of bullion had temporarily ceased to be a piofitable enterprise. No bills of exchange were sent from England after April 6, and the imports of gold came to an abrupt end on June 28. It is significant that about the same time a few of the remittances in payment of the old debts were sent, in the old way once again, in bills of exchange from Lisbon. Thus in the middle of 1762, except for a single shipment in September, 1763, which seems to have been made to seize the chance of a transitory rise in the price of gold during the speculative fluctuations of that year of European post-war credit inflation,[1] the bullion trade ends as abruptly as the woollen trade had before.

There can be little doubt that it was the political circumstances of Europe which caused the trade to end when it did, just as they had encouraged its growth, for, save for this " commission business," the only active relations which still continued between the two firms were those necessary in the winding up of their business connections. By the end of 1763, when the bullion trade ceased, Braund's accounts with them finally closed, and their name never again occurs in his books. In spite, however, of the shock which their prosperity had received in 1755 and the fact that Braund had lost heavily over them, Jackson, Branfill & Goddard did not go bankrupt. Benjamin Branfill remained connected with the firm until his death, and Goddard was his executor. He seems still to have been in Lisbon in partnership in 1765, but by 1767 had returned to London and set up as a Lisbon merchant to run the English side of the business in the same office as his uncle. Here he began a successful business career; the firm of Branfill & Goddard was recognized as Lisbon correspondent of the East India Company,[2] and Branfill himself rose to the position of

[1] There is a reference in *The Gentleman's Magazine* of May, 1763, to the new rise in the price of bullion, which continued with fluctuations for some months (p. 256). " The demand for gold in coin is so great, that the Jews now give 4 guineas an ounce, so that we may soon expect to have that as scarce as silver. The reason is, the Dutch are drawing their money from our funds, in order to accommodate the French, who give 8 per cent."

[2] India Office Library, *East India Company Court Book*, 79, f. 413, March 18, 1771. The firm had done business for the East India Company as early as 1747. See *ibid.*, *Miscellaneous Home Letters Received*, vol. 35, No. 126ª, letter of 11 November, 1749.

director of the Bank of England and manager of the Sun Fire Office, and succeeded to his uncle's estate on his death.

With the closing of his accounts with Jackson, Branfill & Goddard, William Braund, however, severed a connection with the Portuguese trade which had existed for at least twenty years, but when he had dropped his connections in the woollen trade he was already half-way on his change. From pure dealing in bullion to pure finance as a specialized underwriter was a small step, and with the conclusion of his Portuguese trade, Braund left the ranks of the merchant and entered those of the financier. When he left the Portuguese trade he was able to turn both his capital and his enterprise almost entirely into two channels where they had been already running for some time—into the supply of shipping for the East India Company, and into marine insurance at Lloyd's coffee-house. In the former, where he had interests throughout all the years covered by these accounts, his position was that of a more or less passive capitalist, though until 1760 he had been closely associated with his younger brother, Samuel, who was one of the *entrepreneurs* of the business, a prominent member of the powerful class of " ships' husbands." After 1763 he sank more capital in ship-owning, but took no active part in its management. His personal activities, on the other hand, concentrated on his underwriting business at Lloyd's. From the date at which his accounts begin, and clearly for some time before, he had done some underwriting at Lloyd's, as many merchants then did, but it was not till he turned from the woollens trade to the bullion trade, which made far less demands on his time, that he was able to become a steady underwriter, writing (except for week-ends and Mondays) daily at the coffee-house. He gained considerably in the years of war risks and war premiums, though much of his capital was employed in the bullion trade. When he left the bullion trade he was able to turn most of it to insurance, and even in the post-war days of falling premiums and changed estimation of every kind of risk he built himself up a solid, though never a great, place on the insurance market. A " representative merchant," he was also a representative financier, for just as the years of his activities as a woollens and bullion dealer were those of general activity, so the years of his growing underwriting business were formative ones in the rise of Lloyd's.

The change was, moreover, a shrewd one in the circumstances of the time, as the course of the Portuguese trade of the next half-century was to show, for the great days of the Portugal trade were definitely passing away.

EXPORT OF WOOLLENS, 1753.

Date of Shipping.	Goods in Bales.	Numbers.	Date of Net Price.	First Cost and Charges. £ s. d.	Net Price. £ s. d.	Profit. £ s. d.
Feb. 12	6 ord. long ells	405-10	Mar. 21, 1754	286 18 0	300 19 0	14 1 0
Mar. 27	12 long bays	413-24	July 7, 1753	903 6 4	933 7 0	30 0 8
			June 2			
Mar. 27	9 long bays	426-34	June 22, 1753	665 7 6	733 0 0	67 12 6
			July 7			
Mar. 27	2 long bays	435-6	July 7, 1753	172 14 6	190 0 0	17 5 6
Apr. 2	2 Durants	437-8	Mar. 25, 1754	182 0 0	209 0 0	27 0 0
Apr. 2	4 Shalloons	439-42	Mar. 25, 1754	359 9 10	372 4 0	12 14 2
May 10	11 Long Bays	443-53	July 7, 1753	573 5 10	672 10 0	99 4 2
			Nov. 14			
June 8	1 scarlet cloth	454	April 8, 1754	111 11 0	109 6 0	Loss.2 5 0
July 7	1 Durants	455	Dec. 31, 1754	80 3 0	94 0 0	13 17 0
*Aug. 15	5 blankets	(See note)	—	(151 1 0)	—	
Aug. 28	4 long bays	460-3	Nov. 14, 1753	172 16 0	198 4 0	25 8 0
Aug. 28	2 Durants	464-5	Nov. 24, 1753	175 5 9	201 10 0	26 4 3
Aug. 28	1 Shalloons	466	Nov. 24, 1753	83 17 0	84 11 0	0 14 0
Oct. 31	1 scarlet cloth	467	April 8, 1754	111 11 0	131 3 0	19 12 0
Oct. 31	1 blue cloth	468	April 8, 1754	86 13 0	92 10 0	5 17 0
Oct. 31	1 shalloons	469	Dec. 31, 1754	87 19 4	91 0 0	3 0 8
Dec. 13	15 long bays	470-84	April 8, 1754	956 16 4	1,109 13 0	152 16 8
Dec. 13	2 Colchester bays	485-6	April 8, 1754	117 2 8	127 0 0	9 17 4
Dec. 13	6 long bays	487-92	April 8, 1754	335 18 7	374 18 0	39 1 5
Total	86 bales.			5,462 13 8	6,024 15 0	564 6 4

Average profit, approx. 10⅜ per cent.

* NOTE.—For this consignment of blankets, Philip Jackson of London paid cash on August 31, 1753. together with 5s. commission. It was therefore bought and shipped, it is to be presumed, either on his behalf or on that of Jackson, Branfil & Goddard themselves, for whom he may have been acting.

Belvedere House, Erith, Kent.

17

SAMSON GIDEON: EIGHTEENTH CENTURY JEWISH FINANCIER

SAMSON GIDEON,[2] the most noteworthy financier, Jew or Christian, of mid-eighteenth century England, was born in 1699, entered business in 1719 and died in 1762. His active career covered the period in which England, freed from internal political turmoil (though still threatened from time to time, as in 1745, by dynastic revolt) and successful in foreign war, was expanding in wealth and enterprise and was laying the groundwork of her nineteenth century predominance. He gained his prominence despite, not because of, the circumstances of his birth and upbringing, and his position when gained was not one to which the age awarded social recognition. It was gained by mastery in a new, and to his contemporaries a somewhat sinister craft, that of a jobber in the rising market in stocks and shares, and by qualities of mind and character that made him supreme in it. In consequence he appears fitfully in the memoirs, letters and pamphlets of the time as a powerful but somewhat equivocal figure, and we should willingly exchange much of the surviving material about respectable but mediocre peers and minor politicians for that which would enable us to reconstruct fully the career of Samson Gideon. For it epitomizes a very important aspect of the rising forces of finance and of that strange, autonomous organisation the London money market, an institution which, as much as anything, enabled England to survive the eighteenth century wars and ensured her nineteenth century hegemony.

Unfortunately the main source of such information is sealed to us. At the beginning of the nineteenth century John Eardley Wilmot wrote a short memoir entitled *A Memoir of the Life of Samson Gideon Esq. of Spalding Co. Lincoln and Belvedere, Kent,* published in J. Nichols *Illustrations of the Literary History of the Eighteenth Century,* 1817-58.[3] It was based on papers then in the possession of Gideon's son, Lord Eardley, and makes it clear that a great deal of his correspondence and business papers then survived. But with the extinction of the male line they seem to have disappeared, and all attempts to trace them have so far failed. The short memoir based on them, a personal letter in private possession[4] and some correspondence with ministers and others in various collections[5] is all we can call on to support the references in public records, pamphlets,[6] and the casual allusions in contemporary Press and memoirs.

The main events of his life are, however, known. He was a member of the far-flung and distinguished Portuguese Jewish family of Abudiente. His father Rehuel

---

[1] Paper read before the Jewish Historical Society of England on 25th April, 1949.
[2] He spelt his own name thus ; though others frequently wrote of him as Sampson, the spelling which he favoured for his son.
[3] Vol. VI, pp. 277-84.
[4] See below p. 396. This letter is among a small number of family papers preserved at Bedwell Park, Hatfield, Herts., where they came by inheritance with Samson Gideon's collection of pictures from Belvedere in 1847 to Sir Culling Eardley Smith, son of the second daughter of Lord Eardley. Two Kit-Kats of Samson are also preserved there. I am indebted to Col. Fremantle of Bedwell Park for this information and material.
[5] There is a good deal of correspondence in the Newcastle MSS., British Museum and in the correspondence of Sir Thomas Drury, preserved in the papers of the Marquess of Lothian (Historical MSS. Commission Vol. 62).
[6] There are a number of pamphlets, most of them attacking Gideon's financial activities between 1746 and 1751, and he was not spared by pamphleteer or caricaturist during the agitation against the Jewish Naturalization Bill (see I. Solomons', 'Satirical and Political Prints on the Jews Naturalization Bill.' Trans. Jew. Hist. Soc. of Eng. VI).

Abudiente, probably born near Hamburg, came to England from Barbados where the Sephardi Jews had a strong settlement.[1]   He had already anglicized his name for many purposes to Rowland Gideon and he became a freeman[2] of the City of London by redemption in 1698, the year before Samson's birth.   His son described him as a West Indian merchant, and he would seem to have been a man of some wealth.   He died in 1722.   At his death Samson, aged 23, had already been in business for at least three years.   In July 1719, the son estimated his own capital (as he was to do annually thereafter for forty years) at £1,500.   Twelve months later it had grown to £7,901.[3]   There is no sign that on his father's death Samson stepped into a family business.   Indeed, though he seems from time to time to have engaged in mercantile ventures, it is clear from the beginning that he turned his attention to operations of a speculative kind, carried out in Change Alley and at Garraway's and Jonathan's coffee houses, in lottery tickets, in government securities, and in the stocks of the only three joint stock companies then commonly dealt in, the Bank, the East India Company and the South Sea Company.

The events of the South Sea Bubble year of 1720 and its sequel gave him every opportunity and by 1727 he could provide for his two sisters portions of £2,000 apiece, those of well-to-do City girls of the period, and by 1729 he estimated his capital at £25,000.   As a fortune of £50,000 was at that time considered a substantial achievement for a prominent London merchant after a life-time of commercial success, it can be seen that this young man of thirty was doing well and one can understand the suspicion with which jobbers and brokers like him were regarded by the established merchants of the City.   The same year he improved his status by gaining recognition as one of twelve Jewish brokers officially licensed by the City (out of 100 "sworn brokers" so recognised).[4]   By 1740, by a combination of broking and jobbing in English, Dutch, and even in French funds, by marine insurance and other activities, he had raised his fortune to £44,650.

In these years of his life Gideon might have stood for an example of his contemporaries' idea of a 'stock-jobber'—a creature "as savage as their Bulls and Bears,"[5] who by some sinister process made "barren money breed money," as Aristotle and the mediaeval anti-usury writers would have said.   It may be added that much of what he did was, or became, strictly speaking illegal.   By the Act of William III by which the "sworn brokers" were established, they were strictly forbidden to appear on Change Alley or to job in stock themselves.[6]   Neither Gideon nor his contemporaries, Jewish or Christian, paid the slightest attention to this prohibition, nor to the formidable penalties which they were (on paper) risking by ignoring it.   Still more, in 1734 the pressure of the lesser merchants, reinforced by the prejudice of the country gentry and memories of the South Sea disaster, pushed through Parliament a bill intended to prevent "the infamous practice of stock-jobbing."[7]   It prohibited all the dealings in futures on

[1] W. S. Samuel, *The Jewish Colonists in Barbados in the Year* 1680, 1936, pp. 37-8.   He had been for some time, first in Boston and then on the Island of St. Nevis.
[2] *Ibid*.   He was made free of the Painters-Stainers Company.   Mr. Samuel points out that he was in 1702 *Gabay* (Treasurer) of the new Bevis Marks Synagogue, and that his contributions would appear to be those of a wealthy man.   Samson's mother was his second wife, Esther do Porto, whom he married in 1693, and who survived him.
[3] The annual figures quoted are from Eardley Wilmot's study. Nichols, *Literary Anecdotes* VI.
[4] Guildhall Records.   Brokers Admissions, 1708-1869.
[5] T. Mortimer, *Every Man His Own Broker*, 1761, p. xii.
[7] 8 and 9 Wm. III c. 32.
[6] 7 Geo. II c. 8.

which the speculative activities of Gideon and his like were based.   This prohibition was, however, as ineffective as the first.   All that resulted from it was that an extra risk was added to the transactions, since no debt so contracted was recoverable at common law,[1] and that the more disreputable elements in Change Alley were strengthened, until the rise of the organised Stock Exchange after 1772 gradually established the regulations and sanctions which the law had failed to provide.

It was in 1742 that there opened up for Gideon a new and rich field of operations for the skilful jobber.   It arose from the needs of the two great wars, that of the Austrian Succession 1742-8 (with the Jacobite rising of 1745 in the middle), and the Seven Years War, 1756-63.   About this time too, Gideon had set his foot on the social ladder he meant to climb.   Like so many who achieved wealth in the eighteenth century, he formed the ambition of using it to found a family which could take its place among those of the landed classes.   In his case, and in the circumstances of the time, this meant ultimately the cutting himself off from his religion and from the associates of his past. His first step was to marry a Christian wife, one Jane, daughter of Charles Ermell Esq., and to see that each of the children in turn, including his heir, should be, as he boasted, "baptized by the Sub-dean of St. Paul's few days after their birth."[2]   Three children survived, Elizabeth, Susanna and Sampson.

The opportunities provided by war were primarily those resulting from the loans which the Government had to raise to finance it.   The eighteenth century system of taxation was highly inelastic and any unusual strain on the Exchequer led to a recourse to public borrowing.   In Marlborough's wars the form which this borrowing took became standardized into the two forms of the funded loans, each sanctioned by Act of Parliament, and the short term loans and anticipations of revenue which took the form of such instruments (some of them extensions of ordinary peace-time practice) as Exchequer bills, Ordnance Debentures and Navy tickets.

The development of the funded debt was one of England's greatest eighteenth century assets.   It enabled the English Government to mobilize the private wealth not only of its own people, but of the capitalists of Europe.   The Dutch were particularly prominent among them,[3] but by far the greatest source of supply was the City of London. The people from which the subscriptions were raised are of significance for the purpose of this paper.   The Government of the day, and in particular the Treasury, always had to keep up a connexion with the City.   It had to satisfy its normal need of short-term credit through the monied companies, and it always had remittances, contracts and other financial business on hand.   For this purpose a contact between Government and the "monied interest" was maintained with profit to both sides, and at a time when

---

[1] E.g. in the crash of East India Stock in 1769 William Waller wrote to his friend Warren Hastings, 21 November 1769 : "I had an opportunity of serving a rascally broker with broker's equity. After he had delivered in my account, he stopt [i.e. stopped payment], the majority of his principals not being able to pay their differences [margins].   He however to entitle himself to go on with his business offered them a composition of ten shillings in the pound which he paid—and then applied to me and one or two more to pay him our differences.   You must know in these cases if anyone has a good account he never receives and so it is if the broker die, the Executor never pays—in both which cases the principal who has a bad account is not brought to pay.   I pleaded this equity and told Mr. Broker he did not break on my account, but thought I was fool enough to pay . . ." (Brit. Mus. MS. 29132 f 349 v.).   Recovery could in some circumstances, however, be obtained at Equity in the Court of Exchequer.

[2] Brit. Mus. Add MS. 33055 f. 219.

[3] C. Wilson, *Anglo-Dutch Commerce and Finance in the Eighteenth Century*, Cambridge, 1941, pp. 137 seq.

politics was dominated by "management" this interest achieved a strongly political flavour.   The opportunity to subscribe to Government loans or to obtain Government contracts was much prized, and it was recognized by the leading merchants of the City that they were most likely to get these opportunities if they could be useful to ministers in politics as well as finance.   Hence prominent merchants found it worth while to expend considerable sums in buying seats in Parliament, and those to whom contracts went were either such men or the leaders of the great Companies with whom the Treasury wished to keep on terms.   Hence under normal conditions the Jewish community of London, despite their considerable liquid capital and their useful continental connexions, were excluded from this profitable form of business, for the prejudice of the time kept them off the boards of the great companies and they were ineligible for Parliament.

When the needs of war became compelling, however, the Government had to change its attitude, since it needed all the money it could get, and it is here that Samson Gideon first got his chance.   The normal procedure for floating a long-term loan was the "Closed Subscription."   The Treasury invited applications from the individuals with whom they were in touch.   The terms of the loan were discussed and settled and each individual put in an application on behalf of a number of would-be subscribers known as his "list."   Some of them spoke for the foreign and particularly the Dutch subscribers; prominent Government contractors often included a number of M.P's. among the names on their list.[1] Private bankers in touch with Government would submit a list of favoured customers.   The subscriptions were paid then as now in instalments, and as soon as the receipts had been given out the "scrip" began to be the subject of dealings in the market where it was known as "Light Horse"[2] and where the Government followed with anxious eyes the often erratic course of its prices.

The importance which Gideon achieved after the outbreak of the war in 1742 was twofold ; for the first time he brought together and organized a "list" of Jewish sub-scribers whose application was accepted in 1742, and whose participation continued and became more important as the war went on ; he also became increasingly prominent as an adviser of the Government on the floating of loans and all matters concerning their placing on the market.[3]

A document submitted to Ministers by Gideon outlines his contributions to the raising of loans in these years.   For the £3,000,000 loan of 1742, after the declaration of war with Spain, he produced a list of more than £600,000; for that of 1743 his list was for "a much larger sum "; in 1744 £300,000 was allotted to his list ;[4] in 1745, a year of great difficulty, he played a similar role ; in 1746, when the financial panic accompanying the Jacobite rising threatened disaster to the loan, he made himself responsible for subscriptions of no less than £1,070,000 and in 1747 and 1748 he stood behind the nominally "open" subscriptions (i.e. subscriptions open to all who cared to inscribe their names in books laid open for this purpose) sponsored by Sir John Barnard.[5] It is not surprising that by 1745 Gideon's capital had risen from the £44,500 of 1740 to £82,200.   It was the events of 1746 and the succeeding war years, however, which

---

[1] L. B. Namier, *The Structure of Politics at the Accession of George III*, 1929, i, 68 n. 2.
[2] Mortimer, *op. cit.* pp. 147-8.   When more instalments had been paid up it was known as "heavy horse."
[3] I am indebted to Mr. Paul Emden for drawing my attention to the importance of this latter point.
[4] *Gentleman's Magazine*, 1744, p. 225.
[5] Taken from a document (Brit. Mus. Add MS. 33055 ff 219 seq.) which I have reproduced in full in 'Samson Gideon and the Reduction of Interest, 1749-50' *Econ. Hist. Rev.* XVI (1946), pp. 15 seq. See below, pp. 399-413.

were the making of his fortune and which brought him into close personal touch with those responsible for the country's public finance. In 1742 he had some contact with Sandys,[1] then Chancellor of the Exchequer; but it was with Henry Pelham, Sandys' successor and one of the greatest finance ministers of the century, that he had the longest and closest association.

In the second half of 1745 the Young Pretender landed in Scotland, confident of French aid if he could bring about a coup d'état. He was at first successful and advanced as far as Derby before he turned back and was finally defeated. The news of the first reverses caused a panic on the London market—its course can be traced in Gideon's own letters to his client Sir Thomas Drury[2]—there was real danger of a run on the Bank, and a growing disinclination to accept Bank notes. The attempt of the Bank to aid itself by calling on a species of guarantors who then existed, the holders of the so-called "bank circulation"[3] for the circulation of Exchequer Bills merely added to the panic. At this crisis four prominent City men decided to sink their differences and to rally the City. Samson Gideon, Theodore Janssen, later the City's Chamberlain, Sir John Barnard, representative of the lesser merchants and normally a great hater of the great finance interests and of Gideon in particular, and another[4] combined to call a meeting to restore credit. Gideon later claimed that he

> proposed the Subscription for circulating of Bank notes and restoring their credit, and was one of the four persons that carried on that Association, and there is now in Mr. Gideon's hands the original papers and the signatures of above thirteen hundred merchants and others who signed in little more than óne day which had that good effect that should be remembered.[5]

When the danger to the Bank was over, moreover, the crisis still continued. In the first place the Bank who usually advanced the Government money in anticipation of the Land Tax was quite unable to do so, and here once again Gideon took the lead and organized a list of subscribers to fill the gap, though in this he was only partly successful.[6] In the second place at the end of 1745 and beginning of 1746 Pelham was struggling to raise a loan, and the £1,070,000 which Gideon provided was a tribute to the courage as well as the foresight of those who followed his lead. Both were rewarded. When news arrived of the defeat of the rebels near Stirling it was realized that they would clear a very handsome profit, a fact which aroused an uproar in the City, and even led to a demand that the terms of the loan should be altered. Pelham very properly stood out against this demand, but for the loan of the following year (1747) he came to terms with his city critics by agreeing to an "open" subscription under the general management of Sit John Barnard, Gideon's enemy. It was characteristic of Pelham's skill as a negotiator, however, that he succeeded in maintaining the services of Gideon and the rest of the financial interest at the same time, and the combination of these forces brought the loan of 1747 to success, though even their combined efforts could not prevent heavy strain on the weaker subscribers in the loan of 1748, the last year of the war.[7]

Besides his subscriptions to the loans of these years Gideon had performed other

[1] *Ibid.*
[2] Hist. MSS. Comm. Rept. MSS. of Marquess of Lothian. Correspondence of Sir Thomas Drury pp. 148-52.
[3] Cf. J. Clapham, *The Bank of England, A History*, Cambridge, 1944, pp. 68 seq.
[4] I have been unable to identify the fourth.
[5] Quoted "Samson Gideon and the Reduction of Interest" *loc. cit.* p. 400.
[6] *Ibid. loc. cit.* p. 406.
[7] *Ibid.* p. 408.

services. He had signed the loyal address got up by the City in 1745 and served actively on a voluntary committee to supply the soldiers in Scotland with equipment and comforts.[1] He had also put at the Treasury's disposal his financial ingenuity in proposals for making the loans attractive to subscribers, and at least in 1744 he had played a part in the awkward business of floating the loan by the purchase on the market at a critical moment of a number of the lottery tickets which formed part of the loan, to keep up their price.[2] Equally important was the steadying effect of his personality on Change Alley. It is from the crisis of 1745-6 that the well authenticated story arises, that when a private banker, Thomas Snow, affected by the prevailing nervousness, asked him for the repayment of a considerable loan, he sent the sum by return in bank notes wrapped round a bottle of hartshorn.[3] By the end of the war Gideon, the interloper into the ranks of the Government's monied friends, had become one of its chief financial advisers. When Pelham came to undertake his famous Conversion Scheme of 1749-50, Gideon was one of his most active coadjutors.[4]

His private wealth had increased notably as a result of his public services. Between 1745 and 1750 his capital more than doubled, standing at £180,000 in the latter year, and he now began in earnest to establish himself as a country gentleman. In 1747 he obtained a grant of arms.[5] When Belvedere House, Erith, Kent, came on the market after the death of Lord Baltimore he purchased it as his country house (his town house for many years was in Lincoln's Inn Fields), choosing, as merchants were wont, one within easy reach of the City. It was a fine house with superb views over the Thames and one which he improved still further.[6] About the same time he purchased the Manor of Spalding in Lincolnshire, a purchase preceded or accompanied by private Acts necessitated, it would seem, by default of title,—the land formed part of the estate of the Duke of Monmouth, forfeited for high treason.[7] These Acts seem to be the basis of the unfounded tradition that, despite legislation to the contrary, there was still uncertainty about the right of Jews to own land, and that Gideon used his ministerial connexions to obtain special protection.[8] In his will in 1760 he speaks of property in the county of Buckinghamshire as well as in Lincoln[9] and it seems likely he had properties in other counties too.[10] It was at this time too that he began to pay his first tribute to

---

[1] With Theodore Janssen who originated the Committee jointly with him (Brit. Mus. Add MS. 32862 f. 72).
[2] *Hist. MSS. Comm. Rept. loc. cit.* p. 152. Gideon, writing on 23 November 1745, of the low price to which lottery tickets had fallen remarked "The same would have happened last year had I not taken care to prevent it, which might have been done this year by buying about 2,000 tickets, the want of which I wish may not be of fatal consequence in raising the next supplies." It became customary in succeeding years for the Ministry to make arrangements for purchases of tickets and "scrip" in this way by private bankers.
[3] The story often quoted, was told in a letter to Gideon's grandson by Robert the grandson of Thomas Snow on 9 December 1821 and is preserved at Bedwell Park.
[4] "Samson Gideon and the Conversion of Interest" *loc. cit.*
[5] *Anglo-Jewish Notabilities, their Arms and Testamentary Dispositions*, Jew. Hist. Soc. of Eng. 1949, p. 94.
[6] E. Hasted, *History and Topographical Survey of the County of Kent* 1. 198.
[7] Private Acts 22 Geo. II c. 19 (1749) and 23 Geo. II c. 5 (1750).
[8] E.g. J. Picciotto, *Sketches of Anglo-Jewish History* (1875), p. 62.
[9] Somerset House, Caesar 59.
[10] A well-written and charmingly illuminated manuscript survives (Brit. Mus. Add MS. 35172 a and b) entitled "Surveys and Particulars of the Estates of Sir Sampson Gideon, baronet, in the Counties of Cambridge, Lincoln, Huntingdon and Northampton, 1782" by George Maxwell Gravely, Herts., 2 vols. Though there is nothing specifically stated, the introduction would seem to suggest that these properties (some of them reclaimed fenland) had been in the same estate for a period long enough to bring them back to Samson's date. By 1782 the estate had fallen into very bad condition.

the visual arts (as a young man he had shown some literary interests for he was one of the contributors to Daniel Lopez Laguna's poetical translations of the Psalms)[1] and he proceeded to lay the foundations of his collection of pictures which was described as "though not numerous, yet . . . very valuable ; containing none but pieces which are original of the greatest masters, and some of them very capital.[2]"

The time was now coming when he might think of seeking some relief from the unremitting strain of his business. Sometime before 1755 he had decided to withdraw from it altogether.[3] This decision may have been precipitated by his final breach with his co-religionists. In 1753 he formally withdrew from membership of the Portuguese Jewish Synagogue. The immediate cause of the breach was the fiasco of the Jew's Naturalization Bill of that year, which the Government had to withdraw in consequence of violent and factious political agitation. Gideon was no supporter of the bill. As he wrote at the time :—

> The affair you mention does not in the least concern me, having always declared my sentiments against any innovation ; but contrary to my wishes and opinion it was solicited in folly and want of knowledge, granted in levity and good nature as a matter of no consequence, and now prosecuted with malice to serve a political purpose. It would give me concern as an Englishman if I apprehended any danger to my country, but as I look upon it in a trifling light, I am perfectly easy and shall not choose to meddle either way.[4]

He was therefore the more indignant when, as the result of an indiscretion of the Jewish authorities, he became the centre of vituperative public attack,[5] and he retaliated by withdrawing from the Community.[6] This withdrawal was, however, but the culmination of a long process. How complete the breach was can be guessed from the will he drew up later, in which, among a variety of executors and trustees, there is not one Jewish name.[7]

Gideon's intention to retire from business by the comparatively early age of 55 was thwarted by political events and his own ambitions. His old patron, Henry Pelham, of whom he always spoke with respect and affection, had died in 1754, but his 'connexion' remained in power and the Duke of Newcastle and the Duke of Devonshire continued to welcome Gideon's support and advice. In 1755, looking at the ominous international situation, he let the Secretary of the Treasury know that if the Government were obliged to raise a loan for the war which was looming he would be ready, despite his retirement, to assist by "offering any proposition or supporting any one that shall be advised by others."[8] This offer opened up to him a scene of public activity almost as strenuous as that of his earlier war experiences. His new role was, however, rather different. His fortune once again gained greatly from his exertions. By 1759 (the last year in which we have an estimate) it seems to have been about £350,000—but he was no longer struggling to increase it ; he often represented as much the point of view of the holders

[1] A. M. Hyamson. *The Sephardim of England* (1951), p. 129.
[2] Hasted *op. cit.* He bought a number from Robert Walpole's collection at Houghton which Horace Walpole was selling (H. Walpole *Letters* ed. P. Toynbee iii, 60. H. Walpole to H. Mann 18 June, 1751).
[3] See Brit. Mus. Add MS. 32859 f. 9v. J. West to Newcastle 6 September 1755.
[4] Quoted Eardley Wilmot *op. cit.* p. 283.
[5] I. Solomons, "Satirical and Political Prints on the Jews' Naturalization Bill 1753," *Trans Jew. Hist. Soc. of Eng.* Vol. VI.
[6] For this see A. M. Hyamson, *op. cit.* (1951). p. 128 *seq.*
[7] His executors were Beeston Long, West India merchant, Sir Francis Gosling Kt., Alderman and banker, Robert Gosling his partner, and the widow Jane Gideon.
[8] Brit. Mus. Add MS. 32859 f. 9v. J. West to Newcastle, 6 September 1755.

of existing government securities as that of the subscribers to new ones,[1] and he was moreover bent on using his financial power for non-financial ends. He saw his way to bringing to a triumphant conclusion his struggle for position among the landed classes for his family and himself, by obtaining a peerage or baronetcy in exchange for his services.

The Seven Years War was far the most expensive that had yet been fought and imposed heavy strains on the immature fiscal system of the country. Moreover, since the death of Pelham, there was no strong finance minister in control and the unhappy Duke of Newcastle, on whom the main responsibility fell, was constitutionally unfit for the firm and clear-sighted actions necessary in the war's recurrent crises. Each year a loan had to be raised, and in steadily mounting sums. Each year the Duke's nerves threatened indecision in bargaining and weakness in the actual flotation of the loan. Gideon each year made proposals to the Treasury on the terms of the loan, subscribed to it, and, above all, came to the Government's rescue when it ran into difficulties by negotiating with the Bank on its behalf (as in 1756 and 1759).[2] by filling up the subscription (as in 1756)[3] and by steadying the nerve of the Ministers and City alike. The greatest test of his services was in 1759 when the Government was trying to raise what was then the unprecedented sum of £6,600,000.[4] All went well at first in obtaining subscriptions for a loan for the terms of which Gideon was largely responsible;[5] but to attract the large amount required the Treasury had given in to demands that the subscription be an 'open' one,[6] and an unduly high proportion of the subscribers were entirely dependent on credit for the payment of their instalments. An unfortunate coincidence of a heavy drain on specie to meet requirements abroad with demands on the banks for accommodation to meet the third instalment of payments led in March and April to a sudden and alarming credit crisis which threatened both the capacity of the Bank of England to meet demands on it in gold[7] and the receipt of the funds necessary for the prosecution of the war.[8] The Bank was forced to cease discounting bills and to threaten a call on "bank circulation."

The Duke of Newcastle was at his wits' end; he asked advice from all sides, in-including the Bank of England, and received for the most part panicky or impracticable suggestions. That shrewd observer Henry Fox instructed his broker to sell his holding as he had "no opinion of the Subscription : I don't think it will grow much better,

---

[1] *Ibid.* Add MSS. 32859-32938, *passim* especially Add MS. 32890.

[2] The loans passed in 29 Geo. II c. 7 and 32 Geo. II c. 10. With regard to the first Gideon mentions that on 26th January "I waited upon the Governors and Directors of the Bank by orders from the Duke of Newcastle, to assure them and desire they would declare in his Grace's name that no more than two million shd be raised by way of funding, or any *other Lottery* allowed of" (Brit. Mus. Add MS. 32864 f. 44, S. Gideon to J. West 28 March 1756).

[3] On 3 February 1756, Gideon wrote that he would come to town and see Newcastle about the loan, subscriptions for which were coming in slowly; on 5 February he wrote, "Permit me to acquaint Your Grace that I have subscribed £— more and filled the subscription." (Brit. Mus. Add MS. 32862 f. 362). The total of his list for this 2£m loan was £107,960 (*Ibid.* Add MS. 32864 f. 45).

[4] In 1757 £3,000,000 was raised; in 1758 £5,000,000. The sums raised increased to £8,000,000 in 1760 and £12,000,000 in 1761 and 1762.

[5] Brit. Mus. Add MS. 32886-7 *passim*.

[6] *Ibid.* 32890 f. 227. Newcastle to W. Legge 21 April 1759. "To be sure the fatality of giving in to an open subscription has hurt us."

[7] *Ibid.* f. 37v. 12 April 1759, Notes of meeting between Newcastle and representatives of the Bank. "They fear they may be obliged to pay silver; which would be destruction to them."

[8] *Ibid.* f. 288v. Sir John Barnard 23 April 1759, proposing extreme measures concludes that in this way "it may be possible to go on this year with the War."

the Duke of Newcastle consults too many people about it."[1] Gideon's help was very different. He came up from Belvedere to find out the cause of the fall of Stock prices which he thought must be due to bad war news, discovered that a major cause was the fear of a call on "bank circulation," wrote a firm letter to the Governor and Deputy Governor of the Bank reminding them that they were "the very vitals of credit," pointing out the dangers of such a step and suggesting alternative measures,[2] and he kept in close touch with the Secretary of the Treasury.[3] The immediate results were highly satisfactory. His letter to the bank, as he boasted,

> proved an immediate stiptick to the fall of Stocks, they presently rose near three per cent. and the Bank Circulation fifty shillings, as I was credibly informed, for although there might not be a call upon the latter intended, it was courantly so reported upon the Exchange and everywhere for five days without being contradicted till after the receipt of my letter ; perhaps that might apprize and give them an opportunity to declare there was no foundation for such report, which indeed has had an extreem good effect . . .[4]

Equally salutary was his bracing influence upon Newcastle. He strongly deplored any suggestion of improving the terms offered the subscribers. "Should not be surprized" he wrote sardonically, "if some of them should expect a clause, that Parliament will make good to us our losings (if any be) and secure to us a profit at all events."[5] He had already said that, should they lose by this venture, he for one would "eat my pudding and hold my toung (sic)."[6] By the end of the month the crisis was over and the third payment was assured.[7] No-one reading the Duke of Newcastle's correspondence could fail to conclude that the crisis was surmounted largely through Gideon's courage and skill.

This crowning service also brought him the crowning award for his social ambition. In 1757 he had married his daughter Elizabeth to Viscount Gage with a portion of £40,000. In 1758, after winning the royal thanks for his part in raising a loan for the King in his capacity of Elector of Hanover,[8] he approached the Duke of Devonshire with the suggestion that he be given a baronetcy as a reward for his services. It was in support of this demand that he drew up the list of financial services already referred to,[9] and he prefaced it with a statement of what precedents he could find.

> Antonio Lopez Suasso native of Holland professing the Jewish religion was in a Catholic country created a Baron by the King of Spain and the Patent sets forth that the title shall descend to male or female, not withstanding their professing themselves to be Jews.
>
> The Emperor of Germany confirmed the above and granted him a new Patent by the title of Antonio Lopez Suasso Baron de Avernes le Gross.[10]

---

[1] *Ibid.* f. 343. Extract of letter from Henry Fox to his broker, 25 April 1759—sent in to Newcastle by Carrington.
[2] *Ibid.* ff. 164-5. Gideon to Governor and Deputy Governor of the Bank, [17 April 1759].
[3] *Ibid.* f. 162, J. West to Newcastle, 18 April 1759.
[4] *Ibid.* f. 233, S. Gideon to Newcastle, 21 April 1759.
[5] *Ibid.* f. 233v.
[6] *Ibid.* 32888 f. 295, S. Gideon to J. West [2 March 1759].
[7] *Ibid.* 32890 f. 361. Memorandum by Newcastle for the King 27 April 1759.
[8] *Ibid.* 32884 f. 160. Newcastle to S. Gideon, 26 September 1758. Correspondence about this loan may be found throughout the volume. Gideon refers to it in his list of services ('Samson Gideon and the Reduction of Interest' p.401).
[9] P.390, n. 5. above.
[10] In 1676. The title was d'Avernas le Gras, *Jewish Encyclopedia.*

Mr. Diego Pereira de Agular [Aguilar] a merchant and native of Portugal and free denizen in England, professing the Jewish religion and educating all his children in the faith he embraced some years since, was made very lately a Baron of the Empire.[1]

Whereas Samson the son of Rowland Gideon (a West India merchant and a free and livery man of London) was born in England, married an English Protestant, his sons and daughters were all baptized by the Sub-Dean of St. Paul's few days after their birth, were strictly educated and so many of them that are living continue to profess Christianity.

Creations of peerages and baronetcies were still at that time comparatively rare, and were strictly in the King's hands. The award of a title to a notorious stock jobber would have caused comment in itself, his being also a Jew was held to make it quite impossible. The Duke of Devonshire replied with a civil refusal, acknowledging Gideon's services and reporting that

the King seemed extremely well disposed, spoke very handsomely of you and said he should have no objection himself to oblige you, but as you was not bred up in the religion of the country he was afraid it would make a noise and that in a time of confusion and public distress as the present is, he was afraid they would make an ill use of it and therefore desired that I would inform you in the civilest manner that it was not convenient for him to comply with your request.[2]

Gideon accepted the rebuff, but was not diverted from his aim. By December of the same year, while arranging with the Duke of Newcastle for the loan of 1759 he had made a new proposal, that the baronetcy should be bestowed upon his son, and on that date he forwarded a certificate of the latter's baptism.[3] As the negotiations for the loan continued and as Newcastle's fears of failure rose he pressed harder. In January he urged the Minister to press his claims on the King "one word at this crisis will do, which, if neglected, may not be ever recovered, his father has it at heart and dreads being disappointed, be the object of his desire great or small."[4] In April when Gideon came to town to the rescue of the Treasury, the Secretary of the Treasury tells Newcastle that he "is very thankful to your Grace for the continuance of your goodness to him."[5] In May 1759 his son, an thirteen year old boy at Eton, was created a baronet. His father's letter to him on this occasion has been preserved and illustrates clearly and comprehensively the ambitions actuating him.

Belvedere May [1759]

Dear Sampson,

The King as been pleased to order his Letters Patents to promote you to the dignity of a baronet. It is the lowest hereditary honor, but the first step. I have hope that by your *own merit* you will go higher, shall otherwise wish his Majesty had not been so gracious.

I have always recommended to you the practice and title of an honest man. That only will render you honorable with the wise and good, reconcile your conduct to yourself, and be most acceptable to God.

You are allowed to charge your coat with the arms of Ulster which are *in a field argent a hand gules*. Let them be a constant warning before your eyes that if ever you sign a bond, paper, or instrument derogating from truth, your duty to the King, or destructive to your estate, that very moment you commit a crime as much to be detested as a hand in blood.

[1] In 1747. *Ibid* and A. M. Hyamson *op. cit.* pp. 101-2.
[2] Brit. Mus. Add MS. 32886 f. 243-243v, 13 June 1758.
[3] *Ibid.* f. 241. 9 December 1758.
[4] *Ibid.* 32887 f. 276, 21 January 1759.
[5] *Ibid.* 32890 f. 162. J. West to Newcastle, 18 April 1759.

Behave, my dear boy, as you have hitherto towards your Master, school fellows and everybody.

Remember the Proverb "When Pride cometh then cometh Shame, but with the lowly is Wisdom."[1]

Johnson in his farce points at the vice strongly. "Pride is an adder's egg, laid in the breast of every man, but hatched by none but fools."[2]

Mama, Lord and Lady Gage, and Sister Sukey join in joy and love to you.

Your affectionate Father
Samson Gideon.[3]

Gideon had now achieved his ambitions and, though he was only sixty, he was an old man. He continued to assist the Government in its financial measures until a few months before his death of dropsy in October 1762,[4] but his life was drawing to a close. In 1760 he drew up a will[5] which is, from the personal point of view, one of the, most interesting things we know of him. Much of it was concerned with making such provision as he could for the foundation of his family. His lands were preserved from the possibility of dispersal by dissolute heirs by the strictest of strict settlements.[6] Dignified provision was made for his wife, his daughter Lady Gage and her husband and heirs, if any, and for his unmarried daughter. If all other heirs failed the estate was to go (rather surprisingly to our views but less so to his contemporaries)[7] to the Duke of Devonshire. He left legacies to the hospitals on whose boards he sat, to more distant relatives, servants and to charities—characteristically they included both the Sons of the Clergy and a Jewish orphanage. Then came the point of real interest. He left £1,000 to the Portuguese Synagogue of Bevis Marks with a request that he be buried with full and specified rites in the "Jews burial ground of Mile End." If this were refused him he wished for Christian burial at Spalding, and in this event made bequests for the poor of that parish and of Erith. When his request was considered, a member of the community came forward and announced that ever since Gideon's withdrawal, he had made on the latter's behalf an anonymous annual gift equivalent to the dues he would have paid had he remained a member.[8] The intricacies of the human mind are strange; the hard man with his ruthless and worldly ambitions had not succeeded in driving from him some craving for the religion of his fathers nor the desire to rest among them. His desire was fulfilled. The *Gentleman's Magazine* of 1762 describes his funeral:—

His remains were brought in a hearse and six horses from his seat called Belvedere, in Kent, to Pewterer's Hall in Lyme St., where that Company that was to attend the funeral

[1] Prov. ii. 2.
[2] Probably Charles Johnson. I have not been able to trace the reference.
[3] In the possession of Colonel Fremantle of Bedwell Park, Herts., to whom I am indebted for a transcript of the letter and permission to print it. It is indorsed "My Father's Letter: Dated May 1759." The son heeded his father's precepts and was raised to the peerage as Lord Eardley in 1789.
[4] His last letter to the Duke of Newcastle is on 16 May 1762. Add MS. 32938 f. 300. In this he congratulates the Government on their "punctuality" with their creditors and adjures them to respect "the sacredness with which the several funds ought at all times to be maintained."
[5] Somerset House Caesar 59.
[6] The trustees were the Earl of Ashburnham, Earl Gower and the Earl of Bessborough. Trustees for the legacies to the other relatives were the Earl of Bessborough, Beeston Long (West Indian merchant and one of the Executors) and Robert Cliffe (banker).
[7] Horace Walpole, however, seems to have thought it presumptuous (*Letters op. cit.* V. 269-70).
[8] J. Picciotto, *Sketches of Anglo-Jewish History*, 1875, p. 63. Hyamson. *op. cit.* p. 133.

met ; from whence the corps was carried in another hearse, drawn by six horses, and followed by 12 mourning coaches and six to the Jews' burying-ground near Mile End, where the body was interred near noon, agreeable to the rites of the Jewish religion, as directed by his will.

Summing up the evidence of this striking career one can see Samson Gideon as a man of great force and ability, absorbed by a passion for wealth and what wealth can bring. All the tales about him show a forceful and even violent personality—an unhappy official complains that he was "after him . . . like a madman."[1] for his share in the lottery of 1753-4, and his correspondence bears the imprint of an almost savage vigour and contempt of weakness or cowardice. He was uncouth in dress, sardonic in his humour, outwardly a cynic about religion.[2] On the other hand he was clearly an affectionate family man, respected for his honesty in business among a class of dealers where this qualification was then far from common,[3] charitable and capable of that kindness to business associates in misfortune[4] that has always characterized the City. He had also some real, if simple, patriotism and that appreciation of the visual arts which is often the unexpected attribute of successful men of affairs. Nor, though he longed for the aggrandisement of his family, was he subservient to those from whom he sought it. Supreme in his command of a highly-specialized craft and aware of its value to the statesmen he served, he wrote and spoke to them with a blunt outspokenness and assurance oddly at variance with the normal tone of political correspondence of the day. And even when he asked favours, he demanded them, choosing his time to do so with good hopes of success, and did not beg for them.

As a public figure he is significant for what he stood for and for the assurance with which he moved in the financial field before him. His advice was always bold but never rash and, though it was not his way to theorize or introduce generalizations that were not relevant to his immediate purpose, there shines through everything he wrote a clear grasp of the rising credit structure, a grasp of the functions both of the Bank and the money market in this structure, and a consummate mastery of all the day-to-day minutiae of the financial world in which he moved.

---

[1] Brit Mus. Add MS. 32855 f. 468, P. Leheup to Newcastle, 11 June 1755.
[2] A number of these tales are included in an otherwise valueless account of him in J. Francis, *Chronicles and Characters of the Stock Exchange*, 1849, pp. 88 *seq.*
[3] This did not prevent his participation in practices which would not be accepted by later periods, e.g. his implication in the British Museum Lottery scandal of 1753-4. J. Ashton, *The History of English Lotteries*, 1893, p. 70. For this see also Brit. Mus. Add MS. 32855, ff. 467 *seq.*
[4] See Eardley Wilmot *op. cit.* pp. 281-2.

18

SAMSON GIDEON AND THE REDUCTION
OF INTEREST, 1749-50

IN 1758 the Jewish financier Samson Gideon, the most famous stock-jobber at Jonathan's Coffee-house in the first half of the eighteenth century, presented a paper to the Newcastle ministry in which he pushed his claims to a peerage.[2] He had been advancing these claims since at least 1757[3] and he urged in their support the ennoblement of others of his race by various monarchs of Europe: ·

Antonio Lopez Suasso Native of Holland professing the Jewish religion was in a Catholick Country Created a Baron by the King of Spain and the Patent sets forth, that the Title shall decend [sic] to Male or Faemale notwithstanding their professing Themselves to be Jews.

The Emperor of Germany Confirmed the above, and Granted him a New Patent by the title of Antonio Lopez Suasso de Avernes Le Gross.[4]

Mr Diego Periera de Aguilar a merchant and Native of Portugal and Free Denison in England Professing the Jewish Religion and Educating all his Children in the Faith he Embraced some years Since, was made very lately a Baron of the Empire.[5]

Whereas Samson the Son of Rowland Gideon[6] (a West India Merchant and a free and Livery Man of London) was born in England, married an English Protestant,[7] his Sons and Daughters were all Baptized by the Sub Dean of St Paul's, few days after their birth, were Strictly Educated and so many of them that are Living Continu [sic] to Profess Christianity.

His plea was not granted, but a compromise was offered and accepted. In May 1759 his school-boy son, so providently baptized by the Sub-Dean of St Paul's, was made a baronet in his stead. For on one side stood the anti-semitism of English society and of George II, but on the other the desire of the ministry to serve a most useful man.

Of more interest than the ambitions of the financier (which were fulfilled when his son was created Baron Eardley by the younger Pitt in 1789) are the services for which he demanded payment. He lays them out himself in his application.

[1] Since the Manuscript Room of the British Museum is still closed, it has not been possible to check most of the manuscript references in this article.
[2] Brit. Mus. Add. MS. 33055, ff. 219 seq. Date clear from internal evidence.
[3] Letter quoted in 'Memoir of the Life of Sampson Gideon Esq. of Spalding, Co. Lincoln and Belvedere, Kent. by J. E. Wilmot Esq.', in J. Nichols, *Illustrations of the Literary History of the Eighteenth Century* (1817–58), VI, 277–84.
[4] In 1676. The title was really Avernas de Gras. *Jewish Encyclopaedia.*
[5] In 1747. Ibid.
[6] A Portuguese Jew who had changed his name from Abudiente.
[7] Jane, daughter of Charles Ermell.

Anno 1742.   After a declaration of War with Spain Mr Gideon delivered a
Scheme for raising of Three Millions at Three p. cent. and made
himself answerable for the first payment upon upwards of £600,000,
and otherwise assisted to Compleat the Whole; as can be Testified
by the Rt. Honble Lord Sandys Then Chancellor of the Exchequer.[1]

1743.   Delivered a Scheme to the Rt. Honble Henry Pelham Esq.
Chancellor of the Exchequer and, as above, Subscribed and otherwise made himself liable for a much larger Sum than the preceding
year... well known to Mr West.[2]

1744.   Performed the Same when the French Fleets were in the British
Channel and the Publick Funds daily sinking.[3]

1745.   In times of great distress proposed by a New method how to raise
the Supplies and as before constantly attended the progress thereof.[4]

1746.   A scheme was delivered by Messrs Jno Bristow and Gerard Van
Neck just befor the Battle of Culloden. Mr Pelham in Order to be
Secure of part of the sum proposed to be raised, Took Mr Gideon's
Note annexed to a list to be collected by him and by the Chancellor's
order, to be answerable for the first payment of £1,070,000 which
was all distributed among the People as may now be made appear
by the said list and obligation at that time deposited with the
Directors of the Bank.[5]

1746[5]. Proposed the Subscription for Circulating of Bank Notes and
restoring their Credit, and was one of the four persons that Carried
on that Association, and there is now in Mr Gideon's hands the
Original Papers and the Signatures of above thirteen hundred
merchants and others who signed in little more than one Day
which had that good Effect that shou'd be remembered.[6]

1746.   Contributed and promoted the Subscription to the Land Tax, etc.[7]
and during the Rebellion Constantly attended the comee for
Supplying the Soldiers in the North with Necessaries.[8]

1747.   Subscribed largely for himself and friends to the Schemes

---

[1] 15 Geo II, c. 19.   [2] 16 Geo. II, c. 13.
[3] 17 Geo. II, c. 18. The *Gentleman's Magazine* (1744), p. 225, gives the 'lists'
of subscribers to the loan of that year. The 'Treasury's list' (i.e. the subscriptions
made through the three Monied Companies) was £600,000; Gideon's £300,000;
J. Gore, J. Bristow, G. Van Neck £150,000 each; R. Drake, R. Jackson,
J. Edwards, P. Burrell and Henry Lascelles £90,000 each.
[4] 18 Geo. II, c. 9. The 'new method' was presumably the attachment of small
life annuities as 'douceurs" to the lottery tickets, a feature which recurs in 1746
in a scheme in which he was much concerned. On this later occasion it was
much criticized.
[5] 19 Geo. II, c. 12. Gideon is incorrect in dating it 'just before the battle of
Culloden'. The battle took place in April, and the scheme appears to have been
agreed on at the end of December or beginning of January after the defeat at
Falkirk and before the success at Stirling.
[6] Sir Theodore Janssen (Brit. Mus. Add. MS. 32862, ff. 69 seq.) and Sir John
Barnard appear to be two of the 'four persons'. I have not been able to trace
the fourth.
[7] See below, p.406.
[8] With Sir Theodore Janssen the initiator of the Committee (Brit. Mus. Add.
MS. 32862, ff. 69 seq.).

1748. delivered by Sir Jno Barnard.[1]

1749.   Was Imployed by the Right Honble Mr Pelham (as will appear by the Letters now in the hands of Mr Roberts)[2] to bring about the reduction of Interest upon the Funds, subscribed all his own property in them Immediately.

1749.   Seconded the Motion at the Bank and debates arising by arguments contributed to Convince the Proprietors, at their General Court, that it was prudent and Right for that Corporation to accept of Mr Pelham's proposal, notwithstanding they had rejected the same at a former Genl Court. The Earl of Winchilsea was present and has often mentioned Since, that Mr Gideon was Serviceable upon that Occasion.

1751.   The Chancellor of the Exchequer proposed to raise One million at three per cent and the Gentleman that undertook to Compleat the Same delivered a list for only £40,000, and declared he coud do no more as the Three per cent annuities were sold at a Discount at Market. Mr Gideon sent for by Mr Pelham subscribed upwards of £100,000 and declared he woud take more if necessary, and the whole was subscribed for by the Chancellors friends in two days which brought the Foreigners and allmost all the Outstanders into the Second reduction.[3]

1756.   Mr Gideon Subscribed for £107,000 for his own account and begs leave to appeal to the Duke of Newcastle with what difficulty his Grace raised the Supplies that Year.[4]

1757.   Was the first private person that Published to pay a bounty for Recruiting his Majesty's army, which Example was followed by Many not without Success and had the Honor to meet with Royal applause.

1757.   Attended his Grace the Duke of Devonshire to raise the Supplies.[5]

1758.   Mr Gideon had the honor to Attend the Duke of Newcastle and will be glad if his Grace thinks that he was in any way assistant in raising of two Loans for his Majesty's Service in his Ellectoral Capacity.[6]

     Mr Gideon never Asked or had from the Government any Gratuity, fee or Commission, nor will he Accept of any Pecuniary reward.

[1] See below, p.408.

[2] Pelham's papers were left after his death in the keeping of his former secretary Roberts, whose widow appears to have destroyed them. Wm. Coxe, *Pelham Administration* (1829), I, ix.

[3] See below, p.413.

[4] 29 Geo. II, c. 7. For difficulties see Brit. Mus. Add. MS. 32862, ff. 204–365 passim.

[5] The list of subscribers to this loan (30 Geo. II, c. 19) is preserved in the Exchequer Papers (P.R.O. E. 401, 2598), *Subscribers to the £3,000,000 loan for 1757*. Gideon was the largest of the very numerous subscribers, his list standing at £100,000.

[6] Wilmot, op. cit. p. 278, mentions that in 1753 Gideon combined with Bristow and Boehm to lend £90,000 to the City of Danzig, so that he had earlier experience of contributing to loans raised by foreign governments.

The services set out in this list are substantial and all are of some interest to the historian of eighteenth-century public finance. This article is, however, concerned primarily with those entered under the years 1749 and 1751 in connexion with the conversion operation undertaken by Henry Pelham when he was First Lord of the Treasury and from which there emerged the original 3 % Consols.

Little attention has been paid by historians to the means by which this transaction, the most important in Pelham's financial career, was carried out. Some circulation has indeed been given to a facile account of it by Richard ('Leonidas') Glover, a City politician and poet, in his *Memoirs of a Late Literary Character*, in which he attributes the success of the enterprise entirely to Sir John Barnard, the well-known independent City Member, and to himself.[1] It does not require much knowledge of the machinery of eighteenth-century public credit to refute the account of this always unreliable witness. Gideon's claims fall into quite a different class. Both he and Sir John Barnard were in fact, in their different ways, closely connected with the transaction for which, however, the chief credit must go to Pelham himself. All, moreover, played their part within the framework of a credit organization which had gradually been built up during the preceding years and which must be kept clearly in mind if the success of the transaction is to be understood.

Eighteenth-century administrations relied for their fiscal requirements partly on a system of taxation that was from the modern point of view both rigid and unproductive and partly on short- and long-term loans.[2] In raising both they depended on the growing London money market, with the Bank of England rising to a central position in it,[3] and (where long-term loans were concerned) on the power of the London market to mobilize the funds of the *rentier* class, not only in the British Isles but in various Continental countries, particularly in Holland.[4]

As Sir John Clapham has shown,[5] governments throughout this period were relying to an increasing extent on the Bank of England for their short-term credit. For the most part Gideon's services consisted in his assistance in the raising of long-term loans in time of war and in his help, both financial and moral, in bringing to a successful conclusion Pelham's conversion scheme.

The normal Treasury procedure when floating a long-term loan was as follows: applications were invited from individuals with whom the Treasury was in touch. These applicants were drawn from a narrower or wider circle according to the contacts of the Treasury in the City at the time. It was understood that each applicant spoke for a considerable body of would-be subscribers as well as himself; certain of them represented the

---

[1] Edited and published after his death by R. Duppa (1813), p. 38.
[2] E. L. Hargreaves, *The National Debt* (1930).
[3] J. H. Clapham, *The Bank of England: A History*, vol. 1 (Cambridge, 1944).
[4] C. Wilson, *Anglo-Dutch Commerce and Finance in the Eighteenth Century* (Cambridge, 1941).
[5] Op. cit.

foreign subscribers whose importance in the fund-holding body caused from time to time so much public disquiet;[1] prominent government contractors, usually themselves Members of Parliament, had a number of M.P.s among the names on their list;[2] and at this time Samson Gideon's list brought in a Jewish financial element likely otherwise to be omitted. While these proposals were being formulated there was a period of active discussion behind the scenes between the Treasury and the more important of these applicants, in which the First Lord of the Treasury, the Chancellor of the Exchequer and other ministers joined. A meeting was then arranged between the Treasury officials and the applicants, after which no further application was considered. Contemporary references confirm Lord North's description to the House in 1781 of what happened at such a meeting.

The rule of that meeting was to convene the monied men who had made applications and offers and to convene the heads of all the great public companies [often called by contemporaries the 'three monied Companies', i.e. the Bank of England, the East India Company and the South Sea Company] who usually assisted the Government with money, but who never made any applications previous to that meeting; by these gentlemen so collected, the terms were settled and it was always usual to expect that the gentlemen who were present were to take a pretty considerable share of the loan among them.[3]

In fact the loan was nearly always over-subscribed and, after its terms had been passed by parliament, the final list of subscribers was drawn up by the Treasury, who allotted subscriptions at discretion, usually with the advice of some City supporter. The importance of the three monied Companies on the market and the big share usually taken by their representatives made them in many ways the centre of the body negotiating for terms, though they did not subscribe in their corporate capacity.

As soon as the first instalment had been paid and the receipts given out, the 'scrip' began to be the subject of dealings on the market, where it was called 'Light Horse' (fully paid up subscriptions were known as 'Heavy Horse'),[4] and was considered a highly speculative security. The Treasury were wont to justify their discrimination between subscribers and their use of middlemen on the grounds of the danger to public credit which would follow if subscribers proved financially weak and were obliged to sell out precipitately to avoid the later payments. A closely knit financial system with the three monied Companies at its centre both as corporate creditors of the state and as a focus for the interests of individual creditors arose out of these arrangements.

Whatever its advantages, however, it is easy to see that such a system must give rise to dissatisfaction in the City when terms turned out favourable and when any considerable financial interests had been ignored. The

[1] Wilson, op. cit.
[2] L. B. Namier, *Structure of Politics at the Accession of George III* (1929), i, 68.
[3] *Parliamentary History*, xxi, 1355.
[4] T. Mortimer, *Every Man his own Broker* (2nd (enlarged) ed. 1761), pp. 144 seq.

ill-feeling was moreover exacerbated by the fact that the Treasury's choice was not based solely on financial considerations. Participation in the subscription, like a share in a government contract, was often used as an inducement towards or reward for political services. It is not surprising therefore that the 'monied interest' with the three Companies at its centre was often attacked by their less influential fellow-citizens as a sinister oligarchy bolstered up by the corrupt influence of the administration. This feeling, moreover, had political consequences; it was one of the strongest forces driving the main body of City opinion into the arms of any parliamentary opposition which was prepared to make use of them.

Pelham had inherited a peculiarly difficult position in this respect. Opposition to the government in the City had been strong during the parliamentary struggle which ended in the downfall of Walpole. In the City as in parliament, Pelham was able to reconstruct the strong connexion built up by his predecessor only after slow and anxious work and by establishing it on a 'broad bottom'. In the City this was only achieved in 1747. In the years 1744–5 and the earlier part of 1746 in particular, dissatisfaction continued in the City and was centralized by Sir John Barnard, the independent City Member, in an attack on the administration's financial arrangements and a demand for government loans to be raised by 'open subscription' (that is, for arrangements whereby, once the terms had been agreed on, the books would lie open for anyone who wished to subscribe and whereby, in the event of an over-subscription, subscribers would have their share allotted on a *pro rata* basis), in the place of the 'closed subscription' of normal contemporary practice.

An anonymous pamphleteer took Samson Gideon as typical of the monied interest and Sir John Barnard as typical of its opponents.[1] They had certainly been old enemies representing very different aspects of the City's activities. While Gideon was acknowledged as the greatest of stock-jobbers, Sir John Barnard had in 1734 fathered and pushed through an Act which, if enforced, would have prevented speculative dealing in stocks altogether[2] and Gideon's activities at the end of 1745 and the beginning of 1746, when he first came strikingly to the fore, were the object of Sir John's most scathing attacks. Gideon was, however, hardly a typical representative of the monied interest. More typical were such men as John Bristow, M.P.[3] or Sir William Baker, M.P.,[4] government contractors, London merchants of good repute and high on the direction of one or other of the three monied Companies. Gideon, on the other hand, stood rather aloof and as late as 1746 was still considered something of an

---

[1] *An Essay upon Publick Credit, in a Letter to a Friend. Occasioned by the Fall of Stocks* (1748) (Brit. Mus. T. 1143, 11).

[2] 7 Geo. II, c. 8.

[3] Merchant with big interests in the Portugal trade; government contractor; Director of the South Sea Company for many years, Deputy Governor in 1754 and Sub-Governor in 1759.

[4] Alderman; West India and America Merchant; Director of the East India Company for many years and Chairman in 1749 and 1752.

interloper.[1] His religion debarred him from rendering the political services that received their reward in profitable government contracts, and made him an object of suspicion. He was also surrounded with the discredit that then attached to the professional stock-jobber.

Wilmot, whose memoir of him was based on the examination of his papers (now lost), claims that in addition to his purely financial activities Gideon could claim the status of a merchant and that he had 'frequently large ventures himself in all parts of the world'.[2] But while we have evidence that he had been sworn in as a Jew broker in 1729,[3] that he dealt in the funds and in the short-term securities of the market, and that he subscribed to the loans raised by his own and other governments, there is no corresponding evidence to suggest that he had any substantial interests as a merchant. There seems no reason to doubt that he was what his contemporaries thought him, a highly skilled jobber and broker and a daring speculator. In 1720, when he was just of age, his father died, leaving him a fortune of £7901. During the South Sea Bubble years he speculated extensively and with success; by 1727 he could give his two sisters portions of £2000 apiece, the dowries of well-to-do girls. By September 1729 his capital had grown to £25,000. In more settled times it took him more than eleven years to double it, but by December 1745 in the depth of the panic induced by the Jacobite Rebellion, it had risen to £82,000 and by 1748 when the depression was over his capital stood at £156,000. From that time on he continued to gain steadily; when he partially retired from business in 1755 he calculated that he was worth £279,000 and £297,000 by July 1759.[4] It seems clear that he won his way into the 'monied interest' by sheer usefulness in time of financial need.

Such a man was a useful friend and a bad enemy for an eighteenth-century administration in time of war or other stress. It was widely believed that he manipulated stock prices to serve his ends; indeed he boasted that in 1744 he had kept up the price of lottery tickets by artificial means[5] and in 1746 Sir John Barnard publicly accused him and his friends of manipulating the price of annuities to suit their plans.[6] In the panic of 1745 when the rebels were marching south, he showed his address and spirit in protecting the joint interest of himself and the public credit. As prices fell he bought openly to the full extent of his resources;[7] he subscribed to the merchants' address of loyalty to the king which did much to steady public opinion and played a prominent part in the association of London

[1] *Gentleman's Magazine* (1746), pp. 191–2 contrasts those subscribing to the loan of that year with the government's 'old friends'.

[2] Nichols, op. cit. p. 277.

[3] Guildhall Records.

[4] Nichols, op. cit. pp. 277–8. He died in 1762 at the age of 63.

[5] Hist. MSS. Comm. Marquess of Lothian, Sect. III, Correspondence of Sir Thomas Drury, pp. 148–53.

[6] Sir John Barnard, *A Defence of Several Proposals for Raising of Three Millions for the Service of the Government for the Year 1746, with a Postscript containing some Notions relating to Publick Credit* 31st May 1746.

[7] Hist. MSS. Comm. op. cit. pp. 153 seq.

merchants who pledged themselves to accept bank notes to avert a threatened run on the Bank in September,[1] and was very active in the attempt, when the ordinary lenders in advance of the Land Tax failed, to raise at least half of the credit required by public subscription, an attempt which was only partially successful.[2]

It was the government loan of 1746, however, that stamped Gideon on the public mind as a leader among the monied interest. In a scheme put forward to the Treasury he says by the well-known contractors Bristow and Vanneck, sometime at the end of December 1745 or early in January 1746 when the outlook was still very threatening, he was the largest subscriber.[3] The news of the Pretender's retreat from Stirling came through to the City about 7 February and as confidence returned it began to become apparent that the terms which the Treasury had been glad to accept were likely to prove very favourable to the subscribers. In the debates on the loan in the Committee of Ways and Means in March, Sir John Barnard voiced the jealousy of the City interests not concerned in the loan, attacking it in unmeasured terms, proposing two alternative methods of meeting the needs of the state and demanding, in the interest of equity and national economy, the introduction of 'open' subscription in the raising of government loans.[4]

If Gideon was a prominent member though not a typical representative of the monied interest, Sir John Barnard was certainly the leader of the popular opposition in the City to it. He had all the reputation which Gideon lacked, and served the City for fifty years as its example of the just man and upright citizen.[5] Standing outside the monied interest he represented the outlook of the ordinary City merchant who formed public opinion there.[6] In the House of Commons he identified himself with all the whiggish doctrines of opposition inherited from the preceding century and which retained their appeal among the political public of the period. He had thus tended to find himself in opposition, though his honesty and independence had prevented his using influence in the City even in the

---

[1] See above, p.400.

[2] See above, p. 400. The names of the subscribers are preserved in a document in the P.R.O. T1/319 (bundle). Sir John Barnard (*Defence of Several Proposals*), trying to explain away the failure of the City to subscribe better to this venture, maintained that the City disliked its sponsors and that a public subscription of that kind should have been undertaken through the Lord Mayor.

[3] See above, p.400.

[4] Sir John Barnard, op. cit.

[5] The anonymous *Memoirs of the late Sir John Barnard* (1776) takes as its motto the couplet:

'Ages were ransack'd for the good and great
Till Barnard came, and made the group compleat.'

[6] He was born at Reading in 1685, a Quaker, but received into the Church of England in 1703. He began his business career as a wine-merchant, but soon turned to underwriting. He represented the City in parliament from 1722–61, was Alderman 1728–58, Lord Mayor in 1737, knighted in 1732, died in 1764. Speaker Onslow who knew him well in the House gives an excellent account of his character and outlook. (Hist. MSS. Comm. Onslow MSS. pp. 469–70.)

height of the attacks on Walpole for the ends of political faction. Though he was often impracticable in his views on government finance and had a robust dislike of politicians, he had a real interest in good government and was not in the least afraid of unpopularity. It was he who in 1737 had made the first unsuccessful attempt to obtain a reduction in the interest on the national debt.[1] When Pelham turned to the pacification of the City he could hardly have hoped for a better leader of the opposition there with whom to deal.

In conformity with the general lines of his policy, Pelham would undoubtedly have sought to win over the opposition in the City as soon as opportunity arose. The Jacobite Rebellion not only gave him his opportunity, but made it essential for him to grasp it. He was able to take advantage of the fact that the greater part of the City opposition, under Sir John Barnard, rallied to the government in the crisis, and that those under the leadership of Alderman Heathcote, who did not, were discredited.[2] To keep their support, however, two concessions were necessary: their financial demands must be met and a long-standing grievance about the form of the City government must be redressed. Pelham was prepared to meet the popular party in the City on both counts.

Their constitutional grievance arose from the recognition in the City of London Elections Act of 1725[3] of the traditional claim of the Court of Aldermen to veto resolutions of the Common Council, the so-called Aldermanic Negative.[4] As late as 1745 an attempt by the popular party to get the relevant clauses of the Act repealed had been defeated by the administration. In January 1746, however, on the presentation of a further petition from the Common Council, leave was given for the introduction of a bill to this effect which passed rapidly through both Houses and received the Royal assent on 19 March.[5]

The debates on 14 March on the 1746 Loan showed, however, that this concession was not in itself sufficient to placate them, and on the financial

---

[1] Hist. MSS. Comm. Earl of Carlisle, p. 182, etc. The feeling against him in the City was so bitter at this time that there was talk of boycotting him as an underwriter.

[2] G. H. Rose, *Selections from the Papers of the Earls of Marchmont* (1831), II, 341–8.

[3] 11 Geo. I, c. 18. For an account of this Act see A. J. Henderson, *London and the National Government* (Durham, North Dakota, 1945), pp. 74–113.

[4] For the attacks on this claim in the first half of the seventeenth century, see A. Beaven, *Aldermen of London* (1913), II, xlvii and M. James, *Social Policy during the Puritan Revolution* (1930), pp. 224 seq. In 1674–8 the Aldermen obtained strong legal support for their claim (R. Sharpe, *London and the Kingdom* (1894), II, 448). In consequence Walpole had a good case for recognizing it in his Bill. The clause was violently opposed in the City and in both Houses, where the cause of the Common Council was taken up by the opposition. Though the Act went through unchanged, agitation against it continued in the City, rising to unusual heights in e.g. 1739, 1744 and 1745. (Wm. Maitland, *History of London* (1756), I, 536 seq. and Guildhall Records, Journal of the Common Council, vols. 58 and 59).

[5] 19 Geo. II, c. 8.

issue too Pelham was prepared to meet them. Though he stood firm on the arrangements for the current year,[1] in the following December when a further loan was under discussion, it was agreed that this should be raised by the 'open' subscription advocated by Sir John Barnard, and that Sir John himself should be the chief organizer of that section of would-be subscribers who had hitherto been excluded. From this time on Barnard became the financial supporter of this and the succeeding administration.

Pelham's diplomatic revolution in the City was thus entirely successful. He had destroyed the opposition there which had become endemic in the preceding years and he did so without detriment to his immediate financial needs. In 1747 the open subscription, carefully guided by Barnard (who took in a quantity of subscriptions at his own house) and supported by the monied interest including Gideon, was an overwhelming success. That the similar subscription of 1748 was not also a success and that the closing dates for the later instalments of the subscriptions had to be extended, does not seem to be due to the method by which it was raised (though pamphleteers accused Barnard of muddling it and Gideon of maliciously undermining it),[2] so much as to the financial difficulties which hastened the negotiations for the peace of Aix-la-Chapelle rather precipitately concluded that year.

Even before the peace was concluded Pelham had made it clear to those in close touch with him that he meant to use his strengthened position in the City as a means to achieving an end and not merely as a relief from embarrassment. In August he told his brother the Duke of Newcastle:

I have one selfish ambition. I was in hopes, by a Peace being soon made, and by proper economy in the administration of Government afterwards, to have been the author of such a plan as might in time to come, have relieved the nation from the vast load of debt they now labour under; and even in my own time had the satisfaction of demonstrating to the knowing part of the world, that the thing was not impossible; here I own lay my ambition, but a very little more delay will render it impracticable; for me I am sure it will; and I am apt to fear no one will be better able to bring it about.[3]

In other words he had already determined on the coming of peace to do what Walpole had not dared to do, and to undertake the conversion operation which brought the 4 % debts down to 3½ and then to 3 %. Despite the temporary embarrassment in which the government found itself in the spring of 1748, the financial obstacles to such a course were by no means insuperable. 3 % stock, down to 76 when the peace negotiations began in April 1748, had risen almost to 95 in the following February, four months after the definitive peace was signed, and were up

[1] An administration pamphleteer replied to Sir John Barnard's *Defence of Certain Proposals* in *A Letter to Sir John Barnard, upon his Proposals for raising three Millions of Money for the Year* 1746, *from a Member of the House of Commons.*

[2] *An Essay upon Public Credit,* op. cit. Gideon was also attacked in *A Winter Evening's Conversation in a Club of Jews, Dutchmen, French Refugees and English Stock-Jobbers at a noted Coffee-House in Change Alley* (1748).

[3] Brit. Mus. Add. MS. 32716, f. 13–13v. 4–15 Aug. 1748. Quoted with verbal inaccuracies in Coxe, op. cit. II, 15.

to par by the following June. The political difficulties were, however, redoubtable. A combination among the fund-holders could defeat the government's plans and this was the more probable since the loans from the Bank, the East India Company and the South Sea Company in their corporate capacities were included in the stock affected and might well prove a focus of resistance for the individual fund-holders. It was, moreover, well known that Walpole would have liked to support Barnard's motion for a reduction of interest in 1737, but found it politically impracticable to do so.[1] Pelham, however, felt that the risk could be taken. Fortified by the conviction that 3 % was a rate appropriate to the market and that only a confederacy among the creditors of the state could prevent the success of the operation, he seems to have felt convinced that his powers of negotiation with the Corporations concerned, and the influence which the administration could exert on individuals, would be sufficient to prevent such a confederacy becoming effective. It was of high value in this connexion to be able to call on the services of the two powerful men standing outside the main body of the monied interest, Sir John Barnard with his following among the merchants of moderate means and men of good will, and Samson Gideon with his skill in the manœuvres of the market, the two men of which it was said they were 'a man with as much integrity and...another with as much ability in the Funds as this country has ever produced'.[2] He was prepared to use each of them in the appropriate manner.

Pelham made his preparations systematically. His first care in the spring of 1749 was to maintain taxation for another year at its war-time level, and to fund the greater part of the departmental advances that made up the floating debt.[3] It was, however, useless to reduce the size of and interest on the government's unfunded debt without also taking into account another short-term security, at that time as popular on the market as the government securities themselves, the East India Bonds issued by the East India Company in anticipation of their sales. It is not surprising, therefore, to find on 16 August the Chairman of the East India Company, Sir William Baker, informing the Directors that it would be beneficial to reduce the interest on their bonds,[4] and the next day Samson Gideon and some friends coming forward with a‧fully worked-out scheme in which they undertook the risk of the transaction on reasonable terms. The offer was at once accepted.[5] At the same time Pelham rigidly refused to consider the demands of the King of Poland (strongly backed by the King, and the Duke of Newcastle) to be permitted to raise a loan on the London market,

[1] E.g. Hist. MSS. Comm. Earl of Carlisle, p. 183. Col. C. Howard to Lord Carlisle, 21 April 1737.
[2] Brit. Mus. Add. MS. 32862, f. 204. J. West to Newcastle. 24 Jan. 1756.
[3] 22 Geo. II, c. 23.
[4] India Office MSS. East India Company Court Books, vol. 63, f. 419.
[5] Ibid. f. 427. They offered to be bound for £1,500,000 to facilitate the conversion at 10 %. Individual directors added a further £500,000 to the offer. On 8 Nov. 1749 (f. 503) it was decided that no call need be made on this capital.

on the grounds that it would check the rise in the price of English government securities which was necessary for the success of his plans.[1]

The stage was now set for his great attempt, in which he seems to have had little encouragement from his colleagues. When parliament met in November he announced his intention of introducing a bill, in the preparation of which Sir John Barnard was to be associated, to reduce the interest on the 4 % Funds (the total nominal value of which was £58,703,405) to 3½ % from 1750 to December 1757 and then to 3 %. The bill was introduced in the House and met with little opposition, the landed interest being in general favourable and the monied interest holding their fire.[2] It received the royal assent on 20 December and the fund-holders were given until 28 February 1750 to signify their consent to the reduction of interest by enrolling their names and the particulars of their stock in the books opened for the purpose.

Everyone was aware that the struggle was to come. Though the stock of the three monied Companies affected represented in all only some 26 % of the 4 % stock, the individual fund-holders naturally looked to the Companies for a lead. On 22 November, for instance, the firm of Van Hemerts advised their Dutch correspondents to await the action of the Bank and the East India Company before taking a line.[3] General Courts of the three companies were called for various dates in December and January, and when they met it was clear both that the administration had been seeking to come to terms with their Directors, and that they had only partially succeeded. Even where they had done so, moreover, there was reason to doubt whether the Directors would succeed in carrying the Proprietors with them.

The South Sea Company's General Court was the first to be held on 7 December. The Company not only believed that the government were precluded by the terms of previous statutes from the compulsory redemption of their trading stock, but were also deeply concerned in the result of certain trade negotiations in process with the Court of Spain, and saw no reason to be accommodating to the administration. After a long debate, in which Gideon took an active part, the best result that could be achieved was the postponement of a decision. In the East India Company, things went even worse. At a General Court on 13 December the Directors (with only one dissentient) advised the Proprietors to accept the proposals on condition that legislation was introduced to enable them to fund part of their bond debt.[4] There seems little doubt that the Ministry had agreed to these terms in advance. Opposition arose, however, among the Proprietors, a ballot was demanded[5] and held (after much controversy in the Press) on 3 January, the result of which was the defeat of the Directors'

[1] Coxe, op. cit. II, 76.

[2] Lord Egmont objected at the notice given to the City which would enable them to work up an opposition, but Pelham replied that no measure of such magnitude could be introduced without the advice of men of skill and experience.

[3] Wilson, op. cit. p. 151.

[4] India Office Records. East India Company Court Book, vol. 63, f. 548.

[5] Ibid. f. 557. 19 Dec. 1749.

proposals by 269 to 209. On 31 January the General Court of the Bank of England, after long debates in which Gideon took an active part but the Directors remained silent, turned down by a large majority the motion of the Governor to accept the proposal. Even before this had happened it was generally believed that the measure had failed. Horace Walpole, who had little concern with such things, wrote to Horace Mann on 10 January:

It is plain I am no monied man, as I have forgot till I came to my last paragraph, what a ferment the money changers are in! Mr Pelham...has just miscarried in a scheme for the reduction of interest by the intrigues of the three great Companies and other Usurers.[1]

With only a month before the closing date for acceptance, the Ministry had to take every possible step to reverse the unfavourable trend of events. In press and pamphlet the Ministry sought to drive home their views. Sir John Barnard made a notable contribution in his *Considerations on the Proposals for Reducing the Interest on the National Debt*, published on 6 February. Some years later the claims of a Doctor Thomas were pressed on the Duke of Newcastle for preferment as a reward for services rendered at this time. Lord Kinnoull supporting his claim said:

I told your Grace some years ago that Doctor Thomas had personal merit both with yourself and your late dear brother from the part he was imployed in the scheme for reducing the interest of the Publick debt and the dayly intelligence he gave to Sir John Bernard [*sic*] upon that business, through which channel Mr Pelham had his first information of its taking effect. To this, My Lord, I might add the great pains the Doctor took and the success he met with (though not without many rubbs in the way) in explaining the nature of the scheme to a great many of the Publick creditors, the trouble he was at in attending the press and in dispersing the reasons printed to convince people of the reasonableness of the scheme, and the many wet and dirty journeys he took to Clapham [where Sir John lived] and elsewhere upon that affair.[2]

Of Gideon's activities at this time we have less information (in the absence of Pelham's papers to which he refers) but they were sufficiently prominent for those supporting the measure to be dubbed 'Gideonites'.[3]

By one means or another they succeeded in stemming the tide. No doubt the chief arguments used were those of Sir John Barnard in his pamphlet, viz. that the authority of parliament could not be flouted, that since 3 % was the normal market rate the administration would have no difficulty in raising a loan to pay off those who did not come in, and that those who tried to persuade fund-holders to hold out would be the first to subscribe to such a loan. The fluctuation of fortune might be seen each day in the total subscribed for conversion. The tide probably turned about 15 February, and though by a week later less than £15,000,000 of the £58,700,000 affected seems to have been subscribed, it was known that the battle was won. On 23 February Van Hemerts wrote to their Dutch

[1] H. Walpole, *Letters* (ed. Toynbee), II, 423.
[2] Brit. Mus. Add. MS. 32860, f. 391. Lord Kinnoull to Newcastle, 6 Nov. 1755.
[3] *Old England*, 3 March, quoted in the *London Magazine* (March, 1750), p. 129.

correspondents that 'The generally strong opposition which at first existed here against the Plan for Reduction has changed during the last 8 days into general consent, so that a good sum is already subscribed here'.[1] Finally, to take advantage of the turn of the tide, the requisite number of Proprietors of the Bank of England demanded a further General Court which was summoned on 27 February, and in this a motion, seconded and spoken to by Samson Gideon, was passed by a large majority to accept the proposed terms.[2] It did not matter that the South Sea Company at their postponed General Court held on 26 February had decided to hold out.[3] When the books were closed at midnight on 28 February more than £38,800,000 had been subscribed, and though this covered only some 64 % of the holdings, the scheme might be claimed to be a success.[3]

Now that opposition was broken, steps to make the success more complete were, moreover, immediately undertaken. The uncertainty prevailing throughout January and February had made it particularly difficult for foreign holders to give their agents well-informed instructions. This gave some excuse for an extension of the closing date. As soon as the measure seemed likely to succeed the question of granting such an extension was raised on their behalf. The government felt strong enough to take a fairly high line. First they left the applicants in uncertainty for some time and then offered considerably less favourable terms to those who had failed to take the first opportunity.[4] The results justified their firmness. At the same time they continued their negotiations with the two monied Companies which still held out after the Bank's *volte face*; the East India Company, where they kept open their offer with regard to the funding of the Company's Bond Debt, and the South Sea Company, where the issue remained intimately bound up with the difficult trade negotiations with Spain.[5] The East India Company came into line by accepting these proposals on 25 April.[6] With the South Sea Company terms were not reached until 12 February 1751, and then in consideration of the poor terms which they received from Spain, they were treated more favourably than other fund-holders; the Company was to receive 4 % on its capital stock for seven years before the interest dropped to the 3 % level.[7]

[1] Wilson, op. cit. p. 152.
[2] *General Advertiser* (1750). This result had been forecast by Van Hemert on Feb. 23 (Wilson, op. cit. p. 152). (For Gideon's part, see p. 27 above.) On Feb. 19 the *General Advertiser* reported that the summoning of this General Court was probable and on that and the following day it contained protesting letters complaining that threats were being used against the Bank.
[3] Coxe, op. cit. II, 90 seq. examines a variety of authorities to establish the correct sum.
[4] 23 Geo. II, c. 22. The *London Magazine* (1750) in its 'Account of the Principal Acts passed this Session', gives a short account of the Act and the debates leading up to it. Those subscribing under this arrangement were to obtain $3\frac{1}{2}$ % till December 1755 instead of December 1757.
[5] R. Pares, *War and Trade in the West Indies* (Oxford, 1936), pp. 517–33.
[6] East India Company Court Book, loc. cit. 64, f. 24.
[7] Brit. Mus. Add. MS. 25545, f. 287. Minutes of the General Court of the South Sea Company.

In this way the sum to be paid off was reduced to less than £3,000,000. That the administration should in 1751 have run into difficulties in raising 3 % annuities for £1,000,000 towards this transaction, and have had to rely on Gideon's assistance to support them,[1] shows on how narrow a margin they were working and how easily Pelham's ambition might have been defeated. The measure nevertheless had succeeded and in 1752 the various annuities bearing 3 % interest were consolidated into one stock and the 3 % Consols had come into existence.[2]

Gideon could rightly claim, even though several others could do likewise, that he had been 'serviceable on that occasion'.

[1] See above, p. 401.
[2] 25 Geo. II, c. 27.

Henry Fox, 1st Baron Holland (1705-74)
(After Sir Joshua Reynolds, *c.* 1762)
(National Portrait Gallery)

19

HENRY FOX AS PAYMASTER-GENERAL
OF THE FORCES

(WITH J. BINNEY)

TO be unmistakably identified as the 'Public Defaulter of unaccounted millions'—and in an address presented to the sovereign by a Lord Mayor of London on behalf of the Livery of the City—is not a common experience for an ex-minister of the Crown; but in 1769 it befell the unpopular Henry Fox,[1] who had been Paymaster General of the Forces from 1757 to 1765. It was, indeed, not the first time that he had been attacked on the financial conduct of his office. In 1763, in a debate opened by Sir John Phillips (a prominent tory country gentleman), William Aislabie had raised much the same issue in the house of commons, where it was received with 'loud marks of approbation';[2] but on this occasion little public attention was aroused, and 1769 was the first time that it was taken up with vigour, and outside parliament. The City's address, like a Middlesex petition of the previous month, echoed charges made in the house of commons when Alderman Beckford, the mouthpiece of many popular causes, had asserted that more than forty millions of public money remained unaccounted for in the army Pay Office, and that legal process in regard to this had been issued from the exchequer, but had been suspended by the king's sign manual warrant. Beckford had called upon members of the Treasury Board then present to correct him if he had been misinformed, but not a word had been uttered.[3]

These charges were ultimately dropped, but merit examination, an examination that must be based on some understanding of the nature of Henry Fox's office, and of the procedures relating to army finance and to contemporary law. The office of Paymaster of the

---

[1] Earl of Ilchester, *Henry Fox, first Lord Holland*, 1920, ii. 332. Fox was raised to the baronage in 1763. For the documents and an account of Beckford's speech, see the *Gentleman's Magazine*, 1769, pp. 290, 329 *seqq.*, and 363.

[2] Horace Walpole, *Memoirs of the Reign of George III*, ed. D. le Marchant, 1845, i. 243. William Aislabie was one of the two joint Auditors of the Imprests, to whose office Fox's accounts were to be rendered. As will be seen below, there were sufficient reasons for Fox's accounts not being in the Auditors' hands as early as 1763, and Aislabie ought to have known this.

[3] The date of this is uncertain, but is not unlikely to have been during the debate on the Budget of 1769. The occasion for the attack would seem to be the active part taken by Stephen and Charles James Fox against Wilkes in the Middlesex election. (Ilchester, *op. cit.* ii. 329.)

Forces had a continuous history from 1662, when Henry Fox's own father, Sir Stephen Fox, had been the first tenant. Before his time it had been the custom to appoint Treasurers at War, *ad hoc*, for this or that campaign; the practice of the Protectorate Government foreshadowing, however, a permanent office. Within a generation of the Restoration the status of the Paymastership began to change. In 1692 the then Paymaster, the earl of Ranelagh, was sworn of the privy council; and thereafter every Paymaster, or when there were two Paymasters at least one of them, was sworn of the council if not already a member. From the accession of Queen Anne the Paymaster tended to change with the Ministry, and eighteenth century appointments must be considered as made not upon merit alone, but by merit and political affiliation, the office becoming a political prize and perhaps potentially the most lucrative that a parliamentary career had to offer.

The duty of the Paymaster was to act as sole domestic banker of the army. He received, mainly from the exchequer, the sums voted by parliament for military expenditure, and from other quarters he received fortuitous sums such as those realized by the sale of old stores. He disbursed these sums, by his own hands or by Deputy Paymasters; such disbursements being made under the authority of sign manual warrants as far as related to the ordinary expenses of the army, and under Treasury warrants in the case of the extra-ordinaries, that is to say the expenses unforeseen and unprovided for by parliament. During the whole time in which public money was in his hands, from the day of receipt until the issue of his final discharge, the *Quietus* of the Pipe Office, his private estate was liable for the money in his hands; and failing the *Quietus* this liability remained without limit of time, passing on his death to his legal representatives. *Nullum tempus occurrit regi.*

A necessary preliminary to the issue of a *Quietus* was the audit of accounts by the Auditors of the Imprests in the exchequer. This audit was subject to protracted delay. Since it happened that in 1769 not even Fox's first year's account was as yet finally audited and declared, those who were unacquainted with the working of the administrative machine—or sought to play upon the ignorance of others—could plausibly stigmatize Fox as a 'defaulter'. But it must be said that for such delay there were sufficient explanations, a few of which may be summarized. To begin with, the Pay Office was plagued with excessively complicated book-keeping. In part this was due to the system of statutory appropriation, which not only earmarked the total voted for a given year, confining it to the services incurred in that year, but also analysed the appropriation in some detail according to different heads of service.[1] In part it

---

[1] See the annual Appropriation Acts.

was due to the fact that, especially in war, more or less heavy calls were made on account of the extra-ordinaries, which required distinct accounting. Other causes of complication were services which, although of regular annual occurrence, were nevertheless unprovided for by parliament in the latter's votes and appropriations. Such services were Chelsea Hospital, financed by deducting one day's pay in the year from most military personnel; widows' pensions, found by increasing the establishment of every company by two fictitious men; and administrative expenses, a fund for which was formed by deducting a poundage of 5 per cent. from most of the Paymaster's issues. These matters may be studied in detail in the reports of the commissioners for examining the public accounts, 1780–7,[1] and elsewhere.[2] A most superficial reading carries conviction as to the inevitability of great delay in the Pay Office, especially when it is recollected that eighteenth-century campaigns were conducted overseas, often at great distances, with slow and uncertain communications. It seems that the Pay Office did relatively well in delivering Fox's final accounts to the Auditors only seven years after his resignation, for the accounts of his three peace-time successors were not ready until eleven or twelve years after resignation.[3]

Great delay arose in the Audit Office itself, after the submission of a Paymaster's accounts. This was to a considerable extent beyond the power of the Auditors of the Imprests to remedy, for it was caused by the exacting requirements of the law. By law these two joint Auditors were the sole officers entitled and empowered to examine a Paymaster's accounts, and by law they must be satisfied not only that every disbursement had actually been made, but also that it was duly authorized.[4] In consequence, whatever previous examination might have taken place, the Audit Office had again to compare the accounts with the establishments, warrants, and the like; they were bound to require the production of acquittances vouching every disbursement, and they had to check all arithmetical calculations. If proper documents were wanting, a Paymaster's account could not be closed until the defect had been made good by the issue of a sign manual warrant empowering the Auditors to pass the unvouched items.[5] In the haste and confusion of campaigning, a failure to obtain vouchers, or

---

[1] Reports Nos. 4–7, 9, and 10. These are printed in vols. 38 and 39 of the *Journals of the House of Commons*.

[2] For instance, Public Record Office, Chatham Papers, P.R.O. 30/8, bundle 231, booklet entitled ' Business done at the Treasury '.

[3] *Commissioners for Examining the Public Accounts*, Rep. 4.

[4] Except in the matter of army contracts. The Comptrollers of Army Accounts were responsible for certifying that the terms of these contracts were complied with before the contractors were paid.

[5] See for instance, P.R.O., T. 29/38, Treasury minute of 10 June 1766.

their subsequent loss, was inevitably not infrequent. It must be borne in mind that by the time the Auditors came to do their work many accountable individuals and many of the meaner recipients were dead, or lost sight of; and some, in any case, were foreigners who were not and never had been amenable to English law.

In addition to such inevitable causes of delay, there were others which were within the power of the Auditors to remedy; amongst them what appears to have been a departmental regulation that the accounts of one Paymaster should not be passed until those of his predecessor were completed. It also seems that the exacting demands made by war and its aftermath upon the personnel of the Audit Office were not matched by an adequate increase in staff. This was certainly so in the contemporary navy Pay Office; but, on the other hand, it must be admitted that on at least one occasion (as noticed below), the Treasury Board was satisfied that untrained labour would not be of assistance in the Audit Office. In fairness to the Auditors of the Imprests it should be mentioned that the speed of the Audit Office was not greatly increased by the placing of the joint Auditorships in commission; for the five commissioners, even when urged on by Pitt, did not succeed in overtaking arrears. They failed, for instance, to have Fox's final account ready for declaration until 1788; and the Paymasters' accounts for the period of the American War were being declared, on an average, about ten years after the period to which they related.[1] So far as Fox is concerned we have both the statement that Fox wrote repeatedly to successive Secretaries at War urging haste, (presumably in clearing regimental accounts),[2] and also his executor's testimony that Fox had requested two of his Deputy Paymasters to submit their accounts direct to the Audit Office, to avoid the delay which would have occurred had they been sent to the Pay Office for consolidation there with his own account.[3] Fox was not a defaulter, if that implies that he had retarded the submission of his accounts and vouchers to the Auditors; and if subsequent delays in passing the accounts could have been diminished, the blame (if any) appears to rest rather upon the Audit Office, or the Treasury.

The view that Fox was not blameworthy derives some further support from an investigation of Beckford's charge that legal process had been suspended by 'the King's Sign Manual'. On 19 May 1768 the Treasury Board received a memorial from Lord Holland, as Fox then was, praying to be allowed further time to make up his accounts as late Paymaster. His reasons appeared sufficient, and the Board forthwith directed the preparation of a

[1] See the Declared Accounts in question: P.R.O., A.O. 1, bundles 84–93, Rolls 113–16 and 118–23.

[2] Ilchester, *op. cit.* ii. 335.

[3] *Commissioners for Examining the Public Accounts*, Rep. 4, app. 3.

warrant for stay of process for one year.[1] It does not appear that
this was other than a normal Treasury warrant, nor is it clear why
(supposing that Beckford had his facts correct, or was correctly
reported), a sign manual should have been requisite.   So far from
conniving at delay, the Board at the same time directed John Powell
of the Pay Office to appear before them and explain the cause of the
delay.   He gave as reasons ' the extent and nature of the services, the
bulk of the accounts, and the unusual hurry that was unavoidable
in his office during the late war '.   He added that the accounts of
the years 1757 and 1758 were then before the Auditors, and that
those of 1759 would be delivered in a few weeks.   He also stated
that in preparing the accounts of subsequent years difficulty might
arise ' from several Regiments not being cleared ', and delivered an
account detailing them.   The Board at once ordered a letter to be
written to the Secretary at War requesting the latter to hasten the
clearance of the regimental accounts.[2]   The Board's wish and
intention to speed up the completion of Fox's accounts was further
emphasized a year later when the Deputy Auditors attended,
Powell being summoned again.   Solely to avoid delay, the Board
sanctioned a certain technical procedure which they disliked and
ruled as not permissible in future, and they questioned the Deputy
Auditors as to progress in their office, suggesting to them an
increase in staff.   The Deputies succeeded in satisfying the Board
that new and untrained staff would be of no assistance, and were
dismissed after being recommended in the strongest manner to
exercise all possible despatch.[3]   The Treasury appear to be cleared
of Beckford's imputation of ' going slow '.   The latter seems to
have understood the circumstances only imperfectly, and the episode
illustrates how true was the observation made many years later
by George Rose, one of Pitt's joint Secretaries of the Treasury,
that formerly it had been almost impossible for a true judgement
to be formed on matters connected with public finance, except by
those who had the conduct of them.[4]   If there was blame for delay,
it probably rested mainly on the Audit Office, for it is doubtful
whether at that period [5] the Treasury Board had legal power to
compel an increase of Audit Office staff, should the Auditors not
agree to such a course.

[1] P.R.O., T. 29/39.   Treasury minute of 19 May 1768, and warrant of the same
date, T. 54/40 p. 441.   Ilchester, *op. cit.* ii. 335, states that a six months' stay of process
had already been granted, but this appears to have left no trace in the Treasury minute
and warrant books.
[2] P.R.O., T. 29/39.   Treasury minute of 2 June 1768.
[3] P.R.O., T. 29/40.   Treasury minute of 22 June 1769.   This was upon an application by the Deputy Auditors of the Imprests, and appears to have arisen in the ordinary
course of business.
[4] *A brief examination into the increase of the revenue during Pitt's administration*, 2nd
edn., 1806, p. 1.
[5] I.e. before 25 Geo. III, c. 52, which instituted the Audit Commission in 1785.

In spite of these facts, which go some way towards the exculpation of those concerned, it is not, however, to be denied that at the time of the Address in 1769 Fox continued to retain very large balances of public money; and, as will later be indicated, the uses to which some of these balances were put were of a nature to lay the Governments of the day under some obligation to him.[1] For the retention of these large balances there were, nevertheless, various grounds of justification. It was necessary for him to continue to hold public money because his responsibility for paying services incurred during his period of office continued, whether the demands presented themselves before or after his retirement. It might even be necessary for him, after retirement, to apply for further issues from the exchequer.[2] This appears to have been bound up with legal considerations, for, when in 1782 it was decided to obtain power in future to vest a retiring Paymaster's balance in his successor, to enable the latter to carry on the retiring Paymaster's services and to avoid money lying idle, it was thought necessary to resort to statutory [3] and not administrative action.[4] But when all delayed charges appeared to have been presented, when the practical ground for retaining balances after retirement was no longer of force, the law did not forbid, and custom permitted, their retention, and there were no prompt and convenient sanctions for enforcing their delivery. Before recourse could be had to the Court of Exchequer for this purpose, it was first necessary to ascertain what was the sum of money to be claimed, and, as already indicated, it was a very long time before the exact amount could be known. Further, although it was the practice to issue a writ of distraint for the purpose of enforcing prompt delivery of complete accounts to the Auditors,[5] it was the sensible practice not to issue process for the recovery of balances upon each separate year's account, but to carry forward the balance from one year to the next, until the final account. There does not appear to have been power to enforce payments ' on account ', and when such payments were made they seem to have been made under the authority of a statute, as in 1769.[6] When in 1781 a number of public accountants were to be required to pay in specified balances under an indemnity, a special Act was necessary.[7] Thus it is abundantly clear that the law sanctioned and practice required the retention.

[1] See below, pp. 432-3.

[2] See, for instance, P.R.O., T. 29/38. Treasury minute of 13 February 1767, and other similar minutes.

[3] See 22 Geo. III, c. 81, which is printed in Danby Pickering's edition of *Statutes at Large*, though not in Ruffhead's edition.

[4] I.e. not by Order in Council, Privy Seal, sign manual, or Treasury warrant.

[5] As, for instance, in Fox's case referred to above.

[6] See 10 Geo. III, c. 52.

[7] See 21 Geo. III, c. 48.

The magnitude of the Paymaster's balances raises other considerations, which were of equal force before and after retirement. The public money in the Paymaster's hands was not legally a consolidated fund, any part of which could be drawn on for any purpose. The money voted and issued on account of any year was not available for the service of any other year ; and likewise, the detailed appropriations of the vote of any year were not available for any other head of service than that prescribed in the Appropriation or other Act. Consequently, when a Paymaster had exhausted his receipt on some particular head of service, no matter how much money he might have in hand in respect of other heads, he was compelled to apply for more money on the exhausted head, thus increasing yet further the balances in his hands.[1] Another factor tending to increase the balances was the circumstance that a Paymaster was also *ipso facto* Paymaster of Chelsea Hospital, the establishment having the care of disabled and aged soldiers, both as in-patients within its walls and as out-patients resident all over Great Britain. Money for the out-patients was voted annually by parliament,[2] and funds for the hospital itself were, as already noted, furnished by deducting one day's pay from most active members of the military forces, supplemented also by drawing on the fund of poundage deducted from the Paymaster's issues. But all these revenues were in practice inadequate. The declared accounts of Paymasters of Chelsea Hospital show considerable sums owing to them by the public, and there seems to be no other explanation of the manner in which Paymasters of Chelsea Hospital contrived to pay out far more than they received, than by supposing that they raided for this purpose the balances of the Paymasters of the Forces. This fact has been obscured because the commissioners for examining the public accounts were directed to enquire into the balances of the Paymasters of the Forces, but not into those of the Paymasters of Chelsea Hospital ; and the circumstance seems to have escaped their notice, or at least their publicity. When in January 1783 the Treasury Board, on the authority of the Act of 1781, set about demanding repayment of Fox's balance of £288,529, they were informed that his estate was actually owed £220,521 on account of the hospital, so that the net claim was reduced to £68,008.[3] Thus to finance his deficit on the hospital the Paymaster had, in his capacity as Paymaster of the Forces, to hold larger balances than he need otherwise have done, whilst the nominal amount of his balances represented a fictitious inflation of the sums actually in his hands.

[1] For Lord North on this subject, see William Cobbett's *Parliamentary History*, xxii. col. 211. He was speaking in the debate on the first four reports of the commissioners for examining the public accounts, 10 May 1781.

[2] See the annual Appropriation Acts, *passim*.

[3] P.R.O., T. 29/53. Treasury minute of 14 January 1783.

Yet another factor confusing the true state of the balances was the practice of issuing subsistence in advance, the period varying between one month for the forces at home and twelve months for those in India; and issuing pay for garrisons and staff (and certain other services) from two to eighteen months in arrear— the arrears much exceeding the advances. These withheld arrears were employed as temporary finance for the army extra-ordinaries until such time as parliament voted the amount of the latter, and thus enabled the Treasury to carry out the withheld payments, the money for which had been otherwise applied for the time being.[1]

Although there were all these proper grounds for the holding of large balances, nevertheless, so far as it is possible to judge, the balances which successive Paymasters actually held appear to have been too great to be justified by necessity. The system of management was open to abuse, for while law and custom permitted the employment of balances for the Paymaster's private enrichment, neither law nor custom limited the extent to which this might be practised; provided always that when needed the money was forth-coming. There was, moreover, a sinister distinction between the situation of the Paymaster of the Forces and that of certain other public accountants such as the Treasurers of the Navy and of the Ordnance. With the exception of some relatively small sums re-quired for paying exchequer and Treasury fees on passing accounts, &c., the two latter officers applied to the Treasury for money merely as the mouthpieces of Boards of Commissioners. The Navy, Victual-ling, Sick and Hurt, and Ordnance Boards had no personal incentive to apply for larger sums than were really necessary, for they were not personally the custodians of the cash. It was otherwise with the Paymaster of the Forces, for he not only kept the cash but was the sole authority for deciding when to apply for money and how much to apply for. This was a situation of some delicacy, and it is not difficult to believe that the temptation to apply for more than was really necessary continually presented itself to Fox and his successors, up until the time of the regulation of the Paymaster's office in 1782.[2] The Treasury Board acceded to all such applica-tions, having no information by which to judge their propriety, nor, apparently, any legal power to demand it. That the resulting situa-tion was more satisfactory for the holder of the Paymastership than for the public may be inferred from the zeal with which the Pay-mastership was sought by those politicians who looked to places

[1] For this see especially P.R.O. 30/8, bundle 231, booklet entitled ' Business done at the Treasury '.

[2] Before 1759 it had been the custom to apply every four months for about one-third of the year's vote, but after that period to apply as and when demands for payment were approaching (*Commissioners for Examining the Public Accounts*, Rep. 5).

of profit rather than of power or honour. Richard Rigby, for
instance, Paymaster from 1768 to 1782, was said to have made the
Paymastership the avowed goal of his ambition. Fox's father-in-
law, the duke of Richmond, told the duke of Newcastle in 1747
that, while welcoming the proposal to make Fox Secretary of
State, ' we still wish him the Paymaster's place, as it is less precarious and a better thing, for his family's sake '; [1] and when
Fox achieved it ten years later, it was ' . . . the very thing he
wished '.[2]

The means by which the great gains might be made require
explanation. The Paymaster's letters patent provided for a salary
of £3,000 as Paymaster of the Forces, another £365 as Paymaster
of Chelsea Hospital, and a third salary, also of £365, as one upon
the establishment of General and Staff officers. In addition, he
received an allowance of £600 for the contingencies of his office,
and a further allowance for paying the salaries of his under-officers
and clerks. Fox's allowance under the latter head is uncertain,
but is not likely to have fallen below the £1,500 allowed to Pitt,
nor to have exceeded the £1,760 allowed to Rigby. This gross
receipt was reduced by departmental poundage, already referred to,
by taxes,[3] and by the sums necessary to defray the clerical payroll
and contingent expenses. Comparable calculations based upon a
document in the Chatham Papers [4] and upon figures in the sixth
report of the commissioners for examining the public accounts,
suggest that after all deductions are taken into account the clear
profit of office was about £2,940 in the first case, and about
£2,964 in the second. It is probably not wide of the mark to suggest
that Fox's clear official profit did not greatly exceed £3,000 on the
average. It was, however, the contemporary practice, established
beyond the memory of man, for a Paymaster to supplement his
official emoluments by profitably employing a part of the balances
in his hands and taking that profit to his own use. This was one
of the accepted perquisites of office; nor (despite the applause
which the elder Pitt received for his alleged refusal as Paymaster
to profit by these balances) [5] was there anything approaching public

---

[1] Brit. Mus. Add. MSS. 32,714, fo. 219, quoted by Ilchester, *op. cit.* i. 145.

[2] J. Calcraft to Lord Charles Hay, 9 July 1757, Brit. Mus. Add. MSS. 17,493, fo. 78.

[3] Land Tax, the 1*s.* in the £ ' Pension Duty ', and the 6*d.* in the £ Civil List Duty,
were all payable in respect of Pay Office emoluments, though not every member of
the staff was burdened with all three. It does not seem possible to determine how
much of the gross sum paid for all taxes actually relates to the Paymaster's salaries.

[4] P.R.O. 30/8, bundle 76.

[5] *The English Pericles*, p. 32. This is an anonymous pamphlet apparently written
about the spring of 1759. See also John Almon, *Anecdotes of the Life of the Rt. Hon.
William Pitt, Earl of Chatham*, &c. (6th edn.) 1797, i. 243, for the statement that when
Pitt retired from the Paymastership, the balances belonging to his office were found
intact in the Bank. See also B. Williams, *The Life of William Pitt, Earl of Chatham*
(1915) i. 154-5.

condemnation of the practice until another generation had arisen and until after the great and fruitless expenditure of the American War.[1]

Although it has always been known that the tenure of the Paymastership was, by reason of the magnitude of the sums passing through a Paymaster's hands, a very paying proposition, the actual amount of profit that could be made has hitherto been quite unknown. A corner of the veil is now lifted. Sir Lewis Namier recently drew attention to a set of Henry Fox's private ledgers containing, *inter alia*, accounts relating to his private transactions with public money in his hands, preserved amongst the Bunbury Papers in the Bury St. Edmunds and West Suffolk Record Office.[2] A similar ledger for the short term of office of Fox's successor, Charles Townshend, has been preserved with them and provides useful supplementary information.[3] Fox's ledgers, mostly for a period of twelve months each, cover the years 1758 to 1773; that is to say, they begin a few months after he had taken office, and they continue long after his retirement—indeed to within a few months of his death. The first ledger of the set is unhappily missing, and for lack of the journals and vouchers much in the surviving books is obscure; but their general tenor is informative enough, and, surprisingly, they show that what is termed Fox's 'Private Account' (as distinguished from his 'Office Account'), was actually made up in the Pay Office itself. The fortuitous survival of the ledger for Charles Townshend's 'Private Account' suggests that this was the normal practice of the period.

Each ledger contains what is described as an 'Inventory', which is in effect a balance sheet setting out the commencing balances on those various accounts which constitute the ledger proper. These accounts display the transactions of the year, or other accounting period, which followed after the date of the inventory; the inventory itself revealing the state of affairs at the day on which the ledger opens. On the debtor side of the inventory appear the sums in respect of which Fox was a debtor to the Pay Office or other source of money; and on the creditor side appears the disposition of Fox's indebtedness, the sums advanced to sundry persons (of whom Fox was thus a creditor), the sums invested in public or other securities, and that resting in the form of cash. It

---

[1] Another source of profit which, according to Edmund Burke, his predecessor as Paymaster General (Richard Rigby) had enjoyed, arose upon the contract for clothing the pensioners belonging to Chelsea Hospital. Burke stated the profit, which presumably was annual, at £700. (See John Debrett's *Parliamentary Register*, vii. 277.) No such profit is identifiable in Fox's private ledgers, but this does not necessarily prove that it was not taken. There is no evidence of Fox's having taken a commission on foreign subsidies. For this alleged practice see B. Williams, *op. cit.* i. 155.

[2] Referenced as in boxes E. 18/853(1) and E. 18/853(2). The books would appear to have come into the family's possession through the marriage of a daughter of General Henry Edward Fox, Henry Fox's youngest son, who ultimately took on the duties of administrator of his father's final account.   [3] See Appendix.

is to be noted that the figures brought into the inventory are not always those appearing at the close of the accounts in the previous ledger; investments are sometimes adjusted to their current market value before being entered in the inventory, a process that might involve either ' writing up ' or ' writing down '. Thus the balance on the inventories, which in most cases represents an excess of advances by Fox over and above his indebtedness to the public, is explicable as profits taken credit for in the books but not yet realized by being turned into cash. An exception is the closing balance, which reveals that Fox's indebtedness exceeded the assets available for discharging it, and appears to be connected with the payment of Charles James Fox's debts.

From the inventories have been compiled Tables 1 and 2,

TABLE 1

STATEMENT OF HENRY FOX'S INDEBTEDNESS TO THE PUBLIC, &C.

(Extracted from the inventories in his private ledgers.)

Date	On Pay Office Account &c.	On Crown Land Revenue Account & to Private Persons	Total
	£	£	£
5 Jan. 1759	133,969	7,956	141,925
5 Jan. 1760	188,867	8,356	197,223
5 Jan. 1761	413,087	8,537	421,624
5 Jan. 1762	628,154	8,822	636,976
5 Jan. 1763	800,620	9,177	809,797
18 Jan. 1764	306,080	9,505	315,585
1 Jan. 1765	159,374	5,010	164,384
1 Jan. 1766	289,364	5,452	294,816
1 Jan. 1767	398,937	5,009	403,946
29 Sep. 1767	426,937	5,810	432,747
29 Sep. 1768	498,937	7,985	506,922
29 Sep. 1769	519,465	6,549	526,014
29 Sep. 1770	489,799	6,249	496,048
29 Sep. 1771	484,799	6,409	491,208
25 Dec. 1772	464,974	7,346	472,320
25 Dec. 1773 *	464,397	75,441	539,838

* Built up from the balances carried forward at the close of the last surviving ledger.

which show respectively the money with which Fox was operating and the manner in which it was disposed. The figures of indebtedness on Pay Office account require little comment. Much of the money was drawn out of an account at the Bank of England where, by custom and for convenience, Paymasters were wont to keep army cash, though they were not yet positively required by statute to do so. Smaller sums came through Hoare's Bank, with which Fox had already been banking as a young man.[1] These latter

[1] Ilchester, *op. cit.* i. 25.

represent the proceeds of sales of stores, of repayments by sub-accountants, and remittances in respect of Irish troops employed. In 1760 and 1761 considerable sums were taken in the form of Exchequer Bills which, at that difficult time, were perhaps issued to the Paymaster in lieu of cash. It should always be remembered, however, that the ledgers only deal with money employed by Fox privately, and so represent only a part of the public balances in his hands, the remainder lying at the Bank of England or elsewhere for the current needs of military expenditure. Before passing on from the first Table it may be remarked that the great increase in indebtedness to private persons arising in 1773 is due to a large borrowing from John Powell, and is almost certainly connected with the payment of Charles James Fox's debts.[1]

TABLE 2

ANALYSIS OF HENRY FOX'S ADVANCES, INVESTMENTS, &c.

(Extracted from the inventories in his private ledgers.)

Date	On Mortgage	On Bonds	In Stocks	In Cash	Sundries	Total
	£	£	£	£	£	£
5 Jan. 1759	62,000	42,110	24,960	11,702	3,415	144,187
5 Jan. 1760	63,395	54,540	63,128	15,108	4,812	200,983
5 Jan. 1761	62,000	62,485	302,581	2,581	4,162	433,809
5 Jan. 1762	86,950	36,024	380,990	145,399	4,597	653,960
5 Jan. 1763	100,250	56,140	313,323	367,714	3,157	840,584
18 Jan. 1764	110,950	23,498	249,220	72,220	5,884	461,772
1 Jan. 1765	131,250	30,052	140,055	17,544	5,731	324,632
1 Jan. 1766	132,793	26,750	248,829	34,101	5,334	447,807
1 Jan. 1767	145,451	38,900	320,656	81,899	5,234	592,140
29 Sep. 1767	222,784	29,795	346,495	4,883	20,678	624,635
29 Sep. 1768	260,284	27,937	376,830	10	20,794	685,855
29 Sep. 1769	265,784	34,137	356,204	10	35,116	691,251
29 Sep. 1770	256,784	42,839	295,017	7,186	38,269	640,095
29 Sep. 1771	178,084	41,255	388,166	5,706	38,689	651,900
25 Dec. 1772	148,321	41,967	390,995	—	38,009	619,292
25 Dec. 1773*	150,460	53,405	266,961	—	38,629	509,455

* Built up from the balances carried forward at the close of the last surviving ledger.

Regarding the second Table, a few notes may explain the principal variations. The increase in mortgages in 1767 is accounted for by seven fresh advances; and the fall in 1770–1 by the repayment of a single large one (£53,000) advanced to Sir Blake Delaval and his brothers. The rise in the holding of public funds from 1761 reflects speculations with the loans of that and the following year, a residuum being retained for the interest it brought in, and further purchases and sales being made from time to time. Fox was not a man to leave money long lying idle.[2] As far back

---

[1] For this, see below, pp. 438-9.

[2] A significant exception is to be found during the acute financial crisis of 1759, when between 16 and 19 April he acquired £10,500 in gold specie. This he kept in a chest until 3 November of the same year, when he paid it into Hoare's Bank.

as 1735 he had written : ' I don't see why any more of my money than is necessary for the election should lie dead at Mr. Hoare's '.[1] Consequently, except when Fox has just been speculating on a grand scale (as in 1761 to 1763), or was still varying his investments considerably (as in the following four years), little is lying idle in the form of cash bringing him no return. The increase in the sundries in 1767 and 1768–9 is largely accounted for by advances to his extravagant elder son Stephen, and to his natural son Charles Cooper.

A study of the ledgers indicates that the bulk of Fox's gains was derived from interest on mortgages, bonds, and public investments, though two spectacularly successful *coups* which greatly increased his capital must be described later. The individuals favoured with loans on mortgage or bond fall into various categories. A number of them were personal friends, though other loans were clearly business transactions, sometimes concealed under the name of a nominee such as his nephew, Lord Digby. The mortgages were in nearly all cases for considerable sums, advanced to persons of large landed estate, such as Earl Ferrers, Sir Blake Delaval and his brothers, the earl of Oxford, &c. Interest at the normal mortgage rate of 4 per cent. was payable on the bulk of these, but the advances made in the hard times of 1761 and 1762 were at the higher rate of 5 per cent. The recipients of advances on bond were more various, and considerable loans, at rates of from $3\frac{1}{2}$ per cent. to 5 per cent., were made to such relatives as the duke of Richmond,[2] and the marquis of Kildare ;[3] to his one time patron the duke of Cumberland (an interest-free loan in 1761, and another at 4 per cent. contracted in 1762 and repaid with accumulated interest after their estrangement at the end of that year) ;[4] and to such friends as that man-about-town George Selwyn,[5] who failed to pay up his interest, and Sir George Macartney.[6] Such loans included, no doubt, both investments and the fruits of Fox's generosity to those he held in affection. Some of the smaller loans can clearly not be classed as investments. Such was the loan of £500, on bond at 5 per cent., to William and Edmund Burke, made in 1766 when William Burke had common interests with Fox in East India speculations, on which neither interest nor capital had been paid at Fox's death, and for which the executor was still

---

[1] Ilchester, *op. cit.* i. 25. [2] His wife's brother.

[3] The husband of his wife's sister.

[4] Ilchester, *op. cit.* ii. 176. The amount of the first loan was a thousand guineas, and of the second loan, £8,000.

[5] Selwyn's loan was of £2,000. Interest owed but unpaid at December 1773 may be computed at almost £1,200.

[6] The amount of the loan varied at different times between the limits of £2,000 and £7,000. Interest was paid only intermittently, and £1,120 appears to have been outstanding in December, 1773.

struggling to get satisfaction in 1780 ;[1] or the loan of £1,050 made
in 1773 to Edward Moore, Receiver and Register for the Office of
Hackney Coaches and Chairs, and Index Maker to the house of
commons, who, when pressed for payment pointed out firstly that
he was owed money by Fox's estate both on Fox's account and on
Charles James's, and secondly that 'I formerly was qualified by
holding Lord Holland's stock to vote in the India House. When
the law was altered Lord Holland lent me the £1,050 towards
purchasing an East India qualification, and I did so principally
to oblige his Lordship, who lent it me at 4 per cent. for that
purpose '.[2]

Of particular interest are the large loans which Fox made from
time to time, either directly or through an intermediary, to jobbers
and brokers on the London market, on the security of stock or
scrip, sometimes for a year, or more often for a shorter period, a
practice that throws some light on the embryonic London Stock
Exchange. Thus in 1758, by an intermediary Mr. Tucker, he lent
£25,000 to the broking and jobbing firm of Lejay and Chamier,[3]
and in March 1759 he lent £20,000 for one year at 5 per cent.,
soon after increased by a further £12,000. Renewed in 1760, the
loan of £20,000 was not paid off until April 1761. In 1760, during
the subscription to the government loan of that year, he lent to
unspecified persons £12,000 on the security of stock, and £20,000
on the security of lottery tickets, for three months at the same rate.[4]
In 1765 he lent a total of £21,760 at 5 per cent. to Nathan
Modigliani of Old Bethlem, a Jewish broker and jobber very active
in East India speculation, and £1,500 to Samuel Gardiner of Change
Alley, broker, to carry them over to the next ' Rescounter ', or
quarterly settlement day. In 1766 Modigliani received a loan of
£30,000 between ' Rescounters ' (of which £20,000 was renewed),
and one Dawes received the sum of £10,000 for the same purpose.

[1] Executor's Letter Book, p. 73, Bury St. Edmunds &c. Record Office E.18/360/5.
[2] Executor's Letter Book, p. 70. Moore held a contingent promissory note of
Fox's, liability for which the executor would not admit. The note related to Charles
James's affairs. The ground of the direct debt is significant of Fox's unpopularity.
Fox had asked Moore to make extracts from the house of commons journals of every
entry relating to public accountants ' for the last hundred years ', and had never paid
for the work. Moore's tender of what he considered to be his net legal debt appears
to have been refused.
[3] Anthony Chamier, a successful stockbroker of Huguenot descent. ' He acquired
such a fortune as enabled him, though young, to quit business and become, what
indeed he seemed by nature intended for, a gentleman.' (Sir John Hawkins, *The
Works of Samuel Johnson, LL.D., together with his Life*, &c. (1787) i. 423.) He later
held minor office, and was a friend of Dr. Johnson.
[4] Charles Townshend's ledger shows him making such loans out of his balances
in the same way, though necessarily on a smaller scale. Loans from the Bank of
England on the security of scrip were recognized to be essential to the success of a
subscription, and it seems probable that merchant banks were increasingly rendering
the same service to their clients ; but the whole subject of the finance of the stock
market at this period remains obscure.

In 1770 he lent to ' a friend of Mr. Fisher's ',[1] the sum of £30,500 on the security of £20,000 Bank Stock, and a further £11,000 on the security of £5,000 East India Stock.

Fox employed the services of a number of agents in the transaction of his financial concerns. Until their breach in 1763 [2] John Calcraft, a close friend and associate of many years' standing and the richest of the army commissaries of the day, was clearly working closely with him; Samuel Touchet, a merchant who crashed in a spectacular manner in 1763,[3] did a good deal for him in later years, and a number of lesser men carried out minor operations on his behalf. But his chief man of business throughout the period was John Powell, accountant (and later cashier) of the Pay Office, in whose hands these ledgers show the bulk of Fox's idle cash to have lain. Powell was later to be the only one of Fox's three named executors who consented to act, was himself to become extremely wealthy, and was destined to end his career in disgrace and suicide in 1782, despite the ill-judged attempts of Edmund Burke, Paymaster at the time, to shelter him.[4] Transactions between Fox and Powell, as shown in the ledgers, are extraordinarily numerous and complicated. In the absence of other information they are indeed impossible to unravel, but everything suggests that Powell was fully informed of Fox's proceedings, being perhaps the only man who ever has been or will be.

The sundries in the accounts embrace a miscellaneous variety of transactions such as shares in turnpikes, in a privateer, in an Indiaman (called ' Lord Holland '), and advances to members of his own family.

The two speculative *coups* already referred to demand particular attention for the large capital profits which they brought, for the part they played in causing Fox's intense unpopularity, and for their significance in the financial history of the time. They arose in connexion with the raising of the government loans during the Seven Years' War; and after them must be mentioned lengthy operations connected with speculation in East India stock and the development of political ' management ' in the East India Company from 1763 onward.

The ledgers show, though not always in full detail, Fox's part in the raising of the government loans of 1759, 1760, 1761, and 1762. In 1759, when the duke of Newcastle's attempt to raise the then almost unprecedented sum of £6,600,000 [5]—coinciding with

---

[1] William Fisher of Change Alley, one of the biggest dealers of the day.

[2] The circumstances of their estrangement have never become altogether clear, but Calcraft threw in his lot with Lord Shelburne, and Fox considered him guilty of the blackest treachery and ingratitude.

[3] For him see Alfred P. Wadsworth and J. de L. Mann, *The Cotton Trade and Industrial Lancashire, 1600–1780* (Manchester) 1931, pp. 243 *seq.*

[4] Sir Philip M. Magnus, *Edmund Burke* (1939) pp. 121–3.

[5] Of earlier loans only that of 1748 (£6,930,000), appears to have been greater.

a payments crisis arising from the needs of wartime remittances—
nearly led to disaster in the City,[1] Fox made his first payment on a
subscription of £117,700.   He did little to help the Treasury in its
hour of need, however, as he sold out all but £17,700 before the
second payment became due, and by early May had parted with
the whole, estimating his loss at £644 18s. 3d.   A letter of 27 April
to his broker, which came into the hands of the duke of Newcastle,
ordering the broker to sell all that Fox held, as ' . . . I have no
opinion of the Subscription; I don't think it will grow much better;
the Duke of Newcastle consults too many people about it '.[2]   Fox
formed a somewhat more favourable impression of the prospects
of the 1760 subscription, making a first payment on £260,000, a
second payment on £145,700, a third payment on £130,700, and a
fourth payment on £87,700.   But though he dealt a good deal in
the loan throughout the year, he closed the account in 1761 with
an estimated loss of £182 18s. 5d.

So far his dealings had not proved profitable.   Those in the
loans of 1761 and 1762 had, however, a very different result.   In
1761 Fox put his name down for £300,000 out of the £12,000,000
to be raised, and he paid the first instalment of 15 per cent. on his
subscription.   He then took to purchasing in the market, and in
the first four months of that year paid out, either in his own name
or in the name of others, the enormous total of £773,936—all public
money.   The loan was constituted of three parts: perpetual 3 per
cent. stock, long annuities (for 99 years) at £1 2s. 6d. per cent.,
and lottery tickets.   Fox participated in all three.   He began his
sales in March, almost two months before he ceased purchasing,
which suggests that the market quotations of the three parts were
rising unequally, as buyers preferred and demanded one rather than
another.   By the end of 1761 he had divested himself of all pro-
prietorship in the loan save for long annuities worth £10,000 a
year, and a few lottery tickets.   The reason for his initial subscription may have been creditable; as a member of the Ministry it
may have seemed proper to assist at a time when Pitt's vehement
conduct of the war was making unprecedented demands upon
the public purse and the money market.   But his subsequent
market purchases cannot be regarded as anything but speculative;
they did nothing to assist Government (the subscription list being
already filled), and tended merely to force up the market quotations.
His sales prove his true object, and his memoir suggests that these
transactions were somewhat on his mind, as the stir in the house
of commons about his balances at that time gave good cause.

---

[1] L. S. Sutherland, ' Samson Gideon, Eighteenth Century Financier ', *Transactions
of the Jewish Historical Society of England*, xvii. 86–7. See above, pp. 394-5.
[2] Brit. Mus. Add. MSS. 32,890, fo. 343, quoted by L. S. Sutherland, *loc. cit.* pp.
86–7. See above, pp. 394-5.

The sudden and great rise of the stocks (so he writes) has made me richer than I ever intended or desired to be . . . The Government borrows money at 20 % discount. I am not consulted or concerned in making the bargain. I have, as Paymaster, great sums in my hands which, not applicable to any present use, must either lie dead in the Bank or be employed by me. I lend this to the Government in 1761. A peace is thought certain. I am not in the least consulted, but my very bad opinion of Mr. Pitt makes me think it will not be concluded. I sell out and gain greatly.[1]

It seems not unfair to observe that the amount he lent directly to Government was very small. The outside world was certainly optimistic about a speedy peace—hence the rise in the stocks and the speculative fever. But it is difficult indeed to believe, as Fox would apparently have us do, that in his position he had no inside information as to the progress of negotiations.[2] When the outside world's mistake became evident the market broke, and at the end of the year the market value of Fox's retained long annuities was below their cost to him. But this represented only a temporary recession, and by the end of 1763 he had taken credit for realized and book profits in the neighbourhood of £103,000—little of which, if any, appears to have been lost afterwards.

Success again attended his participation in the loan of 1762. His memoir continues:

In 1762 I lend again; a peace comes, in which again I am not consulted, and I again gain greatly. If anybody should say that I advised a peace, let it be considered that that was in November last. I had no money in the Funds then, and indeed thought that my advice would not be taken, nor was it, but on the contrary a declaration of war with Spain followed.

Readers may wonder at his statement that he had no money in the Funds at this period, since his private ledgers show that he held a large block of long annuities, and never less than £60,000 of the four-per-cents. of 1762, not to mention a great holding of navy bills.[3] However, there is no ground for casting suspicion on his exactitude when he admits to having gained greatly, for by the end of 1764 his ledgers show an actually realized profit on this loan amounting to upwards of £56,000.

[1] Henry Fox's 'Memoir', written in 1763, is printed in the *Life and Letters of Lady Sarah Lennox*, by the countess of Ilchester and Lord Stavordale (1902), i. 3–79. This, with the subsequent passage quoted, appears on p. 72.

[2] It has already been seen that at this period Fox had a close financial association with the stockbroker Anthony Chamier. These great capital gains of Fox's were made at the same period as was Chamier's fortune. Of the latter, Sir John Hawkins, writing in 1787 (*op. cit.* i. 423), stated that it arose by Chamier's 'dealings in the funds, and, it was supposed, with the advantage of intelligence which, previous to the conclusion of the peace before last, he had obtained'.

[3] It may be true that Fox had none of his *private* resources in the Funds, but in view of the use to which the public balances was put, the passage quoted has a certain air of the disingenuous.

Fox's operations in East India stock were more complex, and in the long run less rewarding. Their course is known to us in outline from other sources,[1] and the ledgers serve to fill in some, though not all, of the gaps. In the ten years between 1763 and 1773, when his active concern in East India affairs ceases, he was pursuing in his dealings in the stock two main purposes, sometimes both at the same time. He was furthering the political interests of a series of Governments in obtaining a control over the election of the directors of the great political organization which the East India Company had become, and he was seeking on his own account opportunities of gain in the speculative boom which swept over the Company between 1766 and 1769, as a result of Clive's successes in India. The political interests of Governments necessitated the provision of funds to create votes at the Company's elections, pledged to support candidates favoured by the Administration. The course of these great so-called ' splitting ' campaigns can best be traced from the stock ledgers of the East India Company itself. Neither the Company's stock-ledgers nor these Pay Office private account ledgers give a full picture of Fox's part in the campaigns, since the management of the funds he provided was in the hands of such men as John Calcraft (at first), John Powell and others. The private account ledgers make, however, occasional references to the payment of fees for numerous stock transfers (e.g. thirty-six in the 1764 campaign), and they give more information on Fox's holdings than do the Company's stock ledgers, since they include stock evidently held by him in the names of others. Thus the Company's ledgers show Fox as purchasing £500 on 3 March 1763 (to qualify him as a voter in the first annual election of directors in which Government actively intervened), and as purchasing another £500 later in the year. Before the next election he disposed of this holding in such a way as to create two votes, but does not re-appear as a holder of stock himself until June 1767. In his own ledgers he is shown as buying not £500 but £11,000 on 3 March 1763, and retaining £10,500 of it through 1764, and purchasing much greater holdings in the next two years.

Fox's political activities in the Company fall into two periods, 1763–4 and 1768–73. In the first period his activities require little explanation. His nominees voted, it is true, for the candidates of Laurence Sulivan's party in the election of 1763, and for the candidates of the rival party under Lord Clive in 1764, but this was because Fox was Paymaster both under the Bute Administration and under that of George Grenville, and the two ministers supported different sides in the Company's conflicts. After he relinquished

---

[1] For the course of East India affairs and the evidence of Fox's participation in them, see L. S. Sutherland, *The East India Company in Eighteenth Century Politics* (Oxford) 1952, chaps. vi and vii.

the Paymastership in 1765, however, it might have been expected that Fox's assistance to Government in East India matters would cease. In fact it did so until the autumn of 1768, but at that time he began once again to place some of his balances at the disposal of the Grafton Administration for the same purpose. Men concerned with East India affairs spoke of £25,000 stock administered for this purpose in the contested Company election of 1769; his ledgers suggest that probably at least £30,000 more was being used for this purpose.[1] Though we have no explanation of this renewed employment of his balances on Government's behalf, it may be noted that it coincides with the entry of his two elder sons, Stephen and Charles James, into parliament as active young Government supporters, and with the renewal of his own earlier pressure for an earldom. He continued to provide this assistance until the end of 1772 when, after all the dispositions had been made for the Company election of 1773, his ledgers confirm the evidence of those of the Company that he unexpectedly sold out, thus depriving his nominees of any right to vote—no doubt to the embarrassment of Government. Whether his action was due to the pressure of his sons' debts (soon to reach a crisis), to some disagreement with the Ministry, or to alarm at the fall in the price of East India stock which was badly affected at this time by the financial crisis which hit the London market in 1772, and by the particular difficulties of the Company which led to Lord North's East India regulation next year, no evidence is at present available.

Of Fox's purely speculative activities in the stock, which took place between 1766 and 1769, the ledgers are more informative, though here, too, incidental references in them show that much was done by nominees whose affairs only enter accidentally into these accounts. The great boom in East India stock began when the news reached England that Clive had taken over the Diwani, or financial control, of Bengal. Clive's agent, John Walsh, who was purchasing largely on his principal's instructions, advised Fox to do likewise; and those informed in East India affairs were soon aware that he had made considerable purchases, and was prominent amongst the group of speculators who were ' bulling ' the stock. The Company ledgers, however, retain no trace of these purchases apart from one of £40,000 stock by John Powell on 29 April 1766. Fox's ledgers, on the other hand, show that between 23 and 25 April he added £50,000 (purchased at prices varying between 174 and 181) to a holding of £20,000; that between 14 and 23 May he added £30,000 more (purchased at much the same prices); and that by 16 July he held £115,000. Of this he sold £65,000 between 11 and 12 September, at prices ranging between 207 and 210, and

[1] See below, p.434.

at the end of the year he calculated his gains (realized, and estimated on the current value of his holdings of stock), at £41,958.

The rise in the price of stock which lies behind these gains, considerable though it was, was not so great as the ' bulls ' had hoped, and was partly at least the result of organized pressure from them (pressure exerted with all the technique of the ' splitting ' of votes learned in recent contests), for an increase in the Company's dividend.   It is known that Fox put his holdings at the disposal of the organizers of this pressure group, and it has been estimated that at least 300 votes were created by this group for the Company's quarterly Court on 26 September 1766.   These ledgers throw a striking light on the part Fox's holdings played in this campaign, for on 13 September 1766 there is an entry of payment for forty-three transfers of East India stock, and on 25 September another for no fewer than 118 transfers explicitly stated to be for ' raising the dividend '.

Throughout the vicissitudes of the negotiations of 1767 between Chatham's Administration and the Company, which resulted in the first parliamentary intervention of the century in the Company's affairs, Fox continued to buy and sell on a large scale, and in 1767 and 1768 his speculations continued to be very profitable.   But 1769, the year in which the break came in the inflated stock prices and many speculators crashed, brought to him, too, a reversal of fortune.   At the end of September 1768 his holding stood at £80,000 valued at 274.   At the end of September 1769 he still held £61,000, but he valued it at 225 ; and on the twelve months' operations he wrote off a loss of £17,857 5s.   Part of this loss was no doubt incurred for political reasons.   A purchase of £25,000 stock in February 1769 in joint ownership with John Powell and Clotworthy Upton, and the loan to them of money to purchase another £15,000 each to be held on the same terms, is probably connected with his responsibilities in the creation of votes in support of the Ministry's supporters in the Company elections of that year, and an insurance fund created to guarantee voters against a fall in the value of their stock.[1]   Some of the loss was incurred not by him but by his son Stephen, who had been concerned disastrously in dealing in futures on the inflated market,[2] and whose liabilities he took over ; but it ended the days of his great profits from

[1] Cf. L. S. Sutherland, *The East India Company in Eighteenth Century Politics*, p. 188.

[2] A well-informed contemporary said in August 1769 (I. Barré to Lord Shelburne, *ibid.* p. 192), that Fox had to pay the ' difference ' on £50,000 stock for the jobbing operations of his son Stephen.   Fox's ledgers show that he had paid out well over £15,000 to clear Stephen of his speculative engagements.   He paid £7,810 to the Jewish firm of Fatio & Co., the balance of Stephen's account with the brokers Delafontaine & Brymer, who crashed at this time ; and paid another well-known Jewish jobber, Isaac Ximenes, £4,510 as the difference on £11,000 stock between 267½ and the ruling price of 226½, besides taking over the stock at the current rate.   He later paid Ximenes a further £2,732 15s. 7d. in full settlement of Stephen's account.

dealing in India stock; and his interest in it henceforth, though still considerable, appears to have been confined to that of salvaging the remains of his speculative interests and carrying out his political obligations. Thus although in the years 1766–8 he took credit for realized or book capital profits of over £68,000, when he finally divested himself of his stock in 1773, less than £15,000 remained as a capital gain.

The manner in which Fox invested his capital gains and that part of the profits derived from the employment of his balances which was not required for his current consumption is interesting. Landed property was not only in the nature of a gilt-edged investment but was also a sound foundation for social position. One might not make a fortune from possessing it, but by it one might conserve a fortune or position already made. The ledgers show Fox steadily spending on real estate, into which he put (after allowing for a few small sales credited in the ledgers), a sum which at the end of 1773 aggregated £193,000. The famous Holland House, first leased and afterwards purchased by him, seems mainly to have been bought out of his private means, for no more than £4,000 appears in the books on this account. But Kingsgate, on the north-east coast coast of Kent—a small property which his ageing fancy turned into a costly folly—appears for a total of £14,615. It may be mentioned that he left Kingsgate to his son Charles James who was, inevitably, compelled to sell it, and that the purchaser was the same John Powell whose fortunes were so closely linked with his own. Another purchase was a town house in Piccadilly, formerly Lord Monson's, and bought for £16,000. When sold in 1771 the consideration money did not come back into these ledgers, and it is of course possible that other properties bought with public money were sold and accounted for elsewhere than in the Paymaster's 'private account'. The remaining purchases, some large, some quite small, were scattered about the southern counties, and occasionally they took the form of a purchase of quit rents.[1]

It was not to be expected that with such resources Fox should not live on a correspondingly lavish scale. In addition to anything that may have been paid out of his private income, these ledgers stand charged under the head of 'house-keeping' with a sum that averages, from 1758 to 1773, almost exactly £6,000 a year. At the contemporary purchasing power of money, this indeed seems living like a grandee.[2] It is matched by the scale of his disbursements

[1] A fixed perpetual rent, often nominal, in return for which a tenant went free and quit from all other rents and services. It may be contrasted with a rack rent, or full economic annual worth of a property (which was therefore capable of improvement).

[2] In 1784 the household and miscellaneous expenses of the duke of Portland stood at £4,000 p.a. H. J. Habakkuk, in *The European Nobility in the Eighteenth Century* (1953) p. 10.

when travelling on the Continent as an English Milord.   Expenses
incurred in France during the years 1763 to 1765 totalled £20,620;
and in 1768 and 1769 a further £10,466.   It is hard to resist the
suspicion that these sums include payment of his sons' foreign
debts, but if this is so it must be pointed out that the youths are
shown as receiving still more money in other distinct parts of the
ledgers.   Minor embellishments for Fox's residences are represented
by paintings.   In 1762 he paid twenty guineas apiece to Hogarth
and Ramsay ' for my picture ', and next year he paid a further bill
of Hogarth's for £34 2s. 6d.   Ramsay provided another canvas in
1766, by which time the price had risen to twenty-five guineas, but
the subject is not indicated.   Reynolds was, however, the artist
most patronized, no less than £341 being paid for paintings in
1765.   Of less interest is the fact that the public balances provided
thirty guineas for six places at the coronation of George III, together
with 1,000 guineas for cash lost at Lord Harrington's, with other
small losses of a similar nature.

It is natural to examine the ledgers to see whether they impinge
upon parliamentary life.   They do not suggest any unusually heavy
expenditure on electioneering.   There is a reference in 1759 under
' Promiscuous Payments ' to a sum of £25 for an old election debt
at Windsor, dating, no doubt, from Fox's heavily contested election
there in 1757.[1]   In 1762 there was also a payment to Sir Jacob
Downing of £91 4s. 3d. ' for re-election ', which must be connected
with Downing's interest in the borough of Dunwich, for which
Fox was elected in 1761.[2]   Apart from these minor matters, however, the balances seem to have been drawn on only for advancing
the elections of his sons (and perhaps his nephew), and in connexion with the borough of Malmesbury.

Fox had been elected High Steward of Malmesbury in 1751
and held the position for some years,[3] apparently until the earl of
Suffolk was elected to the office in 1763.[4]   It was an office of importance solely for electoral purposes.   The ruling body of this
borough was described in 1833 as ' self-elected, irresponsible to the
inhabitants of the town, and composed chiefly of labourers without
education and of the least instructed class of retail tradesmen '.
It was also a body ' which has long ceased to exercise any municipal
function but that of returning to Parliament the nominees of the
patron of the borough '.[5]   The High Steward, who was elected

---

[1] *Official Return of Members of Parliament (House of Commons Sessional Paper of 1878*
No. 69–1, vol. 72).   See also J. Calcraft to the earl of Loudoun, 8 July 1757, Brit. Mus.
Add. MSS. 17,493, fo. 73ᵛ.   [2] *Official Return of Members of Parliament.*
   [3] Ilchester, *op. cit.* i. 171.   Sir L. B. Namier, *The Structure of Politics at the Accession of
George III* (1929) i. 538, n. 2.   See also *Correspondence of John, 4th Duke of Bedford,* ii.
243–4.   [4] G. E. C., *Peerage.*
   [5] *1st Report of the Commissioners appointed to enquire into the Municipal Corporations of
England and Wales (House of Commons Sessional Paper of 1835,* No. 116, vol. 23, app.
part 1, p. 75.

annually, was normally a man of importance and exercised a strong influence over the creation of burgesses and the exercise of their votes. In the general election of 1761 the burgesses had evidently given Fox some trouble, as he drafted a scheme for their control which he hoped would ' put an end to those cabals and strugglings in the choice of new Burgesses, which have given Mr. Earle so much trouble and through which he has with great Difficulty, by his honesty, spirit, ability and attention carry'd through this election '.[1] In the same scheme, which he submitted to the earl of Suffolk, who had a strong local family influence, he offered ' to go hand in hand with his Lordship in the choice of Burgesses and Members for that place and hopes his son may have the Honour to do so after him ', but no one connected with him sat there again till 1774 when his son Charles James was elected for the borough.

The Malmesbury account is active during 1759 to 1761, and again from 1769 to 1773. Fox's expenditure in the former period totals about £5,677, but this sum was recouped in its entirety by cash payments of £2,000 from Sir Robert Long, and the balance from Mr. Conolly. Sir Robert Long was brother-in-law of John Tylney, elected for Malmesbury at the general election of 1761 ; Thomas Conolly (brother-in-law to Lady Holland), was elected at a by-election in 1759,[2] and again at the general election of 1761. The disbursements include many items entered as ' loans ', some of which are described as being made to so-and-so, ' a new burgess '. The nature of some other and larger payments is not specified, but notice may be taken of £25 14s. for ' small expenses paid on account of next election ' (which might refer to a parliamentary, a High Steward's, but more probably a burgess's election), and of a disbursement of £100 described as ' Secret Service '. It is tempting to connect this with assistance which, on at least one occasion, Fox obtained from Government to secure the High Stewardship at an annual election, but the connexion with the ledger entry is doubtful.[3] When the

[1] Wilts County Record Office, Trowbridge, No. 88 (Suffolk and Berks MSS.). The manuscript is endorsed ' Paper delivered to Lord Suffolk by Mr. Fox in 1760 '. ' Mr. Earle ' is William Rawlinson Earle of Condwell, Wilts, M.P. for Malmesbury, 1727–47, and subsequently for Cricklade. We are indebted to Miss M. Ransome for a transcript of the document and for this information.

[2] It would appear that in Conolly's absence—perhaps in Ireland—his mother, Lady Anne Conolly, had received from Fox a contingent offer of the seat for her son. ' It strikes me ', wrote Fox, when reporting his action to the duke of Devonshire, ' that Conolly would be very glad to find himself a Member of Parlt., at his arrival '. (4 March 1759, Devonshire MSS. 330, 229.)

[3] See Namier, *loc. cit.* A document on elections amongst the duke of Newcastle's papers, endorsed 12 December 1760, contains a note of ' £1,000 given to elect Mr. Fox High Steward ' of Malmesbury, and continues : ' Q. Whether the £1,000 was the King's money. To speak to Mr. Fox about it.' The document then refers to the members elected for Malmesbury in 1754 (Brit. Mus. Add. MSS. 32,999, fo. 119). The conjunction of this with a repayment by Fox of £356 18s. 6d. for ' remainder

Malmesbury Account is reopened in 1769, it is with a disbursement of £1,100 for bank bills remitted to 'Mr. [Charles] Fox', who over the years 1769 to 1773 received a further £1,460. The only other item is £620 for 'cash paid Mr. Collins draft'. When the last ledger closes the total debit is £3,180 and no recoupment has been received from any quarter. Yet the nature of these transactions becomes fairly clear when it is found that Charles James Fox was elected a member at the next general election, in 1774; his fellow member being William Strahan.

Fox first had occasion to provide for the election of his two elder sons in the general election of 1768. Stephen might, it seems, have secured a safe seat at Stockbridge, and some preparations to this end were made from September 1766,[1] but finally New Sarum was chosen—a borough for which his uncle and grandfather had sat in former years. His election there cost £2,600. Charles James was returned for Midhurst, £3,000 being paid to Lord Montague on this account. It appears that Fox hired this borough jointly with his brother Lord Ilchester, the other elected member being the latter's son, Lord Stavordale.[2]

The expenditure incurred in bringing Fox's elder sons into parliament was the least of the burdens they laid on him, for their extravagance was notorious. The researches of Lord Ilchester have shown the extent of the drain on him.[3] The ledgers give only part of the story, but they show Stephen as receiving over £67,000 in all from the public balances, of which, however, some £50,000 was treated as a debt on which he began to pay interest in 1773.[4] Charles James is shown as costing the still greater sum of £118,718 of which £100,000 was the amount placed in the hands

from Malmesbury' on 24 April 1754 (Brit. Mus. Add. MSS. 33,044, fo. 27), suggests that the assistance was concerned rather with the general election of 1754 than of 1760, and that the repayment closed the account. In must, in any case, be emphasized that the £100 entered in Fox's ledger is a disbursement, not a receipt, and that the whole receipt came to him through the hands of Long and Conolly.

---

[1] In 1756 Fox had, according to Lord Ilchester (*op. cit.* ii. 13–14), leased Sir Robert Henley's interest in this borough for ten years. The account in the ledgers, which dates from after the end of this period, does not mention Sir Robert Henley but is entitled 'Sir George Macartney on account of Stockbridge Election'. Macartney's name does not otherwise appear in the account. £3,600 was advanced directly to Stephen, and £500 previously advanced to a Mr. Harmood was transferred to this account, making in all £4,100. Of this, Harmood refunded £300, and Stephen cleared his £3,600 either by bills to a certain Mr. Moore, or by cash paid by Moore on his behalf. This was possibly the same Moore who has been mentioned above, p. 242. The balance of £200, which would appear to have been part of the advance to Harmood, was written off as a loss.

[2] Ilchester, *op. cit.* ii. 325.   [3] Ilchester, *op. cit.* ii. 351 *seqq.*

[4] The sum also includes some small sums paid in early days to the tutor who was travelling on the Continent with him.

of John Powell to buy off the annuitants [1] (shown in the ledgers to include a high proportion of the more speculative dealers, Jewish and Christian, on the London market) who had been speculating on his chance of succeeding to the family fortunes. In contrast to this disheartening picture the third son Henry Edward cost much less. His father cared for him—and therefore spoiled him—less than his brothers, and he was made of different stuff, for he avoided notoriety and pursued a creditable military career. The public balances helped to start him off, carrying him as far as a lieutenancy of Dragoons for no more than £2,687. Of this, the initial cornetcy cost £1,000, and was sold for just over £1,100. The lieutenancy itself cost £1,365. This son was later to take upon his shoulders voluntarily the task of acting as ' administrator ' of his father's final account as Paymaster. Of Fox's three named executors his son, Charles James, and his nephew, Lord Digby, had declined to act, leaving John Powell to do all the work. After Powell's suicide the house of commons was treated to the spectacle of an attorney-general thirsting for a prosecution in regard to the late Paymaster's balances, but baulked of his prey for lack of any legal representative to prosecute.[2] It was in these circumstances that Henry Edward consented to act as administrator, and it was something like twenty-three years before he was freed from his responsibilities.[3]

If Fox was generous to his legitimate children, he did not forget his natural ones. A son, Charles Cooper, received all told over £11,000, of which £3,000 purchased a colonelcy, and £5,500 was treated as a loan. A daughter, Alicia, was less handsomely treated; but she received £100 for wedding clothes when she was married to Edward Young, who shortly afterwards became bishop of Dromore (and was thence translated to Ferns), in which capacities he enjoyed a moderate accommodation by way of loan on bond. Fox also stood by the widow of John Ayliff, who had been his agent as Receiver General of the Crown Land Revenue for the South Wales district. This agent forged Fox's signature and was hanged for it.[4] The £969 he owed Fox remained in the ledgers, never called in, until they close; and a small annuity helped to rescue Mrs. Ayliff from privation.

[1] Ilchester, *op. cit.* ii. 354. Over £73,000 of this sum was in fact borrowed from Powell (cf. p. 240). It would be interesting to know the source from which a man in Powell's position could have supplied so large a sum. Richard Rigby, the Paymaster at the time, does not appear to have been on very good terms with Fox, but possibly the money came from his balances through Powell. Powell's whole career suggests that he was also able to play with Pay Office money on his own account.

[2] William Cobbett, *Parliamentary History*, xxiv. col. 673, 23 February 1784.

[3] His final payment on account of his father's balances, by which at last Henry Edward became ' Quit ', was made on 1 December 1807, forty-two years after Fox's retirement, and a third of a century after his death. See the last folio of Fox's final Declared Account, P.R.O., A.O. 1, 76, roll 100.

[4] Ilchester, *op. cit.* ii. 112.

The story unfolded by these ledgers is an astonishing one, even though contemporary comment has prepared us for it.   A man of medium fortune took a public office the net worth of which, so far as official emolument is concerned, appears to have been not more than £3,000 a year.   After eight years' tenure he retired; yet as the result of his tenure he continued until the end of his life to receive an income vastly greater than his official profit when he was in office.   The annual average ' unofficial ' profit from within a few months of Fox's taking office until within a few months of his death was £23,657—or more than seven and a half times the net salary.[1]   In a single year, 1766, his profit of £54,851 was over eighteen times the net salary; and altogether he laid out in landed property alone £193,366, or almost sixty-five times the value of the net annual salary.   Further, he was able to save his family from disgrace, and, almost certainly, ruin, by having the means with which to pay his sons' debts without realizing all that he had of his private estate.   Yet there was nothing illegal in what he did, nor, according to the customs and notions of his age anything grossly improper.

Opinion as to the propriety of such gains was, nevertheless, changing.   A beginning in reform was made, in 1782, with the Regulating Act [2] implementing there commendations of the commissioners for examining the public accounts and passed by the Rockingham Administration.   Amongst other things this Act required the Paymaster's cash to be remitted from the exchequer to an official account at the Bank of England, drawings upon that account to be made by warrants stating the service for which the money was required.   A continuation of reform was made shortly afterwards, when Henry Dundas was responsible for a similar Act [3] regulating his office of Treasurer of the Navy, which was another recommendation of the commissioners.   The latter's recommendation that the office of Treasurer of the Ordnance should be similarly regulated was not, however, heeded until after Pitt's death.   How quick was the change in outlook and how far these measures effected their ends is, however, uncertain.   The regulation of the Paymaster's office may have been effectual, but that of the other two offices was not.   Although Dundas, as Lord Melville, was acquitted of his impeachment for alleged irregularities, the impression given by a reading of the evidence at the impeachment is that the condemned self-enrichment had merely been transferred from the Treasurer to a subordinate; and a Treasurer of the Ordnance was detected in improper conduct in the years immediately after the regulation of

---

[1] The *Gentleman's Magazine* printed an obituary notice on Richard Rigby (vol. 58, pp. 369–70), in which the Paymastership, at the time of Rigby's appointment in 1768, is referred to as ' a place, by the lowest computation, then valued at £16,000 p.a. '.

[2] 22 Geo. III, c. 81.   [3] 25 Geo. III, c. 31.

his office.[1] With a civil service tradition as well established as this, and with effective public condemnation so slowly developing, it is not to be expected that in a previous generation public officers should act according to a high standard of conduct unnatural to the age in which they lived.

Nevertheless, the fact remains that Fox was, at least from the sixties onward, acutely unpopular. Various explanations can be adduced for this fact. Some stress has been laid on the contrast presented between his career and that of the elder Pitt. It is likely that contempt for him for his decision to drop out of the struggle for power with Pitt in 1757, and to accept a position of profit rather than of honour, has been more keenly felt by subsequent historians than by his contemporaries; certainly it caused little if any surprise at the time. More important in this connexion probably, as drawing public disfavour on Fox, was the ill-judged pamphleteering carried on on his behalf (and, no doubt, with his connivance) by Dr. Francis in the *Test* against Pitt, the popular hero, during his short-lived Ministry of 1756; and the contrast between the two men was too striking to ignore. But the form taken by the various attacks on Fox makes it plain that the feeling against him arose largely from his Paymaster's balances and the use he made of them. This was partly due to circumstance. To make outstanding gains from the office a Paymaster must hold it for some time and under the conditions of war. Though the profits made under such circumstances by Sir Stephen Fox and Lord Chandos had become legendary, no Paymaster in recent times had both had the chances which were open to Fox and taken advantage of them. Only two men among his more recent precedessors had held it under these conditions, Henry Pelham from 1730–43 and the elder Pitt from 1746–55. The latter, as has already been said, was understood to have refused to employ his balances at all, and the former was known to have died a comparatively poor man. Among his immediate successors Charles Townshend (1765 to 1766), clearly had no such scruples, but he held the office in time of peace and for too short a tenure to make great profits; and the same applied to Lord North and George Cooke, who jointly succeeded Townshend. It was not until the Paymastership of Richard Rigby, during the American War of Independence, that Fox's gains were rivalled. At the time of the attacks on him Fox thus stood in unenviable isolation.

Moreover, the dates at which the two attacks on him were launched, 1763 and 1769, have some relevance when the method by which he made some of his biggest capital gains is considered.

---

[1] *Commissioners of Military Enquiry 1806–12*, Rep. 12. *House of Commons Sessional Paper of 1810*, no. 81, vol. 9. The Regulating Act was 46 Geo. III, c. 45 (1806).

The attack of 1763 followed his great speculative gains in connexion with the Peace, and that of 1769 followed his participation in jobbing and corruption within the East India Company, which had just resulted in a series of painful scandals when the crash in the stock came.   Though the political morality of the eighteenth century was in many ways low, leading politicians, ever since the South Sea scandals, had been careful not to incur the stigma of using their position to speculate on the stock market, and discredit attached to a major political figure who was known to have engaged in the 'infamous practice of stock jobbing'.   The greatness of Fox's balances during the course of the Seven Years' war, his success in employing them to increase his wealth, the evidence of this wealth displayed in his own way of life and that of his family, but above all the means he employed to increase his capital were probably the main causes of his sustained unpopularity.   As Fox himself remarked : 'Obloquy generally attends money so got.' [1]

APPENDIX

CHARLES TOWNSHEND'S LEDGER

The ledger containing the 'Private Account' of Charles Townshend who, as Fox's successor, was Paymaster General of the Forces from June 1765 to August 1766,[2] is smaller than those of Henry Fox, is less elaborately bound and less fairly written.   It contains entries up to 27 July 1769, almost two years after Townshend's death,[3] and then the ledger appears to have been laid aside without any attempt to balance and close the accounts.

Corresponding to the inventories in Fox's ledgers, there are three 'General States', taken at 11 June 1766, 25 December 1766, and 12 September 1767.   These 'General States' show that indebtedness was to the Pay Office alone, and that by June 1766 Townshend was already operating with £99,500 of public money, a figure which had risen to £150,784 at the end of his life.   As in Fox's case, some of this money arose out of remittances for the pay of Irish troops, and some by direct drawing on the Bank of England, which in Townshend's case appears to have been by draft in favour of John Powell.   The bulk arose out of taking Exchequer Bills (probably issued to the Paymaster in lieu of cash), on which Townshend pocketed the accrued interest.

---

[1] Henry Fox's 'Memoir', countess of Ilchester and Lord Stavordale, *op. cit.* i. 72.

[2] In accordance with the usual contemporary practice, Townshend remained Accountant to the Crown in respect of the Pay Office until the close of the current half year in December 1766.

[3] 4 September 1767.

The disposition of the indebtedness shows no advances specifically stated to be on mortgage, but Townshend made sundry advances upon bond; for example, £500 to his brother, the fourth Viscount Townshend, and £1,000 to Chase Price, M.P., both being at 5 per cent., and a further £6,000 to Sir George Yonge, at 4 per cent. Two large advances made on unspecified security were £10,500 to Edward M. D. Howarth (the cash being paid to ' Mr. Woodhouse '), and £20,300 to the duke of Buccleugh (of which the initial £2,300 was 'cash paid to sundry persons '). There is clear evidence of the purchase of real estate in the £3,000 paid for ' Mr. Allenson's estate in Hertfordshire '.

Like his predecessor, Townshend used his balances to speculate on the stock market. In June 1766 he held in Government stocks £66,000 valued at £66,859, and in India stock £5,500 valued at £9,900. He was constantly switching, and at Christmas his Government stocks were down to £45,000 worth £46,013, and his India stocks were up to £17,000 worth £37,400. At his death he had jettisoned all his India stock save the minimum holding of £500 qualifying for a vote; he held £9,000 Bank stock worth £13,320; and his Government stocks were now worth £81,115. The latter included a participation in the Loan of 1767, but as the holding is described as Scrip and not as Omnium, it is probable that he bought it in the market and was not an original subscriber.[1]

City names already familiar in Fox's ledgers appear again in Townshend's as receiving accommodation. Modigliani was lent £10,000 ' to Rescounter in May next ' (a period of three months), and loans on the security of stock were made, as for instance £5,000 to G. Shergold on Bank stock ' to opening ', and the same sum to Modigliani on India stock. Like Fox, Townshend had £1,000 invested in an Indiaman, and like Fox he placed his surplus cash in John Powell's hands, the amount at Townshend's death being £13,628. It may also be noted that his speculation in East India stock occurred at a time when, as chancellor of the exchequer, he was actively concerned in the Chatham Administration's intervention in the Company's affairs.[2]

Owing to the less detailed manner in which the ledger is written up, and the imperfect state in which it was abandoned, it is impossible to calculate Townshend's gains as exactly as it is possible to calculate Fox's. It can, however, be stated that by April 1767 gains of £8,259 were recorded, of which £7,071 arose out of successful East India speculation.

It is clear from this ledger that Townshend employed his balances in the same way as Fox had, and it appears highly probable that, as in Fox's case, Powell of the Pay Office was closely connected with his new chief's operations, and was an important agent in the private profit making of both Paymasters.

[1] The Loan of 1767 consisted of 3 per cent. stock, of which part was issued in accordance with the subscription list, and the remainder was divided amongst the proprietors as determined by a lottery. The united interest was known as the Omnium, and the separate interests as Scrip. Original subscriptions were for Omnium.

[2] L. S. Sutherland, *op. cit.* pp. 151 *seqq.*

20

SIR GEORGE COLEBROOKE'S WORLD CORNER
IN ALUM, 1771-73

Two European crises stand out prominently in the eighteenth century before the financial dislocations of the Revolutionary wars, and prepare the way for the great credit fluctuations of the succeeding century. The first, that of 1763, originated in Amsterdam, had immediate repercussions in Hamburg,[1] and affected, though to a less degree, the other important international money market, London. Its general cause was the end of the credit boom which followed the Seven Years' War; its occasion the spectacular failure of the great Dutch firm of de Neufville, due mainly, as men with knowledge believed, to their concern with the unsound financial expedients of Frederick the Great and his agents, the Jewish firm of Ephraim.[2]

[1] W. P. Sautijn Kluit, *De Amsterdamsche Beurs in* 1763 *en* 1773. Amsterdam, 1865, pp. 12 *seq.*

[2] An interesting letter dealing with this subject is to be found in the Liverpool MSS. (Brit. Mus. Add. MS. 38,201, ff. 193-4 v.) from R. Wolters of Rotterdam, October 14, 1763, agent of the Royal packet boats there, a steady correspondent of Charles Jenkinson on commercial and other matters. "Since last Tuesday I have collected the following particulars upon the late commercial distresses att Amsterdam.

"The origin of the evil is properly to be dated from the beginning of the King of Prussia's distresses. 1. To supply that Prince with the silver necessary to make his case win, the Jew Ephraim combined with the Berlin bankers engaged to procure it from Amsterdam; the merchants of that place were inticed to give into this upon the prospect of a great gain; the payments for the matter furnished were made by drawing and redrawing between Amsterdam, Berlin and Hamborourgh.

2. Most of the contributions which different parts of Saxony engaged to pay to the King of Prussia, payable in terms, were by that Prince sold to merchants att a prodigious advance for ready money, and partly in payment for the specie furnished for his operations for the Mint : the dilatoriness of payment of these contributions, and even non-payment of some, brought the merchants to great straights (*sic*), and obliged them to have recourse to the same expedient of a circulation of paper. This went on till bills being returned upon Aaron Joseph att Amsterdam, obliged him to stop payment; the de Neufvilles followed, the alarm was general, and all discounters of bills stopt their hands not knowing how things would go, and this immediately brought on a total stagnation of credit, whilst a circulation of paper for 4 millions of florins was hanging unpay'd.

"This whole summ is even absorbed in commissions pay'd, and expense and loss of drawing and redrawing. Besides these two causes there is another which was the purchase of the Russian magazines which were bought for 3 millions of florins, and by the peace fell most considerably in their value."

Cf. *Politische Correspondenz : Friedrichs des Grosse*, Vol. XXIII 92 and Vols. XXII and XXIII *passim.*

The second crisis was that of 1772–3.   Its origin was different. It arose at a time when no war finance had disturbed the credit of nations, and it originated not in Amsterdam, but in London, whence it spread after an interval to the European markets.[1] It is a mark of the growing importance of London among the money markets of the world, that the day of retribution which followed its six years of increasingly speculative finance should bring about this international dislocation and dismay.

The causes of the crisis in London are various and complex. Chief among them were probably—the gambling in futures in East India stock in which the money markets of London and Amsterdam had been immersed since 1766, and as a result of which there had already been a serious break in the price of East India stock in May 1769; the heavy losses incurred in 1769 not only by speculators but by the managers of the political " splitting " of East India stock, which had left many members of the London money market badly crippled;[2] the over-issue of credit by the Scottish banks, and the reckless change and rechange of bills with which they and their London correspondents tried to keep up their credit ("swiveling" it was called at the time);[3] and finally such unsound ventures as the ambitious attempt to corner the world supply of alum described in this article, which undermined the stability of important houses both in London and Amsterdam.

The course of the crisis was fairly clear.   Early in the year the Bank of England began restricting its discount of bills in some quarters, feeling, it was believed, some doubt of the soundness of the finance of the Scottish banks and some suspicion of the speculation of stockjobbers.[4]   Its fears were justified, and in June the storm broke.   On June 10, 1772, Alexander Fordyce, a singularly speculative banker with close Scottish connections, suddenly fled the country, and his firm, Neil, James, Fordyce and Down, stopped payment.   Two days later three important firms with Scottish connections closed their doors—John Mackintosh; Charles Fergusson & Co.; Fordyce, Grant & Co.[5]—and it

[1] Kluit, *op. cit.*, pp. 65 *seq.*   For Hamburg cf. *Vierteljahrsschrift f. Sozial und Wirtschaftgeschichte*, Vol. XV, 1919.   E. Baasch, *Aus ein Hamburgischen Fallitensstatistik des 18 Jahrhundert.*

[2] Cf. my article "Lord Shelburne and the East India Company," 1763–69. *E. H. R.*, July 1934.   See above, pp. 177-213.

[3] Letter in the *Public Advertizer*, July 8, 1772.   Cf. Adam Smith, *Wealth of Nations*, ed. Cannan, i. 292 *seqq.*, on the same practice.

[4] *Réflexions sur les Dernières Banqueroutes en Angleterre et Hollande et Conduite du Ministère Anglois à ce sujet.*   London, 1773.

[5] B.M. Hastings MSS.   Add. MS. 29,133, ff. 355-6.   G. Stratton–W. Hastings, January 29, 1773.

was realised that havoc would be wrought in Scotland and that the much-lauded Bank of Ayr [1] in particular, as the chief offender among the Scottish banks, must be in a deplorable position. Though the Scottish gentry and merchants entered into an association to support its credit, and though on June 23 a meeting of merchants in London agreed to subscribe to indemnify the Bank of England for discounting its bills,[2] and at least £50,000 to £60,000 was subscribed,[3] this could not check the run on it in Edinburgh itself, and on July 26 it stopped payment.

Fordyce's failure in itself would have been enough to shake the London market, for his interests were multitudinous, but alarms about the Scottish banks were even more disintegrating. Between June 10 and 22 twenty firms of importance and numbers of lesser firms failed, as contemporaries said, "for millions," and June 22, on which one of the most notable of these firms, Glynn and Halifax, Bankers, shut their doors,[4] was a day of veritable panic throughout the City.

The Bank of England was held up to reproach by the City Press, on the grounds that its policy of restricting credit was the cause of the crisis. It seems arguable that the Directors should have acted sooner. When the panic was on them, however, though they were blamed for not giving credit to all comers, they seem to have pursued on the whole a wise policy. They sat daily, sometimes until five in the afternoon, considering the claims of the merchants for credit,[5] and lent freely when they considered the security sufficient to justify them in so doing. Among the London merchants whose fortunes had been tottering precariously and who were offered at least a reprieve by the Bank was Sir George Colebrooke, head of the firm of Colebrooke, Lesingham and Binns, Bankers of Threadneedle Street.[6] Some of his many activities at this time are the subject of this article.

Thus the worst of the panic passed, but the dangers were not yet over. Men's attentions were soon turned to a financial

[1] Douglas, Heron & Co. For its foundation and aims cf. A. Kerr, *History of Banking in Scotland*, 3rd ed., 1918.

[2] *Public Advertizer*, June 25, 1772, gives the Resolution and the Committee.

[3] The proposers of the subscription expected much more, and a letter in the *Public Advertizer*, June 29, urged merchants to increase the subscription.

[4] The Commission of Bankruptcy against them was shortly afterwards superseded, and with the help of the Bank of England the firm got again on its feet.

[5] *London Evening Post*, June 27–30.

It is noteworthy in the controversial articles, letters and pamphlets of this year, how widely it was assumed that the Bank stood in a peculiar position as the " depository of public credit."

[6] Lesingham and Binns (the latter of whom had formerly been a clerk in the bank) were only nominal partners.

institution only less prominent than the Bank, the East India Company. The paralysis of credit had affected its sales at a moment when a crisis was threatening its financial arrangements, which for six years had been becoming increasingly unsound. The Directors had failed altogether in their attempt to prevent their servants in India drawing on them by bill,[1] so that according to the Directors the Bengal servants alone had drawn on them for more than £8,000,000 in 1772.[2] They found it necessary to renew a temporary loan of £400,000 from the Bank, due as usual to be returned after the September sales, until October 31.[3] At the General Court of September 24 called for the quarterly statement of dividend, the Chairman (the same Sir George Colebrooke, whose own affairs were so uncertain) had to announce that no dividend would be declared, and that the Company was negotiating with the Government for power to raise a loan. The price of stock fell precipitately. On October 2 the Company defaulted in its payment to the Government, and on the 29th the Bank of England refused to renew once more its £400,000 loan.[4] When this situation arose the East Indian investigation of 1772–3 had already begun, and it made Lord North's regulating Act inevitable.[5]

Though the heavy losses suffered by holders of East India stock did not cause any further spectacular failures in London, they deepened the gloom which enveloped the City until the end of the year, and they were directly responsible for the spread of the disorders of the London market to Amsterdam. The interests of the great Dutch houses in speculation in East India stock were extensive, and proved now unfortunate to them. On December 27 the important house of Pieter Clifford and Sons, with its long English connections, stopped payment.[6] The firm

[1] General Letters of 16 Mar. 1768 and 17 Mar. 1769. 9th Report of the Committee of Secrecy, 1783, p. 113.

[2] *Ibid.*, p. 116, General Letter of 24 Nov. 1772.

[3] Copy of Bank's letter B.M. Add. MS. 38,397 f. 228. Liverpool MSS., 10 (?) Sept. 1772.

[4] *Ibid.* Copy of Bank's letter of 29 Oct. f. 240 and Minute of East India Committee of Treasury, 18 Nov. 1772, f. 284–5.

[5] L. Sulivan wrote to Warren Hastings, 28 April, 1773 (B.M. Add. MS. 29,133, ff. 534–4 v.): ". . . our domestic distresses came fast upon us—a general gloom springing from immense bankruptcys had brought public credit almost to stagnate; affected our sales to a deep degree and brought the Bank of England (our single resource) to be seriously cautious—they call'd upon us for their money, and would lend no more . . . we then apply'd to the Minister to extricate the Company and he (perhaps glad to grasp the glorious object) took public ground, and demanded a state of our affairs to be laid before Parliament."

[6] The news was in the English papers on January 2, having been brought by the Dutch mail the day before.

in England closely associated with it, George Clifford and Son, fell with it, and once again panic seized the English market. A connection of the Hopes thought it necessary to write to the *Public Advertizer* on January 5 insisting on the soundness of this firm. In the issue of January 9 there is a letter from " a merchant " dated January 7, insisting that not only Hope's, but Muilman & Sons, Pye, Rich and Wilkinson, Baauw & Co. and Pels & Co. of Amsterdam were in a thoroughly sound position, and suggesting that the Bank of England should assist them and that London merchants should form an Association to support their bills. Once again English firms were threatened, and among the most notable of those affected was Sir George Colebrooke, who had so narrowly escaped in June. In January the King asked anxiously if he were not in a very precarious position.[1] On March 31 he stopped payment. Though his creditors permitted him to reopen his doors, like so many firms in the same position, he never succeeded in liquidating his frozen resources, and on August 8, 1776, he again stopped payment; in February 1777 a bill of bankruptcy was filed against him, and he fled the country.[2]

Sir George was the son of James Colebrooke, a banker who had made a large fortune in the South Sea Bubble years.[3] The son, after two years' commercial training at Leyden,[4] entered his father's business, and with his elder brother Sir James succeeded him in it after his death in 1752, and on his brother's death in 1761 took over its full control. His father and brother had been prominent members of the " moneyed interest " in the City. His father had been a close friend of the Pelham Administration; his brother, too, had increased his wealth by Government contracts and loans.[5] Sir George, at least in the earlier

[1] *The Correspondence of King George III*, ed. J. Fortescue, II. 436.

It was maintained in a contemporary pamphlet, *Réflexions sur les Dernières Banqueroutes en Angleterre et Hollande et Conduite de Ministère Anglois à ce sujet*, 1773, that Cliffords had for years been merely a shadow of its past greatness. On this cf. Sautijn Kluit, *op. cit.*, pp. 98 *seq.*

[2] The action against him was taken by Mary Barwell, the formidable sister of Richard Barwell, the East Indian " nabob." It was claimed by Sir George's descendants that the creditors were ultimately repaid in full. Meantime he lived for some years abroad on his wife's fortune, and must for some time at least have been in poverty, for the East India Company voted him an annuity of £200 a year in 1778 (East India Co. Court Book, 86, f. 605).

In 1781 he obtained an appointment as Senior Merchant in the East India Company (Ct. Bk. 90, f. 104), and though he never proceeded to India he held it at least until 1783 (Ct. Bk. 91, f. 766).

[3] The first reference to the firm seen by F. G. Price (*Handbook of London Bankers*, p. 41) is in 1706.   [4] B.M. Add. MS. 32,712, f. 410.

[5] L.B. Namier, *Structure of Politics at the Accession of George III*, 1. 69.

part of his career, was true to the family connection, but as it was since 1762 generally in opposition, the lines of his career were necessarily different.[1] He seems always to have been an active, speculative man, careless of detail and not over-scrupulous. It was he, apparently, who enlarged the banking business by founding the house of George Colebrooke & Co. in Dublin, of which mention is first found in 1764, which temporarily stopped payment in 1770,[2] and with which he severed his connection at the end of 1772.[3] He had great dealings in East India stock, and from 1767 onwards he began to play an important part in the Company's politics, entering the Direction in that year, being elected Deputy Chairman in 1768 and Chairman in 1769, 1770 and 1772, some of the stormiest years of the Company's history. His activities in East India politics were not thought by his enemies to be altogether independent of his interests as a stockjobber. Accusations were brought against him in the General Court of the Company itself [4] in 1771, when he was a member of a combine dealing anonymously in futures on the Amsterdam market in East India stock, and also in the Press in 1772, when the London papers were full of abuse of the "little stockjobbing baronet" and his party in East India House. At the time of the panic of June 1772 he had transactions in East India stock with the firm of Neil, Fordyce, James and Down alone to the sum of £110,000,[5] and his associates speak of his "great concerns" in that stock. A more unusual activity of his, however, and one which he admitted to be undesirable for a banker, was his indulgence in a form of speculation commoner in Amsterdam than in London at the time, speculation on the wholesale commodity markets. One of his business associates said that he knew that Sir George was

> " a great Adventurer in Articles of Merchandize commonly
> called Articles of Speculation, and that he had oftentimes

---

[1] Sir George retained at least one Government contract till 1765. Brit. Mus. Add. MS. 38,338, ff. 109–11. Liverpool MSS., *State of the Several Subsisting Contracts.*

[2] M. Dillon, *The History and Development of Banking in Ireland from the Earliest Times to the Present Day,* Dublin, 1889, p. 26. J. W. Gilbert, *History of Banking in Ireland,* 1836, pp. 15–16.

[3] *London Evening Post,* March 20–23, 1773.

[4] Reports of the House of Commons. 8th Report of Committee of Secrecy, pp. 394 *seq.*

[5] B.M. Add. MS. 38,208, ff. 160–1. Liverpool MSS., William James-Jenkinson, July 29, 1775, and ff. 176–7, Sept. 14, 1775, complaining that the Bank of England saved " Sir George and a few friends " in 1772 " at our expence " and claiming compensation from the Government.

bought large Quantities of Hemp, Flax, Logwood and other Merchandize with a view to sell the same again for Profit." [1]

When he failed it was said in jest :

" He is in contract for all the alum in Bohemia, all the chip hats in Italy, and the hemp in Russia and other places, so that if he should be ordered to be hanged, no one will have hemp enough to find him a halter." [2]

Possibly because these speculations were deemed improper for a banker, he carried them out through and with his wife's half-brother,[3] Ambrose Lynch Gilbert, a merchant of London, who traded both alone and in partnership with Samuel Justice, and who was believed in both these capacities to be little more than a cover for Sir George Colebrooke himself. The attempt to corner the supply of hemp had failed before the alum speculation began in 1771. On it and other speculations with Gilbert (excluding the corner in alum) it was found by 1773 that Sir George had lost £190,000. Undeterred by this failure, the full extent of which was probably not yet realised, they entered in 1771 an even more ambitious undertaking, an elaborate scheme to corner the world's supply of alum.

Some cases in the Court of Exchequer arising out of his bankruptcy yield valuable information about this venture and have been used as the material for this article. In *Exchequer Bills and Answers George III London and Middlesex*, Bundle 1640, No. 2118 and Bundle 1665, No. 2572, may be found much of the business correspondence of and a great deal of recriminatory abuse between the partners in this ambitious and hazardous attempt.[4] From this business correspondence the whole of its history may be reconstructed. Where no other authority is cited in this article it may be taken that the material is to be found in these Bills and answers and the documents appended to them.

The scheme was attractive for a number of reasons. In the first place, the price of alum was unusually low in 1771. In

[1] Bill of Jonas Brown in E 112. Geo. III, Bundle 1640, No. 2118.

[2] *A Series of Letters of the First Earl of Malmesbury,* ed. the Earl of Malmesbury, 1870, I. 271.

[3] Sir George Colebrooke m. 1754 Mary, daughter and heiress of Peter Gaynor of Antigua.

[4] The former is a case brought by Jonas Brown and Isaac Mallison against Sir George Colebrooke in T. T. 1773 : the latter by John Purling and others against Jonas Brown, Isaac Mallison and others in Easter Term, 1778. Supplementary evidence is found in a case in Chancery brought by the Marchese Lepri and others against Sir George Colebrooke in H. T. 1773 (C. 12, Bundle 73, No. 23).

the second place, the supply was localised.[1] The best alum was produced at Tolfa in the Papal States, where the Papacy farmed out the monopoly of its manufacture, at this time to the Marchese Carlo Ambrosio Lepri and his heirs. An inferior quality was found and commercially exploited in Asia Minor (Smyrna was the distributing centre), in Sweden, in England (Yorkshire and Lancashire), and a poorer quality still was worked around Liège.[2] In the third place, the demand for alum though not heavy was very rigid. Its use in dyeing, in particular, made it a staple product, in constant stock at the dry-salters'. The world's annual consumption is hard to determine; the adventurers believed it to be more than 7,000 tons when they laid their schemes. It was later maintained to be no more than 4,500; the truth probably lay between the two.

The scheme, like all of its kind, had of necessity two sides : the control of production and that of distribution. Control of production was achieved by buying large quantities of alum and by entering into contracts with important alum manufacturers throughout Europe, Asia Minor and England, chiefly through the agency of merchant correspondents abroad. This control was supplemented by the purchase of the lease or freehold of several English alum works, which the adventurers themselves exploited as they worked other mines already in their possession. In England, at least, there was a slight attempt to restrict the output.

Six contracts were made with producers outside England, three for unlimited, and three for limited quantities.[3] There was no attempt to limit output, though in the contract for Roman alum there were clauses whereby they could check its expansion. Of the two contracts for unlimited quantities of alum, the first was made on January 28, 1772, through a correspondent, Albert-Joseph Rahier, for all the alum produced at and around Liège for three years from that spring, estimated at about 12,000 quintals a year.[4] The terms seem to have been very favourable to the producers, since the price offered was nearly £18 a ton, while it could be sold at a reasonable profit, it would appear, at £13 a ton. The second and third contracts for un-

---

[1] The best account of the technique of alum mining at the time is to be found in the *Royal Society Philosophical Transactions*, Vol. XII, 1678, p. 1035.

[2] It was stated to be worth £2 per ton less than English or Swedish alum, and to be used only locally.

[3] The contracts are given in Public Record Office, C. 12, Bundle 73, No. 23 (cf. n. 4, p. 451).

[4] 1 quintal = 100 lbs.

limited quantities were made in Sweden through their correspondent Stephen Kniper of Stockholm. On February 21, 1772, he made an agreement to receive from Frederick von Essen, owner of the *Kaflas* works, all the alum that was lying there and in Stockholm (about 250 barrels in each place) and at Gottenburg (60 barrels), and all further alum produced in a time not here specified. On December 2, 1771, and April 3, 1772, he made a similar arrangement with Charles Augustus Piper, owner of the *Garphytta* and *Andrarum* works, which included the output of another mine called *Beata Christiana*. While the details of these contracts are not recorded, they must have been more favourable to the purchaser, for they are mentioned in the correspondence with special favour.

One of the three contracts for limited quantities was for Smyrna alum. It was arranged on May 6, 1772, by the Smyrna correspondents Van Lennep and Enslie, for 7,000 quintals of alum with a Jewish firm, Solomon and Abraham Alasdrak. The other two contracts for limited quantities were for Roman alum, and are of special interest. In April 1772 the Marchese Giuseppe Lepri, holder of the Papal monopoly at Tolfa, was in London and made a long and detailed agreement with the English partnership. The Papal monopolist was bound to supply the needs of the Papal States; he was also at that time pledged to furnish 6,000 Cantaras [1] a year to France, to Gachon & Cie of Paris. After satisfying these two liabilities, he bound himself to supply the partners with all the alum they wanted at 7 Crowns Roman (of 10 Paolis per Crown) for each Cantara. They on their side guaranteed to take from him 6,000 Cantaras a year for three years and nine months from July 1772, transporting it from Civita Vecchia at their own risk. They promised not to sell Lepri's alum in France; Lepri promised not to sell alum outside the Papal States, except as he was bound by his French contract, and elaborate penalties were laid down on each side in case of breaches of the covenant. Having made this agreement, the partners then set to work, and through and under the guarantee of their Marseilles correspondents, Councler, Rigot and Sollicoffre (who also guaranteed the Liège contracts), they made their third contract for a limited quantity and arranged to purchase from Gachon & Cie the alum with which Lepri was bound to supply them. From them they were to receive 40,000 quintals in four years. Thus they had complete possession of the world's supply of Roman alum.

[1] Roman Cantara = 74¾ lbs. English.

In England contracts were entered into with the following producers :—[1]

Lord Mulgrave and his son the Hon. Constantine Phipps, for 300 tons of British alum a year for five years at £14 10s. a ton, to begin in March 1772.[2]

John Yeoman, 200 tons on terms unknown. Made on December 8, 1771.

Samuel Howlett and John Matthews. 100 tons to be delivered before May 1, 1773, then 200 tons a year for three years. Made February 25, 1772.

George Baker and Ralph Jackson of the *Boulby* works. All present stock to be delivered within thirty days, and from January 1, 1772, 330 to 290 tons to be delivered every year for three years.

Peter Thelluson and John Cossart, merchants, 750 tons of British alum to be delivered in five years, 15 tons a year, at £18 10s. (It is not clear whether they were producers or merely dealers in the product.)

Mallison, Clarke & Co. (See below.[3])

Brown, Cookson, Carr & Co. (See below.[3])

The only important producer with whom no terms were made was Sir Lawrence Dundas.[4] The details of the contracts are known only in the case of the last two firms. Brown, Cookson, Carr & Co. worked two mines, one at Saltwick near Whitby, the other at Shields. On December 28, 1771, they signed an agreement whereby they promised for three years to make alum only at their Saltwick works, and to limit their output in a ratio fixed by the output of the two works owned by Mallison, Clarke & Co., *Stowbrow* and *Peak*. They agreed that they would not increase their works above " five drawing pans, one Slam pan and one other Pan commonly called a Driver or Roaching Pan," unless *Stowbrow* and *Peak* should together use 10 drawing pans, when they could increase their number to 6, or more than 10 when they could increase theirs to 7. In return, they were promised £15 per ton free on board for as much alum as they produced for three years when the market price was not above

[1] The first five of these contracts are given in Public Record Office, C. 12, Bundle 73, No. 23 (cf. n. 4, p. 451). The last two are to be found in E. 112, Bundle 1655, No. 2572, London and Middlesex.

[2] The validity of this contract was afterwards disputed.

[3] For their special position see below, p. 458.

[4] Sir L. Dundas, M.P., " The Nabob of the North," who as Scottish Contractor and Commissary-General made his fortune during the Seven Years' War and controlled several seats in the House of Commons.

£16 10*s*. in London; when it was above £16 10*s*., but below £21, they were promised a price 30*s*. below market price; when it was above £21 they were promised a price 40*s*. below that given on the market. A similar agreement was made with Mallison, Clarke & Co. in January 1772, except that no reference is made to restriction of output. This was probably considered unnecessary, since, as will be shown, the adventurers themselves controlled the greater number of shares in the partnership.

The alum works which they purchased, either freehold or leasehold, were five in number. They bought the freehold of *Ayton* near Guisborough, and the leases of the following :— *Saltburn* in Cleveland, on a seven years' lease; *Guisborough* from William Chaloner, Esq. (the descendant of Sir Thomas Chaloner, who in 1600 was believed first to have discovered alum in England on this very estate),[1] on a seven years' lease for £400 a year; *Goodland Banks* near Whitby, on a three years' lease for £300 a year, and *Pleasington* in Lancashire, on a five years' lease for £40 a year.

In this way was production organised. By these contracts and by considerable purchases on the open market, the adventurers believed that they had " secured nearly the whole quantity of alum made in Europe," and though this belief was later challenged, and it was asserted that they controlled scarcely two-thirds of the supply, the evidence for the first half of 1772 at least seems to bear them out.

The distribution of the alum was organised by a number of correspondents and agents, some of whom were also concerned in the contracts for its supply. The two centres of operations were London and Amsterdam. In London, Ambrose Lynch Gilbert and Sir George Colebrooke themselves controlled finance and general policy, while the two agents, Thomas Carter and William Brooke, arranged some special sales in England and abroad. Amsterdam was a centre only less important than London in the organisation of the venture. From Amsterdam indeed most of the foreign side of the business, commercial and financial, could most easily be transacted. Here the firm of Clifford and Sons, for many years connected in business with the house of Colebrooke, was their agent until its bankruptcy in December 1772, when its place was taken by the other famous house with English connections, Hope & Co. These agents met bills from various centres to a very large sum, carried large stocks of alum, which served as a partial security for the bills

---

[1] A. Kippax, *Biographia Britannica*, II, 1278.

they discounted, and suggested the best markets to which alum should be shipped. The agents and correspondents who took part in the distribution in the less important centres were twenty-six in number :—

Thomas Littledale, Rotterdam.
Cretien Gottlob Frege (or Friege) & Co. Leipzig.
Stephen Kniper, Stockholm.
Sir Trevor Curry & Co., Danzig.
Herman Roossen, Jr., Hamburg.
Glyn and Gilbert, St. Petersburg.
William Collins, Riga.
Caley and Pole (or Poel), Archangel.
Chippendale, Selby & Co., Copenhagen.
Belli and Fonnereau, Leghorn.
Paltiel Semah (?), Leghorn.
Councler, Rigot and Sollicoffre, Marseilles.
Midy & Co., Rouen.
Breame and Collett, Genoa.
Skinner and Fenwick, Bordeaux.
Van Lennep and Enslie, Smyrna.
Daniel Bonfils and Sons, Venice.
Fremin Frères, Paris.
Pierre Babut, Jr., & Co., Nantes.
Ray and Brandenburg, Cadiz.
Bewicke, Timerman and Romer, Cadiz (taking the place of
    Ray and Brandenburg after the middle of 1773).
Grossi, Sinigaglia.[1]
Fuhrer, Wagner and Gilbert, Liverpool.
Edwin Sneyd, Dublin.
Samuel Span, Bristol.
John Woolmer, Halifax.

By means of these correspondents a net of distributors was spread over the most important markets of Europe.

The origin of the scheme is curious. Sir George did not himself originate it. In 1771 the low price of alum inspired one Jonas Brown of Whitby, co-partner with Cookson, Carr[2] and Ellison in two alum works near Whitby, to work out a scheme for restricting the output of alum in England, and for creating a corner in the product by using £10,000 to buy in alum and contracts for its production. His scheme does not seem to have

[1] In the agreement with the Marchese Lepri, Gilbert, Brown & Co. were permitted to store alum at Sinigaglia.
[2] Cookson and Carr were bankers of Newcastle.

involved the foreign market at all. To obtain the necessary financial assistance he approached Sir George Colebrooke, whose speculative interests were well known, and wrote to him giving the outlines of the plan on June 4, 1771. He received a not discouraging reply, and was referred to Ambrose Lynch Gilbert, Sir George's agent.

It was Gilbert who answered his next letter, in terms which must have reassured him as to the reception of his plan, but which must also have shown him that he had put himself into the hands of determined men who might easily prove a match for a Yorkshire mine-owner. Gilbert wrote on June 27.:— [1]

" Sir George Colebrooke, being on his departure for Ireland at the time he received your Letter of the 14th Instant, Communicated to me the Contents with Intention that I should reply to it and carry on the correspondence with you on the subject on which it treats, on account of the same plan having been proposed to me by two Gentlemen almost two months since. I told Sir George I could not with honor correspond with you about it, seeing I was already far engaged with others, and therefore begg'd to decline it. Sir George upon this proposed that I should endeavour to bring about a coalition of Parties, even pressing it as thinking it incumbent on him to be of service to you on Account of your Candour towards him in the detail you are pleased to give concerning the said Alum works, at the same time declining a concern for himself. In consequence of his request I have used my endeavour with the two gentlemen with whom I was engaged, and I have the pleasure to acquaint you that they consent to admit your taking a fourth concern in the Engagement. I must request a reply from you by return of Post, and if the Proposal has been agreeable to you I will write to one concerned who is in the Country to wait on you to discuss the matter at large. I must beg leave to observe to you that it would be highly imprudent in you to decline the offer, as the opposition you will meet with for want of a Junction with my party would totally frustrate all your Endeavours, a consideration which has weight with them for fear of any opposition from you. I must further add that when you come to learn the parties you will be thoroughly satisfied. I cannot but think it fortunate that your scheme has reached my knowledge, for without

[1] Public Record Office. Series E. 112. No. 2572. London and Middlesex.

it we should have acted against each other and perhaps have missed our Aim.   Although Sir George has not expressed to me the least desire to become concerned, yet for these Considerations, Vizt. that he has been accessory in bringing this matter thus far and will be useful to me in raising the Money, none of which will be required from you, I think it would appear well in us to make an offer to him that the half concern reserved for you and myself should be equally divided between the Three.   Your plan is well laid but ours is of a Nature to render the undertaking much more advantageous than what you propose from yours.   However, defer entering on that head till I have the honour of your Reply."

In consequence of this letter Brown came to London and learned that the men who proposed themselves as his future partners, together with Gilbert, were Isaac Mallison, a lawyer of Gray's Inn with an interest in four alum works, and Henry Sowley, a merchant of London with an interest in two alum works.   After several meetings they came to an agreement and on July 12 signed an instrument founding the firm of Ambrose Lynch Gilbert, Brown & Co., Gilbert holding a two-fifths share, Brown, Mallison and Sowley each holding one-fifth.   This firm was to be under the general management of Gilbert, and from an early stage it seems to have been more ambitious in its aims than Brown had been, for it aimed at a corner not of the alum of England alone, but of the world.

Sir George Colebrooke was from the beginning understood to be financing it, and though his name never appeared, both the partners and the public considered him the real power within the firm.   Though he afterwards tried to deny it, there seems no reasonable doubt that one of the two shares in Gilbert's name was held, as Gilbert had already suggested it should be, in trust for him and that Sir George was the dominant partner.

It seems certain, therefore, that Sir George was a partner in the scheme, that he was its financier, Gilbert its manager, and that Brown, Mallison and Sowley provided an interest among the actual producers of alum.   Even among the producers, however, Sir George had an interest.   When the firm of Gilbert, Brown & Co. was founded, at least one of Mallison's four works was let.   The *Peak* alum works at Stainton, in Fylingdales, Yorkshire, had been let on a lease, fifteen years of which were still to run, to William Child of London, merchant, William

Dowson of Southwark, wharfinger,[1] and William Strickland of Southwark, merchant. *Stowbrow* works, also in Fylingdales, were worked by Mallison with four partners, Robert Clarke, Charles Jackson, Edward Windle, and William Forden. Gilbert, Mallison and Sowley decided to buy back the remainder of the lease of the *Peak* works, and it was decided in October to fuse the two works under the title of Mallison, Clarke & Co. : Sowley holding two-fifths (one-fifth in trust for Gilbert), Mallison one-fifth, Clarke and Jackson one-fifth between them and Windle and Forden the remaining fifth between them. The money used to purchase the lease of the *Peak* works, £4,753 in all, was nominally provided by Sowley, but actually came from Sir George.

This was the scheme in its completed form as it was in operation by February 1772. Its obvious weakness lay on the side of production. Beginning as it did at a time when the price of alum was unduly low, it was essential for the success of their corner, not only that the partners should get the greater part of the supply into their own hands, but that they should limit the output. While they were careful to purchase alum as widely as possible they paid quite insufficient attention to the limitation of future output. The case was indeed one of very serious difficulty. Except where Roman alum was concerned, the producers were small and unorganised, and even in England itself an association to limit output seemed unlikely to succeed. Success of an international association for such a purpose was quite inconceivable. It might indeed have been possible, as was later attempted, to limit foreign output by obtaining the co-operation of Amsterdam capitalists who financed at least the Liège works,[2] but even this would have been hard to achieve in a time of rising prices, and incomplete in its results. It seems clear, moreover, that the adventurers did not for some time realise the importance of this difficulty, though it placed them on the horns of a dilemma. It meant that they could either

---

[1] The position of a wharfinger among the owners of this alum work is interesting. The more technical parts of this correspondence suggest a very close connection between alum works and some members of the coal industry around Newcastle, due to the high place taken by coal among the expenses of an alum work. The importance of the London wharfingers in the Newcastle coal trade is well known.

[2] On Dec. 27, 1772, an agent of Sir George Colebrooke, Dr. Charles Irwin, says he waited personally on " the Gentlemen at Amsterdam who had advanced the money to carry on these works, and to convince them of the impossibility of their succeeding." (Public Record Office, E. 112, Bundle 1640, No. 2118. London and Middlesex.)

make contracts with the alum-makers for limited quantities, in which case when they began to force the price up the makers were tempted to produce more and sell their product to rival merchants; or they could contract to purchase all the alum produced by each maker at a fixed price, in the making of which the alum maker was in a strong bargaining position, so that the price would probably be high enough to tempt the alum makers to increase their supply and pour into this ready market an embarrassing amount of a product already over-produced. Under such conditions no monopoly could expect to be more than temporary. The adventurers themselves seem to have hoped for no more than three or four years in which to clear the profit of more than £120,000 on which they fixed their ambitions. Its chances of success rested then on their power to keep on buying up alum until the consumers were forced to purchase, and on the consumers purchasing from them in sufficient quantities to exhaust the stocks they had amassed before the increased output affected the market.

By February 1772 the mechanism had been set up and the operations began. Sir George lent the first instalment of the funds necessary to set them going, and on March 6 guaranteed drafts on Clifford's for the firm up to £20,000, for " the advances they will be obliged to be under till they begin to sell." By July he had advanced over £44,000. Meantime, though only a few sales were taking place, the price rose rapidly. In the *London Evening Post* of April 16–18, a note appeared :

> " How far a little directing B——t is conscientiously qualified to preside over a great Company's affairs may be inferred from his present monopoly of alum. which he in conjunction with one or more of his intimate friends has made so scarce that it is generally imagined in a few weeks it will arise to 30 guineas per ton."

In the issue of August 11–13 a correspondent calling himself " an injured man " calls on him to deny that he has monopolised alum and raised its price from 11–12*s.* a cwt. to 28*s.*, and brands him as a " pest of society, who has injured me and many worthy tradesmen."

If great sums were being spent on buying alum by the partners, however, they were also, it seems, being spent on speculation. It was widely believed that Sir George and Gilbert had taken up speculative policies of insurance on the rise of price. This was openly stated in the Press in April 1772 in general terms, and

John Weskett in his *Complete Digest of the Theory, Laws and Practice of Insurance*, 1781, stated (p. 35) :—

> " Such speculative insurances were made to a large amount in London in 1772 by Sir George Colebrooke and his associates on the rise of the price of alum to 30£ per ton within six months : which they attempted to *monopolise* and thereby raise the price as they pleased, and also to recover from the insurers."

A similar, though slightly different, charge was brought by Brown and Mallison with more precision. They maintained that policies were opened in trust for Sir George Colebrooke and Gilbert, who paid 5 per cent. premium and wagered that £500 tons of alum were sold by August 1, 1772. The premiums paid out were £3,000, so that they stood to win £60,000. They also alleged that, to win these wagers, Gilbert made collusive purchases of alum in Holland, where it is certainly true that he was later found to have considerable quantities to his private account in the hands of two Dutch merchants.[1]

Meantime the firm continued to buy. By September Sir George Colebrooke had advanced £110,000 to pay for it. In October there is a complete statement of accounts.

Dr.	£	Cr.		(cost price) £
To Sir George Colebrooke, about	123,000	By 6894 tons Alum.		147,324
To bills running undischarged .	31,500	By purchase Alum works :		
		Pleasington	£2,898	
To Midy & Co. running on them	6,000	Saltburn	2,340	
		Guisbro'	1,140	
To Thomas Carter on consignment by him	3,000	Ayton	1,250	7,628
To Bonfils & Sons at Venice advanced	900	By deposit :		
		to Marquis Lepri	3,500	
To Skinner & Co. at Bordeaux .	1,000	to Baker & Jackson	1,000	
		to Howlett & Co.	200	4,700
To Curry & Co. at Dantzig .	1,000	By kelp paid .		2,500
		By leading of Coals, etc., duty, etc.		1,000
		By mine burnt, etc.		2,500
		By Interest of Money & Wages, etc.		1,300
	£166,400			£166,952

Balance £552

---

[1] These speculations seem to have failed with everything else when the credit crisis intervened. E. 112, Bundle 1640, No. 2118.

This account is accompanied by a table of the alum in their possession at twenty-six different centres, 6,894 tons in all, and its average cost price in each centre. The general average cost price is worked out as £32 9s. 6d. for Roman alum, and £19 17s. for Levant, Swedish and English alum.

With the price of English alum raised to £28 or even £30 on the London market, this would seem on a summary investigation to be a highly satisfactory balance-sheet. Nevertheless, before it was drawn up disaster had already overtaken the venture. In the first place, sales were slower to begin than they had anticipated. Between February and October little more than 29 tons had been sold in England, and though much larger sales were reported from abroad, notably from Smyrna and from St. Petersburg, where about 209 tons had been sold at a profit of more than £1,000,[1] expectations were nowhere realised. Moreover, though the power of the consumers to hold off was, the partners believed, exhausted by October, the delay had brought into existence a second difficulty. The high price of alum was encouraging the production of more alum. Old works that had ceased to pay were now reopening, and new ones beginning to be worked. Hence their incessant need of funds to keep control of the market. As early as September the partners began to consider the possibility of restricting the output. It is very possible, therefore, that the scheme would have failed through the weakness of their control on the side of production. However, the ruin of the enterprise actually came through the destruction of their financial resources. It failed on account of the financial difficulties into which Sir George fell in the crisis of June and July 1772, difficulties which were due in part to the great sums he had tied up in this venture. An unsecured debt of more than £40,000, and every reason to suppose that he would be asked to pay more or lose all, was not an asset likely to strengthen the position of a speculative banker caught by a crisis on the money market.

In July, therefore, Ambrose Lynch Gilbert (whose private affairs were in a still worse way than his patron's) went to Amsterdam and Paris and tried unsuccessfully to raise a loan on the alum in the firm's possession. At the end of July he was recalled to deal with serious dissensions within the firm itself. Sir George, in his difficulties, had attempted to get some security

---

[1] No complete account of the purchases abroad has been preserved. There was a disagreement as to the profit made at St. Petersburg, some putting it as high as £2000.

for his advances on the alum by obtaining a mortgage on the whole property of the co-partnership. The partners rightly saw this as an attempt to dissociate himself from the venture and to pose as nothing more than their banker, and they opposed him hotly. A reconciliation was effected, but the position of the firm did not improve. Bills continued to be drawn on them; alum to the value of £70,000 went unpaid for, and Sir George's credit remained at a standstill. Even the partners saw that the only hope for them was that Sir George might raise money on the security of the alum. On September 7 an agreement was unwillingly drawn up whereby they mortgaged their property in alum and works to Sir George, and he for his part promised to meet their bills up to a total of £110,000. His attempt to borrow money on this security, however, failed completely, and the demands for money on the partnership were so great that within a few days he had exceeded the total he had promised to lend. That the alum corner was beginning to weaken must also have been becoming obvious to the outer world, for in September correspondents were permitted to reduce the price at which they would sell, in a desperate attempt to obtain some ready money.

By October the position was so serious that Colebrooke decided on still stronger measures. Gilbert was no longer there to advise him. On September 14 he made Sir George Colebrooke and Company his attornies irrevocably for the collection of his debts, and gave them an instrument admitting he owed Sir George £190,000.[1] Sir George and his other advisers agreed that two things alone could save the situation. New capitalists must be interested in the scheme; and some plan for the restriction of output of alum must be devised to put before them. Early in October they were in touch with the two great English producers of alum, Lord Mulgrave (with whom the partners had already had a contract) and Sir Lawrence Dundas. Friends of Sir George who were also mentioned as possible supporters were Sir Gilbert Elliott, Sir Joshua Vanneck and Sir James Cockburn. After a violent scene at the Adelphi Tavern, the partners (of whom Sowley was himself on the verge of bankruptcy) were persuaded to hand over the absolute property in the concern to Sir George. There was indeed nothing else to do. On October 8 he took it over; the following day he suspended payments on

---

[1] Gilbert, who was ill at the time, was later provided by Sir George with a position in India, that haven for the victims of eighteenth-century speculation. The *London Evening Post*, January 5–7, 1773, did not fail to point this out.

the bills drawn on the firm of Gilbert, Brown & Co., though he was careful to assure all the correspondents that this stoppage was only temporary. By the following March he had mortgaged it three times. In this ignominious way ended the original attempt to corner the world supply of alum.

Sir George was not, however, prepared to admit defeat. He still hoped to retrieve the situation, and, as one of his agents said, was " determined to possess the market at any price till his Quantity was disposed of." [1] He concentrated all his efforts on achieving some restriction on the output of alum on the one side, and on the other on preventing the correspondents, whose bills had not been met, from precipitately selling the alum they held to recoup themselves. He therefore followed different policies on the home and foreign markets. On the home market he sought by a violent drop in prices to force producers to agree to the breach of their old contracts and the formation of new ones under less favourable terms. These new contracts he hoped to base on a policy of co-operation in the restriction of output. In consequence he arranged a series of sales of alum in London at which the price fell at a blow from £28 a ton to £14 or less. The same month his agents went to Yorkshire and after some trouble effected the dissolution of all the English contracts except that with his late partners, with whom his relations remained very strained. Abroad, on the other hand, he was anxious to sell at as high a price as was consistent with his need for ready money. On October 23 all correspondents were informed that they could reduce the price of English alum to £21 5s., and that of Roman alum proportionately. On October 30 the minimum was lowered to £16, but the correspondents were assured that " le prix en tout apparence sera tenu ferme par la suitte par accorde avec les fabriquants de cet article," [2] while correspondents anxious for the money they had advanced were urged not to spoil the market. Thus the price was reduced, far more gradually abroad than in England, and the dissolution of the foreign contracts was deferred until affairs were more settled in England.

When the English contracts had almost all been ended, the agents of Sir George turned their attention to the position abroad. As one of them, Irwin explained, the success of any attempt to form an association limiting the output of English alum

---

[1] Public Record Office, E. 112, Bundle 1640, No. 2118. London and Middlesex.
[2] *Ibid.*

" must depend on the laying down or almost total reduction of the foreign works, which, by reason of the price of allum, were not only increased in their make but now are opened in different parts of Europe. It became, therefore, not only necessary to lower the price of Allum at Markett to damp the Spirit of those Enterprizes, but likewise for me to personally wait on the Gentlemen at Amsterdam who had advanced the money to carry on these works, and to convince them of the impossibility of their succeeding. . . . From my intimate knowledge of the state of allum at the foreign ports and the channels through which proprietors must have their money I can with confidence assure you that Sir George will be able to diminish these works and in many parts to cause them to be laid down." [1]

In the meantime, however, the last hope of saving the alum venture had departed. The attempt to form an English association failed. By the end of December Lord Mulgrave made it clear that he had no intention of entering an agreement to keep down the production of alum. Without his co-operation the scheme could not even be attempted. Nothing remained but to get rid of its liabilities as soon as possible and to minimise the inevitable losses.

It does not seem useful to go into the necessarily sordid activities of winding up a speculative venture that had failed. The precariousness of Sir George's own position added to his difficulties. In April, when they learned that he had stopped payment, the creditors, already clamorous, became desperate. Already, however, a crisis had been reached in the affairs of Cliffords', the chief foreign agents. When Sir George took over the business in October 1772, they at once took alarm, and showed every desire to get rid of the concern altogether. It was soon plain that they had reason to be anxious. They had taken a big part in the purchase of alum, and like Sir George himself they found a large debt secured only by a commodity which could not rapidly be sold, a serious incumbrance in a time of financial difficulty. In December they too failed, and even in the following April Justice wrote, " there is yet a large Sum to be advanced to pay Clifford their disburse." At the end of April the balance still due to them was calculated to be fl. 61,484,[2] while the firm of George Clifford & Co. in England

---

[1] Public Record Office, E. 112, Bundle 1640, No. 2118. London and Middlesex.
[2] *i.e.* about £5,940.

had also advanced £5,270 19s. 5d. on their behalf. Thus the speculation in alum played its part, though to a less degree, in weakening the resistance of the Cliffords in Amsterdam as it did that of Colebrooke in London against the shocks of the crisis of 1772–3. Hope's took over the Amsterdam agency on the failure of Cliffords', and the dreary process of winding up the business continued. The contracts with the Swedish works and the Marchese Lepri were simply broken. The former could do nothing but sue the agent, Kniper; the latter, owing (as Sir George complained) to the unwariness of Gilbert in paying a deposit, was able to sue Sir George in Chancery,[1] though he soon gave up the attempt. Two contracts, however, had to be treated with more respect, since they were guaranteed by firms holding quantities of alum in pledge, the value of which far exceeded the sum they guaranteed; that for Liège alum with Rahier, guaranteed in Amsterdam and Marseilles, and that for Roman alum with Gachon & Co., guaranteed in Marseilles. The former they succeeded in annulling at considerable expense, but in the case of the latter both contractor and guarantor displayed true Gallic tenacity, and the correspondence ceases in 1774 with the matter still unsettled.

Thus the great alum venture petered out among litigation, bankruptcies and every kind of vituperation. Of those taking part in it Sir George Colebrooke, Gilbert, and Sowley, and the firm of Cliffords', were ruined, though in no case was alum the sole cause of their ruin. Sir George's creditors calculated his loss on this account at £100,000. It is doubtful if it could have succeeded in any circumstances, for the problem of limiting output was probably insoluble under the conditions of its production. It had no chance, however, to show what it could do, for its course was cut across by a financial crisis that shook the bourses of Europe. It remains, therefore, merely an illustration of a corner that failed, showing what possibilities of international commercial organisation were afforded by the close relations of the London and Amsterdam markets, and illustrating the type of unsound speculations pursued by the great Dutch and English houses, which does much to explain why the crisis of 1772–3 was so damaging to them.

---

[1] Public Record Office, C. 12, Bundle 73, No. 23.

VI
Junius

BIBLIOGRAPHICAL NOTE

CHAPTER 21

The Letters of Junius, ed. J. Cannon (Oxford, 1978), has superseded all previous editions of the correspondence and provided what must be the definitive elucidation of all problems connected with Junius. It incorporates the findings of Dame Lucy and her co-authors.

Sir Philip Francis (1740-1818) (James Lonsdale, 1810)
(National Portrait Gallery)

JUNIUS AND PHILIP FRANCIS: NEW EVIDENCE

(WITH W. DOYLE AND J.M.J. ROGISTER)

IT IS NOW widely assumed that the letters of Junius were the work of Philip Francis. Recently, however, in an article for this journal Dr. J. N. M. Maclean has set out to rebut the most recent argument in favour of Francis and to provide new evidence which, so he writes, 'if accepted, will destroy the Franciscan case once and for all'.[1] Beginning by controverting a suggestion recently thrown out that Philip Francis was the man introduced as Junius by Grant of Blairfindy to the duc d'Aiguillon around May 1773,[2] he goes on to adduce certain evidence intended to support the case against Francis as the author. Whether he has proved that Francis was not Junius depends upon what one considers the weight of his new evidence. Dr. Maclean himself has no doubt that the eleven letters written by Robert Orme's amanuensis, who could not have been Francis, then in India, are in the same hand as those written by or for Junius. He admits, however, that evidence based on handwriting 'is always a matter for argument'.[3] This is an important reservation if the handwriting is that of a person who is still unknown. Dr. Maclean's 'item of more positive evidence',[4] namely Sir David Brewster's *Memor^m. of a convers^n. with Mr. Bell, April 10th 1822* turns not so much upon the reliability of Sir David, which, as a fellow Scot, Dr. Maclean deems unimpeachable, as upon that of the mysterious Mr. Bell when the latter dismisses the idea that Sir Philip Francis had anything to do with Junius.[5] Moreover, whereas Mr. Bell thought Lauchlin Macleane's handwriting had a very considerable general resemblance to that of Junius,[6] it is clear that Dr. Maclean has not been equally convinced that it bears a resemblance to that of Orme's amanuensis.[7]

Dr. Maclean's case against Francis is still not a strong one, and it is further weakened by the recent discovery of an important piece of evidence in the papers of King Louis XVI seized during the Revolution and now kept at the

[1] J. N. M. Maclean, 'Grant of Blairfindy, Junius and Francis', *BIHR*, xli (1968), 73 *et seq.*

[2] Rohan Butler in review of *Correspondance secrète du Comte de Broglie avec Louis XV (1756–74)*, vol. ii, *1767–1775*, ed. D. Ozanam and M. Antoine (Paris, 1961) in *Eng. Hist. Rev.*, lxxix (1964), 794–8. We wish to thank Mr. Butler, who was the first to draw attention to French archives as a line of enquiry on Junius, for his help in preparing this article. We also wish to thank Monsieur and Madame Michel Antoine who greatly facilitated our research at the Archives Nationales.

[3] Maclean, *ubi supra*, p. 83.

[4] *Ibid.*

[5] *Ibid.*, p. 85.

[6] *Ibid.*, p. 84.

[7] *Ibid.*, p. 80: 'It is not possible to discover . . . who this amanuensis was'.

Archives Nationales in Paris.[1] Among a set of letters on matters of state, addressed to the king by various ministers at different times,[2] there is a file containing two unsigned and undated notes.[3] The first note, written on good quality paper,[4] reads as follows:

a few days ago, your Majesty expressed his desire to Know who was the author of Junius's Letters. it was Mr. *fitzpatricK* who lived on his comfortable income. he was a private friend to one Mr. francis a man of parts who was a ClercK in the court offices and from him Mr. fitzpatricK got his best informations. such was the sentiment of his intimate acquaintances and particularly of the famous GarricK who, all of them, were strucK with the liKeness that was between his conversation and the ordinary subject of his letters which dropt off with him; a consideration worthy to be taKen notice of as it strenghtens [*sic*] the information I have the honour to impart to your Majesty.[5]

From what is written on the cover of the file[6] it seems likely that the second

---

[1] Dr. Doyle and Mr. Rogister discovered this evidence in the course of their work on the French *parlements* in the 18th century. They are grateful to Dr. J. M. Roberts for encouraging them to publish their findings, and Mr. Rogister is greatly indebted to the Trustees of the Arnold Historical Essay Prize Fund and to the Research Fund Committee of the University of Durham for grants made to him at different times in connection with visits to France to collect material.

[2] A[rchives] N[ationales], Cartons des Rois, K. 163.

[3] *Ibid.*, nos. 3[4] and [5].

[4] The watermark follows the pattern of a famous Dutch one known from its superscription as the *Pro Patria*. It represents a lion rampant with sword, together with the maid of Holland seated within a palisade and holding a hat on the point of a spear (on *Pro Patria* marks, see W. A. Churchill, *Watermarks in Paper in Holland, France, etc., in the XVIIth and XVIIIth centuries and their interconnection* (Amsterdam, 1935), p. 44, and E. Heawood, *Watermarks, mainly of the 17th and 18th centuries* (Monumenta chartae papyraceae historiam illustrantia, ed. E. J. Labarre, i, Hilversum, 1950), pp. 145–6 and plates 491–6). Lower down there is an N which is probably the mark of the papermaker. Much paper used in England at this time was imported from abroad, and much *Pro Patria* paper came in from Holland (Heawood, p. 27). The mark was also copied by some English papermakers at this time; see A. M. Shorter, *Paper mills and paper makers in England 1495–1800* (Monumenta, vi, 1957), pp. 318–19 and 332–3. However, it is fair to add that, although the French had important paper-making centres of their own and had developed their own distinctive watermarks (Heawood, pp. 24–5), a certain amount of Dutch paper was probably used in France, and some French papermakers may also have copied the *Pro Patria* mark, if only with an eye to the English market. Hence it is difficult to draw any firm conclusions at this stage about the provenance of the Junius note from its watermark. Moreover, a 'β-radiography' of the watermark could not be made available to us.

[5] AN., K. 163, no. 3[4].

[6] 'Note/en anglais que l'on a fait traduire. elle annonce au cid[t]. Roi que l'auteur des Lettres de Junius est m. fitzpatricK'. At the bottom there is a further note, initialled by a revolutionary, which reads: 'liasse de deux pieces / Cotte 0.5[e]'. The *liasse* is referred to in the same terms in an authenticated copy made by the archivist P. A. Laloy of an *Inventaire des Papiers, Registres et Cartons provenant du Comité Diplomatique de la Convention Nationale* drawn up by the Commission of 18 pluviôse de l'an 2 (6 Feb. 1794); see AN., M. 717, no. 2, fo. 34 r. The two notes were then in an eleventh carton, labelled 'Mélange/Ancien Régime' and which was a

note was a translation of the first done at the time when the revolutionaries were making their inventory of the former king's papers. The translation is mediocre and written out on poor quality paper. It runs as follows:

Note d'angleterre au Roi

Il y a peu de jours que Votre Majesté exprimoit son désir de savoir qui étoit l'auteur des Lettres de Junius. C'étoit M. fitzpatricK qui jouissoit d'un revenu honnête, il étoit l'ami intime d'un Mr. nommé francis homme d'esprit qui étoit commis dans les Bureaux de la Cour et de qui M. fitzpatricK avait tiré les meilleurs informations. tel fut le sentiment de ses intimes amis et particulièrement du fameux GarricK, qui comme toutes ses connaissances, fut frappé de la ressemblance qu'il y avait entre sa conversation et celle ordinaire du sujet de ses lettres qui ne terminerent qu'à sa mort. une consideration qui est très digne d'observer, comme il [sic] établi [sic] l'information que j'ai l'honneur de communiquer à Votre Majesté.[1]

The first note is the important one. Unfortunately, nothing is clear about its provenance and it has not yet been possible to identify the writer.[2] The note could be a transcript of a message which had been received in cipher,[3] or it could have been dictated to somebody. Also, Louis XVI may have found the note among his grandfather's papers, and it may even be connected with the enquiry about Junius which the comte de Broglie, the secret agent of Louis XV, proposed to make in the light of the incident involving Grant of Blairfindy. From Broglie's letter to Louis XV describing that incident, it appears that the enquiry was to be conducted by the Chevalier d'Éon, then in England, but possible details about this enquiry have not

hotchpotch of documents containing, amongst other items, some petitions to Louis XV and Louis XVI, a memoir against the *parlements* by Louis XVI's father, and a 'tableau des Remarques Journalières sur le Thermomètre de la Chambre à Coucher de Capet, tenu depuis le premier mai 1792, jusqu'au neuf août suivant'. Many of these documents, together with other papers of Louis XVI mentioned in the inventory, are now scattered throughout series K.

[1] AN., K. 163, no. 3⁵.

[2] There is no mention of the note in Vergennes' correspondence with Louis XVI now in AN., K. 164. No further details could be found in the archives of the French Foreign Ministry where Mr. Rogister looked at the Correspondance Politique; Angleterre, nos. 501 (Jan.–Apr. 1773, letters from Guines, Bourdieu, D'Éon, de Martangis), 502 (May–Sept. 1773, letters from D'Éon), 531 (Jan.–July 1779, 'correspondance diverse et secrète') and 532 (Aug.–Dec. 1779, 'correspondance diverse et secrète' mainly from the agent Vanderhey). He also investigated the handwriting of Grant of Blairfindy, Mante, D'Éon, Beaumarchais, Suard and Nathaniel Parker Forth. Finally, use was made of B. F. Stevens, *Facsimiles of MSS. in European Archives relating to America (1773–83)* (25 vols., 1889–98). The search has not yet been given up.

[3] It is curious that when the note is held up to a light, one notices that something appears to have been written in between the first three lines (from 'a few days' to 'income') and then scratched out, as if the writer had perhaps felt that he should include the cipher in a transcript and had changed his mind: but this is mere guesswork.

been made available.[1] All the same, it is more likely that the note was addressed to Louis XVI himself and not to his predecessor. No translation of it at the time would have been necessary because the king could understand English, unlike his predecessor.[2] Moreover, the writer's use of the past tense in several places suggests, amongst other things, that his note was written after Garrick's death in 1779. Still, the most one can say with assurance is that the writer was not an Englishman. No Englishman would have called a clerk in the War Office 'a ClercK in the Court Offices' or used a Gallicism like 'his best informations'.[3] He would probably not have put a capital where the small letter k was called for, whereas a Frenchman might have done so when writing in English and having, therefore, to make frequent use of a letter which was relatively unfamiliar to him in his own language.[4] The unanswered question remains, however, of why the note was written in English for a French king.

It seems likely that the writer of the note knew very little about who was who in London. He speaks of 'Mr. Fitzpatrick' and 'one Mr. Francis'. Anyone either in England or Paris (where he was quite well-known) would

[1] With his letter to Louis XV of 12 May 1773 (cf. *Correspondance secrète du comte de Broglie*, ii. 402), Broglie enclosed the draft of a letter which he proposed to write to D'Éon to this effect. In Nov. 1966, Sotheby's conducted a sale of the papers which D'Éon had entrusted to his administrator and intended biographer, Thomas William Plummer. They included letters he had received from Broglie and copies of his replies over the period 1763 to 1774 (see Catalogue of the Sotheby's sale held on 7–8 Nov. 1966, item no. 513; 'Lettres, ordres et instructions secrètes de Louis XV, et de son Ministre Secret M. le comte de Broglie &C &C. Au Chevalier D'Éon à Londres', 1763–74). The Paris bookshop which bought these papers agreed to look for some trace of Broglie's letter to D'Éon and of the latter's more important reply, but then went back upon the agreement in a very cavalier fashion. Among some D'Éon papers kept at the Archives Nationales there are two interesting books of addresses in Versailles (for 1777 and 1785) and in London (after 1785). The addresses of Mante, Grant, Francis and Woodfall are not to be found in either of them; AN. 277 AP 1.5.

[2] This may be seen from a passage in the memoirs of J.-N. Moreau in which the author, claiming that Louis XVI was by nature a pessimist, adds the following comment; 'J'ai presque été fâché que mon ami, M. Le Moine de Clermont, qui lui avait appris l'anglais, lui eût prêté les *Mémoires de Clarendon*, qu'il lut dans leur langue originale et qu'il médita beaucoup trop' (see J.-N. Moreau, *Mes souvenirs*, etc. ed. C. Hermelin (Paris, 1898, 1901), ii. 467–8). It has also been claimed that Louis XVI may have translated the first five volumes of Gibbon's *Decline and Fall* which began to appear under the name of Leclerc de Sept-Chênes in 1777; see a garbled account from a life of Louis XVI quoted in the article on Gibbon's work in J.-M. Quérard, *La France littéraire*, etc. (12 vols., Paris, 1827–39), iii. 343. Le Moine de Clermont was *secrétaire de la chambre et des Menus-Plaisirs du Roi*, and Leclerc de Sept-Chênes was a *lecteur du cabinet*; it is possible that one of them may be connected with the note found in the king's papers, but examples of their handwriting have not been traced.

[3] It is perhaps reasonable to assume that the mis-spelling of 'strengthens' was a slip of the pen.

[4] The same quirk appears in Suard's handwriting; see the facsimile of a letter of his to Wilkes in *Lettres inédites de Suard à Wilkes*, ed. G. Bonnot (Univ. of California Publications in Modern Philology, xv, no. 2, Berkeley, 1932).

have assumed the writer to mean the Hon. Richard Fitzpatrick,[1] brother of the earl of Ossory and boon companion of Charles James Fox, and maybe this was intended. But one can easily show that this is so unlikely as to be impossible, that Garrick, who knew Richard Fitzpatrick well, would not have suggested it, and, moreover, that Richard Fitzpatrick was never intimate with Francis. There was, however, a Mr. Fitzpatrick who was intimate with Francis, one Thady Fitzpatrick, an old enemy of Garrick's and an anonymous pamphleteer. He is obviously the Fitzpatrick referred to.

Davies,[2] the early biographer of Garrick, described Thady Fitzpatrick as

a gentleman who lived upon a moderate income left him by his father. His education had given him a taste for the belles lettres, more specially for dramatical writings. He was a frequenter of the coffee-houses about Covent Garden, especially the Bedford.[3]

Thady or Thadaeus Fitzpatrick (1724–71) was indeed a character of some, though minor, note in the London of his time. A tall, white-faced, rather elegant figure, he was of Catholic Irish extraction, the son of Edward and grandson of Thady Fitzpatrick both of Dublin. Both his Christian name and his circumstances suggest that he was a member of one of the branches of the ancient Fitzpatrick family, whose heads had been the dispossessed rebel Lords of Upper Ossory.[4] His education was generally agreed to have been 'polished'[5] and seems to have been acquired privately in London,[6]

[1] Hon. Richard Fitzpatrick (1748–1813).

[2] Thomas Davies (1712 ?–1785), a bookseller.

[3] T. Davies, *Memoirs of the Life of David Garrick* (3rd edn., London, 1781), ii. 15–16. This passage is also to be found in the 1st, 2nd ('new'), and Dublin editions, all of 1780. Further references to Davies's work are taken from the 3rd edition.

[4] Thady was a common name among them. The only attempt to examine the genealogy of the 'ancient branches' was made in 1877–8 by J. F. Shearman in his 'Loca Patriciana and Ossorian genealogy', *Jour. of the Royal Hist. Assoc. of Ireland*, 4th ser., iv. 335–490. There is no recognizable reference to Thady or his father, but the author admits that 'there are other Fitzpatrick families which evidently belong to some of the ancient branches, their pedigrees have not been satisfactorily made out owing to the apathy and neglect of not very remote ancestors'. Thady's father died intestate in 1726, three years after his marriage with Ellinor Lincoln, who married *en secondes noces* Nicholas Lynch of London, merchant. On 23 Sept. 1726 the administration of Edward's estate was granted to his widow and two minor children Thady and Maria (see Index of Prerogative Grants in the Public Record Office, Dublin, and Betham's Abstracts in the same place). Thady was the only surviving child of this first marriage, and he did not himself marry. We are indebted to Dr. John Woods of the University of Leeds for the Irish genealogical evidence included in this note and in p. 476, n. 1.

[5] E.g. a note in J. Foot, *Life of Arthur Murphy* (1811), p. 68. Jesse Foot (1744–1826), executor to Arthur Murphy (1727–1805), based his work on materials left by Murphy.

[6] Thady said of the Rev. Peter Whalley, author and Fellow of St. John's College, that 'it was he who formed my early youth and in Moorfields first taught me what it is to be a man'; see his letter to James Murphy French, 6 Aug. 1748, quoted in Foot, p. 71. As Whalley was only two years the older and had been a scholar at Merchant Taylors' School from 1731 to 1740 and was then elected to a scholarship at St. John's, his influence must have been that of a friend, not of a tutor.

a city which, apart from a long stay in Ireland in 1751 on business connected with a small estate he owned there[1] and a visit to Paris in 1748,[2] he never seems to have left for long. In it he lived the life of a popular, witty and convivial frequenter of coffee-houses and taverns, particularly those favoured by men interested in literature and drama; and here he earned the reputation not only of an excellent talker but of a stylish pamphleteer (when his indolence permitted him to write) and in particular of a dramatic critic.

In his youth he had struck up a close friendship with James Murphy French, elder brother of Arthur Murphy, playwright, pamphleteer and barrister, and, sometime before 1743,[3] he became a member of the coterie of wits, pamphleteers and dramatists which included Arthur Murphy, Samuel Foote, George Coleman and John Bourke (a friend and connection of Edmund Burke). With members of this group David Garrick, as actor-manager and playwright, had close but often stormy relations. To this group too Dr. Philip Francis, chaplain and factotum to Henry Fox (later Lord Holland) and father to the more famous Philip Francis, gravitated, partly through his own unsuccessful aspirations as a playwright, partly as organizer of pamphlet warfare for his patron.[4] Dr. Francis became friendly with Thady, and the friendship was passed on to his brilliant young son when the doctor introduced him into the society in which he moved.[5] All the evidence shows Thady as under normal conditions the most pleasant and easy of companions, and though there were sixteen years between them, the two men became close friends. In the years following Philip Francis's breach with his father over his marriage, Thady was one of the few intimates of this able, proud and awkward young man.

Thady is best known, however, as a result of his relations with Garrick. Enthusiastic as he was about drama and the stage, he was for some years an

[1] On 27 July 1751 he wrote to French from Dublin that his soul 'is on your side of the water, and frequently accompanies you and my other friends to Vauxhall, Ranelagh and Mary-le-Bone', and that he would try to despatch 'the business which is the sole cause of my stay' as soon as possible (quoted *ibid.*, p. 72). The property was an estate of 140 acres in the barony of Ossory in Queen's County, called Longford. A deed in the Dublin Deed Office shows that Thady was in Dublin in Oct. 1751 and that the estate was then let; see 147/408/100739 (1751). In 1759 he sold it for £1,400: *ibid.* 200/523/134162 (1759).

[2] Foot, p. 70, letter, Fitzpatrick to French, Paris, 6 Aug. 1748.

[3] *Ibid.*, p. 69, letter, same to same, London, 15 Sept. 1743. This is the first letter from Fitzpatrick quoted in the biography of Murphy; their association was clearly already well-established.

[4] Foot (p. 107) claimed that Murphy was chiefly responsible for a periodical called *The Test*, published on behalf of Henry Fox. Well-informed contemporaries were certain that Dr. Francis also played a considerable part in it.

[5] On 6 Sept. 1760 Dr. Francis wrote to his son, then on mission at Lisbon; 'I dined last Sunday for the first time this summer at Hampstead and with your friends Mr. Gorman, Mr. Fitzpatrick, Mr. Butler, . . . they said a thousand kind things of you'; quoted in J. Parkes and H. Merivale, *Memoirs of Sir Philip Francis, KCB with Correspondence and Journals* (2 vols., 1867), i. 44.

admirer of Garrick and evidently something of a favourite with him;[1] but Garrick's career was punctuated by quarrels and at least from 1758, Thady was a supporter of Murphy in one of the quarrels which occurred between the two men at regular intervals.[2] At some stage of his growing dislike for Garrick, Thady would seem to have spoken of him at the Shakespeare Club with that arrogance of the gentleman for the actor which always hurt Garrick most deeply,[3] and in 1760 he openly declared war on him in a series of articles which he collected and republished under the title of *An Enquiry into the Real Merit of a Certain Popular Performer in a series of letters first published in the Craftsman or Gray's Inn Journal*, with an introduction addressed to 'D—d. G—k, Esq.'.

As Murphy commented, 'Fitzpatrick had the pen of an elegant writer, and knowing Garrick well, he was able to point his malevolence at the vulnerable parts'.[4] Indeed, as he threatened next winter to show in a series of letters that Garrick 'never did, nor ever could, speak ten successive lines of Shakespeare with grammatical propriety', retaliation by the actor was to be expected. Garrick retorted in 1761 with his lively satirical poem *The Fribbleriad*, which introduced a new personal element into the dispute. In it he pilloried Thady as 'Fizgig' the 'cock Fribble of them all'.

> So dainty, so dev'lish is all that you scribble,
> Not a soul but can see 'tis the spite of a Fribble;
> And all will expect you, when forth you shall come,
> With a round smirking face, and a jut with your bum.[5]

At the beginning of 1763 Garrick's ally Charles Churchill the savage satirist

[1] See A. Murphy, *The Life of David Garrick* (1801), i. 370. Davies believed that Garrick complimented him with the freedom of his playhouse; he states that Thady published favourable reviews of Garrick's productions (Davies, ii. 16). Thady's first known publications are, however, certain articles in Murphy's *Gray's Inn Journal* for 1752–3 (Foot, p. 68). These were largely but not exclusively literary in character. They can best be identified by a comparison of this reference with the edition of the *Gray's Inn Journal* published by A. Murphy in London and Dublin in 1756, though the numbers do not correspond.

[2] *The Private Correspondence of David Garrick with the Most Celebrated Persons of his Time* (2 vols., 1831–2), i. 83–4. Cf. R. W. Lowe, *A Bibliographical Account of English Theatrical Literature* (1888), p. 542.

[3] We know of the incident only from Garrick's partizans. Davies (pp. 17–18) says that at the Shakespeare Club, founded by Garrick and his intimates, Thady met a proposal that business should be deferred till Garrick was present with an expression of surprise that this should be done on account of a member 'who was certainly the most insignificant person that belonged to it'. Garrick called on him for an explanation afterwards but was given none. The date of this incident is not given.

[4] Murphy, i. 370.

[5] *The Fribbleriad* (1761), p. vii. There was also a frontispiece composed of a caricature of Thady labelled 'Fizgig' [*sic*] showing him as a round-faced, smirking, foppish figure. Garrick had already published in the press the lines quoted here.

drove home this attack in a 'cruel caricature', in the 8th edition of his *Rosciad*.[1]

Meantime Thady was carrying the feud still further, and had taken the first step to the 'Half-Price' or Fitzpatrick riots to which he owed his notoriety. In these disturbances Thady who, his friends said, 'had always been distinguished by the most placid manners, became of a sudden the fomentor and leader of a tumultuous riot'[2] first against Garrick at Drury Lane and then against the other manager, Beard, at Covent Garden. The cause was not in itself an unworthy one. The managers were seeking to encroach on the established right of spectators who came in for the later acts of most types of performance to have their seats at half price, a great benefit to the theatre-going tradesmen, apprentices and craftsmen whose hours of work precluded them from seeing the whole performance.[3] On 25 January 1763 Thady issued a flysheet to the 'Frequenters of Theatres' signed 'An Enemy to Imposition' concluding with the words 'NB. The Reason for addressing the Town in this Manner is, that all Communication with the Public, by the Channel of the News Papers is cut off thro' the Influence of one of the Theatrical Managers'.[4] Receiving no satisfaction, he stood up 'to the astonishment of all his acquaintance' as the leader of a violent demonstration in Garrick's theatre. Here, not satisfied with forcing Garrick publicly to rescind his decision, he made him agree to refrain from employing one of his actors, who had angered the crowd, so long as he was under their displeasure.[5] Next night, going on to Covent Garden with the same demand, the crowd, still with Thady at their head, became completely out of hand and did so much damage to property that Beard sued out a warrant against the rioters, and Thady, appearing with others before the chief justice Lord Mansfield, was severely reprimanded by him.[6]

[1] Murphy reported that 'a cruel caricature of him was drawn by Churchill in one of his poems, to gratify the resentments of Garrick' (Foot, p. 68). Among other things Churchill wrote of him

> 'a motley figure of the Fribble Tribe
> Nor Male nor Female; Neither and yet both;
> Of Neuter Gender, though of Irish Growth;
> A six-foot suckling, mincing in its gait;
> Affected, peevish, prim, and delicate.'

[2] Murphy, i. 370.
[3] See *The Letters of David Garrick*, ed. D. M. Little and G. M. Kahrl (3 vols., 1963), i, p. xlvii.
[4] A copy of this flysheet is preserved among the papers of Philip Francis in the British Museum (Add. MS. 40760). The 'Actor Manager' was Garrick whose close connections with the press were well known.
[5] A friend 'very willing and able to bring about a reconciliation between the audience and the actor' later persuaded the good-natured Thady, who 'now began to view his conduct with impartial eyes', to write to Garrick removing the ban on the unfortunate actor, John Moody (Davies, ii. 9–10).
[6] Accounts differ as to whether Thady himself was summoned or 'thought proper' to accompany the rioters to the chief justice's house (Davies, ii. 13–14; Murphy, i. 370). According to Murphy, Lord Mansfield singled him out for reproof: 'You, Sir, look so like a gentleman, that I am astonished to see a person of your appearance

Nevertheless at Covent Garden, too, the rioters succeeded in their aim.

These riots formed something of a crisis for both the chief characters concerned in them. Garrick, though the sympathy of the educated public was with him,[1] was deeply humiliated by the treatment he had received. His two years' foreign tour at the end of the season was undertaken in part at least on doctor's advice to seek a rest which he considered he had 'dearly earn'd',[2] and seven years later he was put to great pains to correct a garbled account of the incident which had been published abroad.[3] Thady's reputation suffered more severely. He was not successful in winning public support for his criticism of Garrick as a Shakespearian actor, and his part in the riots was condemned even by his friends. When Thomas Davies, a supporter of Garrick, published the first edition of his *Life* in 1780, Thady was treated as no more than a ruffian, and though his friends ensured the insertion of a very different account of him in later editions,[4] and Murphy's *Life of Garrick* reiterated the more favourable account,[5] no attempt was made to justify his part in the riots. It is of interest that the first known publication by Philip Francis, an anonymous letter in the *Public Ledger*, is annotated by its author in the copy preserved in his manuscripts in the British Museum

---

involved in such a breach of the peace'. According to Davies, 'the usual paleness of his [Thady's] cheek was rendered perfectly of a livid colour by the dreadful rebuke of Lord Mansfield, who told him solemnly, that if a life was lost in this tumultuous contest, he would be answerable for his own'. The rioters promised not to repeat their performance and the case was not proceeded with.

[1] The sympathies of the poorer playgoers may well have been different. Davies, in his highly partizan account, admitted that the public gained the 'wonderful privilege of seeing two acts of a play at half price, and the exalting of pantomime to a rank superior to tragedy and comedy' but added: 'But I can tell them honestly, they owed this great prerogative to the private resentment of a splenetick man, not to publick spirit or patriotick principles' (ii. 15). The reference to 'pantomime' refers to the fact that seats were not available at half price when pantomimes were played, owing to the high expense of their presentation.

[2] *Letters of David Garrick*, i. 385 : Garrick to Susannah Cibber (*ante* 8 Sept. 1763).

[3] P. J. Grosley, a Swiss writer, published in Lausanne in 1770 his three-volume *Londres* in which, referring to these riots, he stated that Garrick had been forced to beg the pardon of the audience on his knees. Garrick, greatly distressed, published a correction of the account in the *Journal Encyclopédique* of Oct. 1770, and a full account of the correction was published in T. Nugent's English translation of the work; P. J. Grosley, *A Tour to London or New Observations on England, and its Inhabitants* (2 vols., 1772), ii. 292 *et seq.* Grosley, who was in England in 1765, was said to have got his information from 'an English Gentleman'.

[4] Fitzpatrick, he now wrote, 'was much respected by many gentlemen eminent in rank, and distinguished by their literature and taste; they admired and loved his company and conversation, which united frankness of behaviour and freedom of thought, with superior knowledge and elegance of manners' (Davies, ii. 26). It may have been Murphy or Foote who got him to make his amendments. If it were so, then it is possible that the information in the French note came not directly from Garrick but from someone like Murphy who may have quoted Garrick as the source. The reference in the French note to Fitzpatrick's income bears a curious resemblance to that given by Davies.

[5] Murphy, i. 370–1.

'written by me at the Shakespeare Tavern in 1763, to help my friend Thady Fitzpatrick out of a scrape'.[1]

After this episode Thady disappeared from the public view, though he continued his amiable and convivial life. There are some indications that towards the end of his life his estate became involved.[2] Our only information about him comes from the Francis correspondence, which shows him, lively and companionable as ever, as one of Philip Francis's small circle of close friends. The only manuscript letter from him which is known to survive is written to Francis. It is dated 'the glorious first of August and Jubilee-year of the Hanoverian Succession' and in it he regretfully declines an invitation for the next day,

being under a necessity of attending at the Long Room, with Butler, Fremantle & Co. in order to consume the Remains of a Turtle which is dressed there today. If you could conveniently favour us with your Company it would add much to our Jollity; and I flatter myself, that no office-Business is likely to prevent it, as I perceive by the papers that the important Point of preserving the Horses Tails is at length happily settled.[3]

In a letter to his wife on 11 June 1765 Francis wrote 'Your brother [Alexander Makrabie] and Fitz and I went to Foote's last night, and afterwards they supped on Bread and Butter with me'.[4] In 1768 the same Alexander Makrabie wrote from distant Philadelphia to his sister, entreating her 'when you see Mr. Fitzpatrick, Roberts, Marsh and Gravier, give my love to them'.[5] Two years later he wrote to Francis himself: 'I long to make one of your Parties with Dick Tilghman, Fitz, and so forth but the Devil take politics! I'll never debate with either you or Dick'.[6]

Francis was recently returned from a short tour in the country when Thady died unexpectedly on 6 September 1771;[7] a few days before he had

[1] Quoted by Parkes and Merivale, i. 69.

[2] Thady's will, as that of a Catholic, is not preserved at Somerset House, but there is an entry that his mother took out the administration of his estate in March 1772. In Aug. 1777, however, his half-sister Ellinor Lynch took out a further administration. Delay in completing administration is a common sign of an absence of clear assets to administer.

[3] Brit. Mus., Add. MS. 40763 fo. 9. The Long Room was at the Customs House where John Freemantle was at this time Clerk of the Western Ports in England and the Plantations. There is no evidence, however, that Fitzpatrick was employed at the London Customs at this time: his name does not appear on the registers (Series 1 Establishments) of the Board of Customs and Excise that have survived for 1765–6 (cf. P.R.O., Customs 18/301, 302 (wanting), 303, 304 (Christmas 1765 wanting), 305–8). Francis's own work as a clerk at the War Office had no doubt been affected by a controversy which found its way into the press at this time about docking the cavalry horses' tails.

[4] *The Francis Letters, by Sir Philip Francis and other members of the Family*, ed. Beata Francis and Eliza Keary (2 vols., 1901), ii. 71–2.

[5] *Ibid.*, p. 92, letter of 9 March 1768.

[6] *Ibid.*, p. 118, letter from Philadelphia, 9 June 1770. Tilghman was a cousin of Francis.

[7] The *London Evening Post*, 5–7 Sept. 1771 bore the following entry: 'Yesterday at his mother's house in East St., Red Lion Square, Thady Fitzpatrick, Esq'. He

set out they attended a convivial party.[1] On 5 January 1772 Makrabie wrote to Francis that in a letter from his father

He informs me of the death of our Worthy Friend Fitzpatrick—But I shall only distress you by expressing how very much I admired his Character, and how truly concerned I am at such a loss. It has cost honest Tilghman many a sigh.[2]

There is no doubt that Francis and Thady were constant companions and that Francis was sincerely attached to him; he spoke of him with real affection, a rare thing for Francis, even some years after his death.[3]

Why should anyone have suspected Thady Fitzpatrick of being Junius? On general grounds, the only reasons were that he had written anonymous articles which, as Garrick knew to his cost, were well-written and telling, and that he still consorted with people who had gone in for this kind of writing, like Arthur Murphy and Sam Foote. He was also intimate with Philip Francis, but though the latter's father had been active in this line, the son's efforts to date had apparently been kept secret. On the other hand, Fitzpatrick was known to be indolent and, except during his notorious altercation with Garrick between 1758 and 1763, good-natured. His interests were primarily dramatic and literary, and he had no direct access to the kind of political matters dealt with by Junius. Finally, his sudden death at the age of forty-seven occurred on 6 September 1771 and Junius went on writing till 1772.

It would seem, therefore, on general grounds unlikely that Fitzpatrick would be suspected. Why then was Garrick's attention directed to him? The answer would seem almost certainly to lie in his curious brush with Junius in 1771 which began a month after Fitzpatrick's death.[4] On the face of it what happened was that about this time Woodfall, editor of the *Public Advertiser*, told Garrick in a letter that Junius would 'write no more'.[5] Garrick passed this information to a friend at Court as well as to others, and

was buried, as London Catholics often were, in St. Pancras Churchyard and his mother erected a monument to 'a most amiable and worthy son' with a laudatory epitaph. (Reported under 'Miscellaneous Monumental Inscriptions' in the *Gentleman's Magazine*, 1793, ii. 1192.)

[1] 'Fitzpatrick, Tilman, Gravier and I dined yesterday at the Queen's Arms. They drank immoderately; even I, who drank nothing but thimblefulls, grew intoxicated at last'; Francis to Major J. Baggs, 25 June 1771, in Parkes and Merivale, i. 263.

[2] Brit. Mus., Add. MS. 40762 fo. 181.

[3] See his letter to Sir John Day, 20 May 1778: 'Poor Fitzpatrick whom, if you will remember, you ought to revere, often showed that nothing was so dangerous to a man's happiness as prosperity' (Parkes and Merivale, ii. 130).

[4] The crucial letters in the Garrick incident formed part of the Phillipps collection and were sold at Sotheby's in May 1913. They had already been published in an incomplete and inaccurate way by Mason Good and reprinted by John Wade, but the definitive edition of them is that given by Sir Ernest Clarke in 'David Garrick and Junius', *The Nineteenth Century*, lxxv (1914), 180–5.

[5] Clarke, *ubi supra*, p. 183: Garrick to H. S. Woodfall (for Junius), 20 Nov. 1771.

was startled, on 18 November, to receive through Woodfall a savagely threatening letter from Junius. Written in a formal clerkly hand, it read:

To Mr. David Garrick

I am very exactly informed of your practices, and of the information you so busily sent to Richmond, and with what triumph and exultation it was received. I knew every particular of it the next day—Now mark me, vagabond—Keep to your pantomimes, or be assured you shall hear of it. Meddle no more, thou busy informer! It is in my power to make you curse the hour in which you dared to interfere with

JUNIUS[1]

Garrick at once protested his innocence, claiming that Woodfall had told him that Junius would 'write no more' without attaching any secrecy to a piece of information which Garrick had not tried to elicit from him in the first place.[2] Pressed by Garrick and his friends, Woodfall tried unsuccessfully to get Junius to make a satisfactory reply to Garrick's letter.[3] Woodfall himself obviously thought Junius's reaction excessive, and he told one of Garrick's friends that he thought some more deep-rooted resentment towards Garrick lay behind Junius's attack and that 'it does not proceed merely from this little communication'.[4] Garrick was not at all likely to ignore the warning he had received, as he was always much afraid of the effect of press attacks on his theatre. But he was a great collector of information about his world; indeed, Murphy called him a 'whispering gallery',[5] and Thomas Becket, the bookseller who notoriously was his 'runner' for the collection of such news,[6] was at work for him on this occasion.[7] It would seem from the note in Louis XVI's papers that some people began to see some connection and to associate Thady Fitzpatrick's death with Junius's intention to write no more and with the attack made on Garrick for concerning himself with this intention, and that Garrick knew what they were saying and agreed with them.

The note states that Fitzpatrick's 'intimate acquaintances' were 'strucK with the liKeness that was between his conversation and the ordinary subject

---

[1] *Ibid.*, pp. 181–2. As sent by Junius to Woodfall the note for Garrick originally bore the words 'impertinent enquiries' instead of 'practices'. Woodfall did not want to offend either Junius or Garrick and he hesitated to send this letter as directed, and seems to have asked Junius to suppress it or tone it down. In another (undated) letter to Woodfall (*ibid.*, p. 181) Junius insisted that a copy of the note should be sent to Garrick but changed 'impertinent enquiries' to 'practices'. Clarke pointed out that Woodfall must have acquainted Garrick with the original terms of Junius's letter because Garrick uses the very words 'impertinent enquiries' in his rejoinder to Junius of 20 Nov.

[2] Above, p. 481, n. 5.

[3] Clarke, *ubi supra*, p. 183: Woodfall to Thomas à[?] Becket, 23 Nov. 1771.

[4] *Ibid.*

[5] E.g. Murphy, ii. 197.

[6] A. Downer, 'The diary of Benjamin Webster', *Theatre Annual* (1945), p. 64 (quoting Joseph Cradock).

[7] Becket saw Woodfall on Garrick's behalf; see n. 3 above.

of his letters'. It looks as if the idea began to circulate among them that Fitzpatrick was Junius, together with the conclusion that he must have got his information from his close friend Francis. Moreover, these men probably began to notice that after the date of Fitzpatrick's death Junius was writing less than before and on somewhat different topics even before he stopped altogether. Garrick must, of course, have known that the threatening letter he had received was not written by Fitzpatrick, since Fitzpatrick was dead; but the insulting references to his 'pantomimes' echoed some of Thady's attacks on him in the past. Garrick and his friends were familiar with the methods of periodical writing of the time, and they would have assumed that more than one person had been involved; they could have suspected Francis.

They certainly succeeded, however, in keeping their reflections to themselves, Garrick and his friends for obvious reasons, others perhaps because Junius did go on writing for a short while. Apart from the note, the only reference to Thady Fitzpatrick in connection with Junius seems to be a very garbled passage in the *Reminiscences* of Charles Butler,[1] published in 1822. Butler writes of 'an accomplished Irishman, since dead' named Fitzgerald about whom he quotes a complicated account taken from a Scottish gazette. From Butler's own comments, however, it is clear that the name had been muddled and that it is Thady Fitzpatrick who is referred to, as he alludes to his leading part in the 'Half-Price' riots. This, he continued,

exposed him to ridicule, but he was allowed to be a man of learning and elegant pursuits. He resided at Hampstead;[2] one of his most intimate friends was a Mr. Madan,[3] a gentleman who resided in the same place . . . This gentleman, in 1776, mentioned to the Reminiscent, that he always suspected his friend Fitzgerald [*sic*] was the author of Junius's Letters, and thought him more than equal to the composition of them. But such circumstances are light as air, and even this mention of them may be thought to require an apology.[4]

The private correspondence of Junius with Woodfall which they did not know of, strengthens their case. Junius had certainly told Woodfall by October that he would 'write no more' and he had begun to arrange for a complete edition of his letters. His alarm at Garrick's interest was acute; he intensified his security arrangements and showed signs of real panic.[5] In his

[1] Charles Butler (1750–1832), Catholic writer on legal and historical topics.

[2] Though the Somerset House record of the administration of his will states him to be of Great Ormonde Street, the Francis correspondence shows that Fitzpatrick was often at Hampstead, and his only known letter to Francis (see p. 167 above) was addressed from there.

[3] Probably Dr. Martin Madan (1726–90), the author of *Thelyphtora* and a Methodist preacher.

[4] C. Butler, *Reminiscences* ([1st edn.,] 1822), p. 111n.

[5] Clarke, *ubi supra*, p. 181: Junius to Woodfall, undated (but probably written about 10 Nov. 1771): 'I must be more cautious than ever. I am sure I should not survive a discovery three days: or if I did, they wo[d] attaint me by bill. Change [address] to the Somerset Coffee-house, and let no mortal know the alteration'.

published letters he kept up a recently acquired interest in City affairs, and towards the end of the year he developed a fierce attack under the title of Philo-Junius on Lord Mansfield.[1] But his attacks on ministers fell off, and of one of the only two he published on Grafton he remarked that 'D[avid] G[arrick] has literally forced me to break my resolution of writing no more'.[2]

If their suspicions were correct, however, the question remains, what can Fitzpatrick's part have been in these publications ? He was not the amanuensis. Whether or not the handwriting experts succeeded in showing that the letters were written in a feigned hand by Francis, the *same* hand appears before and after Fitzpatrick's death.[3] It is almost superfluous to add that Fitzpatrick's own handwriting bears no resemblance to that of Junius.[4] Equally, if Mr. Ellegård's recent stylistic tests are to be accepted, making up, as they do, a very strong case for Francis,[5] then Fitzpatrick cannot have been the author, nor even the author of some of the letters. It may be, however, that Francis discussed his plans with Fitzpatrick. Here there may be some significance in Junius's letter of 7 September 1769 written in reply to 'Junia', and which he asked his publisher three days later to repudiate by suggesting that it was not authentic. He wished it recalled, he wrote, as 'idle and improper and I assure you printed against my own opinion.'; and he added 'The truth is there are people about me whom I would wish not to contradict, and who had rather see Junius in the papers ever so improperly than not at all'.[6] The cancelled letter was humorous and mildly scurrilous. Woodfall got out of the difficulty by inserting in the *Public Advertiser* a notice that there was reason to think it was 'sent by some one of his waggish friends' who had copied his style. The letter is written in a vein which is reminiscent of Thady,[7] and it may be that it was he who persuaded the author to publish a work which on second thoughts he considered too frivolous for his reputation. But it is possible that Fitzpatrick wrote some of the publications which Junius thought necessary as proper support

----

[1] See Letters lx–lxiii in [*Letters of*] *Junius etc.*, ed. J. Wade (new and enlarged edn., 2 vols., 1850), i. 417–32 *et seq.* (hereafter referred to as Wade).

[2] Clarke, *ubi supra*, pp. 183–4: Junius to Woodfall, undated but probably written about 27 Nov. 1771. The letter to the duke of Grafton (no. lxvii) appeared the next day (Wade, i. 441–5). Both Wade (i. 441–2n) and Clarke (*ubi supra*, p. 180) thought that the next letter (no. lxviii), addressed to Lord Mansfield and published on 21 Jan. 1772, was completed by 8 Nov. 1771, sometime, therefore, before the one to Grafton.

[3] Junius wrote a long private letter to Wilkes on the day after Fitzpatrick's death.

[4] See his letter to Francis, above, p. 480, n. 3.

[5] A. Ellegård, *Method for Determining Authorship: the Junius Letters 1769–1772* (Gothenburg Studies in English, xiii, 1962). Dr. Ellegård does not accept the view that Francis penned the Junian manuscripts. He claims that his stylistic tests demonstrate, however, that Francis could have been the author of the letters; see his other work, *Who was Junius ?* (Uppsala, 1962), pp. 93–5 and 139.

[6] See Junius ('C') to Woodfall, private letter no. 8, in Wade, ii. 22.

[7] It is the Miscellaneous Letter no. lix in Wade, ii. 275.

in the newspapers.[1] It is also possible that he helped in the 'conveyancing' part of the correspondence.[2]

What, then, is the significance of the new evidence? The informant was wrong in thinking that Thady Fitzpatrick was Junius, and so were Garrick and his friends, if such was their opinion. But they were probably right in thinking that he had something to do with Junius, although his exact role has not yet been determined. The chief importance, however, of their identification is that it led them to associate Philip Francis with the letters of Junius. It has generally been accepted that the name of Philip Francis was not associated with the letters until after the publication of Junius's private correspondence with his publisher Woodfall in 1812 and the evidence these contained of his authorship of letters appearing under other names.[3] Hence, the note in Louis XVI's papers is indeed the first known contemporary association of Francis with Junius. The fact that Garrick made the association is particularly interesting because of the hitherto unexplained brush which he had with Junius in 1771. Moreover, the fact that the brush occurred at the time and in the way it did suggests that Garrick had some grounds for the conclusions which the note claims that he drew, besides mere general guesswork.

[1] An illustration of this is given in *The letter of A.B. to the Duke of Grafton* printed in the *London Evening Post* of 7 Nov. 1769, and which Junius ('C') asked Woodfall to reproduce in the *Public Advertiser* as it was 'very material that it should spread', though he had not himself written it (Wade, ii. 23–4, 277 et seq.). There is no suggestion that this letter was written by Fitzpatrick.

[2] That Junius employed a conveyancer at times may be seen from a letter he wrote to Woodfall a year after Thady's death in which he speaks of 'a gentleman who transacts the conveyancing part of our correspondence' (Wade, ii. 54). Now that the question of how the Junian enterprise functioned has been mentioned, it is interesting to recall, as Mr. Rohan Butler did in his review (cf. p. 471 n. 2 above), that another friend of Francis was Philip Rosenhagen. Rosenhagen was on the continent during the better part of the Junian period, but when he was living in Orleans in 1774 he made it no secret there that he was Junius (see an extract from the *Gazetteer* of 24 Jan. 1774 quoted in *Notes and Queries*, 3rd ser., v (1864), 17). It is also claimed that he later tried to make Lord North believe the same story and that he attempted to get a pension from him on an undertaking to write no more. Parkes and Merivale make the cryptic statement that Rosenhagen subsequently intimated such knowledge or suspicion of the real authorship of Junius as to disquiet Francis (Parkes and Merivale, i. 232). It is unlikely that Rosenhagen was connected with the note in Louis XVI's papers; he was certainly in Paris in 1776 (see *Notes and Queries*, 2nd ser., x (1860), 315), but his handwriting is not the same as that of the note (although the information contained in that note may, of course, have been dictated to the person who wrote it).

[3] Unless one is to accept George Woodfall's statement more than forty years later that his father had referred to Francis as the author in or shortly after 1781 (Parkes and Merivale, i. 293–4).

VII

Eighteenth-Century Oxford

BIBLIOGRAPHICAL NOTE

See the forthcoming eighteenth-century volume of *The History of the University of Oxford.*

Worcester College, Oxford (Oxford University Almanac, 1741). Charity kneels before Sir Thomas Cookes, the founder; behind her, figures representing the three faculties, Divinity, Law and Physick, and the Sciences. Bishop Lloyd of Worcester is beside the founder. Dr. Clarke, designer of the new buildings, stands holding a plan of the library on the right, with two other benefactors, Margaret Alcorne and Sarah Eaton. *(Ashmolean Museum, Oxford)*

22

THE UNIVERSITY OF OXFORD
IN THE EIGHTEENTH CENTURY:
A RECONSIDERATION

I MUST begin my lecture this afternoon by thanking my old College for the honour they have done me in asking me to deliver it, and by paying my respects to the memory of that versatile and liberal man of affairs and letters, James Lord Bryce, whom it commemorates. And I should be lacking in piety if I did not also refer—particularly in the light of the subject of my lecture—to my former tutor and colleague, Maude Clarke, sometime Fellow, Tutor, and Vice-Principal of this College, to whom the College and all who have been her pupils owe so much. Maude Clarke would have welcomed the enterprise on which some of us have embarked under the general editorship of Mr. Trevor Aston, the production of a comprehensive and large-scale history of the University; for the study of the institutions which originated in that great era of institution-making, the Middle Ages, was her life work.

Boswell reported an *obiter dictum* of Dr. Johnson's in praise of the University when they were together in Oxford in 1768:

'The tutors are anxious to have their pupils appear well in the college; the colleges are anxious to have their students appear well in the University. There are all opportunities of books and learned men; there are excellent rules of discipline in every college'. 'I objected that the rules and indeed the whole system is very ill observed'. 'Why, Sir', said he, 'that is nothing against the institution. The members of an university may for a season be unmindful of their duty. I am arguing for the excellence of the institution.'[1]

---

[1] *Boswell in Search of a Wife 1766–1769.* Eds. F. Brady and F. A. Pottle, Yale edn. of the private papers of James Boswell, London, 1957, p. 163.

Perhaps I should apologize for choosing, out of all the periods of the University's history, that in which it has been most widely held that 'its members were for a season unmindful of their duty', but I do so, chiefly because the eighteenth century is the period of my own studies, but also because I wish to consider how far the general opinion of eighteenth-century Oxford was justified. I do apologize for the fact that those of us who are working on the subject are still only at the beginning of our task, and there is much which I shall be speaking about of which I am still very ignorant.

The University in the eighteenth century was a very small body, and, despite the increase in the wealth and population of the country as a whole, it was for much of the period stationary in numbers, and in the middle years even declining. It was the nineteenth century which saw the beginning of the increase which has since become such a flood. The researches of Mr. Julian Hill in the University Archives have recently presented us with statistical evidence of the position. In 1724/5, for instance, 272 men matriculated. Many of them were unlikely to take degrees, for in the same year only 190 were admitted B.A. and 82 M.A. Twenty-one years later in 1745/6 matriculations had dropped sharply, from 272 to 197, 135 were admitted B.A. and 74 M.A. Twenty years later again in 1765/6 the decline was still continuing, though it had slowed down. Only 170 men matriculated, 98 were admitted B.A. and 69 M.A.

The members of this small institution were divided among Colleges which varied widely in size, but were all by our standards small, and among the five remaining medieval Halls, which were tiny. In 1745/6, for instance, Christ Church, which always led in numbers, matriculated 25 men; Queen's followed with 19, and Oriel was third with 18. Twelve Colleges matriculated fewer than 10 men apiece, and all the Halls together only 13. Basically each College consisted of its Head and the members of its Foundation, set up and endowed by former benefactors; but by this time all to some, and some to a considerable, extent had added to their numbers and strengthened their finances by admitting what one College (Exeter) still called 'sojourners'—that is, the Commoners who are now the bulk of the undergraduate population, and the Gentlemen Commoners, who have now disappeared.

Though the Colleges were so small, their undergraduate members were sharply stratified. To begin with the most socially distinguished. The University gave special recognition to peers and the sons of peers, including the sons of bishops. Not only were these entitled to wear a gold-laced gown and a golden tuft, they were invited with the Senior Members to all University occasions, and given seats of prominence there, and if they actually wished to take a degree (which they did occasionally) they were excused a year's standing for the purpose.[2] In the Colleges they were not generally distinguished from the other members of an only less honorific class, that of the Gentlemen or Fellow-Commoners.[3] A statute of Lincoln College of 1606 defined them as 'sons of lords, knights and gentlemen of good place in the commonwealth'.[4] They were sharply differentiated from other undergraduates; in most Colleges

[2] If they took degrees at all they were usually made M.A. by creation.

[3] At some Colleges they were called Fellow-Commoners, though at Queen's Fellow-Commoners were quite distinct from Gentlemen Commoners, being Commoners of three years' standing or more, whose good record led the Provost and Fellows to admit them to the High Table and the Fellows' stalls in Chapel (see G. Fothergill—Provost Smith *et al.*, Library of Queen's College, Joseph Smith MSS. 473). The University records called them *superioris ordinis commensales*. At Christ Church 'Noblemen of the House' sat at the High Table.

[4] College Register, vol. 2, fol. 51. Quoted in *V.C.H. Oxfordshire*, iii (1954), 171.

they enjoyed some at least of the privileges of the Fellows, often dining with them and being admitted to their Common Rooms. Despite the efforts of their Colleges, they seldom seem to have submitted themselves to the normal College or University exercises leading to a degree, for they seldom took a degree by normal means. A custom had grown up whereby, if they stayed up for three years, and so wished, they could when they went down be awarded an honorary M.A. by creation.[5] It is characteristic of the eighteenth century that not even the most critical observer of the University saw occasion to object to this (to us) very dubious concession except Thomas Hearne who made the point that it was important that the honorand should be really rich and really distinguished in rank, lest he later used his degree to enter a profession, thus competing with those who had won their qualification by their own efforts.[6] Though Gentlemen Commoners were profitable to Colleges and gave them social prestige, it is to the credit of the Colleges (and perhaps even more to the good sense of parents) that their numbers remained small in the University as a whole. The institution was not popular in most Colleges, and snobbish Commoners or their parents, seeking, as the phrase went, to 'change their gowns' were not encouraged.[7]

[5] The details were specified in a minute of the Hebdomadal Board, 15 June 1798 (University Archives, W.P.Y. 24 (2), Hebdomadal Meetings 1788–1803). It probably represented a rationalization of the custom by that time prevailing. Cases had been dealt with from the beginning of the century *ad hoc*. At first they had been comparatively rare (Convocation Registers) and those put forward had often had five years' residence; but even at an early date there were cases where residence had been less than three years. In 1803 the time was reduced to two and a half years (Hebdomadal Meetings, 2 March 1803).

[6] *Remarks and Collections of Thomas Hearne*, ii, *Oxford Historical Society*, vii (1886), 305.

[7] When Jeremy Bentham's conscientious though unsympathetic tutor misunderstood a message from Bentham's father, and thought he was pressing for his son to be made a Gentleman Commoner, he

The two big undergraduate classes were the Commoners, the other class of 'sojourners', and the undergraduate Foundationers, by whatever name they were known in their respective Colleges. Not all Colleges were prepared to take Commoners—there were none at New College, Magdalen, or Corpus—but others accepted them freely, and at the Halls there were no Foundationers. One of the many things we must find out before we fully understand the eighteenth-century University is the social and economic classes from which the Commoners were drawn. They were certainly very wide-ranging. At the top of the social scale they shaded into that of the Gentlemen Commoners; at the bottom they included some, like Dr. Johnson at Pembroke,[8] whose shaky finances proved inadequate to see them through their course. There was also probably quite a wide spread as between Colleges. We know that in general the Commoners included many sons of country gentry, well-to-do parsons, and professional men, but in 1704 Peter Leigh of Adlestrop, who had been a Commoner at Trinity in his time, warned his widowed sister that, if she sent her son to Trinity, which he described as 'the dearest House in Town', it must be as a Gentleman Commoner since 'none now but sons of inferior clergymen, tradesmen, and substantial countrymen

intended to travel up to London to dissuade him (*Correspondence of Jeremy Bentham*, ed. T. L. S. Sprigge, London, ii (1968), 54). The careful Doctor Thomas Fry (President of St. John's, 1757–72) confided to his Diary his reasons for permitting one Velley, a Commoner, to assume a Gentleman Commoner's gown in 1768. 'Mr. Cleeve his uncle approved of it, and as Mr. Ashfield was soon to take his degree, he would have been left alone, or, what is worse, with Pool, a commoner of very ill character and behaviour.' (I am indebted to Mr. Hargreaves-Mawdsley of Brandon University, Canada, for the reference from this unprinted Diary.)

[8] See *The Correspondence and other papers of James Boswell relating to the making of the Life of Johnson*. Ed. M. Waingrow, Yale edn. of the private papers of James Boswell, London, 1969, pp. 57–8.

are Commoners there'.[9] Which may, or may not, have been true.

The Foundationers, Scholars, or by whatever name they were known in their Colleges, were still regarded as the backbone of the undergraduate body, and in some Colleges provided almost the whole of it. They were in most Colleges predominantly (though by no means universally) destined for the Church, most of the Fellows of Colleges were drawn from their ranks, and many of them were the sons of clergymen. Contemporaries commonly referred to them as poor men, but this was by no means always true, and in any case the poverty was relative. Here, too, much research will be needed before we can form an accurate picture of their social and economic origins; and such research will certainly show wide variations between individuals and still more between Colleges. No one, for instance, assumed that the undergraduate students of Christ Church (whether they were 'Westminsters' or 'Canoneers')[10] were for the most part poor men. Lord Bute, four years after he had resigned from the position of First Minister to the Crown, tried to get a 'canoneer' student-ship for one of his sons, Frederick, the black sheep of the family, on the grounds that he did not wish to submit him to the temptations of 'the nobleman's gown'. In his case he was politely told that there were no vacancies, and entrance as a Gentleman Commoner was offered and accepted.[11] In 1707 the Headmaster of Rugby, advising Sir Justinian Isham, a prominent landowner of Northamptonshire, about the placing of his son, recommended 'Baliol . . . Sir, if you enter Him Commoner; but if

[9] Northamptonshire Record Office, D (CA), 354, fol. 51.

[10] Canoneers were students nominated by the Dean and Canons (E. G. W. Bill and J. F. A. Mason, *Christ Church and Reform*, Christ Church Papers, no. I, Oxford, 1970, pp. 1–13).

[11] S. Barrington to Charles Jenkinson, 19 November 1767, Brit. Mus. Add. MS. 38205, fols. 276–7.

Gentleman Commoner . . . Magdalen; unless you design . . . for a Cannon's [*sic*] nomination for a Student in Christ Church'.[12] Christ Church was throughout the century atypical in this as in most other ways, but there may well have been parallels at others of the 'fashionable' Colleges.

Probably a more typical illustration, however, of the members of this class is provided by the defence of the Foundation as an institution given by Richard Radcliffe, Foundationer and Fellow of Queen's (not at that time a fashionable College) in 1773. He makes it clear that the kind of young man he has in mind is one who intends to enter the Church, is of moderate ambition, and lacks useful family connections, whose father 'can give him some three or four hundred pounds, but has no possibility of providing for him afterwards'. Though he himself, he says, has found advancement within the College, first to a Fellowship and then to the College living to which he aspired, unusually slow (he had spent much of the waiting time serving as a curate in country livings), 'I am still', he asserts, 'in love with the Foundation. . . . It has been the grand comfort of my life—it enabled me to go into the Company of my superiors with the greater pleasure because I was not dependent on them, and made me be received with the greater civility by them because they knew I wanted nothing from them.' In this way he had avoided the ignominies of place-hunting, which he describes for a young parson as either 'A diligent and obsequious attendance upon the squire or lord of the place' or 'The more active and popular qualifications of fox-hunting, drinking and bustling at an election'.[13] Anyone

[12] Northamptonshire Record Office, Isham MSS., no. 2758.

[13] *Letters of Richard Radcliffe and John James of Queen's College, Oxford, 1755–83.* Ed. M. Evans, *Oxford Historical Society*, ix (1888), pp. 31–2. Not everyone was as patient and independent as Radcliffe, see *The Journal of the Rev. William Bagshaw Stevens.* Ed. Georgina Galbraith, Oxford, 1965.

who has read the mass of place-hunting letters in the correspondence of a prominent eighteenth-century patron knows what he is talking about, and how many young men in his situation had to advance themselves by the means he was glad to avoid.

This is, however, by the way. Though there is much we do not know about the eighteenth-century Foundationer, there is one thing we do. It seems clear that at no College could even the most economical undergraduate get through his course on his College emoluments alone. Changes in the value of money and increased University and College charges had made this impossible. The only provision for the really poor was in the small and declining band of servitors who worked their way through the College by undertaking menial tasks. This institution had seen better days: in so class-conscious a society as the eighteenth century their lot was apt to be a hard one— we are told that other undergraduates did not like to be seen with them, and University opinion was hardening against their continuance.[14] Nevertheless, it still had its uses. Dr. Benjamin Kennicott, the greatest Hebrew scholar of his age, began his University career in this class.[15] We do not know whether he experienced slights as an undergraduate; he certainly did not in the long and prosperous career of scholarship to which it was the entry.

So much for the undergraduate members of the Colleges. The senior members consisted of an intermediate

[14] For the discussions which arose on this question after the publication of Hawkins's *Life of Johnson*, see *Gentleman's Magazine*, lvii (1787), pp. 1146–7.

[15] Benjamin Kennicott (1718–83), D.D., F.R.S. His father was a barber and parish clerk at Totnes. He matriculated at Wadham as a servitor in March 1744. Even he, however, depended to some extent on outside support; see his introductory address to his benefactors, whom he lists, in his *Two Dissertations, the First on the Tree of Life in Paradise . . . the Second on the Oblations of Cain and Abel*, Oxford, 1747.

category—often with their own Common Room and social organization, the B.A.s reading for their M.A.s (most of them looking to a Fellowship) and men on the Foundation who had already taken their M.A.s but for whom a Fellowship was not yet available—for succession to Fellowships was becoming very slow in many Colleges. To this intermediate class we should add in some Colleges, where Fellows were numerous, the Junior Fellows who had not the full rights of a Fellow as we know them. Then, finally, there were the Fellows themselves, who, with the Head, governed the College under its statutes. Few of them held what we should call open Fellowships. In the first place those elected to the Foundation as undergraduates had a strong presumptive right to Fellowships as they became vacant. Moreover some Colleges were burdened with preferences for Founders' kin, many had Fellowships attached to those educated at certain schools, and nearly all had some, or all, their Fellowships restricted to certain parts of the country, where their benefactors had been anxious to improve the numbers and quality of the parish clergy. Fellowships had to be vacated on matrimony, on coming into the possession of an estate, and on being presented to livings over a certain value, including the better of those livings whose advowson the College itself held and which were the Fellows' much-prized monopoly. It was obligatory on most, but not all, of them to take Holy Orders after a fixed term of years. But Fellowships could be held in conjunction with a wide variety of paid occupations, the rules of residence were being relaxed in a good many Colleges, with the concurrence of their Visitors, to meet the problems caused by the slowing up of successions to both Fellowships and College livings, and a considerable number of Fellows were non-resident for part or all their tenure of office.

The University itself was a loose confederation of Colleges, held together by certain University institutions, most of them still in existence today, though much changed in character. Some, like the Hebdomadal Board, predecessor of the present Hebdomadal Council, were oligarchic in character, and dated from the sixteenth and seventeenth centuries; others originated in the Middle Ages, and retained the democratic stamp of that epoch. This is the small but complex society, set in an equally small and beautiful, but very dirty and unsalubrious, town, which we are examining today.

Throughout the century and ever since, it has enjoyed a very bad Press. The general histories of the University, and only to a slightly less degree of its Colleges, have tended to pass rapidly and distastefully over it. They have relied heavily on the writings of those who had been bred in the University and had become its critics, and the picture they provide is lamentable. The senior members, from the Vice-Chancellors and Heads of Houses downwards, have been portrayed as sunk in sloth, drunkenness, and personal animosities, galvanized only into occasional activity by the search for personal preferment or the excitements of Parliamentary elections. Even if Fellows escaped the more active forms of impropriety, they are shown as drearily putting in time till a College living came their way, and they could escape to matrimony and the hardly more exciting life of a country parish. The junior members appear in a different but equally unattractive light, as idle young members of the ruling classes, riotous and increasingly extravagant and exclusive.

There is certainly a good deal in this picture which is recognizable, but it is grossly exaggerated and needs correction from other types of evidence. But even where the accusations have truth in them, there are considerations which must be borne in mind in extenuation of the

University's failings; and there are also some items which should be put on the credit side. The cards were heavily stacked against the University as an institution in the eighteenth century. It was basically clerical in an age of growing anti-clericalism. It must not be forgotten that the University still considered its primary educational function to be the 'breeding of godly and learned divines'. It stood at the centre of that pervasive but intangible structure, the eighteenth-century Anglican Church. It was also, through the terms on which Fellowships were held, largely celibate at a time when celibacy was no longer admired (though it was common enough among the younger sons of the ruling classes). The institutions of University and Colleges alike, as well as most of their buildings, were firmly set in a medieval tradition which to contemporaries was 'monkish' and 'papistical'. Even the 'dreaming spires' which were to enchant the nineteenth century won only grudging admiration from the votaries of Palladian architecture (who included by the way the senior members of the University themselves, for they were great builders). But more fundamental, the University suffered, like all the ancient universities of Europe, from the shattering intellectual revolution which we call the Enlightenment, whose leaders despised even their ideals, those of traditional scholarship, as well as their failure to implement them.

In this atmosphere of pervasive hostility Oxford had, moreover, some special handicaps to contend with. In the first place, as the institution which most fully represented the Church, it was forced into the midst of national party politics at a time when these were particularly bitter, and after the Hanoverian succession it was for some forty-five years on end in unwavering hostility to the Government and even to the existing regime. It was only after the accession of George III in 1760 that the University began to lose the sense of being a beleaguered fortress, and in the years before its relief it was threatened on several occasions with what would have amounted to the complete loss of its institutional independence. In the second place, University and Colleges alike were bound by statutes embodying the intentions of founders and benefactors long since dead; but the University was in a particularly unhappy situation. It was bound hand and foot by the Laudian code of Statutes imposed on it in 1636, which were explicitly intended to prevent its changing any of them by its own decision, and which were conceived in such detail that every iota of its curriculum and degree structure and the working of all its institutions were prescribed for it.[16]

That in the second half of the century, when the University began to feel more politically secure, it began to show a growing boldness in interpreting, and even in modifying, these Statutes is due to legal advice it obtained under the influence of one of its greatest figures, the lawyer Sir William Blackstone,[17] and it was in reliance on this advice that it ultimately made radical and long overdue changes in its degrees and curriculum—though in point of fact the legality of these changes was later gravely doubted.[18] There is clearly something to be said for a Corporation thus handicapped and forced for years on to the defensive, that it not only succeeded in riding out its political storms, but also ultimately in reforming its most serious academic

[16] *Statutes of the University of Oxford, codified in the year 1636 under the authority of Archbishop Laud.* Ed. J. Griffiths, Oxford, 1888.

[17] The issue was a reform of the constitution of Convocation (whose membership was not laid down in the Statutes), to prevent its being swamped by non-residents. See *Case of the University with regard to its powers in making, altering and repealing statutes, submitted for the opinion of Counsel* . . . 1759. Also W.P.Y. 22 (1), fols. 4–6 and W.P.Y. 22 (2), Flysheets and Forms of Statutes 1758–9 in the University Archives; Blackstone's draft of the University's case.

[18] By the Royal Commission of 1850–2 among others.

defects, and that by the time the mid-nineteenth-century commissions were set up to reform it from without, it had established such a reputation that, though they sought to change much else, they did not challenge the self-governing institutions which we believe (as did our predecessors) to be the bastions of academic freedom. Nor should we ignore the great work they did in beautifying their city. None of this could have been achieved if their leaders had been worthless sots or their members indifferent to the welfare of the bodies to which they belonged.

The criticisms of the eighteenth-century University cover a wide field. Some of them are of doubtful validity. These include the criticisms directed against its internal administration and its political activities. But a university cannot be defended on the grounds that its administration was (for the time) not incompetent, or that its politics (again for the time) was unusually uncorrupt. Its reputation must stand on the way in which it fulfilled its role as a place of education and learning. And it is precisely here that the attacks on it have been most telling. The main criticisms of the University as distinct from the Colleges have been: that its curriculum was antiquated and sterile, making no demands upon the ability or industry of those taking its degrees; that it had surrendered its teaching responsibilities to the Colleges, becoming little more than an examining body; and that its professors made little or no contribution to learning for the most part, and did not even often lecture. So far as the Colleges were concerned, they have been accused of neglecting their students, while their Fellows frittered away their time in worthless pursuits, they too making little contribution to learning. This is a formidable list of accusations. Some of them are unquestionably justified. What can be said on the other side is that others had less justification or were exaggerated, and that, when all has been said, they do not add up to a full picture of the intellectual life of the University—as I shall hope to show.

There can be no doubt about the validity of the main line of attack on the University's curriculum. Under the iron hand of the Laudian Statutes it was hopelessly out of touch with the needs of the time. It is also true that University teaching for the curriculum had virtually ceased, except in some specialized subjects, such as Oriental Languages, particularly in Hebrew. Nor, though we may say that the University still functioned as an examining body, do we mean this in the sense in which we should today. We do not mean that some days of the academic year were set aside for examinations, nor that certain senior members were appointed to control and correct them. On the contrary, the numerous exercises through which a graduand had to progress towards his degree could be taken, within certain limits, at times of the candidate's own choice, he had great freedom in selection of the details in which he was to be examined, and above all he could select his own examiners.[19] The exercises he had to go through were, as they always had been, purely oral; they took various forms—for the B.A. for instance they included a Latin Declamation and questions on three classical texts of his own choice—but their backbone was a series of scholastic disputations of the kind which had stood the medieval University in such good stead in its great days, but which had become so unfamiliar to the eighteenth century that would-be reformers often felt they had to explain to the public what they were. The strength of the disputation as a means of academic training in its great days was that it was a contest of wits and of the rapid

---

[19] The examiners had to be M.A.s and to be approved by the Masters of the Schools, but this approbation was very much a formality.

application of learned argument, a contest between individuals performed in public, in which those who excelled
could win an academic reputation; and the system
culminated in the excitement of the annual Public Act
when those incepting for their M.A.s or Doctorates disputed before large and critical audiences on subjects on
which serious debate was possible.

But the system had been in decline before the eighteenth
century began, and its vitality had all been drained away.
Men still sometimes enjoyed the clash of argument, and
the rigours of its method can still often be discerned in
the arguments of writers who had gone through its training. Jeremy Bentham, for instance, in whom this is very
marked, wrote after his first disputation in his College
Hall, 'I am sorry that it does not come to my turn to
dispute every disputation day; for my part I can desire no
better sport.'[20] But there was no longer publicity or general
credit to be gained from the exercise, the subjects disputed
had become stereotyped, the senior members presiding
over them indifferent and themselves often none too
skilled. It was notorious that idle men disputing on subjects of their own choice could get them up by the use of
cribs, and the Public Acts which should have been their
culmination had gone for ever.[21] The Encaenia which
gradually took their place served none of the same purpose.

When at the end of the century the University took the
decisive step of reforming its examining system, one of
the most important steps it took (besides introducing
more specialization) was to set up Boards of Examiners to
carry out the examinations and thus to establish standards,

[20] Bentham, *Correspondence*, op. cit., i. 50. According to his own
account he came off triumphantly, 'having fairly beat off not my
proper Antagonist but the Moderator himself: for he was forced to
supply my Antagonist with Arguments, the Invalidity of which I
clearly demonstrated'.

[21] The last Public Act, held after a long intermission, was in 1733.

and to offer the optional class list to give the able man his chance to distinguish himself. It is remarkable how quickly the vivifying effects of this change were seen.

The degradation of the University's examinations was inevitably reflected in the teaching which the Colleges provided for them. They offered stimulus neither to the undergraduate nor to his tutor. It has sometimes even been assumed that, under these discouraging conditions, the teaching in the Colleges too almost ceased. But this is quite untrue. Those who have made this assumption have done so very largely on the strength of some comments made in his *Memoirs* by Edward Gibbon, the most distinguished of the University's academic critics. They deserve consideration in detail. Gibbon spent a few months at Magdalen as a Gentleman Commoner between 1752 and 1753, when his career was abruptly cut short by his temporary (and quite uncharacteristic) conversion to Roman Catholicism. He calls them 'the most idle and unprofitable in my life'.[22] During them, he says, he took part in no College or University exercise, never attended a lecture, and came and went as he pleased, but, above all, he bitterly complained of the incompetence and neglect of his tutors. Of his first tutor Gibbon admits that he was 'a learned and pious man' but adds that 'his learning was of the past rather than the present age' and 'his faculties which were not of the first rate, had been relaxed by the climate'. He soon left for a College living. Gibbon dismissed his second tutor with the lapidary phrase which has since become famous, that he 'well remembered he had a salary to receive, and only forgot he had a duty to perform'. How far was Gibbon's experience typical? Over so considerable a period, and in so many different Colleges, each pursuing its independent course and much less than

[22] E. Gibbon, *Memoirs of my Life*. Ed. G. A. Bonnard, London, 1966, pp. 46 ff.

now affected by the demands of the University curriculum, this is a difficult question to answer. But there is a good deal of miscellaneous evidence to work on in the reminiscences of former undergraduates (to be taken with some caution), letters from undergraduates still in residence (also not always reliable), occasional diaries, and the great mass of College records, by no means all yet fully explored. Though no doubt a great deal more will be turned up, there is already enough evidence to show that, while Gibbon's criticisms of the lack of ability of his first tutor are widely echoed, the total neglect of his second tutor either to teach him or arrange any College exercises for him are not.

I have indeed found so far only one case to be compared with it: the charge made by James Harris (afterwards 1st Earl of Malmesbury, 1746–1820), a Gentleman Commoner at Merton some ten years after Gibbon's time. Harris was a member of a very smart set of young men about town, chiefly from Christ Church but also from other Colleges. He claims that he never saw his tutor 'but during a fortnight when I took into my head to be taught trigonometry',[23] and he implies that his experience was normal. There was only one thing in common between Malmesbury and his gay young friends and the solitary, bookish little Gibbon—they both belonged to the special class of the Gentlemen Commoner: not expected to take degrees, hardly ever in residence for the whole course, often called to Town by their parents, and some of them, no doubt, fairly arrogant towards tutors they considered their social inferiors. Not all Gentlemen Commoners were, of course, so unsatisfactory. One who had been up about 1758, defending his class forty years later, named no fewer than nine who, as he put it, wore 'the silken and golden

[23] *Diaries and Correspondence of James Harris, First Earl of Malmesbury . . .*, ed. Malmesbury (London, 1844), I. ix.

robe' at Christ Church alone who were exemplary,[24] and we know of at least three who were later Ministers of State, Lord North, Lord Shelburne, and Charles James Fox (whenever his over-indulgent father allowed him to be in residence), of whom the same could be said.[25] Colleges, moreover, made efforts from time to time to deal with this difficult but highly conspicuous minority,[26] and Christ Church in particular prided itself on being very good with them. But one can understand that, if they did not seem prepared to co-operate, no great obligation was felt to put pressure on them. Had Gibbon's father, like Jeremy Bentham's, sent him as a Commoner to Queen's instead of as a Gentleman Commoner to Magdalen, he would, no doubt, have been equally critical of his Oxford education; but the interesting thing is that his criticisms would have been quite different.

For none of what he said applied to the great majority of the undergraduates, the Commoners and men on the

[24] *Gentleman's Magazine*, lxviii (1798), 282.

[25] It was said of Lord North when he was at Trinity that he never missed early, and very seldom evening, chapel; *Gentleman's Magazine*, lxviii (1798), 283. He remained throughout his life an elegant scholar. Lord Shelburne, in his Autobiography (E. Fitzmaurice, *Life of William, Earl of Shelburne . . .*, London, 1875, i. 18 ff.), though somewhat critical of his tutor said of him that 'He was not without learning, and certainly laid himself out to be serviceable to me in point of reading', and he describes his reading with him. For Charles James Fox at Hertford see Lord John Russell, *Memorials and Correspondence of Charles James Fox*, London, 1853, i. 21 ff.

[26] Thus at Queen's the regulations drawn up by Provost Smith in 1732 enjoined that they were equally with other undergraduates obliged to attend 'the Classick Exercises in the Hall, as usual, but likewise the Disputations in Logick and Philosophy, and perform their parts therein as it comes to their Turns' (Library of Queen's College, Joseph Smith MSS. 475 (i)). In 1768 Brasenose laid down the same regulations; see evidence quoted in *V.C.H. Oxfordshire*, p. 211. Even at Magdalen in the later years of the century the same applied according to [J. Hurdis] *A word or two in vindication of the University of Oxford and of Magdalen College in particular from the posthumous aspersions of Mr. Gibbon* [1797?]. Reprinted in *Reminiscences of Oxford*, Oxford Historical Society, xxii (1892), 130 ff.

Foundation. Indeed even Gibbon admits that at Magdalen 'some duties may possibly have been imposed on the poor scholars who aspired to the peaceful honours of a Fellowship'.[27] Since there were no Commoners at Magdalen, this means the great majority of its undergraduate members. For such men there is ample evidence that they were generally in regular (if not always welcome) contact with their tutors, and that the Colleges provided a system of educational training of which the tutors were in most cases the centre and which was in reasonable working order throughout the century, though of course in such small societies its operation was inevitably affected from time to time by a few individuals and their idiosyncrasies. The tutors were by this time usually (perhaps always) chosen by the Head of the House. Most Colleges seem to have had one or two of them. The Head tried to choose them from among his senior resident Fellows, though he was not always successful in so doing. In most Colleges there were also regular College lecturers, who, unlike professors, seem to have lectured, though not always with much energy and (unless the Head was firm) sometimes by deputy.[28] Moreover, undergraduates were obliged, under threat of fine, to dispute in Hall and to recite regular Latin Declamations of their own composition there; and what evidence we have suggests that they did so with reasonable conscientiousness.

The complaints made against College tutors and the system of which they formed a part seem not indeed to be so much that these activities were neglected in any obvious way, as that they were frequently so lifeless and mechanical as to be of little value. In many ways what we can see of the system which the College tried to impose

[27] Gibbon, *Memoirs of my Life*, pp. 46 ff.
[28] See the case of Dr. Routh and William Bagshaw Stevens at Magdalen, 1796–8 (E. Galbraith, op. cit., pp. 377 and 464).

(particularly on those in their first year) suggests that they tended to over- rather than under-teach their men. When Jeremy Bentham went up to Queen's in 1760 he and others in their first term had what we should call two classes a day with their tutor, at 11.0 a.m. and 9.0 p.m. and were expected to prepare texts for them in advance. On Tuesdays and Fridays a lecture from the College Greek Lecturer was substituted for one or both of the tutor's classes. In his second term he was kept busy with lectures or classes on Logic, Geography, New Testament in Greek, Cicero's *De Oratore*, and had 'a great deal of Caesar's commentaries to translate into Greek prose' for his tutor, which he found very difficult.[29] He also did Latin Declamations in Hall, but at Queen's at that time men did not dispute in Hall for a couple of terms after they came up. We have evidence from several other Colleges whose system was somewhat different, though not necessarily less onerous. Though the number of set lectures seems to have decreased in undergraduates' later years, they continued. Some Colleges assumed that men continued to see their tutors daily, but this does not seem to have been the case, though they certainly still saw them frequently; and their tutors are still found pressing them to push on with their independent reading.[30] A reasonably conscientious but not bookish man seems to have expected to spend his mornings from 9.30 to 1.0 on College work, and the rest of the day on his own avocations.[31]

[29] Bentham, *Correspondence*, i. 21 and 37.

[30] In July 1761 at the end of his first year Bentham complains that his tutor is 'plaguing me about doing Homer, I did above 3 books and a half in 2 days . . .' (Bentham, *Correspondence*, i. 53). Bentham was later less than just to his tutor, for Bowring quotes him as saying 'I learnt nothing . . . I took to reading Greek of my own fancy, but there was no encouragement'.

[31] See p. 513 below. The impression is confirmed by the verses, probably by J. Skinner of Trinity, *c.* 1790 (Bodl. MS. Top. Oxon. e 41) reproduced in *Reminiscences of Oxford by Oxford Men 1559–1850*, Oxford Historical Society, xxii (1892), 183 ff.

The best side of the system was the effort that was made to get undergraduates to read thoroughly the classical authors with which an educated man of the period was expected to be familiar (it is clear that they never restricted themselves to teaching only the three texts a man had to offer for his B.A.)[32]—and to help him to understand them, though able undergraduates complained of the poverty of the commentaries and background material which was provided. It may be noted that undergraduates seem to have got some satisfaction from their Declamations, particularly those in Latin verse, for they often proudly sent home copies of those which their tutors and they thought were their best. Here at least the University also helped to keep the interest alive. As Encaenia gradually arose to take the place of the Public Act at the end of Trinity Term, a great number of pieces of Latin prose and verse were required for public recital. Encaenias were still held only on special occasions, but when one came it was a marathon affair, requiring some eight to ten Declamations by undergraduates and B.A.s each day.[33] The coming in from 1768 of the Chancellor's prizes for Latin verse (awarded strictly on merit) were an added inducement.[34]

Nevertheless, the teaching was obviously uninspiring and, though the lack of stimulus from the University

---

[32] Jeremy Bentham did this part of his examination in 1763 with a friend from Queen's. He reports 'his Books were, Gr[eek] Testament, Horace and Sallust; mine, Demosthenes, Anacreon and Tusc[ulan] Disp[utation]s' (Bentham, op. cit., i. 72).

[33] Many were delivered by noblemen and other Gentlemen Commoners, and there was no pretence that they wrote them themselves. Colleges also, however, sent in work by able men, and these also had their chance.

[34] These were sent in under a 'motto' by the candidate himself, as now. There was great rejoicing when the prize went to a man not trained at the great classical schools, Westminster, Eton, and Winchester, as when John James, junior, of Queen's, son of the former Headmaster of St. Bee's, won it in 1782 (*Letters of Radcliffe and James*, pp. 222–3).

curriculum was partly to blame, blame must also be attributed to lack of intellectual distinction as well as (perhaps more than) slackness among tutors. There were able men among them, but College Fellows were not generally chosen for intellectual distinction until the last twenty years or so of the century when some Colleges began to attach increasing weight to it, sometimes with striking results. Moreover, a good many Fellows at any one time were not resident and those who were by no means all wanted to take on tutorial responsibilities. There is an entry in the diary of President Fry of St. John's which has a bearing on this. In 1769 he reports a conversation with one of his Fellows, who thought he was making too much fuss about finding a good tutor. 'Mr. Clare', he wrote, 'thought I was too anxious in these things; that in other Colleges they found it very difficult to meet with persons for that office—that at N.C. they had Brs of Arts sometimes and likewise at Ch. Ch. where he mentioned an instance of one Mr. Jackson—that their people notwithstanding did very well'. (Mr. Jackson, it may be noted, was the great Cyril Jackson, later one of Christ Church's most famous Deans. One can imagine that his pupils, even when he was still a B.A., 'did very well'.) Clare continued with a gloomy observation on undergraduates in general that 'very few were capable of improvement, and others 'found things out by themselves'.[35]

I quote this extract both to illustrate the imperfections of the tutorial system, but also for a different reason. Men 'found things out for themselves'. If one were to look solely at the University curriculum and the College teaching of the period one might expect to find undergraduate Oxford a very unintellectual place, and the graduates it turned out dull and uneducated. But as soon as one begins to look

[35] MS. Diary. Quoted in W. C. Costin, *The History of St. John's College Oxford 1598–1860*, Oxford, 1958, p. 219.

round one sees that nothing was further from the truth. Dr. Johnson's 'opportunities of books' and absence of 'avocations' clearly had their effects.

There is indeed ample evidence of diversified intellectual activities among undergraduates both as individuals and groups, some of them intense and having lasting effects. It is also clear from the number of free-lance teachers of music, the arts, and modern languages who congregated in Oxford that there was a demand for their services, and we find the most unlikely undergraduates employing them. There is even the case of William ('Oriental') Jones who, though by no means a rich undergraduate, imported a Syrian into Oxford to help him with his Arabic.[36]

I shall give one illustration of what went on. It is the account of his undergraduate career given by Richard Graves, later D.D., who went up to Pembroke as a scholar in 1732. His mornings he set aside for what he called 'dry' College work, and did so with 'strict regularity'. His evenings were his own. Coming up from school with the reputation, he says, of a 'tolerably good Grecian' he was first recruited into a serious little group who spent their evenings reading Greek texts and drinking water. He was then temporarily seduced into a set of what he calls 'jolly sprightly young fellows' who spent their evenings singing catches and drinking toasts, and even for a time into more raffish society, including some Gentlemen Commoners whom he describes as 'bucks of the first head'; but they were too much for his purse and his constitution. He therefore fell back on what he calls 'a sort of flying squadron of plain, sensible matter-of-fact men, confined to no club', who 'anxiously enquired after the news of the day and the politics of the times' and who 'had come to the university

[36] J. Shore, Baron Teignmouth, *Memoirs of the Life, Writings and Correspondence of Sir William Jones*, London, 1804, i. 33.

on their way to the Temple, or to get a slight smattering of the Sciences before they settled in the country'. But then he became intimate with the poet Shenstone, and they with one or two more began to pursue with passion the study of literature.[37]

Activities of this kind seem to have originated wholly with the undergraduates themselves; but the University, so supine in curricular studies, played a considerably larger part in extra-curricular ones. It was one of the results of the out-dated character of its curriculum, that most of the benefactions it received during this and even earlier periods, were intended for the encouragement of subjects outside the curriculum. And it was in these new fields in particular that professors and others less formally attached to the University began to provide systematic courses of lectures, many of which attracted good audiences and aroused marked interest among under-graduates and young graduates. For most, though not all of them, fees were charged, which went directly to the lecturer.[38] They became more frequent in the second half of the century, but the movement began earlier. Some of these lectures were on the Arts side—like those of the Professors of Poetry and the Vinerian Professor of Common Law;[39] but there were a number on the various

---

[37] [Richard Graves] *Recollections of some particulars in the life of the late William Shenstone*, London, 1788. Quoted in *Reminiscences of Oxford*, pp. 97 ff.

[38] Thereby achieving, at least in part, one of Adam Smith's proposals for ensuring that Oxford professors lectured. *An Inquiry into the Nature and Causes of the Wealth of Nations*. Ed. E. Cannan, London, 1950, ii. 249 ff.

[39] William Blackstone began the famous lectures (later published as the *Commentaries on the Laws of England*) before he was elected to the Vinerian Chair. Dr. E. Bentham, Regius Professor of Divinity in 1764, advertised a free course of lectures on theology for men of three to seven years standing aiming at Holy Orders. The notice warns that 'It is hoped that no person will make his attendance on these lectures a pretence for neglecting any duty or exercise to which he may be

scientific subjects in which educated men were at this time becoming increasingly engrossed,[40] and the interest they elicited was often very strong. Oxford may not, after the early years of the century, have made much contribution to scientific learning, but it certainly played its part in scientific education; and enlightened College authorities encouraged their young men to concern themselves in these new and exciting fields of study. Dr. Markham, Dean of Christ Church, told an undergraduate in 1768 that 'only classical and historical knowledge could make able statesmen' but that 'mathematics and other things were very necessary for a gentleman'.[41]

Something of the same stirrings of interest can be discerned among the resident Fellows of Colleges. Some were no doubt as dull and idle as popular rumour portrayed them,[42] but others (and we should like to know which type predominated) were on the contrary active contributors to literary periodicals and voracious and systematic readers, keeping up with the publications of the day. This may be seen from the extensive purchases which were being made by nearly all College libraries, and even more from such lists as survive of the books they borrowed from them. In 1786, for instance, sixteen Fellows of Exeter (not all resident), three men about to take their M.A.s, a bible clerk, and one Gentleman Commoner (whose borrowings were

called by the rules of his College' (Bodl. G.A. Oxon. (b) (19). These lectures seem to have been continued by his successors and according to Hurdis, op. cit., by the end of the century no young man was admitted to Orders in the Oxford diocese without a certificate that he had attended them.

[40] e.g. Natural Philosophy (Physics), Chemistry, Astronomy, and Anatomy.

[41] The Countess of Minto, *Life and Letters of Sir Gilbert Elliot, first Earl of Minto*, London, 1874, i. 38.

[42] Among these we must count Parson James Woodforde, as shown in his Oxford diary: *Woodforde at Oxford 1759–1776*. Ed. W. N. Hargreaves-Mawdsley, Oxford, 1959.

minimal) took out 233 books between them, some of several volumes, and covering a very wide range of interests.[43]

If, in short, we look at education at Oxford at this time, we are bound to admit the unsatisfactoriness of a situation where the University's intellectual life was carried on so largely outside its formal instruction; but that intellectual life existed there can be no doubt. This was presumably one of the reasons why in the next century, when the English universities were compared with the flourishing Scottish ones, it could be said that, despite the up-to-date virtues of the latter 'the English system is more successful in giving the student the tone and style of learning and literate associations'.[44]

But it is when we come to Oxford's contributions to learning that we see how much it had suffered in morale from the supersession of the old concepts of scholarship and the rise of the confident new ideas of the Enlightenment, and its own failure either to challenge or to adapt itself to them. It may well be that in fact it suffered less than other universities nearer to the epicentre of the storm; but its decline is nevertheless a sad tale. At the beginning of the century it could still feel that it stood in a great scholarly tradition. On the scientific side Wallis and Halley were carrying on the traditions of the Royal Society; and it has been claimed that Gregory was the first scholar to introduce the Newtonian system into university teaching. On the Arts side, there was not only activity in Classical and Theological studies, but Oxford was making a unique contribution to the new study of Anglo-Saxon language and institutions, and (through that remarkable

[43] Exeter College Library.

[44] J. Mac Gilchrist, *The Life and Career of Henry, Lord Brougham*, London, 1863, pp. 23–4. Quoted W. M. Mathews 'The Origins and Occupations of Glasgow Students 1740–1839', *Past and Present*, April 1966, p. 74.

figure Edward Lhuyd) to Celtic studies; while in medieval history Thomas Hearne was producing the great series of editions of English chronicles on which scholars relied until late in the last century.

But there was no sequel to these studies, and by the middle of the century almost all had died away. Though there were many good Latinists in Oxford and some competent students of Greek, it produced no notable Classical scholars. Only Kennicott in Hebrew, with his vast collation of Old Testament Hebrew texts, was carrying on in the old way the old tradition—and he was the only Oxford scholar of his day to have an international reputation, even if a rather controversial one.

Gibbon found worthy of praise only three Oxford scholars of the eighteenth century proper: Robert Lowth, for his 'incomparable *Praelections* of the Poetry of the Hebrews',[45] William Blackstone, for his *Commentaries on the Laws of England*,[46] and William, so-called Oriental, Jones—and this not for his work as father of Sanskrit studies, for this lay far in the future, but for his contributions to Persian and Arabic studies, which are rather slight.[47] To these we should add not only Kennicott, but

[45] Gibbon, *Memoirs*, p. 51. Lowth's book *De Sacra Poesi Hebraeorum* came out in 1753. Friedrich Meinecke in his *Historism* (English tr. by J. E. Anderson, 1972) calls it 'a combination of pure piety with new, original and creative taste' (p. 205) and 'perhaps the most intellectually important of the whole Pre-Romantic movement in England' (p. 206).

[46] Gibbon called the work 'a rational System of the English Jurisprudence, digested into a natural method, and cleared of the pedantry, the obscurity, and the superfluities which rendered it the unknown horror of all men of taste' (*Miscellaneous Works of Edward Gibbon, Esq. . . . .* ed. John, Lord Sheffield, London (1815), ii. 576).

[47] Gibbon said of him, 'He is perhaps the only lawyer equally conversant with the year-books of Westminster, the commentaries of Ulpian, the Attic pleadings of Isaeus, and the sentences of Arabian and Persian cadhis' (*Decline and Fall of the Roman Empire*, ed. J. Bury, iv. 496, n. 173).

another name, that of Thomas Warton, who spent his life
in Trinity, and by his *History of English Poetry, 1774–81*,
and his other works, gave Oxford a prominent part in the
rise of English medieval literary studies in the second half
of the century—a movement which did so much to foster
the Romantic Revival.[48] But it is not an impressive list.

When we come to sum up the eighteenth-century University as a whole we see weaknesses which are only too
obvious, though also some less obvious strengths. It is not
easy to summarize them in one statement. It was clearly
not a period of notable intellectual activity; but neither
was it one of complete intellectual inertia. It had inherited
a formal academic structure badly in need of reform, and,
despite many obstacles, it ultimately did a good deal to
reform it, though built-in inertia, both social and intellectual, obviously remained. But it played its part in producing a conscientious and educated clergy: it maintained
its independence, and it gave to many men, one way or
another, the habits and interests of a liberal education.
Dr. Johnson had undoubtedly seen it in too rosy a light,
but he was wiser than those who thought it incapable of
regeneration.

[48] For Warton see A. Johnston, *Enchanted Ground. The Study of
Medieval Romance in the Eighteenth Century*, London, 1964,
pp. 100 ff.

23

THE ORIGIN AND EARLY HISTORY OF THE LORD ALMONER'S PROFESSORSHIP IN ARABIC AT OXFORD

THE origin and early development of the two Lord Almoner's chairs, the one at Oxford and the other at Cambridge (both now defunct[1]) remain something of a mystery. The records of the Almonry Office, from which their endowment came, survive only from 1724 onward, and the official archives of the two universities are equally silent about them. Their printed *Historical Registers* make no attempt to trace them before 1724 though J. W. Clark in his *Endowments of the University of Cambridge* (1904) makes reference to evidence of an earlier beginning for both chairs.[2] Neither university gives more than minimum information of their role in the university during the eighteenth century or of their relation with the major chairs of Arabic, the Laudian at Oxford and the Sir Thomas Adams's at Cambridge, though the names of those appointed to them are significant on this last point.

Nevertheless, since Hubert Hall published in the *Athenaeum* in 1889[3] the results of his researches into the Treasury Books in the Public Record Office (a formidable piece of work before these records were calendared), a good deal is known about the beginnings of these chairs, and particularly of that at Oxford, before 1724. Further details also appear in letters in particular among the miscellaneous manuscript correspondence in the Bodleian Library. Hall made it clear that both chairs were in existence before 1724, and that the salaries of the 'two Arabic Professors at Oxford and Cambridge' (each £50 a year, less tax on fees) were paid by the Crown out of a grant from the Civil List to the Lord Almoner for the time being ever since a royal warrant of 24 June 1714, though sometimes they fell into arrears. But he also showed that there was a continuing provision of Crown moneys for modern Oriental studies at Oxford from a consider-

[1] The Crown ceased to appoint to these offices in 1904.
[2] p. 193.
[3] 16 Nov. 1889, p. 673, 'The origin of the Lord Almoner's Professorship of Arabic'.

ably earlier date, since a royal warrant was issued by William III in 1699 and the purely personal provisions it embodied were given a more permanent form under the auspices of the Lord Almoner in 1702.

The first that is heard of the personal arrangement is in a couple of letters from James Vernon, Secretary of State, Northern Department, to Thomas Hyde, Regius Professor of Hebrew and Laudian Professor of Arabic at Oxford (as well as being Bodley's Librarian 1665–1701). Hyde gave the Government a good deal of help in the translation of official documents from the Levant, and Vernon's letters show that the Crown was anxious for him to train a successor. Tenison, the Archbishop of Canterbury, a great encourager of Oriental languages, had already approached Hyde who had promised, Vernon reminded him, 'that you would take care to instruct and bring up some young man in the knowledge of the Oriental Languages as they are in modern use; that there may be a succession of such as may serve the public in the same manner you have done'.[1] About a year later a royal warrant was issued for the payment of £100 a year to the Bishop of Oxford, £20 of which was to go to Hyde as the instructor and £40 each a year to what had now become two young men who were to study Arabic and Turkish under him and were to be chosen by the Archbishop of Canterbury for their 'genius in languages'.[2] The two selected were John Wallis, then an M.A. at Magdalen College, a protégé of John Postlethwayt (1650–1713), Chief Master of St. Paul's and a notable Hebraist, who succeeded Hyde as Laudian Professor some four years later, and Benjamin Marshall, then an undergraduate at Christ Church, and nephew and later chaplain of another bishop who was a notable patron of the Eastern studies, William Lloyd, Bishop of Worcester, at that time Lord Almoner.

That the scheme was put into operation is clear not only from the records of Treasury payments, but from private letters. John Wallis wrote to Thomas Smith, the Orientalist, begging for

---

[1] *Calendar of State Papers (Domestic), 1698*, pp. 389 and 392; James Vernon–Thomas Hyde, 20 Sept. and 27 Sept. 1698.

[2] Royal warrant issued at Loo 1/11 Aug. 1699 (*Calendar of Treasury Books*, vol. xv, 1699/1700, p. 121). In *C.S.P. (Dom.), 1699–1700*, p. 90, there is a letter of instruction to the Treasury dated 10 Mar. 1699, containing the full particulars.

books and documents in Turkish which he found difficult to procure.[1] That the arrangements were not an unqualified success is
suggested both by Wallis's complaints that Hyde was ignorant of
Turkish,[1] and by Hyde's dissatisfaction with his salary.[2] Indeed
the Treasury records give reason to think that there was uncertainty whether it would survive the death of William III, its
sponsor, at the accession of Queen Anne. Though some arrears in
what was called the 'pension' got on to the list of liabilities of the
late king which his successor was prepared to honour, a note was
appended in the Exchequer Account 'provided that they were
under instruction so long and [the arrear] not satisfied elsewhere'.[3] There was obviously some discussion about its future,
though all that the Treasury Books show is a decision to transfer
it from its place among the Civil List pensions to the allowance
made to the Lord Almoner for the queen's private pensions and
charities, where it appeared on the new Pension List.[4] At the
same time the study of Turkish as part of the curriculum was
dropped and it was confined to Arabic.

This was not an economy measure, since £100 was added to
the block grant of £800 made to the Lord Almoner for the
queen's private charities and for Maundy money, and was earmarked for this purpose. It was rather an attempt to reform the
administration and represents the passing of the initiative from
the Crown, with its practical needs, to the educationalists. A
letter from Hyde to Postlethwayt of 4 May 1702, about six weeks
before the final settlement, throws some light on what was going
on:

This is to acquaint you that the Bp of Worcester[5] is employing Sr Benj. Bathurst
to speak to the Queen for renewing the Grant of the Arabick Pension, so as to be
payable by the L. Almoner from the Civill List. Therefore you may please with speed
to acquaint my L. of Canterbury what is in doing, that so he may joyn in it, and get
it so ordered that the Teacher may not have less than the Learner. For if its so again
[i.e. a salary of £20 for the Professor], I shall desire to be excused from medling in
it: not so much for the value of a little money, but because the thing is undecent

[1] Bodl. MS. Smith 54, fol. 67, dated 1 Jan. 1700/1.
[2] See below.
[3] *Cal. Treas. Books*, vol. xvii, pt. 2 (1702), p. 967; Exchequer Account at the death of
William III.
[4] Ibid., vol. xviii (1703), p. 214.
[5] Then still Lord Almoner.

[*sic*], and by everybody laughed at and ridiculed, as we have found by experience already: and therefore this I would avoyd. I suppose the Queen will as easily grant the Pension to be a little larger, if its so proposed to her. Though after all, I had rather be wholly excused both from Trouble and Profit.

I am apt to think this business is in agitation without the knowledge of my L. of Canterbury.[1]

Hyde did not get his way, nor is there any evidence that he resigned, and from that time on the grant was the responsibility of the Lord Almoner, by whose title it began to be known. Bishop Lloyd who took this authority over did not, however, long exercise it, the queen dismissing him from his office within the year. A few months later Hyde died and Wallis succeeded him, so further changes must have followed. Unfortunately for the historian, the change in the status of the grant made the evidence about it less informative. Though in the Pension List of June 1702 it was laid down that the extra £100 allocated to the Lord Almoner was 'more for the Arabic Professor at Oxford being 80*l*. per ann. for the support of two youths from time to time to be instructed in that language, and 20*l*. per ann. to the said Professor for his pains in teaching them',[2] the later annual grants were often less specific, and at no time were either the professor or the students named, as they had been under King William's arrangement. We do not at present know whether Wallis succeeded Hyde in this professorship as in the Laudian chair. All we do know is that the 'Declared Accounts' of the queen's charities administered by the Lord Almoner show that the £100 was distributed every year until 1707,[3] and then, after a pause, from 1712 to the end of the reign.[4]

I have so far found no further evidence outside the Treasury papers about the professor and his students throughout the reign of Queen Anne. The next change that occurred came with the accession of George I. In 1714 when the grant got on to the new Pension List, it was unchanged in value, and remained under the umbrella of the Lord Almoner, but was considerably modified in content. All reference to grants to students disappears, and the claims of Cambridge University for the first time appear. The

1 Letter of 4 May 1702 (Bodl. MS. Autogr. c. 10, fol. 125).
2 *Cal. Treas. Books*, vol. xviii (1703), p. 214.
3 P.R.O. E/351/2720; AO/1/1922.
4 Ibid. T 61/21, p. 243.

£100 is simply divided into the equal parts to be paid £50 each to 'an Arabic Professor at Oxford and at Cambridge'.[1]

At this point, however, private correspondence throws light on some new and curious developments in the history of the chairs. The clue to them is given in a letter from Edmund Gibson, then Bishop of Lincoln, to Arthur Charlett, Master of University College, dated 2 January 1720. He wrote, 'When the present Bishop of Derry [William Nicolson, formerly Bishop of Carlisle] was Almoner, I have heard him speak of applying the allowance made by the late Bp. of Worcester to one or more Professors of the Oriental Languages, to a Saxon Lecture'.[2] He did not know the outcome. Bishop Nicolson was Lord Almoner between 1715 and 1718, and this letter explains some correspondence between that remarkable scholar, though unattractive man, David Wilkins,[3] and two of his patrons, Archbishop Wake and Bishop Nicolson, both much concerned in Anglo-Saxon studies. It is to be found in Nicolson's published correspondence and in the Wake manuscripts in Christ Church Library.

On 6 July 1715 approaches were made on Wilkins's behalf to Bishop Nicolson. Wilkins had, his friend lamented, failed in all hopes of preferment through Archbishop Tenison, and unless something were found for him by his influential Whig clerical friends, he must return to Holland. Wilkins proffered himself ready for any work, at home or abroad, with the sword or the gown, but particularly favoured 'a little pension or a less prebend'.[4] Within a year Nicolson had a scheme worked out with the support of Wake (the newly appointed archbishop) whereby the money allocated for the new Cambridge lecturership in Arabic should be used to pay for one in Anglo-Saxon Studies and be given to Wilkins, who would edit and publish a collection of Anglo-Saxon laws with episcopal support.

Wilkins certainly assumed that the Oxford chair would also be affected, though it was already held by another foreign scholar of

---

[1] *Cal. Treas. Books*, vol. xxix, pt. 2, p. 678.

[2] Bodl. MS. Ballard 6, fol. 139.

[3] 1685–1745, a Prussian by origin. His most famous work was the *Concilia Magnae Britanniae et Hiberniae*, 1737.

[4] John Chamberlayne–W. Nicolson, 6 July 1715, in *Letters on various subjects . . . to and from William Nicolson, D.D.*, ed. J. Nichols, 2 vols., 1809, ii. 430.

high repute, Jean Gagnier,[1] formerly a French priest but a convert to Anglicanism and much favoured by the late Archbishop Tenison and Bishop Lloyd of Worcester. His interests were almost wholly in Oriental studies, and he was said to be ignorant of Anglo-Saxon.[2] It seems unlikely that he welcomed the proposal, as Wilkins cheerfully assumed he did; Wilkins, our only source of information here, may have misunderstood the situation.[3] On 5 July 1716 he had written to Nicolson:

> Your Lordship will be so kind as to let me know something particular about it: whether we must have the King's Patent for it, and whether we must begin our Lectures after Michaelmas.[4]

But he obviously received a somewhat discouraging answer for he wrote again on 29 August:

> The sum of the Saxon Pension may be what it will, I am infinitely obliged to your Lordship for bestowing it upon me, and shall strive to deserve it by publishing what your Lordship shall approve of. I do not question, if . . . I could print something in that study worth his Majesty's Dedication, a grant for a perpetual establishment of a Royal Lecturer in both Universities might easier be obtained, than it seems it can now.[5]

and five days later he wrote to Archbishop Wake:

> My Lord Bishop of Carlile [*sic*] has sent me word from Rose Castle that I should be sure of the Royal Pension for the Saxon, if I could shew to the Publick from time to time my proficiency in it, which I hope to do as well as I can, till by printing some thing or other I can make a step towards a Royal Patent and towards establishing a Royal Lecturer or Professor in the Saxon in both Universities.[6]

In fact no steps seem to have been taken to regularize the position, though the money drawn from the Exchequer was regularly paid out, and he presumably drew the salary. In the circumstances his complaint to Nicolson about Gagnier's activities a year later is odd as well as ill natured.

[1] 1670 ?–1741. He had studied Hebrew and Arabic at the College of Navarre. Through Bishop Lloyd of Worcester he had contacts for a number of years in Oxford.

[2] See statement by Wilkins, p. 172.

[3] It would certainly seem from Wilkins's letters to Nicolson that Gagnier knew of the plan and had some contact with both Nicolson and Wilkins about it. He may have thought that the only way to keep his salary was to fall in with it. The information he gave Wilkins about the salary he had been drawing is the only known evidence that he held the chair at this date (Nichols, op. cit., p. 447).

[4] Ibid., p. 446.

[5] Ibid., p. 447.

[6] Wake MSS., Christ Church, vol. 20, fol. 143; Wilkins to Archbishop Wake, 3 Sept. 1716.

Mr. Gagnier, I am afraid, does but little in Saxon. I wonder his friend in London, that receives the pension, affects to call him Arabic Professor, or Lecturer, in the receipt. The best way would be to put him upon some work or other, to get some knowledge of the language for which he enjoys his Majesty's bountiful pension.[1]

Gagnier was in fact continuing his Oriental studies; in 1715 he was also active as deputy for the Regius Professor of Hebrew in Oxford,[2] and in 1718 the then Vice-Chancellor, Dr. John Baron, became exasperated at the persistent absenteeism of John Wallis, Laudian Professor of Arabic, and forced him to appoint Gagnier as his deputy at a fee of £20 a year,[3] a position which he held for some years.[4]

And in the long run Gagnier's interpretation of his position triumphed. There was a long tradition at Cambridge that Archbishop Blackburne of York, when he became Lord Almoner in 1723, created the Cambridge chair and installed Wilkins in it as first holder.[5] What he seems to have done was to regularize the position. When the Almonry Records of 1724 show for the first time the holders of these chairs, they were Jean Gagnier at Oxford and David Wilkins at Cambridge. There is no sign that in fact Wilkins's position was changed. He continued his Anglo-Saxon publications which were to culminate in the *Concilia*. By this time he was also gaining a good deal of preferment. He held the chair for five more years. When he left it in 1729 it was attached to that of the Sir Thomas Adams's chair in Arabic and remained so until 1815. In 1740 the Arabist Thomas Hunt, who had just obtained the Oxford chair from the same Archbishop of York, reported of the Cambridge chair: 'There is another of the

---

[1] Nicolson letters, op. cit., 7 Dec. 1717, p. 470.

[2] T. Hearne, *Collectanea*, v. 137; 12 Nov. 1715.

[3] T. Hunt–Rawlinson, 25 July 1740 (Bodl. MS. Rawl. Lett. 96, fol. 31); A. Charlett–Wake, 26 Oct. 1718 (Wake MSS. at Christ Church, Misc. Papers and Letters, vol. 21, fol. 49).

[4] On 2 Apr. 1723 Stratford wrote to Lord Harley: 'The Vice-Chancellor has lately dismissed poor Gaynier [*sic*] from being deputy to Wallis the Arabic professor, and has put in a young Fellow of Magdalen College. The Fellow knows not the letters . . .' (*H.M.C. Portland MSS.*, vii. 354). He goes on to say that Thomas (later Professor) Hunt and another of Hart Hall showed his ignorance up at his lectures and complained to the Vice-Chancellor. The scholars were persisting in their objections when Stratford wrote, and the Vice-Chancellor Robert Shippen was begging them to desist until his term of office was over, which it was in the following October.

[5] J. W. Clark, *Endowments of the University of Cambridge*, p. 103.

same Value at Cambridge, which his Grace some years ago gave to the Arabic Professor there.'[1]

Thus the only period during the eighteenth century when the Cambridge chair was held by a separate professor would seem to be the years from 1716 to 1729 when in fact it was used as a lectureship in Anglo-Saxon Studies. Developments in Oxford were somewhat different. Gagnier held the chair until 1740, long outliving his usefulness and admittedly senile towards the end. He died about a year after he relinquished it. When the Archbishop of York replaced him by Thomas Hunt, Laudian Professor of Arabic, he was doing much what he had done in 1729 at Cambridge, but he made an effort to inaugurate something of a new deal at the same time. Its nature suggests one of the reasons which made the Lord Almoner's chair so persistently unsatisfactory to those supporting it—the absence of any recognized position for Arabic in the University's curriculum (a situation different from that of Hebrew) and, partly no doubt in consequence, the almost complete absence of students to be taught. So far as Oxford was concerned, the instructions given to Thomas Hunt on his appointment in 1740 set the scene for the Almoner's chair in the eighteenth century and gave it a *raison d'être*, if hardly in the study of Arabic at least in that of Oriental languages.

The evidence of two correspondences among the Bodleian manuscripts bears out this contention. The first is that of Thomas Hunt himself who succeeded Gagnier in 1740, after being since 1738 the Laudian Professor. It is interesting to note that he still called the position by the old-fashioned name of 'King William's Pension'. He was writing on 16 November 1740 to the antiquary Richard Rawlinson, who was collecting biographical material about Oxford scholars:

I have now forgot the precise day I was nominated by A.Bp York[2] to K. William's Arabic Pension in the room of Mr. Gagnier; but I think it was about the 23rd of March 1740. When I waited on his Grace on this Occasion, he desir'd that, tho' the Pension was given for the Encouragement of Arabic, I would begin with reading in Hebrew, (as what would be useful to many young Students) and from thence proceed to Arabic, if any of my Hearers should be dispos'd to learn that Language. Accordingly, having given some Weeks Notice to the Heads and Tutors of Colleges,

[1] See below, p. 527.
[2] Lancelot Blackburne, at that time Lord Almoner.

I began my Hebrew Lecture in the beginning of Act Term, at which were present upwards of 50 Scholars, of whom I sent a List to his Grace. I read to them in our Dining Hall[1] every Tuesday and Thursday Morning between the Hours of 9 and 11. The Pension is 50 Pound a year, but being Subject to Taxes it does not at present bring in more than 40 clear, if so much. There is another of the same Value at Cambridge, which his Grace some Years ago gave to the Arabic Professor there.[2]

When in 1748 he resigned from the lecturership (as it had obviously come to be called—the terms 'lecturer' and 'professor' were largely interchangeable in the early years of the century) he wrote again to Rawlinson:

I hold the Arabick Lecture, [i.e. the Laudian Chair] as my Predecessors Dr. Pocock[3] and Dr. Hyde[4] did; nor did I ever think of resigning it. What you saw advertised in the News-Papers (ostentatiously call'd the Arabic Lecture) is a Pension paid by the L. Almoner, call'd King Williams Pension, of wch. I gave you an Account abt. 6 or 7 years ago, when I succeeded Mr. Gagnier in it. This, on my coming to Christ-Church, I thought fit to resign.[5]

Although he spoke so contemptuously of it, Dr. Richard Browne of Trinity College who succeeded him in 1748, alleged that he gave it up with a reluctance that annoyed the then Lord Almoner, Thomas Sherlock, Bishop of London.[6]

The second source of information on the Lord Almoner's chair during the eighteenth century to be found in private letters comes from his successor Richard Browne, who had a higher opinion than his predecessor of the dignity of his position. He was ultimately (in 1774) also to succeed Hunt in the Regius Chair of Hebrew, though not in the Laudian Chair of Arabic. He wrote to his patron Lord Guilford on 12 March 1763, declaring a reversionary interest in the Hebrew chair when Hunt should vacate it, and appended some hints for his guidance.

All the Professors of Hebrew in Oxford, since the annexing of the Canonry of Christ Church to the Professorship,[7] have been Persons the most distinguished in their times for their knowledge of the Arabic Language, which contains in a manner all

---

[1] At Hart Hall, soon to be Hertford College.

[2] MS. Rawl. Lett. 96, fol. 38.

[3] Edward Pococke held the Regius Chair of Hebrew together with the Laudian Chair of Arabic 1648–91.

[4] Thomas Hyde held the Regius professorship and the Laudian chair 1697–1703.

[5] MS. Rawl. Lett. 96, fol. 291ᵛ, n.d. but endorsed '24 Oct: 1748 Recd by me R+R'.

[6] Browne–Guilford, 12 Mar. 1763 (Bodl. MS. North d. 9 (vol. 6), fols. 101–2).

[7] 1630.

the Learning of the East, and is in a great degree necessary to the perfect understanding of the Hebrew which is in itself but a very small part of Oriental Literature.[1]

Dr. H[unt] was promoted to the Canonry and Hebrew Professorship, for having been useful about six years in the same way Dr. B[rowne] has since been in the Arabic Professorship which Dr. B now has. Dr. B has been L. Almoner's Professor of Arabic fifteen years; has read Lectures, on the Hebrew and Arabic Languages both, constantly to considerable numbers in the University, two of which are now Heads of Colleges and others gentlemen of Standing in the Place. All which time he has taken no money or Present of any of his Scholars (except a trifle once to shew his right to do so) that he might the more effectually encourage the cultivation of Eastern Learning, and as he thought, and was encouraged to think, that should he outlive the now Professor of Hebrew he might probably succeed him in his Professorship and Canonry. He still hopes his Pretensions may be allowed of, as his present Professorship is but forty one pounds five shillings a year clear of Taxes, and a great part of that sum is necessarily sunk for Rent of Chambers, in College and University Fees, and the expences of attendance upon the Duty of the Place.

As the Professors in general do not read Lectures for their Salaries (neither of Dr. H. Predecessors in those Professorships he now has, nor that in which he was succeeded by Dr. B., did so; nor does Dr. H. do so now for either of the Professorships he at present holds) the most effectual method to provide for the due cultivation of Oriental Learning in the University seems to be, to encourage from time to time the Lord Almoner's Professor of Arabic (who is in some sort a King's Professor) to expect, after having properly discharged his Duty, to be promoted upon a vacancy to the Hebrew Professorship and Canonry of Christ Church. No promotion of any other person to that Professorship (though in other respects worthy or even qualified for the Post by his Oriental Learning) can so well, if at all, answer the same purpose.[2]

Browne was not a distinguished scholar, nor, it would appear, an impressive person.[3] The tenor of his letter makes it clear that the rival he feared was a Hebraist of far higher qualifications than himself, Dr. Benjamin Kennicott,[4] though one with no pretension

[1] He is echoing the views of Thomas Hunt (a much finer scholar) in his 'Inauguration Speech' on 23 Feb. 1748, which he outlines to Rawlinson on 15 June 1748 (MS. Rawl. Lett. 96, fol. 288). It was printed at the Oxford Press in the same year: *De usu dialectorum orientalium, ac praecipue Arabicae, in Hebraico Codice interpretando* . . . 5 Dec. 1748 (H. Carter, *A History of the Oxford University Press*, Oxford, 1975, p. 533).

[2] MS. North d. 9, fols. 103–4.

[3] President Fry of St. John's in his diary considered he had 'little or no taste and seems in all respects, to be a low, lick-spittle fellow', 22 May 1771 (from a typescript in the possession of Dr. Hargreaves-Mawdsley, p. 69, which he has kindly permitted me to use).

[4] 1718–83. A Hebrew scholar of great learning, risen from very humble origins by unremitting industry. His chief work was the collation of the texts of the Old Testament. He was Radcliffe Librarian from 1767 to his death, and in 1770 was appointed Canon of Christ Church. Browne was justified in fearing his rivalry. In 1769 the Vice-Chancellor Nathan Wetherell was trying to get the promise of the reversion to this chair for him from

as an Arabist. Whether on account of past tradition, or the support of Lord Guilford and Lord North (which in due time he warmly acknowledged),[1] Browne succeeded in his ambitions, and Kennicott, though he obtained preferment, never held the Regius chair.

The chief interest of Browne's evidence is the information it provides about the prominent part, at least from 1740 onwards, which the chair played in University lecturing. Browne's information about the state of affairs in the early years of the century may not be altogether accurate,[2] but there is ample evidence of the anxiety felt in these years at the decline of Hebrew studies and the lack of vigour shown by the professors. It is to be seen in the efforts of bishops, Vice-Chancellors, and Heads of individual Houses to provide private Hebrew teaching, including the employment of Jewish scholars, to promote what was still felt to be an important part of the University's curriculum. The study of Arabic, which never won a formal place in this curriculum, was an object of less general interest, despite Vice-Chancellor Baron's interposition on its behalf.

It may be noted that lectures in Arabic were long held only in vacation. The *University Almanack* of 1703 gives the times of Arabic lectures as Wednesdays in the vacation.[3] This was still true in 1719;[4] and it would seem safe to assume that when Thomas Hunt in 1743 was coming into Oxford during the Long Vacation only 'to read my Public Lecture on Wednesdays'[5] he meant to lecture in Arabic, since his Hebrew lectures were, as laid down in the Statutes, delivered on Tuesdays and Thursdays and during term.

When Browne obtained the Regius Chair in Hebrew in 1774 he retained the Lord Almoner's chair, but in 1780, on his death, a serious young scholar Henry Ford (married to the niece of the Bishop of Oxford,[6] and who was said to have owed his appoint-

---

the Duke of Grafton, which would 'make him the happiest man living' (letter to Charles Jenkinson, 10 Feb. 1769, Br.Lib., Add. MS. 38306, fol. 102).

[1] MS. North d. 15, fol. 218.
[2] See p. 525 n. 4.
[3] Gough Oxford 31.
[4] A. Bedford–Charlett, 11 Dec. 1719 (MS. Ballard 34, fol. 111).
[5] Hunt–Rawlinson, 26 July 1743 (MS. Rawl. Lett. 96, fol. 107).
[6] Robert Lowth.

ment to the bishop's interposition), was appointed and held the Lord Almoner's chair until 1813. In 1782 we know that he was delivering Hebrew lectures 'at home in a snug private room'[1] and that he was trying to persuade pupils to attend his lectures in Arabic in the following term.[2] Browne had written of the Arabic as well as of the Hebrew lectures he delivered, but in 1771 he had only one student attending his Arabic class.[3] By the end of the century when James Hurdis sought to justify the lecturing activities of the Oxford professors,[4] the Regius Professor of Hebrew was lecturing twice a week in all full terms, but the Laudian professor was not lecturing in Arabic (though he delivered a controversial series of Bampton Lectures in Divinity) and the Lord Almoner's Professor is not mentioned at all.

[1] *Letters of Richard Radcliffe and John James1 755–83*, ed. M. Evans, (O.H.S. ix, 1833), pp. 191–2.

[2] Ibid., p. 192.

[3] President Fry's Diary, p. 68.

[4] [James Hurdis], 'Vindication of Magdalen College' (*c.* 1800) in *Reminiscences of Oxford*, ed. L. Quiller Couch (O.H.S. xxii, 1892), p. 146.

24

THE FOUNDATION OF WORCESTER COLLEGE, OXFORD

I

THE volume on Worcester College in the University of Oxford College Histories series[2] gives a very incomplete account of the complex and long-drawn-out transactions whereby Gloucester Hall changed its name and status to that of Worcester College. This is partly, though not wholly, the result of shortage of material. The College has in its archives a small but important collection of legal documents relating to its final incorporation in 1714, when a decree of Lord Chancellor Harcourt brought the controversial process to an end.[3] It has on the other hand no manuscripts of Benjamin Woodroffe, Canon of Christ Church and Principal of Gloucester Hall,[4] who first conceived the idea of the transformation (apparently in 1697), and who in the years leading up to 1702 almost succeeded in achieving it. It appears to possess not one of the printed publications with which he sought to justify his claim, and indeed the College historian had to depend almost exclusively for his account of the early years of the controversy on a hostile pamphlet produced by Balliol College which was pressing rival claims against him.[5] Quite recently, however, a bundle of manuscripts has been found in Balliol Library which throws much new light on this early period.[6] They are the letters of John Ince, attorney of Fenchurch Street, addressed almost exclusively to the Master of Balliol, Roger Mander, when he was Vice-Chancellor between the years 1700 and 1702 and in the two succeeding years.[7] They are accompanied by copies of letters and other documents collected for legal purposes by Ince who was employed by Mander on behalf both of the University and Balliol to obstruct Woodroffe's claims.

For a later period, the publication of the Calendar of the *Portland Papers* (Hist. MSS. Comm., series 29, vol. VII) which came out the year after the publication of the College *History*, has also drawn attention to much interesting material. From the various sources now available, therefore, it is possible to work out a fuller account of this curious episode, and to bring out a number of points important for the history of the University as well as for the College.

It is well known that Sir Thomas Cookes, Bt., of Bentley Pauncefote in Wor-

---

[1] I am grateful to the master and fellows of Balliol and to the provost and fellows of Worcester for permission to use and quote from their archives, and to their archivists and librarians for their unfailing helpfulness. I wish also to express gratitude to the Leverhulme Trustees for their award of an Emeritus Leverhulme Fellowship with the assistance of which I have carried out this work.

[2] C. H. Daniel and W. R. Barker, *Worcester College* (1900).

[3] Boxes 28 (1) and (2).

[4] For him see Daniel and Barker, op. cit., 128 ff.

[5] See below, Appendix.

[6] These MSS. at Balliol are cited here simply as ' Ince Papers '; there is no pagination. I am indebted to Mr. Vincent Quinn, librarian of Balliol, for drawing my attention to them.

[7] Ince had been active in ecclesiastical circles for many years, having played a prominent part as attorney for the Seven Bishops in their famous trial (Bodl. MS Tanner 28/1, f. 109 ff.). He continued to do legal work for the University and also for Christ Church (Hist. MSS. Comm. 29, *Portland MSS.*, VII, 165).

cestershire, made a will on 19th February 1697[8] under the influence of the then Bishop of Worcester, Edward Stillingfleet.[9] It contained provisions for a benefaction of £10,000 for building in Oxford an ' Ornamentall pyle ' where trustees might ' . . . add raise create or endow such and so many Scholars places and Fellowships as they shall think the product or Yearly revenue . . . will support or Maintain ' or ' add to create raise or endow such other College or Hall in Oxford with such and so many fellowships and so many schollars places there ' as they may think fit, preference being given to certain schools in Worcestershire, and among their scholars to the Founder's kin. Stillingfleet was apparently responsible for the very cumbersome body of trustees who were to carry out the will: the twenty-five Heads of Oxford Colleges and Halls, the Archbishop of Canterbury and the Bishops of Worcester, Oxford, Gloucester and Lichfield.

As soon as knowledge of Cookes's intentions got about, Woodroffe approached Sir Thomas with the proposal that he should attach the benefaction to Gloucester Hall and convert the latter into Worcester College. Woodroffe, a man who had made some mark for himself in scholarship and the Church, was a most enterprising, though exasperatingly unpractical, person. He was unpopular in the University[10] and among his fellow clergy,[11] but he had at this time personal access to William III, and was in touch with prominent Whig politicians including the Duke of Marlborough.[12] No doubt his political affiliations added to his unpopularity in the University, but both his conduct of this affair and the ultimate collapse of his personal fortunes suggest that his critics were right in believing him to be ill-fitted for the position at which he aimed.

The idea of obtaining a charter of incorporation for his Hall had already occurred to Woodroffe some twelve months earlier, but would seem to have foundered on University opposition.[13] A letter from Archbishop Tenison to Stillingfleet dated 24th March 1697 seems to show that Woodroffe was already enlisting his interest,[14] though he himself dates his first letter to Cookes at the beginning of the following August.[15] In the next year a plan was fully developed, with the assistance of the archbishop and Stillingfleet, for absorbing Sir Thomas Cookes's charity. Sir

[8] The will is dated 1696, but also 9 Will. III, so the date follows the legal custom of the time in beginning the year in March; February 1697 is thus the correct date.
   [9] There are xeroxes of transcripts of Stillingfleet's correspondence in Dr. Williams Library, London, MS. 201, 38 and 39.
   [10] When he put in his first petition for incorporation in 1695/6 the Chancellor of the University sent a message to the University that ' his Grace will suffer nothing to be done in it, but as the University shall approve ' (Bodl. MS. Ballard 9, f. 118). For Dr. Prideaux's views of him at Oxford see Daniel and Barker, op. cit., 129 ff.).
   [11] John Ince (not it must be admitted an impartial witness) claimed that ' our London Divines knew him so well at Sion Colledge that they have but meane thoughts of him ', (Ince Papers, Ince–Mander, 20th August 1702).
   [12] *Remarks and Collections of Thomas Hearne*, ed. C. E. Doble, I (O.H.S. II) 282. Hearne reports (8th August 1706) that Woodroffe had just published a sermon preached at Woodstock for the thanksgiving for Marlborough's success, dedicated to the Duke.
   [13] See Bodl. MSS. Ballard 9, f. 118; 21, f. 36 (J. Hough–Charlett, 28th January 1695/6; F. Adams–Same, 22nd January 1695/6).
   [14] He wrote that Woodroffe had been with him and showed him a scheme, promising a ' more perfect draught speedily '. He had not seen nor heard from him for ' some weeks ' and adds ' Having no part of the scheme, I cannot send any pertinent thoughts upon it. When your Lordship opens the matter further, I will give my opinion and assistance with all freedom and readiness '. (Dr. Williams Library, MS. 201, 38, f. 48).
   [15] Quoted in J. Baron, *The Case of Glocester Hall, in Oxford, Rectifying the false Stating thereof by Doctor Woodroffe*, (see Appendix). The author says that a nephew of Sir Thomas's approached him on 25th June 1697 suggesting he should enter into correspondence with Cookes.

Thomas, a curious character who combined two contradictory qualities, an incapacity to reject any personal approach made to him, and an underlying desire to submit himself to episcopal guidance, was attracted both by Woodroffe's proposition and his ecclesiastical backing. There were, however, obstacles to overcome. In the first place the benefactor was not an old man, and his intention was to leave his charity in his will. Woodroffe hoped to persuade him to grant it *inter vivos*, and though Sir Thomas disclaimed such an intention, he was not consistent in so doing, nor did Woodroffe give up hope.

There were various practical difficulties in the way, one that the site on which Gloucester Hall stood was not freehold, but leasehold belonging to St. John's College. The first necessity, however, was to obtain incorporation of the new College and the recognition of its statutes under the Great Seal. The former Woodroffe obtained on 22nd October 1698; the latter on the following 18th November. Letters from Tenison to Stillingfleet show that the combination of Woodroffe's haste and the absence of both William III and the Chancellor of the University, the Duke of Ormonde, in Ireland, led to a good deal of confusion. The charter, the warrant for which the king had signed before he went overseas and which in consequence passed ' without any addition or alteration, presuming all was by consent and thoroughly considered ',[16] was in fact drawn up in a form which was invalid in law. As the attorney general was to point out some four years later,[17] it failed to name any of those incorporated under it except Woodroffe himself. The situation with regard to the statutes was no better. A body of them had indeed been signed by the bishops (the Bishop of Oxford adding his name later)[18] though they were not signed by Sir Thomas. Those which Woodroffe now rushed through, and which were passed under the Great Seal purporting to have been approved by the Founder, differed considerably from the original ones. This was partly, it would seem, through his incurable inaccuracy, but even more because the Duke of Ormonde had insisted on a change of substance, to which Woodroffe had agreed without consulting Sir Thomas, or, probably, either of the bishops. Woodroffe's statutes were to remain in great confusion (ultimately there were four recensions of them in existence, all different)[19] over-ambitious and full of discrepancies. When, in 1714, a committee of Heads of Houses tried to reduce them to enough order to be used as a basis for the statutes of the new College, they had to abandon the attempt in despair.[20]

Woodroffe's intemperate haste was thus building up difficulties for the future. It also defeated his purpose in the short run. The concessions he had been obliged to make to the Duke of Ormonde proved quite unacceptable to Sir Thomas. The statutes approved by the bishops had placed the nomination of all future provosts, after Woodroffe, in the hands of the benefactor and his heirs. Ormonde (his hand

16 Dr. Williams Library, MS. 201, 38, ff. 51–2 (Tenison–Stillingfleet, 4th November 1698).

17 See below, p. 537.

18 For them, see the Ince Papers.

19 They were: (1) the statutes signed by the bishops (1698) which Woodroffe suppressed, and which his enemies, out of consideration for the bishops, passed lightly over. A copy of them in comparison with the later statutes survives, however, in the Ince Papers. (2) The copy passed under the Great Seal (18th November 1698). (3) The copy sent to the University of Oxford by order of the House of Lords (April 1702) and (4) The copy as amended by the Lords in April 1702 and sent down to the House of Commons. None of them, of course, ever came into operation.

20 See below, p. 547.

strengthened apparently by University opinion[21]) insisted that it should remain with the Chancellor, and provision for this was incorporated in the statutes passed under the Great Seal.   As a result Sir Thomas broke off negotiations with Woodroffe, and for some two years all plans for founding the charity at Gloucester Hall were abandoned.

This gave an opening to another claimant, Balliol, one of whose fellows, John Baron (soon to be master) had been in close touch with Worcester affairs, where, as he claimed, he had earlier used his influence to help Woodroffe.[22]   Balliol could not offer what Gloucester Hall could, but they had some different advantages.   There was no chance of the Cookes's fellows taking over Balliol—they would be engrafted on its Foundation, as fellows under similar endowments were elsewhere—but it had a site which was then held to be much more desirable, it had no problems of incorporation or of title to its land, and, though residential buildings would have to be added, it had the supporting college accommodation.   It was also a sound Tory College, well-looked on by the Chancellor who on 15th January 1700 went on record as considering it the ' fittest place ' for the charity.[23]   Sir Thomas undoubtedly took Balliol's claims seriously.   The party feeling, never far below the surface in this controversy, here became open.   William Lloyd, who had succeeded Stillingfleet as Bishop of Worcester in 1699, and his Whig supporters were at this time engaged in political warfare in Worcestershire with the local Tories.   Sir Thomas's incapacity to steer a steady course through these conflicting currents exacerbated the ill-feeling they caused.

Balliol, like Gloucester Hall before, made a good deal of progress.   A copy of Woodroffe's statutes was given to them and, after amendments, was accepted by their Visitor,[24] and on 9th March 1700 an agent of Sir Thomas's assured them that nothing held his employer back but doubt about the archbishop's consent.[25]   To this the archbishop rather sulkily replied on 28th March 1700 that Sir Thomas was under ' *no sort of Obligation to him* ' though he ' *could not tell* what *Vows to God, or Promises to Men, or personal Resolutions, Sir* Thomas *had made* '.[26]   Nevertheless, behind the scenes the archbishop and others were bringing pressure to bear on Ormonde to compromise.   As early as 8th June 1699 Edmund Gibson, much in the archbishop's confidence, wrote from Lambeth to Arthur Charlett, master of University College, ' We now think, that Worcester-College will goe forward: there being (as I hear) some hopes that the Duke of Ormond will recede from his right of Nomination '.[27] He was premature, but by January 1699/1700 Ormonde was offering compromises, and by May the bargainers were not far apart.   Finally Ormonde agreed to waive his claim to the nomination of the provost in return for the position for the Chancellor

---

[21] Tenison believed that he himself had obtained Ormonde's own consent earlier but that the latter had felt obliged to consult the Vice-Chancellor, (Dr. Williams Library, MS. 201, 38, ff. 50–1, Tenison–Stillingfleet, 29th September 1698).

[22] *The Case of Glocester Hall, in Oxford, Rectifying the false Stating thereof*, 44.

[23] Quoted in ' The Case of Sir Thomas Cooks Charity of 10000£ ', Ince Papers (Ormonde–Sir T. Cooke, 15th January 1699/1700).   It must be admitted that since he was at this time engaged in negotiations for a compromise over Gloucester Hall, this statement is somewhat disingenuous.

[24] Henry Compton, Bishop of London.   A copy of the document is among the Ince Papers.

[25] Quoted in *The Case of Glocester Hall*, 45, where however the archbishop's person is disguised under the title of ' one of the most eminent Trustees '.

[26] Ibid.

[27] Bodl. MS. Ballard 5, f. 162.

of Perpetual Visitor of the College, the nomination of one of the original fellows and of a scholar in perpetuity. On 26th August 1700 Sir Thomas wrote triumphantly and gratefully thanking him for ' so Generous a Concession to make way for me to compleat my Charity at Gloster Hall or rather as I now wish your leave [to] Stile it Worcester College '.[28] Gloucester Hall seemed to have triumphed, and Sir Thomas's obstinacy, so much at variance with his usual irresolution, to have paid off.

Unfortunately, however, the story was not finished. Almost a year was to pass before Sir Thomas's premature death, and during that time he took no steps to consolidate his plans for Worcester College, but on the contrary showed some uneasiness about them. He was worried about the question of the title to the land, and he wanted the statutes translated into English so that he could understand them.[29] It is not quite clear when his health began to fail. It is certain that in his later months the interest of all who had hopes from him began to focus above all on his will. So far as Woodroffe and the supporters of Gloucester Hall were concerned, this became of prime necessity, for not only was the will drawn up in terms which gave little encouragement to the hopes of Gloucester Hall, but it was well-known that the majority of the trustees with whom the settlement of the charity would rest were hostile to Woodroffe and his claims. But Sir Thomas, like many weak men, was extremely unwilling to change his will, and evaded attempts to get him to do so even on his death-bed, and amid agitated scenes he died on 8th June 1701 at the age of fifty-two with his will unchanged.

Woodroffe and the supporters of Gloucester Hall were thus, despite their earlier triumph, left in a very doubtful situation. On the other hand the hopes of Balliol were revived, and they were in a strong position to see that their claims were not overlooked, since their master was now Vice-Chancellor. As soon as the will was proved Mander, in this capacity, waited on the archbishop with the request that the Trust be carried out. The archbishop replied evasively that nothing could be done quickly, that he would ' advise with Council both on the Civil and Common Laws ' and would notify the Vice-Chancellor of the result.[30] The next documentary evidence of activity is the introduction of a private bill in the House of Lords on 5 February 1702[31] with the dual purpose of giving statutory sanction to Woodroffe's charter and statutes and of replacing the thirty persons of the Trust set up in the will by a Trust of four; the Archbishop of Canterbury, the Bishop of Worcester, Woodroffe and Sir Thomas's heir and executor (who had been abroad at the time of his death) his nephew, who now took his name being henceforth known as Sir Thomas Cookes Winford. Judging from Woodroffe's account of the events the bill seems to have been sprung on the University, for he records ' That those of the Heads of Houses, who were in Town, had notice to attend at the first meeting of the Committee, and that they attended, and undertook to give notice to the Vice Chancellor, and the other Heads of Houses in the University '.[32]

It has been assumed, on the strength of the statements in the Balliol pamphlet,

---

[28] Ince Papers.
[29] *The Case of Gloucester Hall*, 27.
[30] Copy of *The Case* sent with a letter of Ince–Mander, 11th July 1702 (Ince Papers).
[31] *Journal of the House of Lords*, XVII, 27.
[32] See B. Woodroffe, *A Letter from a Member of the House of Commons*, Postscript, 8; copy in Christ Church Library, see Appendix.

that the responsibility for this move rested entirely with Woodroffe, that it was typical of his erratic judgement, and that it was doomed to failure.   In fact he could never have undertaken it, still less have carried it well on the way to success, had he not acted under influential patronage.   This was certainly provided by the Archbishop of Canterbury and probably also by no less a person than Lord Chancellor Somers himself.   The bill was described at the time as ' preferred by or in the name of his Grace and two other [of] the Trustees . . . and the Executor . . . '.33   The archbishop was chairman of the powerful committee of the Lords who considered it.   The case for superseding the will was based almost entirely on the evidence of the intentions of the deceased given by the Bishop of Worcester, no doubt reinforced from the chair. Lord Somers himself took a considerable part in the business, and he may have been responsible for some amendments made to Woodroffe's chaotic statutes.   At the request of the Heads of Houses present the proposed statutes were sent down to the University who were given twelve days to comment on them.   They did not do so. A deputation headed by the Vice-Chancellor appeared before the committee and gave evidence against the bill but without effect.34   It passed its final reading on 13th April and was sent down to the Commons.35

It was here that the University, in what were now the early days of Queen Anne's reign, began serious opposition to the bill, and even then only after it had passed its first reading on 20th April.   Some surprise was expressed at their in-activity to date, and here again the party aspects of the affair became apparent. Simon Harcourt, at that time an extreme Tory, wrote to Arthur Charlett, Master of University College, on 28th April 1702,

> Since your Bill came into the House of Commons, I have rec'd no other Commands from the University, than such as Doctor Woodruff [*sic*] hath thought proper to deliver, at which I must confess to you, I have been under some Surprize.36

He added that he would be glad to serve the University.   But he was out of date. On the day on which the bill passed its first reading Ince received instructions from the Vice-Chancellor to oppose it on behalf both of the University and of Balliol.37 Ince was obviously not at that time known to the Vice-Chancellor, for the latter got his name wrong and had to be corrected, but the choice was a good one.   Ince was strongly predisposed against Woodroffe personally,38 he became deeply engaged in his clients' interests—particularly those of Balliol–39 and he had personal access to the archbishop, the bishops40 and a number of politicians.   He promptly canvassed the University Members and other prominent Tory M.P.s41 to hold up the bill, produced

33 Ince Papers (copy of *The Case*).
34 The statutes were sent to the Vice-Chancellor by B. Portlock, secretary to the Duke of Ormonde, who had them from Woodroffe (Ince Papers, Portlock–[Mander],10th March 1701/2).   Ormonde did not oppose the bill.
35 *Journal of the House of Commons*, XIII, 857.
36 Bodl, MS. Ballard 10, f. 115.
37 Ince Papers (Ince–Mander, 20th April 1702).
38 ' I am told Woodroffe is a Beggar and tis dangerous to trust him with such a sume or any part of it ', (ibid., Same–Same, 27th April 1702).
39 He said his main purpose was ' getting this charity (sub rosâ) to Balliol if possible ', (ibid., Same–Same, 22nd July [1702]).
40 He claimed to do all the archbishop's ' business at law ' and to know the Bishop of Worcester (Lloyd) ' intimately well ', (ibid., Same–Same, 15th September 1702).
41 Ibid.; see letters of Ince–Mander from 20–27th April 1702.

a petition from a large majority of the Heads of Colleges and Halls asking for time to study the papers[41a], and submitted a petition on his own stressing not only these points but Balliol's claims.[42]

Though the luckless Woodroffe stationed himself in the lobby of the House with bundles of the printed *Case* for his bill under his gown to distribute to Members,[43] and though he insisted that the opposition was not representative of University opinion as a whole, but only of a small group whipped up by Balliol, his bill was defeated in its second reading by forty-three votes to twenty-seven.[44] This result naturally infuriated him and annoyed his supporters. After the House rose he got out a second issue of his printed *Case* and circulated it with an abusive *Letter from a Member of the House of Commons, in Answer to a Letter, from a Member of the University, Enquiring: How the Bill for Settling Sir Thomas Cookes's Charity . . . came to be rejected in their House.*[44a] The Bishop of Gloucester told Ince that the University's intervention was ' unreasonable ',[45] and the Archbishop of Canterbury (already at odds with the Vice-Chancellor over a different subject[46]), expressed his annoyance to Ince, rebutted his personal attacks on Woodroffe[47] and was quite unmoved by the legal opinions against the Gloucester Hall claims which Ince was collecting.[48]

It was on the basis of the case which Ince drew up that the Attorney General, Sir Edward Northey, and another distingusihed barrister, Henry Poley, gave their opinions (which were never challenged) that Woodroffe's charter and statutes were legally invalid, and that therefore no endowment could be settled on Gloucester Hall; they also maintained that a duly attested will over-rode all other expressions of the testator's alleged intentions, and that in consequence the thirty trustees, or the majority of them, could settle the charity anywhere in Oxford they wished.[49] The alleged evidence of Sir Thomas's intentions expressed after he drew up his will became a major point of discussion in the development of the case, and the legal significance to be attached to it became important. So long as the assumption was no more than that this evidence could provide guidance for the trustees in carrying out the terms of the will, it was obviously legally acceptable, but some of the Gloucester Hall supporters, and certainly the archbishop and Woodroffe, believed that this later evidence could over-ride the provisions of the will, and do so not only if it were superseded by Act of Parliament (though this was the preferred method and two attempts were made to procure private Acts to do so), but in Chancery. In 1713 Lord Chancellor Harcourt was to go very near to acting according to this principle;

[41a] There are two lists of subscribing heads, the one containing sixteen names only (an absolute majority of the trustees), probably the earlier; the second containing the same names but bringing up the total by additions to twenty-one out of a possible twenty-five signatories. Only the heads of St. Johns, Wadham, Gloucester Hall and St. Edmund Hall not appearing, (ibid., Petition of the Vice-Chancellor and Heads of Colleges and Halls).

[42] Ibid., copy n.d. endorsed by Ince: ' This was sent in my own name only '.

[43] Ibid. (Ince–Mander, 27th April 1702).

[44] *Journal of the House of Commons*, XIII, 863.

[44a] See below, Appendix. The House was prorogued on 25th May 1702.

[45] Ince Papers (Ince–Mander [1702]).

[46] The refusal of an honorary degree to Dr. Nicholson, Bishop of Carlisle, (ibid., Ince–Mander, 29th August 1702).

[47] He said to him ' ffye man, ffye, you are misinformed '. Ince replied ' that if he would give me leave I would bring those clergymen to him who could satisfy him that the Dr. was both a·Beggar and a Knave ', (ibid.).

[48] Ibid.

[49] Ibid. (8th August 1702).

but it is of some interest that in the event he was not prepared to put the matter to the test.

It is significant of the feeling aroused over the issue that the attorney general thought it wise to advise Ince to urge his clients not to lose time in settling where the charity was to be fixed, lest pressure either from one of the Houses of Parliament or from some ' Great persons, or some powerfull interpositions by way of mediator ' be brought to bear on the trustees to influence their decision.[50]   It was agreed that it was for the archbishop to call a meeting of the trustees, but he took no steps to do so. Moreover, as the issue became more and move controversial, it was difficult to get individual trustees to give a firm undertaking to act.   Worst of all, by the autumn it was also becoming clear that, though there had been little difficulty in getting a majority of Heads of Houses to oppose Woodroffe's bill, and though Balliol had gathered together a number of supporters, they were not likely to be able to muster a majority in the teeth of episcopal disapproval.   When this news was broken to Ince he at first could scarcely believe it.   ' It deadens me mightily, and abates my courage to heare you doubt of a majority—of which I ever thought you were sure ' he wrote to Mander and three days later described himself as ' your sinking drowned Servant ',[51] but lists of supporters, non-starters, and opponents drawn up by experienced University politicians[52] were discouraging.   Neither Ince nor Balliol gave up hope, though Mander lost influence when he ceased to be Vice-Chancellor.   They were active in propaganda in London, Oxford and Worcester,[53] and in 1703 they got out a long and formidably documented pamphlet, *The Case of Glocester Hall . . .* which has always been attributed to John Baron, but which the Ince Papers show owed much to Ince and something to Mander as well.[54]   It is on this pamphlet that the study of Woodroffe's efforts has hitherto been based, and it was used in the attack on the claims of Gloucester Hall throughout the dispute.

But all was to no avail.   The only document on which a majority of the trustees could be found to agree (and they had to do so without any meeting called by the archbishop) was a bill in Chancery engaging the heir to deposit the money of the charity in Chancery, and even this proved ineffective, the heir continuing evasive on the ground that there were disagreements among the trustees.[55]   Mander's successor as Vice-Chancellor was the notorious William Delaune, president of St. John's, who was both too lazy and too anxious for his own ecclesiastical preferment to raise so contentious an issue.   It was not until 1707, when he had been succeeded by a vigorous and competent Vice-Chancellor in the person of William Lancaster, provost of Queen's, that the matter was raised again.   By this time the fate of the charity had become something of a scandal.   On 23rd September [1707] Henry Compton, bishop of London, wrote to Charlett,

50 Ibid. (Ince–Mander, 13th August 1702).

51 Ibid. (letters of 12th and 15th September 1702).

52 Charlett was in touch with Ince about tactics in Worcestershire and he returned lists of supporters, etc. (ibid., Ince–Charlett, 17th December [1702]; Ince–Mander, 29th April [1703]).

53 Ince produced an Address which was sent to the Vice-Chancellor and heads on 14th August 1702 in support of Balliol by the Grand Jury at the Assizes at Worcester.   A note on a later repeated Address of August 1704 to Baron says it is a copy of a document received by the master from Ince ' as proper to stirr up the slow proceedings in this trust . . .' (ibid.).

54 See Appendix.

55 At one point he agreed to pay it in by June 1704, but failed to do so (Worcester College Archives, Box 28 (1), Lord Keeper's Decretal, 31st October 1712).

. . . let me intreat you to consult a little with Mr. Vice Chancellor about Sir Tho. Cookes bounty. There are some that intend, if they can, to defeat the charity, and others are so stiff to their own inclinations, that makes it almost as unhappy on their side. If therefore you do not agree upon some place in the University joyntly, without the nicety of preferring this or that place to another and resolve to be unanimous in resigning up your private inclinations to a common consent, it may quickly be too late to repent you had not so done. This between you and me.[56]

Lancaster had forestalled his advice. On 4th April 1707 he waited on the archbishop, asking for a meeting of the trustees. The archbishop promised to call one at Oxford on 21st, 22nd and 23rd November. Lancaster had prepared the way carefully, and was pleased with the result. He had no intention of giving way to the claims of Gloucester Hall, and he believed he had some success in placating its supporters. He informed Charlett on 10th May 1707,

. . . I hope to bring power enough from my Lord of Cant. at my coming home if I can se (*sic*) Him before I return, for He is very fair and has said lately that He will be concluded by the majority. I do believe my Lord Somers has soften'd him; and my Lord C. J. will be of the same mind . . .[57]

This last point was of some significance, for the archbishop and the heir now claimed to have some new evidence of the benefactor's wishes on which the Lord Chief Justice's opinion was sought.[58] Lancaster asked that this fact be withheld from the Hebdomadal Board, lest Woodroffe, hearing of it, should procure some tampering with the witnesses.[59] The chief justice presumably found no reason to intervene, and this is the last reference in the papers to Woodroffe's personal concern in the issue.

At the meetings at Oxford in November 1707 neither the archbishop nor any of the bishops attended, but nineteen of the twenty-five Heads of Houses did. The plan put before them was, as Bishop Compton had proposed, a compromise. Neither of the original contestants was chosen. It was thought better that the endowment should go to a Hall than to a College since the Halls were poorer, and it was settled on Magdalen Hall rather than on Gloucester Hall, ostensibly because it offered better accommodation and consequently more of the money could be used for educational purposes.[60] This plan was passed by sixteen of the nineteen trustees present, an absolute majority of the trustees as a body. To hold the endowment Magdalen Hall would require a charter of incorporation under the Great Seal, and a decree releasing the funds of the charity since these were, nominally at least, in Chancery.

The defeat of Gloucester Hall now seemed as certain as its victory had seemed seven years earlier. Nevertheless, its supporters made one last effort to save it by parliamentary intervention. On 19th February 1708 Sir Thomas Cookes Winford, now Member for Worcestershire, petitioned the House of Commons for a private bill to settle the charity in the way he maintained his late uncle had intended. The proposal to refer the petition to a committee was debated in a large House, appar-

[56] Bodl. MS. Ballard 9, f. 62. It is not clear what danger he feared.
[57] Ibid. MS. 21, f. 71.
[58] Ibid., f. 69.
[59] Ibid., f. 71.
[60] Worcester College Archives (Box 28 (1), Lord Keeper's Decretal, 31st October 1712).

ently once again on party lines, for the tellers for the majority were Whigs and those for the minority High Tories. The petition was referred to a committee by 118 votes to 87.[61] The committee to which it was referred was, as was usual with private business, large and miscellaneous. Four days later three extra Members were added to it,[62] after which it disappears from sight. All that is known of its proceedings comes from a schedule of the legal expenses incurred by the University (still under the guidance of the indefatigable Ince) in opposing the petition.[63] These expenses were incurred between Michaelmas Term 1707 and Trinity Term 1709. The committee may well have been a casualty of the dissolution of 1710, when the great Tory victory of this year and the general election following completely changed the political scene.

II

The political events of 1710 and the climate of opinion emerging from them would have seemed prima facie favourable to the settlement of a domestic University issue in which the majority of Heads of Houses were in agreement and where the opposition to them had come largely from the Whigs. (As late as the beginning of 1711 John Holland, the new warden of Merton, one of the small groups of Whig Colleges, was being sworn in as a supporter of Gloucester Hall.[64]) But in the event the most dramatic volte-face of the sixteen years' story was to follow. The explanation for this lay in questions of personality, and the volte-face was a by-product of the tensions within the new Tory Administration between Lord Treasurer Harley, Earl of Oxford, supported by the Queen, who stood for moderation in Church and State on the one side, and a group of extremists on the other. Circumstances brought together two of the most intransigent of the latter in Oxford in 1711, where they proceeded not only to attempt to replace the Lord Treasurer's influence but also to build up a much more powerful one of their own. These two men were Simon Harcourt (appointed Lord Keeper in 1710 and Lord Chancellor in 1713) and Francis Atterbury (appointed Dean of Christ Church in August 1711). Both men saw political power in such a University interest; Harcourt also hoped to extend his family interest by obtaining a University seat for his son, he providing the patronage and Atterbury managing it. The Lord Chancellor's powerful position as an ecclesiastical patron was further strengthened in the University at this time by a plan that was afoot to annex prebends to the headships of some of the smaller Colleges.[65] Moreover he and his allies had the benefit of the support of the University's Chancellor, the Duke of Ormonde.

There might have seemed little likelihood that Harcourt's and Atterbury's ambitions in the University would involve them in the controversy over the use to which Sir Thomas's benefaction should be put, and even less that they should emerge

[61] *Journal of the House of Commons*, XV, 554–5.
[62] Ibid. 567.
[63] Worcester College Archives (Box 28 (1)).
[64] Merton College Archives, Register 4.21, Dr. Holland's Register, Entry for 3rd January 1710/11. Answer to a bill in Chancery on ' information of Dr. Lancaster and others '. Holland related that ' I thought Sir Thomas Cook did design to settle his Charite of £10,000 on Gloc. Hall and name it Worcester College '. Sworn before an attorney in Oxford.
[65] See G. V. Bennett, *The Tory Crisis in Church and State, 1688-1730* (1965), 119–60; G. R. Ward, *Georgian Oxford* (1958), 38–51.

as champions of the claims of Gloucester Hall, whose supporters had hitherto been found among the Whigs. Indeed as late as 8th November 1711 Lancaster believed himself to be on good terms with the Lord Keeper and sure of his co-operation in settling the endowment at Magdalen Hall. He wrote to Charlett on that date,

> My Lord Keeper has promised to hear Sir Thomas Cookes Case this Term and nothing delays it now but the want of Mr. Presidents and your Answers. A Commission is ready to prove the Will as soon as you have answer'd and then my Lord Keeper will make an end of it.[66]

But by the time he wrote the situation was beginning to change. Atterbury and the Lord Keeper were running into difficulties in their campaign to impose their will on the University. Quite apart from the difficulties in which Atterbury's strong-arm tactics were involving him in his own College, he found little support among the Heads of Houses he approached. Instead, he found himself opposed by a strong party led by Lancaster and Bernard Gardiner of All Souls (now in 1712 Vice-Chancellor);[67] the former already was, and the latter soon became, an enemy. William Stratford of Christ Church, whose correspondence begins at this stage to provide valuable, if by no means impartial, evidence on University personalities,[68] drew attention even before Atterbury came into residence to the latter's relations with Lancaster. He wrote to Edward Harley on 2nd September 1711 ' It is no secret how they are affected to each other, and that they will oppose each other to the utmost ',[69] and he later reported that he ' owns he designs upon the first opportunity he can meet with to attack Lancaster. They are as well met as any two I know '.[70]

There can be little doubt that the head-on collision which followed between the Lord Keeper in the court of Chancery and the trustees of the charity (who were in effect the Hebdomadal Board) was the outcome of this design. There was, however, a further explanation. A radical change had taken place in the position of Gloucester Hall. Woodroffe had died in August 1711. The nomination of his successor as principal of the Hall rested with Ormonde as Chancellor of the University, and though the Archbishop of Canterbury and the Bishop of Worcester (both now old and infirm)[71] and the heads of a few Whig Colleges might still support its claims almost by habit, it now became of political importance to the High Tories as well, for its head would have a vote on the Hebdomadal Board and his choice was in effect in their hands.

Tactics born of this new situation soon became apparent. So far from finishing the matter off quickly and confirming the settlement of the charity at Magdalen Hall, Chancery began in 1712 a full-scale investigation into the history of the dispute from 1698 onwards.[72]

It was not until 31st October 1712 that the court was ready to sit. When it did

[66] Bodl. MS. Ballard 21, f. 95.

[67] Thomas Braithwaite of New College was Lancaster's immediate successor, but he resigned on moving to the wardenship of Winchester, and was succeeded by Gardiner, a strong and abrasive personality.

[68] Hist. MSS. Comm. 29, *Portland MSS.*, VII, *passim*. He wrote regularly to Lord (Edward) Harley, son of the Lord Treasurer, whom he had known as an undergraduate.

[69] Ibid. 53.

[70] Ibid. 68.

[71] Ibid. 44, 46; Worcester College Archives, Box 28 (1), Archbishop of Canterbury—Vice-Chancellor, 8th December 1713.

[72] See Lord Keeper's Decretal, 31st October 1712 (ibid. Box 28 (1)).

so the decrees issued by the Lord Keeper created a sensation.   From one point of view they were approved by all.   The Lord Keeper was determined to bring the issue at last to a conclusion.   Sir Thomas's heir was ordered to pay the £10,000 bequest into the court, together with five per cent interest from the date at which payment was due under the will.   All parties were to get taxed costs (which by no means covered actual expenses) and the details of a settlement were carefully spelled out.   It was the settlement itself that was sensational.   Without positively asserting the power of Chancery to over-ride the decision of the trustees under the will, the Lord Keeper went within an ace of doing so.   He referred the trustees' decision back to them together with an expression of the wishes of the court couched in the strongest language.   He found that ' although the Testator at the time of making his Will had not determined on what particular Colledge or Hall the said Charity should be fixed or Established, yet it further appeared by undeniable Evidence that the Testator afterwards had come to a fixed and settled Resolution that the same should be established in Gloucester Hall '.[73]   He advised the trustees to examine in detail all the objections which had been raised to Gloucester Hall: the site of the College; its title to the land from St. John's; the cost of restoring its ruinous buildings and making it habitable for a College; the feasibility of Woodroffe's statutes.   Only if the trustees ' find upon the Reconsidering of the said Trust any unanswerable Objections to the setling the said Charity in Gloster Hall ' were they to ' execute such new Appointment as they shall conceive to be most reasonable . . . and they are to Certifye the same to this Court, After which, such further Directions shall be given as shall be just and necessary '.[74]   The decree added to the difficulties in which they would find themselves if they adhered to their decision in favour of Magdalen Hall, by pointing out that that hall could not hold a permanent endowment without incorporation under the Great Seal, and by accepting without question that Wood-roffe's incorporation of Gloucester Hall (which they attributed not to his application but to a non-existent one from Sir Thomas) was valid, ignoring completely the case so laboriously built up against it in 1703 and put forward in the same form in 1707 and in 1712.

Having issued his decrees the Keeper requested the Archbishop of Canterbury to summon a meeting of the trustees, and he permitted the archbishop and bishops to register their votes in absentia for their convenience, and also no doubt with voting strengths in mind.   Had they all taken advantage of this concession, the votes for Gloucester Hall would have been increased by five.   In the event two of the bishops (Lichfield and Gloucester) wished to continue to abstain, so the gain in votes was only three.

At the time when the decrees came out our informant, Canon Stratford, was deeply engaged in other controversial matters arising out of Atterbury's quarrels in Christ Church in which the Lord Keeper had also become involved, and he at first failed to recognize the significance of the attack on the settlement of Sir Thomas's benefaction, and did not apparently expect any resistance.   On 11th November 1712 he wrote to Edward Harley,

73 Ibid.
74 Ibid.

> Your Lordship has heard that my Lord Keeper has set aside the appointment of the Heads, by which Sir Thomas Cooke's benefaction was appointed to Magdalen Hall. It is now thought that it will be settled on Gloucester Hall.[75]

and he went on at once to what seemed to him the chief importance of the decision ' I know not in whom the nomination of the Head will be placed probably in the Chancellor '. He suggested that John Hudson, Bodley's Librarian, a supporter of the administration who had been offered and had refused the principalship of Gloucester Hall on Woodroffe's death, should be offered it again.[76] But a stronger competitor was in the field now that the appointment was intended to carry with it the provostship of the new College. This was Richard Blechynden, fellow of St. John's and chaplain to the Lord Keeper, whose family interest in Oxford he managed, and from whom he had already received substantial preferments.

The first provost of Worcester College has been under-estimated by the College historians on the strength of Hearne's opinion of him as ' good for nothing but drinking and keeping jolly Company '.[77] In fact he proved a very successful ally of those working for Gloucester Hall, and most of the spade-work necessary to translate the court's intentions for Worcester College into practical terms fell on him. Moreover, the easy acceptance of the new College by the University seems to have owed a good deal to his tact. Stratford respected his ability and for that reason thought at first that his appointment was ' very dexterous in Lord Keeper ',[78] though when he saw the reaction to it in the University he changed his mind. ' Blechingden's being made Principal of Gloucester Hall has quite spoiled the credit of the Lord Keeper's decree ' he wrote ' His Lordship disowns his having had any hand in making Blechingden Principal, but [this] nobody will believe '.[79]

The meeting of the trustees to discuss the decrees was fixed for 2nd January 1713. Two things were clear from the beginning: the dominant majority of the Heads of Houses were not prepared to give way without a struggle, and however the Lord Keeper might bluster, he was trying to achieve his end, not by asserting the claims of an over-riding Chancery jurisdiction, but by bringing about, one way or another, a majority among the trustees. The advantage of the challengers was their control over patronage to use for this purpose, their disadvantage, their unpopularity. When Atterbury first set to work he had only two active supporters among the Heads, William Delaune, who was frankly out for what he could get and who was soon being pushed by the Lord Keeper for an Irish bishopric,[80] and Robert Shippen, principal of Brasenose, brother of the Jacobite M.P. ' Honest ' William Shippen, and thus a natural ally. Two new principals of Halls, nominees of the Duke of Ormonde, Blechynden and Hudson (for whom St. Mary Hall providentially fell vacant) were

---

[75] *Portland MSS*, VII, 110.

[76] *Hearne's Collections*, III (O.H.S. XIII, 220).

[77] Ibid. Hearne's judgement was probably affected by Blechynden's close relations with the president of his College, Delaune, but everything suggests that he was a competent and conciliatory man, who served his new College well. He certainly did so in his friendship with the distinguished Sir George Clarke who became a great benefactor (as C. H. Daniel and W. R. Barker point out, *Worcester College*, 185–6).

[78] *Portland MSS*, VII, 115 (Stratford–E. Harley, 29th November 1712).

[79] Ibid. 126 (Same–Same, 13th December 1712).

[80] Ibid. 113, 175 (Same–Same, 20th November 1712; 5th December 1713). Jonathan Edwards, principal of Jesus, was also thought of as a possible ally at the beginning, but he was old and dying. There had been at one time a hope of combining the two biggest Colleges, Christ Church and Magdalen (a feat never achieved in the Century) through the influence of Sacheverell, but that never got off the ground.

soon added to the challengers' ranks, as was a third, Richard Newton, principal of Hart Hall, whom Atterbury warmly supported in his campaign for election as Public Orator.   We have no knowledge of the extent of the patronage which their leaders had freedom to dispose of, but we do know of the plums among it, the prebends which were made available.   It was originally intended that there should be four of these, all to be attached permanently to headships.   It had not been envisaged that they should all be available at the same fixed date, nor indeed were they, promises and half-promises had to be made in advance.   In the event one fell by the wayside,[81] one was awarded to an individual head and not attached to his College, and two only were permanently attached to headships.

When the trustees met on 2nd January 1713,[82] it was apparent that the battle was only beginning.   Fifteen of the twenty-five heads were present, and the archbishop, the Bishop of Worcester and the Bishop of Oxford registered postal votes in favour of Gloucester Hall.   Given the three episcopal votes, thirteen heads had to be found to support the measure if they were to obtain the absolute majority of sixteen. For some days the meeting proceeded by adjournment, but no attempt was made to divide.   After several adjournments, however, the challengers scored a point. Delaune announced on behalf of St. John's that, with their Visitor's permission they were able to alienate the land required for a site for Worcester College, and that they were prepared to do so.   On the strength of this, over a month after the deliberations had begun, a division was attempted on 7th February.   Once again fifteen heads attended (by no means all the same ones as before), and the vote showed that the challengers had made some gains; they now had the votes of nine heads[83] as well as those of the three bishops.   Besides Atterbury's two original supporters, Delaune and Shippen, and the three heads of Halls, Blechynden, Hudson and Newton, whose support had been added in 1711, they could now count on two heads who were promised the coveted prebends, George Carter, provost of Oriel and John Baron, master of Balliol.   The prebend to be held by the latter was personal only.   His new allegiance to the claims of Gloucester Hall, despite the fact that his pamphlet against them was still the major statement of the opposition's case, is an odd development.   The two other recruits who now came in, Thomas Dunster, warden of Wadham, and John Holland, warden of Merton, the two major Whig Colleges in the University at this time, also found themselves in odd company; they were representing the old Whig Gloucester Hall interest in the midst of a new Tory one.

The challengers' tactics had obviously won them some success, but not yet the majority which they required.   They were still short of this by four votes, and at this point they seemed to have shot their bolt.   For several months nothing happened whatever, the supporters of Magdalen Hall simply abstained from attending, the challengers failed to win over further supporters, and there was no quorum at the meetings of the trustees.   Though Blechynden and others managed to get some

---

[81] A prebend at Worcester had been promised to Charlett in which he was disappointed.   He claimed that Harley had assured him that alternative preferment would be given him, a promise which was not carried out (Bodl. MSS. Ballard, 19, 20, *et al.*).   It is not clear that his disappointment was directly concerned with this particular political operation.

[82] Worcester College Archives (Box 28 (1) and (2)); in particular copy of a letter from Gardiner to Harcourt, 18th June 1713.

[83] In Gardiner's letter (see previous note) the figure of eight is given (Shippen's name being omitted) but later he is included as one would expect, making the figure nine.

practical business started which would be useful if a major decision were reached, no further progress could be made. The deadlock was the more embarrassing to Harcourt (now promoted Lord Chancellor) because he and Atterbury were running into difficulties with the University on other points, resulting in a clash between the Chancery and the Vice-Chancellor's court. Harcourt was said to have broken out angrily in open court that there was ' no man in England ' whom he would ' sooner lay by the heels ' than Gardiner of All Souls, the Vice-Chancellor.[84]

He met this further challenge to his authority in the hectoring style characteristic of his dealings with the University. On 18th May 1713 the court issued a further decree, complaining that the deliberations of the trustees had ' been rendered ineffectual by adjournments from time to time by the Vice-Chancellor and some other of the said trustees who are influenced in Defiance of this Court to oppose the establishing the said Charity in Gloucester Hall ',[85] it ordered the Vice-Chancellor to give within a month's time a report to the court of the trustees' deliberations.[86] When he did so in a detailed letter on 18th June, it consisted of a report of no change. The trustees were in complete defiance of the court.

The Lord Chancellor now found himself in a most awkward position. His previous attack on the University's jurisdiction had ended in humiliating defeat,[87] and his own unpopularity was such that all chance of his building up a family interest in the University—then or later—had been blasted. Moreover, Ormonde was beginning to show signs of uneasiness with an alliance which was proving so unpopular in the University,[88] and Atterbury was escaping from the chaos he had created at Christ Church by promotion to the see of Rochester. Neither side had any real interest in Gloucester Hall or Worcester College, but Harcourt had gone too far to turn back. Indeed, those who had been under attack began to show signs of retaliating. It was believed in the University that the majority of the trustees intended to appeal to the House of Lords against his high-handed actions. He decided therefore to press on with the attempt to find the weakest links in the chain of the hostile majority. He instructed the Vice-Chancellor to procure from all those trustees who had not voted for Gloucester Hall letters explaining their attitude, and to lay these before the court on 28th November 1713.

The only consecutive account of the subsequent events we have comes from Stratford. It is no doubt over-dramatized, but it seems in the main to be accurate. On 13th October he wrote to Edward Harley,

> Here are great discontents here, and much talk of an Appeal to the House of Lords against a late order of Chancery about Sir Th. Cook's charity. Somebody is so apprehensive of this, that all means are tried to bring off particular votes, and to prevent a majority of the trustees from concurring in it. Promises of preferment fly as thick as hail. Public notice has been sent that there are orders for settling a prebend of Gloucester on Pembroke, and one of Norwich on Oriel and a vacant prebend of Bristol is to be bestowed on the Master of Balliol. We shall see in a little

[84] *Portland MSS*, VII, 151.
[85] Worcester College Archives, Box 28 (1), Order of 18th May 1713.
[86] Ibid.
[87] *Portland MSS*, VII, 146; see also E. Hamilton–Charlett, 21st May and 6th June 1713 (Bodl. MS. Ballard 36, ff. 113–16v.), Oxford University Archives (SP/A/13/b).
[88] In October 1713, over the election of a chaplain to the Speaker, Ormonde supported the candidate backed by the University against Atterbury and Harcourt (*Portland MSS*, VII, 170, 181–3). He was also said to have been irritated by the handling of the Aldrich case (ibid. 176).

time whether this be given out only to serve a present turn, but there is no expense will be spared to prevent the storm that is feared.[89]

A week later on 7th November he was inclined to believe that this activity was tending to a loss of votes rather than a gain ' More are disobliged than gained by it; some I believe will now declare who before were doubtful '.[90] But by 16th November, twelve days before the sitting of the court, he reported that the challengers had won.   He wrote,

> Since it was perceived that votes were valued, every one was for getting something, a promise at least.   There were persons here who had a full commission to give them, and they have now brought off so many that they have a majority by one, and it was done so openly that some who had given their word desired to be released from it and named the preferment of which they had a promise, if they voted as they were desired in this case.   The storm is stopped I believe that was apprehended, but they have been obliged to pay dear for it.[91]

When the court sat on 28th November the Vice-Chancellor reported that thirteen heads and three bishops had cast their votes for Gloucester Hall, thereby giving it, as Stratford had forecast, an absolute majority, though not a majority of the University voters.   One of the new votes which came in was that of Colwell Brickenden, master of Pembroke to whose headship a prebend of Gloucester was to be attached; two of the new supporters were heads of Halls, Thomas Bouchier, Regius Professor of Civil Law and principal of St. Alban Hall (always an unsteady voter on this topic) and John Brabourne, principal of New Inn Hall.   The last name needed (and received two days before the vote) was that of William Dobson, president of Trinity, whose statement amounted to little more than that he had changed his mind.

The voting is fully documented in the Chancery records.[92]   Five heads abstained from acting, two on the grounds that they had consistently done so in the past, three because their predecessors had cast a vote and they did not believe they could supercede it.   Atterbury, who was among the abstainers, explained his abstention by his ignorance of the history of the case, but his successor Smalridge attributed his own abstention to a prior vote given for Christ Church by Aldrich.   Six heads maintained to the end their support of Magdalen Hall and their opposition to Gloucester Hall.   They were Gardiner, Lancaster, Harwar, president of Magdalen, Paynter, rector of Exeter, Fitzherbert Adams, rector of Lincoln, and Pearson, principal of St. Edmund Hall.   Of the thirteen heads who now voted for Gloucester Hall, eight were among those who had put their hands in 1707 to the decision in favour of Magdalen Hall (Delaune, Dobson, Carter, Brickenden, Shippen, Bouchier, Brabourne and Newton).   Three had been appointed since the 1707 vote was taken (Holland, Blechynden and Hudson).   Two were men who had abstained in 1707 but now entered the arena and were of very different political affiliations (Baron and Dunster).

It was no doubt a humiliating defeat for Lancaster and his party, though not an overwhelming one.   Since the purpose for which the battle had been engaged was

[89] Ibid. 170.
[90] Ibid. 170–1.
[91] Ibid. 171.
[92] Worcester College Archives (Box 28 (2)).

now at an end, it served no immediate political purpose. It had, however, two permanent consequences, a minor one (though of some consequence for the Colleges concerned) the annexation of prebends to the headships of Oriel and Pembroke which continued into the 20th century, and the major one, the foundation of Worcester College. The vote having been taken, the practical arrangements for the incorporation of the new College went on apace.93 The Chancellor gave his consent though only on the terms which Sir Thomas had refused to accept, the nomination of the provost must rest with the Chancellor who was to select him from two candidates sent forward from among the fellows. Terms were reached with St. John's on the alienation of its land. Blechynden, assisted by an informal committee of Heads of Houses, worked out the statutes for a small but viable College (instructions from the court to base them on Woodroffe's statutes proved impracticable). Care was taken that the articles of association were in order, and on 29th July 1714 Letters Patent from Queen Anne gave Worcester its new status. It was not, however, until 24th January 1715 that the Convocation of the University passed a letter from the Chancellor exempting the new corporation from the Aularian Statutes and confirmed that the Society ' under the name of Worcester College be received into the body of the University '.94

APPENDIX

PUBLICATIONS BEARING ON THE CASE OF GLOUCESTER HALL AND WORCESTER COLLEGE 1699–1703

Two Sermons, one full-dress pamphlet, and three shorter publications concerning this controversy have survived.

A. On 1st June 1699 John Baron (later master of Balliol) preached a sermon at Feckenham in Worcestershire before the trustees appointed by Sir Thomas Cookes to manage his charity.1

B. On 23rd May 1700 Benjamin Woodroffe countered in a sermon preached at the same place.2

Both sermons were extremely partizan and provoked some scandal. Woodroffe's in particular aroused adverse comment.3 It exhausted his oratory and his supply of biblical texts to urge the intending benefactor not only to give his charity to Gloucester Hall, but to do so forthwith ' . . . Expose not thy self to *the temptations* of the *Adversary*; Expose not thy self to *the temptations* of any of *his instruments*; Expose not thy self to *the temptations* of *thine own deceitful heart*; Thou knowest not *what a change time*, and *place*, and persons may work thee to . . .'.4

C. In April 1702 Woodroffe printed a single sheet for circulation to Members of the House of Commons in support of the private bill brought to change the terms of the late Sir Thomas Cookes's will, to vest his charity in Gloucester Hall, and to recognize the latter as Worcester College. Anonymous, without date or place of printing, it was headed *The Case*

---

93 Ibid. (Box 28 (1), Record of the Court of Chancery, 22nd December 1713).

94 Oxford University Archives, Register of Convocation, 1703–1730 (N.E.P./Subtus/Register Bd).

1 *A Sermon Preach'd 1 June 1699 at Feckenham, in Worcestershire Before the Trustees appointed by Sir Thomas Cookes, Kt. Bart. To Manage his Charity given to that Place.* John Baron (Oxford, 1699), [1]–[37]. There is a copy in the Bodleian (Bodl. 4° C. 841 Linc.).

2 *A Sermon Preach'd 23rd May 1700 at Feckenham in Worcestershire, Before the Trustees appointed by Sir Thomas Cookes Bart. To Manage his Charity given to that Place. By Benjamin Woodroffe* (Oxford, 1700). There are three copies in Christ Church Library (Sermons Z247; 3.c.80; 2.c.156).

3 Bodl. MS. Ballard 12, f. 142 (G. Hickes—A. Charlett, 18th July 1700).

4 *A Sermon Preach'd 23rd May 1700 . . .* [21].

*of Worcester-Colledge Or Glocester-Hall, changed into Worcester Colledge.*5 John Ince saw Wood-roffe distributing it in the lobby of the House on 27th April 1702, and obtained a copy which he sent to the then master of Balliol.6

After Parliament was prorogued on 25th May 1702, Woodroffe, we are informed

> ... published a Second Edition of the same Case, with some little Alteration in half a Sheet of 4 Pages, Entitling it " *The Case of Worcester Colledge, as it was presented to the Members of the House of Commons* " which was also dispersed about the Town, together with a printed Letter in 4to of 8 Pages calling itself " *A Letter from a Member of the University,*7 *enquiring, how the Bill for Settling Sir Thomas Cookes's Charity of 10,000£ for the Erecting and Endowing of Worcester Colledge in Oxford,* came to be rejected in their House".8

Until very recently no copy of either of these publications was known to exist, but descriptions of them were taken from the pamphlet replying to them (see D. below).   The assistant librarian of Christ Church has, however, now identified copies of both of these among the College's collection of 18th-century Ephemera.9 Ince's correspondence suggests that they became available to readers shortly after 4th July 1702.10

D.   A reply to the above short papers was made in a long and detailed pamphlet, which has hitherto provided most of our knowledge of the controversy.   It was entitled *The Case of Glocester Hall, in Oxford, Rectifying the false Stating thereof by Doctor Woodforde.*11   Its place and date of publication have been tentatively assigned to ' Oxford 1702 ',12 and its authorship has generally been attributed to John Baron of Balliol, who indeed made little attempt to disguise that he played a part in it.

The Ince correspondence makes it clear (a) that it was printed by Thomas James of London;13 (b) that it appeared in print in 1703;14 (c) that a good deal of the material in the pamphlet was collected and put together by Ince but that Baron determined its final form and also provided material and that the master of Balliol was closely associated with its production at all stages.

We also have evidence that the printer was paid £17 2s. 6d. for an edition of 500 copies and for corrections15 and that near the end of April 1703 some sixty copies were sent, on behalf of Baron, to Clements the Oxford bookseller for distribution.16 The order was completed on 12th August when 100 copies in sheets were dispatched to Baron.17

The production of the pamphlet was held up for a variety of reasons.   In the first place Ince had believed for some time that there would be two publications: a reply to

---

5 The only known copy is in the Ince Papers.

6 Ince Papers (Ince–Mander, 27th April 1702).

7 Woodroffe's opponents suggested that he had invented this ' Member ' since no trace of him has been found.

8 This quotation is taken from *The Case of Glocester Hall* ... (see note 11 below), [1].

9 *The Case of Worcester-Colledge, as presented to the Members of the House of Commons* and *A Letter from a Member of the House of Commons, in Answer to a Letter, from a Member of the University, Enquiring: How the Bill for Settling Sir Thomas Cookes's Charity of 10,000£ for the Erecting and Endowing of Worcester-College in Oxford came to be rejected in their House* (Christ Church Pamphlets Miscellany, Z45 (16)).

10 Ince Papers (Ince–Mander, 4th July [1702]).

11 There are three copies of this pamphlet in the Bodleian (C.8.45 (1) Linc. (57 pp.) complete; Gough Oxford 108, with pp. [48] and [53] missing; Gough Oxford 89 (7) with pp. [40]–[45] missing.   See also note 21 below.

12 E. H. Cordeaux and D. H. Merry, *A Bibliography of Printed Works relating to the University of Oxford* (Oxford, 1968), p. 736.

13 Ince Papers (Ince–Baron, 18th August 1702).

14 Ibid. (Ince–Mander, 20th and 29th April 1703).   There were two sizes of paper; the larger sheets were primarily for the trustees.

15 Worcester College Archives, 28 (1): ' A Particular of the Charges and Expenses the Trustees mentioned in Sir Thomas Cookes Will have been att in relation to the saide Trust besides the Costs and Expenses they have been att in this Cause '.   The costs were queried but were considered reasonable by the Bank Printer ' considering the delay and alterations after composing etc. ' (see also Ince Papers (Ince–Mander, 12th August 1703).

16 Ibid. (Ince–Mander, 29th April 1703); *cf.* note 14 above.

17 Ince Papers (Ince–Mander, 12th August 1703).

Woodroffe's *Case* (suitable for presentation in Parliament) and another more combative reply to his *Letter*, and he became alarmed lest his part in the ' vituperative ' pamphlet which it was ultimately decided to produce should become known, and should damage his professional reputation. Judging from the printer's complaint of the length of time it ' tied up his letter' its printing must have begun early in February 1703.[18] The most serious hold-up occurred after the first sixty copies had been received in Oxford in April, when Ince discovered important new material he thought should be incorporated.[19] When this was adjudged impracticable, he sent a specimen copy showing how the absence of it could be off-set by MS marginalia.[20] His advice was not adopted but two of the copies of the pamphlet in the Bodleian[21] are annotated (one apparently in Baron's hand and one in Ince's hand). In both cases the MS marginal notes concern the proposed statutes for the College and both pamphlets have missing pages.

E.   An abridged form of *The Case of Glocester Hall, in Oxford, Rectifying the false Stating thereof by Doctor Woodforde* was printed for use in the House of Commons in 1709, since the original was deemed ' too long for the Members' perusall ',[22] but no trace of this has been found.

---

[18] Ibid.

[19] The pamphlet contains an analysis of three recensions of Woodroffe's statutes. He had now obtained a copy of a fourth, and most important one, the original body drawn up by the archbishop and Bishop Stilling-fleet. This shows that it agrees with none of the texts published by Woodroffe (ibid., Ince–Mander, 9th July 1703).

[20] Ibid. (Ince–Mander, 25th May 1703).

[21] Bodl. Gough Oxford 108 is annotated by [Baron] and Gough Oxford 89 (7) is annotated by [Ince].

[22] Worcester College Archives, 28 (1).

Sir William Blackstone (1723-80)
(Attributed to Sir Joshua Reynolds)
(National Portrait Gallery)

25

WILLIAM BLACKSTONE AND THE LEGAL CHAIRS
AT OXFORD

THIS ESSAY is in no way intended to make a contribution to legal knowledge. Any interest it may possess is as an examination of an episode in the history of the University of Oxford in the eighteenth century, and in the career of William Blackstone, one of the University's most distinguished sons. The scholar to whose memory this volume is dedicated always delighted in the by-ways of biography, and (a devoted alumnus of Oxford) often sat in the Codrington Library of All Souls under the shadow of Bacon's towering statue of the author of the *Commentaries*.

Blackstone has received less than his due attention from biographers, partly because of the breakdown of his friends' plans to provide an adequate memoir as a foreword to the posthumous edition of his *Reports*,[1] partly because he left no corpus of correspondence (though the number of his scattered letters known to survive is mounting), but most of all because so much of his life was bound up with his College and University, the eighteenth-century history of which has been woefully neglected. It has been said that 'the years that Blackstone spent mainly at Oxford, 1753–1761, were the most productive of his life'.[2] They were the years in which, abandoning for the time being the ambition to

---

[1] James Clitherow, Blackstone's executor and the editor of the *Reports of Cases Determined in the Several Courts of Westminster Hall Taken and Compiled by the Honourable Sir William Blackstone Knt.*, 2 vols. (London, 1781), tells us that it had been hoped to print a Memoir with them by his old and intimate friend Benjamin Buckler D.D., Fellow of All Souls, an admirable stylist and a man concerned in many of Blackstone's activities, but ill health prevented this, and James Clitherow himself took over. Though he was a former colleague of Blackstone's, and later his brother-in-law and though he was assisted by the advice of friends and 'a short Abstract of every Circumstance of Consequence in his life written by himself with his accustomed accuracy' he proved a singularly unenterprising biographer.

[2] H. Carter, *A History of the University Press* (Oxford, 1975), i. 408.

make a successful career at the Bar, he concentrated on his career at Oxford, and delivered, first as a private venture and then as the first Vinerian Professor of Common Law, the courses of lectures which when published in 1765–9 as the *Commentaries on the Laws of England* won him international fame. During these years he also made his maximum impact on the University and was without doubt the most powerful and enterprising individual in it. As a leading figure in Oxford his career was far longer. It showed at all stages—in the early years of the reorganization of All Souls, as a reformer and leader in the administration and politics of the University, and (when he had given up all formal contacts with it) in his plans for revolutionizing the road-system of the City[3]— great powers of mind and character, a capacity to exercise influence over friends and colleagues, a passion for order and efficiency, and an immense capacity for hard work, which gave him pre-eminence in the small and closely-knit society in which he found himself. It was in the University that these qualifications gave him as a man of action, a personal status which he was never later to assume.

Nevertheless outside the University and a small group of men distinguished in his profession who saw his potentialities, he was little known, and it is not surprising that after his death a number of stories (often apocryphal) began to circulate about the earlier years of his life. One of the best known of these purports to explain the circumstances in which he decided to deliver the lectures which were to make him famous and to illustrate in a dramatic way the political conditions at the time this decision was reached.

The story first appeared in print in J. Holliday's *Life of William late Earl of Mansfield* (London, 1797).[4] No independent contemporary version of it has been found, though it was widely copied, with slight embellishments, by later writers.[5] Holliday, who knew Mansfield well in his later years, had to depend in his account of his earlier life on accessible public sources, the reminiscences of a few surviving contemporaries, and anecdotes in general circulation

---

[3] For this little-known activity of his see E. de Villiers, *Swinford Toll Bridge 1769–1969*, Eynsham History Group (1969) and the Bertie MSS. in the Bodleian.

[4] pp. 88–9.

[5] The best known of them was Lord Campbell, *The Lives of the Chief Justices of England* (1849), ii. 378–9.

—the kind of evidence which is seldom accurate but often contains some basis of fact. The story runs:

A fair occasion offered, about this period of time, for Mr. Murray[6] to manifest his love of his profession, and an ardent desire to lay a better foundation in one of our universities for initiating and training students in legal knowledge by the fostering hand of an able law-professor. The first duke of Newcastle[7] was the warm friend and patron of Mr. Murray. The civil law professorship in the university of Oxford being then vacant, Mr. Murray took the liberty of expostulating with his Grace who was the Chancellor of the university of Cambridge on the appointment of a successor . . . he then expressed an anxious wish, that an able professor of civil law might be sought for and invited to fill the vacant seat. Dr. Jenner was the person thought of by the Duke of New-castle, yet he paid Mr. Murray the compliment of asking him if he could recommend any gentleman who would fill it with greater ability. Antecedent to the establishment of the Vinerian Professorship, the late Mr. Justice Blackstone, who was then at the bar, and had given proof that he possessed those qualifications which early pointed him out as *the most worthy* to be promoted on this occasion, was by Mr. Murray introduced and warmly commended to the duke of Newcastle, who considered it as part of his duty to probe a little the political principles of the new candidate, by addressing Mr. Blackstone 'Sir, I can rely on your friend Mr. Murray's judgment as to your giving law-lectures in good style, so as to benefit the students; and I dare say, that I may safely rely on you, whenever any thing in the political hemisphere is agitated in that university you will, Sir, exert yourself in our behalf.' The Answer was 'Your Grace may be assured that I will discharge my duty in giving law-lectures to the best of my poor abilities'. 'Aye! Aye!' replied his Grace hastily, 'and your duty in the other branch too'. Unfortunately for the new candidate, he only bowed assent, and a few days afterwards he had the mortification to hear that Dr. Jenner was appointed the civil-law professor.

Holliday goes on to state that this rebuff 'induced Mr. Murray and some other friends of Mr. Blackstone's strongly to recommend and persuade him to sit down at Oxford to read law-lectures to such students as were disposed to attend him, and that his lectures not only had the success which was well-known, but soon after-wards suggested the idea to the mind of Mr. Viner to establish a real law professorship in the university of Oxford.'

[6] William Murray (1705–92) later (1776) 1st Earl of Mansfield; at this time Solicitor-General.

[7] At this time Secretary of State; (1754) 1st Lord of the Treasury.

Holliday did not date his story, though from its position in his book, he apparently attributed it to the late forties. Since it refers to Newcastle's office as Chancellor of the University of Cambridge, it could not have belonged to a time earlier than the end of 1749. In fact, if it occurred, it must be dated some years later. Dr. Henry Brooke, Regius Professor of Civil Law at Oxford, died on 24 November 1752, and (a fact not noticed by some scholars) there was a considerable delay in the appointment of his successor Dr. Robert Jenner, which was not announced until the beginning of April 1754.[8] If Blackstone's interview with Newcastle took place (as the story goes) only a few days before the announcement of Jenner's appointment, it could not have occurred before the latter days of March 1754.

There are several difficulties about accepting this account as it stands. The first is one of interpretation. The reader is obviously intended to assume that Newcastle injected into the question of the appointment the issue of party politics by 'probing' Blackstone's political principles, and that Blackstone was taken aback when he did so. At no date during the vacancy of the Chair would this have been a fair reflection of the position of the two men. The Government and the predominant 'Old Interest' or Tory party in the University had been for years at daggers drawn, and Blackstone, always a staunch supporter of the 'Old Interest' in the University (though never a Jacobite), had since 1750 stood out as perhaps the most powerful leader among the Tory politicians there, a fact of which Newcastle could not fail to be aware, since it was largely through his efforts that the Tory Sir Roger Newdigate (for long to sit for the University in the House of Commons) had been elected in 1751. If Newcastle did at any time sound Blackstone on his political allegiance, it would not have been to discover what it was, but to find out whether he was prepared to abandon it in return for preferment. Still further, though Blackstone may have been disappointed that Murray's personal influence over the Minister did not over-ride political considerations, he would not have been surprised. Under the first two Hanoverians, appointments to the various Regius Chairs were expected to be used for political purposes.[9] Indeed the Regius

---

[8] Such delays were not unusual in royal appointments, but they were apt to suggest that no strong and obvious candidate had presented himself.

[9] After the Chancellor's election in 1759, for instance, Humphrey Sibthorpe

Chairs of Modern History were invented largely for this purpose.[10]

An awkward problem, too, is that of dating. There could be no time less propitious for a deal between Newcastle and this leader of the Oxford Tory opposition than the last days of March 1754, for within a few weeks the country was to go to the polls in the 1754 General Election, including that for the contested election for Oxfordshire, one of the most bitterly fought party conflicts of the century. The centre of the Tory opposition lay in the University[11] and Blackstone was deeply engaged in it. Such a deal would have been too late to affect the County election itself, and would have been seen by the supporters of both parties as the rankest treachery. Chronological difficulties also beset the consequences which were supposed to flow from the choice of Jenner and Blackstone's disappointment thereat. Clearly it cannot be held to have led to Blackstone's decision to return to Oxford and to begin private lectures there, for he had been delivering them already since November 1753, and had announced his intention to do so in the preceding June. Nor can it be held to be the indirect cause of Charles Viner's founding his Professorship in the Common Law (encouraged, it was suggested, by the success of Blackstone's lectures) since, though Viner's last Will was dated December 1755 and was thus drawn up some time after Blackstone had begun his lectures, the benefaction had been planned and incorporated in earlier Wills dating from 1752, well before they were even announced.

Nevertheless, though Holliday's account as a whole can hardly be accepted, many of its constituent parts may well be based on fact. Other contemporary sources refer to the eminent lawyers who backed Blackstone's venture in 1753,[12] and Murray, with whom

---

lost the appointment to the Regius Chair of Medicine, which he had expected, because he failed to support the Government candidate, and it went to Dr. John Kelly of Christ Church, a very dubious appointment. The Dean of Christ Church thanked Newcastle on behalf of the Whigs as it was, he said, good for them 'at this critical time . . . as it is a strong proof of our being countenanced and attended to . . .' (B.L. Add. MS. 32888, fos. 80 and 128).

[10] N. Sykes, *Edmund Gibson Bishop of London 1669–1748* (Oxford, 1926), pp. 94 f.

[11] See W. R. Ward, *Georgian Oxford. University Politics in the Eighteenth Century* (Oxford, 1958), pp. 192 f.

[12] J. Clitherow in his *Memoir* states that at the Courts he 'contracted an Acquaintance with several of the most eminent Men in that Profession, who saw through the then intervening Cloud, that great Genius, which afterwards broke forth with so much Splendor' (*Reports*, I, p. vii).

Blackstone was to have a long friendship, was very likely to be chief among them. There is no doubt of the close links between Murray and Newcastle, particularly in 1752, at the time the Chair became vacant, when, in addition to their political alliance, Newcastle was deeply beholden to Murray for his help in trying to straighten out his desperately confused personal finances.[13] And, though Holliday links Blackstone's disappointment with the publication of Jenner's success, he might have known that his own hopes had been dashed before the position was offered to anyone else. The trouble in trying to reach conclusions has been that there has been no evidence as to what, if anything, did happen, either in the printed sources such as Blackstone's biography, or the manuscripts in the public collections, such as the correspondence between Newcastle and Murray. In consequence everything concerning the matter long remained in the field of conjecture.

Fortunately, however, evidence has more recently come to light in a private manuscript collection, the large body of papers preserved by Sir Roger Newdigate, now deposited in the Warwickshire County Record Office, which throws a good deal of light on events, though it does not enable us to determine precisely what happened. Its source is unimpeachable, for it is Blackstone himself who is writing in a letter to his friend and patron Sir Roger Newdigate. He writes:

Mr Eyre called upon me some Days ago, with the Papers in Mr Ludford's Cause against You and Lady Newdigate . . . in order to consult with me upon them as You had kindly directed. But I declined meddling with them for Reasons which I then gave him, and which I told him I would myself communicate to You. And this I have now the Honour to do, by informing You that I have taken up a Resolution no longer to attend the Courts at Westminster, but to pursue my Profession in a Way more agreeable to me in all respects, by residing at Oxford. And I have been persuaded to engraft upon this Resolution a Scheme which I am told may be beneficial to the University as well as to myself and of which the enclosed Papers will give you the Particulars . . .[14]

---

[13] He drew up an admirable report on them on 5 November 1752 (R. A. Kelch, *Newcastle, a duke without money* . . ., London, 1974, pp. 143 f.). Murray is hardly likely to have been pushing Oxford Tory candidates on the Administration after the early months of 1753, when he was chiefly concerned with rebutting charges of Jacobitism in his youth, in connection with which Oxford was a liability.

[14] Presumably the printed Advertisement he circulated, dated 23 June 1753.

[*here follows some legal advice to Newdigate*]

You will wonder perhaps at the sudden Resolution I have taken. Indeed it is not a sudden One: It has been growing upon me for some Years. My Temper, Constitution, Inclinations, and a Thing called Principle, have long quarreled with active Life, at least the active Life of Westminster-Hall, and have assured me I am not made to rise in it. Besides there are certain Qualifications for being a public Speaker, in which I am very sensible of my own Deficiency; and happy that I am sensible so early. I am therefore withdrawing myself from that Branch of the Profession, in which I can promise myself no considerable Success, the bustling practical Part; in order to be the more at Leisure to cultivate another, in which I have better Prospects, the thinking theoretical Part.

As to my Scheme for Lectures, You will imagine, and very justly, that it had its original from the Thoughts I was taught to entertain of the Professorship; for which also I found I wanted *some* Qualifications; as you rightly guessed, at this time twelvemonth. Having by that means begun to think in this train, it was not easy to leave it off, especially as I found a Pleasure in it; and I have the Satisfaction to find my Design meets with the Approbation of Persons of the greatest Eminence and Learning, as well in the Inns of Court as at Oxford; and if those Gentlemen in the Country, whose Opinion I value, entertain the same favourable Sentiments, my utmost Ambition will be satisfied. I was desired to take the civil law into my Scheme; but, as I had been so much talked of for the Professorship, I thought it would argue Resentment, or at least Disappointment, in me; of both of which I declare myself clear. I therefore judged it more decent to leave that Field open to the Professor Regius, when our Governors, in their great Deliberation, shall think proper to send us one.[15]

Several points of interest arise from this letter. In the first place it contains the first proof positive that Blackstone had been considered for the Regius Chair of Civil Law and that he had been rejected. It makes clear that he had been encouraged to stand by people whose opinion he respected, and that he had been 'much talked of' for it. In the second place it is also clear that by July 1753 it was a thing of the past, though we need not take at its face value his denial of resentment or disappointment. (The tone of his letter lacks the cheerful self-confidence normally characteristic of

[15] Letter of 3 July 1753, Warwickshire County Record Office, Newdigate MSS., CR136/B, 1488. A small part of this letter has been printed under the heading 'Blackstone' in the biographical columns of *The History of Parliament, 1745–90*, ed. L. B. Namier and J. Brooke (1964).

his private correspondence.) Still more interesting is the fact which becomes apparent, that his candidature was planned before the death of the holder of the Chair. Blackstone (the most accurate of men) speaks of plans in connection with it, in which Newdigate had a part, twelve months before the date of his letter, and thus some four months before Brooke's death. It should be noted that when the scheme began there was no question of any contact between Murray and the Duke of Newcastle about it. The Duke was in Hanover with the King, and all business had to be transacted in writing. Murray's letters to the Duke survive and contain no reference to this matter. The Duke was not back in England until a few days before Brooke's death. In order to improve his qualifications for the position (at this time rather slight[16]) Blackstone had set to work on the lectures he would expect to deliver if he were appointed. How soon he knew that his efforts were in vain is not known, but there is a slight piece of evidence which suggests that he was not long kept in uncertainty. Writing to a prominent legal friend (who would presumably know of the candidature so much talked of) on 9 January 1753—that is some six weeks after Brooke's death—he adds in a PS. 'What has become of our Professor of Law?'[17] Hardly the query of a candidate still awaiting his own fate.

There is no indication of the cause of his rejection, but it can hardly, given the mediocrity of the man who was ultimately appointed, be other than political. Perhaps the melancholy suggestion that 'a thing called Principle' stood in his way as a practical man may hint at it. But perhaps the most valuable point to emerge from it is that Blackstone's rejection was early enough to affect his decision to return to Oxford to give private lectures, and that it was the first stage of his preparation of the Civil Law lectures he would have given had he been elected which stimulated his taste for this kind of 'thinking theoretical' work.

There is only one subject on which his account of his motives may be less than complete, the reason why he chose to read his

[16] His *Essay on Collateral Consanguinity 1750*, arguing the case against Founders' Kin at All Souls, depended largely on Civil Law comparisons. In 1753 he was made Assessor of the Vice-Chancellor's Court where the procedure was that of the Civil Law, but he had concentrated his interests, when his work for his degree was finished, on the Common Law.

[17] University Archives WP α 22 (1), fo. 9^v. Notes by Blackstone in a reply to R. Wilbraham, dated All Souls, 9 January 1753.

lectures in Common and not in Civil Law. The explanation he gives is a reasonable one, but it is negative not positive. Much has been claimed by later scholars for his originality in introducing the study of the Common Law[18] into the University. But this is to ignore a matter of significance, Viner's proposed benefaction. The fact that in 1752 Charles Viner, a benefactor already in his seventy-fifth year, had completed plans to foster the study of Common Law at Oxford, where it had been completely neglected; that the core of his scheme was the endowment of a well-paid Professorship to be held, on attractive conditions, by a qualified Civilian who was also a barrister-at-law, and that within a year William Blackstone, an able and ambitious young D.C.L. and barrister (who was also a Fellow of All Souls) should present himself to lecture on his own initiative on precisely this neglected topic, is on the face of it a somewhat surprising series of coincidences. It is indeed sufficiently surprising to justify some examination into the possibility that these facts were connected. That some such connection existed seems virtually certain. It was not, as has been suggested a personal link between Viner and Blackstone—of this there is no evidence[19]—but there is every reason to believe that there was a more indirect one.

When the University received the benefaction after Viner's death in 1756, a vociferous party there maintained that the bene-factor had intended to limit the teaching responsibilities of his Professor to a solemn (or formal) Lecture once a term.[20] The Delegacy of Convocation who were deputed to draw up the scheme for the use of the benefaction, on the other hand, emphatically denied this, and maintained that Viner had intended his Professor to deliver not only these solemn lectures, but regular lectures to students (provided they were given outside the law terms) as Blackstone had then been doing for some years. At this time a document was circulated, based not only on early copies of Viner's Wills, but on his correspondence with 'a Gentleman of Distinction

[18] e.g. W. B. Odgers, 'Sir William Blackstone', *Yale Law Journal*, xxvii (1918), 604.

[19] See G. H. Hanbury, *The Vinerian Chair and Legal Education* (Oxford, 1967), pp. 11–12.

[20] In the scheme for the Vinerian Endowment the term 'Solemn' Lecture was used in a different sense from that usual in the University, where it was a 'term of art' meaning a lecture proper as distinct from the old cursory lecture, or commentary on texts (Stat vi, § 13). In the Vinerian Scheme it meant something more like a present-day inaugural lecture. The benefactor appears to have used it in this sense. See Vinerian Bundle, University Archives.

in this Place' who had 'permitted his Letters to be made use of upon this Occasion'[21] in support of the views adopted by the Delegacy. Evidence in the University Archives shows that this 'Gentleman of Distinction' was Dr. William King,[22] the well-known Tory Principal of St. Mary Hall; it also shows that the document based on his correspondence was compiled by William Blackstone.[23] Since King and Blackstone were friends and close political associates, since King strongly supported his young friend's candidature when the benefaction came in—even celebrating his success in an 'elegant oration' in Convocation[24]—and since Blackstone claimed the support of eminent persons in the University as well as the Inns of Court for his decision to offer his private lectures in Oxford, it is hard to believe that he was ignorant of Viner's benefaction and of the form it was to take. Still further the advice given to Viner by Dr. King in 1752 so closely resembles what we know of Blackstone's views on the use of the benefaction —sometimes even in wording[25]—that it seems by no means unlikely there was consultation between the two men at the time when Viner's earlier Wills were being drawn up.

In these circumstances it is hard not to believe that, among the considerations which led Blackstone to decide to lecture on the Common Law, was the fact that a benefaction for a Chair in this subject would soon be received, and that an experienced lecturer in the University in this unfamiliar subject would be favourably placed to benefit from it. If this were among the calculations of Blackstone and his friends, they certainly proved correct, and (thanks to the remarkable success of his lectures) more so than his

[21] Two versions of this document were printed, one for the use of the Delegacy, summarizing at the end the points at issue (University Archives, Vinerian Documents (V/3/5/4)), the other, without a conclusion, for general circulation (a copy is in Bodl. Gough Oxf. 96 (15a)).

[22] W. S. Holdsworth, *A History of English Law* (1938), xii. 93, first drew attention to this identification.

[23] The compiler of this document stated that the material for it had been deposited with the Vice-Chancellor. This material can be identified in the bundle of Vinerian Documents in the University Archives, where each item is particularized by a capital letter. They are items V/3/1/2–V/3/1/11. Most of them are endorsed in Blackstone's hand, and they are accompanied by a list, also in his hand (V/3/1/12).

[24] Acta Convocationis, B h 35, p. 50.

[25] Particularly in the arguments for placing Viner's Scholars in a Hall rather than a College. For Blackstone's views see Clitherow (*Reports*, 1, p. xvii) and for King's letter to Viner see University Archives, Vinerian Bundle.

most sanguine supporters could have hoped. When the election to the Chair came up in 1758, Blackstone did not step into it without opposition (some of it very heated), but it was his strength that not even his bitterest enemies could challenge his qualifications for it, and it is significant that they did not succeed in finding a candidate to stand against him, though his supporters claimed that they tried.[26] Nevertheless, if Blackstone himself, then at the height of his power as a University politician, had not seized control of the plans for the Foundation, deflecting them by a bold *coup* from the Hebdomadal Board to Convocation[27]—had not controlled from without the activities of the Delegacy of Convocation set up to consider them (on which he could not himself conveniently serve but of which his most intimate All Souls friend Benjamin Buckler was the spokesman) and if he had not fought off a short but ferocious pamphlet campaign by his enemies, the Vinerian Foundation would not have taken the form which it did. The story of this academic battle is too long to be retailed here; but it was one of the most intense of Blackstone's career, and when Viner's estate had been wound up, the Statutes passed, he himself elected without opposition to the new Chair, and when Dr. King had delivered his 'elegant oration' of praise, he did what he never did in any other of the campaigns of these strenuous years—he had something of a nervous breakdown.

Writing on 12 November 1758 to thank Sir Roger Newdigate for his congratulations he told him

The late Hurries, and too great a Quantity perhaps of dyed Tea, have lately put my nervous System a little out of order; (though I assure you the Report of my Death was groundless) but by Spa Water, Abstinence from that jentacular[28] Poison, a Sabbath as to mental Employment, and a regular Use of gentle (very gentle!) Exercise, I am now pretty well

[26] *A View of the Misrepresentations in the Reply to the Examiner* [B. Buckler], 1 July 1758, 'Will all the Managers of the Opposition deny, that Candidates have been searched for to oppose him?' (Bodl. Gough Oxf. 96 (25)).

[27] The account of the beginning of this campaign is best taken from a note by Blackstone himself in his *Letter to the Revd. Dr. Randolph*, 21 May 1757 (reprinted by I. G. Philip, 'William Blackstone and the Reform of the University Press in the Eighteenth Century', *Oxford Bibliographical Society Publications*, N.S. VII, 1955). The Acta Convocationis (never very satisfactory) broke down completely at the height of this controversy. The pamphlet material is considerable, but has the disadvantages inherent in its nature.

[28] 'drunk at breakfast'—from the Latin *jentacula*, first meal of the day. The adjective has not found its way into the Oxford Dictionary.

recovered, and hope to be quite stout in a Week more. Much Writing does not yet agree with me . . .[29]

He could afford to relax, for his election to the Vinerian Chair set the seal on the success of his lectures, and made certain his later fame.

[29] Warwickshire County Record Office, Newdigate MSS., CR136/B, 1496.

26

THE LAST OF THE SERVITORS

On 13 February 1932 there appeared in *The Times* a letter from Edward Talbot, formerly Bishop successively of Rochester, Southwark, and Winchester, and before that, from 1869–1888, first Warden of Keble College. He was a Christ Church man who came up as a Commoner in 1862, and became Student and Lecturer in Law and Modern History before he left to take up his position at Keble.

His letter arose out of other published reminiscences of Christ Church. He wrote

Sir Herbert Maxwell has added one detail to the description of Oxford social life in Christ Church in the middle of last century given by the Warden of New College. He has distinguished the two orders of noblemen ('tufts,' from the gold tassels on their academical caps) and gentlemen-commoners with no distinction of rank, but wearing silk gowns, and having a special table in Hall. But one feature is left incomplete. May I add it from personal memory? Over my head, dwelling, as I then did, as a commoner in an attic (third floor), I had above me in a 'garret' (fourth floor) a modest 'scriv' or 'servitor'. He was one of a small, and I am afraid rather despised, set who had their own table at the bottom end of the Hall, wearing gowns, but socially much apart. They were, no doubt, successors of those who had earlier been 'servitors' in a menial sense, but they now held a humble place within the fringe of the academical body.

This letter called forth on the day of its publication replies from two members of the House aged 85 and 83 respectively, which the Bishop thought of sufficient interest to send on to the college, where they are still preserved. One was written from the Senior Common Room of Christ Church itself, and its writer was an Honorary Canon. He was the Revd. William Gilbert Edwards, who had come up as a chorister in 1854 and matriculated as a servitor in 1864. He wrote in a bold hand:

My dear Lord Bishop,

With all that I owe to the House over a long past and indeed in the present let me offer my thanks for your letter to the Times of this morning, and may I say how it 'hits off' exactly the state of affairs of the years you refer to—and say it from personal experience. And you have a share in what I gratefully acknowledge, because I expect you had a share in producing the great change that was brought about during my time at the House by your trend of thought and personal influence, and you helped me individually when I was reading 'Law and History'. I was reading to you an Essay soon after on the day you received a letter from Dr Pusey (I believe it was) offering you the Wardenship of Keble College.

Now in my 86th year I am the *Last of the Servitors*—and I am venturing to send you an account of my inside knowledge of the life you have described in your letter, and of the changes in the view other men held of the body, to which I am proud to have belonged—before we Servitors became Exhibitioners.

Believe me
My dear Lord Bishop
Yours gratefully
W. Gilbert Edwards

His enclosure ran as follows:

From the Last of the Servitors.

My name was first entered on the books of the House in May 1854, when after an Examination by Dean Gaisford I was admitted as a 'puer symphoniacus'— I think I can therefore say that I am the oldest living to have my name on the books.

In 1864 I was admitted as a 'puer serviens'. The body of Servitors was all to itself—no man called on us of the House, we had nothing to do with the social or athletic side of the community, except of course that we were an integral part of the College more so than the tufts et hoc genus omne you have referred to.

It must have been in the year 1864 that a change began. I made a venture— and called on Senhouse[1] (a 'Varsity oar and Stroke of the House Eight), asked to be allowed to be a member of the Boat Club. You may imagine what a venture it was when I tell you that my nickname henceforth was 'το θρασυ', anglice the 'Bold-un'. Every kindliness was shown me. Next year I stroked the Torpid and two Servitors rowed behind me. We made 4 bumps and but for a slight accident would have gone Head. In the summer Senhouse put me Stroke of the Eight and rowed 'Seven' to me, and asked me to row in the 'Varsity Pairs with him! I won the Silver medal for the Sculls, rowed in the Final Heat of the Diamonds with two other Oxford men, having beaten the Cambridge man. My 'blue' was won in the Athletics V. Cambridge, and I managed to 'scrape' into Honours in Classics and Law and History.

'There's life in the old dog yet'. For I am thankful—sincerely thankful—that I can still work, as I am Hon: Treasurer to the Mothers Union (diocesan); and to the C.E.T.S. [Church of England Temperance Society]; Hon: Sec to the Ox: Clergy Widows & Orphans; and to the Convalescent and Holiday Fund for the Clergy of the diocese; and Chairman of one of the Sub-Committees of the Dioc. Council of Education; act as representative of Betton's Charity;[2] and as you will see by what I am sending you in a separate envelope am 'doing my bit' for the cause of Church Schools in the diocese for our present Bishop. It was Gore[3] who made me Rural Dean of Cuddesdon and Burge[4] who gave me the right to a stall as Hon: Canon.

I hope you won't think me awfully conceited, but I write it solely because I feel proud to be the Last, not of the Mohicans, but of the Servitors.

W. G. E.

The other letter, in a somewhat shaky hand, suggests a less ebullient personality. It came from Clare Cottage, Glengariff Road, Parkstone,

---

1 Humphrey Pocklington Senhouse (1862), son of Joseph Pocklington Senhouse Esq. of Cumberland, at one time High Sheriff. An Etonian.

2 A Charity run by the Ironmongers' Company.

3 Charles Gore, bishop of Oxford 1911–19.

4 Hubert Burge, bishop of Oxford 1919–25.

Dorset, and was written by the Revd. Edward John Gough, Canon of Newcastle Cathedral, now living in retirement. He wrote:

My dear Bishop,

I am very interested in your letter in today's Times—for I am myself a link between the old and the new systems at Ch. Ch.

In April 1868 I gained one of the Careswell Exhibitions at Shrewsbury and was due to go up to the House in October—In May my father died, and, despite my Exhibition of £60 for four years, my widowed Mother could not have managed to send me. Dr Sandford,[1] then Senior Censor asked me if I would accept a College 'Exhibition' of £50 and other advantages (pecuniary) as they were anxious to merge the old Servitorships in what were henceforth to be known as 'Exhibitions' and to do away with the old social disabilities—This I gladly accepted and with those two Exhibitions and another small one which Shrewsbury gave me (The 'Nonely' I think it was called) I managed to support myself without any cost to my dear Mother—1868 to 1872 when I took my degree.

My only son, now Vicar of Tewkesbury Abbey, was at Keble 1896–1900 and I had the other day the pleasure of visiting my second grandson in his rooms at dear Ch: Ch: to which he has gone up with an Exhibition from Lancing.

I may add that they did not put me in a 'garret' but in a 'cellar' in Canterbury Quad, looking on Oriel Lane and later gave me very nice rooms on 3rd floor in Old Library.

I do not think I found any social disadvantages for I had many nice friends from Shrewsbury and elsewhere—and the old gave place to the new to my very great advantage—without this I should never have been in Holy Orders, never preached a Mission in Leeds, been Vicar and Canon of Newcastle etc. Laus Deo —and blessings on Oxford and the House.

Believe me
Very sincerely yours
Edward John Gough

Canon Edwards was right in claiming that the Servitors were an integral part of the college as the noblemen and gentlemen commoners were not. In their early days all colleges either by Statute or custom provided a cheap education (though without a share in the amenities of their corporate life) for a certain number of poor scholars, and some of these they elected or recognized as Servitors. The Servitors obtained a free or very inexpensive education in return for menial services, and though their lives were at first hard and their position among their contemporaries humiliating, they were offered opportunities otherwise closed to them. As time went on colleges received benefactions for Exhibitions for them, and Christ Church was happy in this respect. Nevertheless well before the nineteenth century the Christ Church Servitor had become an anomaly in Oxford.

---

[1] Charles Waldegrave Sandford (1847); Student 1848–72. Rector of Bishopsbourne, Kent 1870–3. Bishop of Gibraltar 1874.

In the first place, an official return of 1804 shows only twenty servitors in the whole University, as many as fifteen of whom were at Christ Church.[1] In the second place the services they were originally intended to perform had been almost all taken over by the regular college servants: even that which lingered longest, the duty of the 'matriculated waiter' at the High Table was almost extinct, and where it survived seems to have become purely ceremonial. The Royal Commission of 1852 reported of the Servitors of Christ Church that within the last twenty years they used 'to bring the first dish into the Hall'. Even their separate table at the bottom of the Hall noted by Bishop Talbot marked the change in their status, for originally servitors did not dine in Hall.

Unfortunately for them, however, the history of their order had left them under a social stigma, which was perpetuated by their distinctive academic dress. Up to 1770 they, alone of all undergraduates, still wore the seventeenth-century round cap or 'bonnet' instead of the square, and though after that date they were freed from this incubus they still until 1855 wore a gown differing in some respects from that of the commoners, and were not permitted a tassel on their squares.

Reference to the events of 1770 shows, nevertheless, that they were not always passive victims. The University Statute of that year which amended the outdated Laudian Statute *de Vestitu et Habitu Scholastico* was the direct outcome of a revolt by the Servitors of Christ Church against their academic dress. In what was then called the Lent Term, as an indignant pamphleteer complained, 'contrary to express statute and immemorial usage' they made a concerted appearance in Scholars' caps and gowns, claiming that they were in effect Exhibitioners and that at a number of colleges (though not at Christ Church) Exhibitioners were accepted as on the Foundation. Their stand touched off a chain reaction which soon involved the Hebdomadal Board, Congregation, and Convocation and led to a pamphlet war and long and acrimonious debates about the academic dress of undergraduates in general. A young Christ Church don—his name is not known—adopted their cause in the interest of humanity and justice, and of the University's duty to 'take off the mark of servility from the sons of Clergymen and other reputable Persons on whom it is illiberal to continue it'. Others took a more conservative tone, and one of them suggested with some justice that 'a little more condescension and countenance from his superiors at home would contribute in far greater proportion to his comfort and decent estimation, than any improvement in his public habit'.[2] But if they won only limited success no one denied their underlying assumptions—though it is hard to say how far their partial victory was due to the strength of their case, and how far to the

---

[1] University Archives WP. Y 2 (5). Several colleges, though not asked to, also returned a few Bible Clerks separately from their Commoners.

[2] *Remarks on some strictures Lately Published, Entitled Observations upon the Statute Tit. XIV . . . with a Brief State of the Controversy which Gave Occasion to Them* (Oxford, 1770).

diplomacy of the then Dean, Dr. Markham.[1] Some of their tactics strike one as likely to have been counter-productive. It was reported 'A servitor, the other day, during an examination . . . had the assurance, after several other Indecorums, to place himself in the Vice-Chancellor's seat: the Regent Masters could not reduce him to order without interrupting the examination, and offering to go for a Proctor.[2]

There were 'bold-uns' among the Christ Church Servitors well before the days of Canon Edwards.

[1] Dr. William Markham, Dean of Christ Church 1767–77. He was credited with drafting the 1770 Statute, which was a compromise: *Reasons for the Non Placet given in the House of Convocation, Tuesday November 26th 1816* (Oxford, 1816).

[2] *Observations* . . . (1770).

INDEX